Chambers
WORD
LISTS

Indispensable general knowledge
references for crosswords

Compiled and edited by
Roger Prebble

Introduction by
Magnus Magnusson

Chambers

Chambers Word Lists
© Keesing International 1991
is published by W & R Chambers Ltd
43-45 Annandale Street, Edinburgh EH7 4AZ
by arrangement with Keesing International
for sale in all countries except USA

ISBN 0-550-19025-2

A catalogue record for this book is available
from the British Library

Phototypeset by Falcon Graphic Art Ltd, Wallington, Surrey
Printed in England by Clays Ltd, St Ives plc

CONTENTS

INTRODUCTION

I have to say this. I'm sorry, but I can't help it. The blunt fact is that crossword puzzle compilers are becoming positively fiendish. I always knew they were devious and wily — that was part of the game, part of the intellectual fencing match they were playing against the solvers. But now! It's no longer a game. It's war, with no holds barred and no quarter given.

No one likes to lose, either in love or war. So when the enemy starts using underhand tricks — like expecting you to be *au fait* with South American cities, Graham Greene novels, African airports and obscure operas (not to mention astronauts, Third World politicians, criminals and snooker players) — it's time for us solvers to rethink our defence strategy and get the benefit of the latest advances in technology.

Chambers Word Lists is precisely that. It rallies the professional computer database to the aid of our own amateur, disorganized brain power. It helps us to home in on the target word with much greater accuracy. The only snag is that it will also draw you off target by tempting you to browse in the thicket of words served up — especially in subjects like geography, music and literature, which have been given particularly in-depth treatment.

With this invaluable book you don't have to be a Mastermind to complete even the most demanding and devilish crossword puzzle. Cheating? Of course it is (although those of more tender susceptibilities can call it 'research' if they like). And why not? As I said, all's fair in love and war — and crossword puzzles.

Magnus Magnusson

HOW TO USE THIS BOOK

Because *Chambers Word Lists* covers such a wide sweep of general knowledge, accessibility is paramount. Frustrated word-puzzlers tend to want solutions rather swiftly!

To this end, every list has been subdivided into word-length order (three to fifteen letters) before being arranged alphabetically. This, coupled with a comprehensive Index at the back of the book, will ensure the instant pinpointing of any individual entry.

Before plunging in, though, a quick read-through of the following information should obviate any possible queries.

Notes

(a) Where any one word has two accepted spellings or names, both are listed with an asterisk (*), denoting that there is a different spelling or alternative name available. The two entries are matched up by the numbers which follow the asterisks (eg, in GEOGRAPHY – TOWNS & CITIES – FRANCE; REIMS *2, RHEIMS *2).

(b) Where abbreviated forms of names or places occur (eg DR WATSON or ST IVES), they appear strictly alphabetically.

(c) Within PEOPLE, LITERARY CHARACTERS and PLAY CHARACTERS, where both surname and full name are listed, the code beside the surname denotes where to find the full name (eg, in PEOPLE – SPORTSPEOPLE – JOCKEYS; CAUTHEN (12S) = full name will be found under 12-letter word-length, letter S – STEVE CAUTHEN). Also, where a full name would be over 15 letters, only the surname is listed.

(d) If you are looking for a particular person, you must refer to PEOPLE, as they are not listed under any other heading (eg, JOHN HURT is not listed under ARTS – CINEMA or THEATRE, but is to be found under PEOPLE – ENTERTAINERS – ACTORS & ACTRESSES).

(e) Mention should be made of the fact that certain subjects can cause contention. Within GEOGRAPHY especially, anglicised spellings, changing political situations, dubious delineations of European Russia, etc., make it notoriously difficult to be definitive. The sectioning of entries, whilst having convenience of access in mind, takes account of the above comment.

Finally, readers' comments and suggestions will be most welcome.

ARTS

CINEMA – CARTOON CHARACTERS

† = Disney

3

DOC *† (Dwarf)*
GUS *†*
JAQ *†*
KAA *†*
NOD *†*
PAN *†*
PEG *†*
TOM

4

BABE *†*
CHIP *†*
CLEO *†*
DALE *†*
FIFI *†*
HUEY *†*
JEFF
JOCK *†*
LADY *†*
SMEE *†*
TONY *†*
TYKE
VIDI *†*

5

ALICE *†*
BABAR
BALOO *†*
BAMBI *†*
BASIL *†*
BIMBO
BLUTO
BONGO *†*
BONZO

BOSKO *†*
BUTCH *†*
CASEY *†*
CYRIL *†*
DAISY *†*
DANNY *†*
DEWEY *†*
DINAH *†*
DOPEY *† (Dwarf)*
DUMBO *†*
EDGAR *†*
GOOFY *†*
HAPPY *† (Dwarf)*
JERRY
LOUIE *†*
MONTE *†*
PABLO *†*
PEDRO *†*
PLUTO *†*
PONGO *†*
QUEEN *†*
SPIKE
SUSIE *†*
TRAMP *†*
WENDY *†*
WIMPY
WITCH *†*

6

BALSAM *†*
BUBBLE
DROOPY
EEYORE *†*
FIDGET *†*
FIGARO *†*
FLOWER *†*
GERTIE
GIDEON *†*

GOPHER *†*
GRUMPY *† (Dwarf)*
HECKLE
JECKLE
JJ FATE *†*
MC BIRD *†*
MERLIN *†*
MORRIS *†*
MOWGLI *†*
PIGLET *†*
PIPEYE
POPEYE
PUPEYE
RABBIT *†*
RANGER *†*
SLEEPY *† (Dwarf)*
SNEEZY *† (Dwarf)*
SQUEAK
TIGGER *†*
TINTIN
TRUSTY *†*
WYNKEN *†*

7

BASHFUL *† (Dwarf)*
BLYNKEN *†*
BRER FOX *†*
CASEY JR *†*
DARLING *†*
DOLORES *†*
DUCHESS *†*
JESSICA
JIM CROW *†*
JIM DEAR *†*
KATRINA *†*
LAMBERT *†*
LUCIFER *†*
MAX HARE *†*

MONSTRO *†*
MR MAGOO
ORVILLE *†*
PEEPEYE
PEGASUS *†*
PERDITA *†*
POOPEYE
RATIGAN *†*
SCAT CAT *†*
SWEE' PEA
THUMPER *†*
TIMOTHY *†*
WISE OWL *†*
WUZZLES *†*

8

BAGHEERA *†*
BENT-TAIL *†*
BRER BEAR *†*
FLANNERY *†*
GEPPETTO *†*
GUS GOOSE *†*
KRAZY KAT
LAMPWICK *†*
LOIS LANE
MADAM MIM *†*
OLIVE OYL
PANCHITO *†*
PETER PAN *†*
PETER PIG *†*
PORKY PIG
SIR GILES *†*
SUPERMAN

9

BABY WEEMS *†*

1

BETTY BOOP
BLUE FAIRY †
BUGS BUNNY
DAFFY DUCK
DAISY DUCK †
DIPPY DAWG †
DREAMY DUD
ELMER FUDD
FERDINAND †
HARPO MARX †
JENNY WREN †
LULUBELLE †
PECOS BILL †
PIED PIPER †
PINOCCHIO †
ROQUEFORT †
SHERE KHAN †
SNOW WHITE †
STROMBOLI †
SYLVESTER
TWEETY PIE

10

BARNEY BEAR
BIG BAD WOLF †
BRER RABBIT †
CASEY JONES †
CHIP AN' DALE †
CINDERELLA †
CLARA CLUCK †
DEPUTY DAWG
DONALD DUCK †
FOXEY LOXEY †
GUMMI BEARS †
HEATHCLIFF
JACK HORNER †
LITTLE LULU
MALEFICENT †
ORANGE BIRD †
PAUL BUNYAN †
PEG LEG PETE †
PERSEPHONE †

ROAD RUNNER
SANTA CLAUS †
TINKER BELL †

11

ARACUAN BIRD †
CAPTAIN HOOK †
CHILLY WILLY
DINKY DOODLE
FELIX THE CAT
FLIP THE FROG †
FRITZ THE CAT
GRASSHOPPER †
JOSÉ CARIOCA †
KING NEPTUNE †
LOOPY DE LOOP
MAGIC MIRROR †
MICKEY MOUSE †
MIGHTY MOUSE
MINNIE MOUSE †
MUTT AND JEFF
PEG LEG PEDRO †
PINK PANTHER
PLUTO JUNIOR †
POOCH THE PUP
ROGER RABBIT
SEVEN DWARFS †
TOM AND JERRY
WILE E COYOTE

12

BAMBI'S MOTHER †
BOOTLE BEETLE †
CRUELLA DE VIL †
ICHABOD CRANE †
LITTLE AUDREY
PROFESSOR OWL †
TIMOTHY MOUSE †
TOBY TORTOISE †
UGLY DUCKLING †

13

CHICKEN LITTLE †
CLARABELLE COW †
EUGENE THE JEEP
JIMINY CRICKET †
J THADDEUS TOAD †
MORTIMER MOUSE †
POOP-DECK PAPPY
PRINCE PHILLIP †
SCROOGE McDUCK †
THOMAS O'MALLEY †
WINNIE-THE-POOH †

14

ALBERT EINSTEIN †
DONALD'S NEPHEWS †
FOGHORN LEGHORN
LUDWIG VON DRAKE †
PRINCESS AURORA †
SPEEDY GONZALEZ
WILLIE THE GIANT †
WILLIE THE WHALE †
WINDWAGON SMITH †

15

BUBBLE AND SQUEAK
CARELESS CHARLIE †
HECKLE AND JECKLE
HUMPHREY THE BEAR †
JOHNNY APPLESEED †
OSWALD THE RABBIT †
OTTO THE BABY BIRD †
THREE LITTLE PIGS †
UGLY STEPSISTERS †
WOODY WOODPECKER

ARTS

CINEMA – FILMS

F = Best Film Oscar   D = Best Director Oscar   † = Best Actor Oscar
†† = Best Actress Oscar
(C) = Cartoon   (M) = Musical

3

BIG
EVA
HUD
  †† (P Neal)
KES
SHE

4

COMA
DR NO
DUEL
DUNE
FAME *(M)*
FURY
GIGI *(M)*
  F/D (V Minnelli)
G MEN
HAIR *(M)*
HELP! *(M)*
JAWS
MAME *(M)*
M*A*S*H
MASK
NUTS
PEPE *(M)*
REDS
  D (W Beatty)
ROPE
STAR!
TAPS
TESS
THEM!
TRON
WILT
ZULU

5

ALFIE
ALIEN
ANGEL
ANNIE *(M)*
BAMBI *(C)*
COBRA
DIGBY
DUMBO *(C)*
EARTH
EL CID
FREUD
GHOST
GIANT
  D (G Stevens)
GILDA
GREED
GYPSY *(M)*
HOTEL
JULIA
KIPPS
KITTY
KLUTE
  †† (J Fonda)
KOTCH
LADY L
LAURA
MAMMY *(M)*
MANDY
MARTY *F/D/†*
  (D Mann/E Borgnine)
OTLEY
PINKY
RAMBO
ROCKY *F/D*
  (J Avildsen)
SALLY *(M)*
SHAFT

SHANE
SLEEP
TOMMY *(M)*
TWINS
WINGS *F*
YANKS
YENTL
ZELIG

6

AGATHA
ALIENS
ALWAYS
ARTHUR
AVANTI!
BATMAN
BECKET
BEN-HUR *F/D/†*
  (W Wyler/C Heston)
BLOW-UP
BRAZIL *(M)*
BUSTER
CARRIE
CHARLY
  † (C Robertson)
COCOON
CONVOY
ESCAPE
EXODUS
FRENZY
GANDHI
  F/D/†
  (R Attenborough/
  B Kingsley)
GOTHIC
GREASE *(M)*
HAMLET
  F/† (L Olivier)

HARVEY
ISHTAR
JIGSAW
KISMET *(M)*
LOLITA
MAD MAX
MARNIE
ODETTE
OLIVER! *(M)*
  F/D (C Reed)
ORPHÉE
PATTON
  F/D/†
  (F Schaffner/
  G Scott)
PICNIC
POPEYE
PORKY'S
PSYCHO
RIFIFI
SLEUTH
SPLASH!
THE FLY
THE FOG
THE KID
THE WIZ *(M)*
TOP GUN
TOP HAT *(M)*
VICTIM
WILSON
XANADU *(M)*

7

AIRPORT
ALGIERS
AMADEUS
  F/D/† (M Forman/
  FM Abraham)

3

ANDROID
BANANAS
BIGGLES
BULLITT
BUS STOP
CABARET *(M)*
D/†† (B Fosse/
L Minnelli)
CAMELOT *(M)*
CAMILLE
CAPRICE
CHARADE
DARLING
†† (J Christie)
DIMPLES
DRACULA
EBB TIDE
FIREFOX
GI BLUES *(M)*
HOG WILD
HOLIDAY
HOUDINI
JEZEBEL
†† (B Davis)
KING RAT
LA RONDE
LET IT BE *(M)*
MACBETH
MIRANDA
MOROCCO
NETWORK
†/†† (P Finch/
F Dunaway)
NIAGARA
OTHELLO
PAL JOEY *(M)*
PIRATES
PLATOON
D (O Stone)
POOR COW
Q PLANES
QUARTET
QUINTET
RAIN MAN
F/D/†
(B Levinson/
D Hoffman)

REBECCA *F*
RED DUST
RIO LOBO
RIO RITA *(M)*
ROBOCOP
ROSALIE *(M)*
SABRINA
SCROOGE *(M)*
SERPICO
SHAMPOO
SLEEPER
THE BLOB
THE CURE
THE HILL
THE OMEN
THE ROBE
THE STUD
THE VIPs
TOOTSIE
TOPKAPI
TRAFFIC
TRAPEZE
ULYSSES
VALMONT
VERTIGO
WHOOPEE! *(M)*

8

ACES HIGH
ADAM'S RIB
AIRPLANE
ALBERT RN
APPLAUSE
BADLANDS
BETRAYAL
BORN FREE
BOYS' TOWN
† (S Tracy)
BRUBAKER
CALIGULA
CAROUSEL *(M)*
CASTAWAY
CIMARRON *F*
CURLY TOP
DEAD CALM

DUCK SOUP
FANTASIA *(C)*
GASLIGHT
†† (I Bergman)
GODSPELL *(M)*
GODZILLA
GREMLINS
HIGH NOON
† (G Cooper)
IT'S A GIFT
JANE EYRE
KEY LARGO
KHARTOUM
KING KONG
KING'S ROW
LIFEBOAT
MIDNIGHT
MOBY DICK
MONA LISA
MON ONCLE
MY GAL SAL *(M)*
NAKED GUN
NAPOLEON
NORMA RAE
†† (S Field)
NOSTROMO
OKLAHOMA! *(M)*
PAPILLON
PETER PAN *(C)*
QUO VADIS
RIO BRAVO
SAYONARA
SCARFACE
SEXTETTE
SHOWBOAT *(M)*
SILKWOOD
STAR WARS
STEAMING
SUPERMAN
THE ALAMO
THE BIRDS
THE BITCH
THE CHASE
THE KNACK
THE MUMMY
THE REBEL
THE SHEIK

THE STING
F/D (GR Hill)
THE SWARM
THE THING
THE TRAMP
TIGER BAY
TOKYO JOE
TOM JONES
F/D (T Richardson)
TONY ROME
TRUE GRIT
† (J Wayne)
TWO WOMEN
†† (S Loren)
VERA CRUZ
WAR GAMES
WATERLOO

9

ANASTASIA
†† (I Bergman)
ANNIE HALL
*F/D/†† (W Allen/
D Keaton)*
ARABESQUE
BEAU GESTE
BILLY LIAR
BLACKMAIL
BOOMERANG
BRIGADOON *(M)*
CAT BALLOU
† (L Marvin)
CAT PEOPLE
CAVALCADE
F/D (F Lloyd)
CHINATOWN
CLEOPATRA
CLOCKWISE
CROSSFIRE
DEATH WISH
DICK TRACY
DR CYCLOPS
EASY RIDER
EVERGREEN *(M)*
FUNNY FACE

FUNNY GIRL
†† (B Streisand)
GALLIPOLI
GENEVIEVE
GET CARTER
HALLOWEEN
HELPMATES
I'M NO ANGEL
JOAN OF ARC
JUNGLE JIM
KAGEMUSHA
LABYRINTH
LIMELIGHT
LOCAL HERO
LOGAN'S RUN
LOVE STORY
MANHATTAN
MOONRAKER
NASHVILLE
NINOTCHKA
NOTORIOUS
OBSESSION
OCTOPUSSY
ODD MAN OUT
OLD GRINGO
ON THE TOWN *(M)*
PALE RIDER
PAPER MOON
PINOCCHIO *(C)*
PYGMALION
RADIO DAYS
REMBRANDT
REPULSION
ROAD TO RIO
ROSE MARIE *(M)*
ROXIE HART *(M)*
SPARTACUS
STAGE DOOR
STRAW DOGS
SUSPICION
†† (J Fontaine)
THE BOWERY
THE DAMNED
THE DEVILS
THE GUVNOR
THE RACKET

UP POMPEII
WHITE HEAT

10

ABSOLUTION
BACK STREET
BARBARELLA
BEING THERE
BLUE HAWAII *(M)*
CASABLANCA
F/D (M Curtiz)
CITY LIGHTS
CITY ON FIRE
COMING HOME
*†/†† (J Voight/
J Fonda)*
CRY FREEDOM
DIRTY HARRY
DR DOLITTLE
EARTHQUAKE
EAST OF EDEN
EASY STREET
EMMANUELLE
FANCY PANTS
FIRST BLOOD
FLASHDANCE *(M)*
FORT APACHE
FRA DIAVOLO
GEORGY GIRL
GOING MY WAY
*F/D/† (L McCarey/
B Crosby)*
GOLDFINGER
GRAND HOTEL *F*
HALLELUJAH
HELLO DOLLY *(M)*
HIGH SIERRA
HOLIDAY INN *(M)*
HOUSE CALLS
HOUSE OF WAX
INTERMEZZO
JAGGED EDGE
JAMAICA INN
JOUR DE FÊTE
JUGGERNAUT

JUNGLE BOOK *(C)*
KID GALAHAD
KING CREOLE *(M)*
KISS ME KATE *(M)*
KITTY FOYLE
 †† (G Rogers)
LADY BE GOOD *(M)*
LADY KILLER
LONDON TOWN *(M)*
METROPOLIS
MOONSTRUCK
 †† (Cher)
MOONWALKER
MRS MINIVER
 F/D/†† (W Wyler/
 G Garson)
MY FAIR LADY
 F/D/† (G Cukor/
 R Harrison)
MY LEFT FOOT
 † (D Day-Lewis)
NIGHT GAMES
NINE TO FIVE
NOW VOYAGER
OH MR PORTER
ON THE BEACH
PARENTHOOD
PILLOW TALK
POOL SHARKS
RAGING BULL
 † (R de Niro)
REAR WINDOW
RED GARTERS *(M)*
ROAD TO BALI
ROLLERBALL
ROUSTABOUT *(M)*
SAFETY LAST
SHENANDOAH
SING AS WE GO
SPELLBOUND
STAGECOACH
TAXI DRIVER
THE ACCUSED
 †† (J Foster)
THE BIG HEAT
THE BLUE MAX

THE CITADEL
THE DRESSER
THE GENERAL
THE HEIRESS
 †† (O de Havilland)
THE HOT ROCK
THE HUSTLER
THE KILLERS
THE LOVE BUG
THE MISFITS
THE MISSION
THE SHINING
THE THIN MAN
THE WILD ONE
TRADER HORN
UP THE FRONT
VIVA ZAPATA!
WALL STREET
 † (M Douglas)
WAY OUT WEST
WHAT'S UP DOC?

11

A CHORUS LINE *(M)*
ALL ABOUT EVE
 F/D (J Mankiewicz)
ARISE MY LOVE
A STAR IS BORN
BABES IN ARMS *(M)*
BARRY LYNDON
BELLE DE JOUR
BLADE RUNNER
BUGSY MALONE
CALL ME MADAM *(M)*
CARMEN JONES *(M)*
CARRY ON CLEO
CARRY ON DICK
CARRY ON JACK
CHU CHIN CHOW *(M)*
CITIZEN KANE
DELIVERANCE
DOCTOR AT SEA
DON'T LOOK NOW
ELEPHANT BOY

ELMER GANTRY
 † (B Lancaster)
ENDLESS LOVE
GOOD OLD SOAK
HELL'S ANGELS
HIGH SOCIETY *(M)*
IRMA LA DOUCE
I WANT TO LIVE
 †† (S Hayward)
JABBERWOCKY
LA DOLCE VITA
LISZTOMANIA
LOST HORIZON
LUST FOR LIFE
MARATHON MAN
MARY POPPINS *(M)*
 †† (J Andrews)
MEET JOHN DOE
MODERN TIMES
MOULIN ROUGE
NIGHT AND DAY *(M)*
NO NO NANETTE *(M)*
OLIVER TWIST
OUR MISS FRED
OUT OF AFRICA
 F/D (S Pollack)
PEYTON PLACE
POLTERGEIST
ROOM SERVICE
SHIP OF FOOLS
SOLDIER BLUE
TEACHER'S PET
THE BANK DICK
THE BIG SLEEP
THE BLUE LAMP
THE CARDINAL
THE CRUEL SEA
THE EXORCIST
THE GRADUATE
 D (M Nichols)
THE KING AND I *(M)*
 † (Y Brynner)
THE MAGIC BOX
THE PALEFACE
THE QUIET MAN
 D (J Ford)

THE RED SHOES
THE RESCUERS *(C)*
THE SHOOTIST
THE THIRD MAN
THE WAY AHEAD
THE WRONG BOX
THUNDERBALL
THUNDER ROCK
TIME BANDITS
TORN CURTAIN
WAR AND PEACE
WOMEN IN LOVE
  †† (G Jackson)
WORKING GIRL

12

ACE IN THE HOLE
ANNA KARENINA
ANYTHING GOES *(M)*
APRIL IN PARIS *(M)*
A VIEW TO A KILL
BATTLEGROUND
BLITHE SPIRIT
BLOOD AND SAND
BRIGHTON ROCK
CALAMITY JANE
CAPRICORN ONE
CAPTAIN BLOOD
CARRY ON CABBY
CARRY ON GIRLS
CARRY ON HENRY
CARRY ON NURSE
CASINO ROYALE
COOL HAND LUKE
DIRTY DANCING
DOCTOR IN LOVE
DONOVAN'S REEF
DRAGONSLAYER
DUEL IN THE SUN
EASTER PARADE *(M)*
FRANKENSTEIN
GHOSTBUSTERS
GUYS AND DOLLS *(M)*
HELLZAPOPPIN'

HOUSE OF CARDS
KEY TO THE CITY
LETHAL WEAPON
LITTLE CAESAR
LOVE AND DEATH
LOVE ME TENDER *(M)*
MAJOR BARBARA
MEMPHIS BELLE
MY MAN GODFREY
NEVER TOO LATE
OF MICE AND MEN
OLIVER'S STORY
ON GOLDEN POND
  †/†† (H Fonda/K Hepburn)
PATHS OF GLORY
PORK CHOP HILL
PRIZZI'S HONOR
QUADROPHENIA *(M)*
REUBEN, REUBEN
ROAD TO UTOPIA
ROMAN HOLIDAY
  †† (A Hepburn)
ROOM AT THE TOP
  †† (S Signoret)
SAILOR BEWARE
SAN FRANCISCO
SANTA FÉ TRAIL
SAVE THE TIGER
  † (J Lemmon)
SERGEANT YORK
  † (G Cooper)
SEVEN SAMURAI
SHALL WE DANCE? *(M)*
SONG OF NORWAY *(M)*
SOUTH PACIFIC *(M)*
STAYING ALIVE
SWEET CHARITY *(M)*
THE APARTMENT
  F/D (B Wilder)
THE BLUE ANGEL
THE BOY FRIEND *(M)*
THE FAMILY WAY
THE FRONT PAGE
THE GO-BETWEEN
THE GODFATHER
  F/† (M Brando)

THE GOOD EARTH
  †† (L Rainer)
THE GREAT RACE
THE KARATE KID
THE MAIN EVENT
THE NAKED CITY
THE NAVIGATOR
THE NUN'S STORY
THE ODD COUPLE
THE UNINVITED
THE WILD BUNCH
THE WILD GEESE
THE YOUNG ONES *(M)*
TORA! TORA! TORA!
VIVA LAS VEGAS *(M)*
WATERLOO ROAD
WE'RE NO ANGELS
WHISKY GALORE
YOUNG AT HEART
YOUNG WINSTON

13

A BRIDGE TOO FAR
A KIND OF LOVING
ALTERED STATES
ANCHORS AWEIGH *(M)*
APOCALYPSE NOW
A TASTE OF HONEY
A TOUCH OF CLASS
  †† (G Jackson)
A WALK IN THE SUN
BOY ON A DOLPHIN
BREAKING GLASS *(M)*
CABIN IN THE SKY *(M)*
CARRY ON ABROAD
CARRY ON BEHIND
CARRY ON COWBOY
CARRY ON DOCTOR
CARRY ON LOVING
CARRY ON MATRON
CARRY ON SPYING
DADDY LONG LEGS *(M)*
DEATH IN VENICE
DOCTOR AT LARGE

DOCTOR ZHIVAGO
DRESSED TO KILL
DR STRANGELOVE
EDUCATING RITA
EIGHT AND A HALF
ERIC THE VIKING
EXPRESSO BONGO
FOR ME AND MY GAL *(M)*
GIVE ME A SAILOR
HALF A SIXPENCE *(M)*
HARRY AND TONTO
  † *(A Carney)*
HEAVEN CAN WAIT
HORSE FEATHERS
HOW I WON THE WAR
ICE COLD IN ALEX
JAILHOUSE ROCK *(M)*
KISSIN' COUSINS *(M)*
LA BÊTE HUMAINE
LES MISÉRABLES
LICENCE TO KILL
LIVE AND LET DIE
LOVE ME TONIGHT
LOVE ON THE DOLE
MA AND PA KETTLE
MAN OF LA MANCHA
NEVER ON SUNDAY
NORTH TO ALASKA
NOTHING SACRED
PARADISE ALLEY
POLICE ACADEMY
PRIVATE ANGELO
RANDOM HARVEST
ROAD TO MOROCCO
ROMAN SCANDALS *(M)*
ROSEMARY'S BABY
RYAN'S DAUGHTER
SEVENTH HEAVEN
  †† *(J Gaynor)*
SILK STOCKINGS *(M)*
SITTING PRETTY
SOME LIKE IT HOT
SOMETHING WILD
SONS AND LOVERS
SOPHIE'S CHOICE
  †† *(M Streep)*

STORMY WEATHER *(M)*
SUMMER HOLIDAY *(M)*
THE ARISTOCATS *(C)*
THE AWFUL TRUTH
THE BIG COUNTRY
THE BLUE LAGOON
THE COTTON CLUB
THE DAM BUSTERS
THE DAWN PATROL
THE DEER HUNTER
  F/D *(M Cimino)*
THE DESERT SONG *(M)*
THE DIRTY DOZEN
THE FALLEN IDOL
THE GHOST TRAIN
THE ITALIAN JOB
THE JAZZ SINGER
THE LAST TYCOON
THE LONGEST DAY
THE MERRY WIDOW *(M)*
THE MISSIONARY
THE NAKED TRUTH
THE PAJAMA GAME *(M)*
THE PAWNBROKER
THE ROSE TATTOO
  †† *(A Magnani)*
THE RUNAWAY BUS
THE SOUTHERNER
THE TENDER TRAP
THE WHISPERERS
THE WICKED LADY
THE WIZARD OF OZ *(M)*
TO BE OR NOT TO BE
TO CATCH A THIEF
TO SIR WITH LOVE
TWO WAY STRETCH
UNDER TWO FLAGS
UP THE JUNCTION
WATERSHIP DOWN *(C)*
WEST SIDE STORY
  F/D *(J Robbins & R Wise)*
WONDERFUL LIFE *(M)*
ZORBA THE GREEK

14

A DAY AT THE RACES
A HANDFUL OF DUST
A HARD DAY'S NIGHT *(M)*
ALL THE KING'S MEN
  F/† *(B Crawford)*
AMERICAN GIGOLO
ANIMAL CRACKERS
A PLACE IN THE SUN
  D *(G Stevens)*
A SHOT IN THE DARK
A TOWN LIKE ALICE
BICYCLE THIEVES
BLAZING SADDLES
BONNIE AND CLYDE
BREAKHEART PASS
BRIEF ENCOUNTER
BRINGING UP BABY
BROADWAY MELODY *(M)*
CARRY ON CAMPING
CARRY ON ENGLAND
CARRY ON TEACHER
CHARIOTS OF FIRE *F*
CHARLIE BUBBLES
DEATH ON THE NILE
DIAL M FOR MURDER
DOCTOR IN CLOVER
ELECTRIC DREAMS
EMPIRE OF THE SUN
ENTER THE DRAGON
EXECUTIVE SUITE
FINDERS KEEPERS *(M)*
FINIAN'S RAINBOW *(M)*
FIVE EASY PIECES
FOLLOW THE FLEET *(M)*
GOODBYE MR CHIPS
  † *(R Donat)*
GO WEST YOUNG MAN
HANGOVER SQUARE
I'M ALL RIGHT JACK
INHERIT THE WIND
IN WHICH WE SERVE
KRAMER vs KRAMER
  F/D/† *(R Benton/D Hoffman,*
LASSIE COME HOME

MIDNIGHT COWBOY
 F/D (J Schlesinger)
MONKEY BUSINESS
NATIONAL VELVET
OF HUMAN BONDAGE
ONLY TWO CAN PLAY
ORDINARY PEOPLE
 F/D (R Redford)
OUR MAN IN HAVANA
PAINT YOUR WAGON *(M)*
PLAY MISTY FOR ME
QUEEN CHRISTINA
REACH FOR THE SKY
ROAD TO HONG KONG
ROAD TO ZANZIBAR
SANDS OF IWO JIMA
SEPARATE TABLES
 † (D Niven)
SERGEANTS THREE
SEVEN DAYS IN MAY
SHADOW OF A DOUBT
TALES OF HOFFMAN *(M)*
THAT'LL BE THE DAY
THE CAINE MUTINY
THE COLOR PURPLE
THE ELEPHANT MAN
THE GAY DIVORCEE *(M)*
THE GOLD DIGGERS *(M)*
THE GOODBYE GIRL
 † (R Dreyfuss)
THE GREAT CARUSO
THE GREAT ESCAPE
THE GREAT GATSBY
THE IPCRESS FILE
THE JOKER IS WILD
THE JOLSON STORY
THE LADYKILLERS
THE LAST EMPEROR
 F/D (B Bertolucci)
THE LIFE OF BRIAN
THE LITTLE FOXES
THE LOST WEEKEND
 F/D/† (B Wilder/R Milland)
THE L-SHAPED ROOM
THE MARK OF ZORRO
THE MUSIC LOVERS
THE OKLAHOMA KID

THE PINK PANTHER
THE PUBLIC ENEMY
THE SEVENTH SEAL
THE SEVENTH VEIL
THE SINGING FOOL
THE WAGES OF FEAR
THIS HAPPY BREED
TROUBLE IN STORE
TWELVE ANGRY MEN
VANISHING POINT
YOUNG MR LINCOLN

15

ABOVE US THE WAVES
ALEXANDER NEVSKY
ANNIE GET YOUR GUN *(M)*
A PASSAGE TO INDIA
BACK TO THE FUTURE
BEDTIME FOR BONZO
BEVERLY HILLS COP
BHOWANI JUNCTION
CALIFORNIA SUITE
CARNAL KNOWLEDGE
CARRY ON CRUISING
CARRY ON SERGEANT
CROCODILE DUNDEE
DOCTOR IN TROUBLE
DOUBLE INDEMNITY
EVIL UNDER THE SUN
FANNY BY GASLIGHT
FANTASTIC VOYAGE
FATAL ATTRACTION
FLYING DOWN TO RIO *(M)*
FORBIDDEN PLANET
FOR YOUR EYES ONLY
FULL METAL JACKET
FUNERAL IN BERLIN
GONE WITH THE WIND
 F/D/†† (V Fleming/V Leigh)
ICE STATION ZEBRA
JOURNEY INTO FEAR
LA CAGE AUX FOLLES
LADY AND THE TRAMP *(C)*
LES BELLES DE NUIT
MEET ME IN ST LOUIS *(M)*

MIDNIGHT EXPRESS
MONSIEUR VERDOUX
MOVE OVER DARLING
ON THE WATERFRONT
 F/D/† (E Kazan/M Brando)
PLANET OF THE APES
PRIVATE BENJAMIN
RAISE THE TITANIC!
REAP THE WILD WIND
RETURN OF THE JEDI
ROAD TO SINGAPORE
SALLY IN OUR ALLEY
SHANGHAI EXPRESS
SHE DONE HIM WRONG
SINGIN' IN THE RAIN *(M)*
STATE OF THE UNION
STRIKE UP THE BAND *(M)*
SUNSET BOULEVARD
TARZAN THE APE MAN
THAT TOUCH OF MINK
THE AFRICAN QUEEN
 † (H Bogart)
THE COLDITZ STORY
THE COLOR OF MONEY
 † (P Newman)
THE FOUR FEATHERS
THE INVISIBLE MAN
THE LADY VANISHES
THE LEMON DROP KID
THE LION IN WINTER
 †† (K Hepburn)
THE SOUND OF MUSIC
 F/D (R Wise)
THE SUNSHINE BOYS
THE TAMARIND SEED
THE VAGABOND KING *(M)*
THREE MEN IN A BOAT
THREE SMART GIRLS
UNDER THE VOLCANO
VON RYAN'S EXPRESS
WATCH ON THE RHINE
 † (P Lukas)
WHERE EAGLES DARE
YANGTSE INCIDENT
YELLOW SUBMARINE *(C)*
YIELD TO THE NIGHT
ZIEGFELD FOLLIES *(M)*

ARTS

LITERATURE –
BOOK CHARACTERS – ANIMALS & BEINGS

3

KAA *(The Jungle Books – Kipling)*
KES *(Kes – Hines)*
NAG *(The Jungle Books – Kipling)*
OWL *(Winnie-the-Pooh series)*
ROO *(Winnie-the-Pooh series)*
THA *(The Jungle Books – Kipling)*

4

BUCK *(The Call Of The Wild – London)*
GRIP *(Barnaby Rudge – Dickens)*
IKKI *(The Jungle Books – Kipling)*
JAWS *(Jaws – Benchley)*
MANG *(The Jungle Books – Kipling)*
MOLE *(The Wind In The Willows – Grahame)*
RANN *(The Jungle Books – Kipling)*
SAHI *(The Jungle Books – Kipling)*
THUU *(The Jungle Books – Kipling)*
TOAD *(6M – The Wind In The Willows – Grahame)*
TOTO *(The Wizard Of Oz – Baum)*

5

AKELA *(The Jungle Books – Kipling)*
ASLAN *(Narnia series – Lewis)*
BABAR *(Babar series – Brunhoff)*
BALOO *(The Jungle Books – Kipling)*
BOXER *(Animal Farm – Orwell)*
(The Cricket On The Hearth – Dickens)
(Watership Down – Adams)
BUNGO *(Wombles series – Beresford)*
DINAH *(Alice In Wonderland – Carroll)*
FIVER *(Watership Down – Adams)*

FLINT *(12C – Treasure Island – Stevenson)*
GROKE *(Moomins series – Jansson)*
HATHI *(The Jungle Books – Kipling)*
HAZEL *(Watership Down – Adams)*
KANGA *(Winnie-the-Pooh series – Milne)*
MIFFY *(Miffy series – Bruna)*
MOPSY *(many – Potter)*
NODDY *(Noddy series – Blyton)*
RATTY *(The Wind In The Willows – Grahame)*
RIBBY *(The Tale Of Samuel Whiskers – Potter)*
SALAR *(Salar The Salmon – Williamson)*
SMAUG *(Lord Of The Rings – Tolkien)*
SNARK *(Through The Looking-Glass – Carroll)*
SNIFF *(Moomins series – Jansson)*
SPOTS *(The Jungle Books – Kipling)*
TARKA *(Tarka The Otter – Williamson)*
TIMMY *(Famous Five series – Blyton)*
TOMSK *(Wombles series – Beresford)*
VIPER *(Cold Comfort Farm – Gibbons)*

6

BADGER *(The Wind In The Willows – Grahame)*
BIGWIG *(Watership Down – Adams)*
BOOJUM *(Through The Looking-Glass – Carroll)*
DAB-DAB *(Dr Dolittle – Lofting)*
DAPPLE *(Don Quixote – Cervantes)*
DARZEE *(The Jungle Books – Kipling)*
EDISON *(Chitty Chitty Bang Bang – Fleming)*

EEYORE *(Winnie-the-Pooh series –*
Milne)
FLICKA *(My Friend Flicka – O'Hara)*
FLOPSY *(many – Potter)*
FRITHA *(The Snow Goose – Gallico)*
FUNGUS *(Fungus The Bogey Man –*
Briggs)
GOLLUM *(Lord Of The Rings –*
Tolkien)
GUB-GUB *(Dr Dolittle – Lofting)*
MOPPET *(many – Potter)*
MR PLOD *(Noddy series – Blyton)*
MR TOAD *(The Wind In The Willows –*
Grahame)
PIGLET *(Winnie-the-Pooh series –*
Milne)
RABBIT *(Winnie-the-Pooh series –*
Milne)
RUPERT *(Rupert Bear series –*
Tourtel/Bestall)
SMILER *(The Jungle Books – Kipling)*
TIGGER *(Winnie-the-Pooh series –*
Milne)
TIN MAN *(The Wizard Of Oz – Baum)*
UNDINE *(Undine – Fouqué)*
YAHOOS *(Gulliver's Travels – Swift)*
ZEPHIR *(Babar series – Brunhoff)*

7

AIMLESS *(Cold Comfort Farm –*
Gibbons)
BAGGINS *(12B, 12F – Lord Of The*
Rings – Tolkien)
BIG EARS *(Noddy series – Blyton)*
BRER FOX *(Uncle Remus stories –*
Harris)
CELESTE *(Babar series – Brunhoff)*
CHEETAH *(Tarzan series – Burroughs)*
GANDALF *(Lord Of The Rings –*
Tolkien)
GRYPHON *(Alice In Wonderland –*
Carroll)
HALCYON *(Tarka The Otter –*
Williamson)

HEMULEN *(Moomins series –*
Jansson)
HOBBITS *(Lord Of The Rings –*
Tolkien)
JUSTICE *(Black Beauty – Sewell)*
KALA NAG *(The Jungle Books –*
Kipling)
MITTENS *(many – Potter)*
MOOMINS *(Moomins series –*
Jansson)
NAGAINA *(The Jungle Books –*
Kipling)
ORINOCO *(Wombles series –*
Beresford)
PHOENIX *(The Phoenix And The*
Carpet – Nesbit)
RED KING *(Through The Looking-Glass*
– Carroll)
SHARDIK *(Shardik – Adams)*
SNUFKIN *(Moomins series – Jansson)*
WOMBLES *(Wombles series –*
Beresford)

8

BAGHEERA *(The Jungle Books –*
Kipling)
BRER WOLF *(Uncle Remus stories –*
Harris)
BULL'S EYE *(Oliver Twist – Dickens)*
DIOGENES *(Dombey And Son –*
Dickens)
DORMOUSE *(Alice In Wonderland –*
Carroll)
FECKLESS *(Cold Comfort Farm –*
Gibbons)
FUZZYPEG *(Fuzzypeg Goes To School*
– Uttley)
ISSI NOHO *(Issi Noho series –*
Chatfield)
MOBY DICK *(Moby Dick – Melville)*
MORLOCKS *(The Time Machine –*
Wells)
MR TUMNUS *(Narnia series – Lewis)*
NAPOLEON *(Animal Farm – Orwell)*

RED QUEEN *(Through The Looking-Glass – Carroll)*
SNOWBALL *(Animal Farm – Orwell)*
TOADFLAX *(Watership Down – Adams)*
WHITE-TIP *(Tarka The Otter – Williamson)*

9

BLACK BESS *(Rookwood – Ainsworth)*
CORNELIUS *(Babar series – Brunhoff)*
GARGANTUA *(Gargantua And Pantagruel – Rabelais)*
GRACELESS *(Cold Comfort Farm – Gibbons)*
MAD HATTER *(Alice In Wonderland – Carroll)*
MARCH HARE *(Alice In Wonderland – Carroll)*
MERRYLEGS *(Black Beauty – Sewell)*
MUNCHKINS *(The Wizard Of Oz – Baum)*
POINTLESS *(Cold Comfort Farm – Gibbons)*
RED KNIGHT *(Through The Looking-Glass – Carroll)*
ROSINANTE *(Don Quixote – Cervantes)*
SCARECROW *(The Wizard Of Oz – Baum)*
SHERE KHAN *(The Jungle Books – Kipling)*
SLOW-SOLID *(The Jungle Books – Kipling)*
TOBERMORY *(Wombles series – Beresford)*
TOM KITTEN *(The Tale Of Tom Kitten – Potter)*
WHITE FANG *(White Fang – London)*
WHITE KING *(Through The Looking-Glass – Carroll)*
WON-TOLLER *(The Jungle Books – Kipling)*

10

BRER RABBIT *(Uncle Remus stories – Harris)*
COTTONTAIL *(many – Potter)*
HOUYHNHNMS *(Gulliver's Travels – Swift)*
HUNCA MUNCA *(The Tale Of Two Bad Mice – Potter)*
JABBERWOCK *(Through The Looking-Glass – Carroll)*
JUBJUB BIRD *(Through The Looking-Glass – Carroll)*
MOCK TURTLE *(Alice In Wonderland – Carroll)*
MOULDIWARP *(The House Of Arden – Nesbit)*
PADDINGTON *(Paddington Bear series – Bond)*
PANTAGRUEL *(Gargantua And Pantagruel – Rabelais)*
REEPICHEEP *(Narnia series – Lewis)*
RUPERT BEAR *(Rupert Bear series – Tourtel/Bestall)*
STIKKERSEE *(Tarka The Otter – Williamson)*
THE PIEBALD *(National Velvet – Bagnold)*
TWEEDLEDEE *(Through The Looking-Glass – Carroll)*
TWEEDLEDUM *(Through The Looking-Glass – Carroll)*
WELLINGTON *(Wombles series – Beresford)*
WHITE QUEEN *(Through The Looking-Glass – Carroll)*
WIZARD OF OZ *(The Wizard Of Oz – Baum)*

11

BLACK BEAUTY *(Black Beauty – Sewell)*
CATERPILLAR *(Alice In Wonderland – Carroll)*

CHESHIRE CAT *(Alice In Wonderland – Carroll)*

MONTMORENCY *(Three Men In A Boat – Jerome)*

MOOMINMAMMA *(Moomins series – Jansson)*

MOOMINPAPPA *(Moomins series – Jansson)*

MOOMINTROLL *(Moomins series – Jansson)*

PETER RABBIT *(The Tale Of Peter Rabbit – Potter)*

SNORK MAIDEN *(Moomins series – Jansson)*

WHITE RABBIT *(Alice In Wonderland – Carroll)*

12

BANDERSNATCH *(Through The Looking-Glass – Carroll)*

BILBO BAGGINS *(Lord Of The Rings – Tolkien)*

CAPTAIN FLINT *(Treasure Island – Stevenson)*

COWARDLY LION *(The Wizard Of Oz – Baum)*

FRODO BAGGINS *(Lord Of The Rings – Tolkien)*

HUMPTY-DUMPTY *(Through The Looking-Glass – Carroll)*

JEREMY FISHER *(The Tale Of Jeremy Fisher – Potter)*

KING OF HEARTS *(Alice In Wonderland – Carroll)*

PIGLING BLAND *(The Tale Of Pigling Bland – Potter)*

PUSHMI-PULLYU *(Dr Dolittle – Lofting)*

13

AUNT PETTITOES *(The Tale Of Pigling Bland – Potter)*

BENJAMIN BUNNY *(The Tale Of Benjamin Bunny – Potter)*

KNAVE OF HEARTS *(Alice In Wonderland – Carroll)*

LITTLE MERMAID *(The Little Mermaid – Andersen)*

QUEEN OF HEARTS *(Alice In Wonderland – Carroll)*

UNCLE BULGARIA *(Wombles series – Beresford)*

WINNIE-THE-POOH *(Winnie-the-Pooh series – Milne)*

14

HATTIFATTENERS *(Moomins series – Jansson)*

MRS TIGGYWINKLE *(The Tale Of Mrs Tiggywinkle – Potter)*

MRS TITTLEMOUSE *(The Tale Of Mrs Tittlemouse – Potter)*

PADDINGTON BEAR *(Paddington Bear series – Bond)*

RIKKI-TIKKI-TAVI *(The Jungle Books – Kipling)*

SAMUEL WHISKERS *(The Tale Of Samuel Whiskers – Potter)*

SQUIRREL NUTKIN *(The Tale Of Squirrel Nutkin – Potter)*

WORZEL GUMMIDGE *(Worzel Gummidge series – Todd)*

15

TABITHA TWITCHIT *(The Tale Of Tom Kitten – Potter)*

ARTS

LITERATURE – BOOK CHARACTERS – DICKENS

(Bleak) = Bleak House   (Carol) = A Christmas Carol
(Chimes) = The Chimes   (Chuzz) = Martin Chuzzlewit
(Cities) = A Tale Of Two Cities   (Cop) = David Copperfield
(Curi) = The Old Curiosity Shop   (Dombey) = Dombey And Son
(Dorrit) = Little Dorrit   (Drood) = The Mystery Of Edwin Drood
(Great) = Great Expectations   (Hard) = Hard Times
(Mudfog) = The Mudfog Papers   (Mutual) = Our Mutual Friend
(Nick) = Nicholas Nickleby   (Pick) = Pickwick Papers
(Rudge) = Barnaby Rudge   (Trav) = The Uncommercial Traveller
(Twist) = Oliver Twist

3

BAR *(Dorrit)*
BEN *(Twist)*
BET *(5B-Twist)*
BIB *(9J-Chuzz)*
BOB *(Dorrit)*
CLY *(8R-Cities)*
FAN *(Carol)*
FEE *(5D, 9D-Mudfog)*
GAY *(9W-Dombey)*
JEM *(Pick)*
JOE *(Carol)*
 (Cities)
 (Dombey)
 (Drood)
 (Pick)
 (Twist)
LIZ *(Bleak)*
NED *(Twist)*
PIP *(Chuzz)*
 (Great)
SAM *(Chuzz)*
TIM *(7T-Carol)*
TIX *(6T-Nick)*
TOM *(Cities)*
 (10C-Great)
 (Nick)
 (Pick)

4

ANNE *(Dombey)*
ANNY *(Twist)*
BAPS *(Dombey)*
BELL *(10K-Mudfog)*
BILL *(Great)*
 (Pick)
 (Twist)
BRAY *(10W, 12M-Nick)*
CLIP *(Mudfog)*
COBB *(7T-Rudge)*
CUTE *(12A-Chimes)*
DICK *(Chuzz)*
 (6M-Cop)
 (Nick)
 (Twist)
DO'EM *(Mudfog)*
DOZE *(13P-Mudfog)*
DUFF *(Twist)*
DULL *(Mudfog)*
EMMA *(Pick)*
FANG *(Twist)*
FERN *(8W, 10L-Chimes)*
FIPS *(Chuzz)*
FISH *(Chimes)*
FOGG *(Pick)*
FRED *(Carol)*
GRUB *(Mudfog)*
 (11G-Pick)

HAWK *(15S-Nick)*
HEEP *(9U-Cop)*
HUGH *(Rudge)*
HUMM *(11A-Pick)*
HUNT *(Pick)*
JACK *(Chuzz)*
JANE *(Chuzz)*
 (Nick)
 (Pick)
JODD *(Chuzz)*
JOEY *(11C-Mutual)*
JOHN *(Dombey)*
 (Pick)
 (Trav)
JOWL *(7J-Curi)*
JUPE *(10S-Hard)*
KAGS *(Twist)*
KATE *(Dombey)*
 (Pick)
KLEM *(Trav)*
KNAG *(12M-Nick)*
LIST *(9I-Curi)*
MARY *(Pick)*
MELL *(11C-Cop)*
MIKE *(Great)*
MUFF *(13P-Mudfog)*
MULL *(13P-Mudfog)*
NOGO *(13P-Mudfog)*
OMER *(10M-Cop)*
OWEN *(8J-Curi)*

PEAK *(Rudge)*
PEGG *(Trav)*
PELL *(11S-Pick)*
PEPS *(6D, 10D-Dombey)*
POTT *(Pick)*
PYKE *(Nick)*
RIAH *(Mutual)*
ROSA *(Bleak)*
RUGG *(13A-Dorrit)*
SLUG *(Mudfog)*
SLUM *(Curi)*
SMIF *(10P-Chuzz)*
TIGG *(12M-Chuzz)*
TIPP *(Cop)*
TOPE *(Drood)*
VECK *(8T, 12M-Chimes)*
WEGG *(9S-Mutual)*
WOLF *(Chuzz)*

5

ADAMS *(Cop)*
    (9J-Dombey)
    (12C-Nick)
ALICE *(Nick)*
ALLEN *(13A, 13B-Pick)*
BATES *(12C-Twist)*
BECKY *(Twist)*
BELLE *(Carol)*
BENCH *(Dorrit)*
BERRY *(Dorrit)*
BETSY *(Pick)*
    (Twist)
BEVAN *(Chuzz)*
BIDDY *(Great)*
BILER *(Dombey)*
BLANK *(Mudfog)*
BLAZO *(12C-Pick)*
BLOGG *(Mutual)*
BLUBB *(Mudfog)*
BOOTS *(Mutual)*
BRASS *(10S, 12S-Curi)*
BRICK *(14J-Chuzz)*
BROWN *(Curi)*
    (Mudfog)

BUFFY *(12W-Bleak)*
BULPH *(Nick)*
CARLO *(Curi)*
CASBY *(Dorrit)*
CHICK *(9J-Dombey)*
CHIPS *(Trav)*
CHOKE *(12G-Chuzz)*
CLARK *(Dombey)*
CLIVE *(Dorrit)*
COBBY *(Trav)*
CROWL *(Nick)*
DAISY *(12S-Rudge)*
DARBY *(Bleak)*
    (Trav)
DAVID *(Nick)*
DINGO *(14P-Bleak)*
DIVER *(12C-Chuzz)*
DOLLS *(7M-Mutual)*
DOYCE *(11D-Dorrit)*
DR FEE *(Mudfog)*
DROOD *(10E-Drood)*
DUMMY *(Mudfog)*
EVANS *(12R-Curi)*
FAGIN *(Twist)*
FIERY *(12C-Mudfog)*
FILER *(Chimes)*
FOLEY *(Dombey)*
FOXEY *(7D, 11D-Mudfog)*
GILES *(Twist)*
GILLS *(12S-Dombey)*
GOWAN *(10H-Dorrit)*
GREEN *(Bleak)*
    (8T-Rudge)
GRIDE *(11A-Nick)*
GRIME *(14P-Mudfog)*
GUPPY *(12W-Bleak)*
HARRY *(Curi)*
    (Twist)
HENRY *(Pick)*
HEXAM *(10J, 11L,*
    12C-Mutual)
ISAAC *(Pick)*
JAMES *(10H-Dombey)*
JANET *(Cop)*
JENNY *(Bleak)*
JERRY *(Curi)*

JINKS *(Pick)*
JOBBA *(Mudfog)*
JONES *(Bleak)*
    (11G-Mutual)
JOPER *(10B-Dombey)*
JORAM *(8J, 11M-Cop)*
KENGE *(Bleak)*
KETCH *(14P-Mudfog)*
KINCH *(11H-Trav)*
KROOK *(Bleak)*
LORRY *(11J-Cities)*
LOUIS *(Trav)*
LUCAS *(12S-Pick)*
LUMMY *(8N-Chuzz)*
MAGGY *(Dorrit)*
'MELIA *(Dombey)*
MERCY *(Trav)*
MILLS *(10J-Cop)*
MISTY *(Mudfog)*
MOBBS *(Nick)*
MOLLY *(Great)*
MONKS *(Twist)*
MOULD *(Chuzz)*
MUDGE *(10J-Pick)*
NAMBY *(Pick)*
NANCY *(Twist)*
NANDY *(15J-Dorrit)*
NEDDY *(Pick)*
NODDY *(Pick)*
NOGGS *(11N-Nick)*
PAYNE *(7D, 11D-Pick)*
PEDRO *(Curi)*
PERCH *(Dombey)*
PINCH *(8T, 9R-Chuzz)*
PIPER *(14P-Chuzz)*
PLUCK *(Nick)*
POLLY *(Bleak)*
PRICE *(Pick)*
PROSS *(12S-Cities)*
QUALE *(Bleak)*
QUILP *(11D-Curi)*
ROKER *(8T-Pick)*
RUDGE *(12B-Rudge)*
SALLY *(Twist)*
SAXBY *(9L-Dombey)*
SCOTT *(8T-Curi)*

SCROO *(Mudfog)*
SHARP *(Cop)*
SIKES *(9B-Twist)*
SLOUT *(Twist)*
SLURK *(Pick)*
SLYME *(10C-Chuzz)*
SMART *(8T-Pick)*
SMIKE *(Nick)*
SMITH *(Mudfog)*
SNIPE *(11W-Pick)*
SNOBB *(Nick)*
SNORE *(14P-Mudfog)*
SQUOD *(9P-Bleak)*
STAGG *(Rudge)*
SUSAN *(Twist)*
TOMMY *(Pick)*
TOOTS *(Dombey)*
TOZER *(Dombey)*
TRABB *(Great)*
TRENT *(9N, 14F-Curi)*
TRUCK *(Mudfog)*
TUGBY *(Chimes)*
TWIST *(11O-Twist)*
VENUS *(Mutual)*
WATTY *(Pick)*
WICKS *(Pick)*

6

AFFERY *(Dorrit)*
AMELIA *(Great)*
BABLEY *(13R-Cop)*
BADGER *(12B-Bleak)*
BAGNET *(11M, 12Q, 13M, 14W-Bleak)*
BAILEY *(14B-Chuzz)* *(13C-Cop)*
BAMBER *(10J-Pick)*
BANTAM *(12A-Pick)*
BARKER *(10P-Twist)*
BARKIS *(Cop)*
BARLEY *(11C, 13O-Great)*
BARNEY *(Twist)*
BARSAD *(10J-Cities)*
BAYTON *(Twist)*
BELLER *(11H-Pick)*

BISHOP *(Dorrit)*
BITZER *(Hard)*
BLIGHT *(Mutual)*
BOCKER *(9T-Mutual)*
BOFFER *(Pick)*
BOFFIN *(15N-Mutual)*
BOGSBY *(11J-Bleak)*
BOLDER *(Nick)*
BOLTER *(12M-Twist)*
BOLTON *(12R-Mudfog)*
BONNEY *(Nick)*
BOODLE *(10L-Bleak)*
BOWLEY *(12M, 15S-Chimes)*
BREWER *(Mutual)*
BRIGGS *(Dombey)*
BROOKS *(Nick)* *(Pick)*
BUCKET *(15I-Bleak)*
BUFFER *(8D, 12D-Mudfog)*
BUFFUM *(11O-Chuzz)*
BULDER *(13C-Pick)*
BUMBLE *(Twist)*
BUNSBY *(13C-Dombey)*
BURTON *(12T-Pick)*
BUZFUZ *(14S-Pick)*
CARKER *(10J, 11J, 13H-Dombey)*
CARTER *(Mudfog)*
CARTON *(12S-Cities)*
CHEGGS *(11A-Curi)*
CICERO *(Chuzz)*
COBBEY *(Nick)*
COCKER *(Trav)*
CODLIN *(12T-Curi)*
CONWAY *(13G-Rudge)*
CRIPPS *(9T-Pick)*
CURDLE *(Nick)*
CUTLER *(Nick)*
CUTTLE *(13C-Dombey)*
DABBER *(Nick)*
DARNAY *(13C-Cities)*
DEMPLE *(12G-Cop)*
DENNIS *(9N-Rudge)*
DEPUTY *(Drood)*
DIBBLE *(13D, 13S-Trav)*
DODSON *(Pick)*

DOMBEY *(10P, 11E, 11F, 14F-Dombey)*
DORKER *(Nick)*
DORRIT *(9A, 9T, 11F, 12E, 12L, 13W, 15F-Dorrit)*
DOWLER *(13C-Pick)*
DR PEPS *(Dombey)*
DUNKLE *(8D, 12D-Chuzz)*
FEEDER *(14R-Dombey)*
FEENIX *(10L-Dombey)*
FIZKIN *(13H-Pick)*
FOLAIR *(Nick)*
GANDER *(Chuzz)*
GEORGE *(Cop)* *(Curi)* *(Nick)*
GORDON *(10E, 10L, 13C-Rudge)*
GRIGGS *(Pick)*
GROPER *(13C-Chuzz)*
GROVES *(11J-Curi)*
GRUEBY *(10J-Rudge)*
GRUNDY *(Pick)*
GUNTER *(Pick)*
GUSHER *(Bleak)*
GUSTER *(Bleak)*
HANNAH *(Nick)*
HARMON *(10J-Mutual)*
HARRIS *(Curi)* *(Pick)*
HAWDON *(13C-Bleak)*
HOWLER *(14R-Dombey)*
HUBBLE *(Great)*
HUNTER *(9L-Pick)*
HUTLEY *(11J-Pick)*
IZZARD *(Chuzz)*
JASPER *(10J-Drood)*
JEMIMA *(Dombey)*
JINGLE *(12A-Pick)*
JOHNNY *(Mutual)*
KETTLE *(15L-Chuzz)*
KIBBLE *(11J-Mutual)*
KIMBER *(Drood)*
LAMMLE *(12A-Mutual)*
LEAVER *(Mudfog)*

LIVELY *(Twist)*
LOBLEY *(Drood)*
LOWTEN *(Pick)*
LUFFEY *(Pick)*
LUMBEY *(8D, 12D-Nick)*
MAGNUS *(11P-Pick)*
MALDON *(10J-Cop)*
MALLET *(Mudfog)*
MARLEY *(11J-Carol)*
MAROON *(13C-Dorrit)*
MARTHA *(Dombey)*
(Twist)
MARTIN *(13C-Dorrit)*
(9T, 10J,
11B-Pick)
MARTON *(Curi)*
MAYDAY *(Trav)*
MAYLIE *(10R, 11H-Twist)*
MERDLE *(Dorrit)*
MIGGOT *(Trav)*
MILLER *(Pick)*
MILVEY *(14R-Mutual)*
MIVINS *(Pick)*
MODDLE *(14A-Chuzz)*
MOONEY *(Bleak)*
MORFIN *(Dombey)*
MR DICK *(Cop)*
MULLIT *(15P-Chuzz)*
MUNTLE *(Nick)*
MUZZLE *(Pick)*
NOAKES *(Mudfog)*
ORLICK *(11D-Great)*
PANCKS *(Dorrit)*
PARKES *(10P-Rudge)*
PARKLE *(Trav)*
PEPPER *(Great)*
PERKER *(Pick)*
PHOEBE *(Nick)*
PHUNKY *(Pick)*
PIDGER *(Cop)*
PIPKIN *(Mudfog)*
(15N-Pick)
PIRRIP *(12P-Great)*
POCKET *(9J, 10J, 11A,*
11F, 11S, 13H,
13M-Great)

PODDER *(Pick)*
POGRAM *(12E-Chuzz)*
PROSEE *(Mudfog)*
PUPKER *(Nick)*
RADDLE *(Pick)*
RAMSEY *(Pick)*
RIGAUD *(Dorrit)*
RUMMAN *(15P-Mudfog)*
SAPSEA *(12T-Drood)*
SAWYER *(Mudfog)*
(9B-Pick)
SCALEY *(Nick)*
SLEARY *(Hard)*
SLINGO *(Dorrit)*
SLOPPY *(Mutual)*
SMOUCH *(Pick)*
SNIGGS *(Mudfog)*
SNIVEY *(Mudfog)*
SOEMUP *(8D, 12D-Mudfog)*
SOPHIA *(Chuzz)*
(Great)
SOWNDS *(Dombey)*
SPECKS *(9J-Trav)*
SPIKER *(11H-Cop)*
SPYERS *(9J-Twist)*
STAPLE *(Pick)*
STRONG *(8D, 12D-Cop)*
STYLES *(Mudfog)*
TACKER *(Chuzz)*
TADGER *(13B-Pick)*
TANGLE *(Bleak)*
TAPLEY *(10M-Chuzz)*
TARTAR *(Drood)*
THOMAS *(Bleak)*
(Nick)
(Pick)
TICKLE *(Mudfog)*
TIFFEY *(Cop)*
TOM TIX *(Nick)*
TOODLE *(11R-Dombey)*
TOOTLE *(9T-Mutual)*
TOPPER *(Carol)*
TUCKLE *(Pick)*
TUNGAY *(Cop)*
TUPMAN *(11T-Pick)*
VARDEN *(11D, 13G-Rudge)*

VHOLES *(Bleak)*
VILLAM *(Pick)*
VUFFIN *(Curi)*
WALKER *(10M-Cop)*
(Pick)
WARDLE *(11E, 13R,*
14I-Pick)
WELLER *(9S, 10T,*
12S-Pick)
WHEEZY *(15P-Mudfog)*
WIGSBY *(Mudfog)*
WILFER *(11B, 13L,*
14R-Mutual)
WILLET *(9J, 10J-Rudge)*
WINKLE *(15N-Pick)*
WOPSLE *(Great)*
YAWLER *(Cop)*

7

AKERMAN *(Rudge)*
ANTONIO *(Trav)*
BARBARA *(Curi)*
BARDELL *(12T, 13M-Pick)*
BATTENS *(Trav)*
BAZZARD *(Drood)*
BELLING *(Nick)*
BELLOWS *(14B-Dorrit)*
BLIMBER *(9D, 13D,*
15C-Dombey)
BLOTTON *(Pick)*
BLOWERS *(Bleak)*
BOBSTER *(Nick)*
BOLDWIG *(14C-Pick)*
BROGLEY *(Dombey)*
BROOKER *(Nick)*
BROWDIE *(11J-Nick)*
BULLAMY *(Chuzz)*
BULLMAN *(Pick)*
CAMILLA *(Great)*
CHARLEY *(Cop)*
(Pick)
CHESTER *(13E, 14S-Rudge)*
CHESTLE *(Cop)*
CHIGGLE *(Chuzz)*
CHILLIP *(9D, 13D-Cop)*

CHIVERY *(11J-Dorrit)*
CHOLLOP *(12M-Chuzz)*
CHOWSER *(14C-Nick)*
CHUFFEY *(Chuzz)*
CLEAVER *(12F-Mutual)*
CLENNAM *(13A, 14G-Dorrit)*
CLUBBER *(11L-Pick)*
CRACKIT *(11T-Twist)*
CREAKLE *(Cop)*
CREWLER *(12S, 15R-Cop)*
CRIMPLE *(12D-Chuzz)*
CROOKEY *(Pick)*
DAWKINS *(11J-Twist)*
DEDLOCK *(11L, 15V-Bleak)*
DEEDLES *(Chimes)*
DEFARGE *(13E, 13M-Cities)*
DOLLOBY *(Cop)*
DRAWLEY *(Mudfog)*
DR FOXEY *(Mudfog)*
DR PAYNE *(Mudfog)*
DRUMMLE *(14B-Great)*
DUBBLEY *(Pick)*
DUMKINS *(Pick)*
DURDLES *(Drood)*
EDMUNDS *(11J-Pick)*
ESTELLA *(Great)*
FIZZGIG *(Pick)*
FLASHER *(14W-Pick)*
FLOPSON *(Great)*
FLOWERS *(Dombey)*
GABELLE *(Cities)*
GARGERY *(10J-Great)*
GARLAND *(11A-Curi)*
GASPARD *(Cities)*
GILBERT *(11M-Rudge)*
GLAMOUR *(10B-Mutual)*
GLOBSON *(12B-Trav)*
GOODWIN *(Pick)*
GRAYPER *(Cop)*
GREGORY *(Cop)*
GRIDLEY *(Bleak)*
GRIMBLE *(Nick)*
GRIMWIG *(Twist)*
GRINDER *(Curi)*
GROFFIN *(13T-Pick)*
GROMPUS *(Mutual)*

GRUBBLE *(Bleak)*
GRUMMER *(13D-Pick)*
HAGGAGE *(9D, 13D-Dorrit)*
HAWKINS *(Mutual)*
HERBERT *(Rudge)*
HEYLING *(13G-Pick)*
HOPKINS *(14C-Cop)*
(11J-Pick)
JACKSON *(14M-Bleak)*
(Dorrit)
(Pick)
JAGGERS *(Great)*
JELLYBY *(12C, 12P,*
15C-Bleak)
JENKINS *(Nick)*
JINKINS *(Chuzz)*
(Pick)
JOBLING *(11T-Bleak)*
(9D, 13D-Chuzz)
JOE JOWL *(Curi)*
JOHNSON *(10T-Dombey)*
(Nick)
JORKINS *(Cop)*
KEDGICK *(14C-Nick)*
KENWIGS *(15M-Nick)*
KWAKLEY *(Mudfog)*
LARKINS *(Cop)*
LAZARUS *(Great)*
LEEFORD *(12E, 13E-Twist)*
LEWSOME *(Chuzz)*
LINSEED *(13D-Mutual)*
MALLARD *(Pick)*
MANETTE *(9D, 12L,*
13D-Cities)
MANNING *(Pick)*
MARKHAM *(Cop)*
MEAGLES *(10P, 13M-Dorrit)*
MELLOWS *(Trav)*
MERCURY *(Bleak)*
MILLERS *(Great)*
MORDLIN *(14B-Pick)*
MORTAIR *(Mudfog)*
MR DOLLS *(Mutual)*
MRS BAPS *(Dombey)*
MRS GILL *(Chuzz)*
MRS HEEP *(Cop)*

MRS KLEM *(Trav)*
MRS MANN *(Twist)*
MRS MELL *(Cop)*
MRS MIFF *(Dombey)*
MRS PIPE *(Bleak)*
MRS POTT *(Pick)*
MRS TOPE *(Drood)*
MULLINS *(11J-Mutual)*
NADGETT *(Chuzz)*
NECKETT *(10T, 11E-Bleak)*
NUBBLES *(10K, 12J-Curi)*
NUPKINS *(13G-Pick)*
PAWKINS *(12M-Chuzz)*
PESSELL *(Mudfog)*
PILKINS *(Dombey)*
PITCHER *(Nick)*
PODSNAP *(11J-Mutual)*
POTKINS *(14W-Great)*
PRUFFLE *(Pick)*
QUINION *(Cop)*
RACHAEL *(Hard)*
RADFOOT *(13G-Mutual)*
RAYMOND *(Great)*
RICHARD *(Chimes)*
(Nick)
ROSA BUD *(Drood)*
SAMPSON *(13G-Mutual)*
SCADDER *(15Z-Chuzz)*
SCROOGE *(15E-Carol)*
SIMMERY *(12F-Pick)*
SIMMONS *(14W-Chuzz)*
SIMPSON *(Pick)*
SKIMPIN *(Pick)*
SLAMMER *(9D, 13D-Pick)*
SLASHER *(Pick)*
SLUMKEY *(13S-Pick)*
SMANGLE *(Pick)*
SMAUKER *(11J-Pick)*
SMITHIE *(Pick)*
SNAGSBY *(Bleak)*
SNAWLEY *(Nick)*
SNEWKES *(Nick)*
SNUBBIN *(15S-Pick)*
SNUFFIM *(Nick)*
SOWSTER *(Mudfog)*
SPARSIT *(Hard)*

SPENLOW *(11D, 14F, 14L, 15C-Cop)*
SQUEERS *(12F, 15W-Nick)*
STABLES *(10B-Bleak)*
STARTOP *(Great)*
STRYVER *(Cities)*
SWOSSER *(14C-Bleak)*
TAMAROO *(Chuzz)*
TIMPSON *(Trav)*
TINKLER *(Dorrit)*
TINY TIM *(Carol)*
TOM COBB *(Rudge)*
TOMKINS *(Nick)*
TOORELL *(9D, 13D-Mudfog)*
TROTTER *(10J-Pick)*
TRUNDLE *(Pick)*
TWEMLOW *(13M-Mutual)*
TWIGGER *(13E-Mudfog)*
UPWITCH *(14R-Pick)*
WAGHORN *(Mudfog)*
WATKINS *(Nick)*
WEMMICK *(11J-Great)*
WHIFFIN *(Pick)*
WILKINS *(11D-Carol)* *(Pick)*
WILLIAM *(Cop)* *(Nick)*
WITHERS *(Dombey)*
WOBBLER *(Dorrit)*

8

ADA CLARE *(Bleak)*
ALPHONSE *(Nick)*
ANDERSON *(12J-Trav)*
ANGELICA *(Trav)*
BAGSTOCK *(13M-Dombey)*
BARNACLE *(12L, 12T, 15W-Dorrit)*
BENJAMIN *(14T-Cop)* *(Rudge)*
BLATHERS *(Twist)*
BOYTHORN *(Bleak)*
BRITTLES *(Twist)*
BROWNLOW *(Twist)*

CAROLINE *(Carol)*
CARSTONE *(15R-Bleak)*
CHADBAND *(Bleak)*
CHILDERS *(Hard)*
CHINAMAN *(12J-Drood)*
CHITLING *(11T-Twist)*
CLAYPOLE *(12N-Twist)*
CLEVERLY *(15W-Trav)*
CLICKETT *(Cop)*
CRATCHIT *(11B, 11T-Carol)*
CRINKLES *(Mudfog)*
CRIPPLES *(14M-Dorrit)*
CRUMMLES *(13P, 14M, 15N, 15V-Nick)*
CRUNCHER *(13J-Cities)*
CRUSHTON *(Pick)*
DAME WEST *(Curi)*
DARK JACK *(Trav)*
DATCHERY *(12D-Drood)*
DR BUFFER *(Mudfog)*
DR DUNKLE *(Chuzz)*
DR LUMBEY *(Nick)*
DR SOEMUP *(Mudfog)*
DR STRONG *(Cop)*
FEZZIWIG *(Carol)*
FLADDOCK *(15G-Chuzz)*
FLEDGEBY *(Mutual)*
FLUGGERS *(Nick)*
FLUMMERY *(Mudfog)*
FRANÇOIS *(Dombey)*
GAMFIELD *(Twist)*
GASHFORD *(Rudge)*
GLIDDERY *(11B-Mutual)*
GRAINGER *(Cop)*
GRANNETT *(Twist)*
GULPIDGE *(Cop)*
HAREDALE *(12E-Rudge)*
HARRISON *(Mutual)*
HAVISHAM *(14A-Great)*
HORTENSE *(Bleak)*
JARNDYCE *(11T, 12J-Bleak)*
JENNINGS *(Mudfog)* *(Nick)*
JOE JORAM *(Cop)*
JOHN OWEN *(Curi)*
JOLTERED *(Mudfog)*

JONATHAN *(Mutual)*
LANDLESS *(14H, 15N-Drood)*
LANGDALE *(Rudge)*
LEDBRAIN *(Mudfog)*
LENVILLE *(14T-Nick)*
LIMBKINS *(Twist)*
LITTIMER *(Cop)*
LOSBERNE *(Twist)*
MAGWITCH *(12A-Great)*
MARGARET *(Pick)*
MARY ANNE *(Great)*
MARY DAWS *(Dombey)*
MAUNDERS *(Curi)*
MICAWBER *(12E, 15W-Cop)*
MISS BOLO *(Pick)*
MISS KITT *(Cop)*
MISS KLEM *(Trav)*
MISS KNAG *(Nick)*
MISS LANE *(Nick)*
MISS WADE *(Dorrit)*
MISS WISK *(Bleak)*
MRS BEVAN *(Nick)*
MRS BOKUM *(Dombey)*
MRS BORUM *(Nick)*
MRS BRICK *(Chuzz)*
MRS BROWN *(Dombey)*
MRS CHICK *(Dombey)*
MRS CLARK *(Nick)*
MRS CRUPP *(Cop)*
MRS DARBY *(Trav)*
MRS GOODY *(Mutual)*
MRS GOWAN *(Dorrit)*
MRS GUPPY *(Bleak)*
MRS JORAM *(Cop)*
MRS LUPIN *(Chuzz)*
MRS MITTS *(Trav)*
MRS MOULD *(Chuzz)*
MRS PERCH *(Dombey)*
MRS POUCH *(Bleak)*
MRS QUILP *(Curi)*
MRS RUDGE *(Rudge)*
MURDERER *(15C-Trav)*
MUTANHED *(12L-Pick)*
NED LUMMY *(Chuzz)*

NICKLEBY *(12K, 13R, 15G-Nick)*
OLD DAVID *(Curi)*
OLD GLUBB *(Dombey)*
OLD LOBBS *(Pick)*
PANGLOSS *(Trav)*
PEARTREE *(Drood)*
PEGGOTY *(11H, 11J, 13C, 14D-Cop)*
PICKWICK *(14S-Pick)*
PLORNISH *(14T-Dorrit)*
PURBLIND *(Mudfog)*
PYEGRAVE *(15C-Cop)*
QUICKEAR *(Trav)*
ROBINSON *(Dombey)*
ROGER CLY *(Cities)*
SCREWZER *(13T-Dombey)*
SHARPEYE *(Trav)*
SKETTLES *(12L, 14B-Dombey)*
SKIMPOLE *(13K, 13L, 14H-Bleak)*
SLADDERY *(Bleak)*
SMIGGERS *(14J-Pick)*
SPARKLER *(14E-Dorrit)*
STIGGINS *(Pick)*
TIMBERED *(Mudfog)*
TIMBERRY *(15S-Nick)*
TOBY VECK *(Chimes)*
TOM GREEN *(Rudge)*
TOM PINCH *(Chuzz)*
TOM ROKER *(Pick)*
TOM SCOTT *(Curi)*
TOM SMART *(Pick)*
TRADDLES *(14T-Cop)*
TREASURY *(Dorrit)*
TRIMMERS *(Nick)*
WESTLOCK *(12J-Chuzz)*
WESTWOOD *(Nick)*
WHIFFERS *(Pick)*
WILL FERN *(Chimes)*
WILLIAMS *(15W-Mutual)*
WRAYBURN *(14E-Mutual)*

9

AMY DORRIT *(Dorrit)*
BERINTHIA *(Dombey)*
BILL SIKES *(Twist)*
BLACK BILL *(Great)*
BLACKPOOL *(Hard)*
BLUNDERUM *(Mudfog)*
BOB SAWYER *(Pick)*
BOUNDERBY *(15J-Hard)*
BULLFINCH *(Trav)*
CARLAVERO *(Trav)*
CHARLOTTE *(Dorrit)* *(Twist)*
CHEERYBLE *(14E, 14F-Nick)*
CHICKWEED *(15C-Twist)*
CHUCKSTER *(Curi)*
CLARRIKER *(Great)*
COMPEYSON *(Great)*
DOCTOR FEE *(Mudfog)*
DR BLIMBER *(Dombey)*
DR CHILLIP *(Cop)*
DR HAGGAGE *(Dorrit)*
DR JOBLING *(Chuzz)*
DR MANETTE *(Cities)*
DR SLAMMER *(Pick)*
DR TOORELL *(Mudfog)*
DUNSTABLE *(Great)*
FLIPFIELD *(12T-Trav)*
GEORGIANA *(Great)*
GRADGRIND *(12T, 13A, 13J, 15L, 15T-Hard)*
GRAYMARSH *(Nick)*
GREGSBURY *(Nick)*
GREWGIOUS *(14H-Drood)*
GRUMMIDGE *(11D, 15D-Mudfog)*
HARTHOUSE *(14J-Hard)*
HEADSTONE *(Mutual)*
ISAAC LIST *(Curi)*
JACK ADAMS *(Dombey)*
JEM SPYERS *(Twist)*
JENKINSON *(Dorrit)*
JOE POCKET *(Great)*

JOE SPECKS *(Trav)*
JOE WILLET *(Rudge)*
JOHN CHICK *(Dombey)*
JULIUS BIB *(Chuzz)*
KINDHEART *(Trav)*
LEO HUNTER *(Pick)*
LIGHTWOOD *(Mutual)*
LILLYVICK *(Nick)*
LONG SAXBY *(Dombey)*
LORD MAYOR *(Rudge)*
LUCY GREEN *(Trav)*
MANTALINI *(15A, 15M-Nick)*
MARY JONES *(Rudge)*
MISS DAWES *(Dorrit)*
MISS FLITE *(Bleak)*
MISS GREEN *(Nick)*
MISS GWYNN *(Pick)*
MISS MIGGS *(Rudge)*
MISS PROSS *(Cities)*
MRS BADGER *(Bleak)*
MRS BAYTON *(Twist)*
MRS BEDWIN *(Twist)*
MRS BOFFIN *(Mutual)*
MRS BOGLES *(Trav)*
MRS BOLTER *(Twist)*
MRS BUCKET *(Bleak)*
MRS BUDGER *(Pick)*
MRS BULDER *(Pick)*
MRS BUMBLE *(Twist)*
MRS COILER *(Great)*
MRS CORNEY *(Twist)*
MRS CURDLE *(Nick)*
MRS CUTLER *(Nick)*
MRS DOWLER *(Pick)*
MRS GEORGE *(Curi)*
MRS HARMON *(Mutual)*
MRS HARRIS *(Chuzz)*
MRS HOMINY *(Chuzz)*
MRS HUBBLE *(Great)*
MRS HUNTER *(Pick)*
MRS JARLEY *(Curi)*
MRS LAMMLE *(Mutual)*
MRS MARKER *(Nick)*
MRS MAYLIE *(Twist)*
MRS MERDLE *(Dorrit)*
MRS MILVEY *(Mutual)*

MRS PEGLER *(Hard)*
MRS POCKET *(Great)*
MRS QUINCH *(Trav)*
MRS RADDLE *(Pick)*
MRS ROGERS *(Pick)*
MRS SPECKS *(Trav)*
MRS SPIKER *(Cop)*
MRS STRONG *(Cop)*
MRS TICKIT *(Dorrit)*
MRS TISHER *(Drood)*
MRS TOODLE *(Dombey)*
MRS VARDEN *(Rudge)*
MRS WARDLE *(Pick)*
MRS WELLER *(Pick)*
MRS WICKAM *(Dombey)*
MRS WILFER *(Mutual)*
MRS WRYMUG *(Nick)*
MRS WUGSBY *(Pick)*
MURDSTONE *(13J,15E-Cop)*
NED DENNIS *(Rudge)*
NEESHAWTS *(11D,*
    15D-Mudfog)
NELL TRENT *(Curi)*
NOCKEMORF *(Pick)*
PARDIGGLE *(14F, 15A, 15E,*
    15O-Bleak)
PASSNIDGE *(Bleak)*
PECKSNIFF *(13S, 14M,*
    15C-Chuzz)
PHIL SQUOD *(Bleak)*
PORKENHAM *(15S-Pick)*
POTTERSON *(12J,*
    14A-Mutual)
PRISCILLA *(Bleak)*
PUGSTYLES *(Nick)*
RIDERHOOD *(14R-Mutual)*
RUTH PINCH *(Chuzz)*
SAM WELLER *(Pick)*
SARAH GAMP *(Chuzz)*
SILAS WEGG *(Mutual)*
SMALLWEED *(13B,*
    15J-Bleak)
SMORLTORK *(14C-Pick)*
SNODGRASS *(Pick)*
STRUGGLES *(Pick)*
SWIVELLER *(13D-Curi)*

TAPPERTIT *(14S-Rudge)*
TAPPLETON *(Pick)*
THE BAGMAN *(Pick)*
THE SEXTON *(Curi)*
TIP DORRIT *(Dorrit)*
TOM BOCKER *(Mutual)*
TOM CRIPPS *(Pick)*
TOM MARTIN *(Pick)*
TOM TOOTLE *(Mutual)*
TOWLINSON *(15T-Dombey)*
TRAMPFOOT *(Trav)*
TULRUMBLE *(Mudfog)*
URIAH HEEP *(Cop)*
VENEERING *(Mutual)*
VERISOPHT *(13L-Nick)*
WALTER GAY *(Dombey)*
WICKFIELD *(14A-Cop)*
WILTSHIRE *(Trav)*
WITHERDEN *(Curi)*
WOODCOURT *(11D,*
    15D-Bleak)

10

AYRESLEIGH *(Pick)*
BANJO BONES *(Trav)*
BETSEY PRIG *(Chuzz)*
BETSY WHITE *(Trav)*
BILLY JOPER *(Dombey)*
BOB GLAMOUR *(Mutual)*
BOB STABLES *(Bleak)*
CAPTAIN TOM *(Great)*
CAVALLETTO *(15A-Dorrit)*
CHEVY SLYME *(Chuzz)*
CHUZZLEWIT *(14T,*
    15J-Chuzz)
COPPERNOSE *(Mudfog)*
CRISPARKLE *(15C-Drood)*
DOCTOR PEPS *(Dombey)*
EDWIN DROOD *(Drood)*
EMMA GORDON *(Hard)*
FLINTWITCH *(Dorrit)*
GALLANBILE *(Nick)*
HENRY GOWAN *(Dorrit)*
HENRY JAMES *(Dombey)*
JACK BAMBER *(Pick)*

JACK MALDON *(Cop)*
JACK MARTIN *(Pick)*
JANE BETSEY *(Dombey)*
JANE DIBABS *(Nick)*
JANE POCKET *(Great)*
JESSE HEXAM *(Mutual)*
JOB TROTTER *(Pick)*
JOE GARGERY *(Great)*
JOHN BARSAD *(Cities)*
JOHN CARKER *(Dombey)*
JOHN GRUEBY *(Rudge)*
JOHN HARMON *(Mutual)*
JOHN JASPER *(Drood)*
JOHN WILLET *(Rudge)*
JONAS MUDGE *(Pick)*
JULIA MILLS *(Cop)*
KIT NUBBLES *(Curi)*
KNIGHT BELL *(Mudfog)*
LADY BOWLEY *(Chimes)*
LILIAN FERN *(Chimes)*
LITTLE EM'LY *(Cop)*
LITTLE NELL *(Curi)*
LORD BOODLE *(Bleak)*
LORD FEENIX *(Dombey)*
LORD GORDON *(Rudge)*
MacSTINGER *(Dombey)*
MARIA LOBBS *(Pick)*
MARK TAPLEY *(Chuzz)*
MARY GRAHAM *(Chuzz)*
MICK WALKER *(Cop)*
MINNIE OMER *(Cop)*
MISS BULDER *(Pick)*
MISS CHEGGS *(Curi)*
MISS CODGER *(Chuzz)*
MISS PANKEY *(Dombey)*
MISS ROGERS *(Nick)*
MISS TOPPIT *(Chuzz)*
MRS BANGHAM *(Dorrit)*
MRS BARBARY *(Bleak)*
MRS BLIMBER *(Dombey)*
MRS BLINDER *(Bleak)*
MRS CLENNAM *(Dorrit)*
MRS CREAKLE *(Cop)*
MRS CREWLER *(Cop)*
MRS EDMUNDS *(Pick)*
MRS GARGERY *(Great)*

MRS GARLAND *(Curi)*
MRS GENERAL *(Dorrit)*
MRS GRAYPER *(Cop)*
MRS GRUDDEN *(Nick)*
MRS HEYLING *(Pick)*
MRS JELLYBY *(Bleak)*
MRS JINIWIN *(Curi)*
MRS JOLLSON *(Dombey)*
MRS KENWIGS *(Nick)*
MRS MEAGLES *(Dorrit)*
MRS NUBBLES *(Curi)*
MRS NUPKINS *(Pick)*
MRS PAWKINS *(Chuzz)*
MRS PERKINS *(Bleak)*
MRS PIPCHIN *(Dombey)*
MRS PODSNAP *(Mutual)*
MRS SAGGERS *(Trav)*
MRS SANDERS *(Pick)*
MRS SIMMONS *(Curi)*
MRS SKEWTON *(Dombey)*
MRS SMITHIE *(Pick)*
MRS SNAGSBY *(Bleak)*
MRS SNAWLEY *(Nick)*
MRS SPARSIT *(Hard)*
MRS SQUEERS *(Nick)*
MRS SWEENEY *(Trav)*
MRS TAPKINS *(Mutual)*
MRS TODGERS *(Chuzz)*
MRS TWIGGER *(Mudfog)*
MRS WACKLES *(Curi)*
MRS WHIMPLE *(Great)*
MURGATROYD *(Mudfog)*
PAUL Dombey *(Dombey)*
PELTIROGUS *(Nick)*
PET MEAGLES *(Dorrit)*
PHIL BARKER *(Twist)*
PHIL PARKES *(Rudge)*
PUTNAM SMIF *(Chuzz)*
QUEERSPECK *(Mudfog)*
ROSA DARTLE *(Cop)*
ROSE MAYLIE *(Twist)*
ROUNCEWELL *(14W-Bleak)*
SALLY BRASS *(Curi)*
SIGNOR JUPE *(Hard)*
SNEVELLICI *(Nick)*
SNIGSWORTH *(14L-Mutual)*

SOWERBERRY *(Twist)*
SPOTTLETOE *(Chuzz)*
STARELEIGH *(Pick)*
STEERFORTH *(15J-Cop)*
THICKNESSE *(Mudfog)*
TOM JOHNSON *(Dombey)*
TOM NECKETT *(Bleak)*
TONY WELLER *(Pick)*
TURVEYDROP *(Bleak)*
WALTER BRAY *(Nick)*
WATERBROOK *(Cop)*
WITITTERLY *(15H-Nick)*

11

ABEL GARLAND *(Curi)*
ALICK CHEGGS *(Curi)*
ALICK POCKET *(Great)*
ANTHONY HUMM *(Rudge)*
ARTHUR GRIDE *(Nick)*
BECKY MORGAN *(Curi)*
BELLA WILFER *(Mutual)*
BETSY MARTIN *(Pick)*
BETTY HIGDEN *(Mutual)*
BLUNDERBORE *(Mudfog)*
BOB CRATCHIT *(Carol)*
BOB GLIDDERY *(Mutual)*
CAPTAIN JOEY *(Mutual)*
CECILIA JUPE *(Hard)*
CHARLES MELL *(Cop)*
CLARA BARLEY *(Great)*
CopPERFIELD *(Cop)*
DANIEL DOYCE *(Dorrit)*
DANIEL QUILP *(Curi)*
DICK WILKINS *(Carol)*
DOCTOR FOXEY *(Mudfog)*
DOCTOR PAYNE *(Pick)*
DOLGE ORLICK *(Great)*
DOLLY VARDEN *(Rudge)*
DORA SPENLOW *(Cop)*
DR GRUMMIDGE *(Mudfog)*
DR NEESHAWTS *(Mudfog)*
DR WOODCOURT *(Bleak)*
EDITH Dombey *(Dombey)*
EMILY WARDLE *(Pick)*
EMMA NECKETT *(Bleak)*

EMMA PEECHER *(Mutual)*
FANNY DOMBEY *(Dombey)*
FANNY DORRIT *(Dorrit)*
FANNY POCKET *(Great)*
GABRIEL GRUB *(Pick)*
GEORGE JONES *(Mutual)*
HAM PEGGOTTY *(Cop)*
HARRY MAYLIE *(Twist)*
HENRY BELLER *(Pick)*
HENRY SPIKER *(Cop)*
HORACE KINCH *(Trav)*
JACK DAWKINS *(Twist)*
JACK HOPKINS *(Pick)*
JACK MULLINS *(Mutual)*
JACOB KIBBLE *(Mutual)*
JACOB MARLEY *(Carol)*
JAMES BOGSBY *(Bleak)*
JAMES CARKER *(Dombey)*
JAMES GROVES *(Curi)*
JANE WACKLES *(Curi)*
JARVIS LORRY *(Cities)*
JEMMY HUTLEY *(Pick)*
JOE PEGGOTTY *(Cop)*
JOHN BROWDIE *(Nick)*
JOHN CHIVERY *(Dorrit)*
JOHN DAWKINS *(Twist)*
JOHN EDMUNDS *(Pick)*
JOHN PODSNAP *(Mutual)*
JOHN SMAUKER *(Pick)*
JOHN WEMMICK *(Great)*
LADY CLUBBER *(Pick)*
LADY DEDLOCK *(Bleak)*
LADY MITHERS *(Cop)*
LADY TIPPINS *(Mutual)*
LINKINWATER *(14T-Nick)*
LIZZIE HEXAM *(Mutual)*
LUCRETIA TOX *(Dombey)*
MALTA BAGNET *(Bleak)*
MARK GILBERT *(Rudge)*
MINNIE JORAM *(Cop)*
MISS BARBARY *(Bleak)*
MISS CREAKLE *(Cop)*
MISS CROPLEY *(Nick)*
MISS DOWDLES *(Nick)*
MISS EDWARDS *(Curi)*
MISS GAZINGI *(Nick)*

23

MRS SMALLWEED *(Bleak)*
MRS TOMLINSON *(Pick)*
MRS TULRUMBLE *(Mudfog)*
MRS VENEERING *(Mutual)*
MRS WOODCOURT *(Bleak)*
MUDDLEBRAINS *(Mudfog)*
NOAH CLAYPOLE *(Twist)*
PEEPY JELLYBY *(Bleak)*
PHILIP PIRRIP *(Great)*
PUMPKINSKULL *(Mudfog)*
QUEBEC BAGNET *(Bleak)*
RICHARD EVANS *(Curi)*
ROBERT BOLTON *(Mudfog)*
SAMPSON BRASS *(Curi)*
SAMUEL WELLER *(Pick)*
SHINY VILLIAM *(Pick)*
SOLOMON DAISY *(Rudge)*
SOLOMON GILLS *(Dombey)*
SOLOMON LUCAS *(Pick)*
SOLOMON PROSS *(Cities)*
SOPHY CREWLER *(Cop)*
SOPHY WACKLES *(Curi)*
STRAUDENHEIM *(Trav)*
SWEET WILLIAM *(Curi)*
SYDNEY CARTON *(Cities)*
THOMAS BURTON *(Pick)*
THOMAS CODLIN *(Curi)*
THOMAS SAPSEA *(Drood)*
TITE BARNACLE *(Dorrit)*
TOM FLIPFIELD *(Trav)*
TOM GRADGRIND *(Hard)*
TOMMY BARDELL *(Pick)*
WILLIAM BUFFY *(Bleak)*
WILLIAM GUPPY *(Bleak)*
WOODENSCONCE *(Mudfog)*

13

ADAM GRADGRIND *(Hard)*
ANASTASIA RUGG *(Dorrit)*
ARABELLA ALLEN *(Pick)*
ARTHUR CLENNAM *(Dorrit)*
AUNT HAWKINSON *(Mutual)*
BART SMALLWEED *(Bleak)*
BENJAMIN ALLEN *(Pick)*

BROTHER TADGER *(Pick)*
CAPTAIN BAILEY *(Cop)*
CAPTAIN BUNSBY *(Dombey)*
CAPTAIN CUTTLE *(Dombey)*
CAPTAIN DOWLER *(Pick)*
CAPTAIN HAWDON *(Bleak)*
CAPTAIN MAROON *(Dorrit)*
CAPTAIN MARTIN *(Dorrit)*
CHARLES DARNAY *(Cities)*
CLARA PEGGOTTY *(Cop)*
COLONEL BULDER *(Pick)*
COLONEL GORDON *(Rudge)*
COLONEL GROPER *(Chuzz)*
DANIEL GRUMMER *(Pick)*
DICK SWIVELLER *(Curi)*
DOCTOR BLIMBER *(Dombey)*
DOCTOR CHILLIP *(Cop)*
DOCTOR HAGGAGE *(Dorrit)*
DOCTOR JOBLING *(Chuzz)*
DOCTOR MANETTE *(Cities)*
DOCTOR SLAMMER *(Pick)*
DOCTOR TOORELL *(Mudfog)*
DOROTHY DIBBLE *(Trav)*
DUKE OF LINSEED *(Mutual)*
EDWARD CHESTER *(Rudge)*
EDWARD LEEFORD *(Twist)*
EDWARD TWIGGER *(Mudfog)*
ERNEST DEFARGE *(Cities)*
FLORA FINCHING *(Dorrit)*
GABRIEL VARDEN *(Rudge)*
GENERAL CONWAY *(Rudge)*
GEORGE HEYLING *(Pick)*
GEORGE NUPKINS *(Pick)*
GEORGE RADFOOT *(Mutual)*
GEORGE SAMPSON *(Mutual)*
HARRIET BEADLE *(Dorrit)*
HARRIET CARKER *(Dombey)*
HERBERT POCKET *(Great)*
HORATIO FIZKIN *(Pick)*
JANE GRADGRIND *(Hard)*
JANE MURDSTONE *(Cop)*
JERRY CRUNCHER *(Cities)*
KIDDERMINSTER *(Hard)*
KITTY SKIMPOLE *(Bleak)*
LADY FINCHBURY *(Dombey)*
LAURA SKIMPOLE *(Bleak)*

LAVINIA WILFER *(Mutual)*
LORD VERISOPHT *(Nick)*
MADAME DEFARGE *(Cities)*
MAJOR BAGSTOCK *(Dombey)*
MARTHA BARDELL *(Pick)*
MATTHEW BAGNET *(Bleak)*
MATTHEW POCKET *(Great)*
M'CHOAKUMCHILD *(Hard)*
MELVIN TWEMLOW *(Mutual)*
MINNIE MEAGLES *(Dorrit)*
MISS BELVAWNEY *(Nick)*
MISS FERDINAND *(Drood)*
MRS CHUZZLEWIT *(Chuzz)*
MRS CRISPARKLE *(Drood)*
MRS KIDGERBURY *(Cop)*
MRS MacSTINGER *(Dombey)*
MRS ONOWENEVER *(Trav)*
MRS RIDGER BEGS *(Cop)*
MRS ROUNCEWELL *(Bleak)*
MRS SNEVELLICI *(Nick)*
MRS SOWERBERRY *(Twist)*
MRS SPOTTLETOE *(Chuzz)*
MRS STEERFORTH *(Cop)*
MRS WATERBROOK *(Cop)*
MRS WITITTERLY *(Nick)*
OLD BILL BARLEY *(Great)*
PEG SLIDERSKEW *(Nick)*
PERCY CRUMMLES *(Nick)*
PROFESSOR DOZE *(Mudfog)*
PROFESSOR MUFF *(Mudfog)*
PROFESSOR MULL *(Mudfog)*
PROFESSOR NOGO *(Mudfog)*
RACHAEL WARDLE *(Pick)*
RALPH NICKLEBY *(Nick)*
RICHARD BABLEY *(Cop)*
SALLY FLANDERS *(Trav)*
SAMUEL SLUMKEY *(Pick)*
SAMPSON DIBBLE *(Trav)*
SETH PECKSNIFF *(Chuzz)*
SLUMMINTOWKEN *(Pick)*
SNUFFLETOFFLE *(Mudfog)*
STILTSTALKING *(Dorrit)*
THOMAS GROFFIN *(Pick)*
TOMMY SCREWZER *(Dombey)*
TROOPER GEORGE *(Bleak)*
WILLIAM DORRIT *(Dorrit)*

14

ABBEY POTTERSON *(Mutual)*
AGNES WICKFIELD *(Cop)*
ARTHUR HAVISHAM *(Great)*
AUGUSTUS MODDLE *(Chuzz)*
BARNET SKETTLES *(Dombey)*
BENJAMIN BAILEY *(Chuzz)*
BENTLEY DRUMMLE *(Great)*
BETSEY TROTWOOD *(Cop)*
BOTTLE-NOSED NED *(Mudfog)*
BROTHER BELLOWS *(Dorrit)*
BROTHER MORDLIN *(Pick)*
CAPTAIN BOLDWIG *(Pick)*
CAPTAIN HOPKINS *(Cop)*
CAPTAIN KEDGICK *(Chuzz)*
CAPTAIN SWOSSER *(Bleak)*
CECILIA BOBSTER *(Nick)*
COLONEL CHOWSER *(Nick)*
COUNT SMORLTORK *(Pick)*
DANIEL PEGGOTTY *(Cop)*
DONNA CHRISTINA *(Pick)*
DR KUTANKUMAGEN *(Mudfog)*
EDMUND SPARKLER *(Dorrit)*
EDWIN CHEERYBLE *(Nick)*
EUGENE WRAYBURN *(Mutual)*
FELIX PARDIGGLE *(Bleak)*
FLORENCE DOMBEY *(Dombey)*
FRANCIS SPENLOW *(Cop)*
FRANK CHEERYBLE *(Nick)*
FREDERICK TRENT *(Curi)*
GILBERT CLENNAM *(Dorrit)*
HAROLD SKIMPOLE *(Bleak)*
HELENA LANDLESS *(Drood)*
HIRAM GREWGIOUS *(Drood)*
ISABELLA WARDLE *(Pick)*
JAMES HARTHOUSE *(Hard)*
JEFFERSON BRICK *(Chuzz)*
JOSEPH SMIGGERS *(Pick)*
LADY SNUPHANUPH *(Pick)*
LAVINIA SPENLOW *(Cop)*
LORD SNIGSWORTH *(Mutual)*
MASTER CRIPPLES *(Dorrit)*
MASTER CRUMMLES *(Nick)*
MELISSA WACKLES *(Curi)*
MERCANTILE JACK *(Trav)*

MERCY PECKSNIFF *(Chuzz)*
MERRY PECKSNIFF *(Chuzz)*
MICHAEL JACKSON *(Bleak)*
MISS ONOWENEVER *(Trav)*
MISS SNEVELLICI *(Nick)*
MISS TWINKLETON *(Drood)*
MORGAN AP KERRIG *(Bleak)*
MRS COPPERFIELD *(Cop)*
OLYMPIA SQUIRES *(Trav)*
PRINCESS PUFFER *(Drood)*
PROFESSOR DINGO *(Bleak)*
PROFESSOR GRIME *(Mudfog)*
PROFESSOR KETCH *(Mudfog)*
PROFESSOR PIPER *(Chuzz)*
PROFESSOR SNORE *(Mudfog)*
REGINALD WILFER *(Mutual)*
REVEREND FEEDER *(Dombey)*
REVEREND HOWLER *(Dombey)*
REVEREND MILVEY *(Mutual)*
RICHARD UPWITCH *(Pick)*
ROGER RIDERHOOD *(Mutual)*
SALLY COMPEYSON *(Great)*
SALLY SPRODGKIN *(Mutual)*
SAMUEL PICKWICK *(Pick)*
SERJEANT BUZFUZ *(Pick)*
SIMON TAPPERTIT *(Rudge)*
SIR JOHN CHESTER *(Rudge)*
THOMAS BENJAMIN *(Cop)*
THOMAS LENVILLE *(Nick)*
THOMAS PLORNISH *(Dorrit)*
THOMAS TRADDLES *(Cop)*
TIM LINKINWATER *(Nick)*
TOBY CHUZZLEWIT *(Chuzz)*
WATT ROUNCEWELL *(Bleak)*
WILKINS FLASHER *(Pick)*
WILLIAM POTKINS *(Great)*
WILLIAM SIMMONS *(Chuzz)*
WOOLWICH BAGNET *(Bleak)*

15

ALFRED MANTALINI *(Nick)*
ALFRED PARDIGGLE *(Bleak)*
ALTRO CAVALLETTO *(Dorrit)*

ANASTASIA WEEDLE *(Trav)*
CANON CRISPARKLE *(Drood)*
CAPTAIN MURDERER *(Trav)*
CAROLINE JELLYBY *(Bleak)*
CHARLEY PYEGRAVE *(Cop)*
CHERRY PECKSNIFF *(Chuzz)*
CLARISSA SPENLOW *(Cop)*
CONKEY CHICKWEED *(Twist)*
CORNELIA BLIMBER *(Dombey)*
DOCTOR GRUMMIDGE *(Mudfog)*
DOCTOR NEESHAWTS *(Mudfog)*
DOCTOR WOODCOURT *(Bleak)*
EBENEZER SCROOGE *(Carol)*
EDWARD MURDSTONE *(Cop)*
EGBERT PARDIGGLE *(Bleak)*
ESTHER SUMMERSON *(Bleak)*
FREDERICK DORRIT *(Dorrit)*
GENERAL FLADDOCK *(Chuzz)*
GODFREY NICKLEBY *(Nick)*
HENRY WITITTERLY *(Nick)*
INSPECTOR BUCKET *(Bleak)*
JAMES STEERFORTH *(Cop)*
JOHN EDWARD NANDY *(Dorrit)*
JONAS CHUZZLEWIT *(Chuzz)*
JOSEPHINE SLEARY *(Hard)*
JOSHUA SMALLWEED *(Bleak)*
JOSIAH BOUNDERBY *(Hard)*
JUDITH SMALLWEED *(Bleak)*
LA FAYETTE KETTLE *(Chuzz)*
LOUISA GRADGRIND *(Hard)*
MADAME BARRONEAU *(Dorrit)*
MADAME MANTALINI *(Nick)*
MARY ANNE PARAGON *(Cop)*
MISS LINKINWATER *(Nick)*
MISS MELVILLESON *(Bleak)*
MISS MONFLATHERS *(Curi)*
MISS WITHERFIELD *(Pick)*
MORLEENA KENWIGS *(Nick)*
MRS GRAZINGLANDS *(Trav)*
NATHANIEL PIPKIN *(Pick)*
NATHANIEL WINKLE *(Pick)*
NEVILLE LANDLESS *(Drood)*
NICODEMUS BOFFIN *(Mutual)*
NINETTA CRUMMLES *(Nick)*
OSWALD PARDIGGLE *(Bleak)*
PAUL SWEEDLEPIPE *(Chuzz)*

PROFESSOR MULLIT *(Chuzz)*
PROFESSOR RUMMAN *(Mudfog)*
PROFESSOR WHEEZY *(Mudfog)*
REVEREND CREWLER *(Cop)*
RICHARD CARSTONE *(Bleak)*
SERJEANT SNUBBIN *(Pick)*
SIDNEY PORKENHAM *(Pick)*
SIR JOSEPH BOWLEY *(Chimes)*
SIR MULBERRY HAWK *(Nick)*
SNITTLE TIMBERRY *(Nick)*
THE ARTFUL DODGER *(Twist)*

THE YOUNG BUTCHER *(Cop)*
THOMAS GRADGRIND *(Hard)*
THOMAS TOWLINSON *(Dombey)*
VINCENT CRUMMLES *(Nick)*
VOLUMNIA DEDLOCK *(Bleak)*
WACKFORD SQUEERS *(Nick)*
WILKINS MICAWBER *(Cop)*
WILLIAM BARNACLE *(Dorrit)*
WILLIAM CLEVERLY *(Trav)*
WILLIAM WILLIAMS *(Mutual)*
ZEPHANIA SCADDER *(Chuzz)*

ARTS

LITERATURE – BOOK CHARACTERS – GENERAL

3

DAN *(Puck of Pook's Hill – Kipling)*
JEM *(To Kill A Mockingbird – H Lee)*
JIM *(7L – Lord Jim – Conrad)*
LEE *(10L – Gentlemen Prefer Blondes – Loos)*
OAK *(10G – Far From The Madding Crowd – Hardy)*
PEW *(8B – Treasure Island – Stevenson)*
PYM *(9M – A Perfect Spy – Le Carré)*
TOM *(The Water Babies – Kingsley)*
VYE *(11E – The Return Of The Native – Hardy)*

4

AHAB *(11C – Moby Dick – Melville)*
ALGY *(Biggles series – Johns)*
BEDE *(8A – Adam Bede – G Eliot)*

BOND *(9J – many – Fleming)*
BOOT *(8J – Scoop – E Waugh)*
BULL *(10J – Billy Bunter series – Richards)*
CARR *(8K – What Katy Did – Coolidge)*
CASS *(9E – Silas Marner – G Eliot)*
CORD *(9J – The Carpetbaggers – Robbins)*
CUFF *(12S – The Moonstone – W Collins)*
DEAN *(9S – The Good Companions – Priestley)*
DEWY *(8D – Under The Greenwood Tree – Hardy)*
DONN *(12A – Jude The Obscure – Hardy)*
EAST *(Tom Brown's Schooldays – T Hughes)*
EASY *(8J – Mr Midshipman Easy – Marryat)*
EYRE *(8J – Jane Eyre – C Brontë)*

FINN *(11P – Phineas Fogg – Trollope)*
(15H – Huckleberry Finn – Twain)

FOGG *(11P – Around The World In Eighty Days – Verne)*

GARP *(The World According To Garp – J Irving)*

GRAY *(10D – The Picture Of Dorian Gray – Wilde)*

GREY *(9A – Agnes Grey – A Brontë)*

GUNN *(7B – Treasure Island – Stevenson)*

HOLT *(9F – Felix Holt – G Eliot)*
(9G – The Cruel Sea – Monsarrat)

HYDE *(10E – Dr Jekyll And Mr Hyde – Stevenson)*

JANE *(Tarzan series – Burroughs)*

JOAD *(7T – The Grapes Of Wrath – Steinbeck)*

KEMP *(8L – Liza Of Lambeth – Maugham)*

KIRK *(10H – The History Man – M Bradbury)*

LAST *(8T – A Handful Of Dust – E Waugh)*

LIME *(9H – The Third Man – Greene)*

LUNG *(8W – The Good Earth – Buck)*

MOND *(12M – Brave New World – A Huxley)*

NEMO *(11C – 20,000 Leagues Under The Sea – Verne)*

NUNN *(9J – The Good Companions – Priestley)*

PYLE *(9A – The Quiet American – Greene)*

REED *(7M – Jane Eyre – C Brontë)*

RICE *(9S – The Small Back Room – Balchin)*

RIDD *(8J – Lorna Doone – Blackmore)*

SEAL *(9B – Put Out More Flags – E Waugh)*

SYME *(11G – The Man Who Was Thursday – Chesterton)*

TAJI *(Mardi – Melville)*

TROY *(12S – Far From The Madding Crowd – Hardy)*

VANE *(11H – Strong Poison – Sayers)*

VOSS *(10J – Voss – White)*

WEIR *(8A – Weir Of Hermiston – Stevenson)*

5

ALICE *(Alice In Wonderland/Through The Looking-Glass – Carroll)*

ATHOS *(The Three Musketeers – Dumas)*

BATES *(Stalky & Co – Kipling)*

BLAKE *(13F – The Moonstone – W Collins)*

BLOOD *(12C – Captain Blood – Sabatini)*

BLOOM *(10M, 12L – Ulysses – Joyce)*

BOOTH *(11A, 12W – Amelia – Fielding)*

BROOK *(10R – many – Wheatley)*

BROWN *(8T – Tom Brown's Schooldays – T Hughes)*
(11F – Father Brown series – Chesterton)
(11V – National Velvet – Bagnold)
(12W – Just William series – Crompton)

CAREY *(11P – Of Human Bondage – Maugham)*

CLARA *(Heidi – Spyri)*

CLARE *(10A – Tess Of The D'Urbervilles – Hardy)*

COHEN *(10M – Daniel Deronda – G Eliot)*

CRANE *(12I – The Legend Of Sleepy Hollow – W Irving)*

DARCY *(Pride And Prejudice – Austen)*

DAWES *(11B – Sons And Lovers – Lawrence)*

DIXON *(8J – Lucky Jim – K Amis)*

DOONE *(10L – Lorna Doone – Blackmore)*

DUBBY *(Phineas Finn – Trollope)*

DUPIN *(12A – many – Poe)*
DUROY *(12G – Bel-Ami – Maupassant)*
FLORA *(Turn Of The Screw – H James)*
FLYNN *(11F – Dubliners – Joyce)*
FLYTE *(14S – Brideshead Revisited – E Waugh)*
FOSCO *(10C – The Woman In White – W Collins)*
GESTE *(9B – Beau Geste – Wren)*
HEIDI *(Heidi – Spyri)*
HOLLY *(11L – She – Haggard)*
JANET *(Beyond This Place – Cronin)*
JONES *(8T – Tom Jones – Fielding)*
KIPPS *(11A – Kipps – Wells)*
KLEIN *(10H – A Severed Head – Murdoch)*
LEIGH *(10A – Westward Ho! – Kingsley)*
LOGAN *(10F – Pursuit Of Love – Mitford)*
MARCH *(7J, 8A, 8M, 9B – Little Women – Alcott)*
MASON *(10P – many – Gardner)*
MERCY *(Pilgrim's Progress – Bunyan)*
MILES *(Turn Of The Screw – H James)*
MITTY *(11W – The Secret Life Of Walter Mitty – Thurber)*
MOORE *(8M – A Passage To India – Forster)*
M'TURK *(Stalky & Co – Kipling)*
O'HARA *(12K – Kim – Kipling)*
            (13S – Gone With The Wind – Mitchell)
PAGET *(9J – A Town Like Alice – Shute)*
PANZA *(11S – Don Quixote – Cervantes)*
PIGGY *(Lord Of The Flies – Golding)*
POLLY *(11A – The History Of Mr Polly – Wells)*
POSTE *(10F – Cold Comfort Farm – Gibbons)*
POTTS *(15C – Chitty Chitty Bang Bang – Fleming)*

PRICE *(10F – Mansfield Park – Austen)*
QUEEG *(12C – The Caine Mutiny – Wouk)*
QUEEN *(11E – many – Queen)*
RALPH *(Lord Of The Flies – Golding)*
READY *(14M – Masterman Ready – Marryat)*
REMUS *(10U – Uncle Remus series – Harris)*
RYDER *(12C – Brideshead Revisited – E Waugh)*
SAMSA *(11G – Metamorphosis – Kafka)*
SCOUT *(To Kill A Mockingbird – H Lee)*
SHARP *(10B – Vanity Fair – Thackeray)*
SINAI *(11S – Midnight's Children – Rushdie)*
SINGH *(11H – Billy Bunter series – Richards)*
SLOPE *(13R – Barsetshire series – Trollope)*
SLOTH *(Pilgrim's Progress – Bunyan)*
SMITH *(12W – 1984 – Orwell)*
SNOWE *(9L – Villette – C Brontë)*
SPADE *(8S – The Maltese Falcon – Hammett)*
SWANN *(12C – Remembrance Of Things Past – Proust)*
TEMPY *(9A – Uncle Remus series – Harris)*
TOPSY *(Uncle Tom's Cabin – Stowe)*
TOWNE *(12L – North West Passage – Roberts)*
TRANT *(14E – The Good Companions – Priestley)*
TRASK *(9A – East Of Eden – Steinbeck)*
TRENT *(11P – many – Bentley)*
TWALA *(King Solomon's Mines – Haggard)*
UNCAS *(Leatherstocking Tales – JF Cooper)*
USHER *(13R – The Fall Of The House Of Usher – Poe)*

VINCY *(11W – Middlemarch – G Eliot)*
WADDY *(Kipps – Wells)*
WAKEM *(11P – The Mill On The Floss – G Eliot)*
WELLS *(10H – Cider House Rules – J Irving)*
WOLFE *(9N – many – Stout)*

6

ADOLPH *(Uncle Tom's Cabin – Stowe)*
AITKEN *(Prester John – Buchan)*
ALLEYN *(14R – many – Marsh)*
ARAMIS *(The Three Musketeers – Dumas)*
ARCHER *(12I – Portrait Of A Lady – H James)*
AYESHA *(She – Haggard)*
BAINES *(12S, 15C – The Old Wives' Tale – Bennett)*
BEETLE *(Stalky & Co – Kipling)*
BENBOW *(Clayhanger – Bennett)*
BENNET *(9M, 10J, 10M, 11L, 15C, 15E – Pride And Prejudice – Austen)*
BOVARY *(12M – Madame Bovary – Flaubert)*
BOWLES *(11S – Goodbye To Berlin – Isherwood)*
BRODIE *(10J – The Prime Of Miss Jean Brodie – Spark)*
BROOKE *(14D – Middlemarch – G Eliot)*
BUMPPO *(11N – Leatherstocking Tales – JF Cooper)*
BUNTER *(11B – Billy Bunter series – Richards)*
BUTLER *(11R – Gone With The Wind – Mitchell)*
CHERRY *(9B – Billy Bunter series – Richards)*
COOLEY *(14B – Kangaroo – Lawrence)*
CROWNE *(12L – Brave New World – A Huxley)*

CRUSOE *(14R – Robinson Crusoe – Defoe)*
DAGGOO *(Moby Dick – Melville)*
DANTES *(12E – The Count Of Monte Cristo – Dumas)*
DOBSON *(13Z – Zuleika Dobson – Beerbohm)*
ELLIOT *(Persuasion – Austen)*
ESMOND *(13C – Henry Esmond – Thackeray)*
FAWLEY *(10J – Jude The Obscure – Hardy)*
FINLAY *(8D, 12D – Beyond This Place – Cronin)*
FIRMIN *(14G – Under The Volcano – Lowry)*
FOSSIL *(10P – Ballet Shoes – Streatfeild)*
FOWLER *(12T – The Quiet American – Greene)*
FRIDAY *(Robinson Crusoe – Stevenson)*
GAGOOL *(King Solomon's Mines – Haggard)*
GANTRY *(11E – Elmer Gantry – S Lewis)*
GATSBY *(9J – The Great Gatsby – Fitzgerald)*
GEORGE *(Of Mice And Men – Steinbeck)*
(Three Men In A Boat – Jerome)
GORDON *(12S – Black Beauty – Sewell)*
GRIMES *(The Water Babies – Kingsley)*
HANNAH *(Little Women – Alcott)*
HANNAY *(13R – many – Buchan)*
HARKER *(14J – Dracula – Stoker)*
HARPER *(9J – The Adventures Of Tom Sawyer – Twain)*
HERZOG *(11M – Herzog – Bellow)*
HOLMES *(13M, 14S – many – Doyle)*
HUDSON *(9M – many – Doyle)*
JACOBS *(The Mill On The Floss – G Eliot)*

JEEVES (many – Wodehouse)
JEKYLL (8D, 12D – Dr Jekyll And Mr Hyde – Stevenson)
JONSEN (High Wind In Jamaica – R Hughes)
JORDAN (12R – For Whom The Bell Tolls – Hemingway)
KETTLE (13C – many – Hyne)
LARKIN (12S – The Darling Buds Of May – Bates)
LAURIE (Little Women – Alcott)
LEGREE (11S – Uncle Tom's Cabin – Stowe)
LENNIE (Of Mice And Men – Steinbeck)
LINTON (11E – Wuthering Heights – E Brontë)
LITTLE (11B – many – Wodehouse)
LOLITA (Lolita – Nabokov)
LYNDON (11B – Barry Lindon – Thackeray)
MACKAY (10M – The Prime Of Miss Jean Brodie – Spark)
MANSON (8D, 12D – The Citadel – Cronin)
MARNER (11S – Silas Marner – G Eliot)
MARPLE (10M – many – Christie)
MOREAU (8D, 12D – The Island Of Dr Moreau – Wells)
MORGAN (9H, 14A – How Green Was My Valley – Llewellyn)
MOWGLI (The Jungle Books – Kipling)
NORRIS (12A – Mr Norris Changes Trains – Isherwood)
NUGENT (11F – Billy Bunter series – Richards)
ODDJOB (Goldfinger – Fleming)
ODETTE (Remembrance Of Things Past – Proust)
OSMOND (13G – Portrait Of A Lady – H James)
PICKLE (15P – Peregrine Pickle – Smollett)
PINKIE (Brighton Rock – Greene)
POIROT (13H – many – Christie)

POOTER (11L, 12C, 13C – Diary Of A Nobody – G & W Grossmith)
PSMITH (many – Wodehouse)
RANDOM (14R – Roderick Random – Smollett)
ROB ROY (Rob Roy – Scott)
ROSTOV (War And Peace – Tolstoy)
SANGER (11T – The Constant Nymph – Kennedy)
SAWYER (9T – The Adventures Of Tom Sawyer – Twain)
SCOBIE (11H – The Heart Of The Matter – Greene)
SEDLEY (12A – Vanity Fair – Thackeray)
SHANDY (14T – Tristram Shandy – Sterne)
SILVER (14L – Treasure Island – Stevenson)
SIMPLE (11P – Peter Simple – Marryat)
SLOPER (8D, 12D – Washington Square – H James)
SMEETH (Angel Pavement – Priestley)
SMILEY (12G – Smiley's People – Le Carré)
SORREL (11H – Adam Bede – G Eliot)
STALKY (Stalky & Co – Kipling)
STREET (11D – many – Gardner)
TARZAN (Tarzan series – Burroughs)
THORNE (8D, 12D – Doctor Thorne – Trollope)
THORPE (14I – Northanger Abbey – Austen)
TILNEY (11H – Northanger Abbey – Austen)
TOOMEY (13K – Earthly Powers – Burgess)
TURKEY (Stalky & Co – Kipling)
TURPIN (10D – Rookwood – Ainsworth)
UMPOPA (King Solomon's Mines – Haggard)
WALKER (10J, 11R, 11S, 11T, 11V – Swallows And Amazons – Ransome)

WATSON *(8D, 12D – many – Doyle)*
WILCOX *(11H – Howards End – Forster)*
WILKES *(11I, 12A – Gone With The Wind – Mitchell)*
WIMSEY *(15L – many – Sayers)*
WOTTON *(10L – The Picture Of Dorian Gray – Wilde)*

7

AMERIGO *(13P – The Golden Bowl – H James)*
ANDREWS *(13J – Joseph Andrews – Fielding)*
(13P – Pamela – Richardson)
BADGERY *(14H – Illywhacker – Carey)*
BALFOUR *(12D – Kidnapped/ Catriona – Stevenson)*
BEN GUNN *(Treasure Island – Stevenson)*
BERTRAM *(11L – Mansfield Park – Austen)*
(12A – Guy Mannering – Scott)
BIGGLES *(Biggles series – Johns)*
BINGLEY *(14C – Pride And Prejudice – Austen)*
BOWLING *(10T – Roderick Random – Smollett)*
BRANDON *(14C – Sense And Sensibility – Austen)*
CAMERON *(9D, 13D – Beyond This Place – Cronin)*
CAMPION *(13A – many – Allingham)*
CLINKER *(14H – Humphry Clinker – Smollett)*
COLLINS *(15R – Pride And Prejudice – Austen)*
CRAWLEY *(14S – Vanity Fair – Thackeray)*
CYPRESS *(Nightmare Abbey – Peacock)*

DANVERS *(10M – Rebecca – D Du Maurier)*
DEDALUS *(14S – Ulysses – Joyce)*
DERONDA *(13D – Daniel Deronda – G Eliot)*
DE SELBY *(The Third Policeman – F O'Brien)*
DESPAIR *(Pilgrim's Progress – Bunyan)*
DETROIT *(13N – Guys And Dolls – Runyon)*
DINMONT *(12D – Guy Mannering – Scott)*
DRACULA *(12C – Dracula – Stoker)*
DURWARD *(14Q – Quentin Durward – Scott)*
ENDERBY *(Inside Mr Enderby – Burgess)*
FAIRFAX *(10M – Jane Eyre – C Brontë)*
(11J – Emma – Austen)
FARFRAE *(13D – The Mayor Of Casterbridge – Hardy)*
FORSYTE *(12F, 12H, 12J, 13J, 13S – The Forsyte Saga – Galsworthy)*
GRANTLY *(Barsetshire series – Trollope)*
GRIFFIN *(The Invisible Man – Wells)*
HARDING *(15S – Barsetshire series – Trollope)*
HARLOWE *(15C – Clarissa – Richardson)*
HAWK-EYE *(Leatherstocking Tales – JF Cooper)*
HAWKINS *(10J – Treasure Island – Stevenson)*
HERRIES *(14F – Rogue Herries – Walpole)*
HOPEFUL *(Pilgrim's Progress – Bunyan)*
HUMBERT *(14H – Lolita – Nabokov)*
ISHMAEL *(Moby Dick – Melville)*
IVANHOE *(Ivanhoe – Scott)*
JENKYNS *(14D – Cranford – Gaskell)*
JO MARCH *(Little Women – Alcott)*

JOSEPH K *(The Trial − Kafka)*
KEELDAR *(14S − Shirley − C Brontë)*
KROESIG *(14A − Pursuit Of Love −*
N Mitford)
LAMBERT *(14C − The Virginians −*
H James)
LAMPTON *(10J − Room At The Top −*
Braine)
LATIMER *(13D − Redgauntlet − Scott)*
LIVESEY *(9D, 13D − Treasure Island −*
Stevenson)
LORD JIM *(Lord Jim − Conrad)*
LOVEDAY *(11J − The Trumpet-Major*
− Hardy)
MAIGRET *(Maigret series − Simenon)*
MARKHAM *(14G − The Tenant Of*
Wildfell Hall − A Brontë)
MARLOWE *(13P − many − Chandler)*
MELDRUM *(Goodbye Mr Chips −*
Hilton)
MELLORS *(13O − Lady Chatterley's*
Lover − Lawrence)
MORLAND *(Northanger Abbey −*
Austen)
MRS REED *(Jane Eyre − C Brontë)*
NEWCOME *(13T − The Newcomes −*
Thackeray)
OAKROYD *(11J − The Good*
Companions − Priestley)
ORLANDO *(Orlando − Woolf)*
OVERTON *(The Way Of All Flesh −*
Butler)
PADDOCK *(The Thirty-Nine Steps −*
Buchan)
PANURGE *(Gargantua And Pantagruel*
− Rabelais)
PERKUPP *(Diary Of A Nobody −*
G & W Grossmith)
PEVERIL *(13J − Peveril Of The Peak −*
Scott)
POLDARK *(11R − Poldark series −*
Graham)
POPPINS *(11M − Mary Poppins series*
− Travers)
PORTHOS *(The Three Musketeers −*
Dumas)

PROUDIE *(10M, 13B − Barsetshire*
series − Trollope)
QUESTED *(12A − A Passage to India −*
Forster)
QUIXOTE *(10D − Don Quixote −*
Cervantes)
RADLETT *(12L − Pursuit Of Love −*
N Mitford)
RAFFLES *(Raffles series − Hornung)*
RAINIER *(14C − Random Harvest −*
Hilton)
RANDALL *(14R − Rebecca of*
Sunnybrook Farm −
Wiggin)
REBECCA *(Rebecca − D Du Maurier)*
(Ivanhoe − Scott)
ROBSART *(10A − Kenilworth − Scott)*
RUMPOLE *(13H − Rumpole series −*
Mortimer)
SANDERS *(Sanders Of The River −*
E Wallace)
SHIPTON *(13M − The Luck Of Roaring*
Camp − Harte)
SIDONIA *(Coningsby − Disraeli)*
ST CLARE *(10E − Uncle Tom's Cabin −*
Stowe)
TEMPLAR *(12S − Saint series −*
Charteris)
TOM JOAD *(The Grapes Of Wrath −*
Steinbeck)
UKRIDGE *(Ukridge series −*
Wodehouse)
VALJEAN *(11J − Les Misérables −*
Hugo)
VRONSKI *(Anna Karenina − Tolstoy)*
WARWICK *(12D − Diana Of The*
Crossways − Meredith)
WESTERN *(10M, 13S − Tom Jones −*
Fielding)
WHARTON *(12H − Billy Bunter series*
− Richards)
WICKHAM *(13G − Pride And Prejudice*
− Austen)
WILLIAM *(Three Men In A Boat −*
Jerome)
WOOSTER *(13B − many − Wodehouse)*

ZHIVAGO *(10U – Dr Zhivago – Pasternak)*

8

ADAM BEDE *(Adam Bede – G Eliot)*
ADAM WEIR *(Weir Of Hermiston – Stevenson)*
AMY MARCH *(Little Women – Alcott)*
ANGELICA *(The Rose And The Ring – Thackeray)*
APOLLYON *(Pilgrim's Progress – Bunyan)*
ARMITAGE *(13J – The Children Of The New Forest – Marryat)*
BEVERLEY *(15C – The Children Of The New Forest – Marryat)*
BLAKENEY *(13P – The Scarlet Pimpernel – Orczy)*
BLIND PEW *(Treasure Island – Stevenson)*
BOLDWOOD *(15W – Far From The Madding Crowd – Hardy)*
BRANGWEN *(11T – The Rainbow/ Women In Love – Lawrence)*
BRITLING *(12H – Mr Britling Sees It Through – Wells)*
CARRAWAY *(11N – The Great Gatsby – Fitzgerald)*
CASAUBON *(Foucault's Pendulum – Eco)*
(14E – Middlemarch – G Eliot)
CATRIONA *(Catriona – Stevenson)*
CHIPPING *(Goodbye Mr Chips – Hilton)*
DALLOWAY *(11M – Mrs Dalloway – Woolf)*
DASHWOOD *(13H – Sense And Sensibility – Austen)*
DE BOURGH *(12L – Pride And Prejudice – Austen)*
DERRIMAN *(14F – The Trumpet-Major – Hardy)*

DE WINTER *(11M – Rebecca – D Du Maurier)*
DICK DEWY *(Under The Greenwood Tree – Hardy)*
DR FINLAY *(Beyond This Place – Cronin)*
DR JEKYLL *(Dr Jekyll And Mr Hyde – Stevenson)*
DR MANSON *(The Citadel – Cronin)*
DR MOREAU *(The Island Of Dr Moreau – Wells)*
DR SLOPER *(Washington Square – H James)*
DR THORNE *(Doctor Thorne – Trollope)*
DRUMMOND *(15B – Bulldog Drummond – Sapper)*
DR WATSON *(many – Doyle)*
DULCINEA *(Don Quixote – Cervantes)*
EARNSHAW *(Wuthering Heights – E Brontë)*
EMMELINE *(Uncle Tom's Cabin – Stowe)*
EVERDENE *(Far From The Madding Crowd – Hardy)*
FAITHFUL *(Pilgrim's Progress – Bunyan)*
FFOULKES *(The Scarlet Pimpernel – Orczy)*
FLAMBEAU *(Father Brown series – Chesterton)*
FLANDERS *(12M – Moll Flanders – Defoe)*
(13J – Jacob's Room – Woolf)
FLASHMAN *(Tom Brown's Schooldays – T Hughes)*
GLENCORA *(12L – Palliser series – Trollope)*
GULLIVER *(14L – Gulliver's Travels – Swift)*
HALLWARD *(13B – The Picture Of Dorian Gray – Wilde)*
HASTINGS *(14A – many – Christie)*
HENCHARD *(15M – The Mayor Of Casterbridge – Hardy)*

HOLCOMBE *(14M − The Woman In White − W Collins)*
JANE EYRE *(Jane Eyre − C Brontë)*
JIM DIXON *(Lucky Jim − K Amis)*
JOHN BOOT *(Scoop − E Waugh)*
JOHN EASY *(Mr Midshipman Easy − Marryat)*
JOHN RIDD *(Lorna Doone − Blackmore)*
JORDACHE *(12A − Rich Man, Poor Man − I Shaw)*
JORROCKS *(Jorrocks series − Surtees)*
KARENINA *(12A − Anna Karenina − Tolstoy)*
KATY CARR *(What Katy Did − Coolidge)*
LESSWAYS *(13H − Clayhanger − Bennett)*
LESTRADE *(many − Doyle)*
LEWISHAM *(14G − Love And Mr Lewisham − Wells)*
LIZA KEMP *(Liza Of Lambeth − Maugham)*
LOCKWOOD *(Wuthering Heights − E Brontë)*
MEG MARCH *(Little Women − Alcott)*
MORIARTY *(many − Doyle)*
MRS MOORE *(A Passage To India − Forster)*
O'FERRALL *(14T − Trilby − G Du Maurier)*
PALLISER *(15A − Palliser series − Trollope)*
PANGLOSS *(10D, 14D − Candide − Voltaire)*
PETERSEN *(12C − Bulldog Drummond − Sapper)*
PRIMROSE *(15C − The Vicar Of Wakefield − Goldsmith)*
QUEEQUEG *(Moby Dick − Melville)*
ROBINSON *(13F − The Swiss Family Robinson − Wyss)*
SAM SPADE *(The Maltese Falcon − Hammett)*
SCYTHROP *(Nightmare Abbey − Peacock)*

STANDISH *(12L − Palliser series − Trollope)*
ST BUNGAY *(Phineas Finn − Trollope)*
STELLING *(The Mill On The Floss − G Eliot)*
SVENGALI *(Trilby − G Du Maurier)*
THATCHER *(13B − The Adventures Of Tom Sawyer − Twain)*
THOMPSON *(13S − Rain − Maugham)*
THWACKUM *(Tom Jones − Fielding)*
TOM BROWN *(Tom Brown's Schooldays − T Hughes)*
TOM JONES *(Tom Jones − Fielding)*
TONY LAST *(A Handful Of Dust − E Waugh)*
TULLIVER *(11T, 14M − The Mill On The Floss − G Eliot)*
UNCLE TOM *(Uncle Tom's Cabin − Stowe)*
VERINDER *(14R − The Moonstone − W Collins)*
WANG LUNG *(The Good Earth − Buck)*
WAVERLEY *(14E − Waverley Novels − Scott)*
WETHERBY *(Goodbye Mr Chips − Hilton)*
WILLIAMS *(12E − Eric or Little By Little − Farrar)*

9

ABBEVILLE *(15H − Cannery Row − Steinbeck)*
ADAM TRASK *(East Of Eden − Steinbeck)*
AGNES GREY *(Agnes Grey − A Brontë)*
ALBEN PYLE *(The Quiet American − Greene)*
ALLWORTHY *(15S − Tom Jones − Fielding)*
AUNT TEMPY *(Uncle Remus series − Harris)*
BARRYMORE *(The Hound Of The Baskervilles − Doyle)*

BASIL SEAL *(Put Out More Flags –*
E Waugh)
BATHSHEBA *(Far From The Madding*
Crowd – Hardy)
BEAU GESTE *(Beau Geste – Wren)*
BETH MARCH *(Little Women – Alcott)*
BOB CHERRY *(Billy Bunter series –*
Richards)
BOLKONSKI *(War And Peace –*
Tolstoy)
BRIDEHEAD *(11S – Jude The*
Obscure – Hardy)
CATHERICK *(13A – The Woman In*
White – W Collins)
CAULFIELD *(15H – Catcher In The*
Rye – Salinger)
CHRISTIAN *(Pilgrim's Progress –*
Bunyan)
DALGLEISH *(13A – many –*
PD James)
D'ARTAGNAN *(The Three Musketeers*
– Dumas)
DR CAMERON *(Beyond This Place –*
Cronin)
DRIFFIELD *(14S – Cakes And Ale –*
Maugham)
DR LIVESEY *(Treasure Island –*
Stevenson)
DRYASDUST *(11D, 15D – The*
Antiquary – Scott)
EPPIE CASS *(Silas Marner – G Eliot)*
ESMERELDA *(Notre Dame De Paris –*
Hugo)
ESTERHAZY *(13T – Smiley's People*
– Le Carré)
FELIX HOLT *(Felix Holt – G Eliot)*
GAVIN HOLT *(The Cruel Sea –*
Monsarrat)
GREYSTOKE *(13L – Tarzan series –*
Burroughs)
HARRY LIME *(The Third Man –*
Greene)
HARTRIGHT *(15W – The Woman In*
White – W Collins)
HUW MORGAN *(How Green Was My*
Valley – Llewellyn)

INDIAN JOE *(The Adventures Of Tom*
Sawyer – Twain)
INGLEWOOD *(15S – Rob Roy –*
Scott)
JAMES BOND *(many – Fleming)*
JAY GATSBY *(The Great Gatsby –*
Fitzgerald)
JEAN PAGET *(A Town Like Alice –*
Shute)
JIMMY NUNN *(The Good Companions*
– Priestley)
JOE HARPER *(The Adventures Of Tom*
Sawyer – Twain)
JOLLIFANT *(14I – The Good*
Companions – Priestley)
JONAS CORD *(The Carpetbaggers –*
Robbins)
KNIGHTLEY *(15G – Emma – Austen)*
LUCY SNOWE *(Villette – C Brontë)*
MAGNUS PYM *(A Perfect Spy –*
Le Carré)
MANNERING *(12G – Guy Mannering*
– Scott)
MARCHMAIN *(13L – Brideshead*
Revisited – E Waugh)
MERRILIES *(12M – Guy Mannering –*
Scott)
MEURSAULT *(L'Étranger – Camus)*
MRS BENNET *(Pride And Prejudice –*
Austen)
MRS HUDSON *(many – Doyle)*
NERO WOLFE *(many – Stout)*
PENDENNIS *(15A – Pendennis –*
Thackeray)
PONDEREVO *(15E – Tono-Bungay –*
Wells)
QUASIMODO *(Notre Dame De Paris –*
Hugo)
REMINGTON *(The New Machiavelli –*
Wells)
ROCHESTER *(15E – Jane Eyre –*
C Brontë)
SAMMY RICE *(The Small Back Room*
– Balchin)
SMALLWAYS *(13B – War In The Air –*
Wells)

SOUTHDOWN *(Vanity Fair –
    Thackeray)*
SUSIE DEAN *(The Good Companions
    – Priestley)*
TOM SAWYER *(The Adventures Of
    Tom Sawyer – Twain)*
TRELAWNEY *(15S – Treasure Island
    – Stevenson)*
UNCLE TOBY *(Tristram Shandy –
    Sterne)*
WENTWORTH *(Persuasion – Austen)
    (The Europeans –
    H James)*
WOODHOUSE *(13E – Emma –
    Austen)*
YEOBRIGHT *(13C – The Return Of The
    Native – Hardy)*
YOSSARIAN *(Catch-22 – Heller)*

10

AMYAS LEIGH *(Westward Ho! –
    Kingsley)*
AMY ROBSART *(Kenilworth – Scott)*
ANGEL CLARE *(Tess Of the
    D'Urbervilles – Hardy)*
BECKY SHARP *(Vanity Fair –
    Thackeray)*
BELLEGARDE *(The American –
    H James)*
CHALLENGER *(The Lost World –
    Doyle)*
CHATTERLEY *(14L – Lady
    Chatterley's Lover –
    Lawrence)*
CLAYHANGER *(15E – Clayhanger –
    Bennett)*
COUNT FOSCO *(The Woman In White
    – W Collins)*
CRIMSWORTH *(The Professor –
    C Brontë)*
CROUCHBACK *(13G – Men At Arms
    – E Waugh)*

DICK TURPIN *(Rookwood – Ainsworth)*
DON QUIXOTE *(Don Quixote –
    Cervantes)*
DORIAN GRAY *(The Picture Of Dorian
    Gray – Wilde)*
DR PANGLOSS *(Candide – Voltaire)*
EARWHICKER *(Finnegans Wake –
    Joyce)*
EDWARD HYDE *(Dr Jekyll And Mr
    Hyde – Stevenson)*
EVA ST CLARE *(Uncle Tom's Cabin –
    Stowe)*
FANNY LOGAN *(Pursuit Of Love –
    N Mitford)*
FANNY PRICE *(Mansfield Park –
    Austen)*
FAUNTLEROY *(14L – Little Lord
    Fauntleroy – Burnett)*
FLORA POSTE *(Cold Comfort Farm –
    Gibbons)*
FRIEDEMANN *(Little Herr Friedemann
    – Mann)*
GABRIEL OAK *(Far From The
    Madding Crowd –
    Hardy)*
GOLDFINGER *(15A – Goldfinger –
    Fleming)*
HEATHCLIFF *(Wuthering Heights –
    E Brontë)*
HOMER WELLS *(Cider House Rules –
    J Irving)*
HONOR KLEIN *(A Severed Head –
    Murdoch)*
HORNBLOWER *(Hornblower series –
    Forester)*
HOWARD KIRK *(The History Man –
    M Bradbury)*
HUNTINGDON *(15H – The Tenant Of
    Wildfell Hall –
    A Brontë)*
JANE BENNET *(Pride And Prejudice –
    Austen)*
JEAN BRODIE *(The Prime Of Miss
    Jean Brodie – Spark)*
JIM HAWKINS *(Treasure Island –
    Stevenson)*

JOE LAMPTON *(Room At The Top – Braine)*

JOHANN VOSS *(Voss – White)*

JOHNNY BULL *(Billy Bunter series – Richards)*

JOHN WALKER *(Swallows And Amazons – Ransome)*

JUDE FAWLEY *(Jude The Obscure – Hardy)*

LORD WOTTON *(The Picture Of Dorian Gray – Wilde)*

LORELEI LEE *(Gentlemen Prefer Blondes – Loos)*

LORNA DOONE *(Lorna Doone – Blackmore)*

MARY BENNET *(Pride And Prejudice – Austen)*

MIRAH COHEN *(Daniel Deronda – G Eliot)*

MISS MACKAY *(The Prime Of Miss Jean Brodie – Spark)*

MISS MARPLE *(many – Christie)*

MOLLY BLOOM *(Ulysses – Joyce)*

MONEYPENNY *(14M – many – Fleming)*

MRS DANVERS *(Rebecca – D Du Maurier)*

MRS FAIRFAX *(Jane Eyre – C Brontë)*

MRS PROUDIE *(Barchester series – Trollope)*

MRS WESTERN *(Tom Jones – Fielding)*

PERRY MASON *(many – Gardner)*

PETULENGRO *(Lavengro – Borrow)*

POSY FOSSIL *(Ballet Shoes – Streatfeild)*

QUATERMAIN *(15A – King Solomon's Mines – Haggard)*

RASSENDYLL *(The Prisoner Of Zenda – Hope)*

ROGER BROOK *(many – Wheatley)*

STARKADDER *(14A, 14S – Cold Comfort Farm – Gibbons)*

STRICKLAND *(The Moon And Sixpence – Maugham)*

TELLWRIGHT *(14A – Anna Of The Five Towns – Bennett)*

TOM BOWLING *(Roderick Random – Smollett)*

UNCLE REMUS *(Uncle Remus series – Harris)*

URI ZHIVAGO *(Dr Zhivago – Pasternak)*

VAN DER VALK *(many – Freeling)*

WIDMERPOOL *(A Dance To The Music Of Time – Powell)*

WILLOUGHBY *(14J – Sense And Sensibility – Austen)*

11

ADDENBROOKE *(Raffles series – Hornung)*

ALFRED POLLY *(The History Of Mr Polly – Wells)*

AMELIA BOOTH *(Amelia – Fielding)*

ARTHUR KIPPS *(Kipps – Wells)*

AUNT ADA DOOM *(Cold Comfort Farm – Gibbons)*

BARRY LYNDON *(Barry Lyndon – Thackeray)*

BAXTER DAWES *(Sons And Lovers – Lawrence)*

BILLY BUNTER *(Billy Bunter series – Richards)*

BINGO LITTLE *(many – Wodehouse)*

CAPTAIN AHAB *(Moby Dick – Melville)*

CAPTAIN NEMO *(20,000 Leagues Under The Sea – Verne)*

DELLA STREET *(many – Gardner)*

DR DRYASDUST *(The Antiquary – Scott)*

D'URBERVILLE *(15A – Tess Of The D'Urbervilles – Hardy)*

DURBEYFIELD *(15T – Tess Of The D'Urbervilles – Hardy)*

EDGAR LINTON *(Wuthering Heights – E Brontë)*

ELLERY QUEEN *(many – Queen)*

ELMER GANTRY *(Elmer Gantry –
S Lewis)*
EUSTACIA VYE *(The Return Of The
Native – Hardy)*
FATHER BROWN *(Father Brown series
– Chesterton)*
FATHER FLYNN *(Dubliners – Joyce)*
FRANK NUGENT *(Billy Bunter series –
Richards)*
GABRIEL SYME *(The Man Who Was
Thursday –
Chesterton)*
GREGOR SAMSA *(Metamorphosis –
Kafka)*
HARRIET VANE *(Strong Poison –
Sayers)*
HENRY SCOBIE *(The Heart Of The
Matter – Greene)*
HENRY TILNEY *(Northanger Abbey –
Austen)*
HENRY WILCOX *(Howards End –
Forster)*
HETTY SORREL *(Adam Bede – G Eliot)*
HURREE SINGH *(Billy Bunter series –
Richards)*
INDIA WILKES *(Gone With The Wind –
Mitchell)*
JANE FAIRFAX *(Emma – Austen)*
JEAN VALJEAN *(Les Misèrables –
Hugo)*
JESS OAKROYD *(The Good
Companions –
Priestley)*
JOHN LOVEDAY *(The Trumpet-Major
– Hardy)*
LADY BERTRAM *(Mansfield Park –
Austen)*
LUDWIG HOLLY *(She – Haggard)*
LUPIN POOTER *(Diary Of A Nobody –
G & W Grossmith)*
LYDIA BENNET *(Pride And Prejudice
– Austen)*
MARY POPPINS *(Mary Poppins series
– Travers)*
MAX DE WINTER *(Rebecca –
D Du Maurier)*

MOSES HERZOG *(Herzog – Bellow)*
MRS DALLOWAY *(Mrs Dalloway –
Woolf)*
NATTY BUMPPO *(Leatherstocking
Tales – W Irving)*
PETER SIMPLE *(Peter Simple –
Marryat)*
PHILEAS FOGG *(Around The World In
Eighty Days – Verne)*
PHILIP CAREY *(Of Human Bondage –
Maugham)*
PHILIP TRENT *(many – Bentley)*
PHILIP WAKEM *(The Mill On The Floss
– G Eliot)*
PHINEAS FINN *(Phineas Finn –
Trollope)*
RASKOLNIKOV *(Crime And
Punishment –
Dostoevsky)*
REDGAUNTLET *(Redgauntlet – Scott)*
RHETT BUTLER *(Gone With The Wind
– Mitchell)*
ROSS POLDARK *(Poldark series –
Graham)*
SALEEM SINAI *(Midnight's Children –
Rushdie)*
SALLY BOWLES *(Goodbye To Berlin
– Isherwood)*
SANCHO PANZA *(Don Quixote –
Cervantes)*
SCARAMOUCHE *(Scaramouche –
Sabatini)*
SILAS MARNER *(Silas Marner –
G Eliot)*
SIMON LEGREE *(Uncle Tom's Cabin –
Stowe)*
SUSAN WALKER *(Swallows And
Amazons –
Ransome)*
TESSY SANGER *(The Constant Nymph
– Kennedy)*
TITTY WALKER *(Swallows And
Amazons – Ransome)*
TOM BRANGWEN *(The Rainbow/
Women In Love –
Lawrence)*

TOM TULLIVER *(The Mill On The Floss – G Eliot)*

VELVET BROWN *(National Velvet – Bagnold)*

VICKY WALKER *(Swallows And Amazons – Ransome)*

VON STALHEIN *(Biggles series – Johns)*

WALTER MITTY *(The Secret Life Of Walter Mitty – Thurber)*

WALTER VINCY *(Middlemarch – G Eliot)*

12

ADELA QUESTED *(A Passage To India – Forster)*

ALLAN BERTRAM *(Guy Mannering – Scott)*

AMELIA SEDLEY *(Vanity Fair – Thackeray)*

ANNA KARENINA *(Anna Karenina – Tolstoy)*

ARABELLA DONN *(Jude The Obscure – Hardy)*

ARTHUR NORRIS *(Mr Norris Changes Trains – Isherwood)*

ASHLEY WILKES *(Gone With The Wind – Mitchell)*

AUGUSTE DUPIN *(many – Poe)*

AXEL JORDACHE *(Rich Man, Poor Man – I Shaw)*

BRECKINRIDGE *(Myra Breckinridge – Vidal)*

BROCKLEHURST *(Jane Eyre – C Brontë)*

CAPTAIN BLOOD *(Captain Blood – Sabatini)*

CAPTAIN QUEEG *(The Caine Mutiny – Wouk)*

CARL PETERSEN *(Bulldog Drummond – Sapper)*

CARRIE POOTER *(Diary Of A Nobody – G & W Grossmith)*

CHARLES RYDER *(Brideshead Revisited – E Waugh)*

CHARLES SWANN *(Remembrance Of Things Past – Proust)*

CHINGACHGOOK *(Leatherstocking Tales – JF Cooper)*

COUNT DRACULA *(Dracula – Stoker)*

DANDY DINMONT *(Guy Mannering – Scott)*

DAVID BALFOUR *(Kidnapped/ Catriona – Stevenson)*

DIANA WARWICK *(Diana Of The Crossways – Meredith)*

DOCTOR FINLAY *(Beyond This Place – Cronin)*

DOCTOR JEKYLL *(Dr Jekyll And Mr Hyde – Stevenson)*

DOCTOR MANSON *(The Citadel – Cronin)*

DOCTOR MOREAU *(The Island Of Dr Moreau – Wells)*

DOCTOR SLOPER *(Washington Square – H James)*

DOCTOR THORNE *(Doctor Thorne – Trollope)*

DOCTOR WATSON *(many – Doyle)*

EDMOND DANTES *(The Count Of Monte Cristo – Dumas)*

ERIC WILLIAMS *(Eric or Little By Little – Farrar)*

FLEUR FORSYTE *(The Forsyte Saga – Galsworthy)*

FRANKENSTEIN *(14D – Frankenstein – M Shelley)*

GEORGES DUROY *(Bel-Ami – Maupassant)*

GEORGE SMILEY *(Smiley's People – Le Carré)*

GUY MANNERING *(Guy Mannering – Scott)*

HARRY WHARTON *(Billy Bunter series – Richards)*

HOLLY FORSYTE *(The Forsyte Saga – Galsworthy)*
HUGH BRITLING *(Mr Britling Sees It Through – Wells)*
ICHABOD CRANE *(The Legend Of Sleepy Hollow – W Irving)*
ISABEL ARCHER *(Portrait Of A Lady – H James)*
JAMES FORSYTE *(The Forsyte Saga – Galsworthy)*
JOLLY FORSYTE *(The Forsyte Saga – Galsworthy)*
KIMBALL O'HARA *(Kim – Kipling)*
LADY DE BOURGH *(Pride And Prejudice – Austen)*
LADY GLENCORA *(Palliser series – Trollope)*
LADY STANDISH *(Palliser series – Trollope)*
LANGDON TOWNE *(North West Passage – Roberts)*
LENINA CROWNE *(Brave New World – A Huxley)*
LEOPOLD BLOOM *(Ulysses – Joyce)*
LINDA RADLETT *(Pursuit Of Love – N Mitford)*
MADAME BOVARY *(Madame Bovary – Flaubert)*
MEG MERRILIES *(Guy Mannering – Scott)*
MOLL FLANDERS *(Moll Flanders – Defoe)*
MUSTAPHA MOND *(Brave New World – A Huxley)*
OSBALDISTONE *(Rob Roy – Scott)*
PASSEPARTOUT *(Around The World In Eighty Days – Verne)*
PENNYFEATHER *(Decline And Fall – E Waugh)*
RIP VAN WINKLE *(The Sketch Book – W Irving)*
ROBERT JORDAN *(For Whom The Bell Tolls – Hemingway)*

SERGEANT CUFF *(The Moonstone – W Collins)*
SERGEANT TROY *(Far From The Madding Crowd – Hardy)*
SIDNEY LARKIN *(The Darling Buds Of May – Bates)*
SIMON TEMPLAR *(Saint series – Charteris)*
SOPHIA BAINES *(The Old Wives' Tale – Bennett)*
SQUIRE GORDON *(Black Beauty – Sewell)*
SUE BRIDEHEAD *(Jude The Obscure – Hardy)*
THOMAS FOWLER *(The Quiet American – Greene)*
WILLIAM BOOTH *(Amelia – Fielding)*
WILLIAM BROWN *(Just William series – Crompton)*
WINSTON SMITH *(1984 – Orwell)*

13

ADAM DALGLEISH *(many – PD James)*
ALBERT CAMPION *(many – Allingham)*
ANNE CATHERICK *(The Woman In White – W Collins)*
BASIL HALLWARD *(The Picture Of Dorian Gray – Wilde)*
BECKY THATCHER *(The Adventures Of Tom Sawyer – Twain)*
BERTIE WOOSTER *(many – Wodehouse)*
BERT SMALLWAYS *(War In The Air – Wells)*
BISHOP PROUDIE *(Barsetshire series – Trollope)*
CAPTAIN KETTLE *(many – Hyne)*

CHARLES POOTER *(Diary Of A Nobody – G & W Grossmith)*

CLYM YEOBRIGHT *(The Return Of the Native – Hardy)*

COLONEL ESMOND *(Henry Esmond – Thackeray)*

DANIEL DERONDA *(Daniel Deronda – G Eliot)*

DARSIE LATIMER *(Redgauntlet – Scott)*

DOCTOR CAMERON *(Beyond This Place – Cronin)*

DOCTOR LIVESEY *(Treasure Island – Stevenson)*

DONALD FARFRAE *(The Mayor Of Casterbridge – Hardy)*

EMMA WOODHOUSE *(Emma – Austen)*

FRANKLIN BLAKE *(The Moonstone – W Collins)*

FRITZ ROBINSON *(The Swiss Family Robinson – Wyss)*

GEORGE WICKHAM *(Pride And Prejudice – Austen)*

GILBERT OSMOND *(Portrait Of A Lady – H James)*

GUY CROUCHBACK *(Men At Arms – E Waugh)*

HENRY DASHWOOD *(Sense And Sensibility – Austen)*

HERCULE POIROT *(many – Christie)*

HILDA LESSWAYS *(Clayhanger – Bennett)*

HORACE RUMPOLE *(Rumpole series – Mortimer)*

JACOB ARMITAGE *(The Children Of The New Forest – Marryat)*

JACOB FLANDERS *(Jacob's Room – Woolf)*

JOLYON FORSYTE *(The Forsyte Saga – Galsworthy)*

JULIAN PEVERIL *(Peveril Of The Peak – Scott)*

KENNETH TOOMEY *(Earthly Powers – Burgess)*

LADY MARCHMAIN *(Brideshead Revisited – E Waugh)*

LORD GREYSTOKE *(Tarzan series – Burroughs)*

LORD MARCHMAIN *(Brideshead Revisited – E Waugh)*

MYCROFT HOLMES *(many – Doyle)*

NATHAN DETROIT *(Guys And Dolls – Runyon)*

OLIVER MELLORS *(Lady Chatterley's Lover – Lawrence)*

PAMELA ANDREWS *(Pamela – Richardson)*

PERCY BLAKENEY *(The Scarlet Pimpernel – Orczy)*

PHILIP MARLOWE *(many – Chandler)*

PRINCE AMERIGO *(The Golden Bowl – H James)*

REVEREND SLOPE *(Barsetshire series – Trollope)*

RICHARD HANNAY *(many – Buchan)*

RODERICK USHER *(The Fall Of The House Of Usher – Poe)*

SADIE THOMPSON *(Rain – Maugham)*

SCARLETT O'HARA *(Gone With The Wind – Mitchell)*

SOAMES FORSYTE *(The Forsyte Saga – Galsworthy)*

SOPHIA WESTERN *(Tom Jones – Fielding)*

SQUIRE WESTERN *(Tom Jones – Fielding)*

THOMAS NEWCOME *(The Newcomes – Thackeray)*

TOBY ESTERHAZY *(Smiley's People – Le Carré)*

ZULEIKA DOBSON *(Zuleika Dobson – Beerbohm)*

AMOS STARKADDER *(Cold Comfort Farm – Gibbons)*

ANGHARAD MORGAN *(How Green Was My Valley – Llewellyn)*

ANNA TELLWRIGHT *(Anna Of The Five Towns – Bennett)*

ANTHONY KROESIG *(Pursuit Of Love – N Mitford)*

ARTHUR HASTINGS *(many – Christie)*

BENJAMIN COOLEY *(Kangaroo – Lawrence)*

CHARLES BINGLEY *(Pride And Prejudice – Austen)*

CHARLES RAINIER *(Random Harvest – Hilton)*

COLONEL BRANDON *(Sense And Sensibility – Austen)*

COLONEL LAMBERT *(The Virginians – Thackeray)*

DEBORAH JENKYNS *(Cranford – Gaskell)*

DOCTOR PANGLOSS *(Candide – Voltaire)*

DOROTHEA BROOKE *(Middlemarch – G Eliot)*

DR FRANKENSTEIN *(Frankenstein – M Shelley)*

EDWARD CASAUBON *(Middlemarch – G Eliot)*

EDWARD WAVERLEY *(Waverley novels – Scott)*

ELIZABETH TRANT *(The Good Companions – Priestley)*

FESTUS DERRIMAN *(The Trumpet-Major – Hardy)*

FRANCIS HERRIES *(Rogue Herries – Walpole)*

GEOFFREY FIRMIN *(Under The Volcano – Lowry)*

GEORGE LEWISHAM *(Love And Mr Lewisham – Wells)*

GILBERT MARKHAM *(The Tenant Of Wildfell Hall – A Brontë)*

HERBERT BADGERY *(Illywhacker – Carey)*

HUMBERT HUMBERT *(Lolita – Nabokov)*

HUMPHRY CLINKER *(Humphry Clinker – Smollett)*

INIGO JOLLIFANT *(The Good Companions – Priestley)*

ISABELLA THORPE *(Northanger Abbey – Austen)*

JOHN WILLOUGHBY *(Sense And Sensibility – Austen)*

JONATHAN HARKER *(Dracula – Stoker)*

LADY CHATTERLEY *(Lady Chatterley's Lover – Lawrence)*

LEMUEL GULLIVER *(Gulliver's Travels – Swift)*

LONG JOHN SILVER *(Treasure Island – Stevenson)*

LORD FAUNTLEROY *(Little Lord Fauntleroy – Burnett)*

MAGGIE TULLIVER *(The Mill On The Floss – G Eliot)*

MARIAN HOLCOMBE *(The Woman In White – W Collins)*

MASTERMAN READY *(Masterman Ready – Marryat)*

MISS MONEYPENNY *(many – Fleming)*

QUENTIN DURWARD *(Quentin Durward – Scott)*

RACHEL VERINDER *(The Moonstone – W Collins)*
REBECCA RANDALL *(Rebecca Of Sunnybrook Farm – Wiggin)*
ROBINSON CRUSOE *(Robinson Crusoe – Defoe)*
RODERICK ALLEYN *(many – Marsh)*
RODERICK RANDOM *(Roderick Random – Smollett)*
ROSIE DRIFFIELD *(Cakes And Ale – Maugham)*
SEBASTIAN FLYTE *(Brideshead Revisited – E Waugh)*
SETH STARKADDER *(Cold Comfort Farm – Gibbons)*
SHERLOCK HOLMES *(many – Doyle)*
SHIRLEY KEELDAR *(Shirley – C Brontë)*
SIR PITT CRAWLEY *(Vanity Fair – Thackeray)*
STEPHEN DEDALUS *(Ulysses – Joyce)*
TRILBY O'FERRALL *(Trilby – G Du Maurier)*
TRISTRAM SHANDY *(Tristram Shandy – Sterne)*
WORLDLY-WISEMAN *(Pilgrim's Progress – Bunyan)*

15

ADMIRAL PALLISER *(Palliser series – Trollope)*
ALEC D'URBERVILLE *(Tess Of The D'Urbervilles – Hardy)*
ALLAN QUATERMAIN *(King Solomon's Mines – Haggard)*
ARTHUR PENDENNIS *(Pendennis – Thackeray)*
AURIC GOLDFINGER *(Goldfinger – Fleming)*
BULLDOG DRUMMOND *(Bulldog Drummond – Sapper)*
CARACTACUS POTTS *(Chitty Chitty Bang Bang – Fleming)*
CATHERINE BENNET *(Pride And Prejudice – Austen)*
CHARLES MUSGROVE *(Persuasion – Austen)*
CHARLES PRIMROSE *(The Vicar Of Wakefield – Goldsmith)*
CLARISSA HARLOWE *(Clarissa – Richardson)*
COLONEL BEVERLEY *(The Children Of The New Forest – Marryat)*
CONSTANCE BAINES *(The Old Wives' Tale – Bennett)*
DOCTOR DRYASDUST *(The Antiquary – Scott)*
EDWARD PONDEREVO *(Tono-Bungay – Wells)*
EDWARD ROCHESTER *(Jane Eyre – C Brontë)*
EDWIN CLAYHANGER *(Clayhanger – Bennett)*
ELIZABETH BENNET *(Pride And Prejudice – Austen)*
GEORGE KNIGHTLEY *(Emma – Austen)*
HELEN HUNTINGDON *(The Tenant Of Wildfell Hall – A Brontë)*
HOLDEN CAULFIELD *(Catcher In The Rye – Salinger)*
HORACE ABBEVILLE *(Cannery Row – Steinbeck)*

HUCKLEBERRY FINN *(Huckleberry Finn — Twain)*
LORD PETER WIMSEY *(many — Sayers)*
MICHAEL HENCHARD *(The Mayor Of Casterbridge — Hardy)*
PEREGRINE PICKLE *(Peregrine Pickle — Smollett)*
REVEREND COLLINS *(Pride And Prejudice — Austen)*
RUPERT OF HENTZAU *(Ruritania series — Hope)*
SEPTIMUS HARDING *(Barsetshire series — Trollope)*

SQUIRE ALLWORTHY *(Tom Jones — Fielding)*
SQUIRE INGLEWOOD *(Rob Roy — Scott)*
SQUIRE TRELAWNEY *(Treasure Island — Stevenson)*
TESS DURBEYFIELD *(Tess Of The D'Urbervilles — Hardy)*
WALTER HARTRIGHT *(The Woman In White — W Collins)*
WILLIAM BOLDWOOD *(Far From The Madding Crowd — Hardy)*

ARTS

LITERATURE — BOOKS

* = Alternative title

3

ADA *(Nabokov)*
BOY *(Hanley)*
KES *(Hines)*
KIM *(Kipling)*
OIL! *(Sinclair)*
SHE *(Haggard)*
WEB *(Wyndham)*

4

CLEA *(L Durrell)*
COMA *(Cook)*

DAWN *(Haggard)*
DRED *(Stowe)*
DUNE *(F Herbert)*
EMMA *(Austen)*
GIGI *(Colette)*
JAWS *(Benchley)*
NANA *(Zola)*
N OR M? *(Christie)*
OMOO *(Melville)*
PNIN *(Nabokov)*
RAIN *(Maugham)*
RUTH *(Gaskell)*
SIDO *(Colette)*
SOLO *(Higgins)*
SONS *(Buck)*

SS-GB *(Deighton)*
TARR *(W Lewis)*
TUNC *(L Durrell)*
VOSS *(P White)*
WATT *(Beckett)*
WILT *(Sharpe)*

5

ASSEZ *(Beckett)*
BAMBI *(Salten)*
BANCO *(Charrière)*
BELLA *(J Cooper)* *(Giraudoux)*

ARTS – LITERATURE – BOOKS

BLISS *(Mansfield)*
CHÉRI *(Colette)*
CLASS *(J Cooper)*
ÉMILE *(Rousseau)*
EMILY *(J Cooper)*
FOCUS *(A Miller)*
HEIDI *(Spyri)*
HOTEL *(Hailey)*
KALKI *(Vidal)*
KIPPS *(Wells)*
LIBRA *(Delillo)*
MARDI *(Melville)*
MINGO *(JC Harris)*
MONEY *(M Amis)*
MOODS *(Alcott)*
MOTHS *(Ouida)*
MR PIM *(Milne)*
MR PYE *(Peake)*
MYRON *(Vidal)*
NEXUS *(H Miller)*
PROOF *(Francis)*
ROOTS *(Haley)*
SAPHO *(Daudet)*
SCOOP *(E Waugh)*
SEXUS *(H Miller)*
SMOKE *(Turgenev)*
SPACE *(Michener)*
SYBIL *(Disraeli)*
TEXAS *(Michener)*
TO LET *(Galsworthy)*
TOPAZ *(Uris)*
TYPEE *(Melville)*
WANDA *(Ouida)*
YEAST *(Kingsley)*
ZADIG *(Voltaire)*

FERGUS *(B Moore)*
GROWTH *(Tarkington)*
HELENA *(E Waugh)*
HERZOG *(Bellow)*
I, ROBOT *(Asimov)*
ISLAND *(A Huxley)*
JEREMY *(HS Walpole)*
JULIAN *(Vidal)*
JURGEN *(Cabell)*
LOLITA *(Nabokov)*
MEDUSA *(H Innes)*
MURPHY *(Beckett)*
NAUSEA *(Sartre) *1
NO NAME *(W Collins)*
OTHMAR *(Ouida)*
PAMELA *(Richardson)*
PELHAM *(Bulwer-Lytton)*
PENROD *(Tarkington)*
PHROSO *(Hope)*
PIERRE *(Melville)*
PLEXUS *(H Miller)*
RIDERS *(J Cooper)*
RIENZI *(Bulwer-Lytton)*
ROB ROY *(W Scott)*
ROMOLA *(G Eliot)*
ROXANA *(Defoe)*
SHOGUN *(Clavell)*
SHOSHA *(Singer)*
SYLVIA *(Sinclair)*
THE FOG *(J Herbert)*
THE FOX *(DH Lawrence)*
TRILBY *(G Du Maurier)*
UNGAVA *(Ballantyne)*
WALDEN *(Thoreau)*

CECILIA *(Burney)*
COUPLES *(Updike)*
CRY WOLF *(W Smith)*
CURTAIN *(Christie)*
DOLORES *(Compton-Burnett)*
DRACULA *(Stoker)*
EREWHON *(Butler)*
EUPHUES *(Lyly)*
EVELINA *(Burney)*
FARAWAY *(Priestley)*
HARRIET *(J Cooper)*
HOW IT IS *(Beckett)*
HYPATIA *(Kingsley)*
IVANHOE *(W Scott)*
JOCELYN *(Galsworthy)*
JUSTINE *(L Durrell)*
            (Sade)
KING RAT *(Clavell)*
LA CHUTE *(Camus) *2
LA PESTE *(Camus) *3
LEONORA *(Bennett)*
LORD JIM *(Conrad)*
LOTHAIR *(Disraeli)*
MINE BOY *(Abrahams)*
NEMESIS *(Christie)*
NUNQUAM *(L Durrell)*
OBLOMOV *(Goncharov)*
OCTAVIA *(J Cooper)*
ORLANDO *(Woolf)*
PAL JOEY *(O'Hara)*
POOR COW *(Dunn)*
REBECCA *(D Du Maurier)*
REDBURN *(Melville)*
SALAMBO *(Flaubert)*
SAVILLE *(Storey)*
SECRETS *(Steel)*
SHARDIK *(R Adams)*
SHIRLEY *(C Brontë)*
SKYLARK *(EE Smith)*
SUCCESS *(M Amis)*
TANCRED *(Disraeli)*
THEATRE *(Maugham)*
THE BELL *(Murdoch)*
THE DEEP *(Benchley)*
            (Spillane)
THE FALL *(Camus) *2

6

AMELIA *(Fielding)*
BEL-AMI *(Maupassant)*
BEN-HUR *(L Wallace)*
CARRIE *(King)*
CHOCKY *(Wyndham)*
DEMIAN *(Hesse)*
EMPIRE *(Vidal)*
ESTHER *(H Adams)*

7

AIRPORT *(Hailey)*
ARCADIA *(Sidney)*
ARMANCE *(Stendhal)*
BABBITT *(S Lewis)*
CALYPSO *(McBain)*
CAMILLA *(Burney)*
CANDIDE *(Voltaire)*
CAPRICE *(Firbank)*

TRINITY *(Uris)*
TRISTAN *(Mann)*
TYPHOON *(Conrad)*
UKRIDGE *(Wodehouse)*
ULYSSES *(Joyce)*
VENETIA *(Disraeli)*

8

ADAM BEDE *(G Eliot)*
ANTIC HAY *(A Huxley)*
ATHERTON *(MR Mitford)*
CARNIVAL *(Mackenzie)*
CATRIONA *(Stevenson)*
CLARISSA *(Richardson)*
CONSUELO *(Sand)*
CRANFORD *(Gaskell)*
DOCTOR NO *(Fleming)*
ENDYMION *(Disraeli)*
FANSHAWE *(Hawthorne)*
FICTIONS *(Borges)*
FREE FALL *(Golding)*
FRESCOES *(Ouida)*
GERMINAL *(Zola)*
GOLD MINE *(W Smith)*
I, THE JURY *(Spillane)*
JAILBIRD *(Vonnegut)*
JANE EYRE *(C Brontë)*
KANGAROO *(DH Lawrence)*
LADY ANNA *(Trollope)*
LA NAUSÉE *(Sartre)* *1
LAVENGRO *(Borrow)*
LUCKY JIM *(K Amis)*
MAKING DO *(Goodman)*
MOBY DICK *(Melville)*
NICE WORK *(Lodge)*
NOON WINE *(Porter)*
NOSTROMO *(Conrad)*
OVERLOAD *(Hailey)*
PALE FIRE *(Nabokov)*
PAPILLON *(Charrière)*
POET'S PUB *(Linklater)*
RASSELAS *(S Johnson)*
ROOKWOOD *(Ainsworth)*
SANDITON *(Austen)*

SCRUPLES *(Krantz)*
SEPTIMUS *(Hawthorne)*
SEVEN MEN *(Beerbohm)*
SIR NIGEL *(Doyle)*
SPEAK NOW *(Yerby)*
SPY STORY *(Deighton)*
SWAN SONG *(Galsworthy)*
THE ABBOT *(W Scott)*
THE BIRDS *(D Du Maurier)*
THE IDIOT *(Dostoevsky)*
THE JUDGE *(R West)*
THE MAGUS *(Fowles)*
THE TRIAL *(Kafka)*
THE WAVES *(Woolf)*
TOM JONES *(Fielding)*
TRIAL RUN *(Francis)*
VALPERGA *(M Shelley)*
VILLETTE *(C Brontë)*
VITTORIA *(Meredith)*
WAVERLEY *(W Scott)*
WILLIWAW *(Vidal)*

9

AARON'S ROD *(DH Lawrence)*
AFTER DARK *(W Collins)*
AGNES GREY *(A Brontë)*
A LOT TO ASK *(PH Newby)*
BALTHAZAR *(L Durrell)*
BEAU GESTE *(Wren)*
BILLY BUDD *(Melville)*
BILLY LIAR *(Waterhouse)*
BLACK ROBE *(B Moore)*
BLIND LOVE *(Pritchett)*
BONE CRACK *(Francis)*
CIRCUS BOY *(Manning-Sanders)*
CONINGSBY *(Disraeli)*
DEAD SOULS *(Gogol)*
DEMOCRACY *(H Adams)*
DODSWORTH *(S Lewis)*
DREAM DAYS *(Grahame)*
DUBLINERS *(Joyce)*
EAST LYNNE *(Wood)*
FANNY HILL *(Cleland)*
FELIX HOLT *(G Eliot)*

FIRST LOVE *(Turgenev)*
FORTITUDE *(HS Walpole)*
GOOD WIVES *(Alcott)*
GORKY PARK *(MC Smith)*
GUY RIVERS *(Simms)*
HARD TIMES *(Dickens)*
HARLEQUIN *(M West)*
HAWKSMOOR *(Ackroyd)*
I, CLAUDIUS *(Graves)*
KIDNAPPED *(Stevenson)*
L'ÉTRANGER *(Camus)* *4
LITTLE MEN *(Alcott)*
LOVE STORY *(Segal)*
MEN AT ARMS *(E Waugh)*
MOONRAKER *(Fleming)*
NIGHTFALL *(Asimov)*
ON THE ROAD *(Kerouac)*
ORLEY FARM *(Trollope)*
OUR STREET *(Thackeray)*
PASSENGER *(Keneally)*
PENDENNIS *(Thackeray)*
POTTERISM *(R Macaulay)*
RABBIT, RUN *(Updike)*
RADCLIFFE *(Storey)*
ROGUE MALE *(Household)*
ROMANY RYE *(Borrow)*
SAINT JACK *(Theroux)*
'SALEM'S LOT *(King)*
SEVENTEEN *(Tarkington)*
SOME DO NOT *(Ford)*
STALKY & CO *(Kipling)*
STAYING ON *(P Scott)*
THE CASTLE *(Kafka)*
THE CHIMES *(Dickens)*
THE CLOCKS *(Christie)*
THE DEVILS *(Dostoevsky)*
THE EGOIST *(Meredith)*
THE HEROES *(Kingsley)*
THE HOBBIT *(Tolkien)*
THE MEMBER *(Galt)*
THE PLAGUE *(Camus)* *3
THE SÉANCE *(Singer)*
THE VICTIM *(Bellow)*
THE WARDEN *(Trollope)*
VENUSBERG *(Powell)*
VICE VERSA *(Anstey)*

WHITE FANG *(London)*
WHOSE BODY? *(Sayers)*
WILD WALES *(Borrow)*
WORLD'S END *(Sinclair)*

10

A LAODICEAN *(Hardy)*
ALICE ADAMS *(Tarkington)*
ALTON LOCKE *(Kingsley)*
ANIMAL FARM *(Orwell)*
ANNABEL LEE *(Poe)*
BLEAK HOUSE *(Dickens)*
BULLET PARK *(Cheever)*
CANCER WARD *(Solzhenitsyn)*
CANNERY ROW *(Steinbeck)*
CAT'S CRADLE *(Vonnegut)*
CENTENNIAL *(Michener)*
CHATTERTON *(Ackroyd)*
CLAYHANGER *(Bennett)*
DEAD BABIES *(M Amis)*
DON QUIXOTE *(Cervantes)*
EAST OF EDEN *(Steinbeck)*
EAST OF SUEZ *(Maugham)*
ETHAN FROME *(Wharton)*
EUGENE ARAM *(Bulwer-Lytton)*
FER-DE-LANCE *(Stout)*
GAUDY NIGHT *(Sayers)*
GOLDFINGER *(Fleming)*
GOOD AS GOLD *(Heller)*
HOTEL DU LAC *(Brookner)*
HOWARDS END *(Forster)*
IN CHANCERY *(Galsworthy)*
JACOB'S ROOM *(Woolf)*
JAKE'S THING *(K Amis)*
JAMAICA INN *(D Du Maurier)*
JOSH LAWTON *(Bragg)*
KENILWORTH *(W Scott)*
LABYRINTHS *(Borges)*
LORNA DOONE *(Blackmore)*
MARTIN EDEN *(London)*
MARY BARTON *(Gaskell)*
MELINCOURT *(Peacock)*
MOUNTOLIVE *(L Durrell)*
NOBLE HOUSE *(Clavell)*
ON THE BEACH *(Shute)*

PERELANDRA *(CS Lewis)*
PERSUASION *(Austen)*
POSSESSION *(Byatt)*
RED HARVEST *(Hammett)*
ROUGHING IT *(Twain)*
RURAL RIDES *(Cobbett)*
SALMAGUNDI *(W Irving)*
SAVAGE GOLD *(Fuller)*
SUNSET PASS *(Grey)*
TAKE IT EASY *(Runyon)*
THE CITADEL *(Cronin)*
THE GOLD BUG *(Poe)*
THE MARTIAN *(G Du Maurier)*
THE MONSTER *(Crane)*
THE PRAIRIE *(JF Cooper)*
THE PROVOST *(Galt)*
THE RAINBOW *(DH Lawrence)*
THE RED PONY *(Steinbeck)*
THE SHINING *(King)*
THE THIN MAN *(Hammett)*
THE WATSONS *(Austen)*
THE WRECKER *(Stevenson)*
THREE LIVES *(Stein)*
TITUS ALONE *(Peake)*
TITUS GROAN *(Peake)*
TONO-BUNGAY *(Wells)*
UNCLE REMUS *(JC Harris)*
VANITY FAIR *(Thackeray)*
VESTAL FIRE *(Mackenzie)*
VILE BODIES *(E Waugh)*
VIRGIN SOIL *(Turgenev)*
VIVIAN GREY *(Disraeli)*
WESTWARD HO! *(Kingsley)*
WOLF SOLENT *(JC Powys)*

11

A MAN LAY DEAD *(N Marsh)*
ANN VERONICA *(Wells)*
A PERFECT SPY *(Le Carré)*
AS I LAY DYING *(Faulkner)*
A TALE OF A TUB *(Swift)*
BALLET SHOES *(Streatfeild)*
BARRY LYNDON *(Thackeray)*
BLACK BEAUTY *(Sewell)*

BLACK BRYONY *(TF Powys)*
BLACK SPRING *(H Miller)*
BOGLE CORBET *(Galt)*
BOULE DE SUIF *(Maupassant)*
BURIED ALIVE *(Bennett)*
BURMESE DAYS *(Orwell)*
CAKES AND ALE *(Maugham)*
COLONEL JACK *(Defoe)*
CORAL ISLAND *(Ballantyne)*
CROME YELLOW *(A Huxley)*
DAISY MILLER *(H James)*
DANGLING MAN *(Bellow)*
ELMER GANTRY *(S Lewis)*
ELUSIVE EARL *(Cartland)*
GORMENGHAST *(Peake)*
GREENMANTLE *(Buchan)*
GRIFFIN'S WAY *(Yerby)*
HARRIET SAID *(Bainbridge)*
HENRY ESMOND *(Thackeray)*
ILLYWHACKER *(Carey)*
IN A PROVINCE *(Van Der Post)*
KANE AND ABEL *(Archer)*
LITTLE WOMEN *(Alcott)*
LOST HORIZON *(Hilton)*
MARATHON MAN *(Goldman)*
MARTHA QUEST *(Lessing)*
MARTIN FABER *(Simms)*
MEMENTO MORI *(Spark)*
MEN AND WIVES *(Compton-Burnett)*
MICAH CLARKE *(Doyle)*
MIDDLEMARCH *(G Eliot)*
MRS DALLOWAY *(Woolf)*
NO COMEBACKS *(Forsyth)*
OLIVER TWIST *(Dickens)*
PETER SIMPLE *(Marryat)*
PEYTON PLACE *(Metalious)*
PHINEAS FINN *(Trollope)*
PRESTER JOHN *(Buchan)*
RABBIT REDUX *(Updike)*
REDGAUNTLET *(W Scott)*
RODNEY STONE *(Doyle)*
SCARAMOUCHE *(Sabatini)*
SHIP OF FOOLS *(Porter)*
SHORT FRIDAY *(Singer)*
SILAS MARNER *(G Eliot)*
SILVER BLAZE *(Doyle)*

SNOW COUNTRY *(Kawabata)*
STEPPENWOLF *(Hesse)*
SWITCH BITCH *(Dahl)*
TATTERED TOM *(Alger)*
THE AMERICAN *(H James)*
THE BERTRAMS *(Trollope)*
THE BIG SLEEP *(Chandler)*
THE CRUEL SEA *(Monsarrat)*
THE DEER PARK *(Mailer)*
THE HIRED MAN *(Bragg)*
THE HIRELING *(Hartley)*
THE HUMAN AGE *(W Lewis)*
THE IRON HEEL *(London)*
THE LEVANTER *(Ambler)*
THE LOVED ONE *(E Waugh)*
THE MEMORIAL *(Isherwood)*
THE MIMIC MEN *(Naipaul)*
THE NEWCOMES *(Thackeray)*
THE ODD WOMEN *(Gissing)*
THE OPEN BOAT *(Crane)*
THE SATANIST *(Wheatley)*
THE STRANGER *(Camus)* *4
THE TALISMAN *(W Scott)*
THE THIRD MAN *(Greene)*
THE TOLL GATE *(Heyer)*
THE WRONG BOX *(Stevenson)*
THE YEMASSEE *(Simms)*
THUNDERBALL *(Fleming)*
TOBACCO ROAD *(Caldwell)*
TWO ON A TOWER *(Hardy)*
UNDER THE NET *(Murdoch)*
WAR AND PEACE *(Tolstoy)*
WAR IN THE AIR *(Wells)*
WHAT KATY DID *(Coolidge)*
WOMEN IN LOVE *(DH Lawrence)*

12

A BAR OF SHADOW *(Van Der Post)*
AFTERNOON MEN *(Powell)*
ANNA KARENINA *(Tolstoy)*
A SEVERED HEAD *(Murdoch)*
BARNABY RUDGE *(Dickens)*
BEND SINISTER *(Nabokov)*
BRIGHTON ROCK *(Greene)*

BUDDENBROOKS *(Mann)*
CAPTAIN BLOOD *(Sabatini)*
CASINO ROYALE *(Fleming)*
DEAD MAN'S ROCK *(Quiller-Couch)*
DOCTOR THORNE *(Trollope)*
DOMBEY AND SON *(Dickens)*
DOUBLE DOUBLE *(Queen)*
ESTHER WATERS *(G Moore)*
EUGENE ONEGIN *(Pushkin)*
FEAR IS THE KEY *(Maclean)*
FEAR OF FLYING *(Jong)*
FISH DEFERRED *(Wodehouse)*
FOMA GORDEYEV *(Gorki)*
FRANKENSTEIN *(M Shelley)*
GUY MANNERING *(W Scott)*
GUYS AND DOLLS *(Runyon)*
HANDLEY CROSS *(Surtees)*
HEADLONG HALL *(Peacock)*
HOLD THE DREAM *(Taylor-Bradford)*
HOLY DEADLOCK *(AP Herbert)*
HUNTINGTOWER *(Buchan)*
IN A FREE STATE *(Naipaul)*
ISRAEL POTTER *(Melville)*
LE GRAND ÉCART *(Cocteau)*
LE PETIT CHOSE *(Daudet)*
LIFE AT THE TOP *(Braine)*
LITTLE DORRIT *(Dickens)*
LONDON FIELDS *(M Amis)*
LOVE FOR LYDIA *(Bates)*
LUCIANO'S LUCK *(Higgins)*
MADAME BOVARY *(Flaubert)*
MAIDEN CASTLE *(JC Powys)*
MIGUEL STREET *(Naipaul)*
MOLL FLANDERS *(Defoe)*
MURDER IS EASY *(Christie)*
MY LIFE AS A MAN *(Roth)*
NOT TO DISTURB *(Spark)*
OF MICE AND MEN *(Steinbeck)*
OLD MORTALITY *(W Scott)*
ORPHAN ISLAND *(R Macaulay)*
PHINEAS REDUX *(Trollope)*
PRATER VIOLET *(Isherwood)*
RESURRECTION *(Tolstoy)*
RHODA FLEMING *(Meredith)*
ROGUE HERRIES *(HS Walpole)*
ROOM AT THE TOP *(Braine)*

RUNNING BLIND *(Bagley)*
SISTER CARRIE *(Dreiser)*
STRONG POISON *(Sayers)*
THE ANTIQUARY *(W Scott)*
THE CHOIR BOYS *(Wambaugh)*
THE COLLECTOR *(Fowles)*
THE COMEDIANS *(Greene)*
THE DECAMERON *(Boccaccio)*
THE DOGS OF WAR *(Forsyth)*
THE EUROPEANS *(H James)*
THE FLYING INN *(Chesterton)*
THE GINGER MAN *(Donleavy)*
THE GO-BETWEEN *(Hartley)*
THE GODFATHER *(Puzo)*
THE GOLDEN AGE *(Grahame)*
THE GOOD EARTH *(Buck)*
THE GRASS HARP *(Capote)*
THE LOST WORLD *(Doyle)*
THE LOVING CUP *(Graham)*
THE MAN WITHIN *(Greene)*
THE MARY DEARE *(H Innes)*
THE MONASTERY *(W Scott)*
THE MOONSTONE *(W Collins)*
THE OLD DEVILS *(K Amis)*
THE PROFESSOR *(C Brontë)*
THE SCAPEGOAT *(D Du Maurier)*
THE SEA, THE SEA *(Murdoch)*
THE SNOW GOOSE *(Gallico)*
THE TWO TOWERS *(Tolkien)*
THE WHITE DEER *(Thurber)*
TOO MANY COOKS *(Stout)*
TORTILLA FLAT *(Steinbeck)*
TRAGIC GROUND *(Caldwell)*
WATCH AND WARD *(H James)*
WESTERN UNION *(Grey)*
WHISKY GALORE *(Mackenzie)*
WILD CONQUEST *(Abrahams)*

13

A BURNT-OUT CASE *(Greene)*
A HOUSE DIVIDED *(Buck)*
A KIND OF LOVING *(Barstow)*
ALMAYER'S FOLLY *(Conrad)*
A MODERN COMEDY *(Galsworthy)*

A MODERN UTOPIA *(Wells)*
ANGEL PAVEMENT *(Priestley)*
A SPARROW FALLS *(W Smith)*
BRAVE NEW WORLD *(A Huxley)*
CALL OF THE WILD *(London)*
CARRY ON, JEEVES! *(Wodehouse)*
CHILDHOOD'S END *(Clarke)*
COUSIN PHILLIS *(Gaskell)*
DANIEL DERONDA *(G Eliot)*
DOCTOR AT LARGE *(Gordon)*
DOCTOR FAUSTUS *(Mann)* *5
DOCTOR ZHIVAGO *(Pasternak)*
DOKTOR FAUSTUS *(Mann)* *5
EARTHLY POWERS *(Burgess)*
ENGLAND MADE ME *(Greene)*
EYELESS IN GAZA *(A Huxley)*
FAME IS THE SPUR *(Spring)*
FEMALE FRIENDS *(Weldon)*
FINNEGANS WAKE *(Joyce)*
GIMPEL THE FOOL *(Singer)*
HATTER'S CASTLE *(Cronin)*
HELD IN BONDAGE *(Ouida)*
HILDA LESSWAYS *(Bennett)*
HUMBOLDT'S GIFT *(Bellow)*
JACOB FAITHFUL *(Marryat)*
JOSEPH ANDREWS *(Fielding)*
JUST SO STORIES *(Kipling)*
LADDERS TO FIRE *(Nin)*
LES MISÉRABLES *(Hugo)*
LIGHT IN AUGUST *(Faulkner)*
LIVE AND LET DIE *(Fleming)*
LIZA OF LAMBETH *(Maugham)*
LOSER TAKES ALL *(Greene)*
MANSFIELD PARK *(Austen)*
METAMORPHOSIS *(Kafka)*
NEW GRUB STREET *(Gissing)*
NORTH AND SOUTH *(Gaskell)*
PETER IBBETSON *(G Du Maurier)*
PICTURE PALACE *(Theroux)*
PINCHER MARTIN *(Golding)*
POSTERN OF FATE *(Christie)*
PRINCE CASPIAN *(CS Lewis)*
PRIVATE ANGELO *(Linklater)*
PURSUIT OF LOVE *(N Mitford)*
RANDOM HARVEST *(Hilton)*
RIGHT HO, JEEVES! *(Wodehouse)*

SANDRA BELLONI *(Meredith)*
SATANIC VERSES *(Rushdie)*
SCHINDLER'S ARK *(Keneally)*
SELF-CONDEMNED *(W Lewis)*
SKETCHES BY BOZ *(Dickens)*
SMILEY'S PEOPLE *(Le Carré)*
SOLDIERS THREE *(Kipling)*
SONS AND LOVERS *(DH Lawrence)*
STAMBOUL TRAIN *(Greene)*
SWORD OF HONOUR *(E Waugh)*
SYLVIA'S LOVERS *(Gaskell)*
TARKA THE OTTER *(Williamson)*
THE ABC MURDERS *(Christie)*
THE BLACK ARROW *(Stevenson)*
THE BLACK TOWER *(PD James)*
THE BLUE LAGOON *(Stacpoole)*
THE BOSTONIANS *(H James)*
THE CHRYSALIDS *(Wyndham)*
THE CLAVERINGS *(Trollope)*
THE COMFORTERS *(Spark)*
THE DAISY CHAIN *(Yonge)*
THE DEAD SECRET *(W Collins)*
THE DEERSLAYER *(JF Cooper)*
THE EDWARDIANS *(Sackville-West)*
THE GOLDEN BOWL *(H James)*
THE GOLDEN KEEL *(Bagley)*
THE HIGH WINDOW *(Chandler)*
THE HISTORY MAN *(M Bradbury)*
THE INHERITORS *(Golding)*
THE JEALOUS GOD *(Braine)*
THE LAST BATTLE *(CS Lewis)*
THE LASY TYCOON *(FS Fitzgerald)*
THE MAID OF SKER *(Blackmore)*
THE MARBLE FAUN *(Hawthorne)*
THE METROPOLIS *(Sinclair)*
THE NEGOTIATOR *(Forsyth)*
THE ODESSA FILE *(Forsyth)*
THE ONION FIELD *(Wambaugh)*
THE PATHFINDER *(JF Cooper)*
THE PLAGUE DOGS *(R Adams)*
THE RAJ QUARTET *(P Scott)*
THE RAZOR'S EDGE *(Maugham)*
THÉRÈSE RAQUIN *(Zola)*
THE SIGN OF FOUR *(Doyle)*
THE SKETCH BOOK *(W Irving)*
THE SPOILT CITY *(Manning)*

THE THORN BIRDS *(McCullough)*
THE TRAGIC MUSE *(H James)*
THE TRIPLE ECHO *(Bates)*
THE TWO SISTERS *(Bates)*
THE VIRGINIANS *(Thackeray)*
THE WINDS OF WAR *(Wouk)*
THE WIZARD OF OZ *(Baum)*
THE YOUNG LIONS *(I Shaw)*
TIME FOR A TIGER *(Burgess)*
TOLD BY AN IDIOT *(R Macaulay)*
UNDER TWO FLAGS *(Ouida)*
UP THE JUNCTION *(Dunn)*
WATERSHIP DOWN *(R Adams)*
WINNIE-THE-POOH *(Milne)*
ZULEIKA DOBSON *(Beerbohm)*

14

ABSALOM, ABSALOM! *(Faulkner)*
A HANDFUL OF DUST *(E Waugh)*
A MAN OF PROPERTY *(Galsworthy)*
ANOTHER COUNTRY *(Baldwin)*
A ROOM OF ONE'S OWN *(Woolf)*
A ROOM WITH A VIEW *(Forster)*
A SHIP OF THE LINE *(Forester)*
A TEMPORARY LIFE *(Storey)*
A TOWN LIKE ALICE *(Shute)*
AT SWIM-TWO-BIRDS *(F O'Brien)*
BERNARD QUENAIS *(Maurois)*
CASTLE RACKRENT *(Edgeworth)*
CASTLE RICHMOND *(Trollope)*
CHANGING PLACES *(Lodge)*
CIDER WITH ROSIE *(L Lee)*
CLAUDIUS THE GOD *(Graves)*
COMÉDIE HUMAINE *(Balzac)*
COMING UP FOR AIR *(Orwell)*
CROTCHET CASTLE *(Peacock)*
DALKEY ARCHIVES *(F O'Brien)*
DEAD MAN LEADING *(Pritchett)*
DEATH ON THE NILE *(Christie)*
DECLINE AND FALL *(E Waugh)*
DIARY OF A NOBODY *(G & W Grossmith)*
EVAN HARRINGTON *(Meredith)*
EXCELLENT WOMEN *(Pym)*

FRANNY AND ZOOEY *(Salinger)*
GOD'S LITTLE ACRE *(Caldwell)*
GOODBYE MR CHIPS *(Hilton)*
HOLLYWOOD WIVES *(J Collins)*
HUMPHRY CLINKER *(Smollett)*
ISLAND IN THE SUN *(AR Waugh)*
JUDE THE OBSCURE *(Hardy)*
LE MORTE D'ARTHUR *(Malory)*
LESS THAN ANGELS *(Pym)*
LORD HORNBLOWER *(Forester)*
LORD OF THE FLIES *(Golding)*
LORD OF THE RINGS *(Tolkien)*
MASTERMAN READY *(Marryat)*
MODERN CHIVALRY *(Brackenridge)*
MY COUSIN RACHEL *(D Du Maurier)*
MY FRIEND FLICKA *(O'Hara)*
NATIONAL VELVET *(Bagnold)*
NIGHTMARE ABBEY *(Peacock)*
OF HUMAN BONDAGE *(Maugham)*
ONE PAIR OF HANDS *(M Dickens)*
OUR MAN IN HAVANA *(Greene)*
PICKWICK PAPERS *(Dickens)*
QUENTIN DURWARD *(W Scott)*
RICH MAN, POOR MAN *(I Shaw)*
RITES OF PASSAGE *(Golding)*
ROBINSON CRUSOE *(Defoe)*
RODERICK HUDSON *(H James)*
RODERICK RANDOM *(Smollett)*
SALAR THE SALMON *(Williamson)*
SEA OF FERTILITY *(Mishima)*
THE ADVENTURERS *(Robbins)*
THE AMBASSADORS *(H James)*
THE CAINE MUTINY *(Wouk)*
THE DOCTOR'S WIFE *(B Moore)*
THE FIRST CIRCLE *(Solzhenitsyn)*
THE FORSYTE SAGA *(Galsworthy)*
THE FOUR JUST MEN *(E Wallace)*
THE GARDEN PARTY *(Mansfield)*
THE GOOD SOLDIER *(Ford)*
THE GREAT GATSBY *(FS Fitzgerald)*
THE HUMAN FACTOR *(Greene)*
THE JUNGLE BOOKS *(Kipling)*
THE KRAKEN WAKES *(Wyndham)*
THE LONG GOODBYE *(Chandler)*
THE LOOM OF YOUTH *(AR Waugh)*
THE L-SHAPED ROOM *(Banks)*

THE MALCONTENTS *(Snow)*
THE NINE TAILORS *(Sayers)*
THE PAINTED VEIL *(Maugham)*
THE SILVER CHAIR *(CS Lewis)*
THE SILVER SPOON *(Galsworthy)*
THE TIME MACHINE *(Wells)*
THE WATER BABIES *(Kingsley)*
THE WHITE MONKEY *(Galsworthy)*
THE WOODLANDERS *(Hardy)*
TREASURE ISLAND *(Stevenson)*
TRENT'S LAST CASE *(Bentley)*
TRISTRAM SHANDY *(Sterne)*
TROPIC OF CANCER *(H Miller)*
TURN OF THE SCREW *(H James)*
UNCLE TOM'S CABIN *(Stowe)*
WAR OF THE WORLDS *(Wells)*
WAVERLEY NOVELS *(W Scott)*
WHAT MAISIE KNEW *(H James)*

15

A CHRISTMAS CAROL *(Dickens)*
A FAREWELL TO ARMS *(Hemingway)*
ALLAN QUATERMAIN *(Haggard)*
A MATTER OF HONOUR *(Archer)*
AN AMERICAN DREAM *(Mailer)*
A PAIR OF BLUE EYES *(Hardy)*
A PASSAGE TO INDIA *(Forster)*
A STUDY IN SCARLET *(Doyle)*
BEYOND THIS PLACE *(Cronin)*
BRACEBRIDGE HALL *(W Irving)*
BULLDOG DRUMMOND *(Sapper)*
CARDS ON THE TABLE *(Christie)*
CASTLE DANGEROUS *(W Scott)*
CATCHER IN THE RYE *(Salinger)*
CIDER HOUSE RULES *(J Irving)*
CLOUDS OF WITNESS *(Sayers)*
COLD COMFORT FARM *(Gibbons)*
EUSTACE AND HILDA *(Hartley)*
EVIL UNDER THE SUN *(Christie)*
FOR YOUR EYES ONLY *(Fleming)*
FRENCHMAN'S CREEK *(D Du
Maurier)*
GONE WITH THE WIND *(Mitchell)*

ARTS – LITERATURE – BOOKS

GOODBYE TO BERLIN *(Isherwood)*
HEMLOCK AND AFTER *(A Wilson)*
HENRIETTA TEMPLE *(Disraeli)*
HEREWARD THE WAKE *(Kingsley)*
HUCKLEBERRY FINN *(Twain)*
ICE STATION ZEBRA *(Maclean)*
INNOCENTS ABROAD *(Twain)*
INSIDE MR ENDERBY *(Burgess)*
LEAVE IT TO PSMITH *(Wodehouse)*
LE ROUGE ET LE NOIR *(Stendhal)*
LOVE IN AMSTERDAM *(Freeling)*
MONSIEUR QUIXOTE *(Greene)*
NORTHANGER ABBEY *(Austen)*
ORMEROD'S LANDING *(L Thomas)*
OSCAR AND LUCINDA *(Carey)*
OUR MUTUAL FRIEND *(Dickens)*
PATH OF DALLIANCE *(A Waugh)*
PEREGRINE PICKLE *(Smollett)*
PORTERHOUSE BLUE *(Sharpe)*
PORTRAIT OF A LADY *(H James)*
PREMATURE BURIAL *(Poe)*
PUCK OF POOK'S HILL *(Kipling)*
PUDD'NHEAD WILSON *(Twain)*
PUT OUT MORE FLAGS *(E Waugh)*
QUEEN SHEBA'S RING *(Haggard)*
RETURN OF THE KING *(Tolkien)*
RIOTOUS ASSEMBLY *(Sharpe)*
RUPERT OF HENTZAU *(Hope)*
STRANGE CONFLICT *(Wheatley)*
SUMMER LIGHTNING *(Wodehouse)*
TARZAN OF THE APES *(Burroughs)*
THE ASPERN PAPERS *(H James)*

THE CAVES OF STEEL *(Asimov)*
THE COUNTRY GIRLS *(E O'Brien)*
THE FAR PAVILIONS *(Kaye)*
THE GLASS-BLOWERS *(D Du Maurier)*
THE GREAT FORTUNE *(Manning)*
THE HOUSE OF MIRTH *(Wharton)*
THE INVISIBLE MAN *(Wells)*
THE KING'S GENERAL *(D Du Maurier)*
THE MALLEN STREAK *(Cookson)*
THE MUDFOG PAPERS *(Dickens)*
THE NURSERY ALICE *(Carroll)*
THE OLD WIVES' TALE *(Bennett)*
THE SECRET GARDEN *(Burnett)*
THE SILMARILLION *(Tolkien)*
THE SPECKLED BAND *(Doyle)*
THE THINKING REED *(R West)*
THE TRUMPET-MAJOR *(Hardy)*
THE VALLEY OF FEAR *(Doyle)*
THE WHITE COMPANY *(Doyle)*
THE WHITE PEACOCK *(DH Lawrence)*
THE WOMAN IN WHITE *(W Collins)*
THE WOULDBEGOODS *(Nesbit)*
THREE MEN IN A BOAT *(Jerome)*
TO THE LIGHTHOUSE *(Woolf)*
TROPIC OF RUISLIP *(L Thomas)*
UNDER THE VOLCANO *(Lowry)*
UNNATURAL CAUSES *(PD James)*
WEIR OF HERMISTON *(Stevenson)*
WHERE EAGLES DARE *(Maclean)*
WIDE SARGASSO SEA *(Rhys)*

ARTS

LITERATURE – POEMS

* = Alternative title

3

BAT *(DH Lawrence)*
EVE *(Hodgson)*
FOG *(Sandburg)*
GOG *(Hughes)*
MAY *(W Barnes)*
NAN *(Masefield)*
NOW *(Thwaite)*
WAR *(Apollinaire)*
  (Dryden)
YES *(Joyce)*

4

ALMA *(Prior)*
CROW *(Hughes)*
DAWN *(Lorca)*
DAYS *(Larkin)*
DIDO *(Ashbery)*
DUST *(Brooke)*
HERE *(Larkin)*
  (RS Thomas)
JEAN *(Burns)*
LARA *(Byron)*
LOVE *(Coleridge)*
MAUD *(Tennyson)*
ODES *(Horace)*
PIKE *(Hughes)*
RAIN *(E Thomas)*
SAUL *(Browning)*
SNOW *(MacNeice)*
SONG *(Donne)*
THAW *(E Thomas)*
THEY *(RS Thomas)*
WIND *(Hughes)*

5

AARON *(Herbert)*
A COAT *(Yeats)*
A SONG *(Shakespeare)*
A WAVE *(Ashbery)*
BABEL *(de la Mare)*
BOOKS *(Crabbe)*
BOOTS *(Kipling)*
CAIRO *(Thwaite)*
COMUS *(Milton)*
DADDY *(Plath)*
DELAY *(Jennings)*
DORIS *(Congreve)*
DRAKE *(Noyes)*
ELEGY *(Gray)*
EVANS *(RS Thomas)*
FANCY *(Keats)*
FOOLS *(Jonson)*
GOING *(Larkin)*
GREEN *(W Barnes)*
HÉLAS! *(Wilde)*
IMAGE *(Hulme)*
ILIAD *(Homer)*
ITALY *(Byron)*
LAMIA *(Keats)*
LIMBO *(Coleridge)*
ROADS *(E Thomas)*
SNAKE *(DH Lawrence)*
TOADS *(Larkin)*
TOMMY *(Kipling)*
WANTS *(Larkin)*
WATER *(Larkin)*
YPRES *(Binyon)*
ZIMIR *(Dryden)*

6

A DITTY *(Sidney)*
ADVICE *(Bierce)*

A FEVER *(Donne)*
AFRICA *(Plutarch)*
ANGELS *(Abse)*
APPLES *(Swift)*
ARABIA *(de la Mare)*
ASLEEP *(Owen)*
AUGUST *(MacNeice)*
AUTUMN *(de la Mare)*
BADGER *(Clare)*
BEAUTY *(Sappho)*
CANTOS *(Pound)*
CLOUDS *(Brooke)*
COMING *(Larkin)*
DAPHNE *(Lyly)*
DREAMS *(Breton)*
DUBLIN *(MacNeice)*
HASSAN *(Flecker)*
HUNGER *(Binyon)*
LAMENT *(Flint)*
LEAVES *(Binyon)*
LESBIA *(Catullus)*
LONDON *(Blake)*
  (Jonson)
MARINA *(TS Eliot)*
MILTON *(Blake)*
NATURE *(Emerson)*
RETURN *(Cavafy)*
RIZPAH *(Tennyson)*
SENLIN *(Aiken)*
SLOUGH *(Betjeman)*
SPLEEN *(Baudelaire)*
THE ANT *(Nash)*
THE DAY *(Fuller)*
TOKENS *(W Barnes)*
WOLVES *(MacNeice)*

7

ABISHAG *(Rilke)*
ADONAIS *(Shelley)*

ALASTOR *(Shelley)*
AMERICA *(Ginsberg)*
ANIMULA *(TS Eliot)*
ARCADES *(Milton)*
AT GRASS *(Larkin)*
A VISION *(Clare)*
A WREATH *(Herbert)*
BEOWULF *(?)*
BIRCHES *(Frost)*
CAELICA *(Greville)*
CALAMUS *(Whitman)*
CARGOES *(Masefield)*
CHICAGO *(Sandburg)*
CONTENT *(B Barnes)*
DOLORES *(Swinburne)*
DON JUAN *(Byron)*
ELEGIES *(Donne)*
FATIGUE *(Belloc)*
FLORIDA *(Abse)*
FOREVER *(Carver)*
INFERNO *(Dante)*
IT RAINS *(E Thomas)*
JANUARY *(RS Thomas)*
KILMENY *(Hogg)*
LEPANTO *(Chesterton)*
LIMITED *(Sandburg)*
LULLABY *(Auden)*
LYCIDAS *(Milton)*
MANFRED *(Auden)*
MARIANA *(Tennyson)*
MARMION *(Scott)*
MAZEPPA *(Byron)*
MICHAEL *(Wordsworth)*
MISS GEE *(Auden)*
MISSING *(Auden)*
MISS LOO *(de la Mare)*
MUSEUMS *(MacNeice)*
NEW YORK *(Lorca)*
OCTOBER *(D Thomas)*
ODYSSEY *(Homer)*
PAULINE *(Browning)*
REMAINS *(Greville)*
SHINGLE *(Nicholson)*
SONNETS *(Shakespeare)*
SUCCESS *(Brooke)*
TARTARY *(de la Mare)*

THE BAIT *(Donne)*
THE BARD *(Gray)*
THE BULL *(Hodgson)*
THE DEAD *(Brooke)*
THE FLEA *(Donne)*
THE HILL *(Brooke)*
THE LAMB *(Blake)*
THE OXEN *(Hardy)*
THE PIKE *(Blunden)*
THE TASK *(Cowper)*
TO A LADY *(Pope)*
TO CELIA *(Jonson)*
TZIGANI *(Pushkin)*
ULYSSES *(Tennyson)*
UP THERE *(Auden)*

8

A PEASANT *(RS Thomas)*
A RAPTURE *(Carew)*
AUGURIES *(Blake)*
CADENCES *(Flint)*
CUT GRASS *(Larkin)*
DISABLED *(Owen)*
ENDYMION *(Keats)*
FAIR INES *(Hood)*
FERN HILL *(D Thomas)*
FULL MOON *(Sappho)*
FUTILITY *(Owen)*
GEDICHTE *(Heine)*
GUNGA DIN *(Kipling)*
HESPERUS *(Clare)*
HIAWATHA *(Longfellow)*
HUDIBRAS *(Butler)*
HYPERION *(Keats)*
ISABELLA *(Keats)*
I SAW A MAN *(Crane)*
L'ALLEGRO *(Milton)*
LUCY GRAY *(Wordsworth)*
LUPERCAL *(Hughes)*
MALACODA *(Beckett)*
MANDALAY *(Kipling)*
PARADISO *(Dante)*
POLITICS *(Yeats)*
POOR POLL *(Bridges)*

PORTRAIT *(Cummings)*
PRELUDES *(TS Eliot)*
RELIGION *(Vaughan)*
SEA FEVER *(Masefield)*
SELF PITY *(DH Lawrence)*
SNOWDROP *(Hughes)*
SORDELLO *(Browning)*
THE ALTAR *(Herbert)*
THE BRIDE *(DH Lawrence)*
THE CLOUD *(Shelley)*
THE DREAM *(Donne)*
THE GHOST *(de la Mare)*
THE GLORY *(E Thomas)*
THE GLOVE *(Browning)*
THE HEART *(Crane)*
THE MOUND *(Hardy)*
THE PEARL *(Herbert)*
THE RAVEN *(Poe)*
THE RELIC *(Donne)*
THE ROVER *(Scott)*
THE SNAIL *(Lovelace)*
THE SWARM *(Plath)*
THE TAXIS *(MacNeice)*
THE TYGER *(Blake)*
THE WORLD *(Raine)*
          (Vaughan)
THE WOUND *(Gunn)*
THE YACHT *(Catullus)*
THISTLES *(Hughes)*
TO A MOUSE *(Burns)*
TO AUTUMN *(Keats)*
VALUABLE *(S Smith)*

9

A BOY'S WILL *(Frost)*
ADLESTROP *(E Thomas)*
ALMSWOMEN *(Blunden)*
A PASSER-BY *(Bridges)*
A PASTORAL *(Daniel)*
BIOGRAPHY *(Masefield)*
BYZANTIUM *(Yeats)*
CHRISTMAS *(Betjeman)*
CYPRESSES *(DH Lawrence)*
DEJECTION *(Coleridge)*

EAST COKER *(TS Eliot)*
EXCELSIOR *(Longfellow)*
EXECUTIVE *(Betjeman)*
FIAMMETTA *(Boccaccio)*
GERONTION *(TS Eliot)*
JERUSALEM *(Blake)*
KUBLA KHAN *(Coleridge)*
MARRIAGES *(Thwaite)*
MIDDLESEX *(Betjeman)*
MID-WINTER *(Rossetti)*
MONT BLANC *(Shelley)*
MOONLIGHT *(Apollinaire)*
MR BLEANEY *(Larkin)*
NIGHT MAIL *(Auden)*
ROSABELLE *(Scott)*
ROSALYNDE *(Lodge)*
RURAL LIFE *(Crabbe)*
SKUNK HOUR *(Lowell)*
SNOW-BOUND *(Whittier)*
THE CHOICE *(Yeats)*
THE COLLAR *(Herbert)*
THE DONKEY *(Chesterton)*
THE 'EATHEN *(Kipling)*
THE EXILES *(Auden)*
THE GARDEN *(Marvell)*
THE HORSES *(Muir)*
THE OUTLAW *(Scott)*
THE PULLEY *(Herbert)*
THE TEMPLE *(Herbert)*

10

AE FOND KISS *(Burns)*
ANNABEL LEE *(Poe)*
BRIGHT STAR *(Keats)*
CASABIANCA *(Hemans)*
CHERRY-RIPE *(Campion)*
CHRISTABEL *(Coleridge)*
CORRUPTION *(Vaughan)*
CRADLE SONG *(MacNeice)*
DOVER BEACH *(Arnold)*
ENOCH ARDEN *(Tennyson)*
EVANGELINE *(Longfellow)*
FAMOUS POET *(Hughes)*
HESPERIDES *(Herrick)*

IN MEMORIAM *(Tennyson)*
IN TENEBRIS *(Hardy)*
JOHN GILPIN *(Cowper)*
LONDON SNOW *(Bridges)*
MAN AND WIFE *(Lowell)*
MUTABILITY *(Wordsworth)*
NEXT, PLEASE *(Larkin)*
OZYMANDIAS *(Shelley)*
PIED BEAUTY *(Hopkins)*
POLY-OLBION *(Drayton)*
PROMETHEUS *(Goethe)*
PURGATORIO *(Dante)*
ROSE AYLMER *(Landor)*
ST AGNES EVE *(Tennyson)*
THE BOROUGH *(Crabbe)*
THE COOL WEB *(Graves)*
THE CORSAIR *(Byron)*
THE DUNCIAD *(Pope)*
THE ECSTASY *(Donne)*
THE FLOWERS *(Kipling)*
THE FUNERAL *(Donne)*
THE GENERAL *(Sassoon)*
THE LAST LAP *(Kipling)*
THE PRELUDE *(Wordsworth)*
THE RETREAT *(Vaughan)*
THE SCHOLAR *(Southey)*
THE SKATERS *(Ashbery)*
THE SOLDIER *(Brooke)*
THE TEMPEST *(Vaughan)*
THE VILLAGE *(Crabbe)*
TO A SKYLARK *(Shelley)*
                    (Wordsworth)
TO THE MUSES *(Blake)*
UP THE RHINE *(Hood)*
VIEW OF A PIG *(Hughes)*
WHOROSCOPE *(Beckett)*

11

A RED RED ROSE *(Burns)*
A LOVER'S PLEA *(Campion)*
AND YOU, HELEN *(Hughes)*
AURORA LEIGH *(Barrett-Browning)*
BASE DETAILS *(Sassoon)*
CLAIR DE LUNE *(Verlaine)*

ARTS – LITERATURE – POEMS

DANNY DEEVER *(Kipling)*
DUBLINESQUE *(Larkin)*
FELIX RANDAL *(Hopkins)*
HIGH WINDOWS *(Larkin)*
HOME IS SO SAD *(Larkin)*
IL PENSEROSO *(Milton)*
INTIMATIONS *(Wordsworth)*
JABBERWOCKY *(Carroll)*
LADY LAZARUS *(Plath)*
MAC-FLECKNOE *(Dryden)*
MARY MORISON *(Burns)*
MATLOCK BATH *(Betjeman)*
MEN AND WOMEN *(Browning)*
MORNING SONG *(Plath)*
MR APPOLINAX *(TS Eliot)*
OCTOBER DAWN *(Hughes)*
ON BEN JONSON *(Shakespeare)*
PETER GRIMES *(Crabbe)*
PIPPA PASSES *(Browning)*
RESIGNATION *(Chatterton)*
SCAFELL PIKE *(Nicholson)*
SCOTS WHA HAE *(Burns)*
SISTER HELEN *(Rossetti)*
STONY LIMITS *(MacDiarmid)*
TALL NETTLES *(Larkin)*
TAM O'SHANTER *(Burns)*
THE BAD THING *(Wain)*
THE CASTAWAY *(Cowper)*
THE COLOSSUS *(Plath)*
THE DESERTER *(Housman)*
THE EXCURSION *(Wordsworth)*
THE FOUR ZOAS *(Blake)*
THE HOCK CART *(Herrick)*
THE JUMBLIES *(Lear)*
THE OLD FOOLS *(Larkin)*
THE RUBAIYAT *(Omar Khayyám)*
THE SICK ROSE *(Blake)*
THE SUNSHADE *(Hardy)*
THE TWO TREES *(Yeats)*
TO AN OLD LADY *(Empson)*
TO DAFFODILS *(Herrick)*

12

ABOVE THE DOCK *(Hulme)*
A GAME OF CHESS *(TS Eliot)*

AIR AND ANGELS *(Donne)*
ASH WEDNESDAY *(TS Eliot)*
AULD LANG SYNE *(Burns)*
BLACK JACKETS *(Gunn)*
BONNIE LESLEY *(Burns)*
CHILDE HAROLD *(Byron)*
DEATH AND LOVE *(Jonson)*
DEATH BY WATER *(TS Eliot)*
DOES IT MATTER? *(Sassoon)*
DRUMMER HODGE *(Hardy)*
EPITHALAMION *(Spenser)*
EVERYONE SANG *(Sassoon)*
FAREWELL, LOVE *(Wyatt)*
FLOWER-DE-LUCE *(Tennyson)*
HA'NACKER HILL *(Belloc)*
HAWK ROOSTING *(Hughes)*
HOLY THURSDAY *(Blake)*
INFANT SORROW *(Blake)*
LE BATEAU IVRE *(Rimbaud)* *1
LOCKSLEY HALL *(Tennyson)*
LOVE'S ALCHEMY *(Donne)*
MAGGIE LAUDER *(Burns)*
MORTE D'ARTHUR *(Tennyson)*
NOBLE NUMBERS *(Herrick)*
NO SECOND TROY *(Yeats)*
OLD FURNITURE *(Hardy)*
PARADISE LOST *(Milton)*
PROTHALAMION *(Spenser)*
REINEKE FUCHS *(Goethe)*
SCOTS UNBOUND *(MacDiarmid)*
SONG OF MYSELF *(Whitman)*
THE ALBATROSS *(Baudelaire)*
THE BLACKBIRD *(Drinkwater)*
THE COOK'S TALE *(Chaucer)*
THE EXPLOSION *(Larkin)*
THE FISHERMAN *(Yeats)*
THE HOLLOW MEN *(TS Eliot)*
THE HOURGLASS *(Jonson)*
THE LONG TRAIL *(Kipling)*
THE MONK'S TALE *(Chaucer)*
THE QUIET LIFE *(Pope)*
THE WASTE LAND *(TS Eliot)*
THE WINDHOVER *(Hopkins)*
THE WITNESSES *(Auden)*
TINTERN ABBEY *(Wordsworth)*
TULLOCHGORUM *(Burns)*

ARTS – LITERATURE – POEMS

FAIRGROUND MUSIC *(Fuller)*
HARROW-ON-THE-HILL *(Betjeman)*
IDYLLS OF THE KING *(Tennyson)*
LORD COZENS HARDY *(Betjeman)*
MEN WHO MARCH AWAY *(Hardy)*
MID-WINTER WAKING *(Graves)*
NO CHANGE OF PLACE *(Auden)*
PORTRAIT OF A LADY *(TS Eliot)*
SAMSON AGONISTES *(Milton)*
STELLA'S BIRTHDAY *(Swift)*
SUMMONED BY BELLS *(Betjeman)*
THE DIVINE COMEDY *(Dante)* *2

THE EVE OF ST AGNES *(Keats)*
THE FAERIE QUEENE *(Spenser)*
THE FOUR QUARTETS *(TS Eliot)*
THE HIPPOPOTAMUS *(TS Eliot)*
THE ILLUSIONISTS *(Fuller)*
THE SCHOLAR GIPSY *(Arnold)*
THE SECOND COMING *(Yeats)*
THE SHIPMAN'S TALE *(Chaucer)*
THE SORROW OF LOVE *(Yeats)*
THE WHITE GODDESS *(Graves)*
THIS LUNAR BEAUTY *(Auden)*
WAKING IN THE BLUE *(Lowell)*

ARTS

MUSIC – BALLETS

3

JOB *(Vaughan Williams)*

4

AGON *(Stravinsky)*
JEUX *(Debussy)*
JINX *(Britten)*

5

CHOUT *(Prokofiev)*
MANON *(Massenet)*
RODEO *(Copland)*

6

APOLLO *(Stravinsky)*

BOLÉRO *(Ravel)*
FAÇADE *(Walton)*
HAMLET *(Tchaikovsky)*
JEWELS *(Fauré)*
KHAMMA *(Debussy)*
ONDINE *(Henze)*
PARADE *(Satie)*
SYLVIA *(Delibes)*
TOY-BOX *(Debussy)*
TRACES *(Mahler)*

7

BALLADE *(Debussy)*
BARABAU *(Rieti)*
CIRCLES *(Berio)*
FANFARE *(Britten)*
GISELLE *(Adam)*
NAMOUNA *(Lalo)*
ORPHEUS *(Stravinsky)*
REVENGE *(Verdi)*

8

ADAM ZERO *(Bliss)*
CARNAVAL *(Schumann)*
COPPÉLIA *(Delibes)*
FIREBIRD *(Stravinsky)*
LA SOURCE *(Delibes)*
LES NOCES *(Stravinsky)*
RAYMONDA *(Glazunov)*
SERENADE *(Tchaikovsky)*
STIMMUNG *(Stockhausen)*
SWAN LAKE *(Tchaikovsky)*

9

BLUEBEARD *(Offenbach)*
CAPRICHOS *(Bartók)*
CARD PARTY *(Stravinsky)*
CHECKMATE *(Bliss)*
FANCY FREE *(Bernstein)*

LES BICHES *(Poulenc)*
MOVEMENTS *(Stravinsky)*
SOLITAIRE *(Arnold)*
SPARTACUS *(Khatchaturian)*
THE GUESTS *(Blitzstein)*

LES SYLPHIDES *(Chopin)*
PILLAR OF FIRE *(Schönberg)*
RITE OF SPRING *(Stravinsky)*
SCHEHERAZADE *(Rimsky-Korsakov)*
THE DYING SWAN *(Saint-Saëns)*
THE PIED PIPER *(Copland)*

10

AT MIDNIGHT *(Mahler)*
CINDERELLA *(Prokofiev)*
DON QUIXOTE *(Minkus)*
LA BAYADÈRE *(Minkus)*
LA SYLPHIDE *(Schneitzhoeffer)*
LE CORSAIRE *(Adam)*
LES FORAINS *(Sauguet)*
PETROUCHKA *(Stravinsky)*
THE BIG CITY *(Tansman)*

13

ILLUMINATIONS *(Britten)*
PINEAPPLE POLL *(Sullivan)*
THE FAIRY'S KISS *(Stravinsky)*
THE NUTCRACKER *(Tchaikovsky)*

14

BALLET IMPERIAL *(Tchaikovsky)*
ROMEO AND JULIET *(Prokofiev)*
SCÈNES DE BALLET *(Stravinsky)*
SLEEPING BEAUTY *(Tchaikovsky)*
THE NIGHTINGALE *(Stravinsky)*
THE STONE FLOWER *(Prokofiev)*

11

APPARITIONS *(Liszt)*
BILLY THE KID *(Copland)*
NIGHT SHADOW *(Rieti)*
OLD KING COLE *(Vaughan Williams)*
PRODIGAL SON *(Prokofiev)*

15

DAPHNIS AND CHLOË *(Ravel)*
LE BAISER DE LA FÉE *(Stravinsky)*
THE WOODEN PRINCE *(Bartók)*

12

LES PATINEURS *(Meyerbeer)*

ARTS

MUSIC – CLASSICAL PIECES

(A) = Aria   (CA) = Cantata   (CO) = Concerto   (E) = Étude
(F) = Fugue   (M) = Mass   (OR) = Oratorio   (OV) = Overture   (PI) = Piece
(PR) = Prelude   (Q4) = Quartet   (Q5) = Quintet   (R) = Rhapsody
(SO) = Sonata   (SU) = Suite   (SY) = Symphony   (TP) = Tone poem
(V) = Variations   (W) = Waltz
* = Alternative name

3

HEN *(SY-Haydn)*
JOB *(OR-Parry)*
TOY *(SY-Haydn)*

4

ALTO *(R-Brahms)*
BEAR *(SY-Haydn)*
BIRD *(Q4-Haydn)*
ECHO *(CO-Vivaldi)*
EDEN *(OR-Stanford)*
FEAR *(PR-Chopin)*
FIRE *(SY-Haydn)*
FROG *(Q4-Haydn)*
HOPE *(PI-Mendelssohn)*
HUNT *(Q4-Mozart)*
        (SY- Haydn)
LARK *(Q4-Haydn)*
LINZ *(SY-Mozart)*
LOSS *(PR-Chopin)*
MELK *(CO-Haydn)*
MIMI *(A-Puccini)*
RAIN *(SO-Brahms)*
RUTH *(OR-Cowen)*
SAUL *(OR-Handel)*
THUN *(SO-Brahms)*

5

ANTAR *(SU-Rimsky-*
        Korsakov)

CLOCK *(SY-Haydn)*
CREDO *(M-Mozart)*
FAUST *(OV-Wagner)*
        (SY-Liszt)
GRIEF *(E-Chopin)*
LA MER *(PI-Debussy)*
LARGO *(PI-Handel)*
LYRIC *(SU-Berg)*
        (SY-Bruckner)
OCEAN *(E-Chopin)*
        (SY-Rubinstein)
PARIS *(SY-Haydn)*
        (SY-Mozart)
RAZOR *(Q4-Haydn)*
RUGBY *(PI-Honegger)*
SADKO *(PI-Rimsky-*
        Korsakov)
STORM *(SY-Haydn)*
TASSO *(TP-Liszt)*
TROUT *(Q5-Schubert)*
WEDGE *(F-Bach)*
WELSH *(R-German)*

6

AFRICA *(PI-Saint-Saëns)*
ALPINE *(SY-R Strauss)*
BOLÉRO *(PI-Ravel)*
CAN-CAN *(PI-Offenbach)*
CHORAL *(SY-Beethoven)*
        (SY-Holst)
COFFEE *(CA-Bach)*
COLOUR *(SY-Bliss)*
DORIAN *(F-Bach)*

EGMONT *(OV-Beethoven)*
ELIJAH *(OR-Mendelssohn)*
ENGEDI *(OR-Beethoven)*
ENIGMA *(V-Elgar)*
EROICA *(SY-Beethoven)*
ESTHER *(OR-Handel)*
FAÇADE *(SU-Walton)*
FRENCH *(SU-Bach)*
GERMAN *(SU-Bach)*
GIGUES *(PI-Debussy)*
HAMLET *(OV-Tchaikovsky)*
        (TP-Liszt)
IBÉRIA *(PI-Debussy)*
IMAGES *(PI-Debussy)*
JOSEPH *(OR-Handel)*
JUDITH *(OR-Parry)*
LAUDON *(SY-Haydn)*
LODRON *(CO-Mozart)*
LONDON *(SY-Haydn)*
        (SY-Vaughan Williams)
NELSON *(M-Haydn)*
NORDIC *(SY-Hanson)*
OXFORD *(SY-Haydn)*
POLISH *(SY-Tchaikovsky)*
PRAGUE *(SY-Mozart)*
ROB ROY *(OV-Berlioz)*
ROCOCO *(PI-Haydn)*
SAMSON *(OR-Handel)*
SCARBO *(PI-Ravel)*
SCOTCH *(SY-Mendelssohn)*
SEVERN *(SU-Elgar)*
SIESTA *(PI-Walton)*
SPRING *(SO-Beethoven)*
        (SY-Schumann)

TAMARA *(TP-Balakirev)*
THUNER *(SO-Brahms)*
TRAGIC *(OV-Brahms)*
　　　(SY-Schubert)
TRIPLE *(OV-Dvořák)*
UNDINE *(TP-Strong)*
WARSAW *(CO-Addinsell)*

7

ATHALIE *(PI-Mendelssohn)*
BALLADE *(PI-Chopin)*
CORELLI *(F-Bach)*
DON JUAN *(TP-R Strauss)*
EMPEROR *(CO-Beethoven)*
　　　(Q4-Haydn)
ENGLISH *(SU-Bach)*
FLORIDA *(SU-Delius)*
HAFFNER *(SU-Mozart)*
　　　(SY-Mozart)
HOLBERG *(SU-Grieg)*
ITALIAN *(CO-Bach)*
　　　(SY-Mendelssohn)
JEPHTHA *(OR-Handel)*
JUPITER *(SY-Mozart)*
KARELIA *(SU-Sibelius)*
KINGDOM *(OR-Elgar)*
LA VALSE *(TP-Ravel)*
LE GIBET *(PI-Ravel)*
LEONORA *(OV-Beethoven)*
LUCIFER *(TP-Hadley)*
MACBETH *(TP-R Strauss)*
MANFRED *(SY-Tchaikovsky)*
　　　(TP-Schumann)
M'APPARÌ *(A-Flotow)*
MASS IN D *(M-Beethoven)* *1
MÁ VLAST *(TP-Smetana)* *2
MERCURY *(SY-Haydn)*
MESSIAH *(OR-Handel)*
NAME-DAY *(OV-Beethoven)*
NURSERY *(SU-Elgar)*
OCTOBER *(SY-Shostakovich)*
ORPHEUS *(TP-Liszt)*
OTHELLO *(OV-Dvořák)*
PASSION *(SY-Haydn)*

PEASANT *(CA-Bach)*
PHAËTON *(TP-Saint-Saëns)*
POLONIA *(OV-Elgar)*
　　　(OV-Wagner)
REQUIEM *(M-Berlioz)*
　　　(M-Dvořák)
　　　(M-Fauré)
　　　(M-Mozart)
　　　(M-Palestrina)
　　　(M-Verdi)
RHENISH *(SY-Schumann)*
RUSSIAN *(Q4-Haydn)*
SCAPINO *(OV-Walton)*
SINTRAM *(SY-Strong)*
SPANISH *(SY-Lalo)*
SUICIDE *(PR-Chopin)*
SUNRISE *(Q4-Haydn)*
SUSANNA *(OR-Handel)*
TAPIOLA *(TP-Sibelius)*
THE DUEL *(PR-Chopin)*
THERESA *(M-Haydn)*
TRUMPET *(OV-Mendelssohn)*
VICTORY *(SY-Beethoven)*

8

ADELAIDE *(CA-Beethoven)*
　　　(CO-Mozart)
ALLELUIA *(SY-Haydn)*
AMERICAN *(Q4-Dvořák)*
APOSTLES *(OR-Elgar)*
BERCEUSE *(PI-Chopin)*
CARNAVAL *(PI-Schumann)*
CARNIVAL *(OV-Dvorák)*
　　　(OV-Glazunov)
CAT WALTZ *(Chopin)*
CHRISTUS *(OR-Liszt)*
CREATION *(OR-Haydn)*
DOG WALTZ *(Chopin)*
DOMESTIC *(SY-R Strauss)*
DRUM-ROLL *(SY-Haydn)*
EGYPTIAN *(CO-Saint-Saëns)*
ESTAMPES *(PI-Debussy)*
FALSTAFF *(PI-Elgar)*
FAREWELL *(SY-Haydn)*

FÜR ELISE *(Pl-Beethoven)*
GOLDBERG *(V-Bach)*
GOTHIQUE *(SY-Widor)*
HEBRIDES *(OV-Mendelssohn) *3*
HIAWATHA *(SU-Coleridge-Taylor)*
HORSEMAN *(Q4-Haydn)*
HUNGARIA *(TP-Liszt)*
IMPERIAL *(M-Haydn)*
      (SY-Haydn)
JEREMIAH *(SY-Bernstein)*
KING LEAR *(OV-Berlioz)*
      (Pl-Debussy)
KING OLAF *(CA-Elgar)*
KING SAUL *(OR-Parry)*
KREUTZER *(SO-Beethoven)*
MAY FIRST *(SY-Shostakovich) *4*
MILITARY *(SY-Haydn)*
MOUNTAIN *(SY-Liszt)*
MOURNING *(SY-Haydn)*
NEW WORLD *(SY-Dvořák)*
ODE TO JOY *(Pl-Beethoven)*
PASTORAL *(Pl-Bliss)*
      (SO-Beethoven)
      (SY-Beethoven)
      (SY-Handel)
      (SY-Vaughan Williams)
PEER GYNT *(SU-Grieg)*
PRÉLUDES *(Pl-Debussy)*
      (TP-Liszt)
PRUSSIAN *(Q4-Mozart)*
QUO VADIS *(OR-Dyson)*
RAINDROP *(PR-Chopin)*
ROMANTIC *(SY-Bruckner)*
      (SY-Hanson)
SAD WALTZ *(Schubert)*
SCYTHIAN *(SU-Prokofiev)*
SERENADE *(SU-Britten)*
SURPRISE *(SY-Haydn)*
SWAN SONG *(Pl-Schubert)*
THE BIRDS *(SU-Respighi)*
THE DREAM *(Q4-Haydn)*
THE OCEAN *(SY-Rubinstein)*
      (TP-Hadley)
THEODORA *(OR-Handel)*
THE TITAN *(SY-Mahler)*
THE WASPS *(Pl-Vaughan Williams)*

TINTAGEL *(TP-Bax)*
WAVERLEY *(OV-Berlioz)*

9

ALLA BREVE *(F-Bach)*
ALLA TURCA *(SO-Mozart)*
ANTARTICA *(SY-Vaughan Williams)*
BRIGG FAIR *(R-Delius)*
BUTTERFLY *(Pl-Chopin)*
CASTA DIVA *(A-Bellini)*
CAT'S FUGUE *(Scarlatti)*
CHRISTMAS *(OR-Bach)*
CIELO E MAR *(A-Ponchielli)*
COX AND BOX *(Pl-Sullivan)*
CREDO MASS *(Mozart)*
DUMKY TRIO *(Pl-Dvořák)*
EL CAPITÁN *(Pl-Sousa)*
FINLANDIA *(TP-Sibelius)*
FIREWORKS *(Pl-Stravinsky)*
FLOS CAMPI *(SU-Vaughan Williams)*
FROISSART *(OV-Elgar)*
GHOST TRIO *(Pl-Beethoven)*
GRENADIER *(Pl-Haydn)*
IMPROMPTU *(Pl-Chopin)*
      (Pl-Schubert)
KING DAVID *(OR-Honegger)*
KING ENZIO *(OV-Wagner)*
LENINGRAD *(SY-Shostakovich)*
MOONLIGHT *(SO-Beethoven)*
NOCTURNES *(Pl-Debussy)*
OCEANIDES *(TP-Sibelius)*
ORGAN MASS *(Bach)*
ORGAN SOLO *(M-Mozart)*
PASTORALE *(see PASTORAL)*
POLONAISE *(Pl-Chopin)*
PRINTEMPS *(Pl-Milhaud)*
      (SU-Debussy)
QUIET CITY *(Pl-Copland)*
RIO GRANDE *(Pl-Lambert)*
ROSAMUNDE *(OV-Schubert)*
SATYRICON *(OV-Ireland)*
THE LITTLE *(F-Bach)*
THE VISION *(Pl-Mendelssohn)*
WALDSTEIN *(SO-Beethoven)*

A HERO'S LIFE *(TP-R Strauss)*
AMEN CHORUS *(Handel)*
ANGE SI PURE *(A-Donizetti)*
APPALACHIA *(Pl-Delius)*
BAB BALLADS *(Pl-Gilbert)*
BARCAROLLE *(Pl-Chopin)*
　　　　　　 (Pl-Offenbach)
BENEDICITE *(Pl-Vaughan Williams)*
BRUCKENTAL *(SY-Haydn)*
CAMPANELLA *(Pl-Liszt)*
CARACTACUS *(CA-Elgar)*
CORIOLANUS *(OV-Beethoven)*
CORONATION *(M-Mozart)*
DON QUIXOTE *(TP-R Strauss)*
EGDON HEATH *(TP-Holst)*
FESTKLANGE *(TP-Liszt)*
FIRST OF MAY *(SY-Shostakovich)* *4
FLOWER SONG *(A-Bizet)*
FUNERAL ODE *(CA-Bach)*
GIANT FUGUE *(Bach)*
GREAT FUGUE *(Beethoven)*
IMPATIENCE *(PR-Chopin)*
IMPROVVISO *(A-Giordano)*
IN THE SOUTH *(OV-Elgar)*
LA ROXOLANE *(SY-Haydn)*
LE CORSAIRE *(OV-Berlioz)*
LES ÉOLIDES *(TP-Franck)*
LIFE'S DANCE *(TP-Delius)*
LITURGIQUE *(SY-Honegger)*
LYRIC SUITE *(Berg)*
MAGNIFICAT *(Pl-Bach)*
　　　　　　 (Pl-Vaughan Williams)
MASS OF LIFE *(Delius)*
MOZARTIANA *(SU-Tchaikovsky)*
NELSON MASS *(Haydn)*
NUTCRACKER *(SU-Tchaikovsky)*
OCCASIONAL *(OR-Handel)*
ODE TO DEATH *(CA-Holst)*
OEDIPUS REX *(OR-Stravinsky)*
ONE FINE DAY *(A-Puccini)*
PATHÉTIQUE *(SO-Beethoven)*
　　　　　　 (SY-Tchaikovsky)
PROMETHEUS *(OV-Beethoven)*
　　　　　　 (TP-Liszt)

RAIN SONATA *(Brahms)*
REDEMPTION *(OR-Gounod)*
SABRE DANCE *(Pl-Khatchaturian)*
SPRING SONG *(Pl-Mendelssohn)*
THE FESTINO *(OV-Haydn)*
THE KINGDOM *(OR-Elgar)*
THE MIRACLE *(SY-Haydn)*
THE PASSION *(SY-Haydn)*
THE PLANETS *(SU-Holst)* *5
THE TEMPEST *(Pl-Purcell)*
　　　　　　 (Pl-Sibelius)
　　　　　　 (Pl-Sullivan)
THUN SONATA *(Brahms)*
UNFINISHED *(SY-Schubert)*
WAR REQUIEM *(M-Britten)*
WATER MUSIC *(SU-Handel)*
WEDGE FUGUE *(Bach)*

AIR DES ROSES *(A-Berlioz)*
ANVIL CHORUS *(Verdi)*
APOCALYPTIC *(SY-Bruckner)*
BIRD QUARTET *(Haydn)*
BRANDENBURG *(CO-Bach)*
CELESTE AÏDA *(A-Verdi)*
CLAIR DE LUNE *(Pl-Debussy)*
DESPERATION *(PR-Chopin)*
DORIAN FUGUE *(Bach)*
FINGAL'S CAVE *(OV-Mendelssohn)* *3
FOUR SEASONS *(SU-Vivaldi)*
FROG QUARTET *(Haydn)*
GRAND CANYON *(SU-Grofé)*
HEN SYMPHONY *(Haydn)*
HOMAGE MARCH *(Wagner)*
HUNT QUARTET *(Mozart)*
HYMN OF JESUS *(Pl-Holst)*
IN TIME OF WAR *(M-Haydn)*
LARK QUARTET *(Haydn)*
L'ARLÉSIENNE *(Pl-Bizet)*
L'ÎLE JOYEUSE *(Pl-Debussy)*
MINUTE WALTZ *(Chopin)*
NESSUN DORMA *(A-Puccini)*
PENTHESILEA *(SY-Wolf)*
PHILOSOPHIC *(SY-Bruckner)*

ARTS – MUSIC – CLASSICAL PIECES

PINES OF ROME *(TP-Respighi)*
PLANET SUITE *(Holst)* *5
REFORMATION *(SY-Mendelssohn)*
SEVERN SUITE *(Elgar)*
SHEHERAZADE *(OV-Ravel)*
      (SU-Rimsky-Korsakov)
SHEPHERD BOY *(E-Chopin)*
THE APOSTLES *(OR-Elgar)*
THE CREATION *(M-Haydn)*
THE HOLY CITY *(OR-Gaul)*
THE IMPERIAL *(SY-Haydn)*
THERESA MASS *(Haydn)*
TOY SYMPHONY *(Haydn)*
WAND OF YOUTH *(SU-Elgar)*
WENLOCK EDGE *(PI-Vaughan Williams)* *6
WILLIAM TELL *(OV-Rossini)*

12

AGE OF ANXIETY *(SY-Bernstein)*
ALBUMBLÄTTER *(PI-Schumann)*
ALTO RHAPSODY *(Brahms)*
APPASSIONATA *(SO-Beethoven)*
ARCHDUKE TRIO *(PI-Beethoven)*
A SEA SYMPHONY *(Vaughan Williams)*
BEAR SYMPHONY *(Haydn)*
BRIDAL CHORUS *(Wagner)* *7
CORELLI FUGUE *(Bach)*
DANSE MACABRE *(TP-Saint-Saëns)*
DI QUELLA PIRA *(A-Verdi)*
FESTIVAL SONG *(PI-Mendelssohn)*
FIRE SYMPHONY *(Haydn)*
FLORIDA SUITE *(Delius)*
FRENCH SUITES *(Bach)*
FUNERAL MARCH *(Chopin)*
      (Mendelssohn)
GERMAN SUITES *(Bach)*
HAFFNER SUITE *(Mozart)*
HOLBERG SUITE *(Grieg)*
HUNT SYMPHONY *(Haydn)*
IMPERIAL MASS *(Haydn)*
IN LONDON TOWN *(OV-Elgar)*

JEUX D'ENFANTS *(SU-Bizet)*
KARELIA SUITE *(Sibelius)*
LINZ SYMPHONY *(Mozart)*
LONGING WALTZ *(Schubert)*
MASS IN B MINOR *(Bach)*
MASS IN G MINOR *(Vaughan Williams)*
MY FATHERLAND *(TP-Smetana)* *2
NON PIÙ ANDRAI *(A-Mozart)*
NURSERY SUITE *(Elgar)*
PAGAN REQUIEM *(M-Delius)*
RÁKÓCKY MARCH *(Berlioz)*
RAZOR QUARTET *(Haydn)*
RESURRECTION *(SY-Mahler)*
SALUT, DEMEURE *(A-Gounod)*
SCHOOLMASTER *(SY-Haydn)*
SPRING SONATA *(Beethoven)*
THE DYING SWAN *(PI-Saint-Saëns)*
THE UNCEASING *(OR-Hindemith)*
TROUT QUINTET *(Schubert)*
WEDDING MARCH *(Mendelssohn)*
      (Wagner) *7
WINTER DREAMS *(SY-Tchaikovsky)*

13

ACTUS TRAGICUS *(CA-Bach)*
A SONG OF SUMMER *(TP-Delius)*
CARMINA BURANA *(CA-Orff)*
CLOCK SYMPHONY *(Haydn)*
COFFEE CANTATA *(Bach)*
COUPERIN'S TOMB *(SU-Ravel)*
CROWN IMPERIAL *(PI-Walton)*
DUMBARTON OAKS *(CO-Stravinsky)*
ENGLISH SUITES *(Bach)*
FAUST OVERTURE *(Wagner)*
FAUST SYMPHONY *(Liszt)*
FUNERAL HEROID *(TP-Liszt)*
HAMMERKLAVIER *(SO-Beethoven)*
HAROLD IN ITALY *(SY-Berlioz)*
HYMN OF TRIUMPH *(PI-Brahms)*
LARK ASCENDING *(TP-Vaughan Williams)*
LITTLE RUSSIAN *(SY-Tchaikovsky)*
LYRIC SYMPHONY *(Bruckner)*
MAID OF THE MILL *(SU-Schubert)*
MARIA THÉRESIA *(SY-Haydn)*

MISSA SOLEMNIS *(M-Beethoven)* *1
MORGENBLÄTTER *(W-J Strauss)*
MORNING HEROES *(SY-Bliss)*
MOUNT OF OLIVES *(OR-Beethoven)*
OCEAN SYMPHONY *(Rubinstein)*
ODE TO NAPOLEON *(CA-Schönberg)*
ON WENLOCK EDGE *(Pl-Vaughan
            Williams)* *6
ORB AND SCEPTRE *(Pl-Walton)*
ORGAN SOLO MASS *(Mozart)*
PARIS SYMPHONY *(Mozart)*
POEM OF ECSTASY *(SO-Scriabin)*
RUINS OF ATHENS *(OV-Beethoven)*
RUSSIAN EASTER *(OV-Rimsky-
            Korsakov)*
SCYTHIAN SUITE *(Prokofiev)*
SONG OF THE FLEA *(Pl-Mussorgsky)*
STORM SYMPHONY *(Haydn)*
THE BÉATITUDES *(OR-Franck)*
THE BLUE DANUBE *(W-J Strauss)*
THE LIFE OF MARY *(Pl-Hindemith)*
VESTI DI GIUBBA *(A-Leoncavallo)*
WELSH RHAPSODY *(German)*
WINTER JOURNEY *(Pl-Schumann)*

14

A GERMAN REQUIEM *(OR-Brahms)*
ALLA BREVA FUGUE *(Bach)*
ALPINE SYMPHONY *(R Strauss)*
BELLS OF ZLONICE *(SY-Dvořák)*
CARNAVAL ROMAIN *(OV-Berlioz)*
CHORAL SYMPHONY *(Beethoven)*
            (Holst)
COLOUR SYMPHONY *(Bliss)*
CORONATION MASS *(Mozart)*
EGMONT OVERTURE *(Beethoven)*
EIGHTEEN-TWELVE *(OV-Beethoven)*
EMPEROR QUARTET *(Haydn)*
EROICA SYMPHONY *(Beethoven)*
FIREWORKS MUSIC *(SU-Handel)*
FOURTH OF AUGUST *(Pl-Elgar)*
HAMLET OVERTURE *(Tchaikovsky)*
KREUTZER SONATA *(Beethoven)*
LA DONNA È MOBILE *(A-Verdi)*

LAUDON SYMPHONY *(Haydn)*
LODRON CONCERTO *(Mozart)*
LONDON SYMPHONY *(Haydn)*
            *(Vaughan
            Williams)*
NORDIC SYMPHONY *(Hanson)*
PASTORAL SONATA *(Beethoven)*
PEASANT CANTATA *(Bach)*
POET AND PEASANT *(Pl-Suppé)*
POLISH SYMPHONY *(Tchaikovsky)*
PRAGUE SYMPHONY *(Mozart)*
RHAPSODY IN BLUE *(TP-Gershwin)*
ROB ROY OVERTURE *(Berlioz)*
ROMAN FESTIVALS *(SU-Respighi)*
ROMEO AND JULIET *(OV-
            Tchaikovsky)*
            (SY-Berlioz)
RUSTLE OF SPRING *(Pl-Sinding)*
SCOTCH SYMPHONY *(Mendelssohn)*
SIEGFRIED IDYLL *(Pl-Wagner)*
SLAVONIC DANCES *(Dvořák)*
SPRING SYMPHONY *(Schumann)*
SUNRISE QUARTET *(Haydn)*
THE BEE'S WEDDING *(Pl-
            Mendelssohn)*
THE LIGHT OF LIFE *(OR-Elgar)*
THE MUSIC MAKERS *(TP-Elgar)*
THE PRODIGAL SON *(OR-Sullivan)*
THE WISE VIRGINS *(SU-Walton)*
TRAGIC OVERTURE *(Brahms)*
TRAGIC SYMPHONY *(Schubert)*
TRIPLE OVERTURE *(Dvořák)*
VERKLÄRTE NACHT *(Pl-Schönberg)*
WALPURGIS NIGHT *(Pl-Mendelssohn)*
WARSAW CONCERTO *(Addinsell)*
WASHINGTON POST *(Pl-Sousa)*

15

AIR ON THE G STRING *(Pl-Bach)*
ALEXANDER NEVSKY *(CA-Prokofiev)*
ALEXANDER'S FEAST *(Pl-Handel)*
AMERICAN QUARTET *(Dvořák)*
DEAD MARCH IN SAUL *(OR-Handel)*
EMPEROR CONCERTO *(Beethoven)*

ARTS – MUSIC – CLASSICAL PIECES

FOUNTAINS OF ROME *(TP-Respighi)*
HAFFNER SYMPHONY *(Mozart)*
HORSEMAN QUARTET *(Haydn)*
IN WINDSOR FOREST *(CA-Vaughan Williams)*
ITALIAN CONCERTO *(Bach)*
ITALIAN SYMPHONY *(Mendelssohn)*
JUDAS MACCABAEUS *(OR-Handel)*
JUPITER SYMPHONY *(Mozart)*
LET'S MAKE AN OPERA *(SU-Britten)*
LINCOLN PORTRAIT *(Pl-Copland)*
MANFRED SYMPHONY *(Tchaikovsky)*
MARCHE MILITAIRE *(Pl-Schubert)*
MEPHISTO WALTZES *(Liszt)*
MERCURY SYMPHONY *(Haydn)*
MOONLIGHT SONATA *(Beethoven)*
NAME-DAY OVERTURE *(Beethoven)*
NUTCRACKER SUITE *(Tchaikovsky)*

OCTOBER SYMPHONY *(Shostakovich)*
OTHELLO OVERTURE *(Dvořák)*
PARIS SYMPHONIES *(Haydn)*
PASSION SYMPHONY *(Haydn)*
PETER AND THE WOLF *(Pl-Prokofiev)*
RAINDROP PRELUDE *(Chopin)*
RHENISH SYMPHONY *(Schumann)*
RICHARD THE THIRD *(Pl-German)*
RUSSIAN QUARTETS *(Haydn)*
SINTRAM SYMPHONY *(Strong)*
SPANISH SYMPHONY *(Lalo)*
THE PROMISED LAND *(OR-Saint-Saëns)*
THE ROSE OF SHARON *(OR-Mackenzie)*
TRUMPET OVERTURE *(Mendelssohn)*
VICTORY SYMPHONY *(Beethoven)*
WALDSTEIN SONATA *(Beethoven)*

ARTS

MUSIC – OPERAS

(C) = Opera cycle
* = Alternative title

4

AÏDA *(Verdi)*
IRIS *(Mascagni)*
LULU *(Berg)*
NERO *(Boito) *1*
RING *(C-Wagner)*
ZAZA *(Leoncavallo)*

5

ALEKO *(Rachmaninov)*

FAUST *(Gounod)*
          (Spohr)
HALKA *(Moniuszko)*
KITEJ *(Rimsky-Korsakov)*
LAKMÉ *(Delibes)*
LE CID *(Massenet)*
MANON *(Massenet)*
MAVRA *(Stravinsky)*
NORMA *(Bellini)*
ORFEO *(Monteverdi)*
SADKO *(Rimsky-Korsakov)*
SAPHO *(Gounod)*
THAÏS *(Massenet)*

TOSCA *(Puccini)*

6

ALMIRA *(Handel)*
ANIARA *(Blomdahl)*
ARMIDE *(Gluck)*
BIANCA *(Hadley)*
CARMEN *(Bizet)*
ERNANI *(Verdi)*
FEDORA *(Giordano)*
FIGARO *(Mozart) *2*
KOANGA *(Delius)*

LOUISE *(Charpentier)*
MARTHA *(Flotow)*
MIGNON *(Thomas)*
NATOMA *(Herbert)*
NERONE *(Boito)* *1
OBERON *(Weber)*
OTELLO *(Verdi)* *3
RIENZI *(Wagner)*
SALOME *(R Strauss)*
THE BAT *(J Strauss)* *4
THE ZOO *(Sullivan)*

7

BLODWEN *(Parry)*
COLOMBA *(Mackenzie)*
DIARMID *(MacCunn)*
DIE FEEN *(Wagner)* *5
DINORAH *(Meyerbeer)*
ELEKTRA *(R Strauss)*
FIDELIO *(Beethoven)*
IVANHOE *(Sullivan)*
LEONORA *(Fry)*
LE VILLI *(Puccini)*
MACBETH *(Verdi)*
NABUCCO *(Verdi)*
OTHELLO *(Verdi)* *3
RINALDO *(Handel)*
SAVITRI *(Holst)*
TEODORA *(Scarlatti)*
THE RING *(C-Wagner)*
THESPIS *(Gilbert & Sullivan)*
TIGRANE *(Scarlatti)*
WERTHER *(Massenet)*
WOZZECK *(Berg)*

8

ALCESTIS *(Gluck)*
ALKESTIS *(Broughton)*
ARABELLA *(R Strauss)*
DJAMILEH *(Bizet)*
FALSTAFF *(Verdi)*
GLORIANA *(Britten)*

GOYESCAS *(Granados)*
GRISELDA *(Scarlatti)*
HERODIAS *(Massenet)*
IOLANTHE *(Gilbert & Sullivan)*
          (Tchaikovsky)
LA BOHÈME *(Puccini)*
LE COQ D'OR *(Rimsky-Korsakov)*
MARITANA *(Wallace)*
MIREILLE *(Gounod)*
PARSIFAL *(Wagner)*
PATIENCE *(Gilbert & Sullivan)*
PÉNÉLOPE *(Fauré)*
RUSSALKA *(Dvořák)*
TANCREDI *(Rossini)*
THE MAYOR *(Wolf)* *6
TOM JONES *(German)*
TURANDOT *(Busoni)*
         (Puccini)

9

ABU HASSAN *(Weber)*
BILLY BUDD *(Britten)*
BOCCACCIO *(Suppé)*
CAPRICCIO *(R Strauss)*
CARDILLAC *(Hindemith)*
DON CARLOS *(Verdi)*
EURYANTHE *(Weber)*
HÁRY JÁNOS *(Kodály)*
IL TABARRO *(Puccini)*
KING PRIAM *(Tippett)*
LA RONDINE *(Puccini)*
LA VESTALE *(Spontini)*
PIQUE DAME *(Tchaikovsky)* *7
RIGOLETTO *(Verdi)*
ROBIN HOOD *(Koven)*
RUDDIGORE *(Gilbert & Sullivan)*
SIEGFRIED *(Wagner)*
THE MIKADO *(Gilbert & Sullivan)*
VÉRONIQUE *(Messager)*

10

ARTAXERXES *(Arne)*
CINDERELLA *(Massenet)*
           (Rossini)

ARTS – MUSIC – OPERAS

DIE WALKÜRE *(Wagner)*
IL TRITTICO *(C-Puccini)*
INTERMEZZO *(R Strauss)*
I PAGLIACCI *(Leoncavallo)*
LA FAVORITA *(Donizetti)*
L'AFRICAINE *(Meyerbeer)*
LA GIOCONDA *(Ponchielli)*
LA TRAVIATA *(Verdi)*
LE PROPHÈTE *(Meyerbeer)*
LES TROYENS *(Berlioz)* *8
MERRY MOUNT *(Hanson)*
NIGHT IN MAY *(Rimsky-Korsakov)*
PERSÉPHONE *(Stravinsky)*
PRINCE IGOR *(Borodin)*
SAVONAROLA *(Stanford)*
TANNHÄUSER *(Wagner)*
THE FAIRIES *(Wagner)* *5
THE TROJANS *(Berlioz)* *8

DAS RHEINGOLD *(Wagner)*
EUGENE ONEGIN *(Tchaikovsky)*
JULIUS CAESAR *(Handel)*
LA SONNAMBULA *(Bellini)*
LES HUGUENOTS *(Meyerbeer)*
MANON LESCAUT *(Puccini)*
MOSES IN EGYPT *(Rossini)*
PARADISE LOST *(Penderecki)*
PORGY AND BESS *(Gershwin)*
SHAMUS O'BRIEN *(Stanford)*
SUOR ANGELICA *(Puccini)*
THE GRAND DUKE *(Gilbert & Sullivan)*
THE ISLAND GOD *(Menotti)*
THE NORTH STAR *(Meyerbeer)*
THE OLYMPIANS *(Bliss)*

11

A MASKED BALL *(Verdi)*
DOCTOR FAUST *(Busoni)*
DON GIOVANNI *(Mozart)*
DON PASQUALE *(Donizetti)*
HMS PINAFORE *(Gilbert & Sullivan)*
IL TROVATORE *(Verdi)*
IVAN SUSANIN *(Glinka)*
L'AMICO FRITZ *(Mascagni)*
LA VIDE BREVE *(Falla)*
PETER GRIMES *(Britten)*
PRINCESS IDA *(Gilbert & Sullivan)*
THE MARKSMAN *(Weber)* *9
THE SORCERER *(Gilbert & Sullivan)*
TRIAL BY JURY *(Gilbert & Sullivan)*
WAR AND PEACE *(Prokofiev)*
WILLIAM TELL *(Rossini)*

12

BEGGAR'S OPERA *(Gay & Pepusch)*
BORIS GODUNOV *(Mussorgsky)*
CHRISTMAS EVE *(Rimsky-Korsakov)*
COSI FAN TUTTE *(Mozart)*

13

ALBERT HERRING *(Britten)*
ANDREA CHÉNIER *(Giordano)*
DER CORREGIDOR *(Wolf)* *6
DER FREISCHÜTZ *(Weber)* *9
DIDO AND AENEAS *(Purcell)*
DIE FLEDERMAUS *(J Strauss)* *4
HUGH THE DROVER *(Vaughan
          Williams)*
LA BELLE HÉLÈNE *(Offenbach)*
LA SCALA DI SETA *(Rossini)*
L'ELISIR D'AMOUR *(Donizetti)*
MERRIE ENGLAND *(German)*
MOSES AND AARON *(Schönberg)*
NOZZE DI FIGARO *(Mozart)* *2
QUEEN OF SPADES *(Tchaikovsky)* *7
SIR JOHN IN LOVE *(Vaughan Williams)*
THE CZAR'S BRIDE *(Rimsky-
          Korsakov)*
THE GONDOLIERS *(Gilbert & Sullivan)*
THE MAGIC FLUTE *(Mozart)* *10
THE MERRY WIDOW *(Lehár)*
THE SNOW MAIDEN *(Rimsky-
          Korsakov)*
THE TENDER LAND *(Copland)*
UTOPIA LIMITED *(Gilbert & Sullivan)*

ARIADNE ON NAXOS (R Strauss) *11
CONTRABANDISTA (Sullivan)
DIE ZAUBERFLÖTE (Mozart) *10
FLYING DUTCHMAN (Wagner)
GIANNI SCHICCHI (Puccini)
LUCREZIA BORGIA (Donizetti)
NEBUCHADNEZZAR (Verdi)
RIDERS TO THE SEA (Vaughan
                        Williams)
ROMEO AND JULIET (Gounod)
SAMSON ET DALILA (Saint-Saëns)
THE BEAUTY STONE (Sullivan)

ARIADNE AUF NAXOS (R Strauss) *11
BARBER OF SEVILLE (Rossini)
DOWN IN THE VALLEY (Weill)
FAIR MAID OF PERTH (Bizet)
GÖTTERDÄMMERUNG (Wagner)
HÄNSEL AND GRETEL (Humperdinck)
LE NOZZE DI FIGARO (Mozart) *2
MADAME BUTTERFLY (Puccini)
ORFEO ET EURIDICE (Gluck)
TALES OF HOFFMANN (Offenbach)
THE IMMORTAL HOUR (Broughton)
THE PEARL FISHERS (Bizet)
THE ROSE OF PERSIA (Sullivan)
THREEPENNY OPERA (Weill)

ARTS

MUSIC – SONGS – POPULAR

(v) = various artists

3

ABC (Jackson Five)
ASK (Smiths)
BAD (Michael Jackson)
BEN (v)
BOY (Lulu)
CRY (v)
FBI (Shadows)
IDA (v)
IVY (v)
JET (Paul McCartney)
MAN (Rosemary Clooney)
NOW (Val Doonican)
         (Al Martino)
RIO (Duran Duran)

SHE (Charles Aznavour)
SOS (Abba)
TOY (Casuals)
WAR (Edwin Starr)
WHY (Anthony Newley)
         (Donny Osmond)
WOW (Kate Bush)
YOU (v)

4

ALGY (Vesta Tilley)
ARIA (Acker Bilk)
BLUE (v)
BOYS (Kim Wilde)

CARS *(Gary Numan)*
CO-CO *(Sweet)*
DON'T *(Elvis Presley)*
EASY *(Commodores)*
EMMA *(Hot Chocolate)*
FAME *(Irene Cara)*
FIRE *(Crazy World of Arthur Brown)*
FREE *(Deniece Williams)*
GENO *(Dexy's Midnight Runners)*
GIGI *(Maurice Chevalier)*
GIRL *(St Louis Union)*
GLOW *(Spandau Ballet)*
GOLD *(Spandau Ballet)*
HELP! *(Beatles)*
HOME *(v)*
HURT *(Manhattans)*
JA-DA *(Johnny & the Hurricanes/v)*
JUMP *(Van Halen)*
KING *(UB40)*
LAZY *(v)*
LIES *(Status Quo/v)*
LIZA *(v)*
LOLA *(Kinks)*
LOVE *(v)*
MAMA *(Dave Berry)*
        (Connie Francis)
MAY I *(v)*
MINE *(v)*
MORE *(Perry Como)*
        (Jimmy Young)
MR WU *(George Formby)*
PEPE *(Duane Eddy)*
RAIN *(Cult)*
        (Status Quo/v)
SOON *(v)*
STAR *(v)*
STAY *(Hollies/v)*
SWAY *(Dean Martin)*
TILL *(Tom Jones)*
        (Dorothy Squires)
TRUE *(Spandau Ballet)*
TUSK *(Fleetwood Mac)*
WAIT *(v)*
WHAT *(Soft Cell)*
WHEN *(Kalin Twins)*
        (Showaddywaddy)

YMCA *(Village People)*
ZOOM *(Fat Larry's Band)*

5

ALFIE *(Cilla Black)*
ALONE *(v)*
ANGEL *(v)*
ANGIE *(Rolling Stones)*
ANGRY *(v)*
BIRTH *(Peddlers)*
BITCH *(Rolling Stones)*
CLAIR *(Gilbert O'Sullivan)*
C MOON *(Paul McCartney)*
CRAZY *(Patsy Cline)*
        (Mud)
CRYIN' *(Roy Orbison)*
CUPID *(Johnny Cash)*
        (Sam Cooke)
DADDY *(v)*
DENIS *(Blondie)*
DIANA *(Paul Anka)*
DIANE *(Bachelors/v)*
DINAH *(v)*
DIZZY *(Tommy Roe)*
DONNA *(10 CC)*
        (Marty Wilde)
DREAM *(v)*
ERNIE *(Benny Hill)*
FEVER *(Peggy Lee)*
FLASH *(Queen)*
FRESH *(Kool & the Gang)*
GET IT *(Darts)*
GO NOW *(Moody Blues)*
HELLO *(Lionel Richie)*
HONEY *(Bobby Goldsboro/v)*
HUMAN *(Human League)*
IDAHO *(v)*
I WILL *(Billy Fury)*
        (Ruby Winters)
I WISH *(Stevie Wonder)*
KITES *(Simon Dupree & the Big Sound)*
LA MER *(Charles Trenet)*
LAURA *(v)*
LAYLA *(Eric Clapton)*
        (Derek & the Dominos)

LOVER *(v)*
MAMMY *(Al Jolson)*
MANDY *(Eddie Calvert)*
        (Barry Manilow)
MARIA *(v)*
MARIE *(Bachelors/v)*
MARTA *(Bachelors)*
        (Arthur Tracy)
MAYBE *(v)*
MISTY *(Johnny Mathis)*
        (Ray Stevens)
MY BOY *(Elvis Presley)*
MY WAY *(Elvis Presley)*
        (Sex Pistols)
        (Frank Sinatra/v)
NANCY *(v)*
NEVER *(v)*
OH BOY *(Crickets)*
        (Mud)
PARTY *(Elvis Presley)*
RELAX *(Frankie goes to Hollywood)*
ROMEO *(Petula Clark)*
        (Mr Big)
ROSIE *(Don Partridge)*
SALLY *(Gracie Fields)*
SANDY *(John Travolta)*
SHAFT *(Isaac Hayes)*
SHOUT *(Lulu)*
        (Tears For Fears)
SMILE *(Nat 'King' Cole/v)*
SO DO I *(Kenny Ball & his Jazzmen)*
SOLID *(Ashford & Simpson)*
START *(Jam)*
STILL *(Commodores)*
        (Ken Dodd)
STOMP *(Brothers Johnson)*
SUGAR *(v)*
SUNNY *(Boney M)*
        (Bobby Hebb/v)
TABOO *(v)*
TAMMY *(Debbie Reynolds)*
TEARS *(Ken Dodd)*
TERRY *(Twinkle)*
TORCH *(Soft Cell)*
TRACY *(Cufflinks)*
TRULY *(Lionel Richie)*

UNTIL *(v)*
VENUS *(Bananarama)*
        (Shocking Blue)
VOGUE *(Madonna)*
WOMAN *(José Ferrer)*
        (John Lennon)
WORDS *(Bee Gees)*
        (FR David)
WORLD *(Bee Gees)*
YOURS *(v)*

6

AFRICA *(Toto)*
AGADOO *(Black Lace)*
ALWAYS *(v)*
ANGELO *(Brotherhood of Man)*
APACHE *(Shadows)*
ATOMIC *(Blondie)*
BEAT IT *(Michael Jackson)*
BEND IT *(Dave Dee, Dozy, Beaky, Mick & Tich)*
BIG MAN *(Four Preps)*
BRAZIL *(Edmundo Ros)*
BUT I DO *(Clarence 'Frogman' Henry)*
CALL ME *(Blondie/v)*
CARRIE *(Cliff Richard)*
CHAINS *(Beatles)*
CHERIE *(v)*
CHI MAI *(Ennio Morricone)*
COME ON *(Rolling Stones)*
CONVOY *(CW McCall)*
CRYING *(Don McLean)*
DA DA DA *(Trio)*
DANIEL *(Elton John)*
DON'T GO *(Yazoo)*
DR LOVE *(Tina Charles)*
DUM DUM *(Brenda Lee)*
ELOISE *(Damned)*
        (Barry Ryan)
EL PASO *(Marty Robbins)*
EXODUS *(Ferrante & Teicher)*
FEET UP *(Guy Mitchell)*
FIGARO *(Brotherhood of Man)*
GALAXY *(War)*
GHOSTS *(Japan)*

GREASE *(Frankie Valli)*
GUILTY *(Pearls/v)*
HEY JOE *(Jimi Hendrix Experience)*
HI HI HI *(Paul McCartney)*
HOLD ME *(PJ Proby)*
HOWZAT *(Sherbet)*
IF I WAS *(Midge Ure)*
I GO APE *(Neil Sedaka)*
I'M A BOY *(Who)*
I'M A MAN *(Chicago)*
      (Spencer Davis Group)
I'M FREE *(Roger Daltrey)*
IT'S YOU *(Freddie Starr)*
JOANNA *(Kool & the Gang)*
      (Scott Walker)
JULIET *(Four Pennies)*
LATELY *(Stevie Wonder)*
LOUISE *(Maurice Chevalier)*
MAÑANA *(v)*
MARGIE *(Fats Domino/v)*
MEMORY *(Elaine Paige)*
MICKEY *(Toni Basil)*
MILORD *(Edith Piaf)*
      (Frankie Vaughan)
MOBILE *(Ray Burns)*
MOVE IT *(Cliff Richard)*
MY GIRL *(Madness)*
      (Otis Redding/v)
MY LOVE *(Petula Clark/v)*
MY OH MY *(Slade)*
NADINE *(Chuck Berry)*
NIKITA *(Elton John)*
NURSIE *(Elsie Carlisle)*
OH MAMA *(Dave Berry/v)*
OH WELL *(Fleetwood Mac)*
PEOPLE *(Tymes)*
PICNIC *(v)*
POOR ME *(Adam Faith)*
RABBIT *(Chas & Dave)*
RAMONA *(Bachelors/v)*
RAVE ON *(Buddy Holly)*
REWARD *(Teardrop Explodes)*
ROCKET *(Mud)*
ROCK ON *(David Essex)*
SAILOR *(Petula Clark)*
      (Anne Shelton)

SAVE ME *(Dave Dee, Dozy, Beaky,*
      Mick & Tich)
      (Queen)
SEE YOU *(Depeche Mode)*
SHAZAM! *(Duane Eddy)*
SH-BOOM *(v)*
SHEILA *(Tommy Roe)*
SHERRY *(Four Seasons)*
SHY BOY *(Bananarama)*
SORROW *(David Bowie)*
      (Merseys)
SWANEE *(Al Jolson)*
SYLVIA *(Focus)*
TAXMAN *(Beatles)*
THINGS *(Bobby Darin)*
TOO SHY *(Kajagoogoo)*
US MALE *(Elvis Presley)*
VIENNA *(Ultravox)*
VOLARE *(Dean Martin/v)*
WANTED *(Dooleys)*
      (Perry Como)
WHO AM I? *(Adam Faith)*
WORD UP *(Cameo)*
XANADU *(Olivia Newton-John & ELO)*
YEH YEH *(Matt Bianco)*
      (Georgie Fame)

7

ADELINE *(v)*
AIRPORT *(Motors)*
ALL OF ME *(v)*
AMERICA *(Trini Lopez)*
      (Nice/v)
AM I BLUE? *(v)*
ARIZONA *(v)*
AS USUAL *(Brenda Lee)*
BAD BOYS *(Wham!)*
BAD TO ME *(Billy J Kramer & the*
      Dakotas)
BALI HAI *(v)*
BIRD DOG *(Everly Brothers)*
BOYS CRY *(Eden Kane)*
BUS STOP *(Hollies)*
CABARET *(Louis Armstrong)*
      (Frankie Vaughan/v)

CANDIDA *(Dawn)*
CARAVAN *(Barbara Dickson)*
CARIOCA *(v)*
CECILIA *(v)*
CHANGES *(Imagination)*
        (Crispian St Peters)
CHERISH *(Kool & the Gang)*
CHICAGO *(Frank Sinatra)*
CIRCLES *(New Seekers)*
COLOURS *(Donovan)*
COMPLEX *(Gary Numan)*
CONTACT *(Edwin Starr)*
CRY WOLF *(A-Ha)*
DANCE ON *(Kathy Kirby)*
        (Shadows)
'DEED I DO *(v)*
DELILAH *(Tom Jones)*
DIMPLES *(John Lee Hooker)*
DIVORCE *(Billy Connolly)*
DREAMIN' *(Johnny Burnette)*
        (Cliff Richard)
        (Status Quo)
EBB TIDE *(Frank Chacksfield)*
        (Jerry Colonna)
ELECTED *(Alice Cooper)*
FALLING *(Roy Orbison)*
FASHION *(David Bowie)*
FLOAT ON *(Floaters)*
FRANKIE *(Sister Sledge)*
FREEDOM *(Wham!)*
FRENESI *(v)*
GAMBLER *(Madonna)*
GET AWAY *(Georgie Fame)*
GET BACK *(Beatles)*
GET DOWN *(Gilbert O'Sullivan)*
GET IT ON *(T Rex)*
GOODBYE *(Mary Hopkin/v)*
GRANADA *(Frankie Laine)*
        (Frank Sinatra/v)
GRANDAD *(Clive Dunn)*
GREY DAY *(Madness)*
GROOVIN' *(Young Rascals)*
HEY BABY *(Bruce Channel)*
HEY JUDE *(Beatles)*
HOLIDAY *(Madonna)*
HOLY COW *(Lee Dorsey)*

HOMBURG *(Procol Harum)*
HOTLEGS *(Rod Stewart)*
HOT LOVE *(T Rex)*
I LIKE IT *(Gerry & the Pacemakers)*
I'M A FOOL *(Slim Whitman)*
IMAGINE *(John Lennon)*
I'M ALIVE *(Hollies)*
I'M SORRY *(Brenda Lee)*
I'M YOURS *(v)*
INDIANA *(v)*
IN ZAIRE *(Johnny Wakelin)*
IT'S LATE *(Rick Nelson)*
IT'S OVER *(Roy Orbison)*
I WONDER *(Brenda Lee)*
        (Dickie Valentine)
JACKSON *(Nancy Sinatra)*
JANUARY *(Pilot)*
JEZEBEL *(Marty Wilde)*
JOSHU-AH *(Clarice Mayne)*
K-K-K-KATY *(v)*
KON-TIKI *(Shadows)*
LET IT BE *(Beatles)*
LET ME IN *(Osmonds)*
LIKE I DO *(Maureen Evans)*
LUCILLE *(Everly Brothers)*
        (Little Richard)
        (Kenny Rogers)
MA BAKER *(Boney M)*
MAIS OUI *(King Brothers)*
MICHAEL *(Highwaymen)*
MISS YOU *(Rolling Stones)*
        (Jimmy Young)
MS GRACE *(Tymes)*
NAIROBI *(Tommy Steele)*
NEAR YOU *(Migil Five/v)*
OH CAROL *(Neil Sedaka)*
OH JULIE *(Shakin' Stevens)*
OLD SHEP *(Elvis Presley)*
ONE KISS *(v)*
ONE OF US *(Abba)*
ONLY YOU *(Flying Pickets)*
        (Platters)
        (Yazoo/v)
OVER YOU *(Freddie & the Dreamers)*
        (Roxy Music)
PATCHES *(Clarence Carter)*

PIE JESU *(Sarah Brightman & Paul Miles-Kingston)*
POPCORN *(Hot Butter)*
PRETEND *(Nat 'King' Cole)*
(Alvin Stardust/v)
RAG DOLL *(Four Seasons)*
RAINBOW *(Marmalade)*
RAPTURE *(Blondie)*
RAT RACE *(Specials)*
RAT TRAP *(Boomtown Rats)*
RAWHIDE *(Frankie Laine)*
RESPECT *(Aretha Franklin)*
RIO RITA *(v)*
RIP IT UP *(Bill Haley & his Comets)*
(Little Richard)
(Orange Juice)
(Elvis Presley)
ROSETTA *(Fame & Price)*
ROXANNE *(Police)*
RUNAWAY *(Del Shannon)*
SAILING *(Rod Stewart)*
SHA LA LA *(Manfred Mann)*
SHINDIG *(Shadows)*
SHIRLEY *(Shakin' Stevens)*
SIR DUKE *(Stevie Wonder)*
SKYLARK *(v)*
SOMEDAY *(Kenny Ball & his Jazzmen)*
(Gap Band/v)
SOMEONE *(Johnny Mathis)*
SO TIRED *(v)*
SUGAR ME *(Lynsey De Paul)*
SULTANA *(Titanic)*
TAMPICO *(v)*
TEACHER *(Jethro Tull)*
TELL HIM *(Billie Davis)*
(Hello)
TELSTAR *(Tornados)*
TEQUILA *(Champs)*
(Ted Heath/v)
THE BUMP *(Kenny)*
TOCCATA *(Sky)*
TOM HARK *(Elias & his Zigzag Jive Flutes)*
(Piranhas)
TONIGHT *(Shirley Bassey)*
(Kool & the Gang)
(Move/v)

TOO MUCH *(Elvis Presley)*
TOUCH ME *(Samantha Fox)*
TRAGEDY *(Bee Gees)*
TRAPPED *(Colonel Abrams)*
UPTIGHT *(Stevie Wonder)*
VANESSA *(Ted Heath)*
VICTIMS *(Culture Club)*
VINCENT *(Don McLean)*
VISIONS *(Cliff Richard)*
WAR BABY *(Tom Robinson)*
WAY DOWN *(Elvis Presley)*
WEEKEND *(Eddie Cochran)*
WIDE BOY *(Nik Kershaw)*
WILL YOU? *(Hazel O'Connor)*
WIMOWEH *(Karl Denver)*
WIPE OUT *(Surfaris)*
WISHING *(Buddy Holly)*
ZABADAK! *(Dave Dee, Dozy, Beaky, Mick & Tich)*
ZAMBESI *(Lou Busch)*
(Eddie Calvert/v)

8

ANSWER ME *(Barbara Dickson)*
(Frankie Laine)
(David Whitfield)
AQUARIUS *(Fifth Dimension)*
ATLANTIS *(Shadows)*
AT THE HOP *(Danny & the Juniors)*
AVE MARIA *(Shirley Bassey/v)*
BABY FACE *(Little Richard)*
BABY JANE *(Rod Stewart)*
BABY LOVE *(Supremes)*
BACK HOME *(England World Cup Squad)*
BARBADOS *(Typically Tropical)*
BE A CLOWN *(v)*
BE MY BABY *(Ronettes)*
BE MY LOVE *(Mario Lanza)*
BLESS YOU *(Tony Orlando)*
BLUE MOON *(Marcels/v)*
BREAKOUT *(Swing Out Sister)*
BUSY LINE *(Rose Murphy)*
CANDY MAN *(Brian Poole & the Tremeloes)*

CAROLINA (v)
CHEROKEE (v)
CHIQUITA (v)
COMING UP (Paul McCartney)
DAY BY DAY (v)
DAYDREAM (Lovin' Spoonful)
DELAWARE (Perry Como)
DE-LOVELY (v)
DOWN DOWN (Status Quo)
DOWNTOWN (Petula Clark)
DREAMING (Blondie)
(Flanagan & Allen)
DRY BONES (v)
DYNAMITE (Cliff Richard)
EVERYDAY (Slade)
EYE LEVEL (Simon Park)
FEELINGS (Morris Albert)
FERNANDO (Abba)
GIRL TALK (Jack Jones)
GIVE IT UP (KC & the Sunshine Band)
HANDY MAN (Jimmy Jones)
HEATWAVE (v)
HEY PAULA (Paul & Paula)
HEY THERE (Rosemary Clooney)
(Johnnie Ray/v)
HIGH NOON (Frankie Laine)
HIGH TIME (Paul Jones)
HONEY BUN (v)
HOOTS MON (Lord Rockingham's XI)
HOUND DOG (Elvis Presley)
I BELIEVE (Bachelors)
(Frankie Laine/v)
IF NOT YOU (Dr Hook)
I'LL GET BY (v)
I LOVE YOU (Cliff Richard)
(Donna Summer/v)
I'M A TIGER (Lulu)
I'M IN LOVE (Fourmost)
I'M ON FIRE (5000 Volts)
(Bruce Springsteen)
I'M THE ONE (Gerry & the
Pacemakers)
IN DREAMS (Roy Orbison)
IN SUMMER (Billy Fury)
I PRETEND (Des O'Connor)
IT'LL BE ME (Cliff Richard)

IT'S MAGIC (v)
JEALOUSY (Billy Fury/v)
JEEPSTER (T Rex)
JESAMINE (Casuals)
JUDY TEEN (Steve Harley & Cockney
Rebel)
KAYLEIGH (Marillion)
KENTUCKY (v)
LADY JANE (Rolling Stones)
LAVENDER (Marillion)
LET'S DO IT (Noël Coward/v)
LOLLIPOP (Mudlarks)
LOOK AWAY (Big Country)
LOST JOHN (Lonnie Donegan)
LOVE ME DO (Beatles)
MAD WORLD (Tears For Fears)
MAGIC FLY (Space)
MAMMA MIA (Abba)
MARCHÉTA (v)
MICHELLE (Beatles)
(Overlanders)
MONA LISA (Conway Twitty)
MONY MONY (Tommy James & the
Shondells)
MOONGLOW (v)
MRS MOORE (Lily Morris)
MY GAL SAL (v)
MY OLD MAN (Marie Lloyd)
MY PRAYER (Platters)
NINETEEN (Paul Hardcastle)
NO CHARGE (JJ Barrie)
OH ME! OH MY! (George Formby)
OKLAHOMA! (v)
ONE NIGHT (Elvis Presley)
OUR HOUSE (Madness)
PAPER SUN (Traffic)
PASADENA (Temperance Seven)
PEEK-A-BOO (New Vaudeville Band)
PEGGY SUE (Buddy Holly)
PERFIDIA (Shadows)
(Ventures/v)
PHYSICAL (Olivia Newton-John)
PIPELINE (Chantays)
PRECIOUS (Jam)
PROBLEMS (Everly Brothers)
PROMISES (Buzzcocks)
(Ken Dodd)

QUESTION *(Moody Blues)*
RASPUTIN *(Boney M)*
RESTLESS *(v)*
ROBOT MAN *(Connie Francis)*
ROULETTE *(Russ Conway)*
RUN TO HIM *(Bobby Vee)*
SAMANTHA *(Kenny Ball & his
    Jazzmen)*
SAM'S SONG *(v)*
SEARCHIN' *(Hazel Dean)*
    (Hollies)
SEXY EYES *(Dr Hook)*
SHANGHAI *(v)*
SHIP AHOY *(Hetty King)*
SIDESHOW *(Barry Biggs)*
SKIN DEEP *(Duke Ellington)*
    (Ted Heath)
SOMETIME *(v)*
SONNY BOY *(Al Jolson)*
STARDUST *(Nat 'King' Cole)*
    (David Essex/v)
STEWBALL *(Lonnie Donegan)*
SUCU SUCU *(Ted Heath)*
    (Laurie Johnson)
    (Joe Loss)
SUKIYAKI *(Kenny Ball & his Jazzmen)*
    (Kyu Sakamoto)
SUN ARISE *(Rolf Harris)*
TAKE FIVE *(Dave Brubeck Quartet)*
TAKE ON ME *(A-Ha)*
TEEN BEAT *(Sandy Nelson)*
TENDERLY *(v)*
THE BOXER *(Simon & Garfunkel)*
THRILLER *(Michael Jackson)*
TICO TICO *(v)*
TOMORROW *(Johnny Brandon)*
    (Sandie Shaw/v)
TOO YOUNG *(Donny Osmond/v)*
TRUE BLUE *(Madonna)*
TRUE LOVE *(Bing Crosby & Grace
    Kelly)*
UMBRIAGO *(Jimmy Durante)*
VALENCIA *(v)*
WALK AWAY *(Matt Monro)*
WALK ON BY *(Leroy Van Dyke)*
    (Dionne Warwick)

WALK TALL *(Val Doonican)*
WAR PAINT *(Brook Brothers)*
WATERLOO *(Abba)*
WILD BOYS *(Duran Duran)*
WILD ROSE *(v)*
WILD WIND *(John Leyton)*
YOUR SONG *(Elton John)*
ZIGEUNER *(v)*

9

A FOGGY DAY *(v)*
ALBATROSS *(Fleetwood Mac)*
ALL THE WAY *(Frank Sinatra)*
ANGEL EYES *(Roxy Music/v)*
ANGIE BABY *(Helen Reddy)*
APRIL LOVE *(Pat Boone)*
A TEAR FELL *(Teresa Brewer)*
BACKSTAGE *(Gene Pitney)*
BED SITTER *(Soft Cell)*
BEWITCHED *(v)*
BLACK GIRL *(Four Pennies)*
BLUE BAYOU *(Roy Orbison)*
BLUE PETER *(Mike Oldfield)*
BLUE SKIES *(Bing Crosby/v)*
BO DIDDLEY *(Buddy Holly)*
BREAKAWAY *(Springfields)*
    (Tracey Ullman/v)
BUONA SERA *(Acker Bilk)*
BUTTERFLY *(Andy Williams)*
CANDY GIRL *(Four Seasons)*
    (New Edition)
CAN THE CAN *(Suzi Quatro)*
C'EST SI BON *(Conway Twitty)*
CHAIN GANG *(Sam Cooke)*
CHARMAINE *(Bachelors/v)*
CHINA GIRL *(David Bowie)*
CLAUDETTE *(Everly Brothers)*
COME PRIMA *(Marino Marini)*
CONFESSIN' *(Frank Ifield)*
COOL WATER *(Frankie Laine)*
DAISY BELL *(Katie Lawrence)*
DANCE AWAY *(Roxy Music)*
DELTA LADY *(Joe Cocker)*
DO IT AGAIN *(Beach Boys)*
DOMINIQUE *(Singing Nun)*

DOWN UNDER *(Men At Work)*
DO YOU MIND? *(Anthony Newley)*
DREAM BABY *(Roy Orbison)*
DREAMBOAT *(Alma Cogan)*
EDELWEISS *(Vince Hill)*
ETERNALLY *(Nat 'King' Cole)*
  (Jimmy Young/v)
FOOTLOOSE *(Kenny Loggins)*
FOOTSTEPS *(Steve Lawrence)*
FUNKYTOWN *(Lipps Inc)*
FUNNY FACE *(v)*
GALVESTON *(Glen Campbell)*
GHOST TOWN *(Specials)*
GOODBYE-EE *(Peter Cook & Dudley
  Moore)*
  (Florrie Forde)
GOOD TIMES *(Chic)*
GOOD TIMIN' *(Jimmy Jones)*
GOOGLE EYE *(Nashville Teens)*
GREEN DOOR *(Shakin' Stevens)*
  (Frankie Vaughan)
HAPPINESS *(Ken Dodd)*
HAPPY FEET *(v)*
HAPPY HOUR *(Housemartins)*
HAPPY TALK *(Captain Sensible/v)*
HEARTBEAT *(Buddy Holly)*
  (Ruby Murray)
  (Showaddywaddy)
HE'S A REBEL *(Crystals)*
HE'S IN TOWN *(Rockin' Berries)*
HE'S SO FINE *(Chiffons)*
HOLD ME NOW *(Thompson Twins)*
HOLD TIGHT *(Dave Dee, Dozy, Beaky,
  Mick & Tich)*
HOLY SMOKE *(Iron Maiden)*
I FEEL FINE *(Beatles)*
I FEEL LOVE *(Donna Summer)*
IF I HAD YOU *(v)*
I GOT IT BAD *(v)*
I GOT STUNG *(Elvis Presley)*
I HAVE EYES *(v)*
I'LL BE HOME *(Pat Boone)*
I'M YOUR MAN *(Wham!)*
INSIDE OUT *(Odyssey)*
IN THE MOOD *(Joe Loss)*
  (Glenn Miller)

IN THE NAVY *(Village People)*
IT'S FOR YOU *(Cilla Black)*
JAMBALAYA *(Fats Domino)*
  (Jo Stafford/v)
JIMMY MACK *(Martha Reeves & the
  Vandellas)*
LAZY BONES *(v)*
LAZY RIVER *(Bobby Darin)*
LET IT ROCK *(Chuck Berry)*
  (Rolling Stones)
LET'S DANCE *(David Bowie)*
  (Chris Montez)
LIMELIGHT *(Frank Chacksfield)*
LONELY BOY *(Paul Anka)*
LOUISIANA *(v)*
LOVE HURTS *(Jim Capaldi)*
LOVE TRAIN *(O'Jays)*
LOVING YOU *(Minnie Riperton/v)*
LUCKY LIPS *(Cliff Richard)*
MAGGIE MAY *(Rod Stewart)*
MALAGUEÑA *(v)*
MANHATTAN *(Ella Fitzgerald)*
MAYBE BABY *(Crickets)*
METAL GURU *(T Rex)*
MIRROR MAN *(Human League)*
MISTY BLUE *(Dorothy Moore)*
MOON RIVER *(Greyhound)*
  (Danny Williams/v)
MR BLUE SKY *(ELO)*
MR SANDMAN *(Chordettes)*
  (Four Aces)
  (Dickie Valentine)
MULE TRAIN *(Frank Ifield/v)*
NATURE BOY *(Bobby Darin/v)*
NO REGRETS *(Edith Piaf)*
  (Midge Ure)
  (Walker Brothers)
NUT ROCKER *(B Bumble & the
  Stingers)*
ONE VISION *(Queen)*
ONION SONG *(Marvin Gaye & Tammi
  Terrell)*
O SUPERMAN *(Laurie Anderson)*
OUT OF TIME *(Chris Farlowe)*
OVER THERE *(v)*
PAPER DOLL *(Mills Brothers)*

PENNY LANE *(Beatles)*
PIED PIPER *(Crispian St Peters)*
POISON IVY *(Coasters)*
           (Lambrettas)
           (Rolling Stones)
PUPPY LOVE *(Donny Osmond)*
RADIO GAGA *(Queen)*
REBEL YELL *(Billy Idol)*
RELEASE ME *(Engelbert Humperdinck)*
ROCKET MAN *(Elton John)*
ROSE MARIE *(Slim Whitman)*
ROW ROW ROW *(v)*
SACRIFICE *(Elton John)*
SATIN DOLL *(v)*
SEA OF LOVE *(Marty Wilde)*
SEE THE DAY *(Dee C Lee)*
SEPTEMBER *(Earth Wind And Fire)*
SIMON SAYS *(1910 Fruitgum Co)*
SOLILOQUY *(v)*
SOLITAIRE *(Carpenters)*
           (Andy Williams)
SOME GIRLS *(Racey)*
SOMETHING *(Shirley Bassey)*
           (Beatles)
SOMETIMES *(Erasure)*
SOMEWHERE *(PJ Proby/v)*
STAND BY ME *(Ben E King)*
           (John Lennon)
STARMAKER *(Kids From Fame)*
STEAM HEAT *(v)*
STROLLING *(Flanagan & Allen)*
SUGAR BUSH *(Eve Boswell)*
SUGAR TOWN *(Nancy Sinatra)*
SURRENDER *(Elvis Presley)*
SUSPICION *(Elvis Presley)*
SWISS MAID *(Del Shannon)*
TARZAN BOY *(Baltimora)*
TEA FOR TWO *(Tommy Dorsey)*
           (Joe Loss/v)
TEARDROPS *(Shakin' Stevens)*
TEDDY BEAR *(Elvis Presley)*
           (Red Sovine)
THAT'S LIFE *(Frank Sinatra)*
THE HUSTLE *(Van McCoy)*
THE REFLEX *(Duran Duran)*

THERE IT IS *(Shalamar)*
THE RIDDLE *(Nik Kershaw)*
THE STREAK *(Ray Stevens)*
TIGER FEET *(Mud)*
TOM DOOLEY *(Lonnie Donegan)*
           (Kingston Trio)
TWO TRIBES *(Frankie goes to Hollywood)*
WE LOVE YOU *(Rolling Stones)*
WHAT'D I SAY *(Jerry Lee Lewis)*
WHAT DO I DO *(Phil Fearon & Galaxy)*
WHAT'LL I DO *(v)*
WIG-WAM BAM *(Sweet)*
WILD THING *(Troggs)*
WOLD WORLD *(Jimmy Clift)*
WILLIE CAN *(Alma Cogan/v)*
WOODSTOCK *(Matthews Southern Comfort)*
WUNDERBAR *(v)*
YESTERDAY *(Beatles)*
           (Ray Charles)
           (Matt Monro/v)
YOUNG GIRL *(Gary Puckett & the Union Gap)*
YOUNG GUNS *(Wham!)*
YOUNG LOVE *(Tab Hunter)*
           (Donny Osmond)

10

ADIOS AMIGO *(Jim Reeves)*
A GOOD HEART *(Feargal Sharkey)*
ALL SHOOK UP *(Elvis Presley)*
ANNIE'S SONG *(John Denver)*
           (James Galway)
ANY OLD IRON *(Harry Champion/v)*
ARE YOU SURE? *(Allisons)*
ARMS OF MARY *(Sutherland Brothers)*
ATMOSPHERE *(Russ Abbot)*
BAND OF GOLD *(Freda Payne)*
BARBARA ANN *(Beach Boys)*
BAREFOOTIN' *(Robert Parker)*
BEATNIK FLY *(Johnny & the Hurricanes)*
BE BOP A LULA *(Gene Vincent)*
BERNADETTE *(Four Tops)*

BIG BAD JOHN *(Jimmy Dean)*
BIG SPENDER *(Shirley Bassey)*
BILL BAILEY *(v)*
BILLIE JEAN *(Michael Jackson)*
BLACK NIGHT *(Deep Purple)*
BLUE HAWAII *(Elvis Presley)*
BOBBY'S GIRL *(Susan Maughan)*
BRAHN BOOTS *(Stanley Holloway)*
BRIGHT EYES *(Art Garfunkel)*
BROWN SUGAR *(Rolling Stones)*
BYE BYE BABY *(Bay City Rollers)*
BYE BYE LOVE *(Everly Brothers)*
CALIFORNIA *(Al Jolson/v)*
CARRIE-ANNE *(Hollies)*
CHARLESTON *(v)*
CHICK-A-BOOM *(v)*
CHIQUITITA *(Abba)*
CLOSE TO YOU *(Carpenters)*
CONSTANTLY *(Cliff Richard)*
COPACABANA *(Barry Manilow)*
COPENHAGEN *(Danny Kaye)*
COZ I LUV YOU *(Slade)*
DAYDREAMER *(David Cassidy)*
DAY TRIPPER *(Beatles)*
DEEP PURPLE *(Nino Tempo & April
            Stevens/v)*
DESAFINADO *(Stan Getz & Charlie
            Byrd)*
DEVIL WOMAN *(Marty Robbins)*
DID YOU EVER? *(Nancy Sinatra & Lee
            Hazlewood)*
DREAM LOVER *(Bobby Darin)*
DRESS YOU UP *(Madonna)*
FANCY PANTS *(Kenny)*
FAR FAR AWAY *(Slade)*
FOOT TAPPER *(Shadows)*
FUNKY MOPED *(Jasper Carrott)*
GAMBLIN' MAN *(Lonnie Donegan)*
GEORGY GIRL *(Seekers)*
GOLDFINGER *(Shirley Bassey)*
GONE FISHIN' *(Louis Armstrong)*
            (Bing Crosby)
GOODY GOODY *(v)*
HAPPY HEART *(Andy Williams)*
HAVA NAGILA *(Spotnicks)*
HEARTACHES *(Patsy Cline/v)*

HELLO DOLLY *(Louis Armstrong)*
            (Frankie Vaughan/v)
HIGH ENERGY *(Evelyn Thomas)*
HI LILI HI LO *(Alan Price/v)*
HOLD MY HAND *(v)*
HOT DIGGITY *(Perry Como)*
            (Michael Holliday)
HOUSE OF FUN *(Madness)*
I APOLOGISE *(PJ Proby/v)*
I CAN'T LET GO *(Hollies)*
I GET AROUND *(Beach Boys)*
I GOT RHYTHM *(Ethel Merman/v)*
I HEAR MUSIC *(v)*
I LOVE PARIS *(Maurice Chevalier/v)*
IL SILENZIO *(Nini Rosso)*
I NEVER KNEW *(v)*
INTERMEZZO *(v)*
ISRAELITES *(Desmond Dekker & the
            Aces)*
IT'S MY PARTY *(Lesley Gore)*
            *(Dave Stewart &
            Barbara Gaskin)*
IT'S RAINING *(Darts)*
            (Shakin' Stevens)
IT TAKES TWO *(Marvin Gaye & Kim
            Weston)*
I WONDER WHY *(Showaddywaddy/v)*
I WON'T DANCE *(v)*
JEALOUS GUY *(John Lennon)*
            (Roxy Music)
JOHNNY WILL *(Pat Boone)*
JUST IN TIME *(v)*
KING CREOLE *(Elvis Presley)*
LET'S GROOVE *(Earth Wind And Fire)*
LET'S HANG ON *(Four Seasons)*
LIFE ON MARS *(David Bowie)*
LIVE TO TELL *(Madonna)*
LIVING DOLL *(Cliff Richard)*
            *(Cliff Richard & the
            Young Ones)*
LIVIN' THING *(ELO)*
MARIA ELENA *(Los Indios Tabajaras)*
MASQUERADE *(v)*
MELTING POT *(Blue Mink)*
MODERN LOVE *(David Bowie)*
MONTEGO BAY *(Bobby Bloom)*

MOOD INDIGO *(Duke Ellington)*
MOVE CLOSER *(Phyllis Nelson)*
MY MIND'S EYE *(Small Faces)*
MY OLD DUTCH *(Albert Chevalier)*
MY OLD PIANO *(Diana Ross)*
MY SON MY SON *(Vera Lynn)*
NELLIE DEAN *(Gertie Gitana)*
NEVER NEVER *(Assembly)*
NEW ORLEANS *(Gary 'US' Bonds/v)*
NICE PEOPLE *(v)*
NIGHT FEVER *(Bee Gees)*
NO HONESTLY *(Lynsey De Paul)*
OFF THE WALL *(Michael Jackson)*
OH HAPPY DAY *(Edwin Hawkins Singers)*
OH JOHNNY OH! *(v)*
OH MEIN PAPA *(Eddie Calvert)*
 (Eddie Fisher)
OH MR PORTER *(Marie Lloyd)*
OL' MAN RIVER *(Paul Robeson)*
ONE MAN BAND *(Leo Sayer)*
ON THE BEACH *(Cliff Richard)*
PAPER ROSES *(Kaye Sisters)*
 (Marie Osmond)
PORTSMOUTH *(Mike Oldfield)*
PRETTY BABY *(v)*
PS I LOVE YOU *(Beatles)*
PURPLE HAZE *(Jimi Hendrix Experience)*
PURPLE RAIN *(Prince & the Revolution)*
RED RED WINE *(UB40)*
REET PETITE *(Jackie Wilson)*
RETURN TO ME *(Dean Martin)*
RING MY BELL *(Anita Ward)*
ROCK-A-BILLY *(Guy Mitchell)*
ROLL ME OVER *(v)*
ROSE GARDEN *(Lynn Anderson)*
 (New World)
RUBBER BALL *(Avons)*
 (Bobby Vee)
 (Marty Wilde)
SCHOOL'S OUT *(Alice Cooper)*
SECRET LOVE *(Doris Day)*
 (Kathy Kirby)
SEVEN TEARS *(Goombay Dance Band)*

SHANG-A-LANG *(Bay City Rollers)*
SHE'S NOT YOU *(Elvis Presley)*
SIDE BY SIDE *(Kay Starr/v)*
SIDE SADDLE *(Russ Conway)*
SILLY GAMES *(Janet Kay)*
SILVER LADY *(David Soul)*
SIMPLE GAME *(Four Tops)*
SING AS WE GO *(Gracie Fields)*
SLEIGH RIDE *(v)*
SLOOP JOHN B *(Beach Boys)*
SOLDIER BOY *(Shirelles)*
SOME PEOPLE *(Carol Deene/v)*
SONG FOR GUY *(Elton John)*
STARRY EYED *(Michael Holliday)*
STAY WITH ME *(Faces)*
 (Blue Mink/v)
STEREOTYPE *(Specials)*
STONED LOVE *(Supremes)*
STREET LIFE *(Crusaders)*
 (Roxy Music)
STUCK ON YOU *(Elvis Presley)*
 (Lionel Richie/v)
SUBSTITUTE *(Clout)*
 (Liquid Gold)
 (Who)
SUCH A NIGHT *(Johnnie Ray)*
SUGAR SUGAR *(Archies)*
SUMMERTIME *(v)*
SUNDAY GIRL *(Blondie)*
'S WONDERFUL *(v)*
TELL ME WHEN *(Applejacks)*
TEMPTATION *(Everly Brothers)*
 (Heaven 17/v)
THAT'S AMORE *(Dean Martin)*
THE SHUFFLE *(Van McCoy)*
THE WAR SONG *(Culture Club)*
THE WEDDING *(Julie Rogers)*
TOO DARN HOT *(v)*
TWEEDLE DEE *(Little Jimmy Osmond)*
UPTOWN GIRL *(Billy Joel)*
VOULEZ-VOUS? *(Abba)*
WALK OF LIFE *(Dire Straits)*
WATER WATER *(Tommy Steele)*
WHAT A MOUTH *(Tommy Steele)*
WHAT A WASTE *(Ian Dury & the Blockheads)*

WHAT IS LOVE *(Howard Jones)*
WHISPERING *(Bachelors/v)*
WITCHCRAFT *(Frank Sinatra)*
WITHOUT YOU *(Nilsson)*
YOU GOT SOUL *(Johnny Nash)*
YOU ME AND US *(Alma Cogan)*
YOU'RE A LADY *(Peter Skellern)*

11

ALL ALONE AM I *(Brenda Lee)*
ALL BY MYSELF *(Eric Carmen/v)*
ALL CRIED OUT *(Alison Moyet)*
ALL FALL DOWN *(Five Star)*
　　　　　　　　(Lindisfarne/v)
ALL MY LOVING *(Beatles)*
ALL OF MY LIFE *(Diana Ross)*
ALL RIGHT NOW *(Free)*
ALMOST THERE *(Andy Williams)*
ALWAYS YOURS *(Gary Glitter)*
AMERICAN PIE *(Don McLean)*
ANGELA JONES *(Michael Cox)*
AS TEARS GO BY *(Marianne Faithfull)*
BACHELOR BOY *(Cliff Richard)*
BAKER STREET *(Gerry Rafferty)*
BESAME MUCHO *(Jet Harris/v)*
BLOCKBUSTER *(Sweet)*
BLOWING WILD *(Frankie Laine)*
BODY AND SOUL *(v)*
BRAND NEW KEY *(Melanie)*
BROKEN WINGS *(Mr Mister)*
　　　　　　　　(Stargazers)
　　　　　　　　(Dickie Valentine/v)
BULL AND BUSH *(Florrie Forde)*
BURNING LOVE *(Elvis Presley)*
BYE BYE BLUES *(Bert Kaempfert/v)*
CANDY KISSES *(v)*
CATHY'S CLOWN *(Everly Brothers)*
CHEATIN' ON ME *(v)*
COME OUTSIDE *(Mike Sarne)*
COOL FOR CATS *(Squeeze)*
CRAZY HORSES *(Osmonds)*
CRAZY PEOPLE *(v)*
CRAZY RHYTHM *(v)*
CRY ME A RIVER *(Julie London)*

DANCING TIME *(v)*
DANCIN' PARTY *(Showaddywaddy)*
DAY IN, DAY OUT *(v)*
DECK OF CARDS *(Wink Martindale)*
DON'T BE CRUEL *(Elvis Presley)*
DON'T BLAME ME *(Frank Ifield/v)*
DOO-WACKA-DOO *(v)*
DO YOU LOVE ME *(Dave Clark Five)*
　　　　　　　　(Brian Poole & the
　　　　　　　　Tremeloes)
EASY GOING ME *(Adam Faith)*
ENDLESS LOVE *(Diana Ross & Lionel*
　　　　　　　　Richie)
FASCINATION *(v)*
FIRE BRIGADE *(Move)*
FOOLS RUSH IN *(Rick Nelson)*
FORGET ME NOT *(Eden Kane)*
FOR YOUR LOVE *(Yardbirds)*
FOX ON THE RUN *(Manfred Mann)*
　　　　　　　　(Sweet)
FRIEND OF MINE *(v)*
FROM ME TO YOU *(Beatles)*
FUNKY GIBBON *(Goodies)*
GIRLS ON FILM *(Duran Duran)*
GIRLS' SCHOOL *(Paul McCartney)*
GLAD ALL OVER *(Dave Clark Five)*
GLAD RAG DOLL *(v)*
GLORY OF LOVE *(Pete Cetera)*
GOLDEN BROWN *(Stranglers)*
GOOD MORNING *(v)*
GREEN ONIONS *(Booker T & the MGs)*
GUITAR TANGO *(Shadows)*
HIGH SOCIETY *(Louis Armstrong)*
HOLD ME CLOSE *(David Essex)*
HOME COOKING *(Bing Crosby)*
I FEEL FOR YOU *(Chaka Khan)*
IF I HAD MY WAY *(v)*
IF I LOVED YOU *(v)*
IF NOT FOR YOU *(Olivia Newton-John)*
I GOT YOU BABE *(Sonny & Cher)*
　　　　　　　　(UB40)
I HAVE A DREAM *(Abba)*
I LOVE TO LOVE *(Tina Charles)*
I'M A BELIEVER *(Monkees)*
IMAGINATION *(v)*
I'M CONFESSIN' *(v)*

I'M NOT IN LOVE *(10 CC)*
IN THE GHETTO *(Elvis Presley)*
I SEE THE MOON *(Stargazers)*
ISLE OF CAPRI *(v)*
I THINK OF YOU *(Merseybeats)*
IT'S A MIRACLE *(Culture Club)*
JAPANESE BOY *(Aneka)*
JAZZ ME BLUES *(v)*
JEALOUS MIND *(Alvin Stardust)*
JUST ONE LOOK *(Hollies)*
KILLER QUEEN *(Queen)*
KNOCK ON WOOD *(David Bowie)*
    (Eddie Floyd)
    (Amii Stewart/v)
LA CUCARACHA *(v)*
LADY ELEANOR *(Lindisfarne)*
LADY MADONNA *(Beatles)*
LADY OF SPAIN *(Frankie Laine/v)*
LAMBETH WALK *(v)*
LIGHT MY FIRE *(José Feliciano)*
    (Amii Stewart)
LIKE A VIRGIN *(Madonna)*
LILY THE PINK *(Scaffold)*
LIZA JOHNSON *(Kate Carney)*
LOVE FOR SALE *(v)*
LOVE LETTERS *(Ketty Lester)*
    (Elvis Presley)
LOVE MACHINE *(Miracles)*
LOVE PLUS ONE *(Haircut 100)*
MAGGIE'S FARM *(Bob Dylan)*
    (Specials)
MANIC MONDAY *(Bangles)*
ME AND MY GIRL *(v)*
MIGHTY QUINN *(Manfred Mann)*
MISSISSIPPI *(Bobbie Gentry)*
    (Pussycat)
MOULIN ROUGE *(Mantovani)*
MRS ROBINSON *(Simon & Garfunkel)*
MR WONDERFUL *(Peggy Lee)*
MY COO-CA-CHOO *(Alvin Stardust)*
MY DING-A-LING *(Chuck Berry)*
MY HEART AND I *(v)*
MY SWEET LORD *(George Harrison)*
NIGHT AND DAY *(v)*
NIGHT OF FEAR *(Move)*
NO NO NANETTE *(v)*

NO ONE BUT YOU *(Billy Eckstine)*
NO OTHER LOVE *(Ronnie Hilton)*
    *(Edmund
    Hockridge/v)*
OLIVER'S ARMY *(Elvis Costello & the
    Attractions)*
ON A CAROUSEL *(Hollies)*
ONE MEAT BALL *(v)*
ON HORSEBACK *(Mike Oldfield)*
ONLY SIXTEEN *(Craig Douglas/v)*
PERSONALITY *(Anthony Newley)*
    (Lloyd Price)
PETITE FLEUR *(Chris Barber's Jazz
    Band)*
POOR MAN'S SON *(Rockin' Berries)*
PRETTY PAPER *(Rob Orbison)*
QUE SERA SERA *(Doris Day/v)*
RAIN OR SHINE *(Five Star)*
RAMBLIN' ROSE *(Nat 'King' Cole)*
REFLECTIONS *(Supremes)*
REMINISCING *(Buddy Holly)*
ROCK AND ROLL *(Gary Glitter)*
ROCKIN' ROBIN *(Michael Jackson)*
ROCK THE BOAT *(Forrest)*
    (Hues Corporation)
ROSES ARE RED *(Ronnie Carroll)*
    (Bobby Vinton)
RUBY TUESDAY *(Melanie)*
    (Rolling Stones)
RUNNING BEAR *(Johnny Preston)*
SAVE A PRAYER *(Duran Duran)*
SAY IT ISN'T SO *(v)*
SAY YOU, SAY ME *(Lionel Richie)*
SHE LOVES YOU *(Beatles)*
SHRIMP BOATS *(v)*
SILHOUETTES *(Herman's Hermits)*
SIXTEEN TONS *(Tennessee Ernie
    Ford)*
    (Frankie Laine)
SPACE ODDITY *(David Bowie)*
SPANISH EYES *(Al Martino)*
SPANISH FLEA *(Herb Alpert)*
SPECIAL BREW *(Bad Manners)*
STAYIN' ALIVE *(Bee Gees)*
STRANGE BREW *(Cream)*
STREET DANCE *(Break Machine)*

STUPID CUPID *(Connie Francis)*
SUNNY SIDE UP *(Jessie Matthews)*
TAINTED LOVE *(Soft Cell)*
TELEGRAM SAM *(T Rex)*
THAT'S MY HOME *(Acker Bilk)*
THE FLEET'S IN *(v)*
THE GOOD LIFE *(Tony Bennett)*
THE JONES BOY *(v)*
THE LAST TIME *(Rolling Stones)*
THE MAN I LOVE *(v)*
THE NEXT TIME *(Cliff Richard)*
THE STRANGER *(Shadows)*
THE WANDERER *(Dion)*
　　　　　　　(Status Quo)
TIME IS TIGHT *(Booker T & the MGs)*
TOY BALLOONS *(Russ Conway)*
UKULELE LADY *(v)*
UP ON THE ROOF *(Kenny Lynch/v)*
UP, UP AND AWAY *(Johnny Mann*
　　　　　　　Singers)
VOODOO CHILE *(Jimi Hendrix*
　　　　　　　Experience)
WABASH BLUES *(v)*
WALK DON'T RUN *(John Barry)*
　　　　　　　(Ventures)
WALK RIGHT IN *(Rooftop Singers)*
WAND'RIN' STAR *(Lee Marvin)*
WAYWARD WIND *(Frank Ifield)*
　　　　　　　(Tex Ritter/v)
WE ARE FAMILY *(Sister Sledge)*
WELCOME HOME *(Peters & Lee)*
WELL I ASK YOU *(Eden Kane)*
WE'RE THROUGH *(Hollies)*
WE SAW THE SEA *(v)*
WISHING WELL *(Free)*
WITCH DOCTOR *(Don Lang)*
WOMAN IN LOVE *(Four Aces)*
　　　　　　　(Barbra Streisand)
　　　　　　　(Three Degrees)
WOODEN HEART *(Elvis Presley)*
YELLOW RIVER *(Christie)*
YIP I ADDY I AY *(v)*
YOU DON'T KNOW *(Helen Shapiro)*
YOU'RE NO GOOD *(Swinging Blue*
　　　　　　　Jeans)
YOU'RE SO VAIN *(Carly Simon)*

YOU'RE THE ONE *(Petula Clark)*
　　　　　　　(Kathy Kirby)
YOU TAKE ME UP *(Thompson Twins)*
Y VIVA ESPAÑA *(Sylvia)*

12

A BLOSSOM FELL *(v)*
A FINE ROMANCE *(v)*
A FOOL SUCH AS I *(Elvis Presley)*
AFRICAN WALTZ *(Johnny Dankworth)*
AFTER THE BALL *(Vesta Tilley)*
AIN'T SHE SWEET *(Beatles/v)*
ALABAMY BOUND *(Al Jolson)*
A LITTLE PEACE *(Nicole)*
ALL I ASK OF YOU *(Cliff Richard &*
　　　　　　　Sarah Brightman)
ALL NIGHT LONG *(Rainbow/v)*
ALL OR NOTHING *(Small Faces)*
AMAZING GRACE *(Judy Collins)*
　　　　　　　(Royal Scots
　　　　　　　Dragoon Guards)
A MESS OF BLUES *(Elvis Presley)*
ANGEL FINGERS *(Wizzard)*
ANTHING GOES *(Harpers Bizarre/v)*
APRIL IN PARIS *(v)*
APRIL SHOWERS *(v)*
ASHES TO ASHES *(David Bowie)*
AS TIME GOES BY *(Dooley Wilson/v)*
AUTUMN LEAVES *(v)*
A VIEW TO A KILL *(Duran Duran)*
A WINTER'S TALE *(David Essex)*
A WOMAN IN LOVE *(Frankie Laine)*
BABY I LOVE YOU *(Dave Edmunds)*
　　　　　　　(Kenny)
　　　　　　　(Ramones)
　　　　　　　(Ronettes/v)
BAND ON THE RUN *(Paul McCartney)*
BAT OUT OF HELL *(Meat Loaf)*
BEING WITH YOU *(Smokey Robinson)*
BLACK IS BLACK *(Los Bravos)*
BORN IN THE USA *(Bruce*
　　　　　　　Springsteen)
BORN TO BE WILD *(Steppenwolf)*
BOTH SIDES NOW *(Judy Collins)*

CALENDAR GIRL *(Neil Sedaka)*
CAPTAIN BEAKY *(Keith Michell)*
CARELESS LOVE *(v)*
CAROLINA MOON *(v)*
CATCH THE WIND *(Donovan)*
CHAPEL OF LOVE *(Dixie Cups)*
CHARLIE BROWN *(Coasters)*
CHEEK TO CHEEK *(Fred Astaire)*
CINDY OH CINDY *(Eddie Fisher)*
COME ON EILEEN *(Dexy's Midnight Runners)*
COME TOMORROW *(Manfred Mann)*
DANCING QUEEN *(Abba)*
DISTANT DRUMS *(Jim Reeves)*
DOCTOR DOCTOR *(Thompson Twins)*
EASTER PARADE *(Fred Astaire)*
ELEANOR RIGBY *(Beatles)*
EXCUSE ME BABY *(Magic Lanterns)*
FATTIE BUM BUM *(Carl Malcolm)*
FOR ALL WE KNOW *(Shirley Bassey/v)*
FREIGHT TRAIN *(Charles McDevitt Skiffle Group & Nancy Whiskey)*
GARDEN OF EDEN *(Gary Miller) (Frankie Vaughan/v)*
GHOSTBUSTERS *(Ray Parker Jr)*
GIRL DON'T COME *(Sandie Shaw)*
GOD ONLY KNOWS *(Beach Boys)*
HANG ON SLOOPY *(McCoys)*
HAPPY HOLIDAY *(v)*
HEART AND SOUL *(v)*
HEARTBREAKER *(Dionne Warwick)*
HEART OF GLASS *(Blondie)*
HEART OF STONE *(Kenny) (Rolling Stones)*
HELLO GOODBYE *(Beatles)*
HELLO MARY LOU *(Rick Nelson)*
HELP YOURSELF *(Tom Jones)*
HERE I GO AGAIN *(Hollies)*
HEY NEIGHBOUR *(v)*
HOLE IN MY SHOE *(Neil) (Traffic)*
HORSEY HORSEY *(v)*
HOW ABOUT THAT? *(Adam Faith)*

HOW DO YOU DO IT? *(Gerry & the Pacemakers)*
HOW MANY TEARS *(Bobby Vee)*
HOW SWEET IT IS *(Marvin Gaye) (Junior Walker & the All-Stars)*
I CAN'T EXPLAIN *(Who)*
I CRIED FOR YOU *(Ricky Stevens/v)*
I LOVE A LASSIE *(Harry Lauder)*
IN A SHADY NOOK *(Donald Peers)*
INKA-DINKA-DOO *(Jimmy Durante)*
INSTANT KARMA *(John Lennon)*
IN THE ARMY NOW *(Status Quo)*
INVISIBLE SUN *(Police)*
I REMEMBER YOU *(Frank Ifield)*
IT AIN'T ME BABE *(Bob Dylan)*
ITCHYCOO PARK *(Small Faces)*
IT HAD TO BE YOU *(v)*
I WANNA GO HOME *(Lonnie Donegan)*
I WILL SURVIVE *(Gloria Gaynor)*
JIMMY UNKNOWN *(Lita Roza)*
JOHNNY REGGAE *(Piglets)*
JUST ONE SMILE *(Gene Pitney)*
KEEP A KNOCKIN' *(Little Richard)*
LADY IS A TRAMP *(Buddy Greco) (Frank Sinatra/v)*
LET ME GO LOVER *(Teresa Brewer) (Kathy Kirby) (Dean Martin) (Ruby Murray/v)*
LILLI MARLENE *(Marlene Dietrich)*
LILY OF LAGUNA *(Eugene Stratton)*
LITTLE ARROWS *(Leapy Lee)*
LITTLE BOY SAD *(Johnny Burnette)*
LITTLE DARLIN' *(Diamonds)*
LITTLE DONKEY *(Beverley Sisters) (Nina & Frederick/v)*
LITTLE SISTER *(Elvis Presley)*
LITTLE THINGS *(Dave Berry)*
LONG LIVE LOVE *(Sandie Shaw)*
LOST IN FRANCE *(Bonnie Tyler)*
LOVE ME TENDER *(Elvis Presley)*
MACK THE KNIFE *(Louis Armstrong) (Bobby Darin) (Ella Fitzgerald)*
MAGIC MOMENTS *(Perry Como/v)*

MAKIN' WHOOPEE *(Eddie Cantor)*
MAN OF MYSTERY *(Shadows)*
MATERIAL GIRL *(Madonna)*
MAY YOU ALWAYS *(McGuire Sisters)*
                    (Joan Regan/v)
MEXICALI ROSE *(Karl Denver)*
                  (Jim Reeves)
MONDAY MONDAY *(Mamas & the
                  Papas)*
MOONLIGHTING *(Leo Sayer)*
MORE THAN THIS *(Roxy Music)*
MOTHER OF MINE *(Neil Reid)*
MY BLUE HEAVEN *(Frank Sinatra/v)*
MY GENERATION *(Who)*
MY KIND OF GIRL *(Matt Monro)*
NEVERTHELESS *(v)*
NICE ONE CYRIL *(Cockerel Chorus)*
NOBODY'S DIARY *(Yazoo)*
NO MATTER WHAT *(Badfinger)*
NOW IS THE HOUR *(v)*
OB-LA-DI OB-LA-DA *(Marmalade)*
OH LADY BE GOOD *(v)*
OL' BLACK MAGIC *(Billy Daniels)*
OLD DEVIL MOON *(v)*
ONCE-A-YEAR DAY *(v)*
ONCE IN A WHILE *(v)*
ONE FOR MY BABY *(Frank Sinatra)*
ONE MORE NIGHT *(Phil Collins)*
ONLY ONE WOMAN *(Marbles)*
ON THE REBOUND *(Floyd Kramer)*
PAINT IT BLACK *(Rolling Stones)*
PIPES OF PEACE *(Paul McCartney)*
PLEASE DON'T GO *(KC & the
                    Sunshine Band)*
                    (Donald Peers)
PRETTY VACANT *(Sex Pistols)*
RAGS TO RICHES *(David Whitfield)*
RAZZLE DAZZLE *(Bill Haley & his
                  Comets)*
RED RIVER ROCK *(Johnny & the
                   Hurricanes)*
ROCKING GOOSE *(Johnny & the
                  Hurricanes)*
ROCK ME GENTLY *(Andy Kim)*
ROCK YOUR BABY *(George McCrae)*
RUNAROUND SUE *(Dion)*
                  (Racey)
                  (Doug Sheldon)

RUN RABBIT RUN *(Flanagan & Allen)*
SAN FRANCISCO *(Scott McKenzie)*
SATISFACTION *(Otis Redding)*
                 (Rolling Stones)
SEE EMILY PLAY *(Pink Floyd)*
SHA LA LA LA LEE *(Small Faces)*
SHE'S NOT THERE *(Santana)*
                    (Zombies/v)
SHOESHINE BOY *(v)*
SING BABY SING *(Stylistics)*
SMALLTOWN BOY *(Bronski Beat)*
SOFTLY SOFTLY *(Ruby Murray)*
SONG SUNG BLUE *(Neil Diamond)*
SORRY SUZANNE *(Hollies)*
SPLISH SPLASH *(Bobby Darin)*
                  (Charlie Drake)
ST LOUIS BLUES *(Bessie Smith/v)*
STOP STOP STOP *(Hollies)*
STRANGE FRUIT *(Billie Holiday)*
SUMMER NIGHTS *(John Travolta &
                  Olivia Newton-John)*
SUPERSTITION *(Stevie Wonder)*
SUPER TROUPER *(Abba)*
SWEET ADELINE *(v)*
SWEET VIOLETS *(v)*
SYSTEM ADDICT *(Five Star)*
THE HAPPENING *(Supremes)*
THE LADY IN RED *(Chris De Burgh)*
THE LAST WALTZ *(Engelbert
                   Humperdinck)*
THE SMURF SONG *(Father Abraham &
                   the Smurfs)*
THEY DON'T KNOW *(Tracey Ullman)*
THE YOUNG ONES *(Cliff Richard)*
THIS IS MY SONG *(Petula Clark)*
                    (Harry Secombe)
THIS OLE HOUSE *(Billie Anthony)*
                   (Rosemary Clooney)
                   (Shakin' Stevens)
TICKET TO RIDE *(Beatles)*
TRAVELLIN' MAN *(Rick Nelson)*
TRUE LOVE WAYS *(Buddy Holly)*
                   (Peter & Gordon)
                   (Cliff Richard)
TUBBY THE TUBA *(Danny Kaye)*
TUMBLING DICE *(Rolling Stones)*

TWILIGHT TIME *(Platters)*
UNDER MY THUMB *(Wayne Gibson)*
 (Rolling Stones/v)
VIVA BOBBY JOE *(Equals)*
VIVA LAS VEGAS *(Elvis Presley)*
WALKIN' THE DOG *(Rufus Thomas/v)*
WALK LIKE A MAN *(Four Seasons)*
WEDDING BELLS *(Eddie Fisher)*
 (Godley & Creme)
WE DON'T HAVE TO *(Jermaine Stewart)*
WE'RE ALL ALONE *(Rita Coolidge)*
WEST END GIRLS *(Pet Shop Boys)*
WHAT WOULD I BE? *(Val Doonican)*
WHEELS CHA CHA *(Joe Loss)*
WHITE WEDDING *(Billy Idol)*
WHO'S SORRY NOW? *(Connie Francis)*
 (Johnnie Ray)
WHO'S THAT GIRL *(Eurythmics)*
WITHOUT A SONG *(v)*
YESTERDAY MAN *(Chris Andrews)*
YING TONG SONG *(Goons)*
YOU BELONG TO ME *(Helen Morgan)*
YOU NEED HANDS *(Max Bygraves)*
YOUNG AT HEART *(Bluebells)*
 (Frank Sinatra)
YOU'RE MY WORLD *(Cilla Black)*
YOU'RE SIXTEEN *(Johnny Burnette)*
 (Ringo Starr)
YOU SEXY THING *(Hot Chocolate)*

13

A CERTAIN SMILE *(Johnny Mathis)*
ALICE BLUE GOWN *(v)*
A LITTLE LOVING *(Fourmost)*
ANCHORS AWEIGH *(v)*
AND I LOVE YOU SO *(Perry Como)*
A PICTURE OF YOU *(Joe Brown)*
ASK A POLICEMAN *(James Fawn)*
A TASTE OF HONEY *(Beatles)*
 (Acker Bilk)
BABY I DON'T CARE *(Buddy Holly)*
BACK IN THE USSR *(Beatles)*

BAD MOON RISING *(Creedence Clearwater Revival)*
BAGGY TROUSERS *(Madness)*
BALLIN' THE JACK *(Danny Kaye)*
BEAT SURRENDER *(Jam)*
BECAUSE OF LOVE *(Billy Fury)*
BEND ME SHAPE ME *(Amen Corner)*
BIG YELLOW TAXI *(Joni Mitchell)*
BITS AND PIECES *(Dave Clark Five)*
BLACKBERRY WAY *(Move)*
BLUEBERRY HILL *(Fats Domino)*
BLUE CHRISTMAS *(Elvis Presley)*
BOOM BANG-A-BANG *(Lulu)*
BRASS IN POCKET *(Pretenders)*
CABIN IN THE SKY *(Lena Horne)*
CAN'T BUY ME LOVE *(Beatles)*
 (Ella Fitzgerald)
CARAVAN OF LOVE *(Housemartins)*
CARELESS HANDS *(Des O'Connor)*
CHAIN REACTION *(Diana Ross)*
CHANSON D'AMOUR *(Manhattan Transfer)*
CHANTILLY LACE *(Big Bopper)*
CLUB TROPICANA *(Wham!)*
C'MON EVERYBODY *(Eddie Cochran)*
CROCODILE ROCK *(Elton John)*
CUMBERLAND GAP *(Lonnie Donegan)*
DEADWOOD STAGE *(Doris Day)*
DEATH OF A CLOWN *(Dave Davies)*
DON'T BRING LULU *(Dorothy Provine)*
DON'T FENCE ME IN *(Andrews Sisters)*
 (Bing Crosby)
DON'T LAUGH AT ME *(Norman Wisdom)*
DON'T TALK TO HIM *(Cliff Richard)*
DON'T YOU WANT ME *(Human League)*
EBONY AND IVORY *(Paul McCartney & Stevie Wonder)*
EINSTEIN A GO-GO *(Landscape)*
EMBARRASSMENT *(Madness)*
END OF THE WORLD *(Skeeter Davis)*
ENGLAND SWINGS *(Roger Miller)*

ENJOY YOURSELF *(v)*
EVERY DAY HURTS *(Sad Café)*
EYE OF THE TIGER *(Survivor)*
FANTASY ISLAND *(Tight Fit)*
FARAWAY PLACES *(Bachelors/v)*
FORGIVE ME GIRL *(Detroit Spinners)*
FOR ME AND MY GAL *(v)*
GIPSY IN MY SOUL *(v)*
GOODBYE MY LOVE *(Glitter Band)*
                          (Searchers/v)
GOOD LUCK CHARM *(Elvis Presley)*
GOODY TWO SHOES *(Adam & the*
                          Ants)
GOSSIP CALYPSO *(Bernard Cribbins)*
GRANDMA'S PARTY *(Paul Nicholas)*
HAPPY BIRTHDAY *(Altered Images)*
                          (Stevie Wonder)
HAPPY WANDERER *(Obernkirchen*
                          Children's Choir)
                          (Stargazers)
HARBOUR LIGHTS *(Platters)*
HARLEM SHUFFLE *(Bob & Earl)*
                          (Rolling Stones)
HAVE I THE RIGHT *(Honeycombs)*
HERE IN MY HEART *(Al Martino)*
HOMEWARD BOUND *(Simon &*
                          Garfunkel)
HONG KONG BLUES *(Hoagy*
                          Carmichael)
HOW CAN I BE SURE? *(David*
                          Cassidy)
I CAN HEAR MUSIC *(Beach Boys)*
IF I HAD A HAMMER *(Trini Lopez)*
INTO THE GROOVE *(Madonna)*
IT'S A HEARTACHE *(Bonnie Tyler)*
IT'S ALL OVER NOW *(Rolling Stones)*
IT'S A LOVE THING *(Whispers)*
IT'S IMPOSSIBLE *(Perry Como)*
IT'S NOT UNUSUAL *(Tom Jones)*
IT'S NOW OR NEVER *(Elvis Presley)*
JAILHOUSE ROCK *(Elvis Presley)*
JOHNNY ONE NOTE *(Cleo Laine/v)*
JUNE IN JANUARY *(v)*
JUST LIKE EDDIE *(Heinz)*
JUST LOVING YOU *(Anita Harris)*
KEEP ON RUNNING *(Spencer Davis*
                          Group)

KIDS IN AMERICA *(Kim Wilde)*
KING OF THE ROAD *(Roger Miller)*
KISSIN' COUSINS *(Elvis Presley)*
LAST CHRISMAS *(Wham!)*
LESSONS IN LOVE *(Allisons)*
                          (Level 42)
LET YOURSELF GO *(v)*
LITTLE OLD LADY *(v)*
LITTLE SIR ECHO *(v)*
LONG TALL SALLY *(Little Richard)*
LOVE IS THE DRUG *(Roxy Music)*
LOVESICK BLUES *(Frank Ifield)*
MACARTHUR PARK *(Richard Harris)*
                          (Donna Summer)
MAMBO ITALIANO *(Rosemary*
                          Clooney)
MAN OF THE WORLD *(Fleetwood*
                          Mac)
MARY'S BOY CHILD *(Harry Belafonte)*
MASSACHUSETTS *(Bee Gees)*
MATTHEW AND SON *(Cat Stevens)*
MOTHER MACHREE *(John*
                          McCormack)
MULL OF KINTYRE *(Paul McCartney)*
MUSKRAT RAMBLE *(Freddy Cannon)*
MY BOY LOLLIPOP *(Millie)*
MY BROTHER JAKE *(Free)*
MY CHERIE AMOUR *(Stevie Wonder)*
NAME OF THE GAME *(Abba)*
NEVER ON SUNDAY *(v)*
NO MORE THE FOOL *(Elkie Brooks)*
NORWEGIAN WOOD *(Beatles)*
OH NO NOT MY BABY *(Manfred*
                          Mann)
                          (Rod Stewart)
OH PRETTY WOMAN *(Roy Orbison)*
ONE DAY AT A TIME *(Lena Martell)*
ONLY THE LONELY *(Roy Orbison)*
PINBALL WIZARD *(Elton John)*
                          (Who)
PRIVATE DANCER *(Tina Turner)*
RAINBOW VALLEY *(Love Affair)*
RIGHT SAID FRED *(Bernard Cribbins)*
ROAD TO MOROCCO *(Bing Crosby &*
                          Bob Hope)
ROCK A HULA BABY *(Elvis Presley)*

ROCK ME AMADEUS *(Falco)*
RUBBER BULLETS *(10 CC)*
RUNNING SCARED *(Roy Orbison)*
RUN TO THE HILLS *(Iron Maiden)*
SAND IN MY SHOES *(v)*
SCARLETT O'HARA *(Jet Harris & Tony Meehan)*
SEE MY BABY JIVE *(Wizzard)*
SEPARATE LIVES *(Phil Collins & Marilyn Martin)*
SEPTEMBER SONG *(v)*
SHAKIN' ALL OVER *(Johnny Kidd & the Pirates)*
SHORT'NIN' BREAD *(Paul Robeson/v)*
SOMETHING ELSE *(Sex Pistols)*
SON OF MY FATHER *(Chicory Tip)*
SO YOU WIN AGAIN *(Hot Chocolate)*
SPANISH HARLEM *(Aretha Franklin)*
(Jimmy Justice)
STORMY WEATHER *(Lena Horne/ Ethel Waters/v)*
STRAY CAT STRUT *(Stray Cats)*
SUGAR AND SPICE *(Searchers)*
SUGAR BABY LOVE *(Rubettes)*
SUMMER HOLIDAY *(Cliff Richard)*
SWEET CAROLINE *(Neil Diamond)*
SYLVIA'S MOTHER *(Dr Hook)*
TAKE THE A TRAIN *(Duke Ellington)*
TEARS OF A CLOWN *(Beat)*
(Smokey Robinson & the Miracles)
THE BIRDIE SONG *(Tweets)*
THE BREEZE AND I *(Fentones/v)*
THE CAT CREPT IN *(Mud)*
THE CRYING GAME *(Dave Berry)*
THE ETON RIFLES *(Jam)*
THE FOLK SINGER *(Tommy Roe)*
THE LOCOMOTION *(Little Eva)*
(Kylie Minogue)
THE LOOK OF LOVE *(ABC/v)*
THE TENDER TRAP *(Frank Sinatra)*
THE TIDE IS HIGH *(Blondie)*
THORN IN MY SIDE *(Eurythmics)*
TIME AFTER TIME *(Cyndi Lauper/v)*
TOO SOON TO KNOW *(Roy Orbison)*

TOP OF THE WORLD *(Carpenters)*
TWIST AND SHOUT *(Beatles)*
(Brian Poole & the Tremeloes)
TWO LITTLE BOYS *(Rolf Harris)*
UNDER PRESSURE *(Queen & David Bowie)*
UNFORGETTABLE *(Nat 'King' Cole)*
UP THE JUNCTION *(Squeeze)*
VALLEY OF TEARS *(Fats Domino)*
(Buddy Holly)
VIRGINIA PLAIN *(Roxy Music)*
VISIONS IN BLUE *(Ultravox)*
WALK AWAY RENÉE *(Four Tops)*
WALK RIGHT BACK *(Everly Brothers)*
WE ARE THE WORLD *(USA For Africa)*
WE'LL MEET AGAIN *(Vera Lynn)*
WHAT DO YOU WANT *(Adam Faith)*
WHAT NOW MY LOVE *(Shirley Bassey)*
WIRED FOR SOUND *(Cliff Richard)*
YOU BELONG TO ME *(Jo Stafford)*
YOU CAN DO MAGIC *(Limmie & the Family Cookin')*
YOU DON'T KNOW ME *(Ray Charles)*
YOU GO TO MY HEAD *(v)*
YOU WEAR IT WELL *(Rod Stewart)*
ZIP-A-DEE-DOO-DAH *(v)*

14

AFTER YOU'VE GONE *(v)*
AGAINST ALL ODDS *(Phil Collins)*
A HARD DAY'S NIGHT *(Beatles)*
AIN'T MISBEHAVIN' *(Tommy Bruce)*
(Johnnie Ray)
(Fats Waller)
AIN'T THAT A SHAME *(Pat Boone)*
(Fats Domino)
(Four Seasons)
A LITTLE BIT MORE *(Dr Hook)*
A PUB WITH NO BEER *(Slim Dusty)*
AROUND THE WORLD *(Bing Crosby)*
(Gracie Fields)
(Ronnie Hilton/v)
ART FOR ART'S SAKE *(10 CC)*

A-TISKET A-TASKET *(Ella Fitzgerald)*
AUF WIEDERSEHEN *(Vera Lynn)*
A WALKIN' MIRACLE *(Limmie & the Family Cookin')*
BABY MAKE IT SOON *(Marmalade)*
BANANA BOAT SONG *(Harry Belafonte) (Shirley Bassey)*
BANANA REPUBLIC *(Boomtown Rats)*
BE STILL MY HEART *(v)*
BETTE DAVIS EYES *(Kim Carnes) (Rod Stewart)*
BLUE SUEDE SHOES *(Carl Perkins) (Elvis Presley)*
BOLL WEEVIL SONG *(Brook Benton)*
BROADWAY MELODY *(v)*
BROTHERS IN ARMS *(Dire Straits)*
BUTTONS AND BOWS *(v)*
C'EST MAGNIFIQUE *(v)*
CHARIOTS OF FIRE *(Vangelis)*
COME BACK MY LOVE *(Darts)*
CONFIDENTIALLY *(Reg Dixon)*
DEVIL GATE DRIVE *(Suzi Quatro)*
DONKEY SERENADE *(Allan Jones)*
DON'T EVER CHANGE *(Crickets)*
DON'T GIVE UP ON US *(David Soul)*
EIGHT DAYS A WEEK *(Beatles)*
ELECTRIC AVENUE *(Eddy Grant)*
EMBRACEABLE YOU *(v)*
EVERYBODY KNOWS *(Dave Clark Five)*
EVERY LOSER WINS *(Nick Berry)*
EVERYTHING I OWN *(Ken Boothe)*
FLY ME TO THE MOON *(Frank Sinatra/v)*
FRIDAY ON MY MIND *(Easybeats)*
FRIGHTENED CITY *(Shadows)*
GENTLE ON MY MIND *(Dean Martin)*
GIVE ME YOUR WORD *(v)*
GOODNIGHT IRENE *(v)*
GOOD VIBRATIONS *(Beach Boys)*
HANDFUL OF SONGS *(Tommy Steele)*
HARRY LIME THEME *(Anton Karas)*
HAVE A DRINK ON ME *(Lonnie Donegan)*

HAVE YOU SEEN HER *(Chi-Lites)*
HEART OF MY HEART *(v)*
HI-DIDDLE-DEE-DEE *(v)*
HIS LATEST FLAME *(Elvis Presley)*
HIT THE ROAD JACK *(Ray Charles)*
HOME ON THE RANGE *(Bing Crosby/v)*
HONKY TONK WOMEN *(Rolling Stones)*
I AIN'T GOT NOBODY *(v)*
IF I ONLY HAD TIME *(John Rowles)*
IF YOU KNEW SUZIE *(v)*
I KNOW HIM SO WELL *(Elaine Paige & Barbara Dickson)*
I'LL BE SEEING YOU *(Bing Crosby) (Liberace)*
I'LL SEE YOU AGAIN *(Noël Coward/v)*
I'M AN OLD COW-HAND *(Bing Crosby)*
I'M OLD-FASHIONED *(v)*
I'M STILL WAITING *(Diana Ross)*
INDIAN LOVE CALL *(Slim Whitman) (Anne Zeigler & Webster Booth)*
ISLAND IN THE SUN *(Harry Belafonte)*
ISLAND OF DREAMS *(Springfields)*
I'VE GOT SIXPENCE *(v)*
I WANT TO BE HAPPY *(v)*
JENNIFER ECCLES *(Hollies)*
JUST AN ILLUSION *(Imagination)*
JUST LIKE A WOMAN *(Bob Dylan) (Manfred Mann)*
KARMA CHAMELEON *(Culture Club)*
KUNG FU FIGHTING *(Carl Douglas)*
LEGEND OF XANADU *(Dave Dee, Dozy, Beaky, Mick & Tich)*
LET'S TWIST AGAIN *(Chubby Checker)*
LET THERE BE LOVE *(Nat 'King' Cole)*
LIMEHOUSE BLUES *(v)*
LITTLE BROWN JUG *(Glenn Miller)*
LITTLE CHILDREN *(Billy J Kramer)*
LIVIN' ON A PRAYER *(Bon Jovi)*
LOOK AT THAT GIRL *(Guy Mitchell)*
LOVELY TO LOOK AT *(v)*

MAD ABOUT THE BOY *(Noël Coward)*
MAKE ME AN ISLAND *(Joe Dolan)*
MEAN WOMAN BLUES *(Roy Orbison)*
MELANCHOLY BABY *(v)*
MORE THAN A WOMAN *(Tavares)*
MOULDY OLD DOUGH *(Lieutenant Pigeon)*
MRS WORTHINGTON *(Noël Coward)*
MULTIPLICATION *(Bobby Darin)*
MY SPECIAL ANGEL *(Malcolm Vaughan)*
NEEDLES AND PINS *(Searchers)*
NOT RESPONSIBLE *(Tom Jones)*
ONE AND ONE IS ONE *(Medicine Head)*
ONE STEP FURTHER *(Bardo)*
ON THE ROAD AGAIN *(Canned Heat)*
OVER MY SHOULDER *(Jessie Matthews)*
OVER THE RAINBOW *(Judy Garland)*
PAPA DON'T PREACH *(Madonna)*
PART OF THE UNION *(Strawbs)*
PASS THE DUTCHIE *(Musical Youth)*
PICKIN' A CHICKEN *(Eve Boswell)*
PICK YOURSELF UP *(v)*
PICTURES OF LILY *(Who)*
PLEASE PLEASE ME *(Beatles)*
POETRY IN MOTION *(Johnny Tillotson)*
POPPA PICCOLINO *(Diana Decker)*
PRETTY BLUE EYES *(Craig Douglas)*
PRETTY FLAMINGO *(Manfred Mann)*
PRINCE CHARMING *(Adam & the Ants)*
QUARTER TO THREE *(Gary 'US' Bonds)*
RETURN TO SENDER *(Elvis Presley)*
RIDE A WHITE SWAN *(T Rex)*
RIDERS IN THE SKY *(Ramrods)* *(Shadows)*
ROCK ISLAND LINE *(Lonnie Donegan)*
ROSES OF PICARDY *(Vince Hill/v)*
SAVED BY THE BELL *(Robin Gibb)*
SCARLET RIBBONS *(Harry Belafonte)*
SECOND HAND ROSE *(Barbra Streisand)*
SHADDAP YOU FACE *(Joe Dolce Music Theatre)*

SHAPES OF THINGS *(Yardbirds)*
SHE WEARS MY RING *(Solomon King)*
SHOTGUN WEDDING *(Roy 'C')*
SMOOTH CRIMINAL *(Michael Jackson)*
SOMEBODY HELP ME *(Spencer Davis Group)*
SOMEBODY TO LOVE *(Queen/v)*
SOMETHIN' STUPID *(Nancy & Frank Sinatra)*
SOUND AND VISION *(David Bowie)*
SPEEDY GONZALES *(Pat Boone)*
SPIRIT IN THE SKY *(Doctor & the Medics)* *(Norman Greenbaum)*
STAND BY YOUR MAN *(Tammy Wynette)*
STAY WITH ME BABY *(Walker Brothers)* *(David Essex)*
STEP INSIDE LOVE *(Cilla Black)*
STRAWBERRY FAIR *(Anthony Newley)*
SULTANS OF SWING *(Dire Straits)*
SUMMERTIME CITY *(Mike Batt)*
SUNNY AFTERNOON *(Kinks)*
SUSSEX BY THE SEA *(v)*
SWEET TALKIN' GUY *(Chiffons)*
T'AIN'T WHAT YOU DO *(v)*
TEENAGE RAMPAGE *(Sweet)*
TENNESSEE WALTZ *(v)*
THAT'LL BE THE DAY *(Buddy Holly)*
THAT OLD FEELING *(v)*
THE BITCH IS BACK *(Elton John)*
THE BLACK BOTTOM *(v)*
THE CHICKEN SONG *(Spitting Image)*
THE CONTINENTAL *(Fred Astaire & Ginger Rogers)*
THE FLORAL DANCE *(Brighouse & Rastrick Brass Band)* *(Peter Dawson)* *(Terry Wogan)*
THE HEART OF A MAN *(Frankie Vaughan)*

THEME FOR A DREAM *(Cliff Richard)*
THEME FROM DIXIE *(Duane Eddy)*
THE MORE I SEE YOU *(Chris Montez/v)*
THEN HE KISSED ME *(Crystals)*
THE POWER OF LOVE *(Frankie goes to Hollywood)* *(Huey Lewis & the News)* *(Jennifer Rush)*
THE PRICE OF LOVE *(Everly Brothers)*
THE TIME HAS COME *(Adam Faith)*
THE TROLLEY SONG *(Judy Garland)*
THE WONDER OF YOU *(Elvis Presley)*
TIME IS ON MY SIDE *(Rolling Stones)*
TRAVELLIN' LIGHT *(Cliff Richard)*
TUXEDO JUNCTION *(Glenn Miller)*
UNDER YOUR THUMB *(Godley & Creme)*
WADE IN THE WATER *(Ramsey Lewis)*
WALK HAND IN HAND *(Ronnie Carroll)* *(Tony Martin)*
WATERLOO SUNSET *(Kinks)*
WE CAN WORK IT OUT *(Beatles)*
WE'RE IN THE MONEY *(v)*
WHISKY IN THE JAR *(Thin Lizzy)*
WHITE CHRISTMAS *(Bing Crosby)* *(Mantovani/v)*
WICHITA LINEMAN *(Glen Campbell)*
WISHIN' AND HOPIN' *(Merseybeats)*
WITH ALL MY HEART *(Petula Clark)*
WONDERFUL WORLD *(Sam Cooke)* *(Herman's Hermits)*
YOU CAN CALL ME AL *(Paul Simon)*
YOU'LL NEVER KNOW *(Shirley Bassey/v)*
YOU REALLY GOT ME *(Kinks)*
YOU'RE IN MY HEART *(Rod Stewart)*
YOUR LOVE IS KING *(Sade)*

15

A COUPLE OF SWELLS *(Fred Astaire & Judy Garland)*

ALL OVER THE WORLD *(Françoise Hardy)*
A LOVER'S CONCERTO *(Toys)*
A MAN WITHOUT LOVE *(Engelbert Humperdinck)*
A STRING OF PEARLS *(Glenn Miller)*
A TEENAGER IN LOVE *(Craig Douglas)* *(Marty Wilde)*
A WHITE SPORT COAT *(Terry Dene)* *(King Brothers)*
BACK OFF BOOGALOO *(Ringo Starr)*
BEAR NECESSITIES *(Phil Harris)*
BEGIN THE BEGUINE *(Julio Iglesias/v)*
BELL BOTTOM BLUES *(Alma Cogan)*
BIG GIRLS DON'T CRY *(Four Seasons)*
BIRTH OF THE BLUES *(v)*
BLOWIN' IN THE WIND *(Bob Dylan)* *(Peter, Paul & Mary/v)*
BLUE IS THE COLOUR *(Chelsea FC)*
BYE BYE BLACKBIRD *(v)*
CALIFORNIA GIRLS *(Beach Boys)*
CARELESS WHISPER *(George Michael)*
CHEERIE BEERIE BE *(v)*
COCKTAILS FOR TWO *(Spike Jones/v)*
COME BACK AND STAY *(Paul Young)*
CONGRATULATIONS *(Cliff Richard)*
DE CAMPTOWN RACES *(v)*
DEVIL IN DISGUISE *(Elvis Presley)*
DO WAH DIDDY DIDDY *(Manfred Mann)*
DOWN ON THE STREET *(Shakatak)*
DO YOU WANNA DANCE *(Cliff Richard)*
END OF ME OLD CIGAR *(Harry Champion)*
EVERLASTING LOVE *(Love Affair)*
FEEL THE NEED IN ME *(Detroit Emeralds)*
FLYING DOWN TO RIO *(Fred Astaire & Ginger Rogers)*

FOR OLD TIMES' SAKE *(Millie Lindon)*
FOR ONCE IN MY LOVE *(Stevie Wonder)*
FOR THE GOOD TIMES *(Perry Como)*
GEORGIA ON MY MIND *(Ray Charles/v)*
GIMME SOME LOVING *(Spencer Davis Group)*
GIRL FROM IPANEMA *(Stan Getz & Joao Gilberto) (Astrud Gilberto)*
GIRLS GIRLS GIRLS *(Sailor)*
GIVE A LITTLE LOVE *(Bay City Rollers)*
GOODNIGHT VIENNA *(Jack Buchanan)*
GREASED LIGHTNIN' *(John Travolta)*
GREEN TAMBOURINE *(Lemon Pipers)*
HARD HEADED WOMAN *(Elvis Presley)*
HARPER VALLEY PTA *(Jeannie C Riley)*
HEARTBREAK HOTEL *(Elvis Presley)*
HELLO LITTLE GIRL *(Fourmost)*
HERE COMES SUMMER *(Jerry Keller)*
HOLE IN THE BUCKET *(Harry Belafonte & Odetta)*
HOTEL CALIFORNIA *(Eagles)*
I DON'T WANNA DANCE *(Eddy Grant)*
IF I WERE A RICH MAN *(Topol)*
IF YOU LEAVE ME NOW *(Chicago)*
I LOVE YOU BECAUSE *(Jim Reeves)*
I'M GONNA BE STRONG *(Gene Pitney)*
I'M STILL STANDING *(Elton John)*
IN THE SUMMERTIME *(Mungo Jerry)*
I PUT A SPELL ON YOU *(Alan Price) (Nina Simone)*
ISLE OF INNISFREE *(Bing Crosby)*
I TALK TO THE TREES *(v)*
IT'S ALL IN THE GAME *(Tommy Edwards) (Four Tops) (Cliff Richard)*

IT'S GOOD NEWS WEEK *(Hedgehoppers Anonymous)*
I WANNA BE YOUR MAN *(Rolling Stones)*
JANUARY FEBRUARY *(Barbara Dickson)*
JEEPERS CREEPERS *(Hayley Mills/v)*
JENNIFER JUNIPER *(Donovan)*
KITTEN ON THE KEYS *(v)*
KNOCK THREE TIMES *(Dawn)*
LEADER OF THE PACK *(Shangri-Las)*
LET'S GET TOGETHER *(Hayley Mills)*
LET THERE BE DRUMS *(Sandy Nelson)*
LIGHTNIN' STRIKES *(Lou Christie)*
LITTLE RED MONKEY *(v)*
LITTLE WHITE BULL *(Tommy Steele)*
LITTLE WHITE LIES *(v)*
LOVE AND MARRIAGE *(Frank Sinatra/v)*
LOVE IS ALL AROUND *(Troggs)*
LOVE ME OR LEAVE ME *(Sammy Davis Jr/v)*
MEET ME IN ST LOUIS *(Judy Garland)*
MOCKINGBIRD HILL *(Migil Five)*
MONEY FOR NOTHING *(Dire Straits)*
MONEY MONEY MONEY *(Abba)*
MORE THAN I CAN SAY *(Leo Sayer) (Bobby Vee)*
MORNINGTOWN RIDE *(Seekers)*
MOVE OVER DARLING *(Doris Day) (Tracey Ullman)*
MR TAMBOURINE MAN *(Byrds) (Bob Dylan)*
MUSIC MUSIC MUSIC *(v)*
MY EYES ADORED YOU *(Frankie Valli/v)*
NO MORE MR NICE GUY *(Alice Cooper)*
OLD FATHER THAMES *(v)*
OUTSIDE OF HEAVEN *(Eddie Fisher)*
PAPERBACK WRITER *(Beatles)*
PICK UP THE PIECES *(Average White Band)*

PLEASE DON'T TEASE *(Cliff Richard)*
PLEASE MR POSTMAN *(Beatles)*
(Carpenters)
PUPPET ON A STRING *(Sandie Shaw)*
PUTTIN' ON THE RITZ *(Fred Astaire)*
REASON TO BELIEVE *(Rod Stewart)*
RIVERS OF BABYLON *(Boney M)*
SAD SWEET DREAMER *(Sweet Sensation)*
SEALED WITH A KISS *(Brian Hyland)*
SEA OF HEARTBREAK *(Don Gibson)*
SEASONS IN THE SUN *(Terry Jacks)*
SEND IN THE CLOWNS *(Judy Collins)*
(Glynis Johns)
SEVEN SEAS OF RHYE *(Queen)*
SHE'S OUT OF MY LIFE *(Michael Jackson)*
SILENCE IS GOLDEN *(Tremeloes)*
SINGING THE BLUES *(Guy Mitchell)*
(Tommy Steele)
SINGIN' IN THE RAIN *(Gene Kelly)*
SOME OF THESE DAYS *(v)*
SPEAK TO ME PRETTY *(Brenda Lee)*
STAND AND DELIVER *(Adam & the Ants)*
STREETS OF LONDON *(Ralph McTell)*
SUMMER IN THE CITY *(Lovin' Spoonful)*
SUMMER NIGHT CITY *(Abba)*
SUMMERTIME BLUES *(Eddie Cochran)*
SUSPICIOUS MINDS *(Fine Young Cannibals)*
(Elvis Presley)
SWINGING ON A STAR *(Big Dee Irwin)*
TAKE A CHANCE ON ME *(Abba)*
TEARS ON MY PILLOW *(Johnny Nash)*
THAT LUCKY OLD SUN *(Paul Robeson/v)*
THE BAND PLAYED ON *(v)*
THE BOAT THAT I ROW *(Lulu)*
THE CLAPPING SONG *(Shirley Ellis)*
THE EDGE OF HEAVEN *(Wham!)*
THE FERRY BOAT INN *(v)*
THE PEANUT VENDOR *(v)*
THE PUSHBIKE SONG *(Mixtures)*

THERE MUST BE A WAY *(Frankie Vaughan)*
THE ROSE OF TRALEE *(v)*
THE SHEIK OF ARABY *(v)*
THE SHOW MUST GO ON *(Leo Sayer)*
THREE TIMES A LADY *(Commodores)*
TOOT-TOOT-TOOTSIE *(Al Jolson)*
TOWER OF STRENGTH *(Frankie Vaughan)*
TURNING JAPANESE *(Vapors)*
TWO SLEEPY PEOPLE *(v)*
UNA PALOMA BLANCA *(Jonathan King)*
UNCHAINED MELODY *(Al Hibbler)*
(Liberace)
(Jimmy Young/v)
UNION OF THE SNAKE *(Duran Duran)*
WALK UP THE AVENUE *(Fred Astaire & Judy Garland)*
WE SHALL OVERCOME *(Joan Baez)*
WHATEVER YOU WANT *(Status Quo)*
WHEN I FALL IN LOVE *(Nat 'King' Cole)*
WHEN YOU ARE A KING *(White Plains)*
WHERE THE BOYS ARE *(Connie Francis)*
WHIFFENPOOF SONG *(v)*
WHISPERING GRASS *(Windsor Davies & Don Estelle/v)*
WHOLE LOTTA WOMAN *(Marvin Rainwater)*
YELLOW SUBMARINE *(Beatles)*
YOU ARE MY DESTINY *(Paul Anka)*
YOU DON'T HAVE TO GO *(Chi-Lites)*
YOU DRIVE ME CRAZY *(Shakin' Stevens)*
YOU'LL ANSWER TO ME *(Cleo Laine/v)*
YOUNG AND HEALTHY *(v)*
YOU'VE GOT A FRIEND *(James Taylor)*
YOU WERE ON MY MIND *(Crispian St Peters)*
YUMMY YUMMY YUMMY *(Ohio Express)*

ARTS

MUSIC – SONGS – TRADITIONAL

(H) = Hymn/carol (NA) = National anthem (NR) = Nursery rhyme

5

DIXIE

6

SUNSET
TE DEUM *(H)*
TOM, TOM *(NR)*

7

AEGUKKA *(NA-South Korea)*
O CANADA *(NA-Canada)*

8

AVE MARIA *(H)*
BILLY BOY
DANNY BOY
DAY BY DAY *(H)*
ELWATINI *(NA-Swaziland)*
HATIKVAH *(NA-Israel)*
KIMIGAYO *(NA-Japan)*
KUM BA YAH *(H)*
LAST POST
MARY, MARY *(NR)*
MY BONNIE
OH UGANDA *(NA-Uganda)*
O SOLE MIO
PAT-A-CAKE *(NR)*
QASSAMAN *(NA-Algeria)*
THANK YOU *(H)*

9

GALWAY BAY
JACK SPRAT *(NR)*

JERUSALEM *(H)*
OH FREEDOM *(H)*
RORY O'MORE
TIPPERARY
WILHELMAS *(NA-Netherlands)*

10

AND CAN IT BE *(H)*
BELL ANTHEM
BLESS 'EM ALL
CHOPSTICKS
CLEMENTINE
HAIL TO FIJI *(NA-Fiji)*
HOKEY COKEY
LA CONCORDE *(NA-Gabon)*
LOVE DIVINE *(H)*
LUCY LOCKET *(NR)*
MAGNIFICAT *(H)*
ONS HÉMÉCHT *(NA-Luxembourg)*
ROCK OF AGES *(H)*
ROBIN ADAIR
TANNENBAUM
TIEN QUAN CA *(NA-Vietnam)*
TREI CULORI *(NA-Romania)*

11

ABIDE WITH ME *(H)*
ANNIE LAURIE
A PORTUGUESA *(NA-Portugal)*
BAY OF BISCAY
HEARTS OF OAK
HIMAT AL HIMA *(NA-Tunisia)*
JACK AND JILL *(NR)*
JINGLE BELLS *(H)*
KDE DOMOV MŮJ *(NA-Czechoslovakia)*

LAMBETH WALK
MOTHER GOOSE *(NR)*
OLD KING COLE *(NR)*
QUAMI TARANI *(NA-Pakistan)*
SCOTS WHA HAE
SILENT NIGHT *(H)*
SIMPLE SIMON *(NR)*
SWANEE RIVER
WHAT A FRIEND *(H)*

12

AMAZING GRACE *(H)*
ANGOLA AVANTE *(NA-Angola)*
AULD LANG SYNE
DING DONG BELL *(NR)*
FATSHE LA RONA *(NA-Botswana)*
GREENSLEEVES
HOLY, HOLY, HOLY *(H)*
HOT CROSS BUNS *(NR)*
HUMPTY DUMPTY *(NR)*
INNO DI MAMELI *(NA-Italy)*
ISTIKÂL MARSI *(NA-Turkey)*
JANA-GANA-MANA *(NA-India)*
KONG KRISTIAN *(NA-Denmark)*
KYRIE ELEISON *(H)*
LAVENDER BLUE
L'ABIDJANAISE *(NA-Ivory Coast)*
LILLIBURLERO
LITTLE BO PEEP *(NR)*
LONDON BRIDGE *(NR)*
NUNC DIMITTIS *(H)*
ODE TO FREEDOM *(NA-Cyprus)*
SKYE BOAT SONG
SOROUD-E-MELLI *(NA-Afghanistan)*
THE LOST CHORD
WE THREE KINGS *(H)*
YANKEE DOODLE

13

ADESTE FIDELES *(H)*
AWAY IN A MANGER *(H)*
DU GAMLA, DU FRIA *(NA-Sweden)*

GEORGIE PORGIE *(NR)*
HAPPY BIRTHDAY
INDONESIA RAYA *(NA-Indonesia)*
LA BRABANÇONNE *(NA-Belgium)*
LAND OF THE GODS *(NA-Belize)*
LITTLE BOY BLUE *(NR)*
NAMO NAMO MATHA *(NA-Sri Lanka)*
O GUD VORS LANDS *(NA-Iceland)*
PINA EA SECHABA *(NA-Lesotho)*
RULE BRITANNIA!
SOLOMON GRUNDY *(NR)*
VOLGA BOAT SONG

14

BLACK-EYED SUSAN
BLESS THIS HOUSE
BYE, BABY BUNTING *(NR)*
GOD SAVE THE KING *(NA-Britain)*
GUATEMALA FELIZ *(NA-Guatemala)*
INTERNATIONALE
JOHN BROWN'S BODY
LA MARSEILLAISE *(NA-France)*
LONDONDERRY AIR
LORD OF THE DANCE *(H)*
OLD FOLKS AT HOME
PAMBANSANG AWIT *(NA-Philippines)*
THREE BLIND MICE *(NR)*

15

AMAR SONAR BANGLA *(NA-Bangladesh)*
AMHRÁN NA BHFIANN *(NA-Indonesia)*
ARISE ALL YOU SONS *(NA-Papua New Guinea)*
FOR ALL THE SAINTS *(H)*
GOD BLESS AMERICA
GOD SAVE THE QUEEN *(NA-Britain)*
HEY DIDDLE DIDDLE *(NR)*
HOW GREAT THOU ART *(H)*
HOW SWEET THE NAME *(H)*
HYMNE MONÉGASQUE *(NA-Monaco)*
LA DESSALINIENNE *(NA-Haiti)*

LAND OF MY FATHERS *(NA-Wales)*
LEAD, KINDLY LIGHT *(H)*
LONG LIVE THE KING *(NA-Jordan)*
NAHNU DJUNDULLAH *(NA-Sudan)*

RISING OF THE LARK
SCARBOROUGH FAIR
THE SOLDIER'S SONG *(NA-Eire)*
WALTZING MATILDA

ARTS

PAINTINGS

(E) = Etching/engraving   (S) = Sculpture/statue
* = Alternative title   (v) = various artists

3

DAY *(S-Epstein)*
PAN *(Böcklin)*

4

NOAH *(Bellini)*
RAPE *(Cézanne)*
RIMA *(F-Epstein)*

5

CUPID *(S-Michelangelo/v)*
DANAË *(Titian)*
DAVID *(S-Donatello)*
       (S-Michelangelo/v)
DIANA *(S-Houdon)*
ENNUI *(Sickert)*
MOSES *(S-Michelangelo)*
NIGHT *(S-Epstein)*
PIETÀ *(S-Bellini)*
       (S-Michelangelo/v)
VENUS *(v)*
WHAAM! *(Lichtenstein)*

6

AURORA *(Guercino)*
         (Reni)
DELUGE *(Uccello)*
IRISES *(Van Gogh)*
MURDER *(Cézanne)*
PINKIE *(Lawrence)*
SALOME *(S-Donatello/v)*
SHRIEK *(Munch)*
SLAVES *(S-Michelangelo)*
SPRING *(Botticelli)*
THE WAR *(Dix)*

7

ANGELUS *(Millet)*
AU PIANO *(Whistler)*
BACCHUS *(S-Michelangelo/v)*
BLUE BOY *(Gainsborough)*
BUBBLES *(Millais)*
CALVARY *(Chagall)*
COOKHAM *(Spencer)*
ERASMUS *(Holbein)*
HAY WAIN *(Constable)*
LA BELLA *(Titian)*

LAOCOÖN *(S-v)*
MADONNA *(v)*
MERCURY *(S-Bologna)*
NEPTUNE *(S-Ammanati)*
OLYMPIA *(Manet)*
PERSEUS *(Burne-Jones)*
         (S-Cellini)
QUERINI *(Tiepolo)*
RAINBOW *(Rubens)*
REQUIEM *(S-Hepworth)*
SUICIDE *(Grosz)*
THE KISS *(Hayez)*
         (S-Rodin)
THE MILL *(Rembrandt)*
UGOLINO *(S-Carpeaux)*

8

ADMIRALS *(Lely)*
BEAUTIES *(Lely)*
GUERNICA *(Picasso)*
MILLBANK *(Turner)*
MISERERE *(E-Rouault)*
MONA LISA *(Leonardo)* *1
MORPHEUS *(S-Houdon)*

MR TRUMAN *(Gainsborough)*
PARADISE *(Tintoretto)*
TA MATETE *(Gauguin)*
THE DREAM *(Rousseau)*
THE ROOKS *(Staël)*
TWO NUDES *(Picasso)*
VOLTAIRE *(S-Houdon)*

SHRIMP GIRL *(Hogarth)*
SUNFLOWERS *(Van Gogh)*
THE SKATERS *(Breughel)*
THE THINKER *(S-Rodin)*
VISITATION *(Albertinelli)*

9

ATOM PIECE *(S-Moore)*
A YOUNG MAN *(Andrea)*
CHURCHILL *(Sutherland)*
DONI TONDO *(Michelangelo)*
FORTITUDE *(Botticelli)*
HAYSTACKS *(Monet)*
HENRY VIII *(Holbein)*
HET PELSKE *(Rubens)*
LONGCHAMP *(Picasso)*
NORTH WIND *(S-Moore)*
ODALISQUE *(Ingres)*
         (Matisse)
PARNASSUS *(Appiani)*
PRIMAVERA *(Botticelli)*
PYGMALION *(Burne-Jones)*
SHIPWRECK *(Turner)*
STAG AT BAY *(Landseer)*
THE MACNAB *(Raeburn)*
THE WINDOW *(Bonnard)*

11

AU CHAT BOTTÉ *(Nicholson)*
CORNARD WOOD *(Gainsborough)*
CRUCIFIXION *(v)*
DEMOISELLES *(Picasso)*
DOG ON A LEASH *(Balla)*
DRUNKEN FAUNS *(S-Sergel)*
JOIE DE VIVRE *(Matisse)*
LE JARDINIER *(Cézanne)*
MALVERN HALL *(Constable)*
MOULIN ROUGE *(Toulouse-Lautrec)*
PEACE AND WAR *(Rubens)*
SHIP OF FOOLS *(Bosch)*

12

AUTUMN RHYTHM *(Pollock)*
BEATA BEATRIX *(Rossetti)*
CAPTAIN CORAM *(Hogarth)*
CHILL OCTOBER *(Millais)*
DANCE OF DEATH *(Munch)*
DEATH OF WOLFE *(West)*
DOGE LOREDANO *(Bellini)*
FLATFORD MILL *(Constable)*
ICONOGRAPHIA *(E-Van Dyck)*
LOS CAPRICHOS *(E-Goya)*
MRS DAVENPORT *(Romney)*
OÙ ALLONS-NOUS *(Gauguin)*
PEASANT DANCE *(Breughel)*
RAPE OF EUROPA *(Titian)*
SARDANAPALUS *(Delacroix)*
THE ANGRY SWAN *(Asselyn)*
THE NAKED MAUA *(Goya)*
THE NIGHTMARE *(Fuseli)*
THE SCAPEGOAT *(Hunt)*
THREE DANCERS *(Picasso)*
TWO GENTLEMEN *(Reynolds)*
VIEW OF TOLEDO *(El Greco)*

10

AN INTERIOR *(Hooch)*
BEGGAR BOYS *(Murillo)*
CALAIS PIER *(Turner)*
CONFESSION *(Poussin)*
DEPOSITION *(Raphael)*
DULLE GRIET *(Breughel)*
LA DESSERTE *(Matisse)*
LA GIACONDA *(Leonardo)* *1
MISS FARREN *(Lawrence)*
MISS LINLEY *(Gainsborough)*
MRS SIDDONS *(Gainsborough)*
NIGHT WATCH *(Rembrandt)*

ARTS – PAINTINGS

13

A BIGGER SPLASH *(Hockney)*
ANATOMY LESSON *(Rembrandt)*
BENOIS MADONNA *(Leonardo)*
DUCHESS OF ALBA *(Goya)*
GROSVENOR HUNT *(Stubbs)*
MADDALENA DONI *(Raphael)*
MAISON DE PENDU *(Cézanne)*
PLACE DU TERTRE *(Utrillo)*
RAKE'S PROGRESS *(E-Hogarth)*
THE ASSUMPTION *(Titian/v)*
THE LAST SUPPER *(Leonardo/v)*
VENUS OF URBINO *(Titian)*
WOMAN WITH A FAN *(Rembrandt)*

14

ANSIDEI MADONNA *(Raphael)*
DANCER AT THE BAR *(Degas)*
DISASTERS OF WAR *(E-Goya)*
HALT IN THE CHASE *(Watteau)*
L'EGLISE D'AUVERS *(Van Gogh)*
MYSTIC NATIVITY *(Botticelli)*
NEBUCHADNEZZAR *(Blake)*
PEASANT WEDDING *(Breughel)*
PORT OF ST MARTIN *(Utrillo)*

PROGRESS OF LOVE *(Fragonard)*
SISTINE MADONNA *(Raphael)*
THE CARD PLAYERS *(Cézanne)*
THE ROKEBY VENUS *(Velasquez)*
THE THREE GRACES *(Reynolds)*
VIEW ON THE STOUR *(Constable)*

15

ABSINTHE DRINKER *(Manet)*
APOLLO AND DAPHNE *(S-Bernini)*
EARTHLY PARADISE *(Bosch)*
LIFE OF ST FRANCIS *(Giotto)*
LIGHT OF THE WORLD *(Hunt)*
MADONNA AND CHILD *(S-Moore/v)*
MARRIAGE À LA MODE *(E-Hogarth)*
STATUE OF LIBERTY *(S-Bartholdi)*
THE BIRTH OF VENUS *(Botticelli)*
                              (Rubens/v)
THE GUITAR-PLAYER *(Vermeer)*
THE LAST JUDGMENT
                    (Michelangelo/v)
THE POTATO EATERS *(Van Gogh)*
THE TRIBUTE MONEY *(Titian)*
TRANSFIGURATION *(Raphael)*

ARTS

TELEVISION & RADIO PROGRAMMES

(R) = Radio   NB: (T) = TV only used for joint entries

3		4				
	OTT		FURY	JANE	SWAT	
	QED		HOAX *(R)*	LACE	TAXI	
HOW!	SAM	BOON	I SPY	M*A*S*H	TV-am	AGONY
OSS	UFO	FAME	ITMA *(R)*	SOAP		ARENA

BILKO
BRASS
CHiPs
CRANE
CRIBB
DEF II
DOTTO
DR WHO
EBONY
HOTEL
KOJAK
MITCH
MOGUL
NANNY
OH BOY
RHODA
ROOTS
SORRY!
TENKO
TODAY *(R)*
TV EYE
WINGS
WOGAN
Z CARS
ZORRO

6

ANGELS
BATMAN
BENSON
BOYD QC
BUDGIE
CALLAN
CANNON
CHEERS
CINEMA
CONNIE
DALLAS
F TROOP
GUN LAW
HARRY O
HAZELL
HI-DE-HI!
HI GANG *(R)*

JIGSAW
KUNG FU
LASSIE
LILLIE
MAGPIE
MANNIX
MINDER
MY WORD *(R)*
PARADE
POPEYE
QUINCY
RAPIDO
REDCAP
SAILOR
SHOGUN
SUNDAY *(R)*
TARZAN
T.H.E. CAT
THE FBI
TOP CAT
TOP TEN *(R)*
WHACKO!
WIDOWS
YOU BET!

7

AIRWOLF
ALL HALE *(R)*
BANACEK
BIG DEAL
BIG TIME *(R)*
BONANZA
CAMPION
CHIGLEY
COLDITZ
COMPACT
COWBOYS
DAKTARI
DEE TIME
DRAGNET
DYNASTY
FLIPPER
HAVE A GO *(R)*
HIGHWAY

HOLIDAY
HORIZON
IN TOUCH *(R)*
IVANHOE
JUSTICE
KESSLER
LARAMIE
LAUGH-IN
LEAVING
LOVEJOY
MAIGRET
MANHUNT
McCLOUD
MIDWEEK
MONITOR
MY MUSIC *(R/T)*
OMNIBUS
OPEN AIR
OUTLOOK *(R)*
POLDARK
QUILLER
RAWHIDE
SEA HUNT
SHELLEY
TAGGART
THE BILL
THE LUMP
THE TUBE
TONIGHT
TOP TOWN *(R)*
TOYTOWN *(R)*
WARSHIP
WHO'S WHO *(R)*
ZOO TIME

8

AIR RAIDS *(R)*
'ALLO 'ALLO
AQUARIUS
BAND CALL *(R)*
BEN CASEY
BERGERAC
BULLSEYE
CASANOVA
CASUALTY

C.A.T.S. EYES
CHEYENNE
CITIZENS *(R)*
DAD'S ARMY
DUTY FREE
EVERYMAN
FEEDBACK *(R)*
FILM TIME *(R)*
FOXY LADY
GUNSMOKE
HADLEIGH
HOSPITAL
IN THE AIR *(R)*
IRONSIDE
JAZZ CLUB *(R)*
LIFELINE
LOU GRANT
LUCKY DIP *(R)*
MAGNUM PI
MAN ALIVE
MATT HELM
MAVERICK
MISTER ED
MONEY BOX *(R)*
MR AND MRS
NEW FACES
NEWSBEAT *(R)*
NEWS VIEW
NEWSWEEK
ONE BY ONE
OPEN DOOR
PANORAMA
PORRIDGE
POT BLACK
RADIO FUN *(R)*
SCRUPLES
SHOWTIME *(R)*
STARBILL *(R)*
STAR TREK
STINGRAY
SUPERCAR
SUPERMAN
SURVIVAL
TALKBACK
THE A-TEAM
THE BARON

ARTS — TELEVISION & RADIO PROGRAMMES

THE CREZZ
THE HERBS
THE SAINT
THE VISIT
THIS WEEK
TJ HOOKER
TRIANGLE
TRUMPTON
WE LOVE TV
WHIPLASH
YOGI BEAR
ZOO QUEST

9

ALBUM LEAF (R)
AMOS 'N' ANDY
ANDY PANDY
BANDWAGON (R)
BERYL'S LOT
BEWITCHED
BLIND DATE
BLUE PETER
BOOKSHELF (R)
BREAKAWAY (R)
BROOKSIDE
BURKE'S LAW
CATCHWORD
CATWEAZLE
CHRONICLE
CIRCUS BOY
CLUB NIGHT (R)
COUNTDOWN
DAN AUGUST
DANGER MAN
DANGER UXB
DID YOU SEE?
DOOMWATCH
DR KILDARE
EMMERDALE
FELL TIGER
GENTLE BEN
GET SOME IN
GOING LIVE
HAPPY DAYS
HIT PARADE (R)
HOLOCAUST

I, CLAUDIUS
I LOVE LUCY
JASON KING
JENNY'S WAR
JUNGLE JIM
LIMELIGHT (R)
LOGAN'S RUN
LOOSE ENDS (R)
MAKING OUT
MANY A SLIP (R)
METROLAND
MIAMI VICE
MOVIE TIME (R)
MURDER BAG
MUSIC HALL (R)
NAKED CITY
NEWS AT TEN
NEWSNIGHT
NEWSROUND
NEWS STAND (R)
NIGHTRIDE (R)
OPEN HOUSE (R)
OVER TO YOU (R)
PALM COURT (R)
PLEASE SIR
POTTY TIME
PUBLIC EAR (R)
PUBLIC EYE
QUIZ PARTY (R)
RIN TIN TIN
RIVERBOAT
SCRAPBOOK (R)
SECRET WAR
STAGE DOOR (R)
SUPERGRAN
THAT'S LIFE
THE COLBYS
THE FAMILY
THE GAFFER
THE LOVERS
TIMEWATCH
TOP TWENTY (R)
TWIN PEAKS
ULTRA QUIZ
UP POMPEII
UP THE POLE (R)
WAR SCHOOL

10

AFTER HENRY (R/T)
ANY ANSWERS (R)
ARTHUR'S INN (R)
BAND PARADE (R)
BAND WAGGON (R)
BOTANIC MAN
BRASS TACKS
CANNONBALL
CASEY JONES
CHILD'S PLAY
CLAYHANGER
COMEDY QUIZ (R)
CROSSROADS
CROWN COURT
DEAR LADIES
DEPUTY DAWG
DICK BARTON (R)
DON'T WAIT UP
EASTENDERS
ELIZABETH R
FACE TO FACE
GIDEON'S WAY
GRAND HOTEL (R)
GRANDSTAND
GRANGE HILL
HART TO HART
HELLO THERE (R)
HOWARDS' WAY
JIM'LL FIX IT
MASTERMIND
MISS MARPLE
NATIONWIDE
NEIGHBOURS
NO, HONESTLY
OFF THE CUFF (R)
ON THE BUSES
PERRY MASON
PETROCELLI
POLICE FIVE
QUATERMASS
RAY'S A LAUGH (R)
RECORD TIME (R)
ROBIN'S NEST
ROUNDABOUT (R)

RISING DAMP
SCIENCE NOW (R)
SECRET ARMY
SHOESTRING
SHOW PARADE (R)
SPORTS DESK
SPORTSVIEW
STARGAZING (R)
STREETHAWK
STYLE TRIAL
THAT'S MY BOY
THE ARCHERS (R)
THE BIG TIME
THE CHARMER
THE FALL GUY
THE GOODIES
THE IRISH RM
THE LARKINS
THE MONKEES
THE SWEENEY
THE WALTONS
THE WAR GAME
THE WOMBLES
VAN DER VALK
WACKY RACES
WAGON TRAIN
WEEK ENDING (R)
WHAT'S YOURS? (R)
WHO DO YOU DO?
WISH ME LUCK
WOMAN'S HOUR (R)

11

ADAM ADAMANT
ALL STAR GANG (R)
BAKER'S DOZEN (R)
BEGGIN' YOURS (R)
BEST SELLERS
BILL AND BEN
BILLY BUNTER
BIONIC WOMAN
BLAKE'S SEVEN
BUTTERFLIES
CALL MY BLUFF

COME DANCING
COOL MILLION
CRACKERJACK
CRAZY PEOPLE
DANIEL BOONE
DAYTIME LIVE
DEPARTMENT S
DOWN YOUR WAY *(R)*
ELLERY QUEEN
FALCON CREST
FRAGGLE ROCK
FREEDOM ROAD
FUTTOCK'S END
GIVE US A CLUE
GOING PLACES *(R)*
HAWAII FIVE-O
HOME AND AWAY
HOME TO ROOST
JUKE BOX JURY
JULIET BRAVO
JUST A MINUTE *(R)*
JUST WILLIAM
KNIGHT RIDER
LATE STARTER
LIFE ON EARTH
LIVING WORLD *(R)*
LOST IN SPACE
MAX HEADROOM
MEDICINE NOW *(R)*
MY THREE SONS
ON YOUR MARKS *(R)*
OUTSIDE EDGE
PEYTON PLACE
POLICE WOMAN
RAINBOW ROOM *(R)*
ROCK FOLLIES
SECOND HOUSE *(R)*
SHADOWLANDS
SPORT ON FOUR *(R)*
SPORTSNIGHT
SPOT THE TUNE
ST ELSEWHERE
STOP THE WEEK *(R)*
THE ARMY GAME
THE AVENGERS
THE BROTHERS

THE CISCO KID
THE FUGITIVE
THE GOOD LIFE
THE GOON SHOW *(R)*
THE INFORMER
THE INVADERS
THE MUNSTERS
THE NAVY LARK *(R)*
THE OTHER 'ARF
THE PRACTICE
THE PRISONER
THE RAG TRADE
THE RIFLEMAN
THE THIRD MAN
TOM AND JERRY
TWO'S COMPANY
WHAT'S MY LINE? *(R/T)*
WHIRLYBIRDS
WHITE HUNTER
WONDER WOMAN
YES, MINISTER
YOU AND YOURS *(R)*

12

A FAMILY AT WAR
A FINE ROMANCE
A LIFE OF BLISS *(R)*
ANY QUESTIONS *(R)*
ANYTHING GOES *(R)*
ASK THE FAMILY
BARNABY JONES
BBC DANCE CLUB
BEYOND OUR KEN *(R)*
BLOCKBUSTERS
BRUSH STROKES
BOY MEETS GIRL
CANDID CAMERA
CAN YOU BEAT IT *(R)*
CINEMAGAZINE *(R)*
CITIZEN SMITH
CIVILIZATION
CRIMEWATCH UK
DAILY SERVICE *(R)*
FACE THE MUSIC
FACE THE PRESS

FARMING TODAY *(R)*
FAWLTY TOWERS
FORTY MINUTES
GOING FOR GOLD
HOGAN'S HEROES
HOUSE OF CARDS
HULBERT HOUSE *(R)*
I MARRIED JOAN
IN YOUR GARDEN *(R)*
IT'S A KNOCKOUT
JOHNNY GO HOME
JOINT ACCOUNT
JUNIOR CHOICE *(R)*
KALEIDOSCOPE *(R)*
KNOTS LANDING
LONDON LIGHTS
LOVE FOR LYDIA
LYTTON'S DIARY
MAPP AND LUCIA
MERRY-GO-ROUND *(R)*
MOONLIGHTING
MORK AND MINDY
MORNING STORY *(R)*
MOVIE-GO-ROUND *(R)*
NAME THAT TUNE
OPEN ALL HOURS
PLAY FOR TODAY
POETRY PLEASE *(R)*
POINTS OF VIEW
PUZZLE CORNER *(R)*
QUESTION TIME
RECORD REVIEW *(R)*
RIGHT TO REPLY
RIPPING YARNS
ROUGH JUSTICE
ROUND THE BEND *(R)*
ROVING REPORT
RUGBY SPECIAL
SATURDAY CLUB *(R)*
SERGEANT CORK
SESAME STREET
SOFTLY SOFTLY
SPORTS REPORT *(R)*
START THE WEEK *(R)*
TAKE YOUR PICK *(R/T)*
TELLY ADDICTS

THE BIG VALLEY
THE COMEDIANS
THE CHAMPIONS
THE EQUALIZER
THE FLYING NUN
THE NEARLY MAN
THE ODD COUPLE
THE PALLISERS
THE POWER GAME
THE SOOTY SHOW
THE VIRGINIAN
THE YOUNG ONES
THUNDERBIRDS
TIME FOR CRIME *(R)*
TONIGHT AT SIX *(R)*
TOP OF THE BILL *(R)*
TOP OF THE FORM *(R)*
TOP OF THE POPS
TOP OF THE TOWN *(R)*
TREASURE HUNT
TREBLE CHANCE *(R)*
TUGBOAT ANNIE
WEEKEND WORLD
WILL O' THE WISP
WORLD OF SPORT
YOU RANG, M'LORD?

13

ABIGAIL'S PARTY
ACCENT ON YOUTH *(R)*
AFRICAN PATROL
A SENSE OF GUILT
AT THE BLACK DOG *(R)*
BARMITZVAH BOY
BEYOND COMPÈRE *(R)*
BLANKETY BLANK
BLESS ME FATHER
BREAKFAST CLUB *(R)*
BREAKFAST TIME
CATHY COME HOME
CHILDREN'S HOUR *(R)*
CRIME MAGAZINE *(R)*
CURRY AND CHIPS
EMMERDALE FARM
FANTASY ISLAND

GAME FOR A LAUGH
GENTLY BENTLEY *(R)*
GOING STRAIGHT
HELLO CHILDREN *(R)*
HIGH CHAPARRAL
HIGHWAY PATROL
IN TOWN TONIGHT *(R/T)*
IT TAKES A THIEF
KILVERT'S DIARY
LOOKS FAMILIAR
MARCUS WELBY MD
MATCH OF THE DAY
MRS DALE'S DIARY *(R)*
MUFFIN THE MULE
NEVER THE TWAIN
NO HIDING PLACE
NORTH AND SOUTH
ONE PAIR OF EYES
PETTICOAT LANE *(R)*
PICK OF THE POPS *(R)*
PICK OF THE WEEK *(R)*
PICTURE PARADE *(R)*
POLICE SURGEON
READY STEADY GO!
ROUND THE HORNE *(R)*
SHE KNOWS Y'KNOW *(R)*
SONGS OF PRAISE
SPECIAL BRANCH
SPITTING IMAGE
STARLIGHT HOUR *(R)*
STARLIGHT ROOF *(R)*
STARLIGHT SHOW *(R)*
STARS ON SUNDAY
STEPTOE AND SON
STRIKE IT LUCKY
THE AIR-DO-WELLS *(R)*
THE BLACK ADDER
THE BRADEN BEAT
THE BUCCANEERS
THE GOLDEN SHOT
THE LIKELY LADS
THE LIVER BIRDS
THE LONE RANGER
THE MAIN CHANCE
THE MUPPET SHOW
THE ONEDIN LINE

THE PERSUADERS
THE PROTECTORS
THE RANGE RIDER
THE SKY AT NIGHT
THE TWO RONNIES
THE UPCHAT LINE
THE WINDS OF WAR
THE WOODENTOPS
THE WORLD AT ONE *(R)*
THE WORLD AT WAR
WAGGONER'S WALK *(R)*
WE BEG TO DIFFER *(R)*
WE'LL MEET AGAIN
WHAT DO YOU KNOW *(R)*
WHICKER'S WORLD
WILDLIFE ON ONE
WORLD IN ACTION

14

A BOOK AT BEDTIME *(R)*
ACCENT ON RHYTHM *(R)*
ACK-ACK BEER-BEER *(R)*
AMERICA CALLING *(R)*
ANNA AND THE KING
BLESS THIS HOUSE
BRAIN OF BRITAIN *(R)*
BUSMAN'S HOLIDAY
CAGNEY AND LACEY
CHARLIE'S ANGELS
CRISS CROSS QUIZ
EDGE OF DARKNESS
ENEMY AT THE DOOR
FOLLOW THE STARS *(R)*
FROCKS ON THE BOX
GARDENERS' WORLD
HAPPY EVER AFTER
HELLO PLAYMATES *(R)*
HOW'S YOUR FATHER *(R)*
IN AT THE DEEP END
IN LOVING MEMORY
INSPECTOR MORSE
MICROBES AND MEN
MORNING SERVICE *(R)*
MURDER SHE WROTE

MY WIFE NEXT DOOR
NINE O'CLOCK NEWS
NOT ONLY, BUT ALSO
ONLY WHEN I LAUGH
OPEN UNIVERSITY
PARADISE STREET *(R)*
QUEENIE'S CASTLE
RICH MAN, POOR MAN
SHERLOCK HOLMES
SIX-FIVE SPECIAL
SOUNDS FAMILIAR *(R)*
TAKE IT FROM HERE *(R)*
TELFORD'S CHANGE
THAT MAN CHESTER *(R)*
THE ASCENT OF MAN
THE BRAINS TRUST *(R)*
THE CLOTHES SHOW
THE CUCKOO WALTZ
THE FLINTSTONES
THE FORSYTE SAGA
THE FOUR JUST MEN
THE GENTLE TOUCH
THE GOLDEN GIRLS
THE GOOD OLD DAYS
THE GROVE FAMILY
THE HOT SHOE SHOW
THE HUMAN JUNGLE
THE NEW AVENGERS
THE PLANE MAKERS
THE PYRAMID GAME
THE WATER MARGIN
THE WHOOPEE CLUB *(R)*

THIS IS YOUR LIFE
THREE UP, TWO DOWN
TOMORROW'S WORLD
TO THE MANOR BORN
VARIETY BANDBOX *(R)*
WORZEL GUMMIDGE

15

ALMOST AN ACADEMY *(R)*
ARMCHAIR THEATRE
ASPEL AND COMPANY
A WORD IN EDGEWAYS *(R)*
BBC CONCERT PARTY *(R)*
BIRDS OF A FEATHER
CALLING THE STARS *(R)*
CAMBERWICK GREEN
CHILDREN'S CHOICE *(R)*
DOUBLE YOUR MONEY
EDUCATING ARCHIE *(R)*
FABIAN OF THE YARD
GARRISON THEATRE *(R)*
HILL STREET BLUES
INTERPOL CALLING
IT'S A SQUARE WORLD
IT'S THAT MAN AGAIN *(R)*
JESUS OF NAZARETH
JUST GOOD FRIENDS
LAND OF THE GIANTS
MAGIC ROUNDABOUT
MAN FROM ATLANTIS
McMILLAN AND WIFE

MEET THE HUGGETTS *(R)*
MIDDAY MUSIC HALL *(R)*
NEVER A CROSS WORD
PEBBLE MILL AT ONE
PLANET OF THE APES
REMINGTON STEELE
SPEND, SPEND, SPEND
STARSKY AND HUTCH
TAKE THE HIGH ROAD
TAKING THE WATERS *(R)*
THE ADDAMS FAMILY
THE CLITHEROE KID *(R)*
THE FLYING DOCTOR
THE GREAT EGG RACE
THE INVISIBLE MAN
THE LATE LATE SHOW
THE LIVING PLANET
THE MAN FROM UNCLE
THE NATURAL WORLD
THE PARADISE CLUB
THE PRICE IS RIGHT
THE TRIALS OF LIFE
THE TWILIGHT ZONE
THE UNTOUCHABLES
THE VALIANT YEARS
THE YOUNG DOCTORS
TWENTY QUESTIONS *(R)*
WHERE IN THE WORLD?
WHERE THERE'S LIFE
WISH YOU WERE HERE?
WOODY WOODPECKER
WORKERS' PLAYTIME *(R)*

ARTS

THEATRE – PLAY CHARACTERS – GENERAL

3

BEN *(The Dumb Waiter – Pinter)*
CAT *(10C – Under Milk Wood – D Thomas)*
GUS *(The Dumb Waiter – Pinter)*
LOB *(Dear Brutus – Barrie)*
MAX *(The Homecoming – Pinter)*
UBU *(Ubu-Roi – Jarry)*

4

ANYA *(The Cherry Orchard – Chekhov)*
BETH *(Dry Rot – J Chapman)*
BOON *(10W – You Never Can Tell – GB Shaw)*
CARR *(9H – Travesties – Stoppard)*
CLOV *(Endgame – Beckett)*
FACE *(The Alchemist – Jonson)*
HAMM *(Endgame – Beckett)*
HOOK *(11C – Peter Pan – Barrie)*
HOPE *(9H – The Iceman Cometh – O'Neill)*
JANE *(The Reluctant Debutante – Douglas-Home)*
KATE *(Bedroom Farce – Ayckbourn)*
LAKE *(9D, 11K – French Without Tears – Rattigan)*
LANE *(The Importance Of Being Earnest – Wilde)*
LOAM *(The Admirable Crichton – Barrie)*
LUKA *(The Lower Depths – Gorki)*
NAGG *(Endgame – Beckett)*
NANA *(Peter Pan – Barrie)*
NELL *(Endgame – Beckett)*
NORA *(A Doll's House – Ibsen)*
OLGA *(Three Sisters – Chekhov)*
PAGE *(11F – The Deep Blue Sea – Rattigan)*

PUFF *(The Critic – Sheridan)*
RICE *(10A – The Entertainer – Osborne)*
RITA *(Educating Rita – W Russell)*
SMEE *(Peter Pan – Barrie)*
WYKE *(10A – Sleuth – A Shaffer)*

5

ACRES *(8B – The Rivals – Sheridan)*
ALICE *(A Woman Of No Importance – Wilde)*
ARGAN *(Le Malade Imaginaire – Molière)*
BLACK *(9J – Under Milk Wood – D Thomas)*
BLISS *(10D, 11J – Hay Fever – Coward)*
BOYLE *(9J – Juno And The Paycock – O'Casey)*
CLARK *(11W – The Sunshine Boys – Simon)*
DOYLE *(10L – John Bull's Other Island – GB Shaw)*
DUMBY *(Lady Windermere's Fan – Wilde)*
ELYOT *(Private Lives – Coward)*
FAUST *(Faust – Goethe)*
FEERS *(The Cherry Orchard – Chekhov)*
FELIX *(The Odd Couple – Simon)*
FOWLE *(The Dock Brief – Mortimer)*
FRANK *(Educating Rita – W Russell)*
GOOLE *(14I – An Inspector Calls – Priestley)*
HELEN *(A Taste Of Honey – Delaney)*
HIRST *(No Man's Land – Pinter)*
INDRA *(A Dream Play – Strindberg)*
IRINA *(Three Sisters – Chekhov)*
KRAPP *(Krapp's Last Tape – Beckett)*
LEEDS *(9N – Strange Interlude – O'Neill)*

LEWIS *(7A – The Sunshine Boys – Simon)*
LOMAN *(10W – Death Of A Salesman – A Miller)*
LUCKY *(Waiting For Godot – Beckett)*
MAHON *(12C – Playboy Of The Western World – Synge)*
MASHA *(Three Sisters – Chekhov)*
MASON *(An Ideal Husband – Wilde)*
MOSCA *(Volpone – Jonson)*
OSCAR *(The Odd Couple – Simon)*
PAULA *(The Second Mrs Tanqueray – Pinero)*
PETER *(A Taste Of Honey – Delaney)*
POZZO *(Waiting For Godot – Beckett)*
PRISM *(9M – The Importance Of Being Earnest – Wilde)*
ROWAN *(12R – Exiles – Joyce)*
SKIPS *(12M – The Lady's Not For Burning – Fry)*
SNEER *(The Critic – Sheridan)*
SONYA *(Uncle Vanya – Ibsen)*
SWABB *(8M – Habeas Corpus – A Bennett)*
SYBIL *(Private Lives – Coward)*
TWINE *(13G – Rookery Nook – Travers)*
VANYA *(Uncle Vanya – Ibsen)*
VASKA *(The Lower Depths – Gorki)*

6

ACARTI *(12M – Blithe Spirit – Coward)*
AMANDA *(Private Lives – Coward)*
ARCHER *(13F – The Beaux' Stratagem – Farquhar)*
BARDIN *(12Z – Enemies – Gorki)*
BOSOLA *(Duchess Of Malfi – Webster)*
CARDEW *(12C – The Importance Of Being Earnest – Wilde)*
DANGLE *(The Critic – Sheridan)*
DuBOIS *(13B – A Streetcar Named Desire – T Williams)*
DYSART *(12M – Equus – P Shaffer)*

EGMONT *(11C – Egmont – Goethe)*
ELVIRA *(Pizarro – Sheridan)*
FISHER *(11B – Billy Liar – Waterhouse/Hall)*
GORING *(14V – An Ideal Husband – Wilde)*
GURTON *(12G – Gammer Gurton's Needle – ?)*
HORNER *(The Country Wife – Wycherley)*
HUNTER *(11P, 13F – No Sex Please, We're British – Marriott/Foot)*
JACOMO *(The Jew Of Malta – Marlowe)*
KELVIL *(A Woman Of No Importance – Wilde)*
MAGNUS *(10K – The Apple Cart – GB Shaw)*
MANGAN *(12A – Heartbreak House – GB Shaw)*
MARKBY *(10L – An Ideal Husband – Wilde)*
MORELL *(13C, 14R – Candida – GB Shaw)*
MORGAN *(11O – Under Milk Wood – D Thomas)*
ONDINE *(Ondine – Giraudoux)*
PARKER *(Lady Windermere's Fan – Wilde)*
PHIPPS *(An Ideal Husband – Wilde)*
PORTER *(11J – Look Back In Anger – Osborne)*
SALOMÉ *(Salomé – Wilde)*
SLOANE *(Entertaining Mr Sloane – Orton)*
STRANG *(10A – Equus – P Shaffer)*
TANNER *(10J – Man And Superman – GB Shaw)*
TAPLOW *(The Browning Version – Rattigan)*
TEAZLE *(10L, 15S – The School For Scandal – Sheridan)*
TINDLE *(10M – Sleuth – A Shaffer)*
VICTOR *(Private Lives – Coward)*
WARREN *(9M – Mrs Warren's Profession – GB Shaw)*

YELENA *(Uncle Vanya – Chekhov)*

7

AIMWELL *(13T – The Beaux'
        Strategem – Farquhar)*
ALCESTE *(Le Misanthrope – Molière)*
AL LEWIS *(The Sunshine Boys –
        Simon)*
ALLMERS *(12E – Little Eyolf – Ibsen)*
ALLONBY *(10M – A Woman Of No
        Importance – Wilde)*
ARSINOE *(Le Misanthrope – Molière)*
BARABAS *(The Jew Of Malta –
        Marlowe)*
CANDOUR *(10M – The School For
        Scandal – Sheridan)*
CHESNEY *(11J – Charley's Aunt –
        B Thomas)*
DARLING *(10M, 11J, 12W, 14M –
        Peter Pan – Barrie)*
DUDGEON *(14R – The Devil's Disciple
        – GB Shaw)*
ELIANTE *(Le Misanthrope – Molière)*
FAIRFAX *(The Importance Of Being
        Earnest – Wilde)*
FAUSTUS *(9D, 13D – Doctor Faustus
        – Marlowe)*
HIGGINS *(12H – Pygmalion –
        GB Shaw)*
LOVEWIT *(The Alchemist – Jonson)*
LUMPKIN *(11T – She Stoops To
        Conquer – Goldsmith)*
MALCOLM *(Bedroom Farce –
        Ayckbourn)*
MANDERS *(13P – Ghosts – Ibsen)*
MARLOWE *(She Stoops To Conquer –
        Goldsmith)*
MOULTON *(The Importance Of Being
        Earnest – Wilde)*
OEDIPUS *(Oedipus Rex – Sophocles)*
PROTEUS *(13J – The Apple Cart –
        GB Shaw)*
ROSALIE *(Lady Windermere's Fan –
        Wilde)*

SOLNESS *(14H – The Master Builder
        – Ibsen)*
SOLVEIG *(Peer Gynt – Ibsen)*
SPOONER *(No Man's Land – Pinter)*
SURFACE *(The School For Scandal –
        Sheridan)*
TORVALD *(A Doll's House – Ibsen)*
TROTTER *(15S – The Mousetrap –
        Christie)*
VOLPONE *(Volpone – Jonson)*
WINSLOW *(13R – The Winslow Boy –
        Rattigan)*
WORSLEY *(13H – A Woman Of No
        Importance – Wilde)*
WOYZECK *(Woyzeck – Büchner)*
WYKEHAM *(14C – Charley's Aunt –
        B Thomas)*

8

ABSOLUTE *(15A – The Rivals –
        Sheridan)*
ANTIGONE *(Antigone – Anouilh)
        (Antigone – Cocteau)
        (Antigone – Sophocles)*
BACKBITE *(The School For Scandal –
        Sheridan)*
BEVERLEY *(Abigail's Party – Leigh)
        (14E – The Rivals –
        Sheridan)*
BIG DADDY *(Cat On A Hot Tin Roof –
        T Williams)*
BOB ACRES *(The Rivals – Sheridan)*
BONIFACE *(Hotel Paradiso –
        Feydeau)*
BREWSTER *(12A, 14M – Arsenic And
        Old Lace – Kesselring)*
CARLISLE *(12L – Lady Windermere's
        Fan – Wilde)*
CÉLIMÈNE *(Le Misanthrope – Molière)*
CHASUBLE *(The Importance Of Being
        Earnest – Wilde)*
CHILTERN *(12L, 14R – An Ideal
        Husband – Wilde)*
CRABTREE *(The School For Scandal
        – Sheridan)*

CRICHTON *(12B – The Admirable Crichton – Barrie)*
DELAHAYE *(Spider's Web – Christie)*
ESTRAGON *(Waiting For Godot – Beckett)*
HASTINGS *(She Stoops To Conquer – Goldsmith)*
JOKANAAN *(Salomé – Wilde)*
JOURDAIN *(Le Bourgeois Gentilhomme – Molière)*
LANGUISH *(13L – The Rivals – Sheridan)*
MALAPROP *(11M – The Rivals – Sheridan)*
MERRIMAN *(The Importance Of Being Earnest – Wilde)*
MIRABELL *(The Way Of The World – Congreve)*
MRS SWABB *(Habeas Corpus – A Bennett)*
PEER GYNT *(Peer Gynt – Ibsen)*
PETER PAN *(Peter Pan – Barrie)*
RANEVSKY *14M – The Cherry Orchard – Chekhov)*
ROBINSON *(14V – Man And Superman – GB Shaw)*
SHOTOVER *(15C – Heartbreak House – GB Shaw)*
STANHOPE *(15C – Journey's End – Sherriff)*
VLADIMIR *(Waiting For Godot – Beckett)*
VULLIAMY *(The Fascinating Foundling – GB Shaw)*
WAGSTAFF *(11M, 15C – Dry Rot – J Chapman)*
WORTHING *(12J – The Importance Of Being Earnest – Wilde)*

9

ANDROCLES *(Androcles And The Lion – GB Shaw)*
BABBERLEY *(13L – Charley's Aunt – B Thomas)*

BARNADINE *(The Jew Of Malta – Marlowe)*
BOUNTIFUL *(13L – The Beaux' Stratagem – Farquhar)*
BRACKNELL *(13L – The Importance Of Being Earnest – Wilde)*
BROADBENT *(12T – John Bull's Other Island – GB Shaw)*
CAVERSHAM *(15E – An Ideal Husband – Wilde)*
DIANA LAKE *(French Without Tears – Rattigan)*
DOOLITTLE *(14E, 15A – Pygmalion – GB Shaw)*
DR FAUSTUS *(Doctor Faustus – Marlowe)*
ESSENDINE *(14G – Present Laughter – Coward)*
HARRY HOPE *(The Iceman Cometh – O'Neill)*
HENRY CARR *(Travesties – Stoppard)*
JACK BLACK *(Under Milk Wood – D Thomas)*
JUNO BOYLE *(Juno And The Paycock – O'Casey)*
KOSTILYOV *(The Lower Depths – Gorki)*
MILLAMANT *(The Way Of The World – Congreve)*
MISS PRISM *(The Importance Of Being Earnest – Wilde)*
MONCRIEFF *(The Importance Of Being Earnest – Wilde)*
MRS WARREN *(Mrs Warren's Profession – GB Shaw)*
NINA LEEDS *(Strange Interlude – O'Neill)*
PICKERING *(Pygmalion – GB Shaw)*
POLYDAMUS *(Marriage À La Mode – Dryden)*
SNEERWELL *(13L – The School For Scandal – Sheridan)*
TANQUERAY *(14P, 15A – The Second Mrs Tanqueray – Pinero)*

TIGER LILY *(Peter Pan – Barrie)*
TRELAWNEY *(13R – Trelawney Of The Wells – Pinero)*
WAYNFLETE *(13L – Captain Brassbound's Conversion – GB Shaw)*
WICKSTEED *(11D, 15D – Habeas Corpus – A Bennett)*
WINGFIELD *(15A – Glass Menagerie – T Williams)*

10

ALAN STRANG *(Equus – P Shaffer)*
ANDREW WYKE *(Sleuth – A Shaffer)*
ARCHIE RICE *(The Entertainer – Osborne)*
BLUNTSCHLI *(Arms And The Man – GB Shaw)*
BRASSBOUND *(Captain Brassbound's Conversion – GB Shaw)*
CAPTAIN CAT *(Under Milk Wood – D Thomas)*
DARLINGTON *(14L – Lady Windermere's Fan – Wilde)*
DAVID BLISS *(Hay Fever – Coward)*
DONNA LUCIA *(Charley's Aunt – B Thomas)*
EARL OF LOAM *(The Admirable Crichton – Barrie)*
HARDCASTLE *(13M – She Stoops To Conquer – Goldsmith)*
HUNSTANTON *(14L – A Woman Of No Importance – Wilde)*
JOHN TANNER *(Man And Superman – GB Shaw)*
KING MAGNUS *(The Apple Cart – GB Shaw)*
LADY MARKBY *(An Ideal Husband – Wilde)*
LADY TEAZLE *(The School For Scandal – Sheridan)*

LARRY DOYLE *(John Bull's Other Island – GB Shaw)*
LICKCHEESE *(Widowers' Houses – GB Shaw)*
MANNINGHAM *(Gaslight – Hamilton)*
MARCHBANKS *(Candida – GB Shaw)*
MILO TINDLE *(Sleuth – A Shaffer)*
MORGENHALL *(The Dock Brief – Mortimer)*
MRS ALLONBY *(A Woman Of No Importance – Wilde)*
MRS CANDOUR *(The School For Scandal – Sheridan)*
MRS DARLING *(Peter Pan – Barrie)*
PONTEFRACT *(14L – A Woman Of No Importance – Wilde)*
SEMPRONIUS *(The Apple Cart – GB Shaw)*
TINKERBELL *(Peter Pan – Barrie)*
UNDERSHAFT *(Major Barbara – GB Shaw)*
WALTER BOON *(You Never Can Tell – GB Shaw)*
WILLY LOMAN *(Death Of A Salesman – A Miller)*
WINDERMERE *(14L – Lady Windermere's Fan – Wilde)*
ZARECHNAYA *(14N – The Seagull – Chekhov)*

11

BILLY FISHER *(Billy Liar – Waterhouse/Hall)*
CAPTAIN HOOK *(Peter Pan – Barrie)*
COUNT EGMONT *(Egmont – Goethe)*
DR WICKSTEED *(Habeas Corpus – A Bennett)*
FREDDIE PAGE *(The Deep Blue Sea – Rattigan)*
ILLINGWORTH *(15L – A Woman Of No Importance – Wilde)*
JACK CHESNEY *(Charley's Aunt – B Thomas)*

JIMMY PORTER *(Look Back In Anger – Osborne)*
JOHN DARLING *(Peter Pan – Barrie)*
JUDITH BLISS *(Hay Fever – Coward)*
KENNETH LAKE *(French Without Tears – Rattigan)*
MRS MALAPROP *(The Rivals – Sheridan)*
MRS WAGSTAFF *(Dry Rot – J Chapman)*
ORGAN MORGAN *(Under Milk Wood – D Thomas)*
PETER HUNTER *(No Sex Please, We're British – Marriott/Foot)*
ROSENCRANTZ *(Rosencrantz And Guildenstern Are Dead – Stoppard)*
SEREBREYAKOV *(Uncle Vanya – Chekhov)*
TAMBURLAINE *(Tamburlaine – Marlowe)*
TONY LUMPKIN *(She Stoops To Conquer – Goldsmith)*
WILLIE CLARK *(The Sunshine Boys – Simon)*

HENRY HIGGINS *(Pygmalion – GB Shaw)*
JOHN WORTHING *(The Importance Of Being Earnest – Wilde)*
LADY CARLISLE *(Lady Windermere's Fan – Wilde)*
LADY CHILTERN *(An Ideal Husband – Wilde)*
MADAME ACARTI *(Blithe Spirit – Coward)*
MARTIN DYSART *(Equus – P Shaffer)*
MATTHEW SKIPS *(The Lady's Not For Burning – Fry)*
RICHARD ROWAN *(Exiles – Joyce)*
TOM BROADBENT *(John Bull's Other Island – GB Shaw)*
WENDY DARLING *(Peter Pan – Barrie)*
ZAKHAR BARDIN *(Enemies – Gorki)*

12

ABBY BREWSTER *(Arsenic And Old Lace – Kesselring)*
ALFRED MANGAN *(Heartbreak House – GB Shaw)*
CECILY CARDEW *(The Importance Of Being Earnest – Wilde)*
CHRISTY MAHON *(Playboy Of The Western World – Synge)*
EYOLF ALLMERS *(Little Eyolf – Ibsen)*
GAMMER GURTON *(Gammer Gurton's Needle – ?)*
GUILDENSTERN *(Rosencrantz And Guildenstern Are Dead – Stoppard)*

13

BLANCHE DuBOIS *(A Streetcar Named Desire – T Williams)*
CANDIDA MORELL *(Candida – GB Shaw)*
DOCTOR FAUSTUS *(Doctor Faustus – Marlowe)*
FRANCES HUNTER *(No Sex Please, We're British – Marriott/Foot)*
FRANCIS ARCHER *(The Beaux' Stratagem – Farquhar)*
GERTRUDE TWINE *(Rookery Nook – Travers)*
HESTER WORSLEY *(A Woman Of No Importance – Wilde)*
JOSEPH PROTEUS *(The Apple Cart – GB Shaw)*

LADY BOUNTIFUL *(The Beaux' Stratagem – Farquhar)*

LADY BRACKNELL *(The Importance Of Being Earnest – Wilde)*

LADY SNEERWELL *(The School For Scandal – Sheridan)*

LADY WAYNFLETE *(Captain Brassbound's Conversion – GB Shaw)*

LORD BABBERLEY *(Charley's Aunt – B Thomas)*

LYDIA LANGUISH *(The Rivals – Sheridan)*

MRS HARDCASTLE *(She Stoops To Conquer – Goldsmith)*

PASTOR MANDERS *(Ghosts – Ibsen)*

RONNIE WINSLOW *(The Winslow Boy – Rattigan)*

ROSE TRELAWNEY *(Trelawney Of The Wells – Pinero)*

THOMAS AIMWELL *(The Beaux' Stratagem – Farquhar)*

14

CHARLES WYKEHAM *(Charley's Aunt – B Thomas)*

DUCHESS OF MALFI *(Duchess Of Malfi – Webster)*

ELIZA DOOLITTLE *(Pygmalion – GB Shaw)*

ENSIGN BEVERLEY *(The Rivals – Sheridan)*

GARRY ESSENDINE *(Present Laughter – Coward)*

HALVARD SOLNESS *(The Master Builder – Ibsen)*

INSPECTOR GOOLE *(An Inspector Calls – Priestley)*

LADY HUNSTANTON *(A Woman Of No Importance – Wilde)*

LADY PONTEFRACT *(A Woman Of No Importance – Wilde)*

LADY WINDERMERE *(Lady Windermere's Fan – Wilde)*

LORD DARLINGTON *(Lady Windermere's Fan – Wilde)*

LORD WINDERMERE *(Lady Windermere's Fan – Wilde)*

MADAME RANEVSKY *(The Cherry Orchard – Chekhov)*

MARTHA BREWSTER *(Arsenic And Old Lace – Kesselring)*

MEPHISTOPHELES *(Doctor Faustus – Marlowe)*

MICHAEL DARLING *(Peter Pan – Barrie)*

NINA ZARECHNAYA *(The Seagull – Chekhov)*

PAULA TANQUERAY *(The Second Mrs Tanqueray – Pinero)*

REVEREND MORELL *(Candida – GB Shaw)*

RICHARD DUDGEON *(The Devil's Disciple – GB Shaw)*

VIOLET ROBINSON *(Man And Superman – GB Shaw)*

VISCOUNT GORING *(An Ideal Husband – Wilde)*

ALFRED DOOLITTLE *(Pygmalion – GB Shaw)*
AMANDA WINGFIELD *(Glass Menagerie – T Williams)*
ANTHONY ABSOLUTE *(The Rivals – Sheridan)*
AUBREY TANQUERAY *(The Second Mrs Tanqueray – Pinero)*
CAPTAIN SHOTOVER *(Heartbreak House – GB Shaw)*
CAPTAIN STANHOPE *(Journey's End – Sherriff)*

COLONEL WAGSTAFF *(Dry Rot – J Chapman)*
DOCTOR WICKSTEED *(Habeas Corpus – A Bennett)*
EARL OF CAVERSHAM *(An Ideal Husband – Wilde)*
LORD ILLINGWORTH *(A Woman Of No Importance – Wilde)*
SERGEANT TROTTER *(The Mousetrap – Christie)*
SIR PETER TEAZLE *(The School For Scandal – Sheridan)*

ARTS

THEATRE – PLAY CHARACTERS – SHAKESPEARE

3

BOY *(Macbeth)*
NYM *(Hen V)*
    (M Wives)
SAY *(7L – Hen VI 2)*
SLY *(14C – T Shrew)*

4

ADAM *(AYLI)*
AJAX *(Tr & Cres)*
ANNE *(8L – Rich III)*
BONA *(Hen VI 3)*
CADE *(8J – Hen VI 2)*
CATO *(9Y – J Caesar)*

DAVY *(Hen IV 2)*
DICK *(Hen VI 2)*
DION *(W Tale)*
DUKE *(AYLI)*
DULL *(L Lab L)*
EROS *(Ant & Cle)*
FANG *(Hen IV 2)*
FORD *(12M – M Wives)*
GREY *(8L – Hen V)*
    (8L – Rich III)
    (13S – Hen V)
HERO *(Much Ado)*
HUME *(8J – Hen VI 2)*
IAGO *(Othello)*
IDEN *(13A – Hen VI 2)*
IRAS *(Ant & Cle)*

JAMY *(Hen V)*
JOHN *(8K – K John)*
    (9F – Rom & Jul)
    (10P – Hen IV 1 & 2)
JUNO *(Tempest)*
LEAR *(8K – K Lear)*
LENA *(12P – J Caesar)*
LUCE *(Com Err)*
LUCY *(Hen VI 1)*
MOTH *(L Lab L)*
    (MN Dream)
PAGE *(11W, 12M – M Wives)*
PETO *(Hen IV 1 & 2)*
PUCK *(MN Dream)*
ROSS *(Macbeth)*
    (8L – Rich II)

SNUG *(MN Dream)*
VAUX *(Hen VIII)*
   (15S – Hen VI 2)
WART *(10T – Hen IV 2)*

5

AARON *(Titus An)*
ALICE *(Hen V)*
ANGUS *(Macbeth)*
ARIEL *(Tempest)*
BAGOT *(Rich II)*
BATES *(Hen V)*
BELCH *(12S – T Night)*
BEVIS *(11G – Hen VI 2)*
BIGOT *(9L – K John)*
BLUNT *(14S – Hen IV 1 & 2)*
BOULT *(Peric)*
BOYET *(L Lab L)*
BUSHY *(Rich II)*
BUTTS *(11D – Hen VIII)*
CAIUS *(Titus An)*
   (11D – M Wives)
CASCA *(J Caesar)*
CELIA *(AYLI)*
CERES *(Tempest)*
CINNA *(J Caesar)*
CLEON *(Peric)*
CORIN *(AYLI)*
COURT *(Hen V)*
CUPID *(Timon)*
CURAN *(K Lear)*
CURIO *(T Night)*
DENNY *(15S – Hen VIII)*
DIANA *(All's Well)*
   (Peric)
EDGAR *(K Lear)*
EGEUS *(MN Dream)*
ELBOW *(M for M)*
EVANS *(12S – M Wives)*
FESTE *(T Night)*
FLUTE *(MN Dream)*
FROTH *(M for M)*
GOBBO *(80, 14L – Mer Ven)*
GOFFE *(12M – Hen VI 2)*

GOWER *(Hen IV 2)*
   (Hen V)
   (Peric)
GREEN *(Rich II)*
HELEN *(Cymbel)*
   (Tr & Cres)
HENRY *(11P – K John)*
   (13H – Hen V)
   (13H – Hen VI 3)
   (14H – Hen IV 1 & 2)
   (14H – Hen VIII)
   (Rich III)
JULIA *(Two Gen)*
LAFEU *(All's Well)*
LEWIS *(Hen V)*
   (K John)
LOUIS *(Hen VI 3)*
LOVEL *(9L – Rich III)*
LUCIO *(M for M)*
MARIA *(L Lab L)*
   (T Night)
MELUN *(K John)*
MENAS *(Ant & Cle)*
MOPSA *(W Tale)*
OSRIC *(Hamlet)*
PARIS *(Rom & Jul)*
   (Tr & Cres)
PERCY *(Hen IV 1 & 2)*
   (9L – Hen IV 1 & 2)
   (10H – Rich II)
   (11T – Hen IV 1)
PETER *(Hen VI 2)*
   (K John)
   (M for M)
   (Rom & Jul)
PHEBE *(AYLI)*
PHILO *(Ant & Cle)*
PINCH *(Com Err)*
POINS *(11E – Hen IV 1 & 2)*
PRIAM *(Tr & Cres)*
REGAN *(K Lear)*
ROBIN *(M Wives)*
ROMEO *(Rom & Jul)*
RUGBY *(M Wives)*
SMITH *(Hen VI 2)*
SNARE *(Hen IV 2)*
SNOUT *(MN Dream)*

SPEED *(Two Gen)*
TIMON *(Timon)*
TITUS *(Timon)*
TUBAL *(Mer Ven)*
VARRO *(J Caesar)*
VIOLA *(T Night)*

6

ADRIAN *(Corio)*
   (Tempest)
AEGEON *(Com Err)*
AENEAS *(Tr & Cres)*
ALEXAS *(Ant & Cle)*
ALONSO *(Tempest)*
AMIENS *(AYLI)*
ANGELO *(Com Err)*
   (M for M)
ANTONY *(Ant & Cle)*
ARTHUR *(K John)*
AUDREY *(AYLI)*
BANQUO *(Macbeth)*
BASSET *(Hen VI 1)*
BIANCA *(Othello)*
   (T Shrew)
BLANCH *(K John)*
BLOUNT *(14S – Rich III)*
BOTTOM *(MN Dream)*
BRUTUS *(12D, 12M –*
   J Caesar)
   (12J – Corio)
BULLEN *(10A – Hen VIII)*
CAESAR *(12J, 14O –*
   Ant & Cle)
   (12J – J Caesar)
CAPHIS *(Timon)*
CASSIO *(Othello)*
CHIRON *(Titus An)*
CICERO *(J Caesar)*
CIMBER *(14M – J Caesar)*
CLITUS *(J Caesar)*
CLOTEN *(Cymbel)*
COBWEB *(MN Dream)*
CURTIS *(T Shrew)*
DENNIS *(AYLI)*
DORCAS *(W Tale)*

DROMIO *(Com Err)*
DUMAIN *(L Lab L)*
DUNCAN *(Macbeth)*
EDMUND *(Hen VI 3)*
         (K Lear)
EDWARD *(Hen VI 2 & 3)*
         (15E − Rich III)
ELINOR *(11Q − K John)*
EMILIA *(Othello)*
         (W Tale)
FABIAN *(T Night)*
FEEBLE *(13F −*
         Hen IV 2)
FENTON *(M Wives)*
GALLUS *(Ant & Cle)*
GEORGE *(Hen VI 3)*
         (Rich III)
GREMIO *(T Shrew)*
GRUMIO *(T Shrew)*
GURNEY *(11J − K John)*
HAMLET *(Hamlet)*
HECATE *(Macbeth)*
HECTOR *(Tr & Cres)*
HELENA *(All's Well)*
         (MN Dream)
HERMIA *(MN Dream)*
HORNER *(12T − Hen VI 2)*
HUBERT *(K John)*
IMOGEN *(Cymbel)*
ISABEL *(Hen V)*
JAQUES *(AYLI)*
JULIET *(M for M)*
         (Rom & Jul)
LAUNCE *(Two Gen)*
LE BEAU *(AYLI)*
LENNOX *(Macbeth)*
LOVELL *(15S − Hen VIII)*
LUCIUS *(J Caesar)*
         (Timon)
         (11C − Cymbel)
         (11Y − Titus An)
MARINA *(Peric)*
MINOLA *(14B − T Shrew)*
MORTON *(Hen IV 2)*
         (10J − Rich III)
MOULDY *(11R − Hen IV 2)*

MUTIUS *(Titus An)*
NESTOR *(Tr & Cres)*
OBERON *(MN Dream)*
OLIVER *(AYLI)*
OLIVIA *(T Night)*
ORSINO *(T Night)*
OSWALD *(K Lear)*
PIERCE *(9S − Rich II)*
PISTOL *(Hen IV 2)*
         (Hen V)
         (M Wives)
POMPEY *(M for M)*
PORTIA *(J Caesar)*
         (Mer Ven)
QUINCE *(MN Dream)*
RIVERS *(10E − Rich III)*
         (10L − Hen VI 3)
RUMOUR *(Hen IV 2)*
SANDYS *(10L − Hen VIII)*
SCALES *(10L − Hen VI 2)*
SCARUS *(Ant & Cle)*
SCROOP *(Hen IV 1 & 2)*
         (Rich II)
         (10L − Hen V)
SEYTON *(Macbeth)*
SHADOW *(11S − Hen IV 2)*
SILIUS *(Ant & Cle)*
SILVIA *(Two Gen)*
SIMPLE *(M Wives)*
SIWARD *(11Y − Macbeth)*
STRATO *(J Caesar)*
TALBOT *(10L − Hen VI 1)*
TAMORA *(Titus An)*
TAURUS *(Ant & Cle)*
THAISA *(Peric)*
THOMAS *(Hen IV 2)*
         (M for M)
THURIO *(Two Gen)*
TRANIO *(T Shrew)*
TYBALT *(Rom & Jul)*
TYRREL *(14S − Rich III)*
URSULA *(Much Ado)*
VERGES *(Much Ado)*
VERNON *(Hen IV 1)*
         (Hen VI 1)
WOLSEY *(14C − Hen VIII)*

7

ABRAHAM *(Rom & Jul)*
ADRIANA *(Com Err)*
AEMILIA *(Com Err)*
AGRIPPA *(Ant & Cle)*
         (15M − Corio)
ALARBUS *(Titus An)*
AMAZONS *(Timon)*
ANTENOR *(Tr & Cres)*
ANTONIO *(Mer Ven)*
         (Much Ado)
         (Tempest)
         (T Night)
         (Two Gen)
BEROWNE *(L Lab L)*
BERTRAM *(All's Well)*
BRANDON *(Hen VIII)*
         (Rich III)
CALCHAS *(Tr & Cres)*
CALIBAN *(Tempest)*
CAMILLO *(W Tale)*
CAPULET *(11L − Rom & Jul)*
CASSIUS *(J Caesar)*
CATESBY *(Rich III)*
CERIMON *(Peric)*
CHARLES *(AYLI)*
         (Hen VI 1)
         (15C − Hen V)
CLAUDIO *(M for M)*
         (Much Ado)
CONRADE *(Much Ado)*
COSTARD *(L Lab L)*
CRANMER *(Hen VIII)*
DIONYZA *(Peric)*
DON JOHN *(Much Ado)*
ELEANOR *(Hen VI 2)*
ESCALUS *(M for M)*
         (Rom & Jul)
ESCANES *(Peric)*
FLAVIUS *(J Caesar)*
         (Timon)
FLEANCE *(Macbeth)*
FRANCIS *(Hen IV 2)*
         (12F − Much Ado)
GONERIL *(K Lear)*

GONZALO *(Tempest)*
GREGORY *(Rom & Jul)*
HELENUS *(Tr & Cres)*
HERBERT *(Rich III)*
HOLLAND *(11J – Hen VI 2)*
HORATIO *(Hamlet)*
HOTSPUR *(Hen IV 1)*
IACHIMO *(Cymbel)*
JESSICA *(Mer Ven)*
LAERTES *(Hamlet)*
LARTIUS *(12T – Corio)*
LAVACHE *(All's Well)*
LAVINIA *(Titus An)*
LEONATO *(Much Ado)*
LEONINE *(Peric)*
LEONTES *(W Tale)*
LEPIDUS *(Ant & Cle)*
  (J Caesar)
LORD SAY *(Hen VI 2)*
LORENZO *(Mer Ven)*
LUCETTA *(Two Gen)*
LUCIANA *(Com Err)*
LYMOGES *(K John)*
MACBETH *(11L – Macbeth)*
MACDUFF *(11L – Macbeth)*
MALCOLM *(Macbeth)*
MARCADE *(L Lab L)*
MARCIUS *(12C, 12Y – Corio)*
MARDIAN *(Ant & Cle)*
MARIANA *(All's Well)*
  (M for M)
MARTEXT *(AYLI)*
MARTIUS *(Titus An)*
MESSALA *(J Caesar)*
MICHAEL *(Hen VI 2)*
  (10S – Hen IV 1)
MIRANDA *(Tempest)*
MONTANO *(Othello)*
MONTJOY *(Hen V)*
MOWBRAY *(11L – Hen IV 2)*
  (13T – Rich II)
NERISSA *(Mer Ven)*
NICANOR *(Corio)*
OCTAVIA *(Ant & Cle)*
OPHELIA *(Hamlet)*
ORLANDO *(AYLI)*

OTHELLO *(Othello)*
PAULINA *(W Tale)*
PERDITA *(W Tale)*
PHYRNIA *(Timon)*
PISANIO *(Cymbel)*
PROTEUS *(Two Gen)*
PROVOST *(M for M)*
PUBLIUS *(J Caesar)*
  (Titus An)
QUICKLY *(14H – Hen IV 1 & 2)*
  (15M – M Wives)
QUINTUS *(Titus An)*
RICHARD *(Hen VI 2 & 3)*
  (Rich II)
  (15R – Rich III)
SALERIO *(Mer Ven)*
SAMPSON *(Rom & Jul)*
SHALLOW *(M Wives)*
  (13R – Hen IV 2)
SHYLOCK *(Mer Ven)*
SILENCE *(Hen IV 2)*
SILVIUS *(AYLI)*
SIMPCOX *(14S – Hen VI 2)*
SLENDER *(M Wives)*
SOLANIO *(Mer Ven)*
SOLINUS *(Com Err)*
STANLEY *(Hen VI 3)*
  (11L – Rich III)
  (15S – Hen VI 2)
THESEUS *(MN Dream)*
THYREUS *(Ant & Cle)*
TITANIA *(MN Dream)*
TRAVERS *(Hen IV 2)*
TRESSEL *(Rich III)*
TROILUS *(Tr & Cres)*
ULYSSES *(Tr & Cres)*
URSWICK *(Rich III)*
VALERIA *(Corio)*
VARRIUS *(Ant & Cle)*
  (M for M)
VAUGHAN *(Rich III)*
VELUTUS *(15S – Corio)*
WILLIAM *(AYLI)*
WITCHES *(Macbeth)*

ABHORSON *(M for M)*
ACHILLES *(Tr & Cres)*
AEMILIUS *(Titus An)*
ANTONIUS *(14M – J Caesar)*
AUFIDIUS *(14T – Corio)*
BARDOLPH *(Hen IV 1)*
    (Hen V)
    (M Wives)
    (12L – Hen IV 2)
BASSANIO *(Mer Ven)*
BEATRICE *(Much Ado)*
BEAUFORT *(Hen VI 2 & 3)*
    (14T – Hen VI 1)
BELARIUS *(Cymbel)*
BENEDICK *(Much Ado)*
BENVOLIO *(Rom & Jul)*
BERKELEY *(Rich III)*
    (12E – Rich II)
BERNARDO *(Hamlet)*
BORACHIO *(Much Ado)*
BULLCALF *(13P – Hen IV 2)*
CAMPEIUS *(Hen VIII)*
CANIDIUS *(Ant & Cle)*
CAPUCIUS *(Hen VIII)*
CHARMIAN *(Ant & Cle)*
CLAUDIUS *(Hamlet)*
    (J Caesar)
CLIFFORD *(12L – Hen VI 3)*
    (13Y – Hen VI 2)
COLVILLE *(15S – Hen IV 2)*
COMINIUS *(Corio)*
CORDELIA *(K Lear)*
CRESSIDA *(Tr & Cres)*
CROMWELL *(Hen VIII)*
DERCETAS *(Ant & Cle)*
DIOMEDES *(Ant & Cle)*
    (Tr & Cres)
DOGBERRY *(Much Ado)*
DON PEDRO *(Much Ado)*
EGLAMOUR *(Two Gen)*
FALSTAFF *(M Wives)*
    (15S – Hen IV 1 & 2)
FASTOLFE *(15S – Hen VI 1)*
FLORIZEL *(W Tale)*

FLUELLEN *(Hen V)*
GADSHILL *(Hen IV 1)*
GARDINER *(Hen VIII)*
GARGRAVE *(Hen VI 1)*
GERTRUDE *(Hamlet)*
GRANDPRÉ *(Hen V)*
GRATIANO *(Mer Ven)*
    (Othello)
GRIFFITH *(Hen VIII)*
HARCOURT *(Hen IV 2)*
HASTINGS *(12L – Hen IV 2)*
    (12L – Hen VI 3)
    (12L – Rich III)
HERMIONE *(W Tale)*
HUMPHREY *(14P – Hen IV 2)*
ISABELLA *(M for M)*
JACK CADE *(Hen VI 2)*
JOHN HUME *(Hen VI 2)*
JOURDAIN *(15M – Hen VI 2)*
KING JOHN *(K John)*
KING LEAR *(K Lear)*
LADY ANNE *(Rich III)*
LADY GREY *(Hen VI 3)*
LAWRENCE *(13F – Rom & Jul)*
LEONARDO *(Mer Ven)*
LEONATUS *(Cymbel)*
LIGARIUS *(J Caesar)*
LODOVICO *(Othello)*
LORD GREY *(Rich III)*
LORD ROSS *(Rich II)*
LUCENTIO *(T Shrew)*
LUCILIUS *(J Caesar)*
    (Timon)
LUCULLUS *(Timon)*
LYSANDER *(MN Dream)*
MAECENAS *(Ant & Cle)*
MALVOLIO *(T Night)*
MARGARET *(Much Ado)*
    (Rich III)
    (13Q – Hen VI 1,
    2 & 3)
MARULLUS *(J Caesar)*
MENELAUS *(Tr & Cres)*
MENTEITH *(Macbeth)*
MERCUTIO *(Rom & Jul)*
MONTAGUE *(12L – Rom & Jul)*

MORTIMER *(12L – Hen IV 1)*
(14E – Hen IV 1)
(14E – Hen VI 1)
(15S – Hen VI 3)
OLD GOBBO *(Mer Ven)*
OVERDONE *(M for M)*
PANDARUS *(Tr & Cres)*
PANDULPH *(K John)*
PANTHINO *(Two Gen)*
PAROLLES *(All's Well)*
PATIENCE *(Hen VIII)*
PERICLES *(Peric)*
PHILARIO *(Cymbel)*
PHILEMON *(Peric)*
PHILOTUS *(Timon)*
PINDARUS *(J Caesar)*
POLONIUS *(Hamlet)*
POMPEIUS *(14S – Ant & Cle)*
PROSPERO *(Tempest)*
RAMBURES *(Hen V)*
RATCLIFF *(Rich III)*
REIGNIER *(Hen VI 1)*
REYNALDO *(Hamlet)*
RODERIGO *(Othello)*
ROSALIND *(AYLI)*
ROSALINE *(L Lab L)*
SELEUCUS *(Ant & Cle)*
STAFFORD *(12L – Hen VI 3)*
(15W – Hen VI 2)
STEPHANO *(Mer Ven)*
(Tempest)
THALIARD *(Peric)*
TIMANDRA *(Timon)*
TITINIUS *(J Caesar)*
TRINCULO *(Tempest)*
VIOLENTA *(All's Well)*
VIRGILIA *(Corio)*
VOLUMNIA *(Corio)*
WHITMORE *(14W – Hen VI 2)*
WILLIAMS *(Hen V)*

9

AGAMEMNON *(Tr & Cres)*
AGUECHEEK *(T Night)*
ALEXANDER *(Tr & Cres)*

ANTIGONUS *(W Tale)*
ANTIOCHUS *(Peric)*
APEMANTUS *(Timon)*
ARCHIBALD *(Hen IV 1)*
ARVIRAGUS *(Cymbel)*
AUTOLYCUS *(W Tale)*
BALTHASAR *(Mer Ven)*
(Much Ado)
(Rom & Jul)
BALTHAZAR *(Com Err)*
BASSIANUS *(Titus An)*
BIONDELLO *(T Shrew)*
BOURCHIER *(Rich III)*
BRABANTIO *(Othello)*
CAITHNESS *(Macbeth)*
CASSANDRA *(Tr & Cres)*
CHATILLON *(K John)*
CLEOMENES *(W Tale)*
CLEOPATRA *(Ant & Cle)*
CONSTANCE *(K John)*
CORNELIUS *(Cymbel)*
(Hamlet)
CYMBELINE *(Cymbel)*
DARDANIUS *(J Caesar)*
DEIPHOBUS *(Tr & Cres)*
DEMETRIUS *(Ant & Cle)*
(MN Dream)
(Titus An)
DESDEMONA *(Othello)*
DOLABELLA *(Ant & Cle)*
DONALBAIN *(Macbeth)*
ELIZABETH *(Rich III)*
ENOBARBUS *(Ant & Cle)*
ERPINGHAM *(Hen V)*
FERDINAND *(L Lab L)*
(Tempest)
FITZWATER *(13L – Rich II)*
FLAMINIUS *(Timon)*
FRANCISCA *(M for M)*
FRANCISCO *(Hamlet)*
(Tempest)
FREDERICK *(AYLI)*
FRIAR JOHN *(Rom & Jul)*
GLANSDALE *(Hen VI 1)*
GLENDOWER *(13O – Hen IV 1)*
GUIDERIUS *(Cymbel)*

GUILDFORD *(Hen VIII)*
HELICANUS *(Peric)*
HIPPOLYTA *(MN Dream)*
HORTENSIO *(T Shrew)*
KATHARINE *(L Lab L)*
        (14Q − Hen VIII)
KATHERINA *(T Shrew)*
KATHERINE *(Hen V)*
LADY PERCY *(Hen IV 1 & 2)*
LORD BIGOT *(K John)*
LORD LOVEL *(Rich III)*
LYCHORIDA *(Peric)*
MACMORRIS *(Hen V)*
MAMILLIUS *(W Tale)*
MARCELLUS *(Hamlet)*
NATHANIEL *(12S − L Lab L)*
PATROCLUS *(Tr & Cres)*
PETRUCHIO *(T Shrew)*
POLIXENES *(W Tale)*
ROTHERHAM *(15T − Rich III)*
SEBASTIAN *(Tempest)*
        (T Night)
SERVILIUS *(Timon)*
SIMONIDES *(Peric)*
SIR PIERCE *(Rich II)*
SOUTHWELL *(13J − Hen VI 2)*
TEARSHEET *(13D − Hen IV 2)*
THERSITES *(Tr & Cres)*
TREBONIUS *(J Caesar)*
VALENTINE *(Titus An)*
        (T Night)
        (Two Gen)
VENTIDIUS *(Ant & Cle)*
        (Timon)
VINCENTIO *(M for M)*
        (T Shrew)
VOLTEMAND *(Hamlet)*
VOLUMNIUS *(J Caesar)*
WOODVILLE *(Hen VI 1)*
YOUNG CATO *(J Caesar)*

10

ALCIBIADES *(Timon)*
ANDROMACHE *(Tr & Cres)*
ANDRONICUS *(15T − Titus An)*
ANNE BULLEN *(Hen VIII)*

ANTIPHOLUS *(Com Err)*
ARCHIDAMUS *(W Tale)*
BARNARDINE *(M for M)*
BRAKENBURY *(Rich III)*
CALPHURNIA *(J Caesar)*
CORIOLANUS *(Corio)*
DON ADRIANO *(L Lab L)*
DUKE OF YORK *(Hen V)*
EARL OF KENT *(Hen IV 2)*
        (K Lear)
EARL RIVERS *(Rich III)*
EUPHRONIUS *(Ant & Cle)*
FORTINBRAS *(Hamlet)*
GOODFELLOW *(15R − MN Dream)*
HENRY PERCY *(Hen IV 1 & 2)*
        (Rich II)
HOLOFERNES *(L Lab L)*
JAQUENETTA *(L Lab L)*
JOHN MORTON *(Rich III)*
LONGAVILLE *(L Lab L)*
LORD RIVERS *(Hen VI 3)*
LORD SANDYS *(Hen VIII)*
LORD SCALES *(Hen VI 2)*
LORD SCROOP *(Hen V)*
LORD TALBOT *(Hen VI 1)*
LYSIMACHUS *(Peric)*
MARGARELON *(Tr & Cres)*
MARK ANTONY *(Ant & Cle)*
MENECRATES *(Ant & Cle)*
MONTGOMERY *(Hen VI 3)*
PRINCE JOHN *(Hen IV 1 & 2)*
PROCULEIUS *(Ant & Cle)*
SATURNINUS *(Titus An)*
SEMPRONIUS *(Timon)*
        (Titus An)
SIR MICHAEL *(Hen IV 1)*
SOMERVILLE *(Hen VI 3)*
STARVELING *(MN Dream)*
THOMAS WART *(Hen IV 2)*
TOUCHSTONE *(AYLI)*
WILLOUGHBY *(14L − Rich II)*

11

ABERGAVENNY *(15L − Hen VIII)*
ARTEMIDORUS *(J Caesar)*

BISHOP OF ELY *(Hen V)*
BOLINGBROKE *(Hen VI 2)*
      (Rich II)
CAIUS LUCIUS *(Cymbel)*
DOCTOR BUTTS *(Hen VIII)*
DOCTOR CAIUS *(M Wives)*
DUKE OF MILAN *(Two Gen)*
EARL OF ESSEX *(K John)*
EDWARD POINS *(Hen IV 1 & 2)*
GEORGE BEVIS *(Hen VI 2)*
JAMES GURNEY *(K John)*
JOHN HOLLAND *(Hen VI 2)*
JOHN OF GAUNT *(Rich II)*
LADY CAPULET *(Rom & Jul)*
LADY MACBETH *(Macbeth)*
LADY MACDUFF *(Macbeth)*
LADY MARSHAL *(Rich II)*
LORD MOWBRAY *(Hen IV 2)*
LORD STANLEY *(Rich III)*
MUSTARDSEED *(MN Dream)*
PHILOSTRATE *(MN Dream)*
PLANTAGENET *(Hen IV 1 & 2)*
PRINCE HENRY *(K John)*
QUEEN ELINOR *(K John)*
RALPH MOULDY *(Hen IV 2)*
ROSENCRANTZ *(Hamlet)*
SIMON SHADOW *(Hen IV 2)*
THOMAS PERCY *(Hen IV 1)*
WILLIAM PAGE *(M Wives)*
YOUNG LUCIUS *(Titus An)*
YOUNG SIWARD *(Macbeth)*

EARL OF SURREY *(Hen IV 2)*
      (Hen VIII)
      (Rich III)
FRIAR FRANCIS *(Much Ado)*
GUILDENSTERN *(Hamlet)*
JOHN BEAUFORT *(Hen VI 1, 2 & 3)*
JULIUS CAESAR *(Ant & Cle)*
      (J Caesar)
JUNIUS BRUTUS *(Corio)*
KING OF FRANCE *(All's Well)*
      (K Lear)
LADY MONTAGUE *(Rom & Jul)*
LADY MORTIMER *(Hen IV 1)*
LORD BARDOLPH *(Hen IV 2)*
LORD CLIFFORD *(Hen VI 2 & 3)*
LORD HASTINGS *(Hen IV 2)*
      (Hen VI 3)
      (Rich III)
LORD STAFFORD *(Hen VI 3)*
MARCUS BRUTUS *(J Caesar)*
MATTHEW GOFFE *(Hen VI 2)*
MISTRESS FORD *(M Wives)*
MISTRESS PAGE *(M Wives)*
PEASEBLOSSOM *(MN Dream)*
POPILIUS LENA *(J Caesar)*
SIR HUGH EVANS *(M Wives)*
SIR NATHANIEL *(L Lab L)*
SIR TOBY BELCH *(T Night)*
THOMAS HORNER *(Hen VI 2)*
TITUS LARTIUS *(Corio)*
WEIRD SISTERS *(Macbeth)*
YOUNG MARCIUS *(Corio)*

12

CAIUS MARCIUS *(Corio)*
DECIUS BRUTUS *(J Caesar)*
DUKE OF ALBANY *(K Lear)*
DUKE OF EXETER *(Hen V)*
      (Hen VI 3)
DUKE OF SURREY *(Rich II)*
DUKE OF VENICE *(Mer Ven)*
      (Othello)
EARL BERKELEY *(Rich II)*
EARL OF OXFORD *(Hen VI 3)*
      (Rich III)

13

ALEXANDER IDEN *(Hen VI 2)*
DOLL TEARSHEET *(Hen IV 2)*
DUCHESS OF YORK *(Rich II)*
      (Rich III)
DUKE OF ALENÇON *(Hen VI 1)*
DUKE OF AUMERLE *(Rich II)*
DUKE OF BEDFORD *(Hen V)*
      (Hen VI 1)
DUKE OF BOURBON *(Hen V)*

DUKE OF NORFOLK *(Hen VI 3)*
(Hen VIII)
(Rich III)
DUKE OF ORLEANS *(Hen V)*
DUKE OF SUFFOLK *(Hen VI 2)*
(Hen VIII)
EARL OF SUFFOLK *(Hen VI 2)*
EARL OF WARWICK *(Hen IV 2)*
(Hen V)
(Hen VI 1, 2 & 3)
FAULCONBRIDGE *(K John)*
FRANCIS FEEBLE *(Hen IV 2)*
FRIAR LAWRENCE *(Rom & Jul)*
HENRY BEAUFORT *(Hen VI 1 & 2)*
HENRY THE FIFTH *(Hen V)*
HENRY THE SIXTH *(Hen VI 1 & 2)*
JOAN LA PUCELLE *(Hen VI 1)*
JOHN SOUTHWELL *(Hen VI 2)*
LORD FITZWATER *(Rich II)*
OWEN GLENDOWER *(Hen IV 1)*
PETER BULLCALF *(Hen IV 2)*
QUEEN MARGARET *(Hen VI 1, 2 & 3)*
ROBERT SHALLOW *(Hen IV 2)*
SIR THOMAS GREY *(Hen V)*
THOMAS MOWBRAY *(Rich II)*
YOUNG CLIFFORD *(Hen VI 2)*

14

BAPTISTA MINOLA *(T Shrew)*
CARDINAL WOLSEY *(Hen VIII)*
CHRISTOPHER SLY *(T Shrew)*
DUKE OF BRITAINE *(Hen V)*
DUKE OF BURGUNDY *(Hen V)*
(Hen VI 1)
(K Lear)
DUKE OF CORNWALL *(K Lear)*
DUKE OF FLORENCE *(All's Well)*
EARL OF PEMBROKE *(Hen VI 3)*
(K John)
EDMUND MORTIMER *(Hen IV 1)*
(Hen VI 1)
HENRY THE EIGHTH *(Hen VIII)*
HENRY THE FOURTH *(Hen IV 1 & 2)*
HOSTESS QUICKLY *(Hen IV 1 & 2)*

LAUNCELOT GOBBO *(Mer Ven)*
LORD WILLOUGHBY *(Rich II)*
MARCUS ANTONIUS *(J Caesar)*
METELLUS CIMBER *(J Caesar)*
OCTAVIUS CAESAR *(Ant & Cle)*
(J Caesar)
PHILIP OF FRANCE *(K John)*
PRINCE HUMPHREY *(Hen IV 2)*
QUEEN KATHARINE *(Hen VIII)*
SAUNDER SIMPCOX *(Hen VI 2)*
SEXTUS POMPEIUS *(Ant & Cle)*
SIR JAMES BLOUNT *(Rich III)*
SIR JAMES TYRREL *(Rich III)*
SIR JOHN STANLEY *(Hen VI 2)*
SIR WALTER BLUNT *(Hen IV 1 & 2)*
SIR WILLIAM LUCY *(Hen VI 1)*
THOMAS BEAUFORT *(Hen VI 1)*
TULLUS AUFIDIUS *(Corio)*
WALTER WHITMORE *(Hen VI 2)*

15

CHARLES THE SIXTH *(Hen V)*
EARL OF CAMBRIDGE *(Hen V)*
EARL OF SALISBURY *(Hen V)*
(Hen VI 1 & 2)
(K John)
(Rich II)
EDMUND OF LANGLEY *(Rich II)*
EDWARD THE FOURTH *(Rich III)*
LORD ABERGAVENNY *(Hen VIII)*
MARGERY JOURDAIN *(Hen VI 2)*
MARQUIS OF DORSET *(Rich III)*
MENENIUS AGRIPPA *(Corio)*
MISTRESS QUICKLY *(M Wives)*
PRINCE OF ARRAGON *(Mer Ven)*
PRINCE OF MOROCCO *(Mer Ven)*
RICHARD THE THIRD *(Rich III)*
ROBIN GOODFELLOW *(MN Dream)*
SICINIUS VELUTUS *(Corio)*
SIR ANTHONY DENNY *(Hen VIII)*
SIR HUGH MORTIMER *(Hen VI 3)*
SIR JOHN COLVILLE *(Hen IV 2)*
SIR JOHN FALSTAFF *(Hen IV 1 & 2)*
(M Wives)
SIR JOHN FASTOLFE *(Hen VI 1)*

SIR JOHN MORTIMER *(Hen VI 3)*
SIR NICHOLAS VAUX *(Hen VIII)*
SIR THOMAS LOVELL *(Hen VIII)*

THOMAS ROTHERHAM *(Rich III)*
TITUS ANDRONICUS *(Titus An)*
WILLIAM STAFFORD *(Hen VI 2)*

ARTS

THEATRE – PLAYS

* = Alternative title

3

FEN *(C Churchill)*
ION *(Euripides)*
RUR *(Capek)*
SUS *(Keeffe)*

4

AJAX *(Gide)*
　　　(Sophocles)
BAAL *(Brecht)*
BENT *(Sherman)*
FAME *(A Miller)*
GOOD *(CP Taylor)*
HOME *(Storey)*
KEAN *(Sartre)*
LEAR *(Bond)*
LENZ *(Büchner)*
LOOT *(Orton)*
NOT I *(Beckett)*
PIAF *(Gems)*
PLAY *(Beckett)*
QUAD *(Beckett)*
ROPE *(Hamilton)*
ROSS *(Rattigan)*

VERA *(Wilde)*
ZACK *(Brighouse)*

5

ASHES *(Rudkin)*
BETZI *(Douglas-Home)*
BRAND *(Ibsen)*
CINNA *(Corneille)*
EH JOE *(Beckett)*
ENJOY *(A Bennett)*
EQUUS *(P Shaffer)*
FAUST *(Goethe)*
HELEN *(Euripides)*
LE CID *(Corneille)*
LIOLA *(Pirandello)*
MEDEA *(Euripides)*
　　　(Seneca)
MÉDÉE *(Anouilh)*
POLLY *(Gay)*
ROOTS *(Wesker)*
SAVED *(Bond)*
TANGO *(Mrozek)*
TANYA *(Arbuzov)*
THARK *(Travers)*
YERMA *(Lorca)*

6

ADVENT *(Strindberg)*
BECKET *(Anouilh)*
BUTLEY *(S Gray)*
CLIZIA *(Machiavelli)*
CLOUDS *(Frayn)*
DEIDRE *(Yeats)*
DRY ROT *(J Chapman)*
EASTER *(Strindberg)*
EGMONT *(Goethe)*
ESCAPE *(Galsworthy)*
EXILED *(Galsworthy)*
EXILES *(Joyce)*
GENEVA *(GB Shaw)*
GHOSTS *(Ibsen)*
HAMLET *(Shakespeare)*
HENRY V *(Shakespeare)*
IVANOV *(Chekhov)*
LUTHER *(Osborne)*
MÉLITE *(Corneille)*
MOTHER *(Capek)*
ONDINE *(Giraudoux)*
ORPHÉE *(Cocteau)*
OWNERS *(C Churchill)*
PHÈDRE *(Racine)*
PLENTY *(Hare)*

PRAVDA *(Hare & Brenton)*
SALOMÉ *(Wilde)*
SLEUTH *(A Shaffer)*
STRIFE *(Galsworthy)*
TARARE *(Beaumarchais)*
UBU-ROI *(Jarry)*
WELDED *(O'Neill)*

THE ROOM *(Pinter)*
VERDICT *(Christie)*
VICTORY *(Barker)*
VOLPONE *(Jonson)*
WOYZECK *(Büchner)*
YONADAB *(P Shaffer)*

THE MAIDS *(Genet) *4*
THE ROVER *(Behn)*
THE TUTOR *(Brecht)*
THE VISIT *(Dürrenmatt)*
THE WASPS *(Aristophanes)*
TOP GIRLS *(C Churchill)*
WRECKERS *(Edgar)*

7

ALL OVER *(Albee)*
AMADEUS *(P Shaffer)*
ATHALIE *(Racine)*
CALVARY *(Yeats)*
CANDIDA *(Shaw)*
CLAVIGO *(Goethe)*
DESTINY *(Edgar)*
ELECTRA *(Euripides)*
        (Sophocles)
ENDGAME *(Beckett)*
ENEMIES *(Gorki)*
EPICENE *(Jonson)*
EUGÉNIE *(Beaumarchais)*
HAPGOOD *(Stoppard)*
HENRY IV *(Shakespeare)*
HENRY VI *(Shakespeare)*
JUMPERS *(Stoppard)*
KNUCKLE *(Hare)*
MACBETH *(Shakespeare)*
MARTINE *(Bernard)*
OEDIPUS *(Seneca)*
ORESTES *(Euripides)*
OTHELLO *(Shakespeare)*
OUR TOWN *(T Wilder)*
PIMPLES *(Bleasdale)*
PIZARRO *(Sheridan)*
PLUNDER *(Travers)*
REVENGE *(Brenton)*
ROCKABY *(Beckett)*
SEJANUS *(Jonson)*
SHEPPEY *(Maugham)*
SILENCE *(Pinter)*
THE BEAR *(Chekhov)*
THE LARK *(Anouilh) *1*
THE ROCK *(TS Eliot)*

8

ALCESTIS *(Euripides)*
ANTIGONE *(Anouilh)*
        (Cocteau)
        (Sophocles)
BÉRÉNICE *(Racine)*
BETRAYAL *(Pinter)*
CATALINA *(Ibsen)*
CATILINE *(Jonson)*
CLARENCE *(Tarkington)*
CRACKERS *(Bleasdale)*
DR BOLFRY *(Bridie)*
DUTCHMAN *(Baraka)*
EDWARD II *(Marlowe)*
FOCO NOVO *(Pomerance)*
GASLIGHT *(Hamilton)*
HAY FEVER *(Coward)*
IRONHAND *(Arden)*
KING JOHN *(Shakespeare)*
KING LEAR *(Shakespeare)*
LE BALCON *(Genet) *2*
LE DINDON *(Feydeau)*
MARY ROSE *(Barrie)*
OLD TIMES *(Pinter)*
OPERETTE *(Coward)*
PEER GYNT *(Ibsen)*
PENELOPE *(Maugham)*
PERICLES *(Shakespeare)*
PETER PAN *(Barrie)*
PLATONOV *(Chekhov)*
SALONIKA *(Page)*
TARTUFFE *(Molière)*
TEA PARTY *(Pinter)*
THE BIRDS *(Aristophanes)*
THE CENCI *(Shelley)*
THE FLIES *(Sartre) *3*
THE FROGS *(Aristophanes)*

9

AGAMEMNON *(Aeschylus)*
ALL MY SONS *(A Miller)*
A NIGHT OUT *(Pinter)*
BILLY LIAR *(Hall &*
        Waterhouse)
BLOOD KNOT *(Fugard)*
CAVALCADE *(Coward)*
CITY SUGAR *(Poliakoff)*
CYMBELINE *(Shakespeare)*
DANDY DICK *(Pinero)*
DIE RÄUBER *(Schiller) *5*
DIRTY WORK *(Travers)*
DR FAUSTUS *(Marlowe)*
FLAREPATH *(Rattigan)*
GETTING ON *(A Bennett)*
HAPPY DAYS *(Beckett)*
HENRY VIII *(Shakespeare)*
IPHIGÉNIE *(Goethe)*
        (Racine)
L'ALOUETTE *(Anouilh) *1*
LA SAUVAGE *(Anouilh) *6*
LES BONNES *(Genet) *4*
LISTENING *(Albee)*
LUNCH HOUR *(Mortimer)*
MISS JULIE *(Strindberg)*
MR WHATNOT *(Ayckbourn)*
NOISES OFF *(Frayn)*
OVERHEARD *(Ustinov)*
OVERRULED *(GB Shaw)*
PHILASTER *(Beaumont &*
        Fletcher)
POETASTER *(Jonson)*
PYGMALION *(GB Shaw)*
QUADRILLE *(Coward)*
RICHARD II *(Shakespeare)*

ARTS – THEATRE – PLAYS

SAINT JOAN *(GB Shaw)*
SANTA CRUZ *(Frisch)*
THE CASTLE *(Barker)*
THE CHAIRS *(Ionesco)*
THE CIRCLE *(Maugham)*
THE CLOUDS *(Aristophanes)*
THE CRITIC *(Sheridan)*
THE DEVILS *(Whiting)*
THE FATHER *(Strindberg)*
THE LESSON *(Ionesco)*
THE RIVALS *(Sheridan)*
THE VORTEX *(Coward)*
TOM AND VIV *(Hastings)*
WHITE LIES *(P Shaffer)*

10

ALCIBIADES *(Otway)*
ALL FOR LOVE *(Dryden)*
AMPHITRYON *(Giraudoux)*
          (Plautus)
ANDROMACHE *(Euripides)*
          (Racine)
AURENG-ZEBE *(Dryden)*
BORSTAL BOY *(Behan)*
CAMINO REAL *(T Williams)*
CHAPTER TWO *(Simon)*
CONFUSIONS *(Ayckbourn)*
CORIOLANUS *(Shakespeare)*
DEAR BRUTUS *(Barrie)*
DIRTY LINEN *(Stoppard)*
EAST OF SUEZ *(Maugham)*
EASY VIRTUE *(Coward)*
GENTLE JACK *(Bolt)*
GHOST TRAIN *(Ridley)*
GUSTAF VASA *(Strindberg)*
HIPPOLYTUS *(Euripides)*
INTERMEZZO *(Giraudoux)*
JAKE'S WOMEN *(Simon)*
LES MOUCHES *(Sartre)* *3
LYSISTRATA *(Aristophanes)*
MARY STUART *(Schiller)* *7
OEDIPUS REX *(Sophocles)*
ON THE ROCKS *(GB Shaw)*
PLAZA SUITE *(Simon)*

PURPLE DUST *(O'Casey)*
RHINOCEROS *(Ionesco)*
RICHARD III *(Shakespeare)*
SPIDER'S WEB *(Christie)*
THE BACCHAE *(Euripides)*
THE BALCONY *(Genet)* *2
THE CHANCES *(Fletcher)*
THE DRESSER *(Harwood)*
THE DYNASTS *(Hardy)*
THE HOSTAGE *(Behan)*
THE KITCHEN *(Wesker)*
THE OLD ONES *(Wesker)*
THE RELAPSE *(Vanbrugh)*
THE ROBBERS *(Schiller)* *5
THE SANDBOY *(Frayn)*
THE SEAGULL *(Chekhov)*
THE TEMPEST *(Shakespeare)*
THE WEDDING *(Chekhov)*
TRAVESTIES *(Stoppard)*
TURKEY TIME *(Travers)*
UNCLE VANYA *(Chekhov)*
WEST OF SUEZ *(Osborne)*

11

A DOLL'S HOUSE *(Ibsen)*
ALL FALL DOWN *(Arden)*
ALL THAT FALL *(Beckett)*
A SLIGHT ACHE *(Pinter)*
AS YOU LIKE IT *(Shakespeare)*
BITTER SWEET *(Coward)*
BLACK COFFEE *(Christie)*
BRITANNICUS *(Racine)*
DEAR OCTOPUS *(D Smith)*
HEDDA GABLER *(Ibsen)*
IBSEN'S GHOST *(Barrie)*
IT IS WRITTEN *(Dürrenmatt)*
JOKING APART *(Ayckbourn)*
JOURNEY'S END *(Sherriff)*
LES DEUX AMIS *(Beaumarchais)*
LITTLE EYOLF *(Ibsen)*
LOVE FOR LOVE *(Congreve)*
LOVE IN A WOOD *(Wycherley)*
LOVE'S COMEDY *(Ibsen)*
MARIA STUART *(Schiller)* *7

MISALLIANCE *(GB Shaw)*
PANDORA'S BOX *(Wedekind)*
PHILOCTETES *(Sophocles)*
PHOTO FINISH *(Ustinov)*
ROOKERY NOOK *(Travers)*
ROSMERSHOLM *(Ibsen)*
TAMBURLAINE *(Marlowe)*
THE BANKRUPT *(Ostrovsky)*
THE BOY DAVID *(Barrie)*
THE CRUCIBLE *(A Miller)*
THE GAMBLERS *(Stoppard)*
THE HOTHOUSE *(Pinter)*
THE PERSIANS *(Aeschylus)*
THE PROPOSAL *(Chekhov)*
THE SKIN GAME *(Galsworthy)*
THE STRONGER *(Strindberg)*
THE WILD DUCK *(Ibsen)*
TIME PRESENT *(Osborne)*
WAY UPSTREAM *(Ayckbourn)*
WOMAN IN MIND *(Ayckbourn)*

12

A FAIR QUARREL *(Middleton & Rowley)*
AFTER THE FALL *(A Miller)*
A MAN OF HONOUR *(Maugham)*
ANNA CHRISTIE *(O'Neill)*
AUTUMN CROCUS *(D Smith)*
BEDROOM FARCE *(Ayckbourn)*
BLITHE SPIRIT *(Coward)*
BLOOD WEDDING *(Lorca)*
BORIS GODUNOV *(Pushkin)*
BUSSY D'AMBOIS *(G Chapman)*
CAUSE CÉLÈBRE *(Rattigan)*
CHARLEY'S AUNT *(B Thomas)*
DOCTOR BOLFRY *(Bridie)*
DONKEY'S YEARS *(Frayn)*
FALLEN ANGELS *(Coward)*
FAMILY VOICES *(Pinter)*
FORTY YEARS ON *(A Bennett)*
HABEAS CORPUS *(A Bennett)*
IT'S A MADHOUSE *(Bleasdale)*
JULIUS CAESAR *(Shakespeare)*
LA MANDRAGOLA *(Machiavelli)*

LES PLAIDEURS *(Racine)* *8
MAJOR BARBARA *(GB Shaw)*
MAKE AND BREAK *(Frayn)*
MAKING TRACKS *(Ayckbourn)*
ONE FOR THE POT *(Cooney)*
PRIVATE LIVES *(Coward)*
SARDANAPALUS *(Byron)*
SIMPLE SPYMEN *(J Chapman)*
STAGS AND HENS *(W Russell)*
THE ALCHEMIST *(Jonson)*
THE ANATOMIST *(Bridie)*
THE APPLE CART *(GB Shaw)*
THE BORDERERS *(Wordsworth)*
THE BROKEN JUG *(Kleist)*
THE CARETAKER *(Pinter)*
THE DOCK BRIEF *(Mortimer)*
THE EUMENIDES *(Aeschylus)*
THE HOUR GLASS *(Yeats)*
THE LITIGANTS *(Racine)* *8
THE MOUSETRAP *(Christie)*
THE ODD COUPLE *(Simon)*
THE PUBLIC EYE *(P Shaffer)*
THE SILVER BOX *(Galsworthy)*
THE WOOD DEMON *(Chekhov)*
THE YOUNG IDEA *(Coward)*
THREE SISTERS *(Chekhov)*
TOTAL ECLIPSE *(Hampton)*
TRANSLATIONS *(Friel)*
TWELFTH NIGHT *(Shakespeare)*
TYRANNIC LOVE *(Dryden)*
ZIGGER ZAGGER *(Terson)*

13

ABIGAIL'S PARTY *(Leigh)*
ABSENT FRIENDS *(Ayckbourn)*
AFTER MAGRITTE *(Stoppard)*
AFTER THE DANCE *(Rattigan)*
A PATRIOT FOR ME *(Osborne)*
ARMS AND THE MAN *(GB Shaw)*
A TASTE OF HONEY *(Delaney)*
A WINTER COMEDY *(Fry)*
BLOOD BROTHERS *(W Russell)*
DESERT HIGHWAY *(Priestley)*
DOCTOR FAUSTUS *(Marlowe)*

EDUCATING RITA *(W Russell)*
FIDDLERS THREE *(Christie)*
GOODBYE HOWARD *(Linney)*
HOBSON'S CHOICE *(Brighouse)*
HOTEL PARADISO *(Feydeau)*
IN CELEBRATION *(Storey)*
LABURNUM GROVE *(Priestley)*
LA VOIX HUMAINE *(Cocteau)*
LE MISANTHROPE *(Molière)* *9
MARCO MILLIONS *(O'Neill)*
NIGHT MUST FALL *(E Williams)*
ON THE HIGH ROAD *(Chekhov)*
PRESS CUTTINGS *(GB Shaw)*
QUALITY STREET *(Barrie)*
RESTLESS HEART *(Anouilh)* *6
TEN TIMES TABLE *(Ayckbourn)*
THE ACHARNIANS *(Aristophanes)*
THE AMEN CORNER *(Baldwin)*
THE CHANGELING *(Middleton &*
                          Rowley)
THE COLLECTION *(Pinter)*
THE DUMB WAITER *(Pinter)*
THE INSECT PLAY *(Capek)*
THE JEW OF MALTA *(Marlowe)*
THE KINGFISHER *(Douglas-Home)*
THE LINDEN TREE *(Priestley)*
THE MAGISTRATE *(Pinero)*
THE MATCHMAKER *(T Wilder)*
THE OLD COUNTRY *(A Bennett)*
THE PRIVATE EAR *(P Shaffer)*
THE ROSE TATTOO *(T Williams)*
THE SPIDER'S WEB *(Christie)*
THE TWIN RIVALS *(Farquhar)*
THE TWO FOSCARI *(Byron)*
THE WHITE DEVIL *(Webster)*
THE WINSLOW BOY *(Rattigan)*
TIMON OF ATHENS *(Shakespeare)*
TORQUATO TASSO *(Goethe)*
UNDER MILK WOOD *(D Thomas)*
VENUS OBSERVED *(Fry)*

A PIECE OF MY MIND *(Nichols)*
BOESMAN AND LENA *(Fugard)*
DUCHESS OF MALFI *(Webster)*
GETTING MARRIED *(GB Shaw)*
GLASS MENAGERIE *(T Williams)*
GREAT CATHERINE *(GB Shaw)*
KRAPP'S LAST TAPE *(Beckett)*
LOVE AND A BOTTLE *(Farquhar)*
MAN AND SUPERMAN *(GB Shaw)*
RIDERS TO THE SEA *(Synge)*
ROMEO AND JULIET *(Shakespeare)*
SEPARATE TABLES *(Rattigan)*
THE CORN IS GREEN *(E Williams)*
THE COUNTRY GIRL *(Odets)*
THE COUNTRY WIFE *(Wycherley)*
THE DEEP BLUE SEA *(Rattigan)*
THE ENTERTAINER *(Osborne)*
THE FIRE RAISERS *(Frisch)*
THE GHOST SONATA *(Strindberg)*
THE LITTLE FOXES *(Hellman)*
THE LOWER DEPTHS *(Gorki)*
THE LUCKY CHANCE *(Behn)*
THE MAN FROM HOME *(Tarkington)*
THE MISANTHROPE *(Molière)* *9
THE OLD BACHELOR *(Congreve)*
THE PHILANDERER *(GB Shaw)*
THE QUARE FELLOW *(Behan)*
THE SON OF LIGHT *(Rudkin)*
THE TROJAN WOMEN *(Euripides)*
THE WINTER'S TALE *(Shakespeare)*
THIS HAPPY BREED *(Coward)*
TOAD OF TOAD HALL *(Milne)*
VENICE PRESERV'D *(Otway)*
WIDOWERS' HOUSES *(GB Shaw)*
WITHIN THE GATES *(O'Casey)*
WURZEL-FLUMMERY *(Milne)*

15

AMERICAN BUFFALO *(Mamet)*
BARTHOLOMEW FAIR *(Jonson)*
CALIFORNIA SUITE *(Simon)*
DANGEROUS CORNER *(Priestley)*
DESIGN FOR LIVING *(Coward)*

14

AFORE NIGHT COME *(Rudkin)*
AN IDEAL HUSBAND *(Wilde)*

DOWN THE DOCK ROAD *(Bleasdale)*
EACH IN HIS OWN WAY *(Pirandello)*
FLOWERING CHERRY *(Bolt)*
HEARTBREAK HOUSE *(GB Shaw)*
IN FIVE YEARS' TIME *(Lorca)*
LOOK BACK IN ANGER *(Osborne)*
MARRIAGE À LA MODE *(Dryden)*
NORMAN CONQUESTS *(Ayckbourn)*
PAID ON BOTH SIDES *(Auden)*
PRESENT LAUGHTER *(Coward)*
RICHARD CORK'S LEG *(Behan)*
SPRING AWAKENING *(Wedekind)*
TAKEN IN MARRIAGE *(Babe)*
THE AMOROUS PRAWN *(Kimmins)*
THE BEGGAR'S OPERA *(Gay)*
THE CONSTANT WIFE *(Maugham)*
THE DEVIL IS AN ASS *(Jonson)*

THE DOUBLE-DEALER *(Congreve)*
THE ICEMAN COMETH *(O'Neill)*
THE MAN OF DESTINY *(GB Shaw)*
THE POPE'S WEDDING *(Bond)*
THE PROVOKED WIFE *(Vanbrugh)*
THE SAVAGE PARADE *(A Shaffer)*
THE SILVER TASSIE *(O'Casey)*
THE SUNSHINE BOYS *(Simon)*
THREEPENNY OPERA *(Brecht)*
TITUS ANDRONICUS *(Shakespeare)*
TWO NOBLE KINSMEN *(Shakespeare)*
VASSA SHELESNOVA *(Gorki)*
WAITING FOR GODOT *(Beckett)*
WATCH IT COME DOWN *(Osborne)*
WATCH ON THE RHINE *(Hellman)*
YOU NEVER CAN TELL *(GB Shaw)*

ASTRONOMY

PLANETS & SATELLITES

(A) = Asteroid   (C) = Comet   (S) = Satellite

4

EROS *(A)*
HEBE *(A)*
IRIS *(A)*
ISIS *(A)*
JUNO *(A)*
LEDA *(S-Jupiter)*
MARS
MOON *(S-Earth)*
NYSA *(A)*
PUCK *(S-Uranus)*
RHEA *(S-Saturn)*

5

ARIEL *(S-Uranus)*
ATLAS *(S-Saturn)*
CARME *(S-Jupiter)*
CERES *(A)*
DIONE *(S-Saturn)*
EARTH
ELARA *(S-Jupiter)*
FLORA *(A)*
JANUS *(S-Saturn)*
METIS *(S-Jupiter)*
MIMAS *(S-Saturn)*
PLUTO
THEBE *(S-Jupiter)*
TITAN *(S-Saturn)*
VENUS
VESTA *(A)*

6

ANANKE *(S-Jupiter)*
AUSTIN *(C)*

BIANCA *(S-Uranus)*
BIELA'S *(C)*
CHARON *(S-Pluto)*
CHIRON *(A)*
DAVIDA *(A)*
DEIMOS *(S-Mars)*
EGERIA *(A)*
ENCKE'S *(C)*
EUROPA *(S-Jupiter)*
HELENE *(S-Saturn)*
HYGEIA *(A)*
ICARUS *(A)*
JULIET *(S-Uranus)*
NEREID *(S-Neptune)*
OBERON *(S-Uranus)*
PALLAS *(A)*
PHOBOS *(S-Mars)*
PHOEBE *(S-Saturn)*
PORTIA *(S-Uranus)*
PROKNE *(A)*
PSYCHE *(A)*
SAPPHO *(A)*
SATURN
SINOPE *(S-Jupiter)*
TETHYS *(S-Saturn)*
THALIA *(A)*
TRITON *(S-Neptune)*
URANUS

7

ASTRAEA *(A)*
BELINDA *(S-Uranus)*
CALYPSO *(S-Saturn)*
CAMILLA *(A)*
DONATI'S *(C)*
EUNOMIA *(A)*
EUTERPE *(A)*

FORTUNA *(A)*
HALLEY'S *(C)*
HARMONA *(A)*
HIDALGO *(A)*
HIMALIA *(S-Jupiter)*
IAPETUS *(S-Saturn)*
JUPITER
MERCURY
MIRANDA *(S-Uranus)*
NEPTUNE
OPHELIA *(S-Uranus)*
PANDORA *(S-Saturn)*
TELESTO *(S-Saturn)*
TITANIA *(S-Uranus)*
UMBRIEL *(S-Uranus)*

8

ACHILLES *(A)*
ADRASTEA *(S-Jupiter)*
AMALTHEA *(S-Jupiter)*
CALLISTO *(S-Jupiter)*
CORDELIA *(S-Uranus)*
CRESSIDA *(S-Uranus)*
GANYMEDE *(S-Jupiter)*
HYPERION *(S-Saturn)*
LYSITHEA *(S-Jupiter)*
MASSALIA *(A)*
PASIPHAE *(S-Jupiter)*
ROSALIND *(S-Uranus)*

9

COMET WEST *(C)*
DESDEMONA *(S-Uranus)*
ENCELADUS *(S-Saturn)*
HERCULINA *(A)*
IKEYA-SEKI *(C)*

10

AMPHITRITE *(A)*
EPIMETHEUS *(S-Saturn)*
EUPHROSYNE *(A)*
KOUHOUTEK'S *(C)*
PROMETHEUS *(S-Saturn)*

11

AREND-ROLAND *(C)*

12

PONS-WINNECKE *(C)*

ASTRONOMY

STARS & CONSTELLATIONS

(C) = Constellation   (CL) = Cluster/group   (G) = Galaxy   (N) = Nebula
* = Alternative name

3

ARA *(C) *1*
CUP *(C) *2*
FLY *(C) *3*
FOX *(C) *4*
LEO *(C) *5*
NET *(C) *6*
RAM *(C) *7*
SUN

4

ALYA
APUS *(C) *9*
ARGO *(C)*
BULL *(C) *10*
CAPH
COMA *(CL)*
CONE *(N)*
CRAB *(C) *11, (N)*

CROW *(C) *12*
CRUX *(C) *13*
DOVE *(C) *14*
ENIF
GOAT *(C) *15*
GRUS *(C) *16*
HARE *(C) *17*
IZAR **18*
KEEL *(C) *19*
LION *(C) *5*
LYNX *(C)*
LYRA *(C) *20*
LYRE *(C) *20*
MAIA
MIRA
NAOS
PAVO *(C) *21*
RING *(N)*
SADR
SKAT
SWAN *(C) *22, (N) *23*
VEGA

VEIL *(N)*
VELA *(C) *24*
WOLF *(C) *25*

5

ACRUX
ALCOR
ALGOL
ALTAR *(C) *1*
ARIES *(C) *7*
ARNEB
ARROW *(C) *26*
ATLAS
CETUS *(C) *27*
CRANE *(C) *16*
CURSA
DABIH
DENEB
DRACO *(C) *28*
DUBHE

EAGLE *(C) *29*
ER RAI
GEMMA **30*
HADAR
HAMAL
HARIS
HELIX *(N)*
HOMAM
HYDRA *(C) *31*
INDUS *(C) *32*
LEPUS *(C) *17*
LEVEL *(C) *33*
LIBRA *(C) *34*
LUPUS *(C) *25*
MATAR
MENSA *(C) *35*
MERAK
MIZAR
MUSCA *(C) *3*
NORMA *(C) *33*
NUNKI
OMEGA *(N) *23*

ORION *(C) *36, (N)*
PYXIS *(C) *37*
RIGEL
RIVER *(C) *38*
SABIK
SAILS *(C) *24*
SAIPH
SPICA
STERN *(C) *39*
TWINS *(C) *40*
VIRGO *(C) *41, (G)*
WEZEN
WHALE *(C) *27*
ZOSMA

6

ACAMAR
ADHARA
ALAMAK
ALBALI
ALFIRK
ALGEDI
ALIOTH
ALNAIR
AL NASL
ALTAIR
ALUDRA
ANTLIA *(C) *42*
AQUILA *(C) *29*
ARCHER *(C) *43*
AURIGA *(C) *44*
BOÖTES *(C) *45*
CAELUM *(C) *46*
CANCER *(C) *11*
CARINA *(C) *19*
CASTOR
CHISEL *(C) *46*
CORVUS *(C) *12*
CRATER *(C) *2*
CYGNUS *(C) *22*
DIADEM
DORADO *(C) *47*
DRAGON *(C) *28*
EL NATH

FISHES *(C) *48*
FORNAX *(C) *49*
GEMINI *(C) *40*
GIENAH
HUNTER *(C) *36*
HYADES *(CL)*
HYDRUS *(C)*
INDIAN *(C) *32*
LAGOON *(N)*
LIZARD *(C) *50*
MARKAB
MEGREZ
MENKAR
MEROPE
MIMOSA
MIRACH
MIRZAM
NEKKAR
OCTANS *(C) *51*
OCTANT *(C) *51*
PHECDA
PICTOR *(C) *52*
PISCES *(C) *48*
PLOUGH *(CL)*
POLLUX
PUPPIS *(C) *39*
RUKBAT
SATURN *(N)*
SCALES *(C) *34*
SCHEAT
SCUTUM *(C) *53*
SHIELD *(C) *53*
SIRIUS **54*
SIRRAH **55*
TAURUS *(C) *10*
THUBAN
TOUCAN *(C) *56*
TRIFID *(N)*
TUCANA *(C) *56*
VIRGIN *(C) *41*
VOLANS *(C) *57*

7

ACUBENS

AIR PUMP *(C) *42*
ALBIREO
AL CHIBA
ALCYONE
ALGENIB
ALGIEBA
ALNILAM
ALNITAK
ALPHARD
ALSHAIN
ANTARES
ARRAKIS
BEEHIVE *(CL) *58*
CANOPUS
CAPELLA
CELEANO
CENTAUR *(C) *59*
CEPHEUS
COLUMBA *(C) *14*
COMPASS *(C) *37*
DOG STAR **54*
DOLPHIN *(C) *60*
ELECTRA
ELTANIN
FURNACE *(C) *49*
GIRAFFE *(C) *61*
GOMEISA
LACERTA *(C) *50*
MINTAKA
NASHIRA
PAVONIS **62*
PEACOCK *(C) *21, *62*
PEGASUS *(C) *63*
PERSEUS *(C)*
PHERCAD
PHOENIX *(C)*
PLEIONE
POLARIS **64*
PORRIMA
PROCYON
REGULUS
ROSETTE *(N)*
ROTANEV
SAGITTA *(C) *26*
SCHEDAR
SEA GOAT *(C) *15*

ASTRONOMY – STARS & CONSTELLATIONS

YED POSTERIOR
ZUBENELAKRAB

13

ALPHA CENTAURI
BERENICE'S HAIR *(C)* *86
CANES VENATICI *(C)* *82
COMA BERENICES *(C)* *86
KAFFALJIDHMAH
KAUS AUSTRALIS
NORTHERN CROWN *(C)* *87
OMEGA CENTAURI *(CL)*
PAINTER'S EASEL *(C)* *52
PENDULUM CLOCK *(C)* *81
SERPENT HOLDER *(C)* *77
SOUTHERN CROSS *(C)* *13
SOUTHERN CROWN *(C)* *88

TABLE MOUNTAIN *(C)* *35
ZUBENELGENUBI

14

ARKAB POSTERIOR
BIRD OF PARADISE *(C)* *9
CAMELOPARDALIS *(C)* *61
CORONA BOREALIS *(C)* *87
GHOST OF JUPITER *(N)*
RIGIL KENTAURUS
ZUBENESCHAMALI

15

ASELLUS BOREALIS
CORONA AUSTRALIS *(C)* *88
PISCIS AUSTRALIS *(C)* *85

BIBLE

(B) = Book(s)   (G) = Group   (L) = Location

3

ASA
DAN
DAN *(G)*
ELI
EVE
GAD
GAD *(G)*
GOD
GOG
HAI *(L)*
HAM
HUR
JOB
JOB *(B)*
LOT
JOB *(L)*
NOD *(L)*
NUN
ONO *(L)*
TOI
ZIN *(L)*
ZUR

4

ABEL
ACTS *(B)*
ADAH
ADAM
AHAB
AHAZ
AMOK
AMON
AMOS
AMOS *(B)*
ARAM
ARAM *(L)*
BACA *(L)*
BELA *(L)*

BOAZ
CAIN
CANA *(L)*
CUSH
DOEG
EDOM *(L)*
EHUD
ELAM *(L)*
ELIM *(L)*
ELON
EMIM *(G)*
ENOS
ESAU
EZRA
EZRA *(B)*
GATH *(L)*
GAZA *(L)*
GEBA *(L)*
HELI
HIEL
JAEL
JEHU
JEWS *(G)*
JOAB
JODA
JOEL
JOEL *(B)*
JOHN
JOHN *(B)*
JUDE
JUDE *(B)*
KAIN *(L)*
KISH
LEAH
LEVI
LEVI *(G)*
LOIS
LUKE
LUKE *(B)*
MAGI *(G)*
MAON *(L)*
MARK

MARK *(B)*
MARY
MEAH *(L)*
MICA
MOAB
MYRA *(L)*
NILE *(L)*
OBED
ODED
OMRI
OREB
OZEM
OZNI
PAUL
PEOR *(L)*
REBA
ROME *(L)*
RUTH
RUTH *(B)*
SARA
SAUL
SEBA
SEIR *(L)*
SETH
SHEM
SHEN *(L)*
SHUR *(L)*
SOCO *(L)*
TEMA
TOLA
TYRE *(L)*
ULAI *(L)*
ZELA *(L)*
ZIBA
ZION *(L)*
ZIPH *(L)*
ZOAN *(L)*
ZOAR *(L)*
ZUPH

5

AARON
ABIHU
ABNER
ACCAD *(L)*
ACHOR *(L)*
ADMAH *(L)*
AMASA
AMNON
AMRAM
ANNAS
ARPAD *(L)*
ASHER
ASHER *(G)*
BABEL *(L)*
BALAK
BARAK
CALEB
CHLOE
CYRUS
DAVID
DEMAS
DINAH
EGLON
EGYPT *(L)*
EKRON *(L)*
ELDAD
ELIAB
ELIAS
ELIHU
ENDOR *(L)*
ENOCH
ERECH *(L)*
FELIX
GAIUS
GEBAL *(L)*
GEZER *(L)*
GIHON *(L)*
GOMER
HADAD
HAGAR

HAMAN
HAMOR
HANUN
HARAN
HAZOR *(L)*
HEROD
HIRAM
HOBAB
HOHAM
HORAM
HOSEA
HOSEA *(B)*
IBZAN
ISAAC
JABAL
JABEZ *(L)*
JABIN
JACOB
JAMES
JAMES *(B)*
JASON
JAZIZ
JEBUS *(L)*
JESSE
JESUS
JOASH
JOBAB
JONAH
JONAH *(B)*
JOPPA *(L)*
JORAM
JOSES
JUBAL
JUDAH
JUDAH *(G)*
JUDAH *(L)*
JUDAS
KEDAR *(G)*
KENAN
KINGS *(B)*
KORAH
LABAN

LAHMI
LINUS
LYCIA *(L)*
LYDDA *(L)*
LYDIA
LYDIA *(L)*
MAGOG
MALTA *(L)*
MAMRE *(L)*
MARAH *(L)*
MEDES *(G)*
MERAB
MEROZ
MESHA
MESHA *(L)*
MICAH
MICAH *(B)*
MIZAR *(L)*
MOREH *(L)*
MOSES
MYSIA *(L)*
NABAL
NADAB
NAHOR
NAHUM
NAHUM *(B)*
NAOMI
NEGEB *(L)*
NOGAH
OPHEL *(L)*
OPHIR *(G)*
OPHIR *(L)*
OPHNI *(L)*
ORPAH
PARAN *(L)*
PEKAH
PERGA *(L)*
PETER
PETER *(B)*
RAHAB
RAMAH *(L)*
RAPHA

133

BIBLE

REHOB *(L)*
REKEM
REZIN
REZON
RHODA
RUFUS
SAMOS *(L)*
SARAH
SATAN
SCEVA
SENEH *(L)*
SERAH
SHAUL
SHEBA *(G)*
SHEBA *(L)*
SHEMA *(L)*
SIDON *(L)*
SIHON
SILAS
SIMON
SINAI *(L)*
SODOM *(L)*
SYRIA *(L)*
TABOR *(L)*
TAMAR
TEMAN *(G)*
TERAH
TIMON
TITUS
TITUS *(B)*
TROAS *(L)*
TUBAL *(L)*
URIAH
ZABAD
ZABDI
ZABUD
ZADOK
ZAHAM
ZEBAH
ZEBUL
ZENAS
ZERAH
ZERED *(L)*
ZIDON *(L)*
ZIMRI
ZOHAR

ZORAH *(L)*

6

ABARIM *(L)*
ABIJAH
ACHISH
AGABUS
AHIJAH
ANAKIM *(L)*
ANDREW
AQUILA
ARABAH *(L)*
ARARAT *(L)*
ASHDOD *(L)*
ATHENS *(L)*
BAANAH
BAASHA
BALAAM
BARUCH
BASHAN *(L)*
BETHEL *(L)*
BEULAH *(L)*
BILDAD
BOZRAH *(L)*
CAESAR
CANAAN
CANAAN *(L)*
CARMEL *(L)*
CARPUS
CHEBAR *(L)*
CHIDON *(L)*
CHRIST
CYRENE *(L)*
DANIEL
DANIEL *(B)*
DARIUS
DATHAN
DORCAS
ELIJAH
ELISHA
ELOHIM
ELYMAS
ENGEDI *(L)*
ESHCOL *(L)*

ESTHER
ESTHER *(B)*
EUNICE
EXODUS *(B)*
FESTUS
GADARA *(L)*
GALLIO
GASPAR
GEHAZI
GESHUR *(L)*
GIBEAH *(L)*
GIBEON *(L)*
GIDEON
GILBOA *(L)*
GILEAD
GILEAD *(L)*
GILGAL *(L)*
GOSHEN *(L)*
GREEKS *(G)*
HAGGAI
HAGGAI *(B)*
HAMATH
HANNAH
HASHUM
HATTIN *(L)*
HAURAN *(L)*
HAZAEL
HEBRON *(L)*
HERMAS *(L)*
HERMON *(L)*
HINNOM *(L)*
HOPHNI
HOSHEA
HULDAH
IBLEAM *(L)*
IDUMEA *(L)*
ISAIAH
ISAIAH *(B)*
ISRAEL
ISRAEL *(L)*
JABBOK *(L)*
JABESH
JAIRUS
JASHUB
JEARIM *(L)*
JEMIMA

JETHER
JETHRO
JOANNA
JORDAN *(L)*
JOSEPH
JOSEPH *(G)*
JOSHUA
JOSHUA *(B)*
JOSIAH
JOTHAM
JUDAEA *(L)*
JUDGES *(B)*
JULIUS
KADESH *(L)*
KEDESH *(L)*
KEILAH *(L)*
KENATH *(L)*
KIDRON *(L)*
KISHON *(L)*
KOHATH
LAMECH
LUCIUS
LYSTRA *(L)*
MAACAH
MAHLON
MANOAH
MARTHA
MERARI
MICHAL
MIDIAN
MILCAH
MIRIAM
MIZPAH *(L)*
MNASON
MORIAH *(L)*
NAAMAH
NAAMAN
NABOTH
NACHON *(L)*
NAHASH
NATHAN
NEREUS
NIMROD
NIMSHI
NOAMON *(L)*
OPHRAH

OPHRAH *(L)*
PAPHOS *(L)*
PATMOS *(L)*
PERSIA *(L)*
PHILIP
PHOEBE
PILATE
PISGAH *(L)*
PONTUS *(L)*
PSALMS *(B)*
RAAMAH *(G*
RABBAH *(L)*
RACHEL
RADDAI
RECHAB
RED SEA *(L)*
REUBEN
REUBEN *(G,*
RHODES *(L)*
RIBLAH *(L)*
RIMMON
RIMMON *(L)*
RIZPAH
ROMANS *(B*
ROMANS *(G*
SALMON
SALOME
SAMSON
SAMUEL
SAMUEL *(B)*
SARDIS *(L)*
SARGON
SEIRAH *(L)*
SHAAPH
SHALEM *(L)*
SHAMIR *(L)*
SHARON *(L)*
SHAVEH *(L)*
SHELAH
SHELAH *(L)*
SHEMER
SHIBAH *(L)*
SHIHOR *(L)*
SHILOH *(L)*
SHINAR *(L)*
SHOBAB

SHUNEM *(L)*	AMAZIAH	GOLIATH	MIPHKAD *(L)*	SUSANNA
SILOAM *(L)*	AMITTAI	HAMUTAL	NAHSHON	SYRIANS *(G)*
SIMEON	ANANIAS	HANANEL *(L)*	NICANOR	TAANACH *(L)*
SIMEON *(G)*	ANTIOCH *(L)*	HARSITH *(L)*	NINEVEH *(L)*	TAPHATH
SISERA	ANTIPAS	HAVILAH	NUMBERS *(B)*	TERTIUS
SMYRNA *(L)*	APOLLOS	HAVILAH *(L)*	NYMPHAS	TIMAEUS
STOICS *(G)*	ARAUNAH	HEBREWS *(B)*	OBADIAH	TIMOTHY
SYCHAR *(L)*	ARTEMAS	HEBREWS *(G)*	OBADIAH *(B)*	TIMOTHY *(B)*
SYMEON	ASSYRIA *(L)*	HESHBON *(L)*	OLYMPAS	URBANUS
TABEAL	AZARIAH	HILKIAH	OTHNIEL	VULGATE *(B)*
TALMAI	BABYLON *(L)*	HIVITES *(G)*	PATHROS *(L)*	ZEALOTS *(G)*
TARSUS *(L)*	BENAIAH	ICHABOD	PHARPAR *(L)*	ZEBEDEE
TEKOAH *(L)*	BERNICE	ICONIUM *(L)*	PHRYGIA *(L)*	ZEBIDAH
TERESH	BETHANY *(L)*	ISHMAEL	PISIDIA *(L)*	ZEBULUN
THOMAS	BEZALEL	JAPHETH	PUBLIUS	ZEBULUN *(G)*
TIGRIS *(L)*	CALVARY *(L)*	JEHOASH	PUTEOLI *(L)*	
TIRZAH *(L)*	CANDACE	JEHORAM	QUARTUS	
URIJAH	CHERITH *(L)*	JEHOVAH	RAMESES	
UZZIAH	CLAUDIA	JERICHO *(L)*	REBECCA	**8**
VASHNI	CLEMENT	JETHETH	REBEKAH	
VASHTI	CLEOPAS	JEZEBEL	REPHAIM *(G)*	ABEDNEGO
XERXES	CORINTH *(L)*	JEZREEL *(L)*	SABEANS *(G)*	ABIATHAR
ZEBOIM	CRISPUS	JOHANAN	SALAMIS *(L)*	ABINADAB
ZERESH	DEAD SEA *(L)*	JONADAB	SALECAH *(L)*	ADONIJAH
ZERUAH	DEBORAH	KEDEMAH *(G)*	SALMONE *(L)*	ALPHAEUS
ZERUIA	DELILAH	KENITES *(G)*	SAMARIA *(L)*	AMORITES *(G)*
ZETHAR	DIDYMUS	KERIOTH *(L)*	SEMITES *(G)*	AMRAPHEL
ZIBIAH	ELEAZAR	KETURAH	SERAIAH	ANATHOTH *(L)*
ZIKLAG *(L)*	ELHANAN	LACHISH *(L)*	SHALLUM	APPELLES
ZILLAH	ELIPHAZ	LAZARUS	SHAMGAR	ASHKELON *(L)*
ZILPAH	ELKANAH	LEBANON *(L)*	SHAMMAH	ATHALIAH
ZIPPOR	EMMAEUS *(L)*	MAGADAN	SHAMMUA	BARABBAS
ZOPHAR	EPHESUS *(L)*	MAGDALA *(L)*	SHAPHAN	BARNABAS
	EPHRAIM	MALACHI	SHAPHAT	BEN HADAD
	EPHRAIM *(G)*	MALACHI *(B)*	SHEBUEL	BENJAMIN
	ERASTUS	MALCHUS	SHECHEM *(L)*	BENJAMIN *(G)*
7	ESHTAOL *(L)*	MATTHEW	SHELEPH	BETHESDA *(L)*
	ESSENES *(G)*	MATTHEW *(B)*	SHEPHER *(L)*	BETHPEOR *(L)*
ABIGAIL	EUBULUS	MEGIDDO *(L)*	SHIMEAH	BITHYNIA *(L)*
ABINOAM	EZEKIEL	MEMPHIS *(L)*	SHIMRON	CAESAREA *(L)*
ABISHAI	EZEKIEL *(B)*	MENAHEM	SHITTIM *(L)*	CAIAPHAS
ABRAHAM	GALATIA *(L)*	MERIBAH *(L)*	SHUSHAN *(L)*	CHALDEES *(G)*
ABSALOM	GALILEE *(L)*	MESHACH	SOLOMON	CHORAZIN *(L)*
ADULLAM *(L)*	GENESIS *(B)*	MICAIAH	SOPATER	COLOSSAE *(L)*
AHAZIAH	GERIZIM *(L)*	MICHAEL	STEPHEN	CRESCENS
AHINOAM	GERSHOM	MILETUS *(L)*	SUCCOTH *(L)*	DALMATIA *(L)*
AMARIAH				DAMASCUS *(L)*

BIBLE

DRUSILLA
EDOMITES *(G)*
EMMANUEL
EPAPHRAS
EUTYCHUS
GAMALIEL
GEHENNAH *(L)*
GEMARIAH
GENTILES *(G)*
GOLGOTHA *(L)*
GOMORRAH *(L)*
GRECIANS *(G)*
HABAKKUK
HABAKKUK *(B)*
HACHILAH *(L)*
HAZEROTH *(L)*
HERODIAS
HERODION
HEZEKIAH
HITTITES *(G)*
IMMANUEL
ISSACHAR
ISSACHAR *(G)*
JEHOAHAZ
JEPHTHAH
JEREMIAH
JEREMIAH *(B)*
JEROBOAM
JOCHEBED
JONATHAN
LAODICEA *(L)*
LOT'S WIFE
MADMENAH *(L)*
MAHALATH
MAHANAIM *(L)*
MAKKEDAH *(L)*
MANASSEH
MANASSEH *(G)*
MAONITES *(G)*
MARESHAH *(L)*
MATRITES *(G)*
MATTATHA
MATTHIAS
MELCHIOR
MERAIOTH
MICHMASH *(L)*

MITYLENE *(L)*
MOABITES *(G)*
MORDECAI
NAPHTALI
NAPHTALI *(G)*
NAZARETH *(L)*
NEAPOLIS *(L)*
NEHEMIAH
NEHEMIAH *(B)*
NEPHTOAH *(L)*
NETHANEL
ONESIMUS
OSNAPPAR
PARMENAS
PEKAHIAH
PERGAMUM *(L)*
PERSIANS *(G)*
PHILEMON
PHILEMON *(B)*
PHILETUS
PHILIPPI *(L)*
PHINEHAS
POTIPHAR
PROVERBS *(B)*
REHOBOAM
REHOBOTH *(L)*
REPHIDIM *(L)*
SAPPHIRA
SECUNDUS
SELEUCIA *(L)*
SELEUCUS
SHADRACH
SHAREZER
SHEMAIAH
SHIMSHAI
SIBBECAI
SYNTICHE
TAHPENES
TARSHISH *(L)*
TATTENAI
THADDEUS
THYATIRA *(L)*
TIBERIAS *(L)*
TIBERIUS
TIRHAKAH
TYCHICUS

TYRANNUS
ZARETHAN
ZEBADIAH
ZEDEKIAH
ZEMARAIM *(L)*
ZERAHIAH
ZIPPORAH

9

ABIMELECH
AHASUERUS
AHIMELECH
ALEXANDER
AMMONITES *(G)*
ANTIOCHUS
APOCRYPHA *(B)*
ARCHELAUS
ARCHIPPUS
AREOPAGUS *(L)*
ARIMATHEA *(L)*
BABYLONIA *(L)*
BALTHAZAR
BARSABBAS
BARZILLAI
BASHEMATH
BATHSHEBA
BEER-SHEBA *(L)*
BETHHORON *(L)*
BETHLEHEM *(L)*
BETHPHAGE *(L)*
BETHSAIDA *(L)*
CAPERNAUM *(L)*
CHALDEANS *(G)*
CORNELIUS
DECAPOLIS *(L)*
DEMETRIUS
DIONYSIUS
ELIMELECH
ELISABETH
EPAENETUS
EPHESIANS *(B)*
EPHESIANS *(G)*
EUPHRATES *(L)*
GALATIANS *(B)*

GALATIANS *(G)*
GALILEANS *(G)*
HADADEZER
HAMMURABI
HARARITES *(G)*
HERODIANS *(G)*
HEXATEUCH *(B)*
HYMENAEUS
JASHOBEAM
JEBUSITES *(G)*
JEHOIADAH
JEHOIAKIM
JEHOSHEBA
JERUSALEM *(L)*
KORAHITES *(G)*
LAPPIDOTH
LEVITICUS *(B)*
MACEDONIA *(L)*
MACHPELAH *(L)*
MESHULLAM
MOUNT PEOR *(L)*
MOUNT ZION *(L)*
NATHANAEL
NAZARENES *(L)*
NAZIRITES *(G)*
NICODEMUS
NICOPOLIS *(L)*
PALESTINE *(L)*
PAMPHYLIA *(L)*
PARTHIANS *(G)*
PHARISEES *(G)*
PHOENICIA *(L)*
PHRYGIANS *(G)*
PROCHORUS
QUIRINIUS
RIVER NILE *(L)*
RIVER ULAI *(L)*
SADDUCEES *(G)*
SANBALLAT
SANHEDRIN *(G)*
SCYTHIANS *(G)*
SHEALTIEL
SHELEMIAH
SODOMITES *(G)*
SOSTHENES
STEPHANAS

SUMERIANS *(G)*
TAHPANHES *(L)*
TERTULLUS
THADDAEUS
TIMOTHEUS
TROPHIMUS
ZACCHAEUS
ZACHARIAH
ZALMUNNAH
ZECHARIAH
ZECHARIAH *(B)*
ZEPHANIAH
ZEPHANIAH *(B)*

10

AHITHOPHEL
ALEXANDRIA *(L)*
AMALEKITES *(G)*
AMPHIPOLIS *(L)*
ANDRONICUS
ANTIPATRIS *(L)*
APPII FORUM *(L)*
ARMAGEDDON *(L)*
ARTAXERXES
BARTIMAEUS
BELSHAZZAR
CANAANITES *(G)*
CAPPADOCIA *(L)*
CARCHEMISH *(L)*
CHRISTIANS *(G)*
CHRONICLES *(B)*
COLOSSIANS *(B)*
COLOSSIANS *(G)*
DIOTREPHES
EBEDMELECH
ESARHADDON
EZION GEBER *(L)*
FORTUNATUS
GETHSEMANE *(L)*
HAVOTH JAIR *(L)*
HERMOGENES
ISHBOSHETH
ISRAELITES *(G)*
JEHOIACHIN
KENIZZITES *(G)*

KOHATHITES *(G)*
MALCHI-SHUA
MATTANAIAH
METHUSELAH
MIDIANITES *(G)*
MITHREDATH
MOUNT SINAI *(L)*
MOUNT TABOR *(L)*
NABATHITES *(G)*
OHOLIBAMAH
PELETHITES *(G)*
PENTATEUCH *(B)*
PERIZZITES *(G)*
RECHABITES *(G)*
REVELATION *(B)*
SAMARITANS *(G)*
SAMOTHRACE *(L)*
SEPTUAGINT *(B)*
SIMON MAGUS
SIMON PETER
THEOPHILUS
TROGYLLIUM *(L)*
VIRGIN MARY
ZELOPHEHAD
ZERUBBABEL

11

ARISTARCHUS
ARISTOBULUS
BABYLONIANS *(G)*
BARTHOLOMEW
CHERETHITES *(G)*
CITY OF DAVID *(L)*
CORINTHIANS *(B)*
CORINTHIANS *(G)*
DEUTERONOMY *(B)*
EPHES DAMMIM *(L)*
GENNESARETH *(L)*
ISHMAELITES *(G)*
JAPHLETITES *(G)*
JEHOSHAPHAT
JESUS CHRIST
MELCHIZEDEK
MOUNT ARARAT *(L)*

MOUNT HERMON *(L)*
MOUNT JEARIM *(L)*
MOUNT MORIAH *(L)*
MOUNT PISGAH *(L)*
NEBUZARADAN
ONESIPHORUS
PARAN DESERT *(L)*
PHILIPPIANS *(B)*
PHILIPPIANS *(G)*
PHILISTINES *(G)*
PHOENICIANS *(G)*
RIVER JORDAN *(L)*
RIVER SHIHOR *(L)*
RIVER TIGRIS *(L)*
SENNACHERIB
SHALLECHETH *(L)*
SHALMANESER
SHESH BAZZAR

12

CHEDOR-LAOMER
ECCLESIASTES *(B)*
EPAPHRODITUS
EVIL MERODACH
HEROD AGRIPPA
HEROD ANTIPAS
HINNOM VALLEY *(L)*
JABESH-GILEAD *(L)*
KADESH BARNEA *(L)*
LAMENTATIONS *(B)*
MEPHIBOSHETH
MOUNT SHEPHER *(L)*
NEW TESTAMENT *(B)*
OLD TESTAMENT *(B)*
PHILADELPHIA *(L)*
QUEEN OF SHEBA
RAMOTH-GILEAD *(L)*
SAUL OF TARSUS
SEA OF GALILEE *(L)*
THESSALONICA *(L)*
THREE WISE MEN *(G)*
TOWER OF BABEL *(L)*
VALE OF SIDDIM *(L)*
VALLEY OF SALT *(L)*

BIBLE

BUILDINGS

CASTLES – BRITISH ISLES

All England except: (I) = Ireland   (M) = Isle of Man   (S) = Scotland
(W) = Wales

4

BIRR *(I)*
COCH *(W)*
DEAL
DEAN *(S)*
DRUM *(S)*
FAST *(S)*
HOLT
PEEL *(M)*
RABY
ROSS *(I)*
TRIM *(I)*

5

ADAIR *(I)*
BARRA *(S)*
BLAIR *(S)*
BURGH
CAHIR *(I)*
CHIRK *(W)*
CLARA *(I)*
COITY *(W)*
CONWY *(W)*
CORBY
CORFE
CROFT
DOUNE *(S)*
DOVER
DUART *(S)*
ELCHO *(S)*
EWLOE *(W)*
FLINT *(W)*
GREEN *(I)*
HAGGS *(S)*
HEVER
HOWTH *(I)*
HURST

LEEDS
LEWES
POWIS *(W)*
SLANE *(I)*
TENBY *(W)*
TULLY *(I)*
UPNOR
WHITE *(W)*

6

AIRLIE
BRODIE *(S)*
BROUGH
BUNGAY
BUTLER *(I)*
CAMBER
CASHEL *(I)*
CAWDOR *(S)*
DUBLIN *(I)*
DUDLEY
DUFFUS *(S)*
DUNBOY *(I)*
DURHAM
EDZELL *(S)*
GLAMIS *(S)*
GWYDYR *(W)*
HAILES *(S)*
HUNTLY *(S)*
LUDLOW
LUMLEY
LYMPNE
MAIDEN
MALLOW *(I)*
NENAGH *(I)*
NEWARK *(S)*
NORRIS
NUNNEY

OAKHAM
OGMORE *(W)*
ORFORD
PENHOW *(W)*
PICTON *(W)*
RAGLAN *(W)*
RIPLEY
ROSLIN *(S)*
RUTHIN *(W)*
SKREEN *(I)*
STROME *(S)*
TIORAM *(S)*
TOTNES
WALMER
WEOLEY

7

AFFLECK *(S)*
ALNWICK
ARUNDEL
ATHERNY *(I)*
BALLOCK *(S)*
BARNARD
BEESTON
BELFAST *(I)*
BELVOIR
BLARNEY *(I)*
BRAEMAR *(S)*
BRAMBER
BRODICK *(S)*
BULLOCK *(I)*
CADBURY
CAISTER
CARBURY *(I)*
CARDIFF *(W)*
CHILHAM
COMPTON
CRATHES *(S)*

CULZEAN *(S)*
DENBIGH *(W)*
DONEGAL *(I)*
DOUGLAS *(S)*
DROMORE *(I)*
DUNDRUM *(I)*
DUNLUCE *(I)*
DUNSTER
EASTNOR
FARNHAM
GILLING
GLENAPP *(S)*
HARLECH *(W)*
KISIMUL *(S)*
LINCOLN
LYDFORD
MAYBOLE *(S)*
NORWICH
PENRHYN *(W)*
PENRICE *(W)*
PRUDHOE
QUINTIN *(I)*
SCOTNEY
SIZERGH
SKIPTON
ST MAWES
SUDELEY
TAUNTON
THREAVE *(S)*
TOROSAY *(S)*
TUTBURY
WARDOUR
WARWICK
WEOBLEY *(W)*
WINDSOR

8

ABERDOUR *(S)*

BALMORAL *(S)*
BALVENIE *(S)*
BAMBURGH
BERKELEY
BOLSOVER
BOTHWELL *(S)*
BROUGHAM
BROUGHTY *(S)*
BRYN BRAS *(W)*
BUNCRANA *(I)*
BUNRATTY *(I)*
BURLEIGH *(S)*
CARLISLE
CHEPSTOW *(W)*
CLIFFORD
CORGARFF *(S)*
CRICHTON *(S)*
DELGATIE *(S)*
DRYSLWYN *(W)*
DUNROBIN *(S)*
DUNVEGAN *(S)*
EYNSFORD
FARLEIGH
GIRNIGOE *(S)*
GOODRICH
GROSMONT *(W)*
HADLEIGH
HASTINGS
HELMSLEY
HERTFORD
KIDWELLY *(W)*
KILKENNY *(I)*
KILLINEY *(I)*
LEAMANEH *(I)*
MAYNOOTH *(I)*
MENSTRIE *(S)*
MONMOUTH *(W)*
MOUNTJOY *(I)*
MUCHALLS *(S)*

BUILDINGS – CASTLES – BRITISH ISLES

NEIDPATH *(S)*
PEMBROKE *(W)*
PEVENSEY
PITCAPLE *(S)*
PORTLAND
RHUDDLAN *(W)*
RICHMOND
ROTHESAY *(S)*
SALTWOOD
SINCLAIR *(S)*
SOUTHSEA
ST DONAT'S *(W)*
STIRLING *(S)*
STOKESAY
STORMONT *(I)*
TAMWORTH
THETFORD
TINTAGEL
TIVERTON
URQUHART *(S)*
YARMOUTH

9

ALLINGTON
ARDTERMON *(I)*
BALLYMOON *(I)*
BALLYMOTE *(I)*
BEAUMARIS *(W)*
BICKLEIGH
BLACKBURY
BLACKNESS *(S)*
BORTHWICK *(S)*
BROUGHTON
CARDONESS *(S)*
CARSLUITH *(S)*
CILGERRAN *(W)*
CLEARWELL
CLITHEROE
CRAIGSTON *(S)*
CRICCIETH *(W)*
CROOKSTON *(S)*
CULCREUCH *(S)*
DARTMOUTH
DOLBADARN *(W)*
DONINGTON

DRUMINNOR *(S)*
DUMBARTON *(S)*
DUNGUAIRE *(S)*
DUNIMARIE *(S)*
DUNKERRON *(I)*
DUNNOTTAR *(S)*
EDINBURGH *(S)*
GLENVEAGH *(I)*
GUILDFORD
HERMITAGE *(S)*
INVERARAY *(S)*
INVERNESS *(S)*
KILDRUMMY *(S)*
KIMBOLTON
LANCASTER
LAURISTON *(S)*
LLAWHADEN *(W)*
LOCH LEVEN *(S)*
LOUGHMORE *(I)*
MANORBIER *(W)*
MIDDLEHAM
MUNCASTER
PEMBRIDGE
PENDENNIS
PICKERING
POWDERHAM
RESTORMEL
ROCHESTER
SCALLOWAY *(S)*
SHERBORNE
SKENFRITH *(W)*
SPOFFORTH
STRANRAER *(S)*
TANTALLON *(S)*
TONBRIDGE
URLANMORE *(I)*
WARKWORTH

10

AUGHNANURE *(I)*
BALLYNAHOW *(I)*
CAERNARFON *(W)*
CAERPHILLY *(W)*
CARROWDORE *(I)*
CRAIGIEVAR *(S)*

DEDDINGTON
DONNINGTON
DRUMLANRIG *(S)*
HARTLEBURY
HUNTERSTON *(S)*
INVERLOCHY *(S)*
KENILWORTH
KIRKISTOWN *(I)*
LAUNCESTON
NOTTINGHAM
OKEHAMPTON
PORCHESTER
ROCKINGHAM
SHREWSBURY
ST BRIAVELS
TULLYNALLY *(I)*
WATERMOUTH
WINCHESTER

11

ABERYSTWYTH *(W)*
BALLINLOUGH *(I)*
BERKHAMSTED
CARISBROOKE
CARNASSERIE *(S)*
CASTLE DROGO
CASTLE KIRKE *(I)*
CASTLE OF MEY *(S)*
CHARLEVILLE *(I)*
CONISBROUGH
CRAIGMILLAR *(S)*
CRAIGNETHAN *(S)*
DOLWYDDELAN *(W)*
EILEAN DONAN *(S)*
ENNISKILLEN *(I)*
FRAMLINGHAM
GRIMSTHORPE
LINDISFARNE
LLANSTEPHAN *(W)*
LUDGERSHALL
OYSTERMOUTH
RAVENSBURGH
RAVENSCRAIG *(S)*
SCARBOROUGH
TATTERSHALL
THIRLESTANE *(S)*

12

BACONSTHORPE
BALLINCOLLIG *(I)*
BALLYGRENNAN *(I)*
CAERLAVEROCK *(S)*
CARREG CENNEN *(W)*
CASTLE FRASER *(S)*
CASTLE HOWARD
CASTLE RISING
CHOLMONDELEY
CHRISTCHURCH
DUNSTAFFNAGE *(S)*
DUNSTANBURGH

FOTHERINGHAY
HERSTMONCEUX
HUNTINGTOWER *(S)*
LULLINGSTONE
SISSINGHURST
ST CATHERINE'S

13

BALLYNALACKAN *(I)*
CARRICKFERGUS *(I)*
CHIDDINGSTONE
HAVERFORDWEST *(W)*

KNARESBOROUGH
SHERIFF HUTTON
TOWER OF LONDON

14

ASHBY-DE-LA-ZOUCH
BALLYNACARRIGA *(I)*

15

CASTLE OF OLD WICK *(S)*
DALTON-IN-FURNESS

BUILDINGS

CHURCHES – BRITISH ISLES

(A) = Abbey   (C) = Cathedral   (M) = Minster   (P) = Priory

3

ELY *(C)*

4

BATH *(A)*
DEER *(A)*
IONA *(A)*
PEEL *(C)*
QUIN *(A)*
ROSS *(A)*
SHAP *(A)*
YORK *(M)*

5

BOYLE *(A)*
DERBY *(C)*
DERRY *(C)*
ELGIN *(C)*
FORDE *(A)*
KELSO *(A)*
MOYNE *(A)*
NEATH *(A)*
RIPON *(C)*
ROCHE *(A)*
SELBY *(A)*
TRURO *(C)*
WELLS *(C)*

6

ARMAGH *(C)*
BANGOR *(C)*
BATTLE *(A)*
BAYHAM *(A)*
BEAULY *(P)*
BINHAM *(P)*
BOLTON *(A)*
BRECON *(C)*
BYLAND *(A)*
CASHEL *(C)*
CLEEVE *(A)*
CYMMER *(A)*
DUBLIN *(C)*

DURHAM *(C)*
EWENNY *(P)*
EXETER *(C)*
HEXHAM *(A)*
HINTON *(P)*
LACOCK *(A)*
MILTON *(A)*
NETLEY *(A)*
OXFORD *(C)*
PENMON *(P)*
RAMSEY *(A)*
ROMSEY *(A)*
STRADE *(A)*
TALLEY *(A)*
TRESCO *(A)*

WHITBY *(A)*

7

ARUNDEL *(C)*
BECTIVE *(A)*
BRECHIN *(C)*
BRISTOL *(C)*
CARDIFF *(C)*
CHESTER *(C)*
CULROSS *(A)*
DELAPRÉ *(A)*
DORNOCH *(C)*
DUNKELD *(C)*

141

BUILDINGS – CHURCHES – BRITISH ISLES

EVESHAM *(A)*
FURNESS *(A)*
GLASGOW *(C)*
IXWORTH *(A)*
LEISTON *(A)*
LINCOLN *(C)*
MELROSE *(A)*
NORWICH *(C)*
ST ASAPH *(C)*
ST PAUL'S *(C)*
THORNEY *(A)*
TINTERN *(A)*
WALTHAM *(A)*
WHALLEY *(A)*

8

ABERDEEN *(C)*
ARBROATH *(A)*
BEAULIEU *(A)*
BEVERLEY *(M)*
BRADFORD *(C)*
BUCKFAST *(A)*
BUCKLAND *(A)*
BUILDWAS *(A)*
CARLISLE *(C)*
CLONFERT *(C)*
COVENTRY *(C)*
DRYBURGH *(A)*
DUNBLANE *(C)*
DUNBRODY *(A)*
FINCHALE *(P)*
FORTROSE *(C)*
GLENLUCE *(A)*
HEREFORD *(C)*
INCHCOLM *(A)*
JEDBURGH *(A)*
JERPOINT *(A)*
KIRKWALL *(C)*
MUCKROSS *(A)*
NEWBURGH *(P)*
RIEVAULX *(A)*
ST ALBAN'S *(C)*
ST BENET'S *(A)*

ST DAVID'S *(C)*
ST OLAVE'S *(P)*
THORNTON *(A)*
WAVERLEY *(A)*
WEST ACRE *(P)*
WHITHORN *(P)*
WIMBORNE *(M)*

9

BLACKBURN *(C)*
EDINBURGH *(C)*
FOUNTAINS *(A)*
GUILDFORD *(C)*
HAUGHMOND *(A)*
HOLYCROSS *(A)*
KIRKSTALL *(A)*
LANERCOST *(P)*
LEICESTER *(C)*
LICHFIELD *(C)*
LIVERPOOL *(C)*
LLANTHONY *(P)*
MEDMENHAM *(A)*
MICHELHAM *(P)*
NEWCASTLE *(C)*
PRINKNASH *(A)*
ROCHESTER *(C)*
SALISBURY *(C)*
SHEFFIELD *(C)*
SOUTHWARK *(C)*
SOUTHWELL *(C)*
ST ANDREWS *(C)*
TYNEMOUTH *(P)*
WAKEFIELD *(C)*
WORCESTER *(C)*

10

BIRKENHEAD *(P)*
BIRMINGHAM *(C)*
CANTERBURY *(C)*
CASTLE ACRE *(P)*

CHELMSFORD *(C)*
CHICHESTER *(C)*
DORCHESTER *(A)*
DUNDRENNAN *(A)*
GLOUCESTER *(C)*
INCHMAHOME *(P)*
LILLESHALL *(A)*
MANCHESTER *(C)*
MOTTISFONT *(A)*
PORTSMOUTH *(C)*
PLUSCARDEN *(A)*
STONELEIGH *(A)*
SWEETHEART *(A)*
TEWKESBURY *(A)*
WALSINGHAM *(A)*
WINCHESTER *(C)*

11

GLASTONBURY *(A)*
LAMBERHURST *(P)*
LINDISFARNE *(P)*
PRITTLEWELL *(P)*
SHAFTESBURY *(A)*
VALLE CRUCIS *(A)*
WESTMINSTER *(A/C)*
WHITELADIES *(P)*

12

CLONMACNOISE *(C)*
PETERBOROUGH *(C)*

13

BURY ST EDMUNDS *(C)*

14

STOKE-SUB-HAMDON *(P)*

BUILDINGS

HOUSES – BRITISH ISLES

5

KNOLE
  (Sackville)
STOWE

6

ASCOTT
BOWOOD
ERDDIG
FASQUE
  (Gladstone)
UPPARK

7

ALTHORP
  (Earl Spencer)
BOWHILL
HAWORTH
  (Brontë Sisters)
HILL TOP
  (Beatrix Potter)
IGHTHAM
KAILZIE
KENWOOD
MAX GATE
  (Hardy)
OWLETTS
PLAS TEG
THE VYNE

8

BATEMAN'S
  (Kipling)
BEAULIEU
  (Lord Montagu)
BEAUPARC

CLIVEDEN
CRAGSIDE
DAILMAIN
EYE MANOR
HALE PARK
HAM HOUSE
ICKWORTH
LANGWELL
LONGLEAT
  (Marquess of Bath)
LUTON HOO
LYME PARK
PLAS MAWR
SMEDMORE
SOMERLEY
TONG HALL
WELL VALE

9

ASTON HALL
BEAR STEPS
BRANTWOOD
  (Ruskin)
CHARTWELL
  (Churchill)
CHAVENAGE
CLAREMONT
  (Clive of India)
DEENE PARK
DUFF HOUSE
ELTON HALL
GUNBY HALL
KEW PALACE
KIRBY HALL
LYTES CARY
NEWBY HALL
SPEKE HALL
STOURHEAD
SYON HOUSE
TYTUP HALL

VINE HOUSE

10

ABBOTSFORD
  (Sir Walter Scott)
ALBURY PARK
ARBURY HALL
ASTLEY HALL
BLEAK HOUSE
  (Dickens)
BROADLANDS
  (Earl Mountbatten)
CHATSWORTH
  (Duke of Devonshire)
CLOUDS HILL
  (Lawrence of Arabia)
COBHAM HALL
DYRHAM PARK
FENSTANTON
  (Capability Brown)
FIRLE PLACE
GORHAMBURY
HADDO HOUSE
HADDON HALL
HAGLEY HALL
  (Baron Lyttleton)
HALL'S CROFT
  *(Shakespeare's
   daughter Susanna)*
HEATON HALL
HELMINGHAM
HODNEY HALL
HOLKER HALL
LEVENS HALL
LUCAN HOUSE
LYONS HOUSE
MANDERSTON
MORLEY HALL
PLAS NEWYDD
QUENBY HALL

RAGLEY HALL
  (Marquess of Hertford)
RYDAL MOUNT
  (Wordsworth)
SANDON HALL
SHANDY HALL
  (Laurence Sterne)
TATTON PARK
THORPE HALL
UPTON HOUSE
WALCOT HALL
  (Clive of India)
WESTON PARK

11

ALTON TOWERS
AUBOURN HALL
BANTRY HOUSE
BARDON MANOR
BASING HOUSE
BEESTON HALL
BELTON HOUSE
BOYNTON HALL
BREDE PALACE
CAVICK HOUSE
CHINGLE HALL
CLANDON PARK
CLUMBER PARK
CULTRA MANOR
DOVE COTTAGE
  (Wordsworth)
FENTON HOUSE
GAYTON MANOR
HOLKHAM HALL
  (Sir Edward Coke)
HORTON COURT
LAMPORT HALL
MARLOW PLACE
MARSTON HALL

BUILDINGS — HOUSES — BRITISH ISLES

OAKWELL HALL
ORMESBY HALL
OXBURGH HALL
PINKIE HOUSE
QUEBEC HOUSE
(General Wolfe)
SANDRINGHAM
(Royal Family)
SAWSTON HALL
SCONE PALACE
(Earl of Mansfield)
SEWERBY HALL
SHAW'S CORNER
(GB Shaw)
SHIBDEN HALL
SHIPTON HALL
SHUGBOROUGH
STONOR HOUSE
TARVIT HOUSE
URRAND HOUSE
WILTON HOUSE
WINTON HOUSE
WIMPOLE HALL
WINSLOW HALL
WIVETON HALL
WOBURN ABBEY
(Duke of Bedford)
WOTTON HOUSE

12

ACHESON HOUSE
ARRETON MANOR
ASHDOWN HOUSE
ATHELHAMPTON
BENTHALL HALL
BURNS COTTAGE
(Robert Burns)
CAMERON HOUSE
(Smollett)
CLAYDON HOUSE
CLIFTON HOUSE
CORSHAM COURT
CROXTETH HALL
DANEWAY HOUSE

DENHAM PALACE
DITCHLEY PARK
FELBRIGG HALL
GAULDEN MANOR
GLYNDE PALACE
HAMPTON COURT
(Cardinal Wolsey/Henry VIII)
HARDWICK HALL
HOUGHTON HALL
KENTWELL HALL
MAESMAWR HALL
MANSION HOUSE
(Lord Mayor of London)
NORMANBY HALL
OSBORNE HOUSE
(Queen Victoria)
PARNHAM HOUSE
RAMMERSCALES
ROUSHAM HOUSE
SALTRAM HOUSE
SHELDON MANOR
STANFORD HALL
TEMPLE NEWSAM
(Lord Darnley/Lord Halifax)
THORESBY HALL
THURNHAM HALL
TOSELAND HALL
WEST STOW HALL
WHARTON COURT
WHITTON COURT
WOLLATON HALL
WORTHAM MANOR
WROXTON ABBEY
WYNNSTAY HALL

13

ADLINGTON HALL
ATTINGHAM PARK
BLICKLING HALL
BOSCOBEL HOUSE
(Charles II)
BRADGATE HOUSE
BREAMORE HOUSE
BUCKDEN PALACE

BURGHLEY HOUSE
(Marquess of Exeter)
CARLTON TOWERS
(Duke of Norfolk)
CARLYLE'S HOUSE
(Thomas Carlyle)
CHISWICK HOUSE
CLEVEDON COURT
(Thackeray)
COCKFIELD HALL
COTEHELE HOUSE
COUGHTON COURT
CULROSS PALACE
DUNSLAND HOUSE
EDNASTON MANOR
FOXDENTON HALL
GAD'S HILL PLACE
(Dickens)
GAWTHORPE HALL
GOODWOOD HOUSE
(Duke of Richmond & Gordon)
HARDY'S COTTAGE
(Thomas Hardy)
HAREWOOD HOUSE
(Earl of Harewood)
HATFIELD HOUSE
(Marquess of Salisbury)
HOLYROOD HOUSE
(Royal Family)
HOPETOUN HOUSE
(Marquess of Linlithgow)
KEDLESTON HALL
(Curzon)
LAMBETH PALACE
(Archbishop of Canterbury)
LAMPHEY PALACE
LEIGHTON HOUSE
MELBOURNE HALL
NEWSTEAD ABBEY
(Lord Byron)
NONSUCH PALACE
(Henry VIII)
PACKWOOD HOUSE
PECKOVER HOUSE
PETWORTH HOUSE
POLESDEN LACEY

ROYAL PAVILION
(Prince Regent)
SANDFORD ORCAS
SEATON DELAVAL
SLEDMERE HOUSE
SMITHILLS HALL
SOMERSET HOUSE
SULGRAVE MANOR
(George Washington)
SYDENHAM HOUSE
THRUMPTON HALL
TRAQUAIR HOUSE
(Mary, Queen of Scots)
TREDEGAR HOUSE
(Morgan)
TRETOWER COURT
WESTWOOD MANOR
WOLTERTON HALL

14

ARLINGTON COURT
BADMINTON HOUSE
(Duke of Beaufort)
BALBITHAN HOUSE
BECKINGHAM HALL
BELLAMONT HOUSE
BERRINGTON HALL
BLENHEIM PALACE
(Duke of Marlborough/
Churchill)
BODRHYDDAN HALL
BROUGHTON HOUSE
CARRADALE HOUSE

CHARLSTON MANOR
CHARLECOTE PARK
CLAVERTON MANOR
DALKEITH PALACE
DARTINGTON HALL
DODDINGTON HALL
GODOLPHIN HOUSE
(Earl of Godolphin)
HARVINGTON HALL
HUGHENDEN MANOR
(Disraeli)
KELMSCOTT MANOR
(William Morris)
KNEBWORTH HOUSE
(Lytton)
LANCASTER HOUSE
MAXWELTON HOUSE
MOMPESSON HOUSE
MONTACUTE HOUSE
PAINSWICK HOUSE
PENCARROW HOUSE
PENSHURST PLACE
(Sir Philip Sidney)
RIPPINGTON HALL
RUFFORD OLD HALL
SHERINGHAM HALL
SOUERRYES COURT
STAPLEFORD PARK
ST JAMES'S PALACE
STRAWBERRY HILL
WADDESDON MANOR
WAKEHURST PLACE
WATERSTON MANOR
(Horace Walpole)

WIGHTWICK MANOR
WORLINGHAM HALL

15

BANQUETING HOUSE
(Cardinal Wolsey/
Charles I/George I)
BARRINGTON COURT
CAPESTHORNE HALL
(Bromley-Davenport)
CASTLETOWN HOUSE
COLLACOMBE MANOR
COMPTON WYNYATES
COTHERIDGE COURT
DOWN AMPNEY HOUSE
FARNBOROUGH HALL
GORHAMBURY HOUSE
HEVENINGHAM HALL
INGATESTONE HALL
LANHYDROCK HOUSE
LEVERINGTON HALL
LITTLECOTE HOUSE
LUDDESDOWN COURT
MARY ARDEN'S HOUSE
(Shakespeare's mother)
PARLIAMENT HOUSE
REVOLUTION HOUSE
SCARISBRICK HALL
SOMERLEYTON HALL
STIBBINGTON HALL
TINTINHULL HOUSE
WILDERHOPE MANOR

BUILDINGS

LIGHTHOUSES – BRITISH ISLES

All England except: (CI) = Channel Islands   (I) = Ireland   (M) = Isle of Man
*(S) = Scotland   (W) = Wales   * = Alternative name*

3

NAB

4

ROSS *(S)*
WICK *(S)*

5

BLYTH
DOVER
FIDRA *(S)*
HURST
ORSAY *(S)*
SANDA *(S)*
TROON *(S)*

6

CRINAN *(S)*
CROMER
LIZARD
ORNSAY *(S)*
OXCARS *(S)*
PLADDA *(S)*
SMALLS *(W)*
WHITBY

7

EAST USK *(W)*
FASTNET *(I)*

GODREVY
GRANTON *(S)*
LYBSTER *(S)*
MUMBLES *(W)*
NEEDLES
PENDEEN
TATER-DU
TAYPORT *(S)*
TRWYN-DU *(W)*

8

BAMBURGH
BASS ROCK *(S)*
BELL ROCK *(S) *1*
BULL ROCK *(I)*
CASQUETS *(CI)*
FLATHOLM
HEISKEIR *(S)*
INCHCAPE *(S) *1*
LANGNESS *(M)*
LOOP HEAD *(I)*
LYNMOUTH
MINE HEAD *(I)*
NOSS HEAD *(S)*
PENNINIS
SKELLIGS *(I)*
SKERRIES *(W)*
TEARAGHT *(I)*
WOLF ROCK

9

BARRA HEAD *(S)*
BERRY HEAD
BLACK HEAD *(S)*
BULL POINT

CALF OF MAN *(M)*
CAPE WRATH *(S)*
DUNGENESS
EDDYSTONE
FLEETWOOD
GORLESTON
ISLE OF MAY *(S)*
LES HANOIS *(CI)*
LONGSHIPS
LONGSTONE
LOWESTOFT
NASH POINT *(W)*
ROKER PIER
SLYNE HEAD *(I)*
SOUTHWOLD
SPURN HEAD
ST TUDWAL'S *(W)*

10

AILSA CRAIG *(S)*
ANVIL POINT
BEACHY HEAD
BISHOP ROCK
CAIRN POINT *(S)*
CLOCH POINT *(S)*
EASTER HEAD *(S)*
GIRDLE NESS *(S)*
ILFRACOMBE
LA CORBIÈRE *(CI)*
LUNDY NORTH
LUNDY SOUTH
NEIST POINT *(S)*
ORFORDNESS
POINT LYNAS *(W)*
POINT OF AIR *(W)*
RUBHA RÉIDH *(S)*

SKERRYVORE *(S)*
SOUTH POINT *(S)*
SOUTH STACK *(W)*
ST ABBS HEAD *(S)*
ST ANN'S HEAD *(W)*
START POINT
TARBAT NESS *(S)*
TORY ISLAND *(I)*
WITHERNSEA

11

BUTT OF LEWIS *(S)*
CALDY ISLAND *(W)*
CHICKEN ROCK *(M)*
DOUGLAS HEAD *(M)*
HAPPISBURGH
LADIES' TOWER *(S)*
POINT OF AYRE *(M)*
POINT ROBERT *(CI)*
ROUND ISLAND
SCARBOROUGH
SCURDIE NESS *(S)*
SOUTER POINT
SOUTH BISHOP *(W)*
TOWARD POINT *(S)*
TREVOSE HEAD

12

BURNHAM-ON-SEA
COQUET ISLAND
DAVARR ISLAND *(S)*
FARNE ISLANDS
INISHTRAHULL *(I)*
INNER DOWSING

ISLE OF WALNEY
KILLINGHOLME
LEITH HARBOUR *(S)*
MAUGHOLD HEAD *(M)*
PORTLAND BILL
QUENARD POINT *(CI)*
STRUMBLE HEAD *(W)*
SUMBURGH HEAD *(S)*
TODHEAD POINT *(S)*

13

BARDSEY ISLAND *(W)*

CHANONRY POINT *(S)*
DUNCANSBY HEAD *(S)*
HARTLAND POINT
KINNAIRD'S HEAD *(S)*
LANGATON POINT *(S)*
McARTHUR'S HEAD *(S)*
NORTH FORELAND
PLATTE FOUGÈRE *(CI)*
RATHLIN ISLAND *(I)*
SOUTH FORELAND
ST ANTHONY HEAD
ST MARY'S ISLAND

14

BLACKNORE POINT
GREAT ORME'S HEAD *(W)*
ROYAL SOVEREIGN
SKOKHOLM ISLAND *(W)*

15

ARDTORNISH POINT *(S)*
FLAMBOROUGH HEAD
HUNSTANTON POINT

BUILDINGS

PRISONS

(I) = Ireland   (P) = POW Camp   (R) = Russia   (S) = Scotland
*(SA) = South Africa   (US) = USA   * = Alternative name   † = Former prison*

3

USK

4

DORA *(P)*
FORD
HULL
MAZE *(I)*
SEND

5

CLINK †

DOVER
FLEET †
LEEDS
LEWES
MOUNT
ONLEY
PERTH *(S)*
RANBY
STYAL
TORUN *(P)*
VERNE

6

ALBANY
ATTICA *(US)*

BELSEN *(P)*
CHANGI *(P)*
COLONY
DACHAU *(P)*
DURHAM
EXETER
HASLAR
OXFORD
RADLEY
RISLEY
SHOTTS *(S)*
WYMOTT

7

ASHFORD

ASHWELL
BEDFORD
BELFAST *(I) *1*
BRISTOL
BRIXTON
CARDIFF
CHELMNO *(P)*
COLDITZ *(P)*
CULMHOF *(P)*
FELTHAM
GARTREE
GRENDON
HINDLEY
KIRKHAM
LEYHILL
LINCOLN
NEWGATE †

NEW HALL
NORWICH
PRESTON
READING
RUDGATE
SOBIBOR *(P)*
SPANDAU †
STOCKEN
SUDBURY
SWANSEA
WAYLAND
WHATTON

8

ABERDEEN

BUILDINGS – PRISONS

ALCATRAZ †
BASTILLE †
BIRKENAU (P)
CAMP HILL
DARTMOOR
DEERBOLT
DUNGAVEL (S)
GRINGLEY
HATFIELD
HAVERIGG
HOLLOWAY
KINGSTON
LONG KESH †
LUBYANKA (R)
MAJDANEK (P)
MILLBANK †
MOUNTJOY (I)
NORTHEYE
OSWIECIM (P)
PORTLAND
PRESCOED
SAUGHTON (S)
SING SING (US)
STAFFORD
STUTTHOF (P)
THE MOUNT
THE VERNE
WETHERBY

9

ALDINGTON
AUSCHWITZ (P)
AYLESBURY
BARLINNIE (S)
BROADMOOR
BROCKHILL
CARSTAIRS (S)
DRAKE HALL
ERLESTOKE
FRANKLAND
GLEN PARVA
GUYS MARSH
HIGHPOINT
LANCASTER
LEICESTER

LINDHOLME
LITTLEHEY
LIVERPOOL
LOW NEWTON
MAIDSTONE
MEDOMSLEY
PARKHURST
PETERHEAD (S)
POLLSMOOR (SA)
ROCHESTER
THORP ARCH
TREBLINKA (P)
WAKEFIELD

10

ACKLINGTON
BIRMINGHAM
BLUNDESTON
BUCHENWALD (P)
CANTERBURY
CASTINGTON
CHÂTEAU D'IF †
CHELMSFORD
COLDINGLEY
DORCHESTER
ESTERWEGEN (P)
EVERTHORPE
FOSTON HALL
FULL SUTTON
GLOUCESTER
LONG LARTIN
MAGHABERRY (I)
MAGILLIGAN (I)
MANCHESTER *2
MARSHALSEA †
MORTON HALL
NOTTINGHAM
PORT LAOISE (I)
ROLLESTONE
SAN QUENTIN (US)
SHREWSBURY
SPRING HILL
STOKE HEATH
THORN CROSS

WANDSWORTH
WARREN HILL
WERRINGTON
WINCHESTER

11

BUCKLEY HALL
COOKHAM WOOD
CORNTON VALE (S)
CRUMLIN ROAD (I) *1
HUNTERCOMBE
PENTONVILLE
PORTERFIELD (S)
STRANGEWAYS *2
SWINFEN HALL
WINSON GREEN

12

ASKHAM GRANGE
BULLWOOD HALL
DEVIL'S ISLAND †
EASTWOOD PARK
FEATHERSTONE
HEWELL GRANGE
HOLLESLEY BAY
PUCKLECHURCH
ROBBEN ISLAND (SA)

13

BLANTYRE HOUSE
CHANNINGS WOOD
FINNAMORE WOOD
LOWDHAM GRANGE
NORTHALLERTON
SACHSENHAUSEN (P)
SHEPTON MALLET
STANDFORD HILL

BUILDINGS

SCHOOLS & UNIVERSITIES

All Schools except: (C) = Cambridge college   (E) = European university
(L) = London college   (O) = Oxford college   (R) = Russian university
(S) = When school is also a university or college   (U) = University
(US) = USA university
* = Alternative name   † = Acronym

3

LMH *(O)* †
LSE *(L)* †
WYE *(L)*

4

BATH *(U)*
BONN *(E)*
BURY
CORK
ETON
HULL *(U)*
KENT *(S/U)*
OPEN *(U)*
OSLO *(E)*
PARK

ROME *(E)*
YALE *(US)*
YORK *(U)*

5

ASTON *(U)*
BROWN *(US)*
CAIUS *(C)*
CLARE *(C)*
DERBY
DIJÔN *(E)*
DOVER
EPSOM
ESSEX *(U)*
GREEN *(O)*
HULME
JESUS *(C/O)*
KEBLE *(O)*

KEELE *(U)*
KELLY
KING'S *(C/L/S)*
LEEDS *(U)*
LILLE *(E)*
LYONS *(E)*
MILAN *(E)*
ORIEL *(O)*
PADUA *(E)*
PERSE
REED'S
RUGBY
RYDAL
SOFIA *(E)*
STOWE
TRENT
TRURO
UMIST †
WALES *(U)*

6

ARNOLD
ATHENS *(E)*
BANGOR
BOSTON *(US)*
BRUNEL *(U)*
BUCHAN
CAMDEN
DARWIN *(C)*
DUBLIN *(U)* *1
DUNDEE *(U)*
DURHAM *(S/U)*
ELTHAM
EXETER *(O/S/U)*
FETTES
FOREST
GALWAY
GENEVA *(E)*

BUILDINGS – SCHOOLS & UNIVERSITIES

GIRTON *(C)*
HARROW
HUYTON
HYMERS
LEHIGH *(US)*
LISBON *(E)*
LONDON *(U)*
MADRID *(E)*
MERTON *(O)*
MOSCOW *(E)*
OAKHAM
OUNDLE
OXFORD *(U)*
PRAGUE *(E)*
QUEEN'S *(O/S/U)*
QUEENS' *(C)*
RADLEY
REPTON
SELWYN *(C)*
ST BEES
STONAR
SURREY *(U)*
SUSSEX *(U)*
ULSTER *(U)*
VIENNA *(E)*
WADHAM *(O)*
WARSAW *(E)*
WREKIN

DOWNING *(C)*
DULWICH
ELMSLIE
FELSTED
FERRARA *(E)*
GLASGOW *(U)*
HAMBURG *(E)*
HARVARD *(US)*
HOWELL'S
IPSWICH
IRELAND *(U)*
KIRKHAM
LANCING
LEIPZIG *(E)*
LINACRE *(O)*
LINCOLN *(O)*
LORETTO
MALVERN
MAYNARD
NEW HALL *(C)*
NEWNHAM *(C)*
NORWICH
OAKDENE
PENRHOS
PORTORA
READING *(U)*
REDLAND
ROEDEAN
ROSSALL
RUTGERS *(US)*
SALERNO *(E)*
SALFORD *(U)*
ST ANNE'S *(O/S)*
ST CROSS *(O)*
ST FELIX
ST HUGH'S *(O)*
ST JOHN'S *(C/O)*
ST MARY'S
ST PAUL'S
TAUNTON
THE CITY *(U)*
THE LEYS
TORMEAD
TRINITY *(C/O)*
WARWICK *(S/U)*
WOLFSON *(C/O)*

WORKSOP
YESHIVA *(US)*

8

ABERDEEN *(U)*
ABINGDON
ALL SOULS *(O)*
ARDINGLY
ASHVILLE
BELGRADE *(E)*
BERKELEY *(US)*
BIRKBECK *(L)*
BRADFORD *(S/U)*
BRIGHTON
BRUSSELS *(E)*
BUDAPEST *(E)*
CATERHAM
CHANNING
CHIGWELL
COLSTON'S
COLUMBIA *(US)*
DENSTONE
EDGEHILL
EMMANUEL *(C)*
GONVILLE *(C)*
GRESHAM'S
HELSINKI *(E)*
HERTFORD *(O)*
HEYTHROP *(L)*
HIGHGATE
HOMERTON *(C)*
KINGSLEY
KINGSTON
LAWNSIDE
MAGDALEN *(O)*
MILL HILL
MONMOUTH
NUFFIELD *(O)*
OCKBROOK
PEMBROKE *(C/O)*
PLYMOUTH
RED MAIDS'
RENDCOMB
ROBINSON *(C)*

ROSEMEAD
SEDBERGH
SHEBBEAR
SORBONNE *(E)*
ST ALBAN'S
STAMFORD
ST DAVID'S
ST HELEN'S
ST HILDA'S *(O)*
STIRLING *(U)*
ST PETER'S *(O/S)*
VICTORIA
WADHURST
WHITGIFT
WYCLIFFE

9

AMSTERDAM *(E)*
BANCROFT'S
BARCELONA *(E)*
BLUNDELL'S
BRASENOSE *(O)*
BUCHAREST *(E)*
CAMBRIDGE *(U)*
CHURCHILL *(C)*
CLARE HALL *(C)*
CRANBROOK
DARTMOUTH *(US)*
DAUNTSEY'S
DEAN CLOSE
EDINBURGH *(U)*
ELLERSLIE
ELLESMERE
GODOLPHIN
GRENVILLE
HARROGATE
KIMBOLTON
KINGSWOOD
LANCASTER *(U)*
LEICESTER *(U)*
LIVERPOOL *(S/U)*
LOMONOSOV *(R)*
MAGDALENE *(C)*
MILLFIELD
NEWCASTLE *(U)*

7

ALLEYN'S
ASHFORD
BALLIOL *(O)*
BEDFORD
BLOXHAM
BOLOGNA *(E)*
BOOTHAM
BRISTOL *(S/U)*
CANFORD
CHICAGO *(US)*
CHRIST'S *(C)*
CLIFTON
CORNELL *(US)*
CULFORD

NORTHWOOD
POLAM HALL
PRINCETON *(US)*
QUEEN MARY *(L)*
SEVENOAKS
SHEFFIELD *(U)*
SHERBORNE
SILCOATES
ST ANDREWS *(U)*
ST ANTONY'S *(O)*
ST EDMUND'S *(C/S)*
ST EDWARD'S
ST ELPHIN'S
ST GEORGE'S
STOCKHOLM *(E)*
STOCKPORT
TONBRIDGE
UPPINGHAM
WAKEFIELD
WESTFIELD *(L)*
WESTHOLME
WORCESTER *(O)*

10

AMPLEFORTH
BIRKENHEAD
BIRMINGHAM *(U)*
BROMSGROVE
BUCKINGHAM *(U)*
CHELTENHAM
CLAYESMORE
COBHAM HALL
CROFT HOUSE
DAME ALLAN'S
DOWNE HOUSE
EAST ANGLIA *(U)*
EASTBOURNE
FELIXSTOWE
GLENALMOND
GOLDSMITHS' *(L)*
HAILEYBURY
HEADINGTON
HERIOT-WATT *(U)*
HUGHES HALL *(C)*
LLANDOVERY

MANCHESTER *(S/U)*
MARSEILLES *(E)*
NEW COLLEGE *(O)*
NOTTINGHAM *(S/U)*
PORTSMOUTH
QUEEN ANNE'S
QUEENSWOOD
SHREWSBURY
SOMERVILLE *(O)*
ST COLUMBA'S
ST DUNSTAN'S
ST LAWRENCE
ST MICHAEL'S
STONYHURST
TETTENHALL
UNIVERSITY *(L/O/S)*
UPPER CHINE
WESTONBIRT
WINCHESTER

11

ABBOTSHOLME
ALICE OTTLEY
BATTLE ABBEY
CROHAM HURST
FITZWILLIAM *(C)*
FRAMLINGHAM
GIGGLESWICK
GORDONSTOUN
HUNTERHOUSE
KING EDWARD'S
MARLBOROUGH
MARY ERSKINE
MICKLEFIELD
MILTON ABBEY
NORTHAMPTON
POCKLINGTON
SOUTHAMPTON *(U)*
ST BENEDICT'S
ST MARGARET'S
ST MARY'S HALL
STRATHALLAN
STRATHCLYDE *(U)*
TRINITY HALL *(C)*
WESTMINSTER

12

CHARTERHOUSE
CHEADLE HULME
CHRIST CHURCH *(O)*
CITY OF LONDON
HUNMANBY HALL
KING WILLIAM'S
LEIGHTON PARK
LOUGHBOROUGH
PENNSYLVANIA *(US)*
SAN FRANCISCO *(US)*
SIDNEY SUSSEX *(C)*
ST CATHARINE'S *(C)*
ST CATHERINE'S *(O/S)*
ST EDMUND HALL *(O)*
WEST BUCKLAND
WYCOMBE ABBEY

13

ABBOTS BROMLEY
CORPUS CHRISTI *(C/O)*
GEORGE HERIOT'S
GEORGE WATSON'S
LUCY CAVENDISH *(C)*
SUTTON VALENCE

14

FRANCIS HOLLAND
HURSTPIERPOINT
LORD WANDSWORTH
PRINCESS HELENA
QUEEN MARGARET'S
TRINITY COLLEGE *(U)* *1
WELLINGBOROUGH
WOODHOUSE GROVE

15

MERCHANT TAYLORS'
QUEEN ELIZABETH'S
ST DUNSTAN'S ABBEY
WALTHAMSTOW HALL

BUILDINGS

THEATRES & MUSEUMS

(A) = Art gallery   (C) = Collection   (M) = Museum
(O) = Opera/ballet/concert venue   (T) = Theatre

3

JOS *(M-Nigeria)*

4

BODE *(M-Berlin)*
BURG *(T-Austria)*
FOGG *(A-Cambridge USA)*
GATE *(T-Ireland)*
MOMI *(M-London)*
PARK *(T-New York)*
ROSE *(T-London)*
TATE *(A-Liverpool)*
        (A-London)

5

ABBEY *(T-Dublin)*
BRERA *(A-Milan)*
CIVIC *(O-Chicago)*
CLUNY *(M-Paris)*
CONDE *(M-Chantilly)*
FORD'S *(T-Washington)*
FREER *(A-Washington)*
FRICK *(C-New York)*
GLOBE *(T-London)*
KIROV *(O-Leningrad)*
LAING *(A-Newcastle)*
LYRIC *(T-London)*
OPÉRA *(O-Paris)*
PITTI *(A-Florence)*
PRADO *(A-Madrid)*
SAVOY *(T-London)*
USHER *(M-Lincoln)*
V AND A *(M-London)*

6

ALBERY *(T-London)*
ALLAMI *(O-Budapest)*
APOLLO *(T-London)*
BENAKI *(M-Athens)*
BARODA *(A/M-India)*
BOOTH'S *(T-New York)*
BOWERY *(T-London)*
COMEDY *(T-London)*
DAHLEM *(A-Berlin)*
DELPHI *(M-Delphi)*
FERENS *(A-Hull)*
LOUVRE *(A/M-Paris)*
LYCEUM *(T-London)*
        (T-New York)
MAEGHT *(A-Paris)*
OLD VIC *(T-London)*
PALACE *(T-London)*
QUEEN'S *(T-London)*
STATES *(M-Berlin)*
STRAND *(T-London)*
SUDLEY *(A-Liverpool)*
SYDNEY *(O-Sydney)*
UFFIZI *(A-Florence)*
WALKER *(A-Liverpool)*

7

ACADEMY *(A-Florence)*
ADELPHI *(T-London)*
ALDWYCH *(T-London)*
ASTORIA *(T-London)*
BEAMISH *(M-Gateshead)*
BOLSHOI *(O/T-Moscow)*
BRITISH *(M-London)*
CENTURY *(T-New York)*
DUCHESS *(T-London)*

EPHESUS *(M-Turkey)*

EPHESUS *(M-Turkey)*
FORTUNE *(T-London)*
GARRICK *(T-London)*
HAYWARD *(A-London)*
HERBERT *(A/M-Coventry)*
LA SCALA *(O-Milan)*
MARQUIS *(T-New York)*
MAYFAIR *(T-London)*
MERMAID *(T-London)*
OLIVIER *(T-London)*
PHOENIX *(T-London)*
        (T-New York)
PICASSO *(A-Barcelona)*
SCIENCE *(M-London)*
TOPKAPI *(M-Istanbul)*
VATICAN *(M-Rome)*
WALLACE *(C-London)*
WHITNEY *(A-New York)*

8

BARBICAN *(T-London)*
BORGHESE *(A-Rome)*
CITIZENS' *(T-Glasgow)*
CROMWELL *(M-Huntingdon)*
DOMINION *(T-London)*
FESTIVAL *(T-Ontario)*
        (T-Stratford)
FOLKWANG *(A-Essen)*
LA FENICE *(O-Venice)*
MAJESTIC *(T-New York)*
NATIONAL *(A-London)*
        (O-Prague)
        (T-London)
PERGAMON *(M-Berlin)*
PHILLIPS *(C-Washington)*
WYNDHAM'S *(T-London)*
YOUNG VIC *(T-London)*

9

ACROPOLIS *(M-Athens)*
ALBERTINE *(C-Vienna)*
ASHMOLEAN *(M-Oxford)*
COTTESLOE *(T-London)*
CRITERION *(T-London)*
DRURY LANE *(T-London)*
GROSVENOR *(M-Chester)*
HAYMARKET *(T-London)*
HERMITAGE *(A-Leningrad)*
LYTTLETON *(T-London)*
MARMOTTAN *(A-Paris)*
MARYINSKY *(O-St Petersburg)*
NEW LONDON *(T-London)*
NICHOLSON *(M-Sydney)*
PALLADIUM *(T-London)*
SAN CARLOS *(O-Naples)*
SOUTHWARK *(T-London)*
             (T-Philadelphia)
ST MARTYN'S *(T-London)*
TRETIAKOV *(A-Moscow)*
WHITEHALL *(T-London)*
WHITWORTH *(A-Manchester)*

10

AMBROSIANA *(A-Milan)*
CAPITOLINE *(M-Rome)*
COURTAULD'S *(A-London)*
FUNAMBULES *(T-Paris)*
GEOLOGICAL *(M-London)*
GUGGENHEIM *(A-New York)*
GULBENKIAN *(A-Lisbon)*
PICCADILLY *(T-London)*
ROYAL COURT *(T-London)*
STAATSOPER *(O-Berlin)*
             (O-Munich)
             (O-Vienna)

11

AMBASSADORS *(T-London)*
BRIDGESTONE *(A-Tokyo)*

DUKE OF YORK'S *(T-London)*
FITZWILLIAM *(M-Cambridge)*
HER MAJESTY'S *(T-London)*
IMPERIAL WAR *(M-London)*
POLD PEZZOLI *(A-Milan)*
RIJKSMUSEUM *(A/M-Amsterdam)*
SHAFTESBURY *(T-London)*
WESTMINSTER *(T-London)*
WÜRTTEMBURG *(O/T-Stuttgart)*

12

COVENT GARDEN *(O-London)*
DEUTSCHE OPER *(O-Berlin)*
FESTIVAL HALL *(C/O-London)*
METROPOLITAN *(O-New York)*
NATIONAL ARMY *(M-London)*
REDOUTENSALL *(T-Vienna)*
SADLER'S WELLS *(O/T-London)*
WALNUT STREET *(T-Philadelphia)*

13

FESTSPIELHAUS *(O-Salzburg)*
LINCOLN CENTER *(A/O/T-New York)*
NATIONAL MOTOR *(M-Beaulieu)*
OSKAR REINHART *(A-Switzerland)*
PRINCE OF WALES *(T-London)*
ROYAL AIR FORCE *(M-Hendon)*

14

CARTWRIGHT HALL *(M-Bradford)*
NATURAL HISTORY *(M-London)*
VICTORIA PALACE *(T-London)*

15

BARBER INSTITUTE *(M-Birmingham)*
LEOPOLDERSTADER *(T-Austria)*
NATIONAL RAILWAY *(M-York)*
NATIONAL TRAMWAY *(M-Crich)*

FORENAMES

BOYS' NAMES

3	KEN	**4**	EGON	KARL	RYAN	ANGEL	DACRE	FRANS
	KEV		EMIL	KEIR	SAUL	ANGUS	DAMON	FRANZ
ABE	KIM	ABEL	ERIC	KENT	SEAN	ANTON	DANNY	FRITZ
ABY	KIT	ADAM	ERLE	KING	SETH	ARCHY	DARCY	FULKE
ALF	LEE	ALAN	ERYL	KIRK	STAN	ARTIE	DARYL	GARRY
ALI	LEN	ALEC	ESAU	KURT	SVEN	AUBYN	DAVID	GARTH
ART	LEO	ALED	EVAN	KYLE	THEO	BARRY	DAVIE	GAVIN
ASA	LEV	ALGY	EWAN	LARS	THOR	BASIL	DENIS	GEOFF
BEN	LEW	ALUN	EZRA	LEON	TOBY	BENNY	DENNY	GERRY
BOB	LOU	ALVA	FATS	LIAM	TODD	BEVIS	DENYS	GILES
BUD	MAT	ALYN	FINN	LUKE	TONY	BILLY	DEREK	GLENN
COL	MAX	AMOS	FRED	MARC	TREV	BLAKE	DICKY	GRANT
DAI	MEL	ANDY	FULK	MARK	VERE	BOBBY	DONAL	GRIFF
DAN	NAT	AXEL	GARY	MATT	WALT	BOOTH	DUANE	GUIDO
DEC	NED	BART	GENE	MICK	WILF	BORIS	DWANE	GYLES
DEE	NYE	BERT	GLEN	MIKE	WILL	BRETT	DYLAN	HARRY
DEL	ODO	BILL	GLYN	MORT	WYNN	BRIAN	EAMON	HEINZ
DEN	PAT	BOYD	GREG	MUIR	YVES	BRUCE	EARLE	HENRI
DOD	PIP	BRAM	HANK	NEIL	ZEKE	BRUNO	EDDIE	HENRY
DON	RAY	BRYN	HANS	NERO		BRYAN	EDGAR	HIRAM
ECK	RED	BUCK	HOPE	NICK		BUDDY	EDWIN	HOMER
ELI	REG	BURT	HUEY	NIKI	**5**	BUNNY	ELDON	HORST
ERN	REX	CAIN	HUGH	NOAH		BUSBY	ELIAS	HUMPH
GAY	ROD	CARL	HUGO	NOËL	AARON	CAIUS	ELLIS	HYRAM
GIL	ROG	CARY	IAIN	OLAF	ABDUL	CALEB	ELMER	HYWEL
GUS	ROY	CHAD	IGOR	OLAV	ABNER	CAREW	ELTON	INIGO
GUY	SAM	CHAS	IVAN	OMAR	ABRAM	CAROL	ELVIS	INNES
HAL	SEB	CHAY	IVOR	OTHO	ADOLF	CECIL	ELWYN	ISAAC
HEW	SID	CHIP	JACK	OTIS	AIDAN	CHRIS	EMERY	IZAAK
HUW	SLY	CLEM	JAKE	OTTO	AIREY	CHUCK	EMILE	JABEZ
IAN	TAM	DALE	JEAN	OWEN	ALAIN	CLAUD	EMLYN	JACKY
IKE	TED	DAVE	JEFF	PAUL	ALBAN	CLIFF	EMRYS	JACOB
IRA	TIM	DAVY	JESS	PEPE	ALFIE	CLINT	ENOCH	JAIME
IVO	TOM	DEAN	JOCK	PETE	ALICK	CLIVE	ERNIE	JAMES
JAN	VAL	DICK	JODY	PHIL	ALLAN	CLYDE	ERNST	JAMIE
JAY	VAN	DIRK	JOEL	RENÉ	ALLEN	COLIN	ERROL	JARED
JED	VIC	DION	JOEY	RHYS	ALVIN	CONAN	EWART	JASON
JEM	VIV	DREW	JOHN	RICK	ALWIN	COREY	FELIX	JERRY
JIM	WAT	DUFF	JOSH	ROLF	ALWYN	COSMO	FERDY	JESSE
JOB	WES	DUKE	JOSS	RORY	AMAND	CRAIG	FLANN	JIMMY
JOE	WYN	EARL	JUAN	ROSS	AMYAS	CYRIL	FLOYD	JONAH
JON		EDDY	JUDE	RUSS	ANDRÉ	CYRUS	FRANK	JONAS

JULES	RIDER	ALARIC	DERMOT	HARRIS	LUDWIG	RICHIE
KEITH	ROALD	ALBERT	DERYCK	HARVEY	LUTHER	ROBBIE
KELLY	ROBIN	ALDRED	DÉSIRÉ	HAYDON	MAGNUS	ROBERT
KENNY	RODDY	ALEXIS	DICKIE	HECTOR	MANUEL	RODGER
KEVIN	ROGER	ALFRED	DONALD	HEDLEY	MARCEL	RODNEY
LANCE	ROLLO	ANDREW	DONNIE	HELMUT	MARCUS	ROLAND
LARRY	ROMEO	ANGELO	DOUGAL	HERMAN	MARTIN	RONALD
LEIGH	ROWAN	ANSELM	DUGALD	HILARY	MARTYN	ROWLEY
LENNY	RUBIN	ANTONY	DUGGIE	HILTON	MELVIN	RUDOLF
LEROY	RUFUS	ARCHIE	DUNCAN	HORACE	MELVYN	RUPERT
LEWIN	SACHA	ARMAND	DUNDAS	HOWARD	MERLIN	SAMSON
LEWIS	SANDY	ARNOLD	DWIGHT	HOWELL	MICKIE	SAMUEL
LLOYD	SCOTT	ARTHUR	EAMONN	HUBERT	MILTON	SANCHO
LOUIE	SERGE	ASHLEY	EDMOND	HUGHIE	MORGAN	SEAMAS
LOUIS	SHANE	ASHOKA	EDMUND	IGNACE	MORRIS	SEAMUS
LUCAS	SILAS	AUBREY	EDUARD	INGRAM	MOSTYN	SEFTON
LUIGI	SIMON	AUSTIN	EDWARD	IRVINE	MURPHY	SELWYN
MAJOR	SOLLY	AYLMER	EGBERT	ISAIAH	MURRAY	SEXTON
MICAH	SONNY	AYLWIN	ELDRED	ISODOR	NATHAN	SIDNEY
MICKY	SPIRO	BARNEY	ELLIOT	ISRAEL	NEDDIE	SIMEON
MILES	STEVE	BENITO	ERNEST	JACKIE	NELSON	SIMKIN
MONTY	TAFFY	BENJIE	ESMOND	JARVIS	NICHOL	SOAMES
MOSES	TEDDY	BENNIE	EUGENE	JASPER	NINIAN	STEFAN
MUNGO	TERRY	BERNIE	EVELYN	JEREMY	NORMAN	STEVEN
MURDO	TIBOR	BERTIE	FABIAN	JEROME	NORRIS	STEVIE
NAHUM	TITUS	BRUTUS	FERGUS	JERVIS	OLIVER	STUART
NEDDY	TOMMY	BULWER	FINLAY	JETHRO	ONSLOW	SYDNEY
NEVIL	ULICK	BUSTER	FORBES	JOHANN	OSBERT	THOMAS
NIALL	ULRIC	CAESAR	GARETH	JOHNNY	OSMOND	TOBIAS
NIGEL	ULTAN	CALVIN	GASTON	JOSEPH	OSMUND	TREVOR
NOLAN	URBAN	CARLOS	GAWAIN	JOSHUA	OSWALD	TYBALT
OSCAR	URIAH	CASPAR	GEORGE	JOSIAH	PASCAL	TYRONE
OSMAN	VINCE	CEDRIC	GERALD	JULIAN	PASCOE	VERNON
OSRIC	WAHAB	CLAUDE	GERARD	JULIUS	PAULUS	VICTOR
OSWIN	WALLY	COLLEY	GIDEON	JUSTIN	PEARCE	VIRGIL
PADDY	WAYNE	CONNOR	GODWIN	JUSTUS	PELHAM	VIVIAN
PEDRO	WILLY	CONRAD	GORDON	KIERAN	PERKIN	VYVIAN
PERCY	WOLFE	CUDDIE	GRAEME	KONRAD	PHILIP	WALLIS
PERRY	WOODY	DAMIAN	GRAHAM	LAURIE	PIERCE	WALTER
PETER	WYATT	DANIEL	GROGAN	LAWRIE	PIERRE	WARREN
PIERS		DARREN	GUNTER	LEMUEL	RAMSAY	WESLEY
RALPH	**6**	DARRYL	GWILYM	LESLIE	RANDAL	WILBUR
RAMON		DECLAN	HAMISH	LESTER	RASTUS	WILLIE
RAOUL	ADOLPH	DELROY	HAMLET	LIONEL	RAYNER	XAVIER
RHETT	ADRIAN	DENNIS	HANSEL	LORCAN	REGGIE	YEHUDI
RICKY	AENEAS	DENZIL	HAROLD	LUCIUS	RHODES	

FORENAMES – BOYS' NAMES

7

ABRAHAM
ABSALOM
AINSLEY
ALFONSO
ALISTER
ALMERIC
AMADEUS
AMBROSE
ANATOLE
ANEURIN
ANTHONY
ANTOINE
ANTONIO
ARTEMUS
AUBERON
AUGUSTE
BALDWIN
BAPTIST
BARCLAY
BARNABY
BERNARD
BERTRAM
BRANDON
BRENDAN
BRYNMOR
CAMERON
CARADOC
CASIMIR
CHARLES
CHARLEY
CHARLIE
CHESTER
CLAYTON
CLEMENT
CLINTON
COMPTON
CONNELL
CRISPIN
CYPRIAN
DELBERT
DERRICK
DESMOND
DIGGORY
DOMINIC

DONOVAN
DOUGLAS
EDOUARD
ELEAZER
EPHRAIM
ERASMUS
EUSTACE
EVERARD
EZEKIEL
FEARGAL
FINDLAY
FRANCIS
FRANKIE
FREDDIE
GABRIEL
GEORGIE
GERAINT
GERVASE
GILBERT
GLOSTER
GODFREY
GREGORY
GUSTAVE
HADRIAN
HALBERT
HARTLEY
HERBERT
HERMANN
HILAIRE
HORATIO
HUMBERT
HUMPHRY
INGLEBY
ISIDORE
JACKSON
JACQUES
JEFFREY
JOACHIM
JOCELYN
JOHNNIE
KENNETH
KIMBALL
LACHLAN
LAMBERT
LAZARUS
LEONARD

LEOPOLD
LINDSAY
LORENZO
LUDOVIC
MALACHI
MALCOLM
MATTHEW
MAURICE
MAXWELL
MAYNARD
MERRICK
MICHAEL
MONTAGU
MYRDDIN
NEVILLE
NICOLAS
OBADIAH
OCTAVUS
ORLANDO
ORPHEUS
ORVILLE
OSBORNE
PATRICK
PERSEUS
PHINEAS
QUENTIN
QUINTIN
RANULPH
RAPHAEL
RAYMOND
RAYMUND
REDVERS
REYNARD
REYNOLD
RICHARD
ROYSTON
RUDOLPH
RUDYARD
RUSSELL
SAMPSON
SEYMOUR
SHELDON
SHELLEY
SIGMUND
SOLOMON
SPENCER

STANLEY
STAVROS
STEPHEN
STEUART
STEWART
TARQUIN
TERENCE
TIMOTHY
TORQUIL
TRISTAN
UCHTRED
UGHTRED
ULYSSES
UMBERTO
VAUGHAN
VINCENT
WALLACE
WILFRED
WILFRID
WILHELM
WILLIAM
WINSTON
WYNDHAM
WYNFORD
ZACHARY
ZEBEDEE

8

ACHILLES
ADOLPHUS
ALASDAIR
ALASTAIR
ALGERNON
ALISTAIR
ALOYSIUS
ALPHONSO
ANTONIUS
AUGUSTUS
AURELIUS
BARDOLPH
BARNABAS
BARTLEMY
BENEDICT
BENJAMIN

BERTRAND
BEVERLEY
CAMPBELL
CHRISTIE
CLARENCE
CLAUDIUS
CLIFFORD
CONSTANT
COURTNEY
CRAWFORD
CRISPIAN
CUTHBERT
DINSDALE
DOMINICK
EBENEZER
EMMANUEL
ETHELRED
EUSEBIUS
FARQUHAR
FRANÇOIS
FRANKLIN
FREDERIC
GEOFFREY
GIOVANNI
GIUSEPPE
GREVILLE
GRIFFITH
GUSTAVUS
HAMILTON
HARRISON
HAVELOCK
HERCULES
HEREWARD
HEZEKIAH
HORATIUS
HUMPHREY
IGNATIUS
IMMANUEL
JEDEDIAH
JEREMIAH
JONATHAN
KIMBERLY
KINGSLEY
LANCELOT
LAURENCE
LAWRENCE

LEONIDAS
LLEWELYN
LUDOVICK
LUTWIDGE
MEREDITH
MONTAGUE
MORTIMER
NEHEMIAH
NICHOLAS
OCTAVIUS
OLIPHANT
OUGHTRED
PAULINUS
PERCEVAL
PERCIVAL
PETERKIN
PHILEMON
RANDOLPH
REGINALD
ROBINSON
RODERICK
RUAIRIDH
SALVADOR
SECUNDUS
SEPTIMUS
SHERLOCK
SIEGMUND
SINCLAIR
STAFFORD
SYLVANUS
TERRANCE
THADDEUS
THEOBALD
THEODORE
TRISTRAM
VLADIMIR

9

ALEXANDER
ALPHONSUS
ARCHIBALD
ARISTOTLE
ATHELSTAN
AUGUSTINE

BALTHAZAR	GRENVILLE	RUPPRECHT	**10**	WASHINGTON
BARTIMEUS	JUSTINIAN	SEBASTIAN		WILLOUGHBY
CHRISTIAN	KIMBERLEY	SIEGFRIED	ATHANASIUS	
CORNELIUS	LAUNCELOT	SIGISMUND	ATHELSTANE	
DEMETRIUS	LLEWELLYN	STANISLAS	BARRINGTON	**11**
DIONYSIUS	LUCRETIUS	SYLVESTER	DESIDERIUS	BARTHOLOMEW
ENGELBERT	MACKENZIE	THADDAEUS	HILDEBRAND	CHRISTOPHER
ETHELBERT	MARMADUKE	THEODORIC	MAXIMILIAN	CONSTANTINE
FERDINAND	NATHANIEL	VALENTINE	PIERREPONT	DESIDERATUS
FREDERICK	NICODEMUS	ZACHARIAH	STANISLAUS	GILLEASBUIG
GILLESPIE	PEREGRINE	ZECHARIAH	THEODOSIUS	SACHEVERELL
GRANVILLE	RODRIGUEZ		THEOPHILUS	

FORENAMES

GIRLS' NAMES

3	IDA	PAM	**4**	CHER	ETTY	IONA	LAYA	NANA	SINE	
	INA	PAT		CLEO	EVIE	IRIS	LEAH	NELL	SUKY	
ADA	ISA	PEG	ADDY	CORA	FERN	IRMA	LENA	NINA	SUSY	
ALI	IVY	PEN	AFRA	DALE	FIFI	ISLA	LILY	NITA	SUZI	
AMY	JAN	PIA	AGGY	DANA	FRAN	JADE	LISA	NOËL	TARA	
ANN	JEN	RAE	AIMI	DAWN	GABY	JANE	LITA	NOLA	TESS	
AVA	JOY	RAY	ALLY	DIDO	GAIL	JEAN	LIZA	NONA	THEA	
BEA	KAY	RIA	ALMA	DOLL	GAYE	JESS	LOIS	NORA	TINA	
BEE	KIM	RIO	ALYS	DORA	GENE	JILL	LOLA	OLGA	TRIX	
BET	KIT	SAL	ANNA	EDIE	GERT	JOAN	LUCY	OONA	VERA	
CIS	LEA	SIB	ANNE	EDNA	GIGI	JODI	LULU	PRUE	VIDA	
CYD	LEE	SUE	AVIS	ELLA	GILL	JODY	LYNN	RENA	VIKI	
DEE	LIZ	TIB	BABS	ELMA	GINA	JONI	MARY	RITA	VITA	
DOT	LOU	UNA	BEBE	ELSA	GWEN	JUDY	MAUD	ROMA	ZARA	
EDY	LYN	VAL	BECK	ELSE	HANA	JUNE	META	RONA	ZENA	
ENA	MAI	VIV	BELL	EMMA	HEBE	KATE	MIMA	ROSA	ZOLA	
EVA	MAY	WIN	BESS	EMMY	HOPE	KATH	MIMI	ROSE	**5**	
EVE	MEG	ZIA	BETH	ENID	INES	KATY	MINA	RUBY		ABBIE
FAY	MIA	ZOË	CASS	ERYL	INEZ	KIKI	MOLL	RUTH		ADDIE
FLO	MIN		CATH	ESME	INGA	LALA	MONA	SARA		
GAY	NAN		CERI	ETTA	INGE	LARA	MYRA	SIAN		

FORENAMES — GIRLS' NAMES

ADELA	CIRCE	HAZEL	MADGE	PENNY	**6**	CAROLE	GLORIA
ADÈLE	CISSY	HEIDI	MAEVE	PIPPA		CARRIE	GLYNIS
ADINA	CLAIR	HELEN	MAGDA	POLLY	ADELLA	CECILE	GRACIE
AGGIE	CLARA	HELGA	MAGGY	POPPY	AGATHA	CECILY	GRETEL
AGNES	CLARE	HILDA	MAMIE	RENÉE	AILEEN	CHARIS	GUDRUN
AILIE	CORAL	HOLLY	MANDY	RHIAN	ALEXIS	CHERRY	GUSSIE
AILSA	DAISY	HONOR	MARIA	RHODA	ALICIA	CICELY	GWENDA
ALANA	DEBBY	HULDA	MARIE	RHONA	ALISON	CISSIE	HANNAH
ALEXA	DELIA	HYLDA	MAUDE	ROBIN	ALTHEA	CLAIRE	HATTIE
ALICE	DELLA	ILANA	MAVIS	ROBYN	ALYSSA	CONNIE	HAYLEY
ALINE	DIANA	IRENE	MEAVE	ROSIE	AMABEL	DAPHNE	HEDWIG
AMBER	DIANE	ISOLD	MEGAN	SADIE	AMANDA	DAVINA	HELENA
ANAÏS	DILYS	JANET	MERCY	SALLY	AMELIA	DEANNA	HESTER
ANGEL	DINAH	JANIE	MERLE	SANDY	ANDREA	DEANNE	HILARY
ANGIE	DOLLY	JENNY	MERYL	SARAH	ANGELA	DEBBIE	HONORA
ANITA	DONNA	JILLY	MILLY	SIBYL	ANNEKA	DELYTH	IANTHE
ANNIE	DORIS	JINNY	MINNA	SINDY	ANTHEA	DENISE	IMELDA
ANNIS	EBONY	JODIE	MITZI	SISSY	ARETHA	DIANNE	IMOGEN
ANONA	EDITH	JOSIE	MOIRA	SONIA	ARLEEN	DIONNE	INGRID
APHRA	EFFIE	JOYCE	MOLLY	SONJA	ARLENE	DIVINA	ISABEL
APRIL	ELISE	JULIA	MORAG	STACY	ASTRID	DORCAS	ISOBEL
AVICE	ELIZA	JULIE	MOYNA	SUSAN	AUDREY	DOREEN	ISOLDA
AVRIL	ELLEN	KAREN	MOYRA	SUSIE	AURIEL	DULCIE	ISOLDE
BECKY	ELLIE	KATIE	NANCE	SYBIL	AURORA	EDWINA	JACKIE
BELLA	ELSIE	KELLY	NANCY	TAMMY	AVERIL	EILEEN	JACOBA
BELLE	EMILY	KERRY	NAOMI	TANIA	BABBIE	EITHNA	JANICE
BERYL	EPPIE	KETTY	NELLY	TANYA	BARBIE	ELAINE	JEMIMA
BETSY	ERICA	KITTY	NESSA	TERRY	BEATTY	ELINOR	JENNIE
BETTE	ERIKA	KYLIE	NESTA	TESSA	BENITA	ELOISA	JESSIE
BETTY	ESSIE	LAILA	NETTA	THORA	BERTHA	ELOISE	JOANNA
BIDDY	ETHEL	LAURA	NINON	TILLY	BESSIE	ELUNED	JOANNE
BRIDE	FAITH	LEIGH	NIOBE	TRACY	BIDDIE	ELVIRA	JOLEEN
BUNNY	FANNY	LEILA	NOËLE	TRIXY	BILLIE	EMILIA	JOLENE
BUNTY	FIONA	LETTY	NORAH	TRUDY	BLANCH	ESTHER	JUDITH
CANDY	FLEUR	LIANA	NORMA	UNITY	BOBBIE	EUNICE	JULIET
CARLA	FLORA	LIBBY	NORNA	VENUS	BONITA	EVELYN	KIRSTY
CARLY	FREDA	LILLY	OLIVE	VESTA	BONNIE	FATIMA	LALAGE
CAROL	GABBY	LINDA	OLWEN	VICKY	BRANDY	FELICE	LALLIE
CASEY	GEMMA	LINDY	OLWIN	VIOLA	BRENDA	FINOLA	LAUREN
CATHY	GERDA	LORNA	PADDY	WANDA	BRIDIE	FLAVIA	LEANNE
CELIA	GINNY	LOTTY	PANSY	WENDY	BRIGID	FRIEDA	LEONIE
CHÈRE	GRACE	LUCIA	PATSY	WILMA	BRIONY	GAYNOR	LESLEY
CHLOË	GREER	LYDIA	PATTY	XENIA	BRYONY	GERTIE	LETTIE
CHRIS	GRETA	LYNDA	PAULA	ZELDA	BUNNIE	GINGER	LILIAN
CILLA	GUSSY	LYNNE	PEARL		CARMEL	GLADYS	LILIAS
CINDY	HALEY	MABEL	PEGGY		CARMEN	GLENDA	LILLIE

LINSAY	PERSIS	ULRICA	CAROLYN	HORATIA	MELANIE
LINSEY	PETULA	URSULA	CECILIA	HYPATIA	MELISSA
LIZZIE	PHOEBE	VALERY	CELESTE	ISADORA	MICHÈLE
LORANA	PORTIA	VANORA	CHARITY	ISIDORA	MILDRED
LOTTIE	PSYCHE	VERENA	CHLORIS	JACINTA	MINERVA
LOUISA	PURDIE	VERITY	CLARICE	JACQUIE	MIRABEL
LOUISE	RACHEL	VIOLET	CLARRIE	JANETTA	MIRANDA
LYNSEY	RAMONA	VIVIEN	CLAUDIA	JANETTE	MONIQUE
MAGGIE	REGINA	VYVYEN	CLODAGH	JASMINE	MORGANA
MAISIE	RENATA	WINNIE	COLETTE	JEANNIE	MORWENA
MARCIA	ROBINA	YASMIN	CORALIE	JESSICA	MYFANWY
MARGIE	ROSINA	YVETTE	CORINNE	JILLIAN	NATALIA
MARGOT	ROWENA	YVONNE	CORINNA	JOCELYN	NATALIE
MARIAN	ROXANA	ZILLAH	CRYSTAL	JOHANNA	NATASHA
MARION	SABINA		CYNTHIA	JOSEPHA	NINETTE
MARNIE	SABINE	**7**	DEBORAH	JONQUIL	NOELEEN
MARSHA	SALOME		DEIRDRE	JUANITA	OCTAVIA
MARTHA	SANDIE	ABIGAIL	DÉSIRÉE	JULIANA	OLYMPIA
MATTIE	SANDRA	ADELINA	DOLORES	JUSTINA	OPHELIA
MAXINE	SAPPHO	ADELINE	DORINDA	KATHRYN	OTTILIA
MELODY	SELINA	ADRIANA	DOROTHY	KATRINE	PANDORA
MERIEL	SERENA	ALBERTA	ELEANOR	KATRINA	PASCALE
MHAIRI	SHARON	ALETHEA	ELFLEDA	LAVINIA	PAULINA
MILLIE	SHEENA	ALFREDA	ELFREDA	LEONORA	PAULINE
MINNIE	SHEILA	ANNABEL	ELSPETH	LETITIA	PERDITA
MIRIAM	SHERRY	ANNETTE	ESTELLA	LETTICE	PHILLIS
MOLLIE	SIGRID	ANTONIA	ESTELLE	LILLIAN	PHYLLIS
MONICA	SILVIA	ARIADNE	EUGÉNIA	LILLIAS	QUEENIE
MORVEN	SIMONE	ATHENIA	EUGÉNIE	LISBETH	RAELENE
MURIEL	SINEAD	AUGUSTA	EULALIA	LISETTE	REBECCA
MYRTLE	SOPHIA	AURELIA	EVELINA	LIZBETH	RICARDA
NADINE	SOPHIE	BABETTE	EVELINE	LORETTA	ROBERTA
NELLIE	SORCHA	BARBARA	FELICIA	LORINDA	ROSALIA
NESSIE	STELLA	BEATRIX	FENELLA	LUCILLA	ROSALIE
NETTIE	STEVIE	BELINDA	FIDELIA	LUCILLE	ROSANNA
NICOLA	SYLVIA	BERNICE	FLORRIE	LUCINDA	ROSETTA
NICOLE	TAMARA	BETTINA	FLOSSIE	LUCRECE	ROSHEEN
NOREEN	TAMSIN	BLANCHE	FRANCES	LYNETTE	SABRINA
ODETTE	TERESA	BLODWEN	GEORGIA	MADONNA	SEONAID
OLIVIA	TESSIE	BLOSSOM	GILLIAN	MARGERY	SHELLEY
OONAGH	THALIA	BRIDGET	GWENNIE	MARILYN	SHIRLEY
OTILIE	THECLA	BRONWEN	GWYNETH	MARJORY	SIDONIA
PAMELA	THELMA	BRONWYN	HARRIET	MARLENE	SIOBHAN
PARNEL	TOMINA	CAMILLA	HEATHER	MARTINA	SUSANNA
PATTIE	TRACEY	CANDICE	HELOISE	MATILDA	SUSANNE
PERNEL	TRIXIE	CANDIDA	HILARIA	MAUREEN	SUZANNE

159

FORENAMES – GIRLS' NAMES

SYBILLA
TABITHA
TATIANA
THERESA
THERESE
TIFFANY
VALERIA
VALERIE
VANESSA
VENETIA
YOLANDA
YOLANDE
ZENOBIA

8

ADELAIDE
ADRIANNE
ADRIENNE
ANGELICA
ANGELINA
ANGHARAD
ARABELLA
ATALANTA
BEATRICE
BERENICE
BEVERLEY
BRIGITTE
CARLOTTA
CAROLINA
CAROLINE
CATRIONA
CHARLENE
CHARMIAN
CHRISSIE
CHRYSTAL
CLARINDA
CLARISSA
CLEMENCY
CLOTILDA
CLOTILDE
CONSUELA
CORDELIA
CORNELIA
DANIELLA

DANIELLE
DIONYSIA
DOROTHEA
DRUSILLA
ELEANORE
EMMELINE
ETHELIND
EUPHEMIA
FAUSTINA
FELICITY
FLORENCE
FRANCINE
GEORGINA
GERMAINE
GERTRUDE
GRETCHEN
GRISELDA
GRIZELDA
HERMIONE
HORTENSE
HYACINTH
INGEBORG
ISABELLA
JACINTHA
JACINTHE
JACOBINA
JAMESINA
JEANETTE
JENNIFER
JOCELINE
JULIETTA
JULIETTE
KATERINA
KATHLEEN
KIMBERLY
KIRSTEEN
LAETITIA
LAURETTA
LAURINDA
LAVENDER
LORRAINE
LUCRETIA
MADELINE
MAGDALEN
MARCELLE
MARGARET

MARIANNE
MARIETTA
MARIGOLD
MARJORIE
MICHAELA
MICHELLE
MIREILLE
MORWENNA
MYRTILLA
NATHALIE
PATIENCE
PATRICIA
PENELOPE
PHILIPPA
PHILLIDA
PHYLLIDA
PRIMROSE
PRUDENCE
PRUNELLA
RHIANNON
ROSALIND
ROSALINE
ROSAMOND
ROSAMUND
ROSEANNA
ROSEMARY
SAMANTHA
SAPPHIRE
SHEELAGH
STEPHANA
SUSANNAH
TALLULAH
THEODORA
THERESIA
TRYPHENA
VERONICA
VICTORIA
VIOLETTA
VIRGINIA
VIVIENNE
WINIFRED

9

ALBERTINA

ALBERTINE
ALEXANDRA
ANASTASIA
ANNABELLA
ANNABELLE
BENEDICTA
CASSANDRA
CATHARINE
CATHERINE
CELESTINE
CHARLOTTE
CHARMAINE
CHRISTIAN
CHRISTINA
CHRISTINE
CLEOPATRA
CLOTHILDA
CLOTHILDE
COLUMBINE
CONSTANCE
DESDEMONA
ELISABETH
ELIZABETH
ERNESTINE
ESMERALDA
ETHELDRED
FRANCESCA
FRANÇOISE
FREDERICA
GABRIELLA
GABRIELLE
GENEVIEVE
GEORGETTE
GEORGIANA
GERALDINE
GUINEVERE
GWENDOLEN
HENRIETTA
HEPHZIBAH
HILDEGARD
HORTENSIA
IPHIGENIA
JACQUELYN
JACQUETTA
JESSAMINE
JOSEPHINE

KATHARINE
KATHERINE
KIMBERLEY
MADELEINE
MAGDALENA
MAGDALENE
MARGARITA
MILLICENT
PHILOMENA
PRISCILLA
ROSABELLA
SOPHRONIA
STEPHANIE
THEODOSIA
THOMASINA
VALENTINA
VALENTINE

10

ANTOINETTE
BERNADETTE
CHRISTABEL
CHRISTIANA
CINDERELLA
CLEMENTINA
CLEMENTINE
DESIDERATA
ERMENTRUDE
ETHELDREDA
EVANGELINA
EVANGELINE
GWENDOLINE
IRMENTRUDE
JACQUELINE
MARGHERITA
MARGUERITE
PETRONELLA
PETRONILLA
PHILIPPINA
WILHELMINA

11

ALEXANDRINA

160

GEOGRAPHY

BAYS & SEAS – BRITISH ISLES

(C) = Channel   (F) = Firth   (I) = Ireland   (M) = Isle of Man
(S) = Scotland   (SE) = Sea   (SO) = Sound   (ST) = Strait   (W) = Wales
* = Alternative spelling/name   NB: (E) = England & (B) = Bay only when
waters overlap or one name equals two waters

3

AYR *(S)*
MEY *(S)*
RUM *(S-SO)* *1
RYE
TAY *(S)*
TOR

4

ALUM
BUDE
BUTE *(S-SO)*
CLEW *(I)*
DEER *(S-SO)*
EIGG *(S-SO)*
JURA *(S-SO)*
LORN *(S-F)*
LUCE *(S)*
LYME
MULL *(S-SO)*
NIGG *(S)*
RHOS *(W)*
RHUM *(S-SO)* *1
SPEY *(S)*
TARN
TEES
YELL *(S-SO)*

5

BARRA *(S-SO)*
BROAD *(S)*

BUDLE
CANNA *(S-SO)*
CLYDE *(S-F)*
CONWY *(W)*
DOVER *(ST)*
DULAS *(W)*
ENARD *(S)*
FILEY
FORTH *(S-F)*
GIGHA *(S-SO)*
IRISH *(SE)*
LARGS *(S)*
LAXEY *(M)*
LUNAN *(S)*
MENAI *(W-ST)*
MORAY *(S-F)*
MORTE
NORTH *(I/S-C, SE)*
SLEAT *(S-SO)*
SLIGO *(I)*
START

6

AYR BAY *(S)*
BANTRY *(I)*
BEAULY *(S-F)*
CEMAES *(W)*
CROSBY *(C)*
DINGLE *(I)*
DUNNET *(S)*
GALWAY *(I)*
HARRIS *(S-SO)*
IRVINE *(S)*
LAGGAN *(S)*

LIGGER
MEY BAY *(S)*
MOUNT'S
RAASAY *(S-SO)*
RAMSEY *(M)*
RYE BAY
SHIANT *(S-SO)*
SOLWAY *(E/S-F)*
ST IVES
THURSO *(S)*
TONGUE *(S)*
TOR BAY
TRALEE *(I)*
VERYAN

7

ALUM BAY
ALLONBY
ARISAIG *(S-SO)*
BIGBURY
BRISTOL *(E/W-C)*
BUDE BAY
CLEW BAY *(I)*
CUILLIN *(S-SO)*
CULZEAN *(S)*
DONEGAL *(I)*
DORNOCH *(S-F)*
DUNDALK *(I)*
ENGLISH *(C)*
GOSFORD *(S)*
HOLKHAM
KILLALA *(I)*
LUCE BAY *(S)*
LYME BAY

NIARBYL *(M)*
NIGG BAY *(S)*
OSBORNE
RHOS BAY *(W)*
SANDOWN
SPEY BAY *(S)*
SWANSEA *(W)*
TARN BAY
TEES BAY
THE WASH
WESTRAY *(S-F)*
WIGTOWN *(S)*

8

ALNMOUTH
BARMOUTH *(W)*
BIDEFORD *2
BROAD BAY *(S)*
BUDLE BAY
BURGHEAD *(S)*
CARDIGAN *(W)*
CROMARTY *(S-B/F)*
DRURIDGE
DULAS BAY *(W)*
ENARD BAY *(S)*
FALMOUTH
FILEY BAY
GRUINARD *(S)*
HOLYHEAD *(W)*
IRISH SEA
LARGS BAY *(S)*
LAXEY BAY *(M)*
LUNAN BAY *(S)*
MORTE BAY

NORTH SEA
PENTLAND *(S-F)*
PEVENSEY
RHOSSILI *(W)*
SLIGO BAY *(I)*
SPITHEAD
START BAY
ST BRIDES *(W)*
THE MINCH *(S-ST)*
TREMADOG *(W)*
WHITBURN
WHITSAND

9

BANTRY BAY *(I)*
CEMAES BAY *(W)*
DEER SOUND *(S)*
DINGLE BAY *(I)*
DUNNET BAY *(S)*
FISHGUARD *(W)*
GALWAY BAY *(I)*
HOLLESLEY
INVERNESS *(S-F)*
IRVINE BAY *(S)*
LAGGAN BAY *(S)*
LIGGER BAY
LIVERPOOL
MORECAMBE
MOUNT'S BAY
RAMSEY BAY *(M)*
SCAPA FLOW *(S-ST)*
SINCLAIR'S *(S)*
ST ANDREWS *(S)*
ST AUSTELL
ST GEORGE'S *(I/W-C)*
ST IVES BAY *(S)*
SULLOM VOE *(S-ST)*
THE SOLENT *(ST)*
THURSO BAY *(S)*
TONGUE BAY *(S)*
TRALEE BAY *(I)*
VERYAN BAY
WATERGATE
WHITESAND

WIDEMOUTH
YELL SOUND *(S)*

10

ALLONBY BAY
BALLANTRAE *(S)*
BARNSTAPLE *2
BIGBURY BAY
BLUE ANCHOR
BRANCASTER
BRIDGWATER
CAERNARFON *(W)*
CARMARTHEN *(W)*
CULZEAN BAY *(S)*
DONEGAL BAY *(I)*
DUNDALK BAY *(I)*
FIRTH OF TAY *(S)*
GOSFORD BAY *(S)*
HOLKHAM BAY
INNER SOUND *(S)*
KILBRANNAN *(S-SO)*
KILLALA BAY *(I)*
MEVAGISSEY
MORAY FIRTH *(S)*
NIARBYL BAY *(M)*
NORTH MINCH *(S-ST)*
OSBORNE BAY
ROBIN HOOD'S
SANDOWN BAY
SOUND OF RUM *(S) *1*
SWANSEA BAY *(W)*
WIGTOWN BAY *(S)*

11

ALNMOUTH BAY
BALLYCASTLE *(I)*
BARMOUTH BAY *(W)*
BEAULY FIRTH *(S)*
BIDEFORD BAY *2
BRIDLINGTON
BURGHEAD BAY *(S)*

CARDIGAN BAY *(W)*
CROMARTY BAY *(S)*
DRURIDGE BAY
FALMOUTH BAY
FIRTH OF LORN *(S)*
GRUINARD BAY *(S)*
HOLYHEAD BAY *(W)*
LITTLE MINCH *(S-ST)*
PEVENSEY BAY
RHOSSILI BAY *(W)*
SOLWAY FIRTH *(E/S)*
SOUND OF BUTE *(S)*
SOUND OF EIGG *(S)*
SOUND OF JURA *(S)*
SOUND OF MULL *(S)*
SOUND OF RHUM *(S) *1*
ST BRIDES BAY *(W)*
TREMADOG BAY *(W)*
WHITBURN BAY
WHITSAND BAY

12

CUILLIN SOUND *(S)*
DORNOCH FIRTH *(S)*
EDDRACHILLIS *(S)*
FIRTH OF CLYDE *(S)*
FIRTH OF FORTH *(S)*
FISHGUARD BAY *(W)*
HOLLESLEY BAY
LIVERPOOL BAY
MORECAMBE BAY
NORTH CHANNEL *(I/S)*
SINCLAIR'S BAY *(S)*
SOUND OF BARRA *(S)*
SOUND OF CANNA *(S)*
SOUND OF GIGHA *(S)*
SOUND OF SLEAT *(S)*
ST ANDREWS BAY *(S)*
ST AUSTELL BAY
WATERGATE BAY
WESTRAY FIRTH *(S)*
WHITESAND BAY
WIDEMOUTH BAY

BALLANTRAE BAY *(S)*
BARNSTAPLE BAY *2
BLUE ANCHOR BAY
BRANCASTER BAY
BRIDGWATER BAY
CAERNARFON BAY *(W)*
CARMARTHEN BAY *(W)*
CROMARTY FIRTH *(S)*
CROSBY CHANNEL

MEVAGISSEY BAY
PENTLAND FIRTH *(S)*
ROBIN HOOD'S BAY
SOUND OF HARRIS *(S)*
SOUND OF RAASAY *(S)*
SOUND OF SHIANT *(S)*
STRAIT OF DOVER

14

BALLYCASTLE BAY *(I)*

BRIDLINGTON BAY
BRISTOL CHANNEL *(E/W)*
ENGLISH CHANNEL
INVERNESS FIRTH *(S)*
SOUND OF ARISAIG *(S)*

15

EDDRACHILLIS BAY *(S)*
KILBRANNAN SOUND *(S)*

GEOGRAPHY

BAYS & SEAS – WORLD

(AF) = Africa   *(AM)* = The Americas   *(AN)* = Antarctica   *(AS)* = Asia
(AU) = Australasia   *(E)* = Europe
(BI) = Bight   *(C)* = Channel   *(G)* = Gulf   *(O)* = Ocean   *(SE)* = Sea
(ST) = Strait
* = Alternative spelling/name   NB: *(B)* = Bay only when one name equals two
waters

3

KII *(AS-C)*
MED *(E-SE)*
RED *(AF/AS-SE)*

4

ADEN *(AF/AS-G)*
ARAL *(AS-SE)*
AZOV *(AS-SE)*
BASS *(AS-ST)*
BATE *(AU)*

COOK *(AU-ST)*
DEAD *(AS-SE)*
FOXE *(AM-C)*
JAVA *(AS-SE)*
KARA *(AS-SE)*
KIEL *(E)*
OMAN *(AS-G)*
PALK *(AS-ST)*
RIGA *(E-G)*
ROSS *(AN-SE)*
SAVA *(AS-SE)* *1
SAWU *(AS-SE)* *1
SUEZ *(AF-G)*
SULU *(AS-SE)*

5

AQABA *(AS-G)*
BANDA *(AS-SE)*
BENIN *(AF-BI)*
BLACK *(AS/E-SE)*
BONNY *(AF-BI)*
BUNGO *(AS-C)*
CABOT *(AM-ST)*
CADIZ *(E-G)*
CERAM *(AS-SE)* *2
CHINA *(AS-SE)*
CORAL *(AU-SE)*
DAVIS *(AM-ST)*

FUNDY *(AM)*
GENOA *(E-G)*
HAWKE *(AU)*
IZMIR *(AS-G)*
JAMES *(AM)*
JAPAN *(AS-SE)*
KOREA *(AS-ST)*
LIONS *(E-G)*
LUZON *(AS-ST)*
NORTH *(E-SE)*
PAPUA *(AU-G)*
PRYDZ *(AN)*
SERAM *(AS-SE)* *2
SHARK *(AU)*

SIRTE *(AF-G)*
SUMBA *(AS-ST)*
SUNDA *(AS-ST)*
TAMPA *(AM)*
TIMOR *(AU-SE)*
WHITE *(AS-SE)*

6

AEGEAN *(E-SE)*
ALASKA *(AM-G)*
ANADYR *(AS-G)*
ARCTIC *(O)*
BAFFIN *(AM)*
BALTIC *(E-SE)*
BARROW *(AM-ST)*
BENGAL *(AS)*
BERING *(AM/AS-SE,*
     AM/AS-ST)
BISCAY *(E)*
BOTANY *(AU)*
BROKEN *(AU)*
CAMBAY *(AS-G)*
DANZIG *(E-G)*
DARIEN *(AM-G)*
DRAKE'S *(AM)*
FLORES *(AS-SE)*
GUINEA *(AF-G)*
HORMUZ *(AS-ST)*
HUDSON *(AM-B,*
     AM-ST)
INDIAN *(O)*
IONIAN *(E-SE)*
LAPTEV *(AS-SE)*
LÜBECK *(E)*
MANNAR *(AS-G)*
MEXICO *(AM-G)*
NAPLES *(E)*
PANAMA *(AM-G)*
PLENTY *(AU)*
RED SEA *(AF/AS)*
SCOTIA *(AN-SE)*
TASMAN *(AU-B,*
     AU-SE)
TORRES *(AU-ST)*

UNGAVA *(AM)*
VENICE *(E-G)*
YELLOW *(AS-SE)*

7

ABOUKIR *(AF)*
ANDAMAN *(AS-SE)*
ARABIAN *(AS-SE)*
ARAFURA *(AS-SE)*
ARAL SEA *(AS)*
BARENTS *(AS-SE)*
BATE BAY *(AU)*
BOOTHIA *(AM-G)*
BOTHNIA *(E-G)*
CASPIAN *(AS-SE)*
CELEBES *(AS-SE)*
CHUKCHI *(AS-SE)*
CORINTH *(E-G)*
DEAD SEA *(AS)*
DENMARK *(E-ST)*
FINLAND *(E-G)*
FLORIDA *(AM-ST)*
FORMOSA *(AS-ST)*
FOVEAUX *(AU-ST)*
GALILEE *(AS-SE, also*
       TIBERIAS,
      in LAKES)
GASCONY *(E-G)*
HALIFAX *(AU)*
JAVA SEA *(AS)*
KARA SEA *(AS)*
KIEL BAY *(E)*
LINCOLN *(AM-SE)*
MALACCA *(AS-ST)*
MARMARA *(AS/E-SE)*
MESSINA *(E-ST)*
MIRTOAN *(E-SE)*
MORETON *(AU)*
OKHOTSK *(AS-SE)*
OTRANTO *(E-ST)*
PACIFIC *(O)*
PECHORA *(AS-G)*
PEGASUS *(AU)*
PERSIAN *(AS-G)*

ROEBUCK *(AU)*
ROSS SEA *(AN)*
SALERNO *(E-G)*
SAVA SEA *(AS) *1*
SAWU SEA *(AS) *1*
SPENCER *(AU-G)*
SULU SEA *(AS)*
TARANTO *(E-G)*
TRIESTE *(E-G)*
TRINITY *(AM)*
TSUGARU *(AS-ST)*
WEDDELL *(AN-SE)*
YUCATAN *(AM-ST)*

8

ADRIATIC *(E-SE)*
AMUNDSEN *(AN-SE)*
ATLANTIC *(O)*
BANDA SEA *(AS)*
BEAUFORT *(AM-SE)*
BLACK SEA *(AS/E)*
BOSPORUS *(AS/E-ST)*
CAGLIARI *(E-G)*
CAMPECHE *(AM)*
CERAM SEA *(AS) *2*
CHALEURS *(AM)*
CHINA SEA *(AS)*
CORAL SEA *(AU)*
DELAWARE *(AM)*
FRANKLIN *(AM-ST)*
GEORGIAN *(AM)*
HAMMAMET *(AF-G)*
HAWKE BAY *(AU)*
JAMES BAY *(AM)*
KATTEGAT *(E-ST)*
LIGURIAN *(E-SE)*
MAGELLAN *(AM-ST)*
MAKASSAR *(AS-ST)*
MARTABAN *(AS-G)*
MONTEREY *(AM)*
NORTH SEA *(E)*
PRYDZ BAY *(AN)*
QUIBERON *(E)*
SARGASSO *(AM-SE)*

SERAM SEA *(AS)* *2
SHARK BAY *(AU)*
TAMPA BAY *(AM)*
THAILAND *(AS-G)*
TIMOR SEA *(AU)*
TONGKING *(AS-G)*
VALENCIA *(E-G)*
WHITE SEA *(AS)*

TASMAN BAY *(AU)*
TASMAN SEA *(AU)*
UNGAVA BAY *(AM)*
VENEZUELA *(AM-G)*
YELLOW SEA *(AS)*
ZUIDER ZEE *(E-SE)* *3

9

ADMIRALTY *(AM)*
AEGEAN SEA *(E)*
ANTARCTIC *(O)*
BAFFIN BAY *(AM)*
BALTIC SEA *(E)*
BERING SEA *(AM/AS)*
BONAVISTA *(AM)*
BONIFACIO *(E-ST)*
BOTANY BAY *(AU)*
BROKEN BAY *(AU)*
CARIBBEAN *(AM-SE)*
DISCOVERY *(AU)*
DRAKE'S BAY *(AM)*
EAST CHINA *(AS-SE)*
ENCOUNTER *(AU)*
FLORES SEA *(AS)*
FROBISHER *(AM)*
GALVESTON *(AM)*
GEOGRAPHE *(AU)*
GIBRALTAR *(E-ST)*
GREENLAND *(E-SE)*
HERMITAGE *(AM)*
HUDSON BAY *(AM)*
IONIAN SEA *(E)*
LAPTEV SEA *(AS)*
LÜBECK BAY *(E)*
MACKENZIE *(AM,
AN)*
NORWEGIAN *(E-SE)*
PLACENTIA *(AM)*
SCOTIA SEA *(AN)*
SEA OF AZOV *(AS)*
SHELEKHOV *(AS-G)*
SKAGERRAK *(E-ST)*

10

ABOUKIR BAY *(AF)*
ANDAMAN SEA *(AS)*
ARABIAN SEA *(AS)*
ARAFURA SEA *(AS)*
BARENTS SEA *(AS)*
BAY OF FUNDY *(AM)*
BASS STRAIT *(AU)*
CALIFORNIA *(AM-G)*
CANTERBURY *(AU-BI)*
CASPIAN SEA *(AS)*
CELEBES SEA *(AS)*
CHESAPEAKE *(AM)*
CHUKCHI SEA *(AS)*
COOK STRAIT *(AU)*
GULF OF ADEN *(AF/AS)*
GULF OF OMAN *(AS)*
GULF OF RIGA *(E)*
GULF OF SUEZ *(AF)*
HALIFAX BAY *(AU)*
HELIGOLAND *(E-BI)*
IJSSELMEER *(E-SE)* *3
KII CHANNEL *(AS)*
LINCOLN SEA *(AM)*
MIRTOAN SEA *(E)*
MOÇAMBIQUE *(AF-C)* *4
MOZAMBIQUE *(AF-C)* *4
MORETON BAY *(AU)*
PALK STRAIT *(AS)*
PEGASUS BAY *(AU)*
ROEBUCK BAY *(AU)*
SEA OF JAPAN *(AS)*
SETO NAIKAI *(AS-SE)*
SOUTH CHINA *(AS-SE)*
ST LAWRENCE *(AM-G)*
TRINITY BAY *(AM)*
TYRRHENIAN *(E-SE)*
WEDDELL SEA *(AN)*

11

ADRIATIC SEA *(E)*
AMUNDSEN SEA *(AN)*
ARCTIC OCEAN
BAY OF BENGAL *(AS)*
BAY OF BISCAY *(E)*
BAY OF NAPLES *(E)*
BAY OF PLENTY *(AU)*
BEAUFORT SEA *(AM)*
CABOT STRAIT *(AM)*
CARPENTARIA *(AU-G)*
CHALEURS BAY *(AM)*
DARDANELLES *(AS/E-ST)*
DAVIS STRAIT *(AM)*
DELAWARE BAY *(AM)*
FOXE CHANNEL *(AM)*
GEORGIAN BAY *(AM)*
GULF OF AQABA *(AS)*
GULF OF CADIZ *(E)*
GULF OF GENOA *(E)*
GULF OF IZMIR *(AS)*
GULF OF LIONS *(E)*
GULF OF PAPUA *(AU)*
GULF OF SIRTE *(AF)*
INDIAN OCEAN
KOREA STRAIT *(AS)*
LIGURIAN SEA *(E)*
LUZON STRAIT *(AS)*
MONTEREY BAY *(AM)*
PECHORA GULF *(AS)*
PERSIAN GULF *(AS)*
SARGASSO SEA *(AM)*
SPENCER GULF *(AU)*
SUMBA STRAIT *(AS)*
SUNDA STRAIT *(AS)*
TEHUANTEPEC *(AM-G)*

12

ADMIRALTY BAY *(AM)*
BARROW STRAIT *(AM)*
BERING STRAIT *(AM/AS)*
BIGHT OF BENIN *(AF)*
BIGHT OF BONNY *(AF)*

BONAVISTA BAY *(AM)*
BUNGO CHANNEL *(AS)*
CARIBBEAN SEA *(AM)*
DISCOVERY BAY *(AU)*
EAST CHINA SEA *(AS)*
EAST SIBERIAN *(AS-SE)*
ENCOUNTER BAY *(AU)*
FROBISHER BAY *(AM)*
GALVESTON BAY *(AM)*
GEOGRAPHE BAY *(AU)*
GREENLAND SEA *(E)*
GULF OF ALASKA *(AM)*
GULF OF ANADYR *(AS)*
GULF OF CAMBAY *(AS)*
GULF OF DANZIG *(E)*
GULF OF GUINEA *(AF)*
GULF OF MANNAR *(AS)*
GULF OF MEXICO *(AM)*
GULF OF PANAMA *(AM)*
GULF OF VENICE *(E)*
HERMITAGE BAY *(AM)*
HUDSON STRAIT *(AM)*
MACKENZIE BAY *(AM, AN)*
NORWEGIAN SEA *(E)*
PACIFIC OCEAN
PLACENTIA BAY *(AM)*
SAN FRANCISCO *(AM)*
SEA OF GALILEE *(AS)*
SEA OF MARMARA *(AS/E)*
SEA OF OKHOTSK *(AS)*
TORRES STRAIT *(AU)*

13

ATLANTIC OCEAN
BAY OF CAMPECHE *(AM)*
BAY OF QUIBERON *(E)*
CHESAPEAKE BAY *(AM)*
DENMARK STRAIT *(E)*
FLORIDA STRAIT *(AM)*
FORMOSA STRAIT *(AS)*
FOVEAUX STRAIT *(AU)*

GULF OF BOOTHIA *(AM)*
GULF OF BOTHNIA *(E)*
GULF OF CORINTH *(E)*
GULF OF FINLAND *(E)*
GULF OF GASCONY *(E)*
GULF OF SALERNO *(E)*
GULF OF TARANTO *(E)*
GULF OF TRIESTE *(E)*
MEDITERRANEAN *(E-SE)*
SETO NAIKAI SEA *(AS)*
SHELEKHOV GULF *(AS)*
SOUTH CHINA SEA *(AS)*
TSUGARU STRAIT *(AS)*
TYRRHENIAN SEA *(E)*
YUCATAN STRAIT *(AM)*

14

ANTARCTIC OCEAN
BELLINGSHAUSEN *(AN-SE)*
FRANKLIN STRAIT *(AM)*
GULF OF CAGLIARI *(E)*
GULF OF HAMMAMET *(AF)*
GULF OF MARTABAN *(AS)*
GULF OF THAILAND *(AS)*
GULF OF TONGKING *(AS)*
GULF OF VALENCIA *(E)*
MAGELLAN STRAIT *(AM)*
MAKASSAR STRAIT *(AS)*
STRAIT OF HORMUZ *(AS)*

15

CANTERBURY BIGHT *(AU)*
EAST SIBERIAN SEA *(AS)*
GREAT AUSTRALIAN *(AU-BI)*
GULF OF VENEZUELA *(AM)*
HELIGOLAND BIGHT *(E)*
SAN FRANCISCO BAY *(AM)*
STRAIT OF MALACCA *(AS)*
STRAIT OF MESSINA *(E)*
STRAIT OF OTRANTO *(E)*

GEOGRAPHY

COUNTRIES

(AF) = Africa   (AM) = The Americas   (AS) = Asia   (E) = Europe
*(O) = Oceania   * = Former name/country*

3

DDR *(E)**
GDR *(E)**
UAE *(AS)*
UAR *(AF)*
USA *(AM)*

4

CHAD *(AF)*
CUBA *(AM)*
EIRE *(E)*
FIJI *(O)*
IRAN *(AS)*
IRAQ *(AS)*
LAOS *(AS)*
MALI *(AF)*
OMAN *(AS)*
PERU *(AM)*
SIAM *(AS)**
TOGO *(AF)*
USSR *(AS/E)*

5

BENIN *(AF)*
BURMA *(AS)**
CHILE *(AM)*
CHINA *(AS)*
CONGO *(AF)*
EGYPT *(AF)*
GABON *(AF)*
GHANA *(AF)*
HAITI *(AM)*
INDIA *(AS)*

ITALY *(E)*
JAPAN *(AS)*
KENYA *(AF)*
KOREA *(AS)**
LIBYA *(AF)*
MACAO *(AS)*
MALTA *(E)*
NAURU *(O)*
NEPAL *(AS)*
NIGER *(AF)*
QATAR *(AS)*
SABAH *(AS)*
SAMOA *(O)*
SPAIN *(E)*
SUDAN *(AF)*
SYRIA *(AS)*
TIBET *(AS)**
TONGA *(O)*
WALES *(E)*
YEMEN *(AS)*
ZAÏRE *(AF)*

6

ANGOLA *(AF)*
BELIZE *(AM)*
BHUTAN *(AS)*
BORNEO *(AS)**
BRAZIL *(AS)*
BRUNEI *(AS)*
CANADA *(AM)*
CEYLON *(AS)**
CYPRUS *(AS/E)*
FRANCE *(E)*
GAMBIA *(AF)*
GREECE *(E)*
GUINEA *(AF)*

GUYANA *(AM)*
ISRAEL *(AS)*
JORDAN *(AS)*
KUWAIT *(AS)*
LATVIA *(E)**
MALAWI *(AF)*
MALAYA *(AS)**
MEXICO *(AM)*
MONACO *(E)*
NORWAY *(E)*
PANAMA *(AM)*
PERSIA *(AS)**
POLAND *(E)*
RUSSIA *(AS/E)*
RWANDA *(AF)*
SWEDEN *(E)*
TAIWAN *(AS)*
TURKEY *(AS/E)*
UGANDA *(AF)*
ZAMBIA *(AF)*

7

ALBANIA *(E)*
ALGERIA *(AF)*
ANDORRA *(E)*
ANTIGUA *(AM)*
AUSTRIA *(E)*
BAHAMAS *(AM)*
BAHRAIN *(AS)*
BELGIUM *(E)*
BERMUDA *(AM)*
BOLIVIA *(AM)*
BRITAIN *(E)*
BURUNDI *(AF)*
DAHOMEY *(AF)**
DENMARK *(E)*

ECUADOR *(AM)*
ENGLAND *(E)*
ESTONIA *(E)**
FINLAND *(E)*
FORMOSA *(AS)**
GERMANY *(E)*
GRENADA *(AM)*
HOLLAND *(E)*
HUNGARY *(E)*
ICELAND *(E)*
JAMAICA *(AM)*
LEBANON *(AS)*
LESOTHO *(AF)*
LIBERIA *(AF)*
MOROCCO *(AF)*
MYANMAR *(AS)*
NAMIBIA *(AF)*
NIGERIA *(AF)*
PRUSSIA *(E)**
RIO MUNI *(AF)**
ROMANIA *(E)*
RUMANIA *(E)**
SARAWAK *(AS)*
SENEGAL *(AF)*
SOMALIA *(AF)*
ST LUCIA *(AM)*
SURINAM *(AM)*
TUNISIA *(AF)*
URUGUAY *(AM)*
VANUATU *(O)*
VATICAN *(E)*
VIETNAM *(AS)*

8

ANGUILLA *(AM)*
BARBADOS *(AM)*

GEOGRAPHY — COUNTRIES

BOTSWANA *(AF)*
BULGARIA *(E)*
CAMBODIA *(AS)**
CAMEROON *(AF)*
CAMEROUN *(AF)**
COLOMBIA *(AM)*
DJIBOUTI *(AF)*
DOMINICA *(AM)*
ETHIOPIA *(AF)*
HONDURAS *(AM)*
HONG KONG *(AS)*
KIRIBATI *(O)*
MALAGASY *(AF)**
MALAYSIA *(AS)*
MALDIVES *(AS)*
MONGOLIA *(AS)*
PAKISTAN *(AS)*
PARAGUAY *(AM)*
PORTUGAL *(E)*
RHODESIA *(AF)**
SCOTLAND *(E)*
SRI LANKA *(AF)*
TANZANIA *(AF)*
THAILAND *(AS)*
TOGOLAND *(AF)**
ZANZIBAR *(AF)**
ZIMBABWE *(AF)*

9

ABYSSINIA *(AF)**
ARGENTINA *(AM)*
AUSTRALIA *(O)*
COSTA RICA *(AM)*
GIBRALTAR *(E)*
GOLD COAST *(AF)**
GREENLAND *(AM)*
GUATEMALA *(AM)*
INDO-CHINA *(AS)**
INDONESIA *(AS)*
KAMPUCHEA *(AS)*
LITHUANIA *(E)**
MAURITIUS *(AF)*
NICARAGUA *(AM)*

NYASALAND *(AF)**
PALESTINE *(AS)**
SAN MARINO *(E)*
SINGAPORE *(AS)*
SWAZILAND *(AF)*
VENEZUELA *(AM)*

10

BANGLADESH *(AS)*
BASUTOLAND *(AF)**
EL SALVADOR *(AM)*
IVORY COAST *(AF)*
LUXEMBOURG *(E)*
MADAGASCAR *(AF)*
MAURITANIA *(AF)*
MOÇAMBIQUE *(AF)*
MOZAMBIQUE *(AF)**
NEW ZEALAND *(O)*
NIUE ISLAND *(O)*
NORTH KOREA *(AS)*
PUERTO RICO *(AM)*
SEYCHELLES *(AS)*
SOUTH KOREA *(AS)*
TANGANYIKA *(AF)**
UPPER VOLTA *(AF)**
YUGOSLAVIA *(E)*

11

AFGHANISTAN *(AS)*
BURKINA FASO *(AF)*
COOK ISLANDS *(O)*
DUTCH GUIANA *(AM)**
EAST GERMANY *(E)**
FRENCH CONGO *(AF)**
LINE ISLANDS *(O)*
NETHERLANDS *(E)*
NEW HEBRIDES *(O)**
PHILIPPINES *(AS)*
SAUDI ARABIA *(AS)*
SIERRA LEONE *(AF)*
SOUTH AFRICA *(AF)*

SOVIET UNION *(AS/E)*
SWITZERLAND *(E)*
VATICAN CITY *(E)*
WEST GERMANY *(E)**

12

BECHUANALAND *(AF)**
BELGIAN CONGO *(AF)**
EAST MALAYSIA *(AS)*
EAST PAKISTAN *(AS)**
FRENCH GUIANA *(AM)*
GREAT BRITAIN *(E)*
GUINEA-BISSAU *(AF)*
NEW CALEDONIA *(O)*
ST KITTS-NEVIS *(AM)*
UNITED STATES *(AM)*
WESTERN SAMOA *(O)*
WEST MALAYSIA *(AS)*

13

AMERICAN SAMOA *(O)*
CAYMAN ISLANDS *(AM)*
COMORO ISLANDS *(AF)*
IRISH REPUBLIC *(E)*
KHMER REPUBLIC *(AS)**
LIECHTENSTEIN *(E)*
NORFOLK ISLAND *(O)*
TRUCIAL STATES *(AS)**
TUVALU ISLANDS *(O)*
UNITED KINGDOM *(E)*
VIRGIN ISLANDS *(AM)*
WESTERN SAHARA *(AF)*

14

CZECHOSLOVAKIA *(E)*
GILBERT ISLANDS *(O)**
PAPUA NEW GUINEA *(O)*
PITCAIRN ISLAND *(O)*
SOLOMON ISLANDS *(O)*
SOMALI REPUBLIC *(AF)*

BRITISH HONDURAS *(AM)**
FALKLAND ISLANDS *(AM)*

FRENCH POLYNESIA *(O)*
NORTHERN IRELAND *(E)*
SOUTHERN IRELAND *(E)*
SOUTH WEST AFRICA *(AF)**

GEOGRAPHY

ISLANDS – BRITISH ISLES

(C) = Channel Islands   (E) = England   (I) = Ireland   (M) = Isle of Man
(S) = Scotland   (W) = Wales
† = So-called island   * = Alternative spelling/name

3

ELY *(E)* †
EWE *(S)*
HOY *(S)*
MAN *(M)*
MAY *(S)*
RAT *(E)*
RUM *(S)* *1
SOA *(S)*

4

ARAN *(I)*
BERE *(I)*
BUTE *(S)*
COLL *(S)*
DOGS *(E)* †
EDAY *(S)*
EIGG *(S)*
HERM *(C)*
HOLY *(E)* *2
    (S)
    (W)

IONA *(S)*
JURA *(S)*
MUCK *(S)*
OSEA *(E)*
RHUM *(S)* *1
ROAN *(S)*
RONA *(S)*
SARK *(C)*
SEIL *(S)*
SKYE *(S)*
SOAY *(S)*
TEAN *(E)*
TORY *(I)*
ULVA *(S)*
UNST *(S)*
WIAY *(S)*
YELL *(S)*

5

ANNET *(E)*
ARRAN *(S)*
BARRA *(S)*
BARRY *(W)*

CALDY *(W)*
CANNA *(S)*
CLARE *(I)*
CLEAR *(I)*
EAGLE *(I)*
ENSAY *(S)*
FIDRA *(S)*
FOULA *(S)*
FUDAY *(S)*
GIGHA *(S)*
GRAIN *(E)*
HANDA *(S)*
HORSE *(S)*
ISLAY *(S)*
LUING *(S)*
LUNDY *(E)*
LUNGA *(S)*
NEAVE *(S)*
PABAY *(S)*
RONAY *(S)*
SANDA *(S)*
SHUNA *(S)*
SULLY *(W)*
TIREE *(S)*
WIGHT *(E)*

6

ACHILL *(I)*
ANNAGH *(I)*
BRYHER *(E)*
BURRAY *(S)*
CANVEY *(E)*
DAVARR *(S)*
DURSEY *(I)*
ELMLEY *(E)*
ERISKA *(S)*
FETLAR *(S)*
FLOTTA *(S)*
HESTAN *(S)*
HORSEA *(E)*
HORSEY *(E)*
JERSEY *(C)*
LAMBAY *(I)*
LONGAY *(S)*
MERSEA *(E)*
OLDANY *(S)*
PABBAY *(S)*
PLADDA *(S)*
POTTON *(E)*
PUFFIN *(W)*

RAASAY *(S)*
RAMSEY *(W)*
ROUSAY *(S)*
SANDAY *(S)*
SCARBA *(S)*
SKOMER *(W)*
STAFFA *(S)*
STROMA *(S)*
THANET *(E)* †
TORSAY *(S)*
TRESCO *(E)*
WALNEY *(E)*

7

ARDWALL *(S)*
AXHOLME *(E)* †
BARDSEY *(W)*
BORERAY *(S)*
CRAMOND *(S)*
ERISKAY *(S)*
FLODDAY *(S)*
GOMETRA *(S)*

GRIMSAY *(S)*
HAYLING *(E)*
HYSKEIR *(S)*
IRELAND
KERRERA *(S)*
LISMORE *(S)*
NORTHEY *(E)*
ORKNEYS *(S)*
ORONSAY *(S)*
PORTSEA *(E)*
PURBECK *(E)* †
RATHLIN *(I)*
ROCKALL *(S)*
RUSHLEY *(E)*
SANDRAY *(S)*
SCALPAY *(S)*
SHEPPEY *(E)*
STAFFIN *(S)*
ST AGNES *(E)*
ST KILDA *(S)*
ST MARY'S *(E)*
THORNEY *(E)*
WESTRAY *(S)*
WHALSAY *(S)*

8

ALDERNEY *(C)*
ANGLESEY *(W)*
BARLOCCO *(S)*
BERNERAY *(S)*
BROWNSEA *(E)*
COLONSAY *(S)*
FAIR ISLE *(S)*
FLAT HOLM *(W)*
FOULNESS *(E)*
GRUINARD *(S)*
GUERNSEY *(C)*
HEBRIDES *(S)*
INISHEER *(I)*
MAINLAND *(S)*
MINGULAY *(S)*
PORTLAND *(E)*
SCILLIES *(E)*
SKOKHOLM *(W)*
STRONSAY *(S)*

TARANSAY *(S)*
VALENTIA *(I)*
VATERSAY *(S)*
WALLASEA *(E)*

9

BALESHARE *(S)*
BENBECULA *(S)*
BURNTWICK *(E)*
CALF OF MAN *(M)*
HAVENGORE *(E)*
INCHKEITH *(S)*
INISHMAAN *(I)*
INISHMORE *(I)*
INISHTURK *(I)*
ISLE OF ELY *(E)* †
ISLE OF EWE *(S)*
ISLE OF MAN *(M)*
ISLE OF MAY *(S)*
MUCKLE ROE *(S)*
NORTH UIST *(S)*
SHAPINSAY *(S)*
SHETLANDS *(S)*
SOUTH UIST *(S)*
ST MARTIN'S *(E)*

10

AILSA CRAIG *(S)*
HOLY ISLAND *(E)* *2
           (S)
           (W)
ISLE OF DOGS *(E)* †
ISLE OF SKYE *(S)*
STEEP HOLME *(E)*

11

ARAN ISLANDS *(I)*
BARRY ISLAND *(W)*
INCHMARNOCK *(S)*
ISLE OF GRAIN *(E)*
ISLE OF WIGHT *(E)*
LINDISFARNE *(E)* *2
LUNDY ISLAND *(E)*

PAPA WESTRAY *(S)*
SCILLY ISLES *(E)*

12

BRITISH ISLES
CANVEY ISLAND *(E)*
FARNE ISLANDS *(E)*
GREAT BERNERA *(S)*
GREAT CUMBRAE *(S)*
ISLE OF THANET *(E)* †
MUCKLE FLUGGA *(S)*
PUFFIN ISLAND *(W)*
WALNEY ISLAND *(E)*

13

HAYLING ISLAND *(E)*
INNER HEBRIDES *(S)*
ISLE OF AXHOLME *(E)* †
ISLE OF PURBECK *(E)* †
ISLE OF SHEPPEY *(E)*
LITTLE CUMBRAE *(S)*
MONACH ISLANDS *(S)*
ORKNEY ISLANDS *(S)*
OUTER HEBRIDES *(S)*
RABBIT ISLANDS *(S)*
SALTEY ISLANDS *(I)*
THORNEY ISLAND *(E)*

14

CHANNEL ISLANDS *(C)*
CROWLIN ISLANDS *(S)*
FLANNAN ISLANDS *(S)*
FOULNESS ISLAND *(E)*
NORTH RONALDSAY *(S)*
PORTLAND ISLAND *(E)*
SOUTH RONALDSAY *(S)*

15

COPELAND ISLANDS *(I)*
LEWIS WITH HARRIS *(S)*
SHETLAND ISLANDS *(S)*

GEOGRAPHY

ISLANDS – WORLD

(A) = Atlantic Ocean   (AF) = Africa   (AN) = Antarctic   (AR) = Arctic
(AS) = Asia   (AU) = Australasia   (CA) = Central America   (E) = Europe
(G) = Group (but only when 'Islands' or 'Group' are not part of the entry)
(IN) = Indian Ocean   (M) = Mediterranean   (NA) = North America
(P) = Pacific Ocean   (SA) = South America   (WI) = West Indies
* = Alternative/former spelling/name

3

ADI (AS)
CAT (WI)
FYN (E)
GAN (IN)
IKI (AS)
IOS (M)
KEA (M)
KOS (M)
KRK (M)
MØN (E)
OBI (AS)
RAB (M)
REY (CA)
VIS (M)

4

AMOY (AS) *1
ATKA (NA)
ATTU (NA)
BALI (AS)
BOAC (AS)
BRAČ (M)
BURU (AS)
CEBU (AS)
CRES (M)
CUBA (WI)
ELBA (M)
EVIA (M) *2
FIJI (P-G)

FOGO (AF)
(NA)
FÖHR (E)
GOZO (M)
GUAM (P)
HVAR (M)
JAVA (AS)
KING (AU)
LONG (NA)
MAHÉ (IN)
MARÉ (P)
MAUI (P)
NIAS (AS)
NIUE (P) *3
OAHU (P)
ORTA (M)
PICO (A)
PITT (AU)
RØMØ (E)
ROSS (AN)
SABA (WI)
SIMI (M) *4
SYLT (E)
SYMI (M) *4
TRUK (P)
UVÉA (P)
WAKE (P)

5

ARUBA (WI)
BAKER (P)

BANKS (NA)
BELAU (P-G) *5
BIAKO (AF) *6
BLOCK (NA)
BYLOT (NA)
CAPRI (M)
CHEJU (AS) *7
CHIOS (M) *8
COATS (NA)
COIBA (CA)
CORFU (M) *9
CORVO (A)
CRETE (M) *10
DELOS (M)
DEVON (NA)
DISKO (AR)
ELLIS (NA)
FERRO (A) *11
HOSTE (CA)
HYDRA (M) *12
IBIZA (M)
IDHRA (M) *12
IMROZ (AS) *13
KAUAI (P)
KHOIS (M) *8
KRÍTI (M) *10
LANAI (P)
LEYTE (AS)
LIFOU (P)
LOPUD (M)
LUZON (AS)
MAFIA (AF)
MALTA (M)

MILOS (M)
MLJET (M)
NAURU (P)
NAXOS (M)
NEVIS (WI)
ÖLAND (E)
PANAY (AS)
PAROS (M)
PELEE (NA)
PEMBA (AF)
PERIM (AS)
POROS (M)
QESHM (AS)
RHODE (NA)
RÜGEN (E)
SABLE (NA)
SAMOA (P-G)
SAMOS (M)
SAMSØ (E)
SERAM (AS)
SIROS (M) *14
SUMBA (AS)
SYROS (M) *14
TEXEL (E)
THIRA (M) *15
TIMOR (AS)
TINOS (M)
TONGA (P-G) *16
UMNAK (NA)
UPLOU (P)
UZNAM (E) *17
WOLFE (NA)
ZANTE (M) *18

6

AEGINA *(M)*
ANDROS *(M)*
    (WI)
AZORES *(A-G)*
BAFFIN *(NA)*
BANABA *(P)*
BANGKA *(AS)*
BEAVER *(NA)*
BORKUM *(E)*
BORNEO *(AS)*
BOUNTY *(AU)*
CANTON *(P)*
CEDROS *(SA)*
CERIGO *(M)* *19
CEYLON *(AS)* *20
CHILOE *(SA)*
CYPRUS *(M)*
DJERBA *(AF)*
EASTER *(P)*
EUBOEA *(M)* *2
FAROES *(E-G)* *21
FLORES *(A)*
    (AS)
FRASER *(AU)*
GIGLIO *(M)*
GOMERA *(A)*
GRAHAM *(NA)*
HAINAN *(AS)*
HAWAII *(P)*
HIERRO *(A)* *11
HIVA OA *(P)*
HONSHU *(AS)*
IKARIA *(M)*
IMBROS *(AS)* *13
ISCHIA *(M)*
ITHACA *(M)*
ITURUP *(AS)*
JARVIS *(P)*
KODIAK *(NA)*
KYUSHU *(AS)*
LABUAN *(AS)*
LEMNOS *(M)* *22
LESBOS *(M)* *23
LESVOS *(M)* *23

LEVKAS *(M)*
LIMNOS *(M)* *22
LINOSA *(M)*
LIPARI *(M)*
LOMBOK *(AS)*
MALDEN *(P)*
MANSEL *(NA)*
MARAJO *(SA)*
MIDWAY *(P-G)*
MOOREA *(P)*
NEGROS *(AS)*
NIIHAU *(P)*
OLÉRON *(E)*
PATMOS *(M)*
PELAGI *(M-G)*
PENANG *(AS)* *24
PHILAE *(AF)*
PHUKET *(AS)*
PINANG *(AS)* *24
RAMREE *(AS)*
RHODES *(M)* *25
RHODOS *(M)* *25
ROBBEN *(AF)*
SAIPAN *(P)*
SALINA *(M)*
SAVAGE *(P)* *3
SAVAII *(P)*
SICILY *(M)*
SKIROS *(M)*
STATEN *(NA)*
ST PAUL *(IN)*
SWAINS *(P)*
TAHITI *(P)*
TAIWAN *(AS)* *26
THASOS *(M)*
THOLEN *(E)*
TOBAGO *(WI)*
TROMSÖ *(E)*
TUVALU *(P-G)* *27
UNIMAK *(NA)*
USEDOM *(E)* *17
USHANT *(E)*
USTICA *(M)*
XIAMEN *(AS)* *1

7

ACKLINS *(WI)*
AEGADES *(M-G)*
AMELAND *(E)*
ANJOUAN *(IN)*
ANTIGUA *(WI)*
ASINARA *(M)*
BAHAMAS *(WI-G)*
BAHRAIN *(AS-G)*
BARBUDA *(WI)*
BERKNER *(AN)*
BERMUDA *(A-G)*
BONAIRE *(WI)*
CABRERA *(M)*
CAPRAIA *(M)*
CAPRERA *(M)*
CAVIANA *(SA)*
CELEBES *(AS)* *28
CHEJU DO *(AS)*
CORSICA *(M)*
COZUMEL *(CA)*
CURAÇAO *(WI)*
CURZOLA *(M)* *29
FAEROES *(E)* *21
FALSTER *(E)*
FANNING *(P)*
FEHMARN *(E)*
FORMOSA *(AS)* *26
GOTLAND *(E)*
GRENADA *(WI)*
HIIUMAA *(E)*
HOWLAND *(P)*
HUAHUNE *(P)*
ICELAND *(E)*
ÎLE DE RÉ *(E)*
IWO JIMA *(P)*
JAMAICA *(WI)*
KAMARAN *(AS)*
KANDAVU *(P)*
KÉRKIRA *(M)* *9
KINGMAN *(P)*
KITHÍRA *(M)* *19
KOOLAND *(AU)*
KORČULA *(M)* *29
LAALAND *(E)* *30

LOLLAND *(E)* *30
MADEIRA *(A)*
    (A-G)
MAJORCA *(M)* *31
MALPELO *(SA)*
MARMARA *(AS)*
MASBATE *(AS)*
MAYOTTE *(IN)*
MEHETIA *(P)*
MENORCA *(M)* *32
MIKONOS *(M)* *33
MINDORO *(AS)*
MINORCA *(M)* *32
MOLOKAI *(P)*
MORESBY *(NA)*
MURUROA *(P)*
MYKONOS *(M)* *33
NORFOLK *(P)*
NOSSI-BÉ *(AF)*
NUNIVAK *(NA)*
OCEANIA *(P-G)*
OKINAWA *(AS)*
OMETEPE *(CA)*
PALAWAN *(AS)*
PALMYRA *(P)*
RAIATEA *(P)*
REDONDA *(WI)*
RÉUNION *(WI)*
ROANOKE *(NA)*
SALAMIS *(M)*
SÃO TOMÉ *(AF)*
SHERBRO *(AF)*
SHIKOKU *(AS)*
SIBERUT *(AS)*
SIKINOS *(M)* *34
SOCOTRA *(AF)*
ST CROIX *(WI)*
STEWART *(AU)*
ST KITTS *(WI)*
ST LUCIA *(WI)*
SUMATRA *(AS)*
SUMBAWA *(AS)*
SYKINOS *(M)* *34
TERNATE *(AS)*
TIBURÓN *(CA)*
TORTOLA *(WI)*

TORTUGA *(WI)* *35
TUAMOTU *(P-G)* *36
VANUATU *(P-G)* *37
VULCANO *(M)*
WHIDBEY *(NA)*
WRANGEL *(AS)*
ZEALAND *(E)* *38

<h1>8</h1>

ABU DHABI *(AS)*
AKIMISKI *(NA)*
ALCATRAZ *(NA)*
ANDAMANS *(IN-G)*
ANGUILLA *(WI)*
ANTILLES *(WI-G)*
BARBADOS *(WI)*
BATHURST *(AU)*
          (NA)
BELITUNG *(AS)* *39
BELLE ÎLE *(E)* *40
BILLITON *(AS)* *39
BORNHOLM *(E)*
BUNGURAN *(AS)*
BJÖRNÖYA *(E)*
CANARIES *(A-G)*
CYCLADES *(M-G)*
DOMINICA *(WI)*
EROMANGA *(P)*
FATU HIVA *(P)*
FLINDERS *(AU)*
HOKKAIDO *(AS)*
HONG KONG *(AS)*
JAN MAYEN *(AR)*
KANGAROO *(AU)*
KEY LARGO *(NA)*
KIRIBATI *(P-G)* *41
KOLGUYEV *(AS)*
KRAKATOA *(AS)*
LORD HOWE *(AU)*
MAGERÖYA *(E)*
MALDIVES *(IN-G)*
MALLORCA *(M)* *31
MALVINAS *(SA-G)* *42
MARIANAS *(P-G)*
MELVILLE *(AU)*
          (NA)

MINDANAO *(AS)*
MIQUELON *(NA)*
MOLUCCAS *(AS-G)* *43
MYTILENE *(M)* *23
NAVARINO *(SA)*
NUKU HIVA *(P)*
PITCAIRN *(P)*
PRINCIPE *(AF)*
QUELPART *(AS)* *7
SAAREMAA *(E)*
SAKHALIN *(AS)*
SALSETTE *(AS)*
SAN FÉLIX *(SA)*
SARDINIA *(M)*
SCHOUWEN *(E)*
SKIATHOS *(M)*
SKOPELOS *(M)*
SOMERSET *(NA)*
SPORADES *(M-G)*
SRI LANKA *(AS)* *20
STARBUCK *(P)*
ST HELENA *(A)*
ST MARTIN *(WI)*
ST PIERRE *(NA)*
ST THOMAS *(WI)*
SULAWESI *(AS)* *28
SVALBARD *(AR-G)* *44
TASMANIA *(AU)*
TENERIFE *(A)*
THURSDAY *(AU)*
TRINIDAD *(WI)*
UNALASKA *(NA)*
VICTORIA *(NA)*
VITI LEVU *(P)*
VLIELAND *(E)*
ZANZIBAR *(AF)*

<h1>9</h1>

ALBEMARLE *(SA)* *45
ALEUTIANS *(NA-G)*
ALEXANDER *(AN)*
AMSTERDAM *(IN)*
ANTICOSTI *(NA)*
ASCENSION *(A)*
AUSTRALIA *(AU)*

BALEARICS *(M-G)*
BELLE ISLE *(E)* *40
          (NA)
CAT ISLAND *(WI)*
CHRISTMAS *(IN)*
          (P)
ELEPHANTA *(IN)*
ELEUTHERA *(WI)*
ELLESMERE *(NA)*
ENDERBURY *(P)*
FALKLANDS *(SA-G)* *42
GALAPAGOS *(SA-G)*
GALVESTON *(NA)*
GREENLAND *(AR)*
HALMAHERA *(AS)*
INDONESIA *(AS-G)*
KAHOOLAWE *(P)*
KARPATHOS *(M)* *46
KERGUELEN *(IN-G)*
LAMPEDOSA *(M)*
LANGELAND *(E)*
LANZAROTE *(A)*
MANGARÉVA *(P)*
MANHATTAN *(NA)*
MARGARITA *(WI)*
MARQUESAS *(P-G)*
MAURITIUS *(IN)*
MELANESIA *(P-G)*
NANTUCKET *(NA)*
NEW GUINEA *(AU)*
NORDERNEY *(E)*
POLYNESIA *(P-G)*
RAROTONGA *(P)*
RODRIGUEZ *(IN)*
ROOSEVELT *(AN)*
SAN MIGUEL *(NA)*
SANTA CRUZ *(SA)*
SANTA ROSA *(NA)*
SANTORINI *(M)* *15
SÃO MIGUEL *(A)*
SCARPANTO *(M)* *46
SINGAPORE *(AS)*
SJAELLAND *(E)* *38
STROMBOLI *(M)*
ST VINCENT *(WI)*
TONGATABU *(P)*

VANCOUVER *(NA)*
VANUA LEVU *(P)*
ZAKINTHOS *(M) *18*

10

ARU ISLANDS *(AS)*
ASSATEAGUE *(NA)*
ASSUMPTION *(IN)*
CAPE BARREN *(AU)*
CAPE BRETON *(NA)*
CEPHALONIA *(M) *47*
DIRK HARTOG *(AU)*
DODECANESE *(M-G)*
FERNANDO PO *(AF) *6*
FORMENTERA *(M)*
FOX ISLANDS *(NA)*
GREAT ABACO *(WI)*
GRENADINES *(WI-G)*
GUADELOUPE *(WI)*
HELIGOLAND *(E)*
HISPANIOLA *(WI)*
ÎLE D'OLÉRON *(E)*
ISLA DEL REY *(CA)*
ISLE ROYALE *(NA)*
KEFALLINIA *(M) *47*
KING ISLAND *(AU)*
LACCADIVES *(IN-G)*
LONG ISLAND *(NA)*
MADAGASCAR *(AF)*
MANITOULIN *(NA)*
MARTINIQUE *(WI)*
MASCARENES *(IN-G)*
MICRONESIA *(P-G)*
MONTSERRAT *(WI)*
NEW BRITAIN *(P)*
NEW IRELAND *(P)*
PINE ISLAND *(WI) *48*
PITT ISLAND *(AU)*
PUERTO RICO *(WI)*
ROSS ISLAND *(AN)*
SAMOTHRACE *(M) *49*
SAMOTHRAKI *(M) *49*
SEYCHELLES *(IN-G)*
ST LAWRENCE *(NA)*

WAKE ISLAND *(P)*
WEST INDIES *(WI-G)*

11

BAKER ISLAND *(P)*
BANKS ISLAND *(NA)*
BLOCK ISLAND *(NA)*
BYLOT ISLAND *(NA)*
COOK ISLANDS *(P)*
DEVON ISLAND *(NA)*
ELLIS ISLAND *(NA)*
FLORIDA KEYS *(NA-G)*
GRAN CANARIA *(A) *50*
GRAND BAHAMA *(WI)*
GRAND CANARY *(A) *50*
GREAT INAGUA *(WI)*
GUADALCANAL *(P)*
ISLA DE PINOS *(WI) *48*
ISLA ISABELA *(SA) *45*
KIZIL ADALAR *(AS-G) *51*
LINE ISLANDS *(P)*
LITTLE ABACO *(WI)*
MONTE CRISTO *(M)*
NEW HEBRIDES *(P-G) *37*
NORTH ISLAND *(AU)*
PANTELLERIA *(M)*
PHILIPPINES *(AS-G)*
PINE ISLANDS *(NA)*
RHODE ISLAND *(NA)*
SABLE ISLAND *(NA)*
SAN AMBROSIO *(SA)*
SOUTHAMPTON *(NA)*
SOUTH ISLAND *(AU)*
SPITZBERGEN *(AR-G) *44*
SULA ISLANDS *(AS-G)*
SULU ISLANDS *(AS-G)*

12

ALAND ISLANDS *(E)*
BAFFIN ISLAND *(NA)*
BANDA ISLANDS *(AS)*
BANKS ISLANDS *(P)*

BONIN ISLANDS *(P)*
BOUGAINVILLE *(P)*
BOUNTY ISLAND *(AU)*
CANTON ISLAND *(P)*
COCOS ISLANDS *(IN) *52*
EASTER ISLAND *(P)*
FAROE ISLANDS *(E) *21*
FRASER ISLAND *(AU)*
GRANDE COMORE *(IN)*
INACCESSIBLE *(A)*
JARVIS ISLAND *(P)*
KURIL ISLANDS *(AS)*
LITTLE INAGUA *(WI)*
MALDEN ISLAND *(P)*
MARIE GALANTE *(WI)*
NEW CALEDONIA *(P)*
NEWFOUNDLAND *(NA)*
NOVAYA ZEMLYA *(AS-G)*
PALAU ISLANDS *(P) *5*
PARRY ISLANDS *(NA)*
PEARL ISLANDS *(CA)*
PRINCE EDWARD *(NA)*
RAMREE ISLAND *(AS)*
ROBBEN ISLAND *(AF)*
SAVAGE ISLAND *(P) *3*
SOUTH GEORGIA *(A)*
SOUTH ORKNEYS *(A-G)*
SPICE ISLANDS *(AS) *43*
STATEN ISLAND *(NA)*
ST BARTHÉLEMY *(WI) *53*
ST PAUL ISLAND *(IN)*
SUNDA ISLANDS *(AS)*
SWAINS ISLAND *(P)*
TERSCHELLING *(E)*
TURKS' ISLAND *(WI)*
WESTERN SAMOA *(P-G)*

13

AMERICAN SAMOA *(P-G)*
ANAMBA ISLANDS *(AS)*
BERKNER ISLAND *(AN)*
CAICOS ISLANDS *(WI)*
CALAMIAN GROUP *(AS)*
CANARY ISLANDS *(A)*

CAYMAN ISLANDS *(WI)*
CHAGOS ISLANDS *(IN)*
COMORO ISLANDS *(AF)*
ELLICE ISLANDS *(P) *27*
FAEROE ISLANDS *(E) *21*
FANNING ISLAND *(P)*
FUERTEVENTURA *(A)*
HOWLAND ISLAND *(P)*
IONIAN ISLANDS *(M)*
JUAN FERNANDEZ *(SA-G)*
ILE DE LA TORTUE *(WI) *35*
KINGMAN ISLAND *(P)*
LIPARI ISLANDS *(M) *54*
MIDWAY ISLANDS *(P)*
NEW PROVIDENCE *(WI)*
NORFOLK ISLAND *(P)*
PRINCE CHARLES *(NA)*
PRINCE OF WALES *(NA)*
PRINCES' ISLANDS *(AS) *51*
SANTA CATALINA *(NA)*
ST BARTHOLEMEW *(WI) *53*
STEWART ISLAND *(AU)*
VIRGIN ISLANDS *(WI)*
WESSEL ISLANDS *(AU)*
WRANGEL ISLAND *(AS)*

14

AEOLIAN ISLANDS *(M) *54*
ANDAMAN ISLANDS *(IN)*
APOSTLE ISLANDS *(NA)*
BATHURST ISLAND *(AU)*
    (NA)
BELCHER ISLANDS *(NA)*
CHATHAM ISLANDS *(AU)*
DAMPIER ISLANDS *(AU)*
DIOMEDE ISLANDS *(AS)*
    (NA)
FLINDERS ISLAND *(AU)*
FRANZ JOSEF LAND *(AR-G)*
FRISIAN ISLANDS *(E)*
GAMBIER ISLANDS *(P)*
GILBERT ISLANDS *(P) *41*
SLAS DE LA BAHÍA *(CA)*
KANGAROO ISLAND *(AU)*

KEELING ISLANDS *(IN) *52*
LEEWARD ISLANDS *(WI)*
LESSER ANTILLES *(WI)*
LOFOTEN ISLANDS *(E)*
LORD HOWE ISLAND *(AU)*
LOW ARCHIPELAGO *(P) *36*
LOYALTY ISLANDS *(P)*
LYAKHOV ISLANDS *(AS)*
MALDIVE ISLANDS *(IN)*
MARIANA ISLANDS *(P)*
MELVILLE ISLAND *(AU)*
    (NA)
MINICOY ISLANDS *(IN)*
NICOBAR ISLANDS *(IN)*
PHOENIX ISLANDS *(P)*
PITCAIRN ISLAND *(P)*
SANGIHE ISLANDS *(AS)*
SAN JUAN ISLANDS *(NA)*
SOCIETY ISLANDS *(P)*
SOLOMON ISLANDS *(P)*
SOMERSET ISLAND *(NA)*
SOUTH SHETLANDS *(A-G)*
STARBUCK ISLAND *(P)*
THURSDAY ISLAND *(AU)*
TIERRA DEL FUEGO *(SA-G)*
TRISTAN DA CUNHA *(A)*
VISAYAN ISLANDS *(AS)*
VICTORIA ISLAND *(NA)*

15

ALEUTIAN ISLANDS *(NA)*
ALEXANDER ISLAND *(AN)*
AMINDIVI ISLANDS *(IN)*
AMIRANTE ISLANDS *(IN)*
AMSTERDAM ISLAND *(IN)*
ANGEL DE LA GUARDA *(CA)*
ASCENSION ISLAND *(A)*
AUCKLAND ISLANDS *(AU)*
BALEARIC ISLANDS *(M)*
BISSAGOS ISLANDS *(AF)*
CAROLINE ISLANDS *(P)*
CHRISTMAS ISLAND *(IN)*
    (P)
ELLESMERE ISLAND *(NA)*

FALKLAND ISLANDS *(SA) *42*
FRIENDLY ISLANDS *(P) *16*
FURNEAUX ISLANDS *(AU)*
GREATER ANTILLES *(WI)*
HAWAIIAN ISLANDS *(P)*
KERMADEC ISLANDS *(P)*
MAGDALEN ISLANDS *(NA)*
MARSHALL ISLANDS *(P)*

MARTHA'S VINEYARD *(NA)*
PRIBILOF ISLANDS *(NA)*
ROOSEVELT ISLAND *(AN)*
SANDWICH ISLANDS *(A)*
SEVERNAYA ZEMLYA *(AS-G)*
THOUSAND ISLANDS *(NA)*
VANCOUVER ISLAND *(NA)*
WINDWARD ISLANDS *(WI)*

GEOGRAPHY

LAKES – BRITISH ISLES

All English except: (I) = Irish lough   (S) = Scottish loch
(W) = Welsh lake/llyn
* = Alternative name

3

AWE *(S)*
EIL *(S)*
EWE *(S)*
KEN *(S)*
LEE *(S)*
REE *(I)*
TAY *(S)*

4

ALSH *(S)*
BALA *(W) *1*
BUIE *(S)*
CONN *(I)*
DERG *(I)*
EARN *(S)*
ERNE *(I)*
FYNE *(S)*

GARA *(I)*
GARE *(S)*
GORM *(S)*
HOPE *(S)*
LYON *(S)*
MASK *(I)*
MHOR *(S)*
MORE *(S)*
NESS *(S)*
SHIN *(S)*
WAST

5

ALLEN *(I)*
BROOM *(S)*
CELYN *(W)*
DUICH *(S)*
ETIVE *(S)*
FITTY *(S)*

FOYLE *(I)*
GARRY *(S)*
GLASS *(S)*
HOURN *(S)*
LEANE *(I)*
LEVEN *(S)*
LOCHY *(S)*
LOYAL *(S)*
LOYNE *(S)*
LUSSA *(S)*
MAREE *(S)*
MORAR *(S)*
MUICK *(S)*
NAVER *(S)*
NEAGH *(I)*
OGWEN *(W)*
ORRIN *(S)*
QUIEN *(S)*
RYDAL
SHIEL *(S)*
SWEEN *(S)*

TEGID *(W) *1*
TREIG *(S)*
TUATH *(S)*

6

ARKAIG *(S)*
ASSYNT *(S)*
BRENIG *(W)*
CALDER *(S)*
CORRIB *(I)*
ERICHT *(S)*
LAGGAN *(S)*
LINNHE *(S)*
LOMOND *(S)*
OSSIAN *(S)*
QUOICH *(S)*
SUNART *(S)*
SWILLY *(I)*
TUMMEL *(S)*

VYRNWY *(W)*
WATTEN *(S)*

7

CLUANIE *(S)*
CWELLYN *(W)*
DERWENT
EISHORT *(S)*
ERIBOLL *(S)*
FANNICH *(S)*
GRAFHAM
KATRINE *(S)*
MELFORT *(S)*
MOCHRUM *(S)*
RANNOCH *(S)*
RUTLAND
SNIZORT *(S)*
ST MARY'S *(S)*
STRIVEN *(S)*

8

CONISTON
CRUMMOCK
GRASMERE
LANGAVAT *(S)*
MENTEITH *(S – the only Scottish lake)*
SCRIDIAN *(S)*
SEAFORTH *(S)*
STENNESS *(S)*
TAL-Y-LLYN *(W)*
TORRIDON *(S)*

9

ENNERDALE
ESTHWAITE
KIRBISTER *(S)*
LLANGORSE *(W)*

OCHILTREE *(S)*
THIRLMERE
ULLSWATER
VENNACHAR *(S)*

10

BUTTERMERE
CHEW VALLEY
LOWESWATER
MULLARDOCH *(S)*
RYDAL WATER
STRANGFORD *(I)*
WINDERMERE

11

GLASCARNOCH *(S)*
TRAWSFYNYDD *(W)*

12

DERWENT WATER
GRAFHAM WATER
RUTLAND WATER

13

BASSENTHWAITE
CONISTON WATER
CRUMMOCK WATER

14

ENNERDALE WATER

15

CLATTERINGSHAWS *(S)*

GEOGRAPHY

LAKES – WORLD

(AF) = Africa   (AM) = The Americas   (AS) = Asia   (AU) = Australasia
(E) = Europe
* = Alternative name

3

TUZ *(AS)*
VAN *(AS)*

4

CHAD *(AF)*

COMO *(E)*
DORÉ *(AM)*
ERIE *(AM)*
EYRE *(AU)*
ISEO *(E)*
KIVU *(AF)*
MEAD *(AM)*
NEMI *(E)*
OHAU *(AU)*

OULU *(E)*
TANA *(AF)*
UTAH *(AM)*

5

ABAYA *(AF)*
BAKER *(AM)*
FROME *(AU)*

GARDA *(E)*
GATUN *(AM)*
HURON *(AM)*
INARI *(E)*
KYOGA *(AF)*
LÉMAN *(E) *1*
MINTO *(AM)*
MWERU *(AF)*
NGAMI *(AF)*

NYASA *(AF) *2*
ONEGA *(AS)*
PAYNE *(AM)*
POOPÓ *(AM)*
SEVAN *(AS)*
TAHOE *(AM)*
TAUPO *(AU)*
URMIA *(AS)*
VOLTA *(AF)*

GEOGRAPHY — LAKES – WORLD

6

ALBERT *(AF)*
AUSTIN *(AU)*
BAIKAL *(AS)*
BIWA-KO *(AS)*
DUNDAS *(AU)*
EDWARD *(AF)*
GENEVA *(E) *1*
KARIBA *(AF)*
KHANKA *(AS)*
LADOGA *(AS)*
LOP NOR *(AS)*
LUGANO *(E)*
MACKAY *(AU)*
MALAWI *(AF) *2*
MARION *(AM)*
MARTIN *(AM)*
McLEOD *(AU)*
MÜRITZ *(E)*
NASSER *(AF)*
ONEIDA *(AM)*
PLACID *(AM)*
POWELL *(AM)*
PUKAKI *(AM)*
RUDOLF *(AF)*
SEGURA *(E)*
SHARPE *(AM)*
ST JOHN *(AM)*
STUART *(AM)*
TE ANAU *(AU)*
TEXOMA *(AM)*
VÄNERN *(E)*
WANAKA *(AU)*
XINIÁS *(E)*
ZÜRICH *(E)*

7

ABITIBI *(AM)*
BALATON *(E)*
BOLSENA *(E)*
BOURGET *(E)*
CHAPALA *(AM)*
ETAWNEY *(AM)*

FAGNANO *(AM)*
FRANCIS *(AM)*
KLAMATH *(AM)*
KOKO NOR *(AS)*
MUSKOVA *(AM)*
NIPIGON *(AM)*
ONTARIO *(AM)*
PYRAMID *(AM)*
QUESNEL *(AM)*
RYBINSK *(AS)*
ST CLAIR *(AM)*
TORRENS *(AU)*
TURKANA *(AF)*
VÄTTERN *(E)*

8

AMMERSEE *(E)*
ATTERSEE *(E)*
BALKHASH *(AS)*
BODENSEE *(E) *3*
CHIEMSEE *(E)*
DRUMMOND *(AM)*
FLATHEAD *(AM)*
HORNAVAN *(E)*
ISSYK-KUL *(AS)*
KENTUCKY *(AM)*
KOOTENAY *(AM)*
MAGGIORE *(E)*
MANITOBA *(AM)*
MAUREPAS *(AM)*
MENINDEE *(AU)*
MICHIGAN *(AM)*
REINDEER *(AM)*
SEMINOLE *(AM)*
STEFANIE *(AF)*
STORSJÖN *(E)*
SUPERIOR *(AM)*
TIBERIAS *(AS, also GALILEE, in BAYS & SEAS)*
TITICACA *(AM)*
TONLE SAP *(AS)*
VICTORIA *(AF)*
WAKATIPU *(AU)*
WINNIPEG *(AM)*

9

ARGENTINO *(AM)*
ATHABASCA *(AM)*
BANGWEULU *(AF)*
BRACCIANO *(E)*
CHAMPLAIN *(AM)*
CONSTANCE *(E) *3*
GREAT BEAR *(AM)*
GREAT SALT *(AM)*
HINDMARSH *(AU)*
MAI NDOMBE *(AF)*
MARACAIBO *(AM)*
NEUCHÂTEL *(E)*
NICARAGUA *(AM)*
NIPISSING *(AM)*
THUNERSEE *(E)*
TRASIMENO *(E)*
WOLLASTON *(AM)*

10

BROKOPONDO *(AM)*
CUMBERLAND *(AM)*
GREAT SLAVE *(AM)*
MISTASSINI *(AM)*
OKEECHOBEE *(AM)*
TANGANYIKA *(AF)*

11

DIEFENBAKER *(AM)*
MAR CHIQUITA *(AM)*
YELLOWSTONE *(AM)*

12

WINNIPEGOSIS *(AM)*

13

PONTCHARTRAIN *(AM)*

GEOGRAPHY

MOUNTAIN RANGES

(AF) = Africa   (AM) = The Americas   (AS) = Asia   (AU) = Australasia
(B) = British Isles   (E) = Europe

4

ALPS *(E)*
HARZ *(E)*
JURA *(E)*
NAGA *(AS)*

5

ALTAI *(AS)*
ANDES *(AM)*
ATLAS *(AF)*
DOWNS *(B)*
GHATS *(AS)*
URALS *(AS/E)*
WOLDS *(E)*

6

GALTEE *(B)*
HOOSAC *(AM)*
LENNOX *(B)*
MOURNE *(B)*
OCHILS *(B)*
TAUNUS *(E)*
TAURUS *(AS)*
VOSGES *(E)*

7

BALKANS *(E)*
MENDIPS *(B)*
NILGIRI *(AS)*
ROCKIES *(AM)*

SUDETES *(E)*
WICKLOW *(B)*

8

AUVERGNE *(E)*
CASCADES *(AM)*
CAUCASUS *(AS/E)*
CHEVIOTS *(B)*
MALVERNS *(B)*
PENNINES *(B)*
PYRENEES *(E)*
SPERRINS *(B)*
THE DOWNS *(B)*
THE GHATS *(AS)*
THE WOLDS *(B)*
TIEN SHAN *(AS)*

9

APENNINES *(E)*
BLUE RIDGE *(AM)*
CATSKILLS *(AM)*
CHILTERNS *(B)*
COTSWOLDS *(B)*
DOLOMITES *(E)*
DRUM HILLS *(B)*
FAUCILLES *(E)*
GRAMPIANS *(B)*
HIMALAYAS *(AS)*
HINDU KUSH *(AS)*
NAGA HILLS *(AS)*
QUANTOCKS *(B)*
SNOWDONIA *(B)*
YABLONOVY *(AS)*

10

CAIRNGORMS *(B)*
CARNIC ALPS *(E)*
ERZGEBIRGE *(E)*
JULIAN ALPS *(E)*
OCHIL HILLS *(B)*
THE GLYDERS *(B)*
TOUCH HILLS *(B)*

11

ADIRONDACKS *(AM)*
BERWYN HILLS *(B)*
CANTABRIANS *(E)*
CARPATHIANS *(E)*
CLEISH HILLS *(B)*
COTTIAN ALPS *(E)*
DINARIC ALPS *(E)*
FINTRY HILLS *(B)*
LENNOX HILLS *(B)*
MENDIP HILLS *(B)*
PENNINE ALPS *(E)*
SIDLAW HILLS *(B)*
SIERRA MADRE *(AM)*
SWABIAN ALPS *(E)*

12

APPALACHIANS *(AM)*
BRENDON HILLS *(B)*
CASCADE RANGE *(AM)*
CHEVIOT HILLS *(B)*
CUILLIN HILLS *(B)*
DRAKENSBERGS *(AF)*
ELK MOUNTAINS *(AM)*

GEOGRAPHY – MOUNTAIN RANGES

KILSYTH HILLS *(B)*
LEBANON RANGE *(AS)*
MALVERN HILLS *(B)*
NILGIRI HILLS *(AS)*
PEAK DISTRICT *(B)*
PENNINE RANGE *(B)*
PRESELI HILLS *(B)*
RHAETIAN ALPS *(E)*
RUAHINE RANGE *(AU)*
SIERRA MORENA *(E)*
SIERRA NEVADA *(AM)*
   (E)
SIWALIK HILLS *(AS)*
THE CARNEDDAU *(B)*
VINDHYA HILLS *(AS)*

CAHA MOUNTAINS *(B)*
CHILTERN HILLS *(B)*
COTSWOLD HILLS *(B)*
FLINDERS RANGE *(AU)*
HARZ MOUNTAINS *(E)*
IRON MOUNTAINS *(B)*
JURA MOUNTAINS *(E)*
KONG MOUNTAINS *(AF)*
MASSIF CENTRAL *(E)*
MOORFOOT HILLS *(B)*
PENTLAND HILLS *(B)*
QUANTOCK HILLS *(B)*
RIESENGEBIRGE *(E)*
SIERRA MAESTRA *(AM)*
URAL MOUNTAINS *(AS/E)*

BLACK MOUNTAINS *(AM,*
   (B)
CLEVELAND HILLS *(B)*
FICHTELGEBIRGE *(E)*
GREEN MOUNTAINS *(AM,*
PAMIR MOUNTAINS *(AS)*
ROCKY MOUNTAINS *(AM*
SHEHY MOUNTAINS *(B)*
SNOWY MOUNTAINS *(AU,*
WHITE MOUNTAINS *(AM)*

15

BALKAN MOUNTAINS *(E)*
BERNESE OBERLAND *(E)*
GALTEE MOUNTAINS *(B)*
KILPATRICK HILLS *(B)*
LAMMERMUIR HILLS *(B)*
PARTRY MOUNTAINS *(B)*
RODOPI MOUNTAINS *(AS)*
TAURUS MOUNTAINS *(AS)*

13

ARAVALLI RANGE *(AS)*
BLUE MOUNTAINS *(AM)*
   (AU)

14

ALTAI MOUNTAINS *(AS)*
ATLAS MOUNTAINS *(AF)*
BLACKDOWN HILLS *(B)*

GEOGRAPHY

MOUNTAINS – BRITISH ISLES

All England except: (I) = Ireland   (M) = Isle of Man   (S) = Scotland
(W) = Wales

4

CAHA *(I)*
DRUM *(W)*

RAISE
SAILS
SAWEL *(I)*

6

BEN HEE *(S)*
BEN IME *(S)*
BEN LUI *(S)*

DROSGL *(W)*
TRYFAN *(W)*
YES TOR
YR ARAN *(W)*

7

BEN AVON *(S)*

BEN LEDI *(S)*
BEN MORE *(S)*
BOW FELL
DIFFWYS *(W)*
DOW CRAG
DUN FELL
ESK PIKE
GREY NAG
HAYCOCK

HIGH SPY
ILL BELL
KIPPURE *(I)*
MERRICK *(S)*
PEN Y FAN *(W)*
RED PIKE
SCA FELL
SKIDDAW
SNOWDON *(W)*

5

GODOR *(W)*
KNOTT

TAL Y FAN *(W)*
THE CALF
THE DODD

8

BEN ALDER *(S)*
BEN NEVIS *(S)*
BEN WYVIS *(S)*
BINK MOSS
BLEAK LOW
BROAD LAW *(S)*
BRYN GARW *(W)*
COLD FELL
COMB FELL
CRAG HILL
DALE HEAD
FELL HEAD
GLASGWYM *(W)*
GLYCHEDD *(W)*
GOAT FELL *(S)*
GRASMOOR
GREAT END
HART CRAG
HIGH PIKE
IRON CRAG
KIRK FELL
LINGMELL
MOEL SYCH *(W)*
MWEELREA *(I)*
REST DODD
ROBINSON
SCALD LAW *(S)*
SNAEFELL *(M)*
SWIRL HOW
TARN CRAG
ULLSCARF
WAEN RYDD *(W)*
YARLSIDE

9

BEN DONICH *(S)*
BEN LAWERS *(S)*

BEN LOMOND *(S)*
BLACK FELL
BRAERIACH *(S)*
BRANDRETH
BRANSTREE
CAIRN GORM *(S)*
CAIRN TOUL *(S)*
CARN DEARG *(S)*
CROSS FELL
CUSHAT LAW
FAIRFIELD
FOEL RHUDD *(W)*
GLARAMARA
GRAGARETH
GREAT COUM
GREAT DODD
GREAT RHOS *(W)*
GREY FRIAR
HELVELLYN
HIGH FIELD
HIGH RAISE
HIGH STILE
KNOCK FELL
LAMMER LAW *(S)*
MANGERTON *(I)*
PLACE FELL
ROUND HILL
SCAR CRAGS
SCOAT FELL
SEATALLAN
STOBILIAN *(S)*
THE SADDLE *(S)*
THE WREKIN
WETHERLAM
WHERNSIDE
WHITESIDE
WINDY GYLE *(E/S)*
YEWBARROW

10

ALLEN CRAGS
BEN CHONZIE *(S)*
BEN MACDHUI *(S)*
BEN VORLICH *(S)*
BLENCATHRA

BROWN WILLY
BYNACK MORE *(S)*
CADER IDRIS *(W)*
CATSTYE CAM
CLOUGH HEAD
FIEND'S FELL
FLINTY FELL
GLYDER FAWR *(W)*
GREAT BORNE
GREAT CALVA
GREAT GABLE
HARTER FELL
HIGH STREET
HINDSCARTH
KEEPER HILL *(I)*
MELDON HILL
MURTON FELL
PILLAR FELL
PILSDON PEN
PLYNLIMMON *(W)*
RHINOG FAWR *(W)*
ROGAN'S SEAT
RYDER'S HILL
SEAT SANDAL
SWARTH FELL
THE CHEVIOT
THE COBBLER *(S)*
WETHER HILL

11

BEN CRUACHAN *(S)*
BRANDON HILL *(I)*
BUCKDEN PIKE
CARROCK FELL
DRUMALDRACE
DRYGARN FAWR *(W)*
FAN GIHIRYCH *(W)*
GREAT MIS TOR
KILLHOPE LAW
KINDER SCOUT
LUGNAQUILLA *(I)*
PIKE O'BLISCO
SCAFELL PIKE
SGORR DHEARG *(S)*
VIEWING HILL

12

BOWSCALE FELL
CRINKLE CRAGS
HIGH WILLHAYS
HOPEGILL HEAD
INGLEBOROUGH
LONSCALE FELL
MELMERBY FELL
RANDYGILL TOP
SCHIEHALLION *(S)*
SLIEVE DONARD *(I)*
ST SUNDAY CRAG
STYBARROW DOD

13

BACKSTONE EDGE
BLACK MOUNTAIN *(W)*
CARRANTUOHILL *(I)*
CHAPELFELL TOP
CROAGH PATRICK *(I)*
DUNKERY BEACON
GRISEDALE PIKE
HEDGEHOPE HILL
KNOUTBERRY HAW
PEN-Y-GHENT HILL
SGURR ALASDAIR *(S)*
SHEFFIELD PIKE
STONY COVE PIKE
THE TWELVE PINS

14

BELLBEAVER RIGG
MIDDLEHOPE MOOR
MULLAGHANATTIN *(I)*

15

DOLLYWAGGON PIKE
KILNSHAW CHIMNEY

GEOGRAPHY

MOUNTAINS – WORLD

(AF) = Africa   (AM) = The Americas   (AN) = Antarctica   (AS) = Asia
(AU) = Australasia   (E) = Europe
* = Alternative spelling   † = Volcanic island

3

ELK *(AM)*
IDA *(E)*
KEA *(AM)*

4

AZUL *(AM)*
COOK *(AU)*
DORE *(E)*
EBAL *(AS)*
ETNA *(E)*
FUJI *(AS)*

JAYA *(AS)*
JOMA *(AS)*
MERU *(AF)*
OSSA *(AU)*
       (E)
RIGI *(E)*
ROAN *(AM)*
ROSA *(E)*
VISO *(E)*

5

ADAMS *(AM)*
ASAHI *(AS)*

ATHOS *(E)*
BAKER *(AM)*
BINGA *(AF)*
BLANC *(E)*
CENIS *(E)*
CINTO *(E)*
CORNO *(E)*
COWAN *(AM)*
DENDI *(AF)*
DJAJA *(AS)*
EIGER *(E)*
ELGON *(AF)*
GUGHE *(AF)*
HAYES *(AM)*

HEKLA *(E)*
HUILA *(AM)*
KAMET *(AS)*
LENIN *(AS)*
LOGAN *(AM)*
LYELL *(AM)*
MARCY *(AM)*
MISTI *(AM)*
MÖNCH *(E)*
OVERO *(AM)*
PELÉE *(AM)*
PERDU *(E)*
SINAI *(AF)*
TABOR *(AS)*

6

ARARAT *(AS)*
BOGONG *(AU)*
CARMEL *(AS)*
DUARTE *(AM)*
ELBERT *(AM)*
ELBRUS *(E)* *1
ELBRUZ *(E)* *1
EREBUS *(AN)*
HERMON *(AS)*
HOTAKA *(AS)*
KAILAS *(AS)*
LELIJA *(E)*

MAKALU *(AS)*
MUSALA *(E)*
MUZTAG *(AS)*
ORTLES *(E)*
PISSIS *(AM)*
POWELL *(AM)*
RUNGWE *(AF)*
SAJAMA *(AM)*
SANGAY *(AM)*
TASMAN *(AU)*
TOLIMA *(AM)*
WILSON *(AM)*
YEGUAS *(AM)*
ZIRKEL *(AM)*

8

ADAMELLO *(E)*
ANAI MUDI *(AS)*
COLUMBIA *(AM)*
COTOPAXI *(AM)*
DEMAVEND *(AS)*
DURMITOR *(E)*
FUJIYAMA *(AS)*
ILLIMANI *(AM)*
JUNGFRAU *(E)*
KINABALU *(AS)*
KLINOVEC *(E)*
KRAKATOA *(AS)* †
LICOREIA *(E)*
MAUNA KEA *(AM)*
McKINLEY *(AM)*
MITCHELL *(AM)*
MONT DORE *(E)*
MULHACÉN *(E)*
MURALLÓN *(AM)*
OLIVARES *(AM)*
RUSHMORE *(AM)*
SARAMETI *(AS)*
SMÓLIKAS *(E)*
SNÖHETTA *(E)*
SOKHONDO *(AS)*
ST HELENS *(AM)*
TARAWERA *(AU)*
TOWNSEND *(AU)*
VESUVIUS *(E)*
VICTORIA *(AS)*
WRANGELL *(AM)*

9

ACONCAGUA *(AM)*
ADAM'S PEAK *(AS)*
ANNAPURNA *(AS)*
BLACKBURN *(AM)*
BORAH PEAK *(AM)*
BREITHORN *(E)*
BÜYÜK AGRI *(AS)*
COMMUNISM *(AS)*
DACHSTEIN *(E)*

EMI KOUSSI *(AF)*
GRAN SASSO *(E)*
GRAY'S PEAK *(AM)*
HUASCARÁN *(AM)*
KARAKORAM *(AS)*
KARISIMBE *(AF)*
KING'S PEAK *(AM)*
KOH-I-MAZAR *(AS)*
KOSCIUSKO *(AU)*
LAFAYETTE *(AM)*
LONG'S PEAK *(AM)*
MALADETTA *(E)*
MARMOLADA *(E)*
MONT BLANC *(E)*
MONT CENIS *(E)*
MONTE ROSA *(E)*
MONTE VISO *(E)*
MONT PERDU *(E)*
MUZTAGATA *(AS)*
NANDA DEVI *(AS)*
PARNASSUS *(E)*
PELATSOEU *(AF)*
PIC DU MIDI *(E)*
PIETROSUL *(E)*
PIKE'S PEAK *(AM)*
RAKAPOSHI *(AS)*
RAS DASHAN *(AF)*
STROMBOLI *(E)* †
SUGAR LOAF *(AM)*
TOCORPURI *(AM)*
TONGARIRO *(AU)*
TUPUNGATO *(AM)*
ZUGSPITZE *(E)*

10

BLANCA PEAK *(AM)*
CASTLE PEAK *(AM)*
CHIMBORAZO *(AM)*
DENT DU MIDI *(E)*
DHAULAGIRI *(AS)*
DIABLARETS *(E)*
GONGGA SHAN *(AS)*
GRAND TETON *(AM)*
GRASSY KNOB *(AM)*
KUH-E-TAFTAN *(AS)*

7

BERNINA *(E)*
BOLIVAR *(AM)*
BROCKEN *(E)*
DYKH TAU *(E)*
EVEREST *(AS)*
FORAKER *(AM)*
HARVARD *(AM)*
HOFFMAN *(AM)*
ILLAMPU *(AM)*
JEZERCE *(E)*
KERINCI *(AS)*
LOOKOUT *(AM)*
MARKHAM *(AN)*
OHAKUNE *(AU)*
OLYMPUS *(E)*
PELVOUX *(E)*
PETEROA *(AM)*
POLLINO *(E)*
RAINIER *(AM)*
RORAIMA *(AM)*
SANFORD *(AM)*
SAN JOSÉ *(AM)*
SIMPLON *(E)*
ST ELIAS *(AM)*
THABANA *(AF)*
TIMARUM *(AS)*
TOUBKAL *(AF)*
TRIGLAV *(E)*
WHITNEY *(AM)*

LA MALINCHE *(AM)*
MATTERHORN *(E)*
MERCEDARIO *(AM)*
MINJA KONKA *(AS)*
MONTE CINTO *(E)*
MONTE CORNO *(E)*
ROBSON PEAK *(AM)*
SPRUCE KNOB *(AM)*
TABUN BOGDO *(AS)*
WASHINGTON *(AM)*
WETTERHORN *(E)*
WILDSPITZE *(E)*

11

ASSINIBOINE *(AM)*
DRACHENFELS *(E)*
FAIRWEATHER *(AM)*
GARNETT PEAK *(AM)*
GORA BELUKHA *(AS)*
HOCHSTETTER *(AU)*

KILIMANJARO *(AF)*
KIRKPATRICK *(AN)*
LOOLMALASIN *(AF)*
MUNKU SARDYK *(AS)*
NAMCHA BARWA *(AS)*
NANGA PARBAT *(AS)*
SCHRECKHORN *(E)*
VATNA JÖKULL *(E)*
WHEELER PEAK *(AM)*

12

CITLALTEPETL *(AM)*
GALDHÖPIGGEN *(E)*
GODWIN AUSTEN *(AS)*
GRAN PARADISO *(E)*
LLULLAILLACO *(AM)*
MONTE POLLINO *(E)*
POPOCATEPETL *(AM)*
TINGUIRIRICA *(AM)*

13

CLINGMAN'S DOME *(AM)*
GROSS GLOCKNER *(E)*
JABAL ALCHDHAR *(AS)*
KANGCHENJUNGA *(AS)*
MOUNT OF OLIVES *(AS)*
OJOS DEL SALADO *(AM)*
TABLE MOUNTAIN *(AF)*

14

FINSTERAARHORN *(E)*
MONT AUX SOURCES *(AF)*
PIDURUTALAGALA *(AS)*

15

CHAMPAGNE CASTLE *(AF)*

GEOGRAPHY

REGIONS – BRITISH ISLES (COUNTIES)

All England except: (I) = Irish Republic   (NI) = Northern Ireland
(S) = Scotland   (W) = Wales
* = Former county   (ᴾ) = Province

4

AVON
BUTE *(S)**
CORK *(I)*
DOWN *(NI)*
FIFE *(S)*
KENT
MAYO *(I)*

5

ANGUS *(S)**
CAVAN *(I)*
CLARE *(I)*
CLYWD *(W)*
DEVON
DYFED *(W)*
ESSEX

FLINT *(W)**
GWENT *(W)*
KERRY *(I)*
LAOIS *(I)*
LOUTH *(I)*
MEATH *(I)*
MORAY *(S)**
NAIRN *(S)**
POWYS *(W)*

SALOP ***
SLIGO *(I)*

6

ANTRIM *(NI)*
ARMAGH *(NI)*
CARLOW *(I)*
DORSET

DUBLIN *(I)*
DURHAM
GALWAY *(I)*
OFFALY *(I)*
ORKNEY *(S)*
SURREY
SUSSEX ***
TYRONE *(NI)*
ULSTER *(NI)* ᴾ

7

BORDERS *(S)*
CENTRAL *(S)*
CUMBRIA
DENBIGH *(W)**
DONEGAL *(I)*
GWYNEDD *(W)*
KILDARE *(I)*
LEITRIM *(I)*
LOTHIAN *(S)*
MUNSTER *(I) P*
NORFOLK
RUTLAND *
SUFFOLK
TAYSIDE *(S)*
WEXFORD *(I)*
WICKLOW *(I)*

8

ANGLESEY *(W)**
AYRSHIRE *(S)**
CHESHIRE
CONNACHT *(I) P*
CORNWALL
GRAMPIAN *(S)*
HIGHLAND *(S)*
KILKENNY *(I)*
LEINSTER *(I) P*
LIMERICK *(I)*
LONGFORD *(I)*
MONAGHAN *(I)*
SHETLAND *(S)*
SOMERSET

9

BERKSHIRE
BRECKNOCK *(W)**
CAITHNESS *(S)**
CLEVELAND
FERMANAGH *(NI)*
GLAMORGAN *(W)**

HAMPSHIRE
MERIONETH *(W)**
MIDDLESEX *
ROSCOMMON *(I)*
TIPPERARY *(I)*
WATERFORD *(I)*
WESTMEATH *(I)*
WILTSHIRE
YORKSHIRE *

10

BANFFSHIRE *(S)**
CUMBERLAND *
DERBYSHIRE
DEVONSHIRE *
EAST SUSSEX
HUMBERSIDE
LANCASHIRE
MERSEYSIDE
MIDLOTHIAN *(S)**
MONTGOMERY *(W)**
PERTHSHIRE *(S)**
SHROPSHIRE
SUTHERLAND *(S)**
WEST SUSSEX

11

ARGYLLSHIRE *(S)**
EAST LOTHIAN *(S)**
ISLE OF WIGHT
LANARKSHIRE *(S)**
LONDONDERRY *(NI)*
OXFORDSHIRE
RADNORSHIRE *(W)**
STRATHCLYDE *(S)*
TYNE AND WEAR
WEST LOTHIAN *(S)**
WESTMORLAND *

12

BEDFORDSHIRE
BERWICKSHIRE *(S)**
KINROSS-SHIRE *(S)**
LINCOLNSHIRE
MID GLAMORGAN *(W)*
PEEBLESSHIRE *(S)**
RENFREWSHIRE *(S)**
SELKIRKSHIRE *(S)**
WARWICKSHIRE
WESTERN ISLES *(S)*
WEST MIDLANDS
WIGTOWNSHIRE *(S)**

13

ABERDEENSHIRE *(S)**
CARDIGANSHIRE *(W)**
DUMFRIESSHIRE *(S)**
GREATER LONDON
HEREFORDSHIRE *
HERTFORDSHIRE
MONMOUTHSHIRE *
PEMBROKESHIRE *(W)**
ROXBURGHSHIRE *(S)**
STAFFORDSHIRE
STIRLINGSHIRE *(S)**
WEST GLAMORGAN *(W)*
WEST YORKSHIRE

14

CAMBRIDGESHIRE
DUNBARTONSHIRE *(S)**
INVERNESS-SHIRE *(S)**
LEICESTERSHIRE
NORTHUMBERLAND
NORTH YORKSHIRE
SOUTH GLAMORGAN *(W)*
SOUTH YORKSHIRE
WORCESTERSHIRE *

15

BUCKINGHAMSHIRE
CAERNARVONSHIRE *(W)**
CARMARTHENSHIRE *(W)**

GLOUCESTERSHIRE
HUNTINGDONSHIRE *
KINCARDINESHIRE *(S)**
NOTTINGHAMSHIRE
ROSS AND CROMARTY *(S)**

GEOGRAPHY

REGIONS – NORTH AMERICA (STATES)

(C) = Canadian provinces

4

IOWA
OHIO
UTAH

5

IDAHO
MAINE
TEXAS
YUKON *(C)*

6

ALASKA
HAWAII
KANSAS
NEVADA
OREGON
QUEBEC *(C)*

7

ALABAMA
ALBERTA *(C)*
ARIZONA
FLORIDA
GEORGIA
INDIANA
MONTANA
NEW YORK
ONTARIO *(C)*
VERMONT
WYOMING

8

ARKANSAS
COLORADO
DELAWARE
ILLINOIS
KENTUCKY
MANITOBA *(C)*
MARYLAND
MICHIGAN

MISSOURI
NEBRASKA
OKLAHOMA
VIRGINIA

9

LOUISIANA
MINNESOTA
NEW JERSEY
NEW MEXICO
TENNESSEE
WISCONSIN

10

CALIFORNIA
NOVA SCOTIA *(C)*
WASHINGTON

11

CONNECTICUT

MISSISSIPPI
NORTH DAKOTA
RHODE ISLAND
SOUTH DAKOTA

12

NEW BRUNSWICK *(C)*
NEWFOUNDLAND *(C)*
NEW HAMPSHIRE
PENNSYLVANIA
SASKATCHEWAN *(C)*
WEST VIRGINIA

13

MASSACHUSETTS
NORTH CAROLINA
SOUTH CAROLINA

15

BRITISH COLUMBIA *(C)*

GEOGRAPHY

REGIONS – WESTERN EUROPE

(B) = *Belgian province*   *(F)* = *French department*   *(FR)* = *French region*
(I) = *Italian region*   *(L)* = *Luxembourg district*   *(N)* = *Netherlandic province*
(SP) = *Spanish province*   *(SR)* = *Spanish region*   *(SW)* = *Swiss canton*
(WG) = *West German province*
* = Alternative spelling

3

AIN *(F)*
LOT *(F)*
URI *(SW)*
VAR *(F)*
ZUG *(SW)*

4

AUBE *(F)*
AUDE *(F)*
BERN *(SW)* *1
CHER *(F)*
EURE *(F)*
GARD *(F)*
GERS *(F)*
JURA *(F)*
LEÓN *(SP)*
NORD *(F)*
OISE *(F)*
ORNE *(F)*
TARN *(F)*

5

AISNE *(F)*
BERNE *(SW)* *1
CORSE *(FR)*
DOUBS *(F)*
DRÔME *(F)*
INDRE *(F)*

ISÈRE *(F)*
LAZIO *(I)*
LIÈGE *(B)*
LOIRE *(F)*
MARNE *(F)*
MEUSE *(F)*
NAMUR *(B)*
RHÔNE *(F)*
RIOJA *(SP)*
SOMME *(F)*
YONNE *(F)*

6

ALLIER *(F)*
ALSACE *(FR)*
ARAGÓN *(SP)*
ARIÈGE *(F)*
BAYERN *(WG)* *2
BREMEN *(WG)*
CANTAL *(F)*
CENTRE *(FR)*
CREUSE *(F)*
GLARUS *(SW)*
HESSEN *(WG)*
LANDES *(F)*
LOIRET *(F)*
LOZÈRE *(F)*
MADRID *(SP)*
MANCHE *(F)*
MARCHE *(I)*
MOLISE *(I)*
MURCIA *(SP)*

NIÈVRE *(F)*
PUGLIA *(I)*
SARTHE *(F)*
SAVOIE *(F)*
SCHWYS *(SW)*
UMBRIA *(I)*
VENDÉE *(F)*
VENETO *(I)* *3
VIENNE *(F)*
VOSGES *(F)*
ZÜRICH *(SW)*

7

ABRUZZI *(I)*
ARDÈCHE *(F)*
AVEYRON *(F)*
BAS-RHIN *(F)*
BAVARIA *(WG)* *2
BELFORT *(F)*
BRABANT *(B)*
CASTILE *(SP)*
CORRÈZE *(F)*
CÔTE D'OR *(F)*
DRENTHE *(N)*
ESSONNE *(F)*
GALICIA *(SP)*
GIRONDE *(F)*
HAINAUT *(B)*
HAMBURG *(WG)*
HÉRAULT *(F)*
LIGURIA *(I)*
LIMBURG *(B)*
(N)

LUCERNE *(SW)*
MAYENNE *(F)*
MOSELLE *(F)*
NAVARRE *(SP)*
PICARDY *(FR)* *4
RIVIERA *(FR)*
TOSCANA *(I)* *5
TUSCANY *(I)* *5
UTRECHT *(N)*
VENETIA *(I)* *3
ZEELAND *(N)*

8

ARDENNES *(F)*
ASTURIAS *(SP)*
AUVERGNE *(FR)*
BALEARES *(SP)* *6
BRETAGNE *(FR)* *7
BRITTANY *(FR)* *7
CALABRIA *(I)*
CALVADOS *(F)*
CAMPANIA *(I)*
CANARIAS *(SP)* *8
CANARIES *(SP)* *8
CATALUÑA *(SP)* *9
CHARENTE *(F)*
DIEKIRCH *(L)*
DORDOGNE *(F)*
FLANDERS *(B)* *10
FRIBOURG *(SW)*
HAUT-RHIN *(F)*
LIMOUSIN *(FR)*

LOMBARDY *(I) *11*
LORRAINE *(FR)*
MORBIHAN *(F)*
NORMANDY *(FR) *12*
OBWALDEN *(SW)*
PICARDIE *(FR) *4*
PIEDMONT *(I)*
PROVENCE *(FR)*
SAARLAND *(WG)*
ST GALLEN *(SW)*
VAL D'OISE *(F)*
VALENCIA *(SP)*
VAUCLUSE *(F)*
YVELINES *(F)*

9

ANDALUCIA *(SP)*
ANTWERPEN *(B)*
APPENZELL *(SW)*
AQUITAINE *(FR)*
BALEARICS *(SP) *6*
BASEL-LAND *(SW)*
BOURGOGNE *(FR)*
CANTABRIA *(SP)*
CATALONIA *(SP) *9*
CÔTE D'AZUR *(FR)*
FINISTÈRE *(F)*
FLEVOLAND *(N)*
FRIESLAND *(N)*
GRONINGEN *(N)*
LOMBARDIA *(I) *11*
NIDWALDEN *(SW)*
NORMANDIE *(FR) *12*
PAIS VASCO *(SP)*
PRESIDIOS *(SP)*
PUY-DE-DÔME *(F)*
SOLOTHURN *(SW)*

10

BASEL-STADT *(SW)*
BASILICATA *(I)*
CORSE-DU-SUD *(F)*

COSTA BRAVA *(SR)*
DEUX-SÈVRES *(F)*
EURE-ET-LOIR *(F)*
GELDERLAND *(N)*
HAUTE-CORSE *(F)*
HAUTE-LOIRE *(F)*
HAUTE-MARNE *(F)*
HAUTE-SAÔNE *(F)*
LOIR-ET-CHER *(F)*
LUXEMBOURG *(B)*
            (L)
OVERIJSSEL *(N)*
RHÔNE-ALPES *(FR)*
VAL-DE-MARNE *(F)*
VALLADOLID *(SP)*
VLAANDEREN *(B) *10*

11

BASSES-ALPES *(F)*
CASTILE-LEÓN *(SP)*
COSTA BLANCA *(SR)*
COSTA DEL SOL *(SR)*
COSTA DORADA *(SR)*
CÔTES-DU-NORD *(F)*
ESTREMADURA *(SP)*
HAUTES-ALPES *(F)*
HAUTE-SAVOIE *(F)*
HAUTE-VIENNE *(F)*
ÎLE-DE-FRANCE *(FR)*
LOWER SAXONY *(WG) *13*
PAS-DE-CALAIS *(F)*
VALLE D'AOSTI *(I)*
ZUID HOLLAND *(N) *14*

12

COSTA ALMERIA *(SR)*
FINISTÈRE SUD *(F)*
FRANCHE-COMTÉ *(FR)*
GREVENMACHER *(L)*
HAUTE-GARONNE *(F)*
HAUTS-DE-SEINE *(F)*
INDRE-ET-LOIRE *(F)*
LOT-ET-GARONNE *(F)*

MAINE-ET-LOIRE *(F)*
MIDI-PYRÉNÉES *(FR)*
NOORD BRABANT *(N) *15*
NORTH BRABANT *(N) *15*
NOORD HOLLAND *(N) *16*
NORTH HOLLAND *(N) *16*
SAÔNE-ET-LOIRE *(F)*
SCHAFFHAUSEN *(SW)*
SEINE-ET-MARNE *(F)*
SEINE-ST DENIS *(F)*
SOUTH HOLLAND *(N) *14*
VILLE DE PARIS *(F)*

13

EMILIA-ROMAGNA *(I)*
FINISTÈRE NORD *(F)*
ILLE-ET-VILAINE *(F)*
NIEDERSACHSEN *(WG) *13*
PAYS-DE-LA-LOIRE *(FR)*
SEINE-MARITIME *(F)*
TARN-ET-GARONNE *(F)*

14

ALPES-MARITIMES *(F)*
BASSE-NORMANDIE *(FR)*
BASSES-PYRÉNÉES *(F)*
BOUCHES-DU-RHÔNE *(F)*
HAUTE-NORMANDIE *(FR)*
HAUTES-PYRÉNÉES *(F)*
OOST VLAANDEREN *(B)*
RHEINLAND-PFALZ *(WG)*
WEST VLAANDEREN *(B)*

15

CASTILLE-LA MANCHA *(SP)*
LOIRE-ATLANTIQUE *(F)*
NORD-PAS-DE-CALAIS *(FR)*
POITOU-CHARENTES *(FR)*

GEOGRAPHY

RIVERS – BRITISH ISLES

(I) = Irish Republic   (NI) = Northern Ireland   (S) = Scotland   (W) = Wales
NB: E = England for border rivers

3

ADD *(S)*
ALN
AWE *(S)*
AXE
AYR *(S)*
BOX
CAM
CUR *(S)*
DEE *(E/W)*
DEE *(S)*
DON
DON *(S)*
ESK
ESK *(E/S)*
EWE *(S)*
EXE
EYE
FAL
HIZ
IRT
LEA
LEE
LEE *(S)*
LUD
LYN
MOY *(I)*
NAR
RAY
RIB
ROE *(NI)*
RYE
SOW
TAF *(W)*
TAW
TAY *(S)*
UCK

URE
URR *(S)*
USK *(W)*
WEN *(W)*
WEY
WYE *(E/W)*
YAR
YEO

4

ADUR
AFAN *(W)*
AIRE
ALAW *(W)*
ALDE
ARUN
AVON
AVON *(S)*
BAIN
BANN *(NI)*
BRAY
BRUE
BURE
BUSH *(NI)*
CALE
CHAR
CHET
COLN
CRAY
CREE *(S)*
CULM
DANE
DART
DEEL *(I)*
DERG *(I/NI)*
DOON *(S)*

DOVE
EARN *(S)*
EDEN
EDEN *(S)*
ERME
FOSS
GLEN
HULL
IDLE
INNY
ISLE
IVEL
KENT
LARK
LEAM
LOOE
LUNE
LYME
LYNE
MAIN *(NI)*
MAUN
MEON
MOLE
NENE
NESS *(S)*
NIDD
NITH *(S)*
NORE *(I)*
ONNY
OUSE
PENK
PLYM
REDE
ROBE *(I)*
RUEL *(S)*
SARK *(S)*
SEPH
SLEA

SOAR
SOWE
SPEY *(S)*
SUCK *(I)*
SUIR *(I)*
TAFF *(W)*
TAME
TARF *(S)*
TAVY
TAWE *(W)*
TEES
TEME
TERN
TEST
TILL
TONE
TOVE
TOWY *(W)*
TYNE
TYNE *(S)*
UGIE *(S)*
WEAR
WICK *(S)*
WYRE
YARE

5

AERON *(W)*
ALLAN *(S)*
ALLEN
AMBER
ANKER
ANNAN *(S)*
ARROW
ARROW *(E/W)*
ASHBY

AVICH *(S)*
BEULT
BLYTH
BOVEY
BOYNE *(I)*
BRANT
BREDE
BRIDE *(I)*
BRORA *(S)*
CAMEL
CAREY
CEFNI *(W)*
CHESS
CLARE *(I)*
CLWYD *(W)*
CLYDE *(S)*
COLNE
CONON *(S)*
CONWY *(W)*
DEBEN
DOVEY *(W)*
ELLEN
FEALE *(I)*
FORTH *(S)*
FOWEY
FROME
FRUIN *(S)*
GARRY *(S)*
GWAUN *(W)*
INVER *(S)*
LAGAN *(NI)*
LEVEN *(S)*
LOCHY *(S)*
MAINE *(I)*
MEDEN
MEECE
NAIRN *(S)*
NEATH *(W)*

OGWEN *(W)*
ORCHY *(S)*
OTTER
OUZEL
OYKEL *(S)*
PERRY
RODEN
RYTON
SHIEL *(S)*
STORT
STOUR
SWALE
TAMAR
TEIFI *(W)*
TEIGN
TEISE
TEITH *(S)*
THAME
TIDDY
TORNE
TRENT
TWEED *(E/S)*
WAVER
WISKE
YRFON *(W)*
YTHAN *(S)*

6

AILORT *(S)*
ALMOND *(S)*
BANDON *(I)*
BARROW *(I)*
BEAULY *(S)*
BLYTHE
BORGIE *(S)*
BOURNE
BRAINT *(W)*
BROSNA *(I)*
CALDER
CAMLAD *(E/W)*

CARRON *(S)*
CLOUGH
COCKER
COQUET
DARENT
DWYRYD *(W)*
EAMONT
ERRIFF *(I)*
FESHIE *(S)*
GILPIN
GIRVAN *(S)*
GLAVEN
GRANTA
HODDER
IRVINE *(S)*
IRWELL
ITCHEN
KENNET
KENSEY
LEADON
LIFFEY *(I)*
LLYFNI *(W)*
LODDON
LOSSIE *(S)*
LYNHER
MAIGUE *(I)*
MEDWAY
MERSEY
MONNOW *(E/W)*
MOURNE *(I/NI)*
NADDER
NEVERN *(W)*
ORWELL
OTTERY
RIBBLE
RODING
ROTHER
SEATON
SEIONT *(W)*
SEVERN *(E/W)*
SLANEY *(I)*
SPRINT

STRULE *(NI)*
TEVIOT *(S)*
THAMES
THURSO *(S)*
TUMMEL *(S)*
VYRNWY *(W)*
WEAVER
WENSUM
WHARFE
WISSEY
WITHAM
WREAKE

7

BEESTON
BRATHAY
CHELMER
DERWENT
DEVERON *(S)*
DYSYNNI *(W)*
ENDRICK *(S)*
GARNOCK *(S)*
GIPPING
GLASLYN *(W)*
HUNDRED
IRTHING
LEANNAN *(I)*
MOIDART *(S)*
PARRETT
POULTER
RAWTHEY
RHEIDOL *(W)*
RIVELIN
SHANNON *(I)*
ST ALLEN
WAMPOOL
WAVENEY
WELLAND
WENNING
YSTWYTH *(W)*

8

ANCHOLME
BADACHRO *(S)*
BEAULIEU
BREAMISH
CHERWELL
CUCKMERE
EVENLODE
FINDHORN *(S)*
GLENELLY *(NI)*
MAWDDACH *(W)*
NORTH ESK *(S)*
SALWARPE
SOUTH ESK *(S)*
STEEPING
STINCHAR *(S)*
TORRIDGE
ULLAPOOL *(S)*
WANSBECK
WINDRUSH

9

GREAT OUSE
GWEEBARRA *(I)*
HALLADALE *(S)*
HARBOURNE
HELMSDALE *(S)*
LYMINGTON
NORTH TYNE
SOUTH TYNE

10

BLACKWATER
BLACKWATER *(I/NI)*
GLENWHIRRY *(NI)*
TILLINGHAM
WHITEADDER *(E/S)*

GEOGRAPHY

RIVERS – WORLD

*(AF) = Africa   (AM) = The Americas   (AS) = Asia   (AU) = Australasia
(E) = Europe
* = Alternative name*

3

AIN *(E)*
ARC *(E)*
BUG *(E)*
DON *(E)*
EMS *(E)*
HAY *(AM)*
HUÉ *(AS)*
ILI *(AS)*
INN *(E)*
LEK *(E)*
LOT *(E)*
LYS *(E)*
MUR *(E)*
OKA *(AS)*
TAZ *(AS)*
UME *(E)*
VAR *(E)*

4

AARE *(E)*
ADDA *(E)*
AMUR *(AS)*1*
ARNO *(E)*
AUBE *(E)*
AUDE *(E)*
BACK *(AM)*
BEAS *(AS)*
CHER *(E)*
EBRO *(E)*
ELBE *(E)*
ENNS *(E)*
GILA *(AM)*
GÖTA *(E)*
ISAR *(E)*

JUBA *(AF)*
KAMA *(E)*
KEMI *(E)*
KLAR *(E)*
LECH *(E)*
LENA *(E)*
MAAS *(E)*2*
MAIN *(E)*
NAAB *(E)*
NEVA *(E)*
NILE *(AF)*
ODER *(E)*
OHIO *(AM)*
OHRE *(E)*
OISE *(E)*
PRUT *(E)*
RAVI *(AS)*
RUHR *(E)*
SAAR *(E)*
SAVA *(E)*
SAVE *(AF)*
SWAN *(AU)*
TANA *(AF)*
TARN *(E)*
TISA *(E)*3*
TONE *(AS)*
UNAC *(E)*
URAL *(AS)*
VAAL *(AF)*
WAAL *(E)*
YANA *(AS)*

5

ADIGE *(E)*
ADOUR *(E)*
AISNE *(E)*

ALDAN *(AS)*
ALLER *(E)*
BENUE *(AF)*
CONGO *(AF)*4*
DESNA *(AS)*
DNEPR *(E)*5*
DOUBS *(E)*
DOURO *(E)*
DRAVA *(E)*
DRINA *(E)*
DVINA *(E)*
EIDER *(E)*
GENIL *(E)*
HAVEL *(E)*
INDUS *(AS)*
ISÈRE *(E)*
ISKUR *(E)*
JUCAR *(E)*
JUMNA *(AS)*
KABUL *(AS)*
KARUN *(AS)*
KIZIL *(AS)*
KOTUY *(AS)*
LIARD *(AM)*
LOIRE *(E)*
MARNE *(E)*
MEUSE *(E)*2*
MIAMI *(AM)*
MINHO *(E)*
MULDE *(E)*
NEGRO *(AM)*
NIGER *(AF)*
ONEGA *(E)*
PECOS *(AM)*
PERAK *(AS)*
PLATE *(AM)*6*
PURUS *(AM)*
RANCE *(E)*

REUSS *(E)*
RHINE *(E)*
RHÔNE *(E)*
SAÔNE *(E)*
SEGRE *(E)*
SEINE *(E)*
SHARI *(AF)*
SHIRE *(AF)*
SIRET *(E)*
SOMME *(E)*
SPREE *(E)*
TAGUS *(E)*
TAPTI *(AS)*
TIBER *(E)*
TISZA *(E)*3*
TOBOL *(AS)*
TORNE *(E)*
VOLGA *(E)*
VOLTA *(AF)*
WARTA *(E)*
WESER *(E)*
XIANG *(AS)*
XINGU *(AM)*
YARRA *(AU)*
YONNE *(E)*
YUKON *(AM)*
ZAÏRE *(AF)*4*

6

ALLIER *(E)*
AMAZON *(AM)*
ANGARA *(AS)*
ATBARA *(AF)*7*
BALSAS *(AM)*
BRAZOS *(AM)*
BRENTA *(E)*

CANTON *(AS)*
CARONI *(AM)*
CHENAB *(AS)*
CLUTHA *(AU)*
CREUSE *(E)*
CUANZA *(AF)*
DANUBE *(E)*
DNESTR *(E)*8*
DONETS *(E)*
FRASER *(AM)*
GAMBIA *(AF)*
GANGES *(AS)*
GLOMMA *(E)*
HUDSON *(AM)*
IRTYSH *(AS)*
JAPURÁ *(AM)*
JHELUM *(AF)*
JORDAN *(AS)*
KOLYMA *(AS)*
LOMAMI *(AF)*
MEKONG *(AS)*
MOBILE *(AM)*
MOHAWK *(AM)*
MOLDAU *(E)*9*
MORAVA *(E)*
MOSKVA *(E)*
MURRAY *(AU)*
NECKAR *(E)*
NEISSE *(E)*
NELSON *(AM)*
OFANTO *(E)*
ORANGE *(AF)*
OTTAWA *(AM)*
OURTHE *(E)*
PARANÁ *(AM)*
PLATTE *(AM)*
PRIPET *(E)*10*
RAJANG *(AS)*

RUFIJI *(AF)*
SAMBRE *(E)*
SARTHE *(E)*
SCIOTO *(AM)*
SEGURA *(E)*
SERETH *(E)*
SHACHE *(AS)*
ST JOHN *(AM)*
SUTLEJ *(AS)*
SWANEE *(AM) *11*
TANANA *(AM)*
TIGRIS *(AS)*
UBANGI *(AF)*
USSURI *(AS)*
VARDAR *(E)*
VIENNE *(E)*
VLTAVA *(E)*9*
WABASH *(AM)*

7

ALABAMA *(AM)*
CABRIEL *(E)*
CATAWBA *(AM)*
CAUVERY *(AS)*
CHAMBAL *(AS)*
CUBANGO *(AF)*
DARLING *(AU)*
DNIEPER *(E)*5*
DURANCE *(E)*
FEATHER *(AM)*
FITZROY *(AU)*
GARONNE *(E)*
GUAPORÉ *(AM)*
HELMAND *(AS)*
HOOGHLI *(AS)*12*
HOOGHLY *(AS)*12*
HUANG HE *(AS)*13*
HWANG HO *(AS)*13*
KANAWHA *(AM)*
KRISHNA *(AS)*
LACHLAN *(AU)*
LIMPOPO *(AF)*14*
LUALABA *(AF)*
LUANGWA *(AF)*

MADEIRA *(AM)*
MARAÑON *(AM)*
MARITSA *(E)*
MOSELLE *(E)*
MURGHAB *(AS)*
NIAGARA *(AM)*
OLIFANT *(AF)*
ORINOCO *(AM)*
ORONTES *(AM)*
PECHORA *(E)*
POTOMAC *(AM)*
PRIPYAT *(E)*10*
ROANOKE *(AM)*
RUBICON *(E)*
SALINAS *(AM)*
SALWEEN *(AS)*
SAN JUAN *(AM)*
SCHELDE *(E)*15*
SCHELDT *(E)*15*
SELENGA *(AS)*
SENEGAL *(AF)*
SONGHUA *(AS)*
SPOKANE *(AM)*
ST CLAIR *(AM)*
ST JOHNS *(AM)*
TAPAJÓS *(AM)*
TRINITY *(AM)*
UCAYALI *(AM)*
URUGUAY *(AM)*
VISTULA *(E)*
WAIKATO *(AU)*
WARREGO *(AU)*
YANGTZE *(AS)*16*
YENISEI *(AS)*17*
YENISEY *(AS)*17*
ZAMBESI *(AF)*18*
ZAMBEZI *(AF)*18*

8

AMU DAR'YA *(AS)*
ANGERMAN *(E)*
ARAGUAYA *(AM)*
ARKANSAS *(AM)*
BEREZINA *(E)*

BLUE NILE *(AF)*
BRISBANE *(AU)*
CHINDWIN *(AS)*
COLORADO *(AM)*
COLUMBIA *(AM)*
DELAWARE *(AM)*
DEMERARA *(AM)*
DNIESTER *(E)*8*
DORDOGNE *(E)*
FLINDERS *(AU)*
GASCOYNE *(AU)*
GATINEAU *(AM)*
GODAVARI *(AS)*
GOULBURN *(AU)*
GUADIANA *(E)*
HUMBOLDT *(AM)*
ILLINOIS *(AM)*
KLAIPEDA *(E)*
KLONDIKE *(AM)*
KOOTENAY *(AM)*
MAHANADI *(AS)*
MAZARUNI *(AM)*
MISSOURI *(AM)*
OB-IRTYSH *(AS)*
PARAGUAY *(AM)*
PISUERGA *(E)*
PUTUMAYO *(AM)*
RED RIVER *(AM)*
RIO NEGRO *(AM)*
SAGUENAY *(AM)*
SAVANNAH *(AM)*
SUWANNEE *(AM)*11*
SYR DAR'YA *(AS)*
THOMPSON *(AM)*
TUNGUSKA *(AS)*
WANGANUI *(AU)*

9

ATHABASCA *(AM)*
BLACK NILE *(AF)*7*
CHURCHILL *(AM)*
ESSEQUIBO *(AM)*
EUPHRATES *(AS)*
INDIGIRKA *(AS)*

IRRAWADDY *(AS)*
MACKENZIE *(AM)*
MACQUARIE *(AU)*
PARANAÍBA *(AM)*
PILCOMAYO *(AM)*
RIO BRANCO *(AM)*
RIO GRANDE *(AM)*
ROOSEVELT *(AM)*
SALT RIVER *(AM)*
ST MAURICE *(AM)*
TENNESSEE *(AM)*
TOCANTINS *(AM)*
WHITE NILE *(AF)*
WISCONSIN *(AM)*

10

BLACK RIVER *(AM)*
BLACK VOLTA *(AF)*
BLOOD RIVER *(AF)*
CHANG JIANG *(AS)*16*
CHAO PHRAYA *(AS)*
COURANTYNE *(AM)*
DIAMANTINA *(AU)*
DORA BALTEA *(E)*

ESMERELDAS *(AM)*
GREEN RIVER *(AM)*
HAWKESBURY *(AU)*
MANZANARES *(E)*
PARRAMATTA *(AU)*
PEACE RIVER *(AM)*
RANGITAIKI *(AU)*
SACRAMENTO *(AM)*
SAN JOAQUIN *(AM)*
SHENANDOAH *(AM)*
SNAKE RIVER *(AM)*
ST LAWRENCE *(AM)*
WHITE RIVER *(AM)*
WHITE VOLTA *(AF)*

11

BRAHMAPUTRA *(AS)*
DESAGUADERO *(AM)*
FRENCH RIVER *(AM)*
GUADALAVIAR *(E)*
MISSISSIPPI *(AM)*
SHATT-AL-ARAB *(AS)*
SUSQUEHANNA *(AM)*
YELLOW RIVER *(AS)*13*
YELLOWSTONE *(AM)*

12

BIG HORN RIVER *(AM)*
GUADALQUIVIR *(E)*
HEILONG JIANG *(AS)*1*
MURRUMBIDGEE *(AU)*
PARAÍBA DO SUL *(AM)*
RAPPAHANNOCK *(AM)*
RIO DE LA PLATA *(AM)*6*
SÃO FRANCISCO *(AM)*
SASKATCHEWAN *(AM)*

13

BIG BLACK RIVER *(AM)*
BIG SANDY RIVER *(AM)*
BIG SIOUX RIVER *(AM)*
CANADIAN RIVER *(AM)*
MURRAY-DARLING *(AU)*

14

CROCODILE RIVER *(AF)*14*

GEOGRAPHY

TOWNS & CITIES — AFRICA

(A) = Algeria   (AN) = Angola   (BE) = Benin   (BF) = Burkina Faso
(BO) = Botswana   (BU) = Burundi   (CA) = Cameroon
(CE) = Central African Republic   (CH) = Chad   (CO) = Congo
(D) = Djibouti   (E) = Egypt   (EQ) = Equatorial Guinea   (ET) = Ethiopia
(G) = Gambia   (GA) = Gabon   (GB) = Guinea Bissau   (GH) = Ghana
(GU) = Guinea   (I) = Ivory Coast   (K) = Kenya   (L) = Libya
(LE) = Lesotho   (LI) = Liberia   (M) = Mali   (MA) = Mauritania
(ME) = Moçambique   (MI) = Malawi   (MO) = Morocco
(MR) = Madagascar   (N) = Nigeria   (NA) = Namibia   (NI) = Niger
(R) = Rwanda   (SA) = South Africa   (SE) = Senegal   (SI) = Sierra Leone
(SO) = Somalia   (SU) = Sudan   (SW) = Swaziland   (TA) = Tanzania
(TO) = Togo   (TU) = Tunisia   (UG) = Uganda   (Z) = Zaïre   (ZA) = Zambia
(ZI) = Zimbabwe
* = Alternative name

3

FEZ *(MO)*
QUS *(E)*

4

GAZA *(E)*
GHAT *(L)*
KANO *(N)*
LOMÉ *(TO)*
ORAN *(AL)*
QENA *(E)*
SAFI *(MO)*
SFAX *(TU)*
SUEZ *(E)*

5

ACCRA *(GH)*
ASWAN *(E)*
BEIRA *(ME)*
BENHA *(E)*
CAIRO *(E)*
DAKAR *(SE)*
DE AAR *(SA)*
HARAR *(ET)*
KIFFA *(MA)*
KITWE *(ZA)*
LAGOS *(N)*
LINDI *(TA)*
LUXOR *(E)*
OTAVI *(NA)*
PAARL *(SA)*
RABAT *(MO)*
TUNIS *(TU)*
WAJIR *(K)*
ZOMBA *(MI)*

6

ANNABA *(AL)*
ASMARA *(ET)*
BAMAKO *(M)*
BANGUI *(CE)*
BANJUL *(G) *1*
BENONI *(SA)*
BISSAU *(GB)*
DODOMA *(TA)*
DOUALA *(CA)*
DUMYÂT *(E) *2*
DURBAN *(SA)*
EL GIZA *(E)*
FDÉRIK *(MA)*
HARARE *(ZI)*
IBADAN *(N)*
KIGALI *(R)*
KUMASI *(GH)*
LUANDA *(AN)*
LUSAKA *(ZA)*
MALABO *(EQ)*
MAPUTO *(ME)*
MARQUZ *(L)*
MASERU *(LE)*
MATRUH *(E)*
MEKNÈS *(MO)*
NIAMEY *(NI)*
SEROWE *(BO)*
SOUSSE *(TU)*
SOWETO *(SA)*
TAMALE *(GH)*
TOBRUK *(L) *3*
TUBRUQ *(L) *3*
UMTATA *(SA)*
WANKIE *(ZI)*
WELKOM *(SA)*

7

ABIDJAN *(I)*
ALGIERS *(AL)*
BERBERA *(SO)*
BIZERTE *(TU)*
BRAKPAN *(SA)*
CONAKRY *(GU)*
CRADOCK *(SA)*
EL AAIÚN *(MO)*
EL OBEID *(SU)*
ENTEBBE *(UG)*
GOBABIS *(NA)*
KAMPALA *(UG)*
KANANGA *(Z)*

KISMAYU *(SO)*
LARACHE *(MO)*
MBABANE *(SW)*
MBARARA *(UG)*
MELILLA *(MO)*
MOMBASA *(K)*
NAIROBI *(K)*
ODIENNÉ *(I)*
SPRINGS *(SA)*
ST LOUIS *(MA)*
TANGIER *(MO)*
TOLIARY *(MR)*
TRIPOLI *(L)*
YAOUNDÉ *(CA)*

8

AIN SEFRA *(AL)*
BATHURST *(G)* *1
BENGHAZI *(L)*
BENGUELA *(AN)*
BLANTYRE *(MI)*
BULAWAYO *(ZI)*
CAPE TOWN *(SA)*
DAMIETTA *(E)* *2
DJIBOUTI *(D)*
FREETOWN *(SI)*
GABORONE *(BO)*
HURGHADA *(E)*
KAIROUAN *(TU)*
KHARTOUM *(SU)*
KINSHASA *(Z)*
LILONGWE *(MI)*
LÜDERITZ *(NA)*
MAFEKING *(SA)*
MONASTIR *(TU)*
MONROVIA *(LI)*

N'DJAMENA *(CH)*
OMDURMAN *(SU)*
PORT SAID *(E)*
PRETORIA *(SA)*
TAKORADI *(GH)*
TIMBUKTU *(M)*
WINDHOEK *(NA)*
ZANZIBAR *(TA)*

9

BUJUMBURA *(BU)*
EL ALAMEIN *(E)*
GERMISTON *(SA)*
INHAMBANE *(MO)*
KIMBERLEY *(SA)*
LADYSMITH *(SA)*
MARRAKESH *(MO)*
MOGADISHU *(SO)*
PORTO NOVO *(BE)*
PORT SUDAN *(SU)*
SASSANDRA *(I)*
UITENHAGE *(SA)*
WADI HALFA *(SU)*
WAD MEDANI *(SU)*
WALVIS BAY *(NA)*
WORCESTER *(SA)*

10

ADDIS ABABA *(ET)*
ALEXANDRIA *(E)*
CASABLANCA *(MO)* *4
DAR EL BEIDA *(MO)* *4
EAST LONDON *(SA)*
KLERKSDORP *(SA)*

LIBRÉVILLE *(GA)*
LUBUMBASHI *(Z)*
MALMESBURY *(SA)*
MOÇAMBIQUE *(ME)*
MOSSÂMEDES *(AN)*
MOSSELBAAI *(SA)*
NOUAKCHOTT *(MA)*
OUDTSHOORN *(SA)*
QUEENSTOWN *(SA)*
WELLINGTON *(SA)*

11

BRAZZAVILLE *(CO)*
CONSTANTINE *(AL)*
DAR-ES-SALAAM *(TA)*
KRUGERSDORP *(SA)*
LIVINGSTONE *(ZA)*
OUAGADOUGOU *(BF)*
PIETERSBURG *(SA)*
PORT NOLLOTH *(SA)*
SIDI BARRANI *(E)*
VEREENIGING *(SA)*

12

ANTANANARIVO *(MR)*
BLOEMFONTEIN *(SA)*
GRAAFF REINET *(SA)*
JOHANNESBURG *(SA)*
PORT HARCOURT *(N)*
STELLENBOSCH *(SA)*

13

BOBO DIOULASSA *(BF)*
PORT ELIZABETH *(SA)*
POTCHEFSTROOM *(SA)*

GEOGRAPHY

TOWNS & CITIES – ASIA

*(A) = Afghanistan   (BA) = Bangladesh   (BH) = Bhutan   (C) = China
(E) = Estonia   (H) = Hong Kong   (IN) = India   (IQ) = Iraq   (IR) = Iran
(IS) = Israel   (JA) = Japan   (JO) = Jordan   (K) = Kampuchea
(KU) = Kuwait   (L) = Laos   (LA) = Latvia   (LE) = Lebanon   (LI) = Lithuania
(MA) = Malaysia   (MO) = Mongolia   (MY) = Myanmar (Burma)   (N) = Nepal
(NK) = North Korea   (PA) = Pakistan   (PH) = Philippines   (R) = Russia
(including west of the Urals)   (S) = Singapore   (SA) = Saudi Arabia
(SI) = Sikkim   (SK) = South Korea   (SL) = Sri Lanka   (SY) = Syria
(TH) = Thailand   (TU) = Turkey   (V) = Vietnam   (Y) = Yemen
* = Alternative name*

3

HUÈ *(V)*
KEM' *(R)*
QOM *(IR)*
UFA *(R)*

4

ACRE *(IS)* *1
ADEN *(Y)*
AGRA *(IN)*
'AKKO *(IS)* *1
BAKU *(R)*
DAET *(PH)*
GIFU *(JA)*
HAMA *(SY)*
KIEV *(R)*
LÜ-TA *(C)*
L'VOV *(R)*
OMSK *(R)*
OREL *(R)*
ORSK *(R)*
PERM *(R)*
RIGA *(LA)*
SAN'A *(Y)*
SIBU *(MA)*

TULA *(R)*
TYRE *(LE)*
VINH *(V)*

5

ADANA *(TU)*
AMMAN *(JO)*
AQABA *(JO)*
BASRA *(IQ)*
CHITA *(R)*
DACCA *(BA)*
DAVAO *(PH)*
DELHI *(IN)*
GOMEL' *(R)*
GORKY *(R)*
HAIFA *(IS)*
HANOI *(V)*
HSI-AN *(C)*
IZMIR *(TU)*
JEDDA *(SA)* *2
KABUL *(A)*
KANDY *(SL)*
KIROV *(R)*
KURSK *(R)*
KYOTO *(JA)*
LAOAG *(PH)*

LHASA *(C)*
MECCA *(SA)*
MINSK *(R)*
MOSUL *(IQ)*
OSAKA *(JA)*
PAKSE *(L)*
PATNA *(IN)*
PENZA *(R)*
POONA *(IN)*
PSKOV *(R)*
PUSAN *(SK)*
RASHT *(IR)*
SEOUL *(SK)*
SIDON *(LE)*
SIMLA *(IN)*
SURAT *(IN)*
TARTU *(E)*
TOKYO *(JA)*
TOMSK *(R)*
WU-HAN *(C)*
YALTA *(R)*

6

ABADAN *(IR)*
ALEPPO *(SY)*
ANKARA *(TU)*

BATUMI *(R)*
BEIRUT *(LE)*
BOMBAY *(IN)*
CANTON *(C)*
DA NANG *(V)*
EDIRNE *(TU)*
FRUNZE *(R)*
FU-CHOU *(C)*
HARBIN *(C)*
HOWRAH *(IN)*
INCHŎN *(SK)*
INDORE *(IN)*
JAFFNA *(SL)*
JAIPUR *(IN)*
JIDDAH *(SA)* *2
KAMPOT *(K)*
KANPUR *(IN)*
KAUNAS *(LI)*
LAHORE *(PA)*
MADRAS *(IN)*
MANILA *(PH)*
MATSUE *(JA)*
MEDINA *(SA)*
MEERUT *(IN)*
MERGUI *(MY)*
MOSCOW *(R)* *3
MOSKVA *(R)* *3
MYSORE *(IN)*

NAGOYA *(JA)*
NAGPUR *(IN)*
ODESSA *(R)*
PEKING *(C) *4*
PENANG *(MA)*
QUETTA *(PA)*
RAIPUR *(IN)*
RIYADH *(SA)*
SAIGON *(V) *5*
SENDAI *(JA)*
SUCHOW *(C)*
TABRIZ *(IR)*
TAIPEI *(C)*
TEHRAN *(IR) *6*
YUMEN' *(R)*
VYBORG *(R)*

7

ALMA ATA *(R)*
BAGHDAD *(IQ)*
BANGKOK *(TH)*
BARNAUL *(R)*
BEIJING *(C) *4*
COLOMBO *(SL)*
DAGUPAN *(PH)*
DIPOLOG *(PH)*
DONETSK *(R)*
ISFAHAN *(IR)*
FUKUOKA *(JA)*
GANGTOK *(SI)*
GROZNYY *(R)*
HSÜ-CHOU *(C)*
IRKUTSK *(R)*
IVANOVO *(R)*
IZHEVSK *(R)*
JODHPUR *(IN)*
KALININ *(R)*
KARACHI *(PA)*
KAYSERI *(TU)*
KHARKOV *(R)*
KHERSON *(R)*
KIROVSK *(R)*
KUCHING *(MA)*
KUNMING *(C)*

LAN-CHOU *(C)*
LATAKIA *(SY)*
LUCKNOW *(IN)*
MADURAI *(IN)*
MAGADAN *(R)*
NANKING *(C)*
NIIGATA *(JA)*
OKHOTSK *(R)*
POLTAVA *(R)*
RANGOON *(MY)*
SAPPORO *(JA)*
SARATOV *(R)*
TALLINN *(E)*
TBILISI *(R)*
TEHERAN *(IR) *6*
TEL AVIV *(IS)*
THIMPHU *(BH)*
TRIPOLI *(LE)*
ULAN-UDE *(R)*
URUMCHI *(C)*
ÜSKÜDAR *(TU)*
VILNIUS *(LI)*
VITEBSK *(R)*
VOLOGDA *(R)*
YEREVAN *(R)*
ZHDANOV *(R)*

8

AMRITSAR *(IN)*
CALCUTTA *(IN)*
DAMASCUS *(SY)*
DUSHANBE *(R)*
HAIPHONG *(V)*
HAKODATE *(JA)*
HANG-CHOU *(C)*
ISTANBUL *(TU)*
JABALPUR *(IN)*
KATMANDU *(N) *7*
KISHINEV *(R)*
KUMAMOTO *(JA)*
MANDALAY *(MY)*
MOULMEIN *(MY)*
MURMANSK *(R)*
NAGASAKI *(JA)*

NAZARETH *(IS)*
NOVGOROD *(R)*
PECHENGA *(R)*
PESHAWAR *(IN)*
SHANGHAI *(C)*
SHEN-YANG *(C)*
SHILLONG *(IN)*
SMOLENSK *(R)*
SRINAGAR *(IN)*
TASHKENT *(R)*
TIENTSIN *(C)*
VARANASI *(IN)*
VICTORIA *(H)*
VORONEZH *(R)*
YOKOHAMA *(JA)*

9

AHMADABAD *(IN)*
ALLAHABAD *(IN)*
ARCHANGEL *(R) *8*
ASHKHABAD *(R)*
ASTRAKHAN *(R)*
BANGALORE *(IN)*
BEERSHEBA *(IS)*
BETHLEHEM *(IS)*
CHENG-CHOU *(C)*
CHERNOBYL *(R)*
CHIANG MAI *(TH)*
CHUNGKING *(C)*
GALLIPOLI *(TU)*
HIROSHIMA *(JA)*
HYDERABAD *(IN)*
HYDERABAD *(PA)*
ISLAMABAD *(PA)*
JERUSALEM *(IS)*
KAGOSHIMA *(JA)*
KARAGANDA *(R)*
KATHMANDU *(N) *7*
KRASNODAR *(R)*
KUYBYSHEV *(R)*
LENINGRAD *(R)*
MANGALORE *(IN)*
MUANG UBON *(TH)*
PHNOM PENH *(K)*

GEOGRAPHY – TOWNS & CITIES – ASIA

PYONGYANG *(NK)*
SAMARKAND *(R)*
SINGAPORE *(S)*
ULAN BATOR *(MO)*
VIENTIANE *(L)*
VOLGOGRAD *(R)*
YAROSLAVL' *(R)*

10

CHERNOVTSY *(R)*
CHITTAGONG *(BA)*
DARJEELING *(IN)*
DAUGAVPILS *(LA)*
GEORGE TOWN *(MA)*
KHABAROVSK *(R)*
KUWAIT CITY *(KU)*
QUEZON CITY *(PH)*

SEVASTOPOL *(R)*
SVERDLOVSK *(R)*

11

ARKHANGEL'SK *(R)* *8
CHELYABINSK *(R)*
KALININGRAD *(LI)*
KRASNOYARSK *(R)*
KUALA LUMPUR *(MA)*
NOVOSIBIRSK *(R)*
TRINCOMALEE *(SL)*
VLADIVOSTOK *(R)*

12

BORISOGLEBSK *(R)*
KOTA KINABALU *(MA)*

LUANG PRABANG *(L)*
MAGNITOGORSK *(R)*
NIZHNIY TAGIL *(R)*
NOVOKUZNETSK *(R)*
PETROZAVODSK *(R)*
ROSTOV-NA-DONU *(R)*
XIENG KHOUANG *(L)*

13

HO CHI-MINH CITY *(V)* *5
PETROPAVLOVSK *(R)*

14

DNEPROPETROVSK *(R)*
VOROSHILOVGRAD *(R)*

GEOGRAPHY

TOWNS & CITIES – AUSTRALASIA & INDONESIA

(A) = Australia   (I) = Indonesia   (N) = New Zealand
(P) = Papua New Guinea

3

AYR *(A)*
HAY *(A)*

4

DILI *(I)*
EYRE *(A)*

GORE *(N)*
POSO *(I)*
RABA *(I)*
SALE *(A)*
YORK *(A)*

5

BURRA *(A)*

COLAC *(A)*
DERBY *(A)*
DUBBO *(A)*
JUNEE *(A)*
MEDAN *(I)*
MOORA *(A)*
PERTH *(A)*
QUORN *(A)*
TULLY *(A)*
WEWAK *(P)*

6

ALBANY *(A)*
ALBURY *(A)*
BANGKA *(I)*
BOURKE *(A)*
BROOME *(A)*
CAIRNS *(A)*
CEDUNA *(A)*
COLLIE *(A)*

DARWIN *(A)*
GAWLER *(A)*
HOBART *(A)*
MACKAY *(A)*
MADANG *(P)*
MENADO *(I)*
NAPIER *(N)*
NELSON *(N)*
OAMARU *(N)*
ONSLOW *(A)*

RANGE *(A)*
ADANG *(I)*
ETONE *(N)*
ORONG *(I)*
YDNEY *(A)*
MARU *(N)*
INTON *(A)*

7

ANDUNG *(I)*
ENDIGO *(A)*
UNBURY *(A)*
ENMARK *(A)*
UNEDIN *(N)*
EELONG *(A)*
SWICH *(A)*
SMORE *(A)*
THGOW *(A)*
AKASAR *(I)*
ANUKAU *(N)*
ILDURA *(A)*
ORTHAM *(A)*
ORIRUA *(N)*
OTORUA *(N)*
E KUITI *(N)*
HYALLA *(A)*
OOMERA *(A)*

8

DELAIDE *(A)*
UCKLAND *(N)*
ALLARAT *(A)*
ATHURST *(A)*
LENHEIM *(N)*
RISBANE *(A)*
ANBERRA *(A)*
ESSNOCK *(A)*
JAKARTA *(I)*
ISBORNE *(N)*
OULBURN *(A)*
AMILTON *(N)*
ASTINGS *(N)*
VERELL *(A)*
AITLAND *(A)*

MERREDIN *(A)*
MOUNT ISA *(A)*
ONEHUNGA *(N)*
RANGIORA *(N)*
SEMARANG *(I)*
SOMERSET *(A)*
SURABAYA *(I)*
TAKAPUNA *(N)*
TAMWORTH *(A)*
TAURANGA *(N)*
WANGANUI *(N)*
WESTPORT *(N)*

9

ALEXANDRA *(N)*
BUNDABERG *(A)*
CARNARVON *(A)*
DEVONPORT *(A)*
DEVONPORT *(N)*
DJAJAPURA *(I)*
ELIZABETH *(A)*
ESPERANCE *(A)*
FREMANTLE *(A)*
GERALDTON *(A)*
GLADSTONE *(A)*
GREYMOUTH *(N)*
HUGHENDEN *(A)*
LIVERPOOL *(A)*
LONGREACH *(A)*
LOWER HUTT *(N)*
MASTERTON *(N)*
MELBOURNE *(A)*
NEWCASTLE *(A)*
PALEMBANG *(I)*
PORT PIRIE *(A)*
TOOWOOMBA *(A)*
WATAMPONE *(I)*
WENTWORTH *(A)*
WHAKATANE *(N)*
WHANGAREI *(N)*
WITTENOOM *(A)*

10

BALIKPAPAN *(I)*

BIRDSVILLE *(A)*
BROKEN HILL *(A)*
GOOMALLING *(A)*
JOGJAKARTA *(I)*
KALGOORLIE *(A)*
LAUNCESTON *(A)*
LEIGH CREEK *(A)*
NEW NORFOLK *(A)*
PALMERSTON *(N)*
SHEPPARTON *(A)*
TOWNSVILLE *(A)*
WAGGA WAGGA *(A)*
WOLLONGONG *(A)*

11

BARROW CREEK *(A)*
CASTLEMAINE *(A)*
MARYBOROUGH *(A)*
NEW PLYMOUTH *(N)*
PORT AUGUSTA *(A)*
PORT LINCOLN *(A)*
PORT MORESBY *(P)*
ROCKHAMPTON *(A)*
WARRNAMBOOL *(A)*

12

ALICE SPRINGS *(A)*
BANDJARMASIN *(I)*
CHRISTCHURCH *(N)*
COFF'S HARBOUR *(A)*
INVERCARGILL *(N)*
MOUNT GAMBIER *(A)*
PETERBOROUGH *(A)*

13

VICTOR HARBOUR *(A)*

15

PALMERSTON NORTH *(N)*

GEOGRAPHY

TOWNS & CITIES – BALKAN PENINSULA

(A) = Albania   (B) = Bulgaria   (G) = Greece   (Y) = Yugoslavia
* = Alternative name

3

KRK (Y)
NIŠ (Y)

4

BROD (Y)
FILI (G)
PULA (Y)
RUSE (B) *1
ZARA (Y) *2

5

AGRAM (Y) *3
ARGOS (G)
BERAT (A)
CANEA (G) *4
DRÁMA (G)
KHÍOS (G)
KOPER (Y)
KORSË (A)
KUKËS (A)
LAMIA (G)
PIROT (Y)
SOFIA (B) *5
SPLIT (Y)
SUŠAK (Y)
VARNA (B)
VIDIN (B)
VLORË (A)
VÓLOS (G)
ZADAR (Y) *2

6

ÁNDROS (G)

ATHENS (G) *6
BITOLA (Y)
BURGAS (B)
CANDIA (G) *7
DELPHI (G)
DURRËS (A)
KHANIÁ (G) *4
KOZÁNI (G)
LÁRISA (G)
LINDOS (G)
MOSTAR (Y)
OSIJEK (Y)
PÁTRAI (G) *8
PATRAS (G) *8
PLEVEN (B)
RAGUSA (Y) *9
RHODES (G) *10
RIJEKA (Y)
SÉRRAI (G)
SHUMEN (B)
SKOPJE (Y)
SLIVEN (B)
SOFIYA (B) *5
SPARTA (G) *11
SPÁRTI (G) *11
TIRANA (A) *12
TIRANË (A) *12
VRATSA (B)
XÁNTHI (G)
ZAGREB (Y) *3

7

ATHÍNAI (G) *6
BEOGRAD (Y) *13
CETINJE (Y)
CHALCIS (G) *14

CORINTH (G) *15
GLYFADA (G)
KALÁMAI (G)
KAVÁLLA (G)
KÉRKIRA (G) *16
KHALKÍS (G) *14
NAUPLIA (G) *17
NOVI SAD (Y)
PIRAEUS (G)
PLOVDIV (B) *18
RUSCHUK (B) *1
SALAMÍS (G)
SCUTARI (A) *19
SHKODËR (A) *19
SIBENIK (Y)
SOÚNION (G)
YANNINA (G) *20

8

AGRÍNION (G)
BELGRADE (Y) *13
IOÁNNINA (G) *20
IRÁKLION (G) *7
KARLOVAK (Y)
KASTORÍA (G)
KHASKOVO (B)
KOMOTINÍ (G)
MITILÍNI (G)
NÁUPLION (G) *17
SALONICA (G) *21
SARAJEVO (Y)
SUBOTICA (Y)
TITOGRAD (Y)
TRÍKKALA (G)
TRÍPOLIS (G)

9

BANJA LUKA (Y)
CORFU TOWN (G) *16
DUBROVNIK (Y) *9
KÓRINTHOS (G) *15
LJUBLJANA (Y)
ZÁKINTHOS (G) *22
ZANTE TOWN (G) *22

10

KRAGUJEVAC (Y)
KYUSTENDIL (B)
RHODES TOWN (G) *10

11

GJIROKASTËR (A)
RIJEKA-SUSAK (Y)
STARA ZAGORA (B)

12

THESSALONÍKI (G) *21

13

PHILIPPOPOLIS (B) *18

15

ALEXANDROÚPOLIS (G

GEOGRAPHY

TOWNS & CITIES – BELGIUM & NETHERLANDS

(B) = Belgium   (L) = Luxembourg   (N) = Netherlands
* = Alternative name

3

ATH *(B)*
EDE *(N)*
HAL *(B) *1*
HUY *(B)*
MOL *(B)*
SPA *(B)*

4

BOOM *(B)*
ESCH *(L)*
GAND *(B) *2*
GENK *(B)*
GENT *(B) *2*
LIER *(B) *3*
LUIK *(B) *4*
MONS *(B)*

5

AALST *(B) *5*
ALOST *(B) *5*
ARLON *(B)*
ASSEN *(N)*
BREDA *(N)*
DELFT *(N)*
EEKLO *(B)*
EMMEN *(N)*
EUPEN *(B)*
GHENT *(B) *2*
GILLY *(B)*
GOUDA *(N)*
HALLE *(B) *1*
HEIST *(B)*

HOORN *(N)*
IEPER *(B) *6*
JUMET *(B)*
LIÈGE *(B) *4*
MENEN *(B) *7*
MENIN *(B) *7*
NAMUR *(B)*
RONSE *(B) *8*
TIELT *(B) *9*
VENLO *(N)*
WAVRE *(B)*
YPRES *(B) *6*
ZEIST *(N)*

6

ALMELO *(N)*
ANVERS *(B) *10*
ARNHEM *(N)*
BRUGGE *(B) *11*
BRUGES *(B) *11*
BUSSUM *(N)*
DINANT *(B)*
FURNES *(B) *12*
KAMPEN *(N)*
LEIDEN *(N)*
LEUVEN *(B) *13*
LIERRE *(B) *3*
OSTEND *(B) *14*
RENAIX *(B) *8*
THIELT *(B) *9*
TIENEN *(B) *15*
VELSEN *(N)*
VEURNE *(B) *12*
ZWOLLE *(N)*

7

ALKMAAR *(N)*
ANTWERP *(B) *10*
BRUSSEL *(B) *16*
DEN HAAG *(N) *17*
DE PANNE *(B)*
DIXMUDE *(B) *18*
HAARLEM *(N)*
HASSELT *(B)*
HEERLEN *(N)*
HELMOND *(N)*
HENGELO *(N)*
HOBOKEN *(B)*
LOKEREN *(B)*
LOUVAIN *(B) *13*
MAASEIK *(B)*
MALINES *(B) *19*
MALMÉDY *(B)*
MECHLIN *(B) *19*
MERKSEM *(B)*
OSTENDE *(B) *14*
ROULERS *(B) *20*
SERAING *(B)*
ST TROND *(B) *21*
THOROUT *(B) *22*
TILBURG *(N)*
TONGRES *(B) *23*
TORHOUT *(B) *22*
TOURNAI *(B)*
UTRECHT *(N)*
ZAANDAM *(N)*

8

AARSCHOT *(B)*
BASTOGNE *(B)*

BRUSSELS *(B) *16*
COURTRAI *(B) *24*
DELFZIJL *(N)*
DEVENTER *(N)*
DIEKIRCH *(L)*
ENSCHEDE *(N)*
FLUSHING *(N) *25*
GRAMMONT *(B) *26*
IJMUIDEN *(N)*
KERKRADE *(N)*
KORTRIJK *(B) *24*
LONNEKER *(N)*
MECHELEN *(B) *19*
NIJMEGEN *(N)*
NIVELLES *(B)*
OOSTENDE *(B) *14*
ROERMOND *(N)*
SCHIEDAM *(N)*
TERMONDE *(B) *27*
THE HAGUE *(N) *17*
TONGEREN *(B) *23*
TURNHOUT *(B)*
VERVIERS *(B)*
VOLENDAM *(N)*

9

AMSTERDAM *(N)*
ANTWERPEN *(B) *10*
APELDOORN *(N)*
BOIS-LE-DUC *(N) *28*
BRUXELLES *(B) *16*
CHARLEROI *(B)*
DEN HELDER *(N)*
DIKSMUIDE *(B) *18*
DORDRECHT *(N)*
EINDHOVEN *(N)*

EUROPOORT *(N)*
GORINCHEM *(N)*
GRONINGEN *(N)*
HERENTALS *(B)*
HILVERSUM *(N)*
OLDENZAAL *(N)*
ROESELARE *(B)* *20
ROTTERDAM *(N)*
ST NICOLAS *(B)* *29
ST NIKLAAS *(B)* *29
ST TRUIDEN *(B)* *21
TERNEUZEN *(N)*
TIRLEMONT *(B)* *15
ZEEBRUGGE *(B)*

10

AMERSFOORT *(N)*
HARDERWIJK *(N)*
LE LOUVIÈRE *(B)*
LEEUWARDEN *(N)*
LUXEMBOURG *(L)*
MAASTRICHT *(N)*
NIEUWPOORT *(B)*
OUDENAARDE *(B)*
ROOSENDAAL *(N)*
VLISSINGEN *(N)* *25
WINSCHOTEN *(N)*

11

DENDERMONDE *(B)* *27
DIFFERDANGE *(L)*
NEUFCHATEAU *(B)*
'S-GRAVENHAGE *(N)* *17
VLAARDINGNE *(N)*

12

BERGEN OP ZOOM *(N)*
BLANKENBERGE *(B)*
INGELMUNSTER *(B)*

13

HOOK OF HOLLAND *(N)* *30
KATWIJK ANN ZEE *(B)*
PHILIPPEVILLE *(B)*

14

GERAARDSBERGEN *(B)* *26
HOEK VAN HOLLAND *(N)* *30
'S-HERTOGENBOSCH *(N)* *28

15

MARCHE-EN-FAMENNE *(B)*

GEOGRAPHY

TOWNS & CITIES – CANADA

4

AJAX
HOPE
HULL
NAIN
WAWA

5

GASPÉ
LEDUC
ROUYN
TABER
TRAIL

6

ARVIDA
BIGGAR
DAWSON
GANDER
INUVIK
JASPER
KENORA
LONDON
NAKINA
NELSON
OSHAWA
OTTAWA
QUEBEC
REGINA
SOURIS
SYDNEY
THE PAS

7

BRANDON

CALGARY
CAMROSE
CHATHAM
ESTEVAN
HALIFAX
KELOWNA
KITIMAT
LA RONGE
MELFORT
MONCTON
NANAIMO
QUESNEL
RED DEER
ST JOHN'S
SUDBURY
TIMMINS
TISDALE
TORONTO
WEYBURN
WINDSOR
WYNYARD
YORKTON

8

BATHURST
COCHRANE
CORNWALL
EDMONTON
FLIN FLON
GLACE BAY
GOOSE BAY
HAMILTON
HAY RIVER
HAZELTON
KAMLOOPS
KINGSTON
McMURRAY
MELVILLE
MONTRÉAL

MOOSE JAW
MOOSONEE
NORTH BAY
RIMOUSKI
ROSETOWN
SEPT-ÎLES
THOMPSON
VICTORIA
WINNIPEG

9

BRANTFORD
CHURCHILL
FORT CHIMO
KITCHENER
OWEN SOUND
PENTICTON
SAINT JOAN
SASKATOON
VANCOUVER

10

CHICOUTIMI
DRUMHELLER
EDMUNDSTON
FORT GEORGE
FORT NELSON
FORT ST JOHN
GRAND FALLS
LETHBRIDGE
MAPLE CREEK
NEW GLASGOW
PEACE RIVER
PORT ALFRED
PORT RADIUM
SHAWINIGAN
SHERBROOKE

ST BONIFACE
THUNDER BAY
WETASKIWIN
WHITEHORSE

11

CAMPBELLTON
CORNER BROOK
DAWSON CREEK
FORT MACLEOD
FREDERICTON
KAPUSKASING
LAKE HARBOUR
MEDICINE HAT
NORMAN WELLS
NORTH SYDNEY
ST HYACINTHE
TUKTOYAKTUK
URANIUM CITY
VALLEYFIELD
YELLOWKNIFE

12

KIRKLAND LAKE
LLOYDMINSTER
NIAGARA FALLS
PETERBOROUGH
PRINCE ALBERT
PRINCE GEORGE
PRINCE RUPERT
SIOUX LOOKOUT
ST CATHERINE'S
SWIFT CURRENT

13

BATTLE HARBOUR
CHARLOTTETOWN

FORT McPHERSON
FORT VERMILION
GRANDE PRAIRIE
SCHEFFERVILLE
TROIS RIVIÈRES

14
FORT PROVIDENCE
NEW WESTMINSTER
PORT AUX BASQUES

15
NORTH BATTLEFORD

GEOGRAPHY

TOWNS & CITIES – CENTRAL AMERICA & WEST INDIES

(B) = Belize   (C) = Costa Rica   (E) = El Salvador   (G) = Guatemala
(H) = Honduras   (M) = Mexico   (N) = Nicaragua   (P) = Panama
(W) = West Indies
* = Alternative name

4

APAM *(M)*
BANT *(W)*
LEÓN *(M)*
LEÓN *(N)*
OPAL *(M)*
RUIZ *(M)*
TULA *(M)*

5

AHOME *(M)*
AMECA *(M)*
ARIMA *(W)*
BANES *(W)*
CAYEY *(W)*
COLÓN *(P)*
COLÓN *(W)*
DAVID *(P)*

EL ORO *(M)*
LA PAZ *(M)*
LIMÓN *(C)*
MORÓN *(W)*
PONCE *(W)*
RIVAS *(N)*
SILAO *(M)*
TEPIC *(M)*
TICUL *(M)*

6

ALAMOS *(M)*
ARIZPE *(M)*
BALBOA *(P)*
BELIZE *(B)*
CELAYA *(M)*
CHITRÉ *(P)*
COLIMA *(M)*
CUMPAS *(M)*

GÜINES *(W)*
HABANA *(W) *1*
HAVANA *(W) *1*
IGUALA *(M)*
JACMEL *(W)*
JALAPA *(M)*
LA CRUZ *(M)*
LA VEGA *(W)*
MADERA *(M)*
MAPIMÍ *(M)*
MASAYA *(N)*
MEOQUI *(M)*
MÉRIDA *(M)*
MEXICO *(M)*
NASSAU *(W)*
NICOYA *(C)*
PANAMA *(P)*
PÁNUCO *(M)*
PUEBLA *(M)*
SOLOLÁ *(G)*
ST MARC *(W)*

TOLUCA *(M)*
TONALÁ *(M)*
TUXPAN *(M)*
ZAMORA *(M)*

7

ALLENDE *(M)*
ANTIGUA *(G)*
APIZACO *(M)*
ARECIBO *(W)*
ATLIXCO *(M)*
BARACOA *(W)*
CABORCA *(M)*
CANANEA *(M)*
CARTAGO *(C)*
CHOLULA *(M)*
CORDOBA *(M)*
DURANGO *(M)*
EL MAYOR *(M)*

EL SALTO *(M)*
EL VIEJO *(N)*
EMPALME *(M)*
GRANADA *(N)*
GUAYMAS *(M)*
HEREDÍA *(C)*
HOLGUÍN *(W)*
HUIXTLA *(M)*
JÉRÉMIE *(W)*
JIMÉNEZ *(M)*
LA BARCA *(M)*
LA CEIBA *(H)*
LA UNIÓN *(E)*
LINARES *(M)*
MANAGUA *(N)*
MORELIA *(M)*
NAVAJOA *(M)*
NOGALES *(M)*
OCOTLÁN *(M)*
OJINAGA *(M)*
ORIZABA *(M)*
PACHUCA *(M)*
REYNOSA *(M)*
ROSARIO *(M)*
SABINAS *(M)*
SAHUAYO *(M)*
SAN JOSÉ *(C)*
SAN JUAN *(W)*
SAN LUIS *(M)*
SONOITA *(M)*
ST JOHN'S *(W)*
TAMPICO *(M)*
TEQUILA *(M)*
TIJUANA *(M)*
TIZIMÍN *(M)*
TORREÓN *(M)*
ZIMAPÁN *(M)*

8

ACAJUTLA *(E)*
ACAMBARO *(M)*
ACAPULCO *(M)*
ALAJUELA *(C)*
ALVARADO *(M)*

BARAHONA *(W)*
BELMOPAN *(B)*
CAMAGÜEY *(W)*
CAMPECHE *(M)*
CANATLÁN *(M)*
CARDENAS *(M)*
CASTAÑOS *(M)*
CASTRIES *(W)*
CERRITOS *(M)*
CHETUMAL *(M)*
COATEPEC *(M)*
COMALAPA *(G)*
CULIACÁN *(M)*
EL FUERTE *(M)*
ENSENADA *(M)*
ETZATLAN *(M)*
FREEPORT *(W)*
GONAÏVES *(W)*
IRAPUATO *(M)*
JINOTEGA *(N)*
JUCHITÁN *(M)*
KINGSTON *(W)*
LA ROMANO *(W)*
LES CAYES *(W)*
MATANZAS *(W)*
MAZATLÁN *(M)*
MEXICALI *(M)*
MONCLOVA *(M)*
MOROLEÓN *(M)*
NACOZARI *(M)*
NAVOLATO *(M)*
NUEVITAS *(W)*
PENONOME *(P)*
PLYMOUTH *(W)*
POZA RICA *(M)*
PROGRESO *(M)*
RÍO ABAJO *(P)*
ROSARITO *(M)*
SALTILLO *(M)*
SANTA ANA *(E)*
SANTA ANA *(M)*
SANTIAGO *(P)*
SANTIAGO *(W)*
SAUCILLO *(M)*
TEHUACÁN *(M)*
USULUTÁN *(E)*

VERACRUZ *(M)*
ZOPILOTE *(M)*

9

ACAPONETA *(M)*
CHIHUAHUA *(M)*
CRISTÓBAL *(P)*
ESCUINAPA *(M)*
ESPERANZA *(M)*
GUADALUPE *(M)*
GUATEMALA *(G)*
LOS MOCHIS *(M)*
MACUSPANA *(M)*
MATAGALPA *(N)*
MATAMOROS *(M)*
MATEHUALA *(M)*
MONTERREY *(M)*
QUERÉTARO *(M)*
RÍO GRANDE *(M)*
SAHUARIPA *(M)*
SALAMANCA *(M)*
SAN MIGUEL *(E)*
SONSONATE *(E)*
ST GEORGE'S *(W)*
TAPACHULA *(M)*
TEZIUTLÁN *(M)*
TURRIALBA *(C)*
VILA UNIÓN *(M)*
ZACATECAS *(M)*
ZITÁCUARO *(M)*

10

AGUA PRIETA *(M)*
AHUACHAPÁN *(E)*
BASSETERRE *(W)*
BLUEFIELDS *(N)*
BRIDGETOWN *(W)*
BUSTAMANTE *(M)*
CAP-HAÏTIEN *(W)*
CHINANDEGA *(N)*
CIENFUEGOS *(W)*

CONCEPCIÓN *(M)*
CUAUHTÉMOC *(M)*
CUERNAVACA *(M)*
ECHEVERRÍA *(M)*
EL DESCANSO *(M)*
EL PORVENIR *(M)*
EL PROGRESO *(G)*
GUANTÁNAMO *(W)*
HERMOSILLO *(M)*
MANZANILLO *(M)*
MEXICO CITY *(M)*
MIGUEL AUZA *(M)*
MINATITLÁN *(M)*
MONTEGO BAY *(W)*
ORANJESTAD *(W)*
PORT-DE-PAIX *(W)*
PUERTO KINO *(M)*
PUNTARENAS *(C)*
RIO PIEDRAS *(W)*
SANTA CLARA *(W)*
SOMBRERETE *(M)*
TULANCINGO *(M)*
WILLEMSTAD *(W)*
XOCHIMILCO *(M)*

11

CIUDAD ACUÑA *(M)*
CIUDAD LERDO *(M)*
CIUDAD MANTE *(M)*
GUADALAJARA *(M)*
MAZATENANGO *(G)*
NUEVA ROSITA *(M)*
NUEVO LAREDO *(M)*
OJOCALIENTE *(M)*
PORT OF SPAIN *(W)*
PRINZAPOLCA *(N)*
PUERTO PLATA *(W)*
SALVATIERRA *(M)*
SAN FERNANDO *(W)*
SAN SALVADOR *(E)*
SPANISH TOWN *(W)*
TEGUCIGALPA *(H)*
TEHUANTEPEC *(M)*

GEOGRAPHY — TOWNS & CITIES – CENTRAL AMERICA & WEST INDIES

12

BUENAVENTURA *(M)*
CIUDAD GUZMÁN *(M)*
CIUDAD JUÁREZ *(M)*
CIUDAD MADERO *(M)*
FORT-DE-FRANCE *(W)*
GÓMEZ PALACIO *(M)*
HUAUCHINANGO *(M)*
IXTLAN DEL RIO *(M)*
MONTEMORELOS *(M)*
POINTE-À-PITRE *(W)*
PORT-AU-PRINCE *(W)*
PUERTO CORTÉS *(H)*
SAN FRANCISCO *(W)*
SAN PEDRO SULA *(H)*
SANTA BÁRBARA *(M)*
SANTA ROSALÍA *(M)*

SANTO DOMINGO *(W)*
TAMAZUNCHALE *(M)*
TIERRA BLANCA *(M)*
VILLAHERMOSA *(M)*
ZACATECOLUCA *(E)*

13

CIUDAD CAMARGO *(M)*
CIUDAD IXTEPEC *(M)*
CIUDAD OBREGÓN *(M)*
COATZACOALCOS *(M)*
GUATEMALA CITY *(G)*
PIEDRAS NEGRAS *(M)*
PUERTO BARRIOS *(G)*
PUERTO PENASCO *(M)*
QUEZALTENANGO *(G)*
SAN LUIS POTOSÍ *(M)*

14

AGUASCALIENTES *(M)*
CIUDAD DELICIAS *(M)*
CIUDAD DE VALLES *(M)*
CIUDAD VICTORIA *(M)*
OAXACA DE JUÁREZ *(M)*
SABINAS HIDALGO *(M)*
SANTIAGO DE CUBA *(W)*

15

AUTLÁN DE NAVARRO *(M)*
CIUDAD DEL CARMEN *(M)*
HIDALGO DE PARRAL *(M)*
PUERTO ARMUELLES *(P)*
TUXTLA GUTIÉRREZ *(M)*

GEOGRAPHY

TOWNS & CITIES – EASTERN EUROPE

(C) = Czechoslovakia *(H) = Hungary* *(P) = Poland* *(R) = Romania*
* = Alternative name

4

ARAD *(R)*
BRNO *(C) *1*
CLUJ *(R)*
GYÖR *(H)*
IASI *(R) *2*
LÓDŹ *(P)*
PÉCS *(H)*

5

BRÜNN *(C) *1*
JASSY *(R) *2*
OPAVA *(C)*
PLZEŇ *(C) *3*
POSEN *(P) *4*
PRAHA *(C) *5*
RADOM *(P)*
SIBIU *(R)*
TORUŃ *(P)*

6

BRĂILA *(R)*
CRACOW *(P) *6*
DANZIG *(P) *7*
ELBING *(P) *8*
ELBLAG *(P) *8*
GALATI *(R) *9*
GALATZ *(R) *9*
GDAŃSK *(P) *7*
KIELCE *(P)*

KOŠICE *(C)*
KRAKÓW *(P) *6*
LUBLIN *(P)*
ORADEA *(R)*
PILSEN *(C) *3*
POZNAŃ *(P) *4*
PRAGUE *(C) *5*
SOPRON *(H)*
SZEGED *(H)*
TARNOW *(P)*
TULCEA *(R)*

UJPEST *(H)*
WARSAW *(P) *10*

7

BRESLAU *(P) *11*
CRAIOVA *(R)*
GIURGIU *(R)*
JIHLAVA *(C)*
LEGNICA *(P) *12*
LIBEREC *(C)*
MISKOLC *(H)*
OLOMOUC *(C)*
OSTRAVA *(C)*
STETTIN *(P) *13*
WROCLAW *(P) *11*

8

BROMBERG *(P) *14*

BUDAPEST *(H)*
DEBRECEN *(H)*
KATOWICE *(P)*
LIEGNITZ *(P) *12*
PIOTRKÓW *(P)*
PLOIEŞTI *(R)*
PRZEMYŚL *(P)*
SATU MARE *(R)*
SZCZECIN *(P) *13*
WARSZAWA *(P) *10*

9

BIALYSTOK *(P)*
BUCHAREST *(R) *15*
BUCURESTI *(R) *15*
BYDGOSZCZ *(P) *14*
CONSTANŢA *(R)*
GRUDZIADZ *(P)*
KECSKEMET *(H)*
PARDUBICE *(C)*

PROSTĚJOV *(C)*
SOSNOWIEC *(P)*
TIMIŞOARA *(R)*
WLOCLAWEK *(P)*

10

BÉKESCSABA *(H)*
BRATISLAVA *(C)*
TIRGU MURES *(R)*

11

NAGYKANIZSA *(H)*
NYÍREGYHÁZA *(H)*

15

CESKÉ BUDĚJOVICE *(C)*

GEOGRAPHY

TOWNS & CITIES – ENGLAND

(M) = Isle of Man

3	**4**	ETON	LOOE	WARK	AMBLE	COWES	ESHER
		HALE	LYDD	YARM	BACUP	CREWE	EWELL
ELY	BATH	HOLT	MERE	YORK	BLYTH	CROOK	FILEY
EYE	BRAY	HOVE	PEEL *(M)*		BRIGG	DERBY	FOWEY
RYE	BUDE	HULL	ROSS		CALNE	DOVER	FROME
WEM	BURY	HYDE	RYDE	**5**	CHARD	EGHAM	GOOLE
	CLUN	INCE	SALE		CHEAM	EGTON	HAYLE
	DEAL	IVER	SHAP	ACTON	COLNE	EPSOM	HEDON
	DISS	LEEK	WARE	ALTON	CORBY	ERITH	HYTHE

GEOGRAPHY – TOWNS & CITIES – ENGLAND

LEEDS
LEIGH
LEWES
LOUTH
LUTON
MARCH
OLNEY
OTLEY
POOLE
RIPON
RUGBY
SANDY
SELBY
SOHAM
STOKE
STONE
TEBAY
THAME
TRING
TRURO
WELLS
WIGAN

CANVEY
CARHAM
COBHAM
CROMER
CROSBY
CROWLE
DARWEN
DAWLEY
DIDCOT
DUDLEY
DURHAM
EALING
ECCLES
ELSDON
EPPING
EXETER
FELTON
FORMBY
GORING
HANLEY
HARLOW
HARROW
HAVANT
HEANOR
HENLEY
HEXHAM
HORLEY
HOWDEN
ILFORD
ILKLEY
JARROW
KENDAL
KIRKBY
KNOWLE
LEYTON
LONDON
LOWICK
LUDLOW
LYNTON
LYTHAM
MALDON
MALTON
MARLOW
MASHAM
MERTON
MILLOM

MORLEY
NASEBY
NELSON
NESTON
NEWARK
NEWENT
NEWLYN
NEWTON
NORHAM
NORTON
OAKHAM
OLDHAM
ORFORD
OSSETT
OUNDLE
OXFORD
PENRYN
PEWSEY
PINNER
PUDSEY
PURLEY
PUTNEY
RAMSEY (M)
REDCAR
RIPLEY
ROMSEY
RYHOPE
SCALBY
SEAHAM
SEATON
SELSEY
SETTLE
SLOUGH
SNAITH
ST IVES
STREET
STROOD
STROUD
SUTTON
THIRSK
THORNE
TOTNES
WALMER
WARLEY
WATTON
WELWYN

WHITBY
WIDNES
WIGTON
WILTON
WITNEY
WOKING
WOOLER
WRAGBY
YEADON
YEOVIL

7

ALLONBY
ALNWICK
ANDOVER
APPLEBY
ARUNDEL
ASHFORD
AYLSHAM
BAGSHOT
BALDOCK
BAMPTON
BANBURY
BARKING
BECCLES
BEDFORD
BEESTON
BELFORD
BERWICK
BEWDLEY
BEXHILL
BILSTON
BINGLEY
BIRTLEY
BOWNESS
BRANDON
BRISTOL
BRIXHAM
BROMLEY
BROTTON
BURFORD
BURNHAM
BURNLEY
BURSLEM

BURWELL
CAISTOR
CANNOCK
CARTMEL
CATFORD
CHARING
CHATHAM
CHEADLE
CHEDDAR
CHESHAM
CHESTER
CHOBHAM
CHORLEY
CLACTON
CLIFTON
CONSETT
CRAWLEY
CROYDON
DATCHET
DAWLISH
DEVIZES
DOCKING
DORKING
DOUGLAS (M)
DUNSTER
DURSLEY
EARSDON
ELSTREE
ENFIELD
EVESHAM
EXMOUTH
FAREHAM
FARNHAM
FELTHAM
FLETTON
FRINTON
GLOSSOP
GOSPORT
GRIMSBY
HALIFAX
HAMPTON
HANWELL
HARWICH
HAWORTH
HELSTON
HESWALL

HEYSHAM
HEYWOOD
HINDLEY
HITCHIN
HONITON
HORBURY
HORNSEA
HORSHAM
HORWICH
HOYLAKE
IBSTOCK
IPSWICH
IXWORTH
KESWICK
KINGTON
KIRKHAM
LANCING
LEDBURY
LEISTON
LESBURY
LEYBURN
LEYLAND
LINCOLN
MARGATE
MATLOCK
MORPETH
NEWBURY
NEWPORT
NEWQUAY
NORWICH
OVERTON
PADSTOW
PENRITH
PRESCOT
PRESTON
PRUDHOE
RAINHAM
READING
REDHILL
REDRUTH
REIGATE
ROMFORD
ROYSTON
RUGELEY
RUISLIP
RUNCORN

6

ALFORD
ALSTON
BARNET
BARROW
BATLEY
BATTLE
BAWTRY
BEDALE
BELPER
BEXLEY
BODMIN
BOGNOR
BOLTON
BOOTLE
BOSTON
BOURNE
BRUTON
BUNGAY
BURTON
BUXTON

RUSHDEN	WISBECH	CLEVEDON	LAVENHAM	SIDMOUTH
SALFORD	WORKSOP	CLOVELLY	LECHLADE	SKEGNESS
SALTASH	YOXFORD	CONISTON	LEWISHAM	SLEAFORD
SANDOWN		CORNHILL	LISKEARD	SOLIHULL
SCARTHO	**8**	COVENTRY	LONGTOWN	SOMERTON
SEAFORD		CREDITON	LYNMOUTH	SOUTHEND
SHIFNAL	ABINGDON	DARTFORD	MARYPORT	SPALDING
SHILDON	ALCESTER	DAVENTRY	MELKSHAM	STAFFORD
SHIPLEY	ALFRETON	DEBENHAM	MIDHURST	STAITHES
SHIPTON	ALNMOUTH	DEPTFORD	MINEHEAD	ST ALBANS
SILLOTH	AMERSHAM	DEWSBURY	NANTWICH	STAMFORD
SILSDEN	AMESBURY	EAST LOOE	NEWHAVEN	STANDISH
SKIPTON	AMPTHILL	EASTWOOD	NEW MILLS	STANHOPE
SOUTHAM	ASPATRIA	EGREMONT	NUNEATON	STANWELL
SPILSBY	ATHERTON	FAIRFORD	OLLERTON	STAVELEY
SPITTAL	AXBRIDGE	FAKENHAM	ORMSKIRK	STEYNING
STAINES	AYCLIFFE	FALMOUTH	OSWESTRY	ST HELENS
STANLEY	AYSGARTH	FRODSHAM	PAIGNTON	STOCKTON
STANWIX	BAKEWELL	GARFORTH	PENZANCE	SURBITON
STILTON	BAMBURGH	GARSTANG	PERSHORE	SWAFFHAM
ST NEOTS	BARNSLEY	GOSFORTH	PETERLEE	TAMWORTH
SUDBURY	BASILDON	GRANTHAM	PETWORTH	THETFORD
SUNBURY	BEDWORTH	GRASMERE	PEVENSEY	TINTAGEL
SWANAGE	BEVERLEY	GUISELEY	PLYMOUTH	TIVERTON
SWINDON	BICESTER	HADLEIGH	POLPERRO	TORPOINT
SWINTON	BIDDULPH	HAILSHAM	RADSTOCK	TUNSTALL
TAUNTON	BIDEFORD	HALSTEAD	RAMSGATE	UCKFIELD
TELFORD	BIRSTALL	HASTINGS	RAWMARSH	UXBRIDGE
TETBURY	BLOXWICH	HATFIELD	RAYLEIGH	WALLASEY
THAXTED	BOLSOVER	HELMSLEY	REDDITCH	WALLSEND
TILBURY	BRACKLEY	HEREFORD	RICHMOND	WANSTEAD
TOPSHAM	BRADFORD	HERNE BAY	RINGWOOD	WESTBURY
TORQUAY	BRAMHALL	HERTFORD	ROCHDALE	WEST LOOE
TUXFORD	BRAMPTON	HINCKLEY	ROCHFORD	WETHERAL
TWYFORD	BRAUNTON	HINDHEAD	ROTHBURY	WETHERBY
VENTNOR	BRIDPORT	HOLBEACH	ROTHWELL	WEYMOUTH
WALSALL	BRIGHTON	HOUNSLOW	SALCOMBE	WHITBURN
WALTHAM	BROADWAY	HUCKNALL	SALTBURN	WICKFORD
WANTAGE	BROMYARD	HUNMANBY	SANDBACH	WILLITON
WAREHAM	BROSELEY	ILKESTON	SANDGATE	WILMSLOW
WARWICK	CALDBECK	INGLETON	SANDWICH	WINSFORD
WATCHET	CAMBORNE	KEIGHLEY	SEASCALE	WIVENHOE
WATFORD	CARLISLE	KEMPSTON	SEDBERGH	WOODFORD
WINDSOR	CATERHAM	KEYNSHAM	SHANKLIN	WOOLWICH
WINSLOW	CHERTSEY	KEYWORTH	SHEFFORD	WORTHING
WINSTER	CHESHUNT	KINGSTON	SHOREHAM	YARMOUTH

GEOGRAPHY – TOWNS & CITIES – ENGLAND

9

ALDEBURGH
ALDERSHOT
AMBLESIDE
ASHBOURNE
ASHBURTON
ASHINGTON
ATHERSTON
AVONMOUTH
AXMINSTER
AYLESBURY
BEBINGTON
BLACKBURN
BLACKHILL
BLACKPOOL
BLANDFORD
BLETCHLEY
BOSCASTLE
BRACKNELL
BRAINTREE
BRENTFORD
BRENTWOOD
BRIGHOUSE
BROUGHTON
CAMBERLEY
CAMBRIDGE
CAMELFORD
CARNFORTH
CATTERICK
CHATTERIS
CHINGFORD
CHUDLEIGH
CLITHEROE
COALVILLE
COLESHILL
CONGLETON
CORBRIDGE
CRANBORNE
CRANBROOK
CREWKERNE
CRICKLADE
CUCKFIELD
DARTMOUTH
DEVONPORT
DONCASTER

DROITWICH
DRONFIELD
DUNSTABLE
DYMCHURCH
EASTLEIGH
ELLESMERE
FARINGDON
FAVERSHAM
FLEETWOOD
GATESHEAD
GODALMING
GORLESTON
GRAVESEND
GREENWICH
GREYSTOKE
GUILDFORD
HALESOWEN
HARPENDEN
HARROGATE
HASLEMERE
HAVERHILL
HAWKSHEAD
HODDESDON
HOLMFIRTH
ILCHESTER
ILMINSTER
IMMINGHAM
KETTERING
KIDSGROVE
KING'S LYNN
KNUTSFORD
LANCASTER
LATCHFORD
LEICESTER
LICHFIELD
LIVERPOOL
LONG EATON
LONGRIDGE
LOWESTOFT
LYME REGIS
LYMINGTON
LYNDHURST
MAIDSTONE
MANSFIELD
MIDDLETON
MORECAMBE

NEWCASTLE
NEWMARKET
NEW ROMNEY
NORMANTON
NORTHWICH
ORPINGTON
OTTERBURN
PENISTONE
PICKERING
RADCLIFFE
ROCHESTER
ROSS-ON-WYE
ROTHERHAM
SALISBURY
SALTFLEET
SEAHOUSES
SEVENOAKS
SHEERNESS
SHEFFIELD
SHERBORNE
SMETHWICK
SOUTHPORT
SOUTHWELL
ST AUSTELL
STEVENAGE
STOCKPORT
STOURPORT
STRATFORD
TADCASTER
TARPORLEY
TAVISTOCK
TENTERDEN
THORNBURY
TODMORDEN
TONBRIDGE
TOWCESTER
TYNEMOUTH
ULVERSTON
UP HOLLAND
UPPINGHAM
UTTOXETER
WAINFLEET
WAKEFIELD
WARKWORTH
WESTERHAM
WEYBRIDGE

WIMBLEDON
WINCANTON
WOKINGHAM
WOLVERTON
WOODSTOCK
WORCESTER
WYMONDHAM

10

ACCRINGTON
ALTRINCHAM
BARNSTAPLE
BEAMINSTER
BEDLINGTON
BELLINGHAM
BILLERICAY
BILLINGHAM
BIRKENHEAD
BIRMINGHAM
BRIDGNORTH
BRIDGWATER
BROMSGROVE
BROWNHILLS
BUCKINGHAM
CANTERBURY
CARSHALTON
CASTLE CARY
CASTLEFORD
CASTLETOWN *(M)*
CHELMSFORD
CHELTENHAM
CHICHESTER
CHIPPENHAM
CHULMLEIGH
CINDERFORD
COGGESHALL
COLCHESTER
COTTINGHAM
CULLOMPTON
DARLINGTON
DORCHESTER
DUKINFIELD
EASINGWOLD
EASTBOURNE

ECCLESHALL
EDWINSTOWE
FELIXSTOWE
FOLKESTONE
FRESHWATER
GILLINGHAM
GLOUCESTER
GUNNISLAKE
HALESWORTH
HARTLEPOOL
HASLINGDEN
HEATHFIELD
HILLINGDON
HOLSWORTHY
HORNCASTLE
HUNGERFORD
HUNSTANTON
HUNTINGDON
ILFRACOMBE
KENILWORTH
KINGSCLERE
KIRKNEWTON
LAUNCESTON
LEAMINGTON
LEOMINSTER
LETCHWORTH
LONG SUTTON
MAIDENHEAD
MALMESBURY
MANCHESTER
MEVAGISSEY
MEXBOROUGH
MIDDLEWICH
MILDENHALL
NAILSWORTH
NORTHFLEET
NOTTINGHAM
OAKENGATES
OKEHAMPTON
PEACEHAVEN
PONTEFRACT
PORTISHEAD
PORTSMOUTH
POTTERS BAR
RAMSBOTTOM
RAVENGLASS

SAXMUNDHAM
SCUNTHORPE
SEDGEFIELD
SHEPPERTON
SHERINGHAM
SHREWSBURY
SPENNYMOOR
STALBRIDGE
ST LEONARDS
STOWMARKET
SUNDERLAND
SWANSCOMBE
TEDDINGTON
TEIGNMOUTH
TEWKESBURY
TROWBRIDGE
TWEEDMOUTH
TWICKENHAM
WADEBRIDGE
WALLINGTON
WARMINSTER
WARRINGTON
WASHINGTON
WEDNESBURY
WELLINGTON
WEST MERSEA
WHITCHURCH
WHITEHAVEN
WHITLEY BAY
WHITSTABLE
WHITTLESEY
WILLINGTON
WINCHCOMBE
WINCHELSEA
WINCHESTER
WINDERMERE
WIRKSWORTH
WITHERNSEA
WOLSINGHAM
WOODBRIDGE
WORKINGTON

11

BASINGSTOKE
BERKHAMSTED

BIGGLESWADE
BLITTERLEES
BOGNOR REGIS
BOURNEMOUTH
BOVEY TRACEY
BRIDLINGTON
BROADSTAIRS
BUNTINGFORD
BURGESS HILL
CHORLEYWOOD
CIRENCESTER
CLECKHEATON
CLEETHORPES
COCKERMOUTH
CRAMLINGTON
CROWBOROUGH
EAST DEREHAM
EAST RETFORD
FARNBOROUGH
FRAMLINGHAM
GLASTONBURY
GUISBOROUGH
HALTWHISTLE
HATHERLEIGH
HIGH WYCOMBE
KINGSBRIDGE
LEATHERHEAD
LOSTWITHIEL
LUTTERWORTH
MABLETHORPE
MANNINGTREE
MARKET RASEN
MARLBOROUGH
MUCH WENLOCK
NEW BRIGHTON
NEWTON ABBOT
NORTHAMPTON
PERRANPORTH
PETERSFIELD
POCKLINGTON
RAWTENSTALL
ROTTINGDEAN
SCARBOROUGH
SEATON CAREW
SHAFTESBURY
SOUTHAMPTON

SOUTH MOLTON
STALYBRIDGE
STOURBRIDGE
SWADLINCOTE
TATTERSHALL
WALLINGFORD
WALTHAMSTOW
WEST DRAYTON
WOODHALL SPA

12

ATTLEBOROUGH
BARNOLDSWICK
BEACONSFIELD
BRIERLEY HILL
BURNHAM-ON-SEA
CAISTER-ON-SEA
CHESTERFIELD
CHRISTCHURCH
CLACTON-ON-SEA
GAINSBOROUGH
GREAT HARWOOD
GREAT MALVERN
HAYDON BRIDGE
HEBDEN BRIDGE
HECKMONDWIKE
HETTON-LE-HOLE
HOLMES CHAPEL
HUDDERSFIELD
LONGHAUGHTON
LOUGHBOROUGH
MACCLESFIELD
MILTON KEYNES
NEW ALRESFORD
NORTH SHIELDS
NORTH WALSHAM
OTTERY ST MARY
PETERBOROUGH
PORT SUNLIGHT
SHOEBURYNESS
SKELMERSDALE
SOUTH SHIELDS
STOKE-ON-TRENT
WALTHAM ABBEY

WALTON-LE-DALE
WEST BROMWICH
WIVELISCOMBE

13

ABBOTS BROMLEY
ALLENDALE TOWN
BARNARD CASTLE
BOROUGHBRIDGE
BRIGHTLINGSEA
BUCKFASTLEIGH
BURNHAM MARKET
BURTON LATIMER
BURY ST EDMUNDS
CASTLE CARROCK
CHANDLERS FORD
DOWNHAM MARKET
EAST GRINSTEAD
ELLESMERE PORT
GODMANCHESTER
GRAYS THURROCK
GREAT YARMOUTH
HAYWARDS HEATH
KIDDERMINSTER
KIRKBY STEPHEN
KNARESBOROUGH
LEAMINGTON SPA
LITTLEBOROUGH
LITTLEHAMPTON
LYTHAM ST ANNE'S
MARKET DEEPING
MARKET DRAYTON

MELTON MOWBRAY
MIDDLESBROUGH
NEWARK-ON-TRENT
NORTHALLERTON
OSWALDTWISTLE
RICKMANSWORTH
ROBIN HOOD'S BAY
SAFFRON WALDEN
SEATON DELAVAL
SHEPTON MALLET
SITTINGBOURNE
SOUTHEND-ON-SEA
SOUTH OCKENDON
STOW-ON-THE-WOLD
WESTGATE-ON-SEA
WOLVERHAMPTON

14

ASHBY-DE-LA-ZOUCH
BERWICK-ON-TWEED
BISHOP AUCKLAND
BISHOP'S WALTHAM
BLANDFORD FORUM
CHIPPING NORTON
CHURCH STRETTON
GREAT DRIFFIELD
HEMEL HEMPSTEAD
HENLEY-ON-THAMES
HURSTPIERPOINT
KIRKBY LONSDALE
KIRKBYMOORSIDE
MARKET WEIGHTON
MIDSOMER NORTON

NEWPORT PAGNELL
POULTON-LE-FYLDE
STOCKTON-ON-TEES
STONY STRATFORD
THORNABY-ON-TEES
TUNBRIDGE WELLS
WALTON-ON-THAMES
WELLINGBOROUGH
WOOTTON BASSETT

15

ASHTON-UNDER-LYNE
BARROW-IN-FURNESS
BURNHAM-ON-CROUCH
BURTON-UPON-TRENT
CASTLE DONINGTON
CHAPEL-EN-LE-FRITH
CHESTER-LE-STREET
CHIPPING SODBURY
DALTON-IN-FURNESS
GRANGE OVER SANDS
GREAT TORRINGTON
LEIGHTON BUZZARD
NEWCASTLE-ON-TYNE
NEWTON-LE-WILLOWS
SHIPSTON-ON-STOUR
STRATFORD-ON-AVON
SUNBURY-ON-THAMES
SUTTON COLDFIELD
WALTON-ON-THE-NAZE
WELLS-NEXT-THE-SEA
WESTON-SUPER-MARE
WOTTON-UNDER-EDGE

GEOGRAPHY

TOWNS & CITIES – FRANCE

(C) = Corsica (M) = Monaco
* = Alternative name

3

ARC
DAX
DIE
DOL
GAP
GEX
PAU
VIF

4

AGDE
AGEN
AIRE
ALBI
ALÈS
AUCH
BEHN
CAEN
DÔLE
FOIX
GIEN
LAON
LENS
LEON
LYON *1
METZ
NICE
POIX
PONS
RIOM
ROYE
SÉES
SENS
SÈTE

ST LÔ
TOUL
VIRE

5

ARLES
ARRAS
AURAY
AUTUN
BLOIS
BOURG
BREST
BRIVE
CALVI (C)
CORPS
COUHÉ
CRAON
CRÉCY
CREIL
DIGNE
DIJON
DINAN
DOUAI
DREUX
FEURS
GUISE
LAVAL
LE PUY
LILLE
LYONS *1
MÂCON
MEAUX
MELUN
MENDE
NANCY
NÎMES

NIORT
NOYON
NUITS
PARIS
REDON
REIMS *2
RODEZ
ROUEN
ROYAN
SAMER
SEDAN
ST DIE
ST POL
TOURS
TRANS
TULLE
USSEL
VICHY
VITRÉ
VITRY

6

AMIENS
ANGERS
ARDRES
AUMONT
BASTIA (C)
BAYEUX
BEAUNE
BELLAC
BERNAC
BOLBEC
BOUCAU
BRIARE
CAHORS
CALAIS

CANNES
CARNAC
CASSEL
CHAGNY
CHÂLON
CHINON
CHOLET
COGNAC
COLMAR
DENAIN
DERVAL
DIEPPE
DINARD
ELBEUF
EMBRUN
ÉPINAL
EVREUX
FÉCAMP
FIGEAC
FRÉJUS
GANNAT
GRASSE
GUÉRET
HIRSON
HYÈRES
ISIGNY
JARNAC
JOIGNY
LAIGLE
LE MANS
LODÈVE
LOUDUN
MAURON
MENTON
MILLAN
NANTES
NEVERS
ORANGE

ORTHEZ
POISSY
PRIVAS
RENNES
RETHEL
RHEIMS *2
ROANNE
SALINS
SAUMUR
SENLIS
SERRES
ST CAST
STENAY
ST MALO
ST OMER
TARBES
THIERS
TOULON
TROYES
UGINES
VAIGES
VANNES
VERDUN
VESOUL
VIENNE
VOIRON
YVETOT

7

AJACCIO (C)
ALENÇON
ANTIBES
ARTENAY
AUBAGNE
AUBIGNY
AUXERRE

AVALLON
AVESNES
AVIGNON
BAYONNE
BELFORT
BELLÊME
BÉZIERS
BOURGES
CAMBRAI
CARMAUX
CASTRES
CHABLIS
CHÂLONS
CORBEIL
DESVRES
DUNKIRK *3
ÉPERNAY
ÉTAPLES
FALAISE
FIRMINY
LANGRES
LA ROCHE
LAUTREC
LE BLANC
LE HAVRE
LIMOGES
LISIEUX
LORIENT
LOURDES
MAYENNE
MAZAMET
MÉZIDON
MORLAIX
MOULINS
ORLÉANS
PAIMPOL
PAMIERS
PONTIVY

GEOGRAPHY — TOWNS & CITIES – FRANCE

PROVINS
QUILLAN
QUIMPER
ROMILLY
ROSCOFF
SAINTES
SALBRIS
ST AMAND
ST DENIS
ST FLOUR
ST JUMEN
ST LOUIS
TRÉLAZÉ
UZERCHE
VALENCE
VENDÔME
VIERZON
VOUVRAY

8

AMBÉRIEU
ARCACHON
ARGENTAN
AUBUSSON
AURILLAC
BAILLEUL
BAR LE DUC
BEAUVAIS
BERGERAC
BESANÇON
BIARRITZ
BORDEAUX
BOULOGNE
BRIANÇON
CARENTAN
CHAMBÉRY
CHARTRES
CHAUMONT
CLERMONT
FOUGÈRES
GRENOBLE
GUINGAMP
HAGUENAU
HARFLEUR

HONFLEUR
ISSOUDON
LA CIOTAT
LA FLÈCHE
LAMBALLE
LE CATEAU
LE PORTEL
LE VERDON
LIBOURNE
LONGUYON
LOUVIERS
MARMANDE
MARQUISE
MAUBEUGE
MÉZIÈRES
MORTAGNE
MULHOUSE
NARBONNE
POITIERS
QUIBERON
SÉLESTAT
SOISSONS
SOUILLAC
ST BRIEUC
ST DIZIER
ST MICHEL
ST TROPEZ
ST VALÉRY
TARASCON
TONNERRE
TOULOUSE
VALOGNES
VERNEUIL
VITTEAUX

9

ABBÉVILLE
AGINCOURT
AIGUILLON
AMBRIÈRES
ANGOULÊME
AVRANCHES
BRESSUIRE
BRIGNOGAN
CAVAILLON

CAVALAIRE
CHANTILLY
CHERBOURG
COMPIÈGNE
DEAUVILLE
DUNKERQUE *3
GRANVILLE
LAPALISSE
LA PALLICE
L'ARBRESLE
LE CONQUET
LE CREUSOT
LE QUESNOY
LE TOUQUET
LE TRÉPORT
LUNÉVILLE
MARSEILLE *4
MIRAMBEAU
MONTARGIS
MONTAUBAN
MONTEREAU
MONTLUÇON
MONTREUIL
OCTEVILLE
PARTHENAY
PÉRIGUEUX
PERPIGNAN
PONT L'ABBÉ
PONT LOUIS
QUIMPERLÉ
ROCHEFORT
ROQUEFORT
ST CHAMOND
ST ÉTIENNE
ST NAZAIRE
ST QUENTIN
ST RAPHAEL
TROUVILLE

10

BAR-SUR-AUBE
CARPENTRAS
CASTELLANE
CHÂTEAULIN

DOUARNENEZ
DRAGUIGNAN
FRONTIGNAN
GRAVALINES
HAZEBROUCK
LA ROCHELLE
MARSEILLES *4
MONTCORNET
MONTE CARLO (M)
MONTÉLIMAR
NEUFCHÂTEL
PONTARLIER
ROMORANTIN
STRASBOURG
THIONVILLE
VERSAILLES
VILLENEUVE

11

ARMENTIÈRES
ARROMANCHES
CARCASSONNE
DECAZEVILLE
MONTBELIARD
MONTPELLIER
NEUFCHÂTEAU
NOIRMOUTIER
PONT L'EVÊQUE
PORT VENDRES
ST FLORENTIN
ST JEAN DE LUZ
ST POL DE LEON

12

AIGUES-MORTES
CAYEUX-SUR-MER
MONT DE MARSAN
PORTO VECCHIO (C,
ST PIERRE D'ALB
VALENCIENNES
VILLEFRANCHE
VILLEURBANNE

AIX-EN-PROVENCE
ARGÈLES-SUR-MER
CHÂTEAUBRIANT
CHÂTEAU DU LOIR
CHÂTELLERAULT
FONTAINEBLEAU
LONS LE SAUNIER

MEHUN-SUR-YÈVRE
OLORON ST MARIE

14

BEAUVOIR-SUR-MER
CHÂTEAU THIERRY
LA CHAUX DE FONDS

ROMANS-SUR-ISÈRE

15

BLANGY-SUR-BRESLE
CLERMONT FERRAND
LA ROCHEFOUCAULD
ST GERMAIN EN LAYE

GEOGRAPHY

TOWNS & CITIES – GERMANY

(E) = East Germany until 1990
*† = Divided city until 1990   * = Alternative/former name*

3

HOF
ULM

4

BONN
CHAM
ELZE
GERA (E)
HAMM
KEHL
KIEL
KÖLN *1
LEER
LOHR
PLÖN
PRÜM
UNNA

5

AALEN
BÜNDE
BÜSUM
CELLE
DÜREN
EMDEN
ENGEN
ESSEN
EUTIN
FULDA
FÜRTH
GOTHA (E)
HAGEN
HALLE (E)
HANAU
HEIDE
HUSUM
JEVER

KLEVE
LÜNEN
MAINZ
NEUSS
REGEN
RHEDA
SOEST
TRIER *2
WESEL
WORMS
ZEVEN

6

AACHEN
ALTONA
AMBERG
BASSUM
BERLIN †

BOCHUM
BREMEN
COBURG
DACHAU
DESSAU (E)
DÜLMEN
ERFURT (E)
FÜSSEN
GOSLAR
GRONAU
HAMELN *3
HÖXTER
KASSEL
KASTEL
LANDAU
LEHRTE
LINDEN
LINGEN
LÜBECK
MEPPEN

MÜNDEN
MUNICH *4
MURNAU
PASING
PASSAU
PLAUEN (E)
RHEINE
SEESEN
SIEGEN
SINGEN
SOLTAU
SPEYER
TREVES *2
UELZEN
VECHTA
WEIDEN
XANTEN

GEOGRAPHY – TOWNS & CITIES – GERMANY

7

ALSFELD
ANSBACH
BAD TÖLZ
BAMBERG
BOCHOLT
BOPPARD
BOTTROP
COLOGNE *1
COTTBUS (E)
DETMOLD
DRESDEN (E)
EINBECK
GIESSEN
GIFHORN
HAMBURG
HAMELIN *3
HANOVER *5
HARBURG
HERFORD
HÜNFELD
ITZEHOE
KEMPTEN
KOBLENZ
KORBACH
KREFELD
KRONACH
LASTRUP
LEIPZIG (E)
LIMBURG
LÖRRACH
MARBURG
MEISSEN (E)
MÜLHEIM
MÜNCHEN *4
MÜNSTER
POTSDAM (E)
RINTELN
ROSTOCK (E)
SPANDAU (E)
SPRINGE
WARBURG
WETZLAR
ZWICKAU (E)
ZWIESEL

8

AUGSBURG
BAYREUTH
BIBERACH
CHEMNITZ (E) *6
COESFELD
CUXHAVEN
DIEPHOLZ
DORTMUND
DUISBURG
ELMSHORN
ERLANGEN
FREIBURG
FREISING
GLADBECK
HANNOVER *5
KONSTANZ *7
LANDSHUT
LÖNINGEN
LÜNEBURG
MANNHEIM
MESCHEDE
MÜHLDORF
NIENBURG
NORDHORN
NÜRNBERG *8
RATISBON
ROTTWEIL
SCHWERIN (E)
SOLINGEN
TÜBINGEN
WALDSHUT
WALSRODE
WANDSBEK
WEILHEIM
WITTLICH
WÜNSTORF
WÜRZBURG

9

BIELEFELD
BRUNSWICK *9
BUXTEHUDE

CONSTANCE *6
DARMSTADT
EBERSBERG
EICHSTÄTT
ESSLINGEN
FLENSBURG
FRANKFURT
FRIEDBURG
GÖPPINGEN
GÖTTINGEN
HEILBRONN
KARLSRUHE
KARLSTADT
LAUENBURG
LIPPSTADT
MAGDEBURG (E)
MEMMINGEN
MÜNCHBERG
NUREMBERG *8
OBERWESEL
OFFENBACH
OFFENBURG
OLDENBURG
OSNABRÜCK
PADERBORN
PFORZHEIM
PINNEBERG
REMSCHEID
ROSENHEIM
SCHLESWIG
STRALSUND (E)
STRAUBING
STUTTGART
WIESBADEN
WUPPERTAL

10

BAD AIBLING
BADEN BADEN
BAD PYRMONT
BERNCASTEL
DILLENBURG
DÜSSELDORF
EUSKIRCHEN

HEIDELBERG
HILDESHEIM
IBBENBÜREN
INGOLSTADT
NEUMÜNSTER
OBERHAUSEN
RAVENSBURG
REGENSBURG
REUTLINGEN
SALZGITTER
STADTHAGEN
TRAUNSTEIN
TUTTLINGEN
ÜBERLINGEN
WARNEMÜNDE (E)
WASSERBURG
WEINGARTEN
WITTENBERG (E)

11

BRANDENBURG (E)
BREMERHAVEN
DELMENHORST
LUDWIGSBURG
NEUNKIRCHEN
NEUSTRELITZ (E)
QUAKENBRÜCK
SAARBRÜCHEN
WITTENBERGE (E)
ZWEIBRÜCKEN

12

BAD KREUZNACH
BRAUNSCHWEIG *9
OBERAMMERGAU
SCHWENNINGEN
WILHELMSBURG
WOLFENBÜTTEL

13

AIX-LA-CHAPELLE
ASCHAFFENBURG
BAD LAUTERBERG

BERCHTESGADEN
GELSENKIRCHEN
HEILIGENHAFEN
KARL MARX STADT *(E) *6*
WILHELMSHAVEN

14

BAD REICHENHALL
KAISERSLAUTERN
RECKLINGHAUSEN

15

FRANKFURT AM MAIN
MÖNCHENGLADBACH

GEOGRAPHY

TOWNS & CITIES – IRELAND

(N) = Northern Ireland
* = Alternative name

4

ATHY
BIRR
BRAY
CÓBH
CONG
CORK *1*
GLIN
GORT
INCH
NAAS
RUSH
TARA
TRIM
TUAM

5

ARDEE
AVOCA
BOYLE

CAHIR
CAVAN
CLARA
CROOM
DERRY *(N) *2*
ENNIS
FENIT
FERNS
GOREY
HOWTH
KEADY *(N)*
KELLS *3*
LARNE *(N)*
LOUTH
LUCAN
MOATE
NAVAN *4*
NEWRY *(N)*
OMAGH *(N)*
SLANE
SLIGO
TULLA
TULSK

6

ACLARE
ANTRIM *(N)*
ARDARA
ARKLOW
ARMAGH *(N)*
BANDON
BANTRY
BORRIS
CALLAN
CARLOW
CASHEL
CLONES
CLOUGH *(N)*
CLOYNE
COMBER *(N)*
DALKEY
DINGLE
DUBLIN *5*
DURROW
ELPHIN
FERMOY

FOYNES
GALWAY *6*
KILKEE
KILREA *(N)*
LURGAN *(N)*
MALLOW
MOHILL
NENAGH
NOBBER
OMEATH
ROOSKY
ROSLEA *(N)*
SWORDS
TRALEE
TULLOW

7

AN UAIMH *4*
ARDMORE
ATHENRY
ATHLONE

BALLINA
BELFAST *(N)*
BLARNEY
CLIFDEN
CLOGHAN
CLOGHER *(N)*
CLONMEL
CRUMLIN *(N)*
DONEGAL
DROMARA *(N)*
DROMORE *(N)*
DUNDALK *7*
DUNDRUM *(N)*
DUNGLOE
DUNLEER
DUNMORE
ENFIELD
FINGLAS
FINTONA *(N)*
FOXFORD
GARVAGH *(N)*
GLENARM *(N)*
GRANARD

GEOGRAPHY – TOWNS & CITIES – IRELAND

KANTURK
KENMARE
KILDARE
KILKEEL *(N)*
KILRUSH
KINSALE
LIEXLIP
LIFFORD
LISBURN *(N)*
LISMORE
MACROOM
MAGHERA *(N)*
NEWPORT
NEW ROSS
POMEROY *(N)*
PORTLAW
RATHNEW
ROSCREA
TARBERT
THURLES
TRAMORE
WEXFORD
WICKLOW
YOUGHAL

KINVARRA
LIMAVADY *(N)*
LIMERICK *8
LISTOWEL
LONGFORD
LOUGHREA
MALAHIDE
MAYNOOTH
MIDLETON
MOLLS GAP
MONAGHAN
PETTIGOE
PORTRUSH *(N)*
PORTUMNA
RATHDRUM
ROSSLARE
SKERRIES
STRABANE *(N)*
SWINFORD
TALLAGHT
VIRGINIA
WESTPORT
WOODFORD

8

ARDGLASS *(N)*
BALLYBAY
BALLYGAR
BANAGHER
BUNCRANA
BUNDORAN
CORCAIGH *1
DROGHEDA
DUNBOYNE
DUNGIVEN *(N)*
DUNLAVIN
GAILLIMH *6
GLENTIES
HEADFORD
HOLYWOOD *(N)*
KILKENNY
KILLALOE
KILLIMOR

9

ABBEYLEIX
ATHLEAGUE
BALLYDUFF
BALLYMENA *(N)*
BALLYMOTE
BANBRIDGE *(N)*
BELMULLET
BELTURBET
BUSHMILLS *(N)*
BUTTEVANT
CAPPOQUIN
CARRYDUFF *(N)*
CASTLEBAR
CASTLERAE
CELBRIDGE
COLERAINE *(N)*
COLLOONEY
COOKSTOWN *(N)*
COOTEHILL

CRAIGAVON *(N)*
CUSHENDUN *(N)*
DUNGANNON *(N)*
DUNGARVAN
DUNMANWAY
EDENDERRY
FRESHFORD
GLENBEIGH
GORTAHORK
JOHNSTOWN
KILBEGGAN
KILCORMAC
KILCULLEN
KILLARNEY
KILLYBEGS
LISNASKEA *(N)*
LUIMNEACH *8
MONEYMORE *(N)*
MOUNTRATH
MULLINGAR
NEWBRIDGE *9
NEWCASTLE *(N)*
NEWMARKET
OLDCASTLE
PORTADOWN *(N)*
RATHKEALE
RATH LUIRE *10
ROSCOMMON
ROSTREVOR *(N)*
TANDRAGEE *(N)*
TIPPERARY
TULLAMORE
WATERFORD *11
WHITEHEAD *(N)*

10

ABBEYFEALE
AUGHNACLOY *(N)*
BALBRIGGAN
BALLINROBE
BALLYBOFEY
BALLYMAHON
BALLYMONEY *(N)*
BURTONPORT

CARNDONAGH
CARRICKBOY
CASTLEDERG *(N)*
CLONAKILTY
CLONDALKIN
COALISLAND *(N)*
CREESLOUGH
CROSSHAVEN
CUSHENDALL *(N)*
DONAGHADEE *(N)*
DÚN DEALGAN *7
DUNFANAGHY
ENNISTIMON *12
ENNISTYMON *12
GLENAMADDY
GREYSTONES
KILLORGLIN
KILLYLEAGH *(N)*
KILMALLOCK
KINGSCOURT
MARKETHILL *(N)*
MILLSTREET
MUINE BHEAG *13
OUGHTERARD
PORTAFERRY *(N)*
PORT LÁIRGE *11
PORTLAOISE
RATHMELTON
SHILLELAGH
SKIBBEREEN
STRADBALLY
STRANGFORD *(N)*
TEMPLEMORE
THOMASTOWN
TOBERCURRY *14

11

BALLINASLOE
BALLYBUNION *15
BALLYCASTLE
BALLYCASTLE *(N)*
BALLYGAWLEY *(N)*
BALLYHAUNIS
BALLYRAGGET

BALLYVAGHAN *16
BLESSINGTON
CAHIRCIVEEN *17
CAHIRSIVEEN *17
CASTLECOMER
CASTLEMAINE
CHARLEVILLE *10
CLARECASTLE
CLAREMORRIS
CROSSMAGLEN (N)
DOWNPATRICK (N)
ENNISCORTHY
ENNISKILLEN (N)
GLENGARRIFF
GREENISLAND (N)
IRVINESTOWN (N)
JULIANSTOWN
LETTERKENNY
LONDONDERRY (N) *2
MAGHERAFELT (N)
NEWTOWNARDS (N)
NUTTS CORNER
PORTGLENONE (N)
PORTSTEWART (N)
RANDALSTOWN (N)
RATHFRILAND (N)
STROKESTOWN

TUBBERCURRY *14
WARRENPOINT (N)

12

BAGENALSTOWN *13
BALLYBUNNION *15
BALLYNAHINCH (N)
BALLYSHANNON
BALLYVAUGHAN *16
CASTLEDERMOT
CASTLEISLAND
CASTLEWELLAN (N) *18
CEANANNUS MÓR *3
DROICHEAD NUA *9
DÚN LAOGHAIRE
KILLASHANDRA
LISDOONVARNA
MITCHELSTOWN
MONASTEREVIN
MOUNTMELLICK
NEWTOWNABBEY (N)

13

CARRICKFERGUS (N)
CARRICK-ON-SUIR

CASTLEBLAYNEY
CASTLEPOLLARD
CASTLEWHELLAN (N) *18
MANORHAMILTON
NEWCASTLE WEST
NEWTOWN BUTLER (N)
PORTARLINGTON

14

CARRICKMACROSS
COURTMACSHERRY
EDGEWORTHSTOWN
LEIGHLINBRIDGE
MILLTOWN MALBAY
NEWTOWNSTEWART (N)

15

BAILE ATHA CLIATH *5
BALLAGHADERREEN
COURTOWN HARBOUR
GRAIGUENAMANAGH

GEOGRAPHY

TOWNS & CITIES – ITALY, SWITZERLAND & AUSTRIA

(A) = Austria   (I) = Italy   (L) = Liechtenstein   (S) = Switzerland
(SA) = Sardinia   (SM) = San Marino
* = Alternative name

3

BEX *(S)*
BRA *(I)*
WIL *(S)*

4

ALBA *(I)*
ASTI *(I)*
BARI *(I)*
BERN *(S) *1*
BIEL *(S)*
BRIG *(S)*
CHUR *(S) *2*
COMO *(I)*
FANO *(I)*
GRAZ *(A)*
IMST *(A)*
LINZ *(A)*
LODI *(I)*
NOTO *(I)*
PISA *(I)*
RIED *(A)*
ROMA *(I) *3*
ROME *(I) *3*
WELS *(A)*
WIEN *(A) *4*

5

AARAU *(S)*
ANZIO *(I)*
BADEN *(A)*
BADEN *(S)*

BASEL *(S) *5*
BASLE *(S) *5*
BERNE *(S) *1*
BOZON *(I) *6*
COIRE *(S) *2*
CÚNEO *(I)*
DAVOS *(S)*
FERMO *(I)*
FORLÌ *(I)*
GAETA *(I)*
GENOA *(I) *7*
IMOLA *(I)*
IVREA *(I)*
LECCE *(I)*
LECCO *(I)*
LIENZ *(A)*
LUCCA *(I)*
MILAN *(I) *8*
MURAU *(A)*
OLBIA *(SA)*
OLTEN *(S)*
OSTIA *(I)*
PADUA *(I) *9*
PALMI *(I)*
PARMA *(I)*
PAVIA *(I)*
RIETI *(I)*
SCHIO *(I)*
SIENA *(I)*
STEYR *(A)*
TERNI *(I)*
TURIN *(I) *10*
UDINE *(I)*
VADUZ *(L)*
VEVEY *(S)*

6

ANCONA *(I)*
ANDRIA *(I)*
AREZZO *(I)*
CESENA *(I)*
EMPOLI *(I)*
FAENZA *(I)*
FOGGIA *(I)*
FORMIA *(I)*
GENEVA *(S) *11*
GENÈVE *(S) *11*
GENOVA *(I) *7*
GLARUS *(S)*
LATINA *(I)*
LEOBEN *(A)*
LUGANO *(S)*
LUZERN *(S) *12*
MANTUA *(I) *13*
MERANO *(I)*
MESTRE *(I)*
MILANO *(I) *8*
MODENA *(I)*
NAPLES *(I) *14*
NAPOLI *(I) *14*
NOVARA *(I)*
PADOVA *(I) *9*
PESARO *(I)*
RAGUSA *(I)*
REGGIO *(I)*
RIMINI *(I)*
ROVIGO *(I)*
SAVONA *(I)*
SCHWAZ *(A)*
SCHWYZ *(S)*
THUSIS *(S)*
TIVOLI *(I)*

TORINO *(I) *10*
TRENTO *(I) *15*
TRIENT *(I) *15*
URBINO *(I)*
VARESE *(I)*
VENICE *(I) *16*
VERONA *(I)*
VIENNA *(A) *4*
ZERNEZ *(S)*
ZÜRICH *(S)*

7

BELLUNO *(I)*
BERGAMO *(I)*
BLUDENZ *(A)*
BOLOGNA *(I)*
BOLZANO *(I) *6*
BRESCIA *(I)*
CASERTA *(I)*
CASSINO *(I)*
CATANIA *(I)*
COSENZA *(I)*
CREMONA *(I)*
EBENSEE *(A)*
FERRARA *(I)*
FIDENZA *(I)*
FIRENZE *(I) *17*
FOLIGNO *(I)*
HALLEIN *(A)*
IMPERIA *(I)*
LANDECK *(A)*
L'AQUILA *(I)*
LEGHORN *(I) *18*
LIESTAL *(S)*
LIVORNO *(I) *18*

LOCARNO *(S)*
LUCERNE *(S) *12*
MANTOVA *(I) *13*
MARSALA *(I)*
MESSINA *(I)*
ORVIETO *(I)*
PALERMO *(I)*
PERUGIA *(I)*
PESCARA *(I)*
PISTOIA *(I)*
POTENZA *(I)*
RAVENNA *(I)*
ROSSANO *(I)*
SALERNO *(I)*
SANREMO *(I)*
SASSARI *(SA)*
SONDRIO *(I)*
SPITTAL *(A)*
SULMONA *(I)*
TARANTO *(I)*
TRAPANI *(I)*
TREVISO *(I)*
TRIESTE *(I)*
VENEZIA *(I) *16*
VICENZA *(I)*
VILLACH *(A)*
VITERBO *(I)*
VOGHERA *(I)*
ZERMATT *(S)*

8

AVELLINO *(I)*
BAD ISCHL *(A)*
BARLETTA *(I)*
BRINDISI *(I)*
BURGDORF *(S)*
CAGLIARI *(SA)*
CHIAVARI *(I)*
CHIOGGIA *(I)*
DORNBIRN *(A)*
EISENERZ *(A)*
FLORENCE *(I) *17*

FRIBOURG *(S)*
KLOSTERS *(S)*
KUFSTEIN *(A)*
LA SPEZIA *(I)*
LAUSANNE *(S)*
MONOPOLI *(I)*
MONTREUX *(S)*
PIACENZA *(I)*
PINEROLA *(I)*
PIOMBINO *(I)*
POZZUOLI *(I)*
ROVERETO *(I)*
SALZBURG *(A)*
SIRACUSA *(I) *19*
ST GALLEN *(S)*
ST MORITZ *(S)*
ST PÖLTEN *(A)*
SYRACUSE *(I) *19*
VERCELLI *(I)*

9

AGRIGENTO *(I)*
AMSTETTEN *(A)*
BENEVENTO *(I)*
CATANZARO *(I)*
CATTOLICA *(I)*
FELDKIRCH *(A)*
FOHNSDORF *(A)*
FROSINONE *(I)*
GALLIPOLI *(I)*
INNSBRUCK *(A)*
JUDENBURG *(A)*
NEUCHÂTEL *(S)*
PONTEDERA *(I)*
RORSCHACH *(S)*
SAN MARINO *(SM)*
SOLOTHURN *(S)*
TERRACINA *(I)*

10

BELLINZONA *(S)*
CARAVAGGIO *(I)*

KAPFENBERG *(A)*
KLAGENFURT *(A)*
PORTO TOLLE *(I)*
SENIGALLIA *(I)*
SOLBAD HALL *(A)*
WINTERTHUR *(S)*

11

ALESSÁNDRIA *(I)*
CALTAGIRONE *(I)*
DOMODOSSOLA *(I)*
KNITTELFELD *(A)*
NEUNKIRCHEN *(A)*

12

ASCOLI PICENO *(I)*
BUSTO ARSIZIO *(I)*
MÜRZZUSCHLAG *(A)*

13

BISCHOFSHOFEN *(A)*
BRUCK AN DER MUR *(A)*
CALTANISSETTA *(I)*
CASTELLAMMARE *(I)*
CASTROVILLARI *(I)*
CIVITAVECCHIA *(I)*
TORRE DEL GRECO *(I)*

14

LA CHAUX DE FONDS *(S)*
WIENER NEUSTADT *(A)*

15

TORRE ANNUNZIATA *(I)*

GEOGRAPHY

TOWNS & CITIES – SCANDINAVIA

(F) = Finland   (I) = Iceland   (N) = Norway   (D) = Denmark   (S) = Sweden
* = Alternative name

3

GOL *(N)*
LIT *(S)*
VIK *(I)*
VIK *(N)*

4

ÅNGE *(S)*
BODÖ *(N)*
HÖFN *(I)*
KEMI *(F)*
KØGE *(D)*
LUND *(S)*
MOSS *(N)*
OSLO *(N)*
OULU *(F)*
PORI *(F)*
RENA *(N)*
TANA *(N)*
TORP *(S)*
UMEÅ *(S)*
VOSS *(N)*

5

ÅRHUS *(D)*
BODEN *(S)*
BÖRAS *(S)*
FALUN *(S)*
FLÖRÖ *(N)*
GÄVLE *(S)*
GRENÅ *(D)*
HANGÖ *(F)*
HAMAR *(N)*

INARI *(F)*
KOTKA *(F)*
LAHTI *(F)*
LULEÅ *(S)*
MALMO *(S)*
NAMPA *(F)*
PITEÅ *(S)*
RAAHE *(F)*
SKIEN *(N)*
SKIVE *(D)*
SNÅSA *(N)*
TURKU *(F)*
VAASA *(F)*
VADSÖ *(N)*
VÄXJÖ *(S)*
VEJLE *(D)*
VISBY *(S)*
YSTAD *(S)*

6

ABENRA *(D)*
ÅLBORG *(D)*
ARVIKA *(S)*
ASSENS *(D)*
BERGEN *(N)*
DOMBÅS *(N)*
EKENÄS *(F)*
FÅBORG *(D)*
HORTEN *(N)*
KALMAR *(S)*
KIRUNA *(S)*
KOLARI *(F)*
KORSØR *(D)*
KUOPIO *(F)*
LARVIK *(N)*
MANDAL *(N)*

MOTALA *(S)*
MUONIO *(F)*
NAMSOS *(N)*
NARVIK *(N)*
NYBORG *(D)*
ODENSE *(D)*
OLHAVA *(F)*
ÖREBRO *(S)*
TØNDER *(D)*
TORNIO *(F)*
TROMSÖ *(N)*
VÄNNÄS *(S)*
VIBORG *(D)*

7

ÅLESUND *(N)*
ARENDAL *(N)*
DRAMMEN *(N)*
ESBJERG *(D)*
HERNING *(D)*
HOLBAEK *(D)*
HORSENS *(D)*
HUSAVIK *(I)*
KAJAANI *(F)*
KARUNKI *(F)*
KOKKOLA *(F)*
KOLDING *(D)*
LUDVIKA *(S)*
NAKSKOV *(D)*
NYSÄTRA *(S)*
RANDERS *(D)*
SALTDAL *(N)*
SELFOSS *(I)*
SOLSTAD *(N)*
TAMPERE *(F)*
UPPSALA *(S)*
VARBERG *(S)*

8

AKUREYRI *(I)*
ALINGSÅS *(S)*
ARJEPLOG *(S)*
BLONDUOS *(I)*
BORLÄNGE *(S)*
GÖTEBORG *(S)* *1
HALMSTAD *(S)*
HELSINKI *(F)* *2
HILLERØD *(D)*
HJØRRING *(D)*
HÖNEFOSS *(N)*
JOKKMOKK *(S)*
KARLSTAD *(S)*
KEFLAVIK *(I)*
LYCKSELE *(S)*
NAESTVED *(D)*
NYKØBING *(D)*
NYKÖPING *(S)*
ROSKILDE *(D)*
SLAGELSE *(D)*
STENSELE *(S)*
TÖNSBERG *(N)*
VÄSTERÅS *(S)*
VATNEYRI *(I)*

9

BORGARNES *(I)*
ENONTEKIÖ *(F)*
GÄLLIVARE *(S)*
HADERSLEV *(D)*
HÄRNÖSAND *(S)*
HAUGESUND *(N)*
HELSINGØR *(D)*
JAKOBSTAD *(F)*
JÖNKÖPING *(S)*

JYVÄSKYLÄ *(F)*
KEMIJÄRVI *(F)*
KØPENHAVN *(D) *3*
LINKÖPING *(S)*
ÖSTERSUND *(S)*
REYKJAVIK *(I)*
ROVANIEMI *(F)*
SARPSBORG *(N)*
SAVUKOSKI *(F)*
SILKEBORG *(D)*
SÖDERHAMN *(S)*
STAVANGER *(N)*
STOCKHOLM *(S)*
SUNDSVALL *(S)*
SVENDBORG *(D)*
TRONDHEIM *(N)*
UDDEVALLA *(S)*
VASTERVIK *(S)*

0

BENGTSFORS *(S)*
COPENHAGEN *(D) *3*

DJÚPIVOGUR *(I)*
ESKILSTUNA *(S)*
FREDERICIA *(D)*
GOTHENBURG *(S) *1*
HAMMERFEST *(N)*
KARLSKRONA *(S)*
LANDSKRONA *(S)*
MIDDELFART *(D)*
NORRKÖPING *(S)*
SKELLEFTEÅ *(S)*
SØNDERBORG *(D)*
SUNDBYBERG *(S)*
TRELLEBORG *(S)*

11

ESKIFJÖRDUR *(I)*
FREDRIKSTAD *(N)*
HÄLSINGBORG *(S)*
HELSINGFORS *(F) *2*
LILLEHAMMER *(N)*
VORDINGBORG *(D)*

12

KRISTIANSAND *(N)*
KRISTIANSTAD *(S)*
KRISTIANSUND *(N)*
ÖRNSKÖLDSVIK *(S)*
SANDNESSJÖEN *(N)*
UUSIKAUPUNKI *(F)*

13

FREDERIKSHAVN *(D)*
HAFNARFJÖRDUR *(I)*
SEYDISFJÖRDUR *(I)*

14

CHARLOTTENBERG *(S)*

GEOGRAPHY

TOWNS & CITIES – SCOTLAND

3	4	LUSS	ALYTH	CUPAR	KELSO	PERTH	ALNESS
		OBAN	ANNAN	DALRY	LAIRG	SALEN	ARDLUI
AYR	DAVA	TAIN	AYTON	DENNY	LARGO	SCONE	BEAULY
UIG	DREM	WICK	BANFF	DOUNE	LARGS	TROON	BIGGAR
VOE	DUNS		BEITH	ELGIN	LEITH		BODDAM
	DYCE	5	BRORA	ELLON	LEVEN	6	BO'NESS
	ELIE		CLOVA	GARVE	NAIRN		BUCKIE
	KIRN	ALLOA	CRAIL	KEITH	ONICH	ABOYNE	CAWDOR

GEOGRAPHY – TOWNS & CITIES – SCOTLAND

COMRIE
CRIEFF
DARVEL
DOLLAR
DRYMEN
DUNBAR
DUNDEE
DUNLOP
DUNNET
DUNOON
DYSART
EDZELL
FORFAR
FORRES
GIRVAN
GLAMIS
GRETNA
HAWICK
HUNTLY
IRVINE
KILLIN
LAGGAN
LANARK
LAUDER
LESLIE
METHIL
MOFFAT
RENTON
ROSYTH
STRUAN
THURSO
TONGUE
UPHALL
WATTEN
WISHAW

7

AIRDRIE
ALLOWAY
BALLOCH
BANAVIE
BONHILL
BRAEMAR
BRECHIN
BRODICK

CARLUKE
CUMNOCK
DORNOCH
DOUGLAS
DUNKELD
DURNESS
FALKIRK
GALSTON
GLASGOW
GOLSPIE
GOUROCK
GRANTON
GULLANE
HALKIRK
KENMORE
KILSYTH
KINROSS
LAMLASH
LARBERT
LERWICK
LYBSTER
MACDUFF
MAIDENS
MALLAIG
MAYBOLE
MELROSE
METHVEN
MONKTON
NEW DEER
PAISLEY
PEEBLES
PORTREE
PORTSOY
RENFREW
SCOURIE
SELKIRK
STANLEY
TARBERT
TAYPORT
TOMATIN
TURRIFF
TYNDRUM
UNAPOOL
WIGTOWN

8

ABERDEEN
ABERLADY
ARBROATH
ARMADALE
ARROCHAR
AVIEMORE
BALLATER
BALMORAL
BANCHORY
BARRHEAD
BARRHILL
BATHGATE
BEARSDEN
BEATTOCK
BLANTYRE
BROXBURN
BURGHEAD
CARNWATH
CRAWFORD
CREETOWN
CROMARTY
DALKEITH
DALMALLY
DINGWALL
DOUNREAY
DRUMMORE
DUFFTOWN
DUMFRIES
DUNBEATH
DUNBLANE
EYEMOUTH
FALKLAND
FINDHORN
FORTROSE
GAIRLOCH
GLENLUCE
GREENOCK
HAMILTON
INNELLAN
JEDBURGH
KINBRACE
KINCRAIG
KINGHORN
KIRKWALL

KYLEAKIN
LANGHOLM
LATHERON
LEUCHARS
MILLPORT
MONIAIVE
MONTROSE
MUIRKIRK
NEWBURGH
ROTHESAY
ROXBURGH
SANQUHAR
STIRLING
STRICHEN
ULLAPOOL

9

ABERFELDY
ABERFOYLE
ABERNETHY
ARDROSSAN
BLACKFORD
BROADFORD
BUCHLYVIE
BUCKHAVEN
CALLANDER
CARSTAIRS
CLYDEBANK
DALRYMPLE
DUMBARTON
DUNCANSBY
EDINBURGH
FOCHABERS
GAIRLOCHY
HELMSDALE
INVERARAY
INVERNESS
INVERSHIN
INVERURIE
JOHNSTONE
KILMARTIN
KINGUSSIE
KIRKCALDY
LOCHINVER
LOCKERBIE

MILNGAVIE
MONIFIETH
NEW LANARK
OCHILTREE
PETERHEAD
PITLOCHRY
PRESTWICK
SALTCOATS
SHIELDAIG
SLAMANNAN
ST ANDREWS
STORNOWAY
STRANRAER
STRATHYRE
STROMNESS
STRONTIAN
THORNHILL
TOBERMORY
TOMINTOUL
TURNBERRY
WEMYSS BAY

10

ACHNASHEEN
ALTNAHARRA
ANSTRUTHER
BALLANTRAE
BALLINLUIG
BERRIEDALE
CARNOUSTIE
CARRBRIDGE
CASTLETOWN
COATBRIDGE
COLDSTREAM
CRAIGHOUSE
DALBEATTIE
DALWHINNIE
GALASHIELS
GLENEAGLES
GLENFINNAN
GLENROTHES
HADDINGTON
KILMARNOCK
KILWINNING

KINCARDINE
KINGSBARNS
KINLOCHEWE
KIRKCONNEL
KIRRIEMUIR
LENNOXTOWN
LINLITHGOW
LIVINGSTON
MOTHERWELL
NEW CUMNOCK
NEWTONMORE
PITTENWEEM
PORT ASKAIG
PORTGORDON
PORTOBELLO
ROSEHEARTY
ROSEMARKIE
RUTHERGLEN
SKELMORLIE
STONEHAVEN
STRATHAVEN

11

BANNOCKBURN
BLAIR ATHOLL
BLAIRGOWRIE
BONAR BRIDGE
BURNTISLAND
CAMPBELTOWN
CLACKMANNAN

COUPAR ANGUS
COWDENBEATH
CUMBERNAULD
DUNFERMLINE
ECCLEFECHAN
FORT WILLIAM
FRASERBURGH
GRANGEMOUTH
GRETNA GREEN
HELENSBURGH
INVERBERVIE
INVERGORDON
KIRKPATRICK
LOSSIEMOUTH
MAXWELLTOWN
MUSSELBURGH
NETHYBRIDGE
NEW GALLOWAY
PETERCULTER
PORT GLASGOW
PORTPATRICK
PRESTONPANS
QUEENSFERRY
STRATHBLANE

12

AUCHTERARDER
BALLACHULISH
BOAT OF GARTEN
EAST KILBRIDE
FORT AUGUSTUS

GARELOCHHEAD
INNERLEITHEN
KINLOCHLEVEN
LAURENCEKIRK
MACHRIHANISH
NEWPORT-ON-TAY
NEWTON MEARNS
NORTH BERWICK
PORTNACROISH
STRATHPEFFER
TILLICOULTRY
WEST KILBRIDE

13

BRIDGE OF ALLAN
BROUGHTY FERRY
CASTLE DOUGLAS
COCKBURNSPATH
DALMELLINGTON
DRUMNADROCHIT
INVERKEITHING
KIRKCUDBRIGHT
KIRKINTILLOCH
NEWTON STEWART
STENHOUSEMUIR

14

GRANTOWN-ON-SPEY
KINLOCH RANNOCH
KYLE OF LOCHALSH

GEOGRAPHY

TOWNS & CITIES – SOUTH AMERICA

(A) = Argentina (BO) = Bolivia (BR) = Brazil (CH) = Chile
(CO) = Colombia (E) = Ecuador (FA) = Falklands (FR) = French Guiana
(G) = Guyana (PA) = Paraguay (PE) = Peru (S) = Surinam
(U) = Uruguay (V) = Venezuela

3

ICA *(PE)*
IPU *(BR)*
RIO *(BR)*

SALTO *(U)*
SUCRE *(BO)*
TACNA *(PE)*
TALCA *(CH)*
TUNJA *(CO)*

TEMUCO *(CH)*
VALERA *(V)*
VIEDMA *(A)*
ZÁRATE *(A)*

SÃO JOSÉ *(BR)*
SÃO LUÍS *(BR)*
SULLANA *(PE)*
UBERABA *(BR)*
VITÓRIA *(BR)*

4

AZUL *(A)*
BUGA *(CO)*
CALI *(CO)*
CORO *(V)*
GOYA *(A)*
LIMA *(PE)*
MELO *(U)*
PUNO *(PE)*

5

ARAXÁ *(BR)*
BÁHIA *(BR)*
BAURU *(BR)*
BELÉM *(BR)*
CEARÁ *(BR)*
CUZCO *(PE)*
JUNÍN *(A)*
LA PAZ *(BO)*
NATAL *(BR)*
ORURO *(BO)*
PASTO *(CO)*
PIURA *(PE)*
QUITO *(E)*
ROCHA *(U)*
SALTA *(A)*

6

BOGOTÁ *(CO)*
CALLAO *(PE)*
CAMETA *(BR)*
CAMPOS *(BR)*
CANOAS *(BR)*
CÚCUTA *(CO)*
CUENCA *(E)*
CUIABÁ *(BR)*
CUMANA *(V)*
IBAGUÉ *(CO)*
IBARRA *(E)*
JEQUIE *(BR)*
MACAPÁ *(BR)*
MACEIÓ *(BR)*
MANAUS *(BR)*
MERIDA *(V)*
OBIDOS *(BR)*
OLINDA *(BR)*
OSORNO *(CH)*
PARANÁ *(A)*
POTOSÍ *(BO)*
RECIFE *(BR)*
SANTOS *(BR)*
SOBRAL *(BR)*
TALTAL *(CH)*
TANDIL *(A)*
TARIJA *(BO)*

7

ARACAJU *(BR)*
CARACAS *(V)*
CAYENNE *(FR)*
CHILLAN *(CH)*
CODAJAS *(BR)*
COPIAPÓ *(CH)*
CÓRDOBA *(A)*
CORUMBÁ *(BR)*
DOLARES *(A)*
GOIÂNIA *(BR)*
GUANARE *(V)*
IQUIQUE *(CH)*
IQUITOS *(PE)*
ITABUNA *(BR)*
LA OROYA *(PE)*
LA PLATA *(A)*
LINARES *(CH)*
MATURIN *(V)*
MENDOZA *(A)*
MOSSORÓ *(BR)*
NEUQUÉN *(A)*
NITERÓI *(BR)*
PALMIRA *(CO)*
PELOTAS *(BR)*
PEREIRA *(CO)*
POPAYAN *(CO)*
POSADAS *(A)*
ROSARIO *(A)*

8

ANÁPOLIS *(BR)*
AREQUIPA *(PE)*
ASUNCIÓN *(PA)*
AYACUCHO *(PE)*
BRAGANÇA *(BR)*
BRASILIA *(BR)*
CARÚPANO *(V)*
CHICLAYO *(PE)*
COQUIMBO *(CH)*
CURITIBA *(BR)*
DEMERARA *(G)*
FONTE BOA *(BR)*
JABOATÃO *(BR)*
LA GUAIRA *(V)*
LA SERENA *(CH)*
LONDRINA *(BR)*
MAGANGUE *(CO)*
MEDELLÍN *(CO)*
MERCEDES *(A)*
MOLLENDO *(PE)*
NOVA LIMA *(BR)*
PAMPLONA *(CO)*
PAYSANDÚ *(U)*
RANCAGUA *(CH)*
RIOBAMBA *(E)*
RIO LARGO *(BR)*
RIO TINTO *(BR)*

SALVADOR *(BR)*
SANTAREM *(BR)*
SANTIAGO *(CH)*
SÃO PAULO *(BR)*
SOROCABA *(BR)*
TERESINA *(BR)*
TRUJILLO *(PE)*
VALDIVIA *(CH)*
VALENCIA *(V)*

9

ARAÇATUBA *(BR)*
BARCELONA *(V)*
CAJAMARCA *(PE)*
CANELONES *(U)*
CARTAGENA *(CO)*
CATAMARCA *(A)*
CHIVILCOY *(A)*
CONCORDIA *(A)*
FORTALEZA *(BR)*
GUAYAQUIL *(E)*
LATACUNGA *(E)*
MANIZALES *(CO)*
MARACAIBO *(V)*
OLAVARRÍA *(A)*
PARAGUARI *(PA)*
PERGAMINO *(A)*
RIO BRANCO *(BR)*
RIO GRANDE *(BR)*
SAN FELIPE *(V)*
SANTA CRUZ *(BO)*
SANTA ROSA *(A)*
TOCOPILLA *(CH)*

10

COCHABAMBA *(BO)*

CONCEPCIÓN *(CH)*
CONCEPCIÓN *(PA)*
CORRIENTES *(A)*
ESMERALDAS *(E)*
FRAY BENTOS *(U)*
GEORGETOWN *(G)*
JOÃO PESSOA *(BR)*
JUIZ DE FORA *(BR)*
LAMBAYEQUE *(PE)*
MONTEVIDEO *(U)*
NOVA IGUACA *(BR)*
PARAMARIBO *(S)*
PERNAMBUCO *(BR)*
PETRÓPOLIS *(BR)*
PORTO VELHO *(BR)*
PORTOVIEJO *(E)*
SAN NICOLÁS *(A)*
SANTA MARIA *(BR)*
SANTA MARIA *(CO)*
SETE LAGOAS *(BR)*
TRÊS LAGOAS *(BR)*
VALPARAÍSO *(CH)*
VILLA MARIA *(A)*
VILLARRICA *(PA)*
VIÑA DEL MAR *(CH)*

11

ANTOFAGASTA *(CH)*
BAHÍA BLANCA *(A)*
BUCARAMANGA *(CO)*
BUENOS AIRES *(A)*
CAMPO GRANDE *(BR)*
MAR DEL PLATA *(A)*
PONTA GROSSA *(BR)*
PORTO ALEGRE *(BR)*
PORT STANLEY *(FA)*
PUERTO MONTT *(CH)*

PUNTA ARENAS *(CH)*
RIO GALLEGOS *(A)*

12

BARQUISIMETO *(V)*
BARRANQUILLA *(CO)*
BUENAVENTURA *(CO)*
CERRO DE PASCO *(PE)*
MONTES CLAROS *(BR)*
NEW AMSTERDAM *(G)*
NOVA FRIBURGO *(BR)*
NOVO HAMBURGO *(BR)*
RIO DE JANEIRO *(BR)*
SAN CRISTÓBAL *(V)*
TEÓFILO OTÔNI *(BR)*
VOLTA REDONDA *(BR)*

13

BELO HORIZONTE *(BR)*
CAMPINA GRANDE *(BR)*
CIUDAD BOLIVAR *(V)*
LOMAS DE ZAMORA *(A)*
RIBEIRÃO PRÊTO *(BR)*

14

TRENQUE LAUQUEN *(A)*

15

BAHÍA DE CARÁQUEZ *(E)*

GEOGRAPHY

TOWNS & CITIES – SPAIN & PORTUGAL

(A) = Andorra (G) = Gibraltar (M) = Mallorca (P) = Portugal
* = Alternative name

3
FOZ
OÑA
TUY *(P)*

4
AOIZ
BAZA
BEJA *(P)*
FARO *(P)*
IRUN
JACA
JAÉN
LEÓN
LOJA
LUGO
MULA
OLOT
OVAR *(P)*
REUS
VICH
VIGO

5
AINSA
ALCOY
ALTEA
ATECA
AVILA
BAENA
BÉJAR
BERJA
BRAGA *(P)*

CÁDIZ
CASPE
DENIA
ÉCIJA
ELCHE
ELVAS
EVORA *(P)*
FRAGA
GIJÓN
GRADO
JEREZ
LAGOS *(P)*
LALIN
LIRIA
LORCA
LOULE *(P)*
MIJAS
MORÓN
MUGIA
NAVIA
NERJA
OSUNA
PALMA *(M)*
PORTO *(P) *1*
RIAÑO
RONDA
ROSAS
SALOU
SORIA
SUECA
TOMAR *(P)*
TREMP
UBEDA
VALLS
VISEA *(P)*
YECLA

6
AGUEDA *(P)*
ALCIRA
AVEIRO *(P)*
AZUAGA
BARGAS
BILBAO
BLANES
BURGOS
CAMBRE
CUENZA
ESTEPA
GANDÍA
GERONA
GUADIX
GUARDA *(P)*
HELLÍN
HUELVA
HUESCA
JÁTIVA
LAMEGO *(P)*
LAREDO
LEIRIA
LÉRIDA
LISBOA *(P) *2*
LISBON *(P) *2*
LLANES
LUARCA
MADRID
MÁLAGA
MARTOS
MATARÓ
MÉRIDA
MIERES
MONZÓN
MOTRIL
MURCIA

NAZARÉ *(P)*
OLMEDO
OPORTO *(P) *1*
ORENSE
OVIEDO
PINEDA
PINHEL *(P)*
RIPOLL
SAGRES *(P)*
SILVES *(P)*
SITGES
TAVIRA *(P)*
TERUEL
TOLEDO
TOLOSA
TOTANA
TUDELA
UTRERA
VIELLA
VIVERO
ZAMORA

7
AGUILAS
ALCARAZ
ALJEZUR *(P)*
ALLARIZ
ALMANSA
ALMERÍA
ALSASUA
AMPOSTA
ANDÚJAR
ARACENA
ARGANDA
ASTORGA
AVEINTA

BADAJOZ
CÁCARES
CAMINHA *(P)*
CARMONA
CASCAIS *(P)*
CEHEGIN
COIMBRA
CÓRDOBA
CORUNNA **3*
COVILHÃ *(P)*
CULLERO
DAIMIEL
DURANGO
ESTELLA
ESTORIL *(P)*
GRANADA
IRURZUN
JUMILLA
LA LINEA
LA UNIÓN
LINARES
LOGROÑO
MALGRAT
MANRESA
MAYORGA
MÉRTOLA *(P)*
MOJÁCAR
MONTORO
NOVELDA
PALAMÓS
PLENCIA
PORT BOU
RIBADEO
SAGUNTO
SANTOÑA
SARRIÓN
SEGOVIA
SETÚBAL *(P)*

SEVILLA *4
SEVILLE *4
TAFALLA
TARRASA
TORTOSA
VINAROZ
VITORIA

8

ABRANTES (P)
ALBACETE
ALBORAYA
ALENQUER (P)
ALICANTE
ARANJUEZ
AYAMONTE
BADALONA
BEMBIBRE
BENIDORM
BETANZOS
BRAGANÇA (P) *5
BRAGANZA (P) *5
CARAVACA
CARBALLO
ESTEPONA
ESTREMOS (P)
FIGUERAS
GUERNICA
LA CORUÑA *3
LA GUDIÑA
LAS ROZAS
MARBELLA
MARCHENA
MARQUINA
MAZARRÓN
ORIHUELA
PALENCIA
PAMPLONA
PORTIMÃO
SABADELL
SAN ROQUE
SANTAREM
TARAZONA
TRUJILLO

VALENCIA
VILALLER
VILA REAL (P)
VILLALBA
ZARAGOZA *6

9

ALBUFEIRA
ALGECIRAS
ANTEQUERA
ASTILLERO
BARCELONA
BENAVENTE
BUJARALOZ
CALAHORRA
CALATAYUD
CAÑAVERAL
CARTAGENA
DON BENITO
GIBRALTAR (G)
GUIMARAES (P)
MARMOLEJO
MORATALLA
PEÑÍSCOLA
PLASENCIA
RIBADAVIA
SALAMANCA
SANTANDER
SARAGOSSA *6
TARRAGONA
VILLARCAY

10

CARCAGENTE
CARCAVELOS (P)
CIUDAD REAL
EL ESCORIAL
FONSAGRADA
FUENGIROLA
LA CAROLINA
MANZANARES
ONTENIENTE
PONFERRADA

PONTEVEDRA
PORTALEGRE (P)
POZOBLANCO
SANTILLANA
TOSSA DE MAR
VALDEPEÑAS
VALLADOLID
VILLANUEVA

11

GARROVILLAS
GUADALAJARA
LLORET DE MAR
POLA DE SIERO
PUENTE GENIL
PUERTOLLANO
RIBADESELLA
SAN FERNANDO
TORDESILLAS
TORREBLANCA
TORRELAVEGA

12

ALCALA LA REAL
HUÉRCAL OVERA
SAN SEBASTIAN
TORREMOLINOS
TORRES VEDRAS (P)
VILLAVICIOSA

13

ARANDA DE DUERO
CASTELO BRANCO (P)
CUIDAD RODRIGO
FIGUERIRA DA FOZ
FUENTEOBEJUNA
ROQUETAS DE MAR
SAMA DE LANGREO
VILLARROBLEDO

14

ANDORRA LA VELLA *(A)*
CALDAS DE RAINHA *(P)*

MEDINA DEL CAMPO
TORREDONJIMENO
VIANA DO CASTELO *(P)*

15

MEDINA DE RIOSECO
MONFORTE DE LEMOS

GEOGRAPHY

TOWNS & CITIES – USA

4

ELKO
ERIE
GARY
HILO
LIMA
LYNN
MESA
NOME
RENO
ROME
TROY
WACO
YORK
YUMA

5

AKRON
BAKER
BELEN
BOISE
BUTTE
CRAIG
DOVER

FARGO
FLINT
HAVRE
HURON
MACON
MALTA
MIAMI
MINOT
NEPHI
OGDEN
OMAHA
OZARK
PROVO
SALEM
SELMA
SITKA
TAMPA
TULSA
TYLER
UKIAH
UTICA

6

ALBANY
AUBURN

AURORA
AUSTIN
BANGOR
BILOXI
BOSTON
CAMDEN
CANTON
CASPER
DALLAS
DAYTON
DEL RIO
DENTON
DENVER
DULUTH
DURHAM
ELMIRA
EL PASO
EUGENE
EUREKA
FRESNO
HELENA
ITHACA
JOLIET
JOPLIN
JUNEAU
KAILUA
KODIAK

LAREDO
LAWTON
LOWELL
MOBILE
MOLINE
MONROE
NASHUA
NEWARK
ODESSA
ORANGE
OSWEGO
OXFORD
OXNARD
PAYSON
PEORIA
PIERRE
PUEBLO
QUINCY
RACINE
SEWARD
ST PAUL
TACOMA
TELLER
TOLEDO
TOPEKA
TOWSON
TUCSON

URBANA
WAUSAU
WINONA
YAKIMA

7

ABILENE
ALTOONA
ATLANTA
AUGUSTA
BAY CITY
BOZEMAN
BUFFALO
CHICAGO
CONCORD
CORDOVA
DECATUR
DENISON
DETROIT
DURANGO
ELK CITY
EVERETT
GADSDEN
HAMMOND
HAMPTON

HOUSTON
JACKSON
KEARNEY
KEY WEST
LANSING
LARAMIE
LINCOLN
LUBBOCK
MADISON
MEDFORD
MEMPHIS
MODESTO
NEWPORT
NEW YORK
NORFOLK
OAKLAND
OILDALE
OLYMPIA
ORLANDO
PHOENIX
RALEIGH
READING
REDDING
ROANOKE
ROSWELL
RUTLAND
SAGINAW

SAN JOSÉ
SANTA FÉ
SEATTLE
SPOKANE
ST CLOUD
ST LOUIS
TRENTON
VENTURA
WAHIAWA
WICHITA
YONKERS

NORTHWAY
OAK RIDGE
OGALLALA
PALO ALTO
PASADENA
PATERSON
PORTLAND
RICHMOND
ROCKFORD
SAN DIEGO
SAN MATEO
SANTA ANA
SAVANNAH
SCRANTON
SHERIDAN
STAMFORD
ST JOSEPH
STOCKTON
SUPERIOR
SYRACUSE
WATERLOO
WHEELING

FORT WAYNE
FORT WORTH
FRANKFORT
GALVESTON
HOLLYWOOD
JAMESTOWN
JOHNSTOWN
KALAMAZOO
KNOXVILLE
LAFAYETTE
LANCASTER
LEXINGTON
LONG BEACH
MILES CITY
MILWAUKEE
NANTUCKET
NASHVILLE
NEW LONDON
PALM BEACH
PAWTUCKET
PENSACOLA
PINE BLUFF
POCATELLO
PRINCETON
RAPID CITY
RIVERSIDE
ROCHESTER
SAN ANGELO
SIOUX CITY
SOUTH BEND
TEXARCANA
VANCOUVER
WATERBURY
WORCESTER

CEDAR FALLS
CHARLESTON
CINCINNATI
CUMBERLAND
EVANSVILLE
GRAND FORKS
GRANT'S PASS
GREENSBORO
GREENVILLE
HAGERSTOWN
HARRISBURG
HUNTINGTON
HUNTSVILLE
IDAHO FALLS
JERSEY CITY
KANSAS CITY
LITTLE ROCK
LONG BRANCH
LOS ANGELES
LOUISVILLE
MANCHESTER
MIAMI BEACH
MONTGOMERY
MONTPELIER
NEW BEDFORD
NEW BRITAIN
NEW ORLEANS
OREGON CITY
PETERSBURG
PITTSBURGH
PORT ARTHUR
PORTSMOUTH
PROVIDENCE
ROCK ISLAND
SACRAMENTO
SAN ANTONIO
SANTA MARIA
SHREVEPORT
SIOUX FALLS
TERRE HAUTE
TUSCALOOSA
WASHINGTON
WATERVILLE
WILMINGTON
WOONSOCKET
YOUNGSTOWN

8

ABERDEEN
AMARILLO
ANN ARBOR
BEAUMONT
BERKELEY
BIG DELTA
BILLINGS
BISMARCK
BROCKTON
CHEYENNE
COLUMBIA
COLUMBUS
DEARHORN
FLORENCE
GREEN BAY
GULFPORT
HANNIBAL
HARTFORD
HONOLULU
IOWA CITY
IRONWOOD
LA CROSSE
LAKELAND
LAS VEGAS
LAWRENCE
MERIDIAN
MISSOULA
MONTEREY
MOORHEAD
MUSKOGEE
NEW HAVEN

9

ANCHORAGE
ANNAPOLIS
ARLINGTON
ASHEVILLE
ASHTABULA
BALTIMORE
BETHLEHEM
BIDDEFORD
BLACKFOOT
CAMBRIDGE
CHAMPAIGN
CHARLOTTE
CLEVELAND
DAVENPORT
DES MOINES
DODGE CITY
EAU CLAIRE
FAIRBANKS
FALL RIVER
FORT SMITH

10

ALEXANDRIA
BATON ROUGE
BELLINGHAM
BIRMINGHAM
BRIDGEPORT
BURLINGTON
CARSON CITY

GEOGRAPHY – TOWNS & CITIES – USA

11

ALBUQUERQUE
BAKERSFIELD
BOULDER CITY
BROWNSVILLE
CEDAR RAPIDS
CHATTANOOGA
EAST ST LOUIS
GRAND RAPIDS
JOHNSON CITY
LAKE CHARLES
MINNEAPOLIS
NEWPORT NEWS
PALM SPRINGS
REDWOOD CITY
ROCK SPRINGS
SANTA MONICA
SCHENECTADY
SPRINGFIELD
TALLAHASSEE

12

ATLANTIC CITY
DAYTONA BEACH
FAYETTEVILLE
INDEPENDENCE
INDIANAPOLIS
JACKSONVILLE
KLAMATH FALLS
NEW BRUNSWICK
NIAGARA FALLS
OKLAHOMA CITY
PHILADELPHIA
POUGHKEEPSIE
SALT LAKE CITY
SAN FRANCISCO
SANTA BARBARA
ST PETERSBURG
WICHITA FALLS
WINSTON-SALEM

13

CAPE GIRARDEAU
COUNCIL BLUFFS
CORPUS CHRISTI
JEFFERSON CITY
SAN BERNARDINO
SAN LUIS OBISPO
WEST PALM BEACH

14

FORT LAUDERDALE

15

COLORADO SPRINGS

GEOGRAPHY

TOWNS & CITIES – WALES

= Alternative name

3

HAY
USK

HOLT
MOLD
PYLE
RHÔS
RHYL

4

ABER
BALA

5

BARRY

BORTH
BWLCH
CHIRK
CONWY *1
DINAS
FLINT
MAGOR
NEATH
NEFYN
PORTH

RISCA
TENBY
TOWYN *2
TYWYN *2

6

AMLWCH
BANGOR

BEDWAS
BRECON
CONWAY *1
CORWEN
KILLAY
MARGAM
MATHRY
NELSON
PENNAL
RUABON

RUMNEY
RUTHIN
YSTRAD

7

BLEDDFA
BUCKLEY
CARDIFF

CLYDACH
CWM-AVON
CWMBRAN
DENBIGH
DOWLAIS
HARLECH
HIRWAUN
LOUGHOR
MAESTEG
MUMBLES
NEWGALE
NEWPORT
NEW QUAY
NEWTOWN
NEYLAND
OVERTON
PENARTH
RHONDDA
ST ASAPH
SWANSEA
TINTERN
WREXHAM

HOLYWELL
KIDWELLY
KNIGHTON
LAMPETER
LLANABER
LLANDAFF
LLANELLI
LLANRWST
MONMOUTH
NARBERTH
PEMBROKE
PENYBONT
PWLLHELI
RHAYADER
RHUDDLAN
ST CLEARS
ST DAVID'S
TALGARTH
TREDEGAR
TREGARON
TREMADOC
WHITLAND

GWALCHMAI
LAUGHARNE
LLANBERIS
LLANDEILO
LLANDUDNO
LLANGEFNI
MORRISTON
NEW RADNOR
PONTYPOOL
PORT EYNON
PORTHCAWL
PORTMADOC *4
PRESTATYN
RHOS-ON-SEA
ST MELLONS
TONYPANDY
TRECASTLE
WELSHPOOL

PRESTEIGNE
WHITCHURCH

11

ABERGAVENNY
ABERTILLERY
ABERYSTWYTH
BRITON FERRY
BUILTH WELLS
CONNAH'S QUAY
CRICKHOWELL
LLANTRISANT
MACHYNLLETH
MENAI BRIDGE
MOUNTAIN ASH
PENMAENMAWR
PORTMEIRION
QUEENSFERRY
TRAWSFYNYDD

10

ABERSYCHAN
BEDDGELERT
BETWS-Y-COED
CAERNARFON *5
CAERNARVON *5
CAERPHILLY
CARMARTHEN
CROSS HANDS
FFESTINIOG
LLANDDAROG
LLANDOVERY
LLANDRILLO
LLANDYSSUL
LLANFYLLIN
LLANGOLLEN
LLANIDLOES
MONTGOMERY
NEWBOROUGH
PONTYPRIDD
PORTHMADOG *4
PORT TALBOT

12

DINAS MAWDDWY
LLANUWCHLLYN
MILFORD HAVEN
PEMBROKE DOCK

13

HAVERFORDWEST
LLANTWIT MAJOR
MERTHYR TYDFIL
YSTRAD RHONDDA

14

LLANWRTYD WELLS
NEWCASTLE EMLYN
YSPYTTY YSTWYTH

8

ABERAVON
ABERDARE
ABERGELE
BARMOUTH
BENLLECH
BETHESDA
BRIDGEND
BRYN-MAWR
CADOXTON
CAERLEON
CARDIGAN
CHEPSTOW
EBBW VALE
GOODWICK
HAWARDEN
HAY-ON-WYE
HOLYHEAD

9

ABERAERON *3
ABERAYRON *3
ABERDARON
ABERDOVEY
ABERFFRAW
ABERPORTH
AMMANFORD
BEAUMARIS
BEDWELLTY
BLAENAVON
BURRY PORT
COLWYN BAY
COWBRIDGE
CRICCIETH
DOLGELLAU
FISHGUARD
GORSEINON

HISTORY

BATTLES & WARS

(A) = Air battle   (S) = Sea battle   (W) = War(s)
* = Alternative name

3

ACS *(1849)*
COD *(W-1973)*
GOA *(1511)*
ULM *(1805)*

4

ACRE *(1189, S-1840)*
ALMA *(1854)*
BOER *(W-1899-1902)*
CAEN *(1944)*
CEVA *(1796)*
COLD *(W-1947-1989)*
DEGO *(1796)*
GULF *(W-1980-1988) *1*
(W-1991)
HOLY *(W-1099, 1148,*
1189-1192,
1202) *2
IRUN *(1837)*
IVRY *(1590)*
JAVA *(S-1942)*
JENA *(1806)*
LAON *(1814)*
LENS *(1648)*
LODI *(1796)*
METZ *(1870)*
MONS *(1914)*
NAAS *(1798)*
NILE *(S-1798) *3*
NIVE *(1813)*
NOVI *(1799, 1800)*
ORAN *(S-1940)*
RAAB *(1809)*
ROME *(387BC, 408, 546,*
1527, 1849)

SOHR *(1745, 1866)*
ST LÔ *(1944)*
TARA *(1798)*
TOBA *(1868)*
WAWZ *(1831)*
YALU *(S-1894)*
ZAMA *(202BC)*
ZELA *(47BC)*
ZULU *(W-1879)*

5

ACCRA *(1824)*
ADUWA *(1896)*
AISNE *(1914, 1917, 1918)*
ALAMO *(1836)*
ALLIA *(390BC)*
ANJOU *(1421)*
ANZIO *(1944)*
ARRAS *(1654, 1917)*
AURAY *(1364)*
BANDA *(1858)*
BEREA *(1852)*
BOYNE *(1690)*
BULGE *(1944) *4*
BUXAR *(1764)*
CADIZ *(S-1587)*
CHIOS *(201BC)*
CIVIL *(W-England-1642-1651,*
USA-1861-1865,
Spain-1936-1939,
China-1945-1949,
Greece-1945-1949,
Nigeria-1967-1970,
Pakistan-1971,
Lebanon-1975-
Cambodia/Kampuchea-
1976-

CRÉCY *(1346)*
CRETE *(1941)*
DAK TO *(1967)*
DELHI *(1398, 1803,*
1804, 1857)
DOURO *(1809)*
DOVER *(S-1652, 1653)*
DREUX *(1562)*
DUNES *(1658)*
ELENA *(1877)*
EL TEB *(1884)*
EUTAW *(1781)*
EYLAU *(1807)*
GINGI *(1689)*
GOREY *(1798)*
HANAU *(1813)*
HANGÖ *(S-1714)*
IMOLA *(1797)*
IPSUS *(301BC)*
JASSY *(1620)*
KALKA *(1224)*
KAZAN *(1552, 1774)*
KHART *(1829)*
KOLIN *(1757)*
LAGOS *(1693, S-1759)*
LA PAZ *(1865)*
LARGS *(1263)*
LEWES *(1264)*
LIÉGE *(1914)*
LIGNY *(1815)*
LIPAU *(1434)*
LISSA *(S-1866)*
MAIDA *(1806)*
MARNE *(1914, 1918)*
MAYPO *(1818)*
MORAT *(1476)*
MUDKI *(1845)*
MUNDA *(45BC)*

MURET *(1213)*
MYLEX *(36BC)*
NARVA *(1700)*
NEDAO *(454)*
NIZIB *(1839)*
OLPAE *(426BC)*
OPIUM *(W-1839-1842)*
PARMA *(1734)*
PATAY *(1429)*
PAVIA *(568, 1431, 1525)*
PODOL *(1866)*
PUNIC *(W-264-146BC)*
RAMLA *(1177)*
REVAL *(1790)*
RIETI *(1821)*
ROSES *(W-1455-1485)*
SAMOS *(S-1824)*
SEDAN *(1870)*
SELBY *(1644)*
SESIA *(1524)*
SIRTE *(S-1942)*
SLUYS *(S-1340)*
SOMME *(1916, 1918)*
STOKE *(1487)*
TEXEL *(S-1653)*
TOURS *(732)*
TUNIS *(255BC)*
UCLES *(1109)*
VALMY *(1792)*
VARNA *(1444)*
VASAQ *(1442)*
VILNA *(1831)*
WAVRE *(1815)*
WÖRTH *(1870)*
XERES *(711)*
YPRES *(1914, 1915, 1917, 1918)*
ZENTA *(1697)*
ZNAIM *(1809)*

6

AACHEN *(1944)*
ACTIUM *(S-31BC)*
AFGHAN *(W-1838-1842, 1979-1987)*

ALFORD *(1645)*
ALIWAL *(1846)*
ANGORA *(1402)*
ARBELA *(331BC)*
ARCOLA *(1796)*
ARGAUM *(1803)*
ARKLOW *(1798)*
ARMADA *(S-1588)*
ARNHEM *(1944)*
ARQUES *(1589)*
ARTOIS *(1915)*
ASPERN *(1809)*
ASSAYE *(1803)*
ATBARA *(1898)*
AUNEAU *(1587)*
BALKAN *(W-1912, 1913)*
BARNET *(1471)*
BAYLEN *(1808)*
BERLIN *(1945)*
BOXTEL *(1794)*
BRAILA *(1773)*
BUSACO *(1810)*
CAMDEN *(1780, 1781)*
CANDIA *(1648)*
CANNAE *(216BC)*
CHIARI *(1701)*
CHILOE *(1826)*
CITATE *(1854)*
CYSSUS *(191BC)*
DELIUM *(424BC)*
DENAIN *(1712)*
DIEPPE *(1942)*
DUNBAR *(1296, 1650)*
DÜPPEL *(1864)*
ELINGA *(206BC)*
ENSLIN *(1899)*
FAMARS *(1793)*
FERKEH *(1896)*
GERONA *(1809)*
GUJRÁT *(1849)*
HARLAW *(1411)*
HASHIN *(1885)*
HEXHAM *(1464)*
HIMERA *(409BC)*
HOCHST *(1622)*
HUESCA *(1837)*

INCHON *(1950)*
INGOGO *(1881)*
INGOUR *(1855)*
JARNAC *(1569)*
JHANSI *(1857)*
KAFFIR *(W-1846-1852)*
KALISZ *(1706)*
KOHIMA *(1942)*
KONIEH *(1831)*
KOREAN *(W-1950-1953)*
KURDLA *(1795)*
LANDEN *(1693)*
LANNOY *(1567)*
LEMNOS *(S-1913)*
LIOPPO *(1860)*
LONATO *(1796)*
LÜTZEN *(1632, 1813)*
MAJUBA *(1881)*
MALAGA *(S-1704)*
MALAYA *(1941, W-1948-1960)*
MALDON *(991)*
MANILA *(S-1898)*
MANTUA *(1797)*
MARGUS *(285, 505)*
MIDWAY *(S-1942)*
MINCIO *(1796, 1814)*
MINDEN *(1759)*
MOHACS *(1526, 1687)*
MOSCOW *(1941)*
MUKDEN *(1905, 1948)*
MULTAN *(1848)*
MYCALE *(479BC)*
NACHOD *(1866)*
NÁJARA *(1367)*
NARVIK *(1940, S-1940)*
NASEBY *(1645)*
NESBIT *(1402)*
NOTIUM *(407BC)*
NOVARA *(1849)*
OBIDOS *(1808)*
OPORTO *(1809)*
ORTHEZ *(1814)*
ORTONA *(1943)*
OSWEGO *(1756)*
OULART *(1798)*
PEKING *(1214)*

PINKLE *(1547)*
PLEI ME *(1965)*
PLEVNA *(1877)*
PODOLL *(1866)*
PRAGUE *(1620, 1757)*
RABAUL *(1943)*
RIVOLI *(1797)*
ROCROI *(1643)*
ROLICA *(1808)*
SADOWA *(1866)*
SAIGON *(1968)*
SANGRO *(1943)*
SESKAR *(1790)*
SHILOH *(1862)*
SILPIA *(206BC)*
SINOPE *(S-1853)*
SIX-DAY *(W-1967)*
SUAKIN *(1888)*
TARBES *(1814)*
THABOR *(1799)*
THEBES *(335BC)*
TORGAU *(1760)*
TOWTON *(1461)*
TUDELA *(1808)*
USHANT *(S-1778, S-1794)*
VARESE *(1859)*
VYBORG *(1918)*
WAGRAM *(1809)*
WARSAW *(1656, 1794, 1831,*
1914, 1939, 1943,
1944)
WERBEN *(1631)*
WIAZMA *(1812)*
XIMENA *(1811)*
YARMUK *(636)*
ZAMORA *(901)*
ZÜRICH *(1799)*

7

ABOUKIR *(1799, 1801)*
ABU KLEA *(1885)*
ALARCOS *(1185)*
ALBUERA *(1811)*
ALKMAAR *(1573, 1799)*

ALMANSA *(1707)*
ALNWICK *(1093)*
ANTIOCH *(244BC, 1098)*
ASHDOWN *(871)*
ATHENRY *(1316)*
ATLANTA *(1864)*
AUGHRIM *(1691)*
BADAJOZ *(1812)*
BAPAUME *(1871)*
BARROSA *(1811)*
BASSANO *(1796)*
BAUTZEN *(1813)*
BELMONT *(1899)*
BÉTHUNE *(1707)*
BITONTO *(1734)*
BORISOV *(1812)*
BRECHIN *(1452)*
BRIENNE *(1814)*
BRITAIN *(A-1940)*
BULL RUN *(1861, 1862)*
CARACHA *(1813)*
CARNOUL *(1739)*
CARRHAE *(53BC)*
CASSANO *(1705, 1799)*
CASSINO *(1944)*
CHÂLONS *(366, 451)*
CHOCZIM *(1799)*
CLISSAU *(1702)*
COLENSO *(1899)*
CORINTH *(429BC, 394BC, 1862)*
CORONEL *(S-1914)*
CORUNNA *(1809)*
COUTRAS *(1587)*
CRAONNE *(1814)*
CRAVANT *(1423)*
CREFELD *(1758)*
CRIMEAN *(W-1853-1856)*
CURICTA *(49BC)*
CZASLAU *(1742)*
DEVIZES *(1643)*
DRESDEN *(1813)*
DUNKELD *(1689)*
DUNKIRK *(S-1666, 1940)*
ECKMÜHL *(1809)*
ECNOMUS *(256BC)*
ELK HORN *(1862)*

ESSLING *(1809)*
EVESHAM *(1265)*
FALKIRK *(1298, 1746)*
FERRARA *(1815)*
FLEURUS *(1622, 1690, 1794)*
FLODDEN *(1513)*
FORNOVO *(1495)*
GALICIA *(1914)*
GORARIA *(1857)*
GROCHÓW *(1831)*
HARWICH *(S-1666)*
HASBAIN *(1408)*
HERRERA *(1837)*
HWAI-HAI *(1948)*
IDSTÄDT *(1850)*
IWO JIMA *(1945)*
JUTLAND *(S-1916)*
KALUNGA *(1814)*
KAPOLNA *(1849)*
KILSYTH *(1645)*
KLISSOW *(1702)*
KOSSOVA *(1448)*
KRASNOI *(1812)*
LA HOGUE *(S-1692)*
LEGHORN *(1653)*
LEIPZIG *(1813)*
LEPANTO *(S-1571)*
LEUCTRA *(371BC)*
LEUTHEN *(1757)*
LIBENAU *(1866)*
LINCOLN *(1141, 1217)*
LUZZARA *(1702)*
MAGENTA *(1859)*
MAGNANO *(1799)*
MARENGO *(1800)*
MARGATE *(1387)*
MATAPAN *(S-1941)*
MATCHIN *(1791)*
MEMPHIS *(459BC, 1862)*
MESSINA *(S-1666, 1718)*
MILAZZO *(1860)*
MINORCA *(S-1756)*
MÖCKERN *(1813)*
MONDOVI *(1796)*
NAM DONG *(1964)*
NANKING *(1949)*

NEWBURN *(1640)*
NEWBURY *(1643, 1644)*
NEW ROSS *(1798)*
NIVELLE *(1813)*
OKINAWA *(S-1945)*
ORLÉANS *(1870)*
OURIQUE *(1139)*
PALERMO *(1848)*
PANIPAT *(1526, 1556)*
PLASSEY *(1757)*
PLATAEA *(479BC, 429BC)*
PLOVDIV *(1878)*
POLOTSK *(1812)*
POLTAVA *(1709)*
PRESTON *(1648, 1715)*
PULTUSK *(1703, 1806)*
RAUCOUX *(1746)*
RAVENNA *(729, 1512)*
REDINHA *(1811)*
RIO SECO *(1808)*
ROSTOCK *(1677)*
SABUGAL *(1811)*
SAGUNTO *(1811)*
SAINTES *(1242)*
SAKARIA *(1921)*
SALAMIS *(S-480BC)*
SALERNO *(1943)*
SAMNITE *(W-290BC)*
SEGEWÁR *(1849)*
SEMPACH *(1386)*
SENEFFE *(1674)*
SINUIJU *(1951)*
SKALITZ *(1866)*
SOBRAON *(1846)*
ST DENIS *(1567)*
ST LUCIA *(S-1794)*
TALKHAN *(1221)*
TANAGRA *(457BC)*
TARANTO *(S-1940)*
TELAMON *(225BC)*
THAPSUS *(46BC)*
TICINUS *(218BC)*
TOURNAI *(1581, 1709, 1794)*
TREBBIA *(218BC, 1799)*
TURBIGO *(1859)*
UPPSALA *(1520, 1521)*

VIETNAM *(W-1959-1979)*
VIGO BAY *(1702)*
VILAGOS *(1521)*
VIMIERO *(1808)*
VITEBSK *(1812)*
VITORIA *(1813)*
VOUILLÉ *(507)*
WAITZEN *(1849)*
WARBURG *(1760)*
WEPENER *(1900)*
YASHIMA *(1184)*
ZALLACA *(1086)*

8

ACAPULCO *(1855)*
AIX ROADS *(S-1809)*
AJNADAIN *(634)*
ALBUFERA *(1812)*
ALMENARA *(1710)*
ANTIETAM *(1862)*
ARDENNES *(1944) *4*
ASSUNDUN *(1016)*
AYACUCHO *(1824)*
AZIMGHUR *(1858)*
BASTOGNE *(1944)*
BERESINA *(1812)*
BIR HAKIM *(1942)*
BLENHEIM *(1704)*
BLUEBERG *(1806)*
BORODINO *(1812)*
BOSWORTH *(1485)*
BOUVINES *(1214)*
BROOKLYN *(1776)*
CALDIERO *(1796)*
CARTHAGE *(152BC, 533)*
CASTALLA *(1813)*
CAWNPORE *(1857)*
CHATALJA *(1912)*
CHERITON *(1644)*
CHIPPEWA *(1814)*
CLONTARF *(1014)*
CORAL SEA *(S-1942)*
COURTRAI *(1302)*

CRUSADES *(W-1099, 1148, 1189-1192, 1202) *2*
CULLODEN *(1746)*
CUSTOZZA *(1848, 1866)*
DAMASCUS *(635, 1401, 1918)*
DANNOURA *(S-1185)*
DOMINICA *(S-1782)*
DROGHEDA *(1649)*
DRUMCLOG *(1679)*
EDGEHILL *(1642)*
EDINGTON *(878)*
FAIR OAKS *(1862)*
FLANDERS *(1914, 1915, 1940)*
FLUSHING *(1809)*
FONTENOY *(1745)*
FORMIGNY *(1450)*
GEMBLOUX *(1578)*
GERGOVIA *(52BC)*
GITSCHIN *(1866)*
GÜNZBURG *(1805)*
HASTINGS *(1066)*
HATFIELD *(632)*
HOMILDON *(1402)*
INKERMAN *(1854)*
IRAN-IRAQ *(W-1980-1988) *1*
ITAMARCA *(S-1640)*
JAPAN SEA *(S-1904)*
JEMAPPES *(1792)*
KANDAHAR *(1221, 1648, 1880)*
KATZBACH *(1813)*
KLUSHINO *(1610)*
KULEVCHA *(1829)*
KULIKOVO *(1380)*
KUMANOVO *(1912)*
LAFFELDT *(1747)*
LANDSHUT *(1809)*
LANGPORT *(1645)*
LANGSIDE *(1568)*
LAUFFELD *(1746)*
LEONTINI *(211BC)*
LIAOYANG *(1904)*
LIEGNITZ *(1760)*
MAGNESIA *(190BC)*
MALVALLI *(1799)*
MANTINEA *(418BC, 362BC, 295BC, 207BC)*

MARATHON *(490BC)*
MESSINES *(1917)*
METAURUS *(207BC)*
MOLLWITZ *(1741)*
MONASTIR *(1912)*
MÜHLBERG *(1547)*
NANTWICH *(1644)*
NAVARINO *(S-1827)*
NIQUITAS *(1813)*
NIVELLES *(1813)*
OMDURMAN *(1898)*
PALESTRO *(1859)*
PALO ALTO *(1846)*
PEA RIDGE *(1862)*
PELUSIUM *(525BC, 321BC)*
PESHAWAR *(1001)*
PIACENZA *(1746)*
PHILIPPI *(42BC)*
POITIERS *(1356)*
PORTLAND *(S-1653)*
QUIBERON *(S-1759)*
RICHMOND *(1862)*
ROSAS BAY *(S-1809)*
ROSSBACH *(1757)*
ROVEREDO *(1796)*
SANTAREM *(1834)*
SANTIAGO *(S-1898)*
SARATOGA *(1777)*
SEIDLITZ *(1831)*
SEMINARA *(1495, 1503)*
SHANGHAI *(1937)*
SIMANCAS *(939)*
SMOLENSK *(1708, 1812,*
1941)
SOISSONS *(486)*
SORAUREN *(1813)*
SPION KOP *(1900)*
ST ALBANS *(1455, 1461)*
ST DIZIER *(1814)*
STRATTON *(1643)*
SYRACUSE *(413BC)*
SZEGEDIN *(1849)*
TALAVERA *(1809)*
TALIKOTA *(1565)*
TCHESINÉ *(S-1770)*
TEN YEARS *(W-1868-1878)*

THE DOWNS *(S-1666)*
THETFORD *(870)*
TOULOUSE *(1814)*
TRUELLAS *(1793)*
TSUSHIMA *(1419, 1905)*
TURNHOUT *(1597)*
VALEGGIO *(1848)*
VALTEZZA *(1821)*
VERNEUIL *(1424)*
VILLIERS *(1870)*
WATERLOO *(1815)*
WURSCHEN *(1813)*
ZENDECAN *(1039)*
ZORNDORF *(1758)*

9

AGINCOURT *(1415)*
AGNADELLO *(1509)*
AHMADABAD *(1780)*
AKHALZIKH *(1828)*
ALGECIRAS *(S-1801)*
ANGLO-SIKH *(W-1845-1848)*
ARGINUSAE *(406BC)*
ASTRAKHAN *(1569)*
AUERSTÄDT *(1806)*
AYLESFORD *(455)*
BALACLAVA *(1854)*
BALLYMORE *(1798)*
BENEVENTO *(1266)*
BORGHETTO *(1796)*
BRENTFORD *(1642)*
BYZANTIUM *(318BC)*
CAPE HENRY *(1781)*
CAPORETTO *(1917)*
CARTAGENA *(S-1588)*
CASTILLON *(1453)*
CASTLEBAR *(1798)*
CERIGNOLA *(1503)*
CERISOLES *(1454)*
CHAERONEA *(338BC, 86BC)*
CHALGROVE *(1643)*
CHAMPAGNE *(1915)*
CHAMPLAIN *(S-1814)*
CHEBRËISS *(1798)*
CROSSKEYS *(1862)*

HISTORY – BATTLES & WARS

DENNEWITZ *(1813)*
DETTINGEN *(1743)*
DORYLAEUM *(1097)*
DUNGENESS *(S-1652)*
EDGEWORTH *(1469)*
EL ALAMEIN *(1942)*
ELCHINGEN *(1805)*
ESPIERRES *(1794)*
FALKLANDS *(W-1982)*
FISH CREEK *(1855)*
FRIEDLAND *(1807)*
GALLIPOLI *(1915)*
GIBRALTAR *(1704)*
HALIARTUS *(395BC)*
HÉRICOURT *(1474)*
HOCHKIRCH *(1758)*
HÖCHSTÄDT *(1800)*
INDO-CHINA *(W-1946-1954)*
JERUSALEM *(1187, 1917, 1948)*
KARAMURAN *(1225)*
KISSINGEN *(1866)*
LA BICOCCA *(1522)*
LANSDOWNE *(1643)*
LEXINGTON *(1775, 1861)*
LEYTE GULF *(S-1944)*
LINCELLES *(1793)*
LINKÖPING *(1598)*
LIPPSTÄDT *(1632)*
MANSFIELD *(1864)*
MANZIKERT *(1071)*
MARIGNANO *(1515, 1859)*
MILLESIMO *(1796)*
MÖESKIRCH *(1800)*
MORGARTEN *(1315)*
NAUPACTUS *(429BC)*
NEGAPATAM *(S-1782)*
NUJUFGHUR *(1857)*
OLTENITZA *(1853)*
OTTERBURN *(1388)*
OUDENARDE *(1708)*
PELEKANON *(1326)*
PHARSALUS *(48BC)*
PIRMACENS *(1793)*
PORTO NOVO *(1781)*
PRINCETON *(1777)*
QUISTELLO *(1734)*

RAMILLIES *(1706)*
RATHMINES *(1649)*
RUREMONDE *(1794)*
SALAMANCA *(1812)*
SAMARKAND *(1220)*
SANTA CRUZ *(S-1657, S-1797)*
SANTANDER *(1937)*
SARAGOSSA *(1710, 1809)*
SCHWECHAT *(1848)*
SEDGEMOOR *(1685)*
SEVENOAKS *(1450)*
SHINOWARA *(1183)*
SOLFERINO *(1859)*
ST ANTOINE *(1652)*
STEENKIRK *(1692)*
ST QUENTIN *(1557, 1871)*
ST VINCENT *(S-1693, S-1780, S-1797)*
TARRAGONA *(1811)*
TCHERNAYA *(1855)*
TRAFALGAR *(S-1805)*
TRAUTENAU *(1866)*
TREBIZOND *(1461)*
VALTELINE *(1812)*
VAUCHAMPS *(1814)*
VIMY RIDGE *(1917)*
WAKEFIELD *(1460)*
WANDIWASH *(1760, 1780)*
WHITE OAKS *(1862)*
WORCESTER *(1642, 1651)*
WORLD WAR I *(W-1914-1918)*
WÜRTZBURG *(1796)*
YELLOW SEA *(S-1904)*
YOM KIPPUR *(W-1973)* *5
ZEEBRUGGE *(S-1918)*
ZÜLLICHAU *(1759)*

10

ABOUKIR BAY *(S-1798)* *3
ABYSSINIAN *(W-1935-1936)*
ADRIANOPLE *(323, 378, 1829, 1913)*
ALADJA DAGH *(1877)*
ALEXANDRIA *(642, 1801, S-1882)*

AMPHIPOLIS *(422BC)*
ANGLO-DUTCH *(W-1652-1654,*
1664-1667,
1672-1674)
ARGENTARIO *(378)*
ASPROMONTE *(1862)*
AUSTERLITZ *(1805)*
BEACHY HEAD *(S-1690)*
BENNINGTON *(1777)*
BLORE HEAD *(1459)*
BRANDYWINE *(1777)*
BRUNANBURH *(937)*
BUNKER HILL *(1775)*
CALATAFIMI *(1860)*
CAMPERDOWN *(S-1797)*
CAMPO SANTO *(1743)*
CEDAR CREEK *(1864)*
CHÂTEAUDUN *(1870)*
COLD HARBOR *(1864)*
COPENHAGEN *(S-1801, S-1807)*
DANNEVIRKE *(1331, 1848)*
DOGGER BANK *(S-1781, S-1915)*
DONNINGTON *(1644)*
DUNGAN HILL *(1647)*
ENGLEFIELD *(871)*
FEHRBELLIN *(1675)*
FINISTERRE *(S-1747, S-1805)*
FUTTEYPORE *(1857)*
GAINES' MILL *(1862)*
GERMANTOWN *(1777)*
GETTYSBURG *(1863)*
GRANT'S HILL *(1758)*
GRAVELOTTE *(1870)*
GUADELOUPE *(S-1782, S-1794)*
GUINEGATTE *(1513)*
HASTENBECK *(1757)*
HELIGOLAND *(S-1807, S-1914)*
HOLLABRUNN *(1805)*
ICHINOTANI *(1189)*
IMJIN RIVER *(1951)*
INVERLOCHY *(1645)*
JELLALABAD *(1842)*
JENKINS' EAR *(W-1739)*
KHOJAH PASS *(1842)*
KUNERSDORF *(1759)*
LAING'S NECK *(1881)*

LANDSKRONE *(1676)*
LAS SALINAS *(1528)*
LÜLE BURGAS *(1912)*
LUNDY'S LANE *(1814)*
LÜTZELBERG *(1758)*
MAHARAJPUR *(1843, 1859)*
MALPLAQUET *(1709)*
MARIENDAHL *(1645)*
MARS-LE-TOUR *(1870)*
MASERFIELD *(642)*
MILLI DUZOV *(1829)*
MONTEBELLO *(1800, 1859)*
MONTENOTTE *(1796)*
MOUNT TABOR *(1799)*
NAPOLEONIC *(W-1799-1815)*
NEERWINDEN *(1693, 1793)*
NEW ORLEANS *(S-1862)*
NÖRDLINGEN *(1634, 1645)*
OSTROLENKA *(1831, 1853)*
PAARDEBERG *(1900)*
PALESTRINA *(1849)*
PANDU NADDI *(1857)*
PENINSULAR *(W-1808-1814)*
PORT ARTHUR *(1894)*
QUATRE BRAS *(1815)*
RIVER PLATE *(S-1939)*
ROSEBECQUE *(1382)*
RUMERSHEIM *(1709)*
SANTA LUCIA *(1842)*
SEVASTOPOL *(1854)*
SEVEN PINES *(1862)*
SEVEN WEEKS *(W-1866) *6*
SEVEN YEARS *(W-1756-1763)*
SHREWSBURY *(1403)*
SOLWAY MOSS *(1542)*
STALINGRAD *(1942)*
STOLHOFFEN *(1707)*
STRASBOURG *(1870)*
SUCCESSION *(W-Spanish-1701-1713,*
Austrian-1740-1748)
TANNENBERG *(1410, 1914)*
TEL-EL-KEBIR *(1882)*
TETTENHALL *(910)*
TEWKESBURY *(1471)*
TINCHEBRAI *(1106)*
TRAVANCORE *(1789)*

241

HISTORY — BATTLES & WARS

UTSONOMIYA *(1868)*
VELESTINOS *(1897)*
WARTEMBERG *(1813)*
WORLD WAR II *(W-1939-1945)*
ZIEZICKSEE *(1302)*

11

AEGOSPOTAMI *(S-405BC)*
AQUAE SEXTIA *(S-102BC)*
ARAB-ISRAELI *(W-1973) *5*
BANNOCKBURN *(1314)*
BISMARCK SEA *(S-1943)*
BLANQUEFORT *(1450)*
BRAMHAM MOOR *(1408)*
BRIARS CREEK *(1779)*
CAMELODUNUM *(AD 43)*
CASTELNUOVA *(1796)*
CASTIGLIONE *(1706, 1796)*
CECRYPHALEA *(458BC)*
CHAMPAUBERT *(1814)*
CHATTANOOGA *(1863)*
CHICKAMAUGA *(1863)*
CHILIANWÁLA *(1849)*
CLIFTON MOOR *(1745)*
DEUTSCHBROD *(1422)*
DÜRRENSTEIN *(1805)*
FERRYBRIDGE *(1461)*
GIBBEL RUTTS *(1798)*
GROSS-BEEREN *(1813)*
GUADALAJARA *(1937)*
GUADALCANAL *(1942)*
HALIDON HILL *(1333)*
HEAVENFIELD *(634)*
HELSINGBORG *(1710)*
HENNERSDORF *(1745)*
HOHENLINDEN *(1800)*
ISANDHLWANA *(1879)*
KESSELSDORF *(1745)*
KIRK-KILISSE *(1912)*
LANGENSALZA *(1866)*
LOSTWITHIEL *(1644)*
MARSTON MOOR *(1644)*
MEGALOPOLIS *(331BC)*
MILETOPOLIS *(86BC)*
MILL SPRINGS *(1862)*

MODDER RIVER *(1899)*
MONTCONTOUR *(1569)*
MONTINIRAIL *(1814)*
MOOKERHEIDE *(1574)*
NOISSEVILLE *(1870)*
NORTHAMPTON *(1460)*
PEARL HARBOR *(S-1941)*
PFAFFENDORF *(1760)*
PHILIPHAUGH *(1645)*
PRESTONPANS *(1745)*
QUIBERON BAY *(S-1759)*
RHEINFELDEN *(1638)*
RIETFONTEIN *(1899)*
RORKE'S DRIFT *(1879)*
SAARBRÜCKEN *(1870)*
SAUCHIE BURN *(1488)*
SHERIFFMUIR *(1715)*
SIDI BARRÂNI *(1940)*
STAVRICHANI *(1739)*
TAGLIACOZZO *(1268)*
TAILLEBOURG *(1242)*
THERMOPYLAE *(480BC)*
THIRTY YEARS *(W-1618-1648)*
TRINCOMALEE *(1759, 1782)*
VILLAFRANCA *(1812)*
VINEGAR HILL *(1798)*
WEDNESFIELD *(911)*
WHITE PLAINS *(1776)*
WORLD WAR ONE *(W-1914-1918)*
WORLD WAR TWO *(W-1939-1945)*

12

ALGECIRAS BAY *(S-1801)*
ANGLO-BURMESE *(W-1823-1825,*
                1852-1853)
ARCIS-SUR-AUBE *(1814)*
ATHERTON MOOR *(1643)*
BARQUISIMETO *(1813)*
BRADDOCK DOWN *(1643)*
CARBERRY HILL *(1567)*
CHICKAHOMINY *(1862)*
ELANDSLAAGTE *(1899)*
FLODDEN FIELD *(1513)*
GIBRALTAR BAY *(S-1782)*
HAMPTON ROADS *(S-1862)*

HOMILDON HILL *(1402)*
HUNDRED YEARS *(W-1337-1453)*
ICLISTAVISUS *(AD16)*
INDEPENDENCE *(W-American-
1775-1783,
Greek-1821-1829,
Israeli-1948-1949,
Italian-1859-1870)*
INDO-PAKISTAN *(W-1965, 1971)*
KÖNIGSWARTHA *(1813)*
LYNN HAVEN BAY *(1781)*
MONS-EN-PÉVÈLE *(1304)*
MÜNCHENGRÄTZ *(1866)*
MURFREESBORO *(1862)*
PENOBSCOT BAY *(S-1779)*
PRAIRIE GROVE *(1862)*
RONCESVALLES *(778, 1813)*
RULLION GREEN *(1666)*
RUSSO-SWEDISH *(W-1788-1790)*
RUSSO-TURKISH *(W-1828-1829)*
SARANTOPORON *(1912)*
SERINGAPATAM *(1792)*
SOUTHWOLD BAY *(S-1672)*
SPOTSYLVANIA *(1864)*
SUNGARI RIVER *(1947)*
TET OFFENSIVE *(1968)*
VALENCIENNES *(1566, 1656)*
VILLAVICIOSA *(1710)*
WILLIAMSBURG *(1862)*
WILSON'S CREEK *(1861)*
WROTHAM HEATH *(1554)*

13

AIX-LA-CHAPELLE *(1795)*
BOROUGHBRIDGE *(1322)*
BOSWORTH FIELD *(1485)*
CAPE ST VINCENT *(S-1693, S-1780,
S-1797)*
CASTELFIDARDO *(1860)*
CHESAPEAKE BAY *(S-1781)*
CYNOSCEPHALAE *(197BC)*
FRANKENHAUSEN *(1525)*
GLENMARRESTON *(683)*
GREAT NORTHERN *(W-1700-1721)*

INVERKEITHING *(1317)*
KILLIECRANKIE *(1689)*
LITTLE BIG HORN *(1876)*
MAGERSFONTEIN *(1899)*
MEGALETAPHRUS *(740BC)*
NAVAS DE TOLOSA *(1212)*
NEVILLE'S CROSS *(1346)*
NEWTOWNBUTLER *(1689)*
NORTHALLERTON *(1138)*
NORTH FORELAND *(S-1653, S-1666)*
PASSCHENDAELE *(1917)*
PELOPONNESIAN *(W-431BC-404BC)*
PHILIPPINE SEA *(S-1944)*
PORTO PRAIA BAY *(S-1781)*
SIEVERSHAUSEN *(1553)*
RUSSO-JAPANESE *(W-1904-1905)*
SPANISH ARMADA *(1588)*
THE WILDERNESS *(1864)*
WHITE MOUNTAIN *(1620)*
WHITE OAK SWAMP *(1862)*
YENIDJE VARDAR *(1912)*
ZUSMARSHAUSEN *(1647)*

14

AUSTRO-PRUSSIAN *(W-1866)* *6
BERWICK-ON-TWEED *(1296)*
BOTHWELL BRIDGE *(1679)*
CAMPUS CASTORUM *(AD69)*
CAPE FINISTERRE *(S-1747, S-1805)*
CHÂTEAU THIERRY *(1814, 1918)*
CONSTANTINOPLE *(668, 1261)*
CROPREDY BRIDGE *(1644)*
DRUMMOSSIE MOOR *(1746)*
FRANCO-PRUSSIAN *(W-1870-1871)*
FREDERICKSBURG *(1862, 1863)*
FUENTES DE ONORO *(1811)*
HOHENFRIEDBERG *(1745)*
LA BELLE FAMILLE *(1759)*
MACASSAR STRAIT *(S-1942)*
MORTIMER'S CROSS *(1461)*
NICHOLSON'S NECK *(1899)*
PUSAN PERIMETER *(1950)*
SANTIAGO DE CUBA *(1898)*
SINAI PENINSULA *(1956)*

HISTORY − BATTLES & WARS

STAMFORD BRIDGE *(1066, 1453)*
TONDEMAN'S WOODS *(1754)*
WARS OF THE ROSES *(W-1455-1485)*

15

AMATOLA MOUNTAIN *(1846)*
APPOMATTOX RIVER *(1865)*

BEAUNE-LA-ROLANDE *(1870)*
GROSS-JAGERSDORF *(1757)*
HELIGOLAND BIGHT *(S-1914)*
MEXICAN-AMERICAN *(W-1846-1848)*
PLAINS OF ABRAHAM *(1759)*
PUENTE DE LA REYNE *(1872)*
RESACA DE LA PALMA *(1846)*
SPANISH-AMERICAN *(W-1898)*
TEUTOBURGER WALD *(AD9)*

HISTORY

SIEGES, INCIDENTS & PLOTS

(I) = Incident   (M) =Massacre   (P) = Plot/conspiracy   (R) = Riot(s)
(REB) = Rebellion/rising/revolt   (REV) = Revolution
¶ = Non-wartime siege

4

ACRE *(1189, 1799, 1832, 1840)*
BONN *(1689, 1703)*
COMO *(1127)*
CONI *(1691, 1744)*
JULY *(REV-1830) (P-1944)*
KARS *(1855)*
KEHL *(1796-1797)*
KET'S *(REB-1549)*
METZ *(1552-1553, 1870)*
MONS *(1691, 1709, 1746, 1792)*
NICE *(1705)*
RIGA *(1700, 1710)*
ROME *(1527, 1849)*
SCIO *(1822)*

SUEZ *(I-1956)*
TROY *(c12th C BC)*
YORK *(1644)*

5

ARRAS *(1640)*
BOXER *(REB-1900)*
BREDA *(1625,1793)*
CADE'S *(REB-1450)*
CADIZ *(1812)*
CALVI *(1794)*
CAPUA *(211BC, 1501, 1799)*
CONDÉ *(1676, 1793, 1794)*
CORFU *(1536, 1716-1718)*
CUMAE *(553)*
DANES *(M-1002)*
DELHI *(1857)*

DERBY *(R-1831)*
DOUAY *(1710)*
GAETA *(1707, 1734, 1860-1861)*
GENOA *(1684, 1747, 1800)*
GHENT *(1706)*
GLATZ *(1622, 1742, 1807)*
HERAT *(1837-1838, 1856)*
LEITH *(1560)*
LIÈGE *(1468, 1702, 1914)*
LILLE *(1708, 1792)*
LYONS *(1793)*
MAINZ *(1689, 1793)*
MALTA *(1565, 1798, 1800, 1940-1942)*
MY LAI *(M-1968)*
NAMUR *(1692, 1695)*
PADUA *(1509)*
PANAY *(I-1937)*

PARIS *(885-886, 1594, 1870-1871)*
PAVIA *(1525, 1655)*
ROUEN *(1419, 1449, 1591)*
THORN *(1703)*
TUNIS *(1270, 1535)*
TURIN *(1640, 1706)*
XERES *(1262)*
YPRES *(1648, 1794)*

6

ALESIA *(52BC)*
AMIENS *(1597)*
ANCONA *(1799)*
BATAAN *(1942)*
BERLIN *(1948-1949)*
BILBAO *(1835, 1874, 1937)*
BURGOS *(1812, 1813)*
CALAIS *(1346-1347, 1558, 1596, 1940)*
CANDIA *(1667-1669)*
CHALUS *(1199)*
CRACOW *(1702, 1794)*
DANZIG *(1734, 1793, 1807, 1813-1814)*
DUBLIN *(1170, 1500, 1649)*
EASTER *(REB-1916)*
EXETER *(1136)*
FRENCH *(REV-1789-1795)*
GERONA *(1808-1809)*
GORDON *(R-1780)*
ISMAIL *(1770, 1790)*
JANINA *(1913)*
LANDAU *(1702, 1703, 1793)*
LERIDA *(1647, 1707, 1810)*
LEYDEN *(1574)*
MADRID *(1936-1939)*
MALAGA *(1487)*
MANTUA *(1796-1797)*
MUKDEN *(I-1931)*
NAPLES *(1495, 1799, 1806)*
OLMÜTZ *(1741, 1758)*
ORSINI *(P-1858)*
OSTEND *(1601-1604, 1706, 1745, 1798)*

PLEVNA *(1877)*
POPISH *(P-1678)*
PRAGUE *(1741-1744)*
QUEBEC *(1759)*
RHEIMS *(1359)*
RHODES *(1306-1309, 1480, 1522)*
SLAVES' *(REB-73-71BC)*
TOBRUK *(1941, 1942)*
TOLEDO *(1936)*
TOULON *(1707, 1793)*
VANNES *(1342)*
VENICE *(1849)*
VERDUN *(1792, 1916)*
VIENNA *(1529, 1683, 1848)*
WARSAW *(1831, 1939, 1944)*
WYATT'S *(REB-1554)*
XATIVA *(1246, 1707)*
ZÜRICH *(1544)*

7

ALGIERS *(1682-1683, 1816, 1830)*
ALMEIDA *(1810)*
ALTMARK *(I-1940)*
ANTWERP *(1584-1585, 1832, 1914)*
AVIGNON *(1226)*
BADAJOZ *(1385, 1396, 1542, 1705, 1811, 1812)*
BAGHDAD *(1258)*
BERWICK *(1296, 1333, 1481)*
BETHUNE *(1710)*
BOLOGNA *(1506, 1796, 1799)*
BRESCIA *(1512, 1849)*
BRESLAU *(1807)*
BRISACH *(1638)*
BRISTOL *(R-1831)*
BRIXTON *(R-1981)*
CHESTER *(1643-1646)*
CHILLON *(1536)*
CHINESE *(REV-1911)*
CHITRAL *(1895)*
CORDOBA *(1012)*

HISTORY — SIEGES, INCIDENTS & PLOTS

CORINTH *(1205, 1209)*
COSSACK *(REB-1648-1657)*
CREMONA *(1702)*
CURRAGH *(I-1914)*
DRESDEN *(1756, 1760, 1813)*
DUNKIRK *(1646, 1793)*
FIFTEEN *(REB-1715)*
GLENCOE *(M-1692)*
GRANADA *(1491-1492)*
HAARLEM *(1572-1573)*
HUMAITÁ *(1868)*
KOMÁROM *(1849)*
LA MOTTE *(1634)*
LEIPZIG *(1547, 1642)*
LUCKNOW *(1857)*
MESSINA *(1282, 1719, 1848)*
OCTOBER *(REV-1917)*
ORLÉANS *(1428-1429, 1563)*
QUESNAY *(1793-1794)*
RIDOLFI *(P-1571)*
RUSSIAN *(REV-1917)*
SCUTARI *(1913)*
SEVILLE *(1248)*
ST PAUL'S *(R-1980)*
TORTOSA *(1810-1811)*
TOXTETH *(R-1981)*
TOURNAI *(1340, 1513, 1581,*
1667, 1709, 1792)
ZUTPHEN *(1586)*

CULTURAL *(REV-1965-1967)*
DECEMBER *(REB-1825)*
DROGHEDA *(1649)*
FEBRUARY *(REV-1917)*
FLUSHING *(1809)*
GLORIOUS *(REV-1688)*
HARFLEUR *(1415)*
JACOBITE *(REB-1715, 1745)*
KANDAHAR *(1521, 1839-1842)*
KHARTOUM *(1884-1885)*
LIMERICK *(1651, 1690-1691)*
MAFEKING *(1899-1900)*
MANNHEIM *(1793)*
MONMOUTH *(REB-1685)*
MOSS SIDE *(R-1981)*
NAGASAKI *(I-1945)*
NO POPERY *(R-1780)*
NUMANTIA *(134-133BC)*
OFFICERS' *(P-1944)*
OLIVENZA *(1811)*
PAMPLONA *(1813)*
PEASANTS' *(REB-1381)*
PETERLOO *(M-1819)*
RICHMOND *(1864-1865)*
ROXBURGH *(1460)*
RYE HOUSE *(P-1683)*
SAGUNTUM *(219BC)*
SMOLENSK *(1611, 1812)*
TEMESVAR *(1716)*
TOULOUSE *(c848, 1229)*
VALENCIA *(1812)*
YORKTOWN *(1781)*

8

AMRITSAR *(R-1919)*
ARMENIAN *(M-1895)*
BASTILLE *(I-1789)*
BELGRADE *(1456, 1521,*
1717, 1789)
BESANÇON *(1668, 1674)*
BORDEAUX *(1451, 1453)*
BOUCHAIN *(1711)*
BOULOGNE *(1544)*
BRUSSELS *(1695, 1746)*
BUDAPEST *(1541, 1686,*
1944-1945)
CHARTRES *(1568)*

9

ALGECIRAS *(1342-1344)*
BABINGTON *(P-1586)*
BARCELONA *(1471, 1697, 1705,*
1706, 1714)
BAY OF PIGS *(I-1961)*
BELLE ISLE *(1761)*
BOIS-LE-DUC *(1601, 1603, 1794)*
BOMARSUND *(1854)*
CARTAGENA *(1706, 1873-1874)*
CHARLEROI *(1672, 1690)*

CHERBOURG *(1418, 1758)*
COMPIÈGNE *(1430)*
EDINBURGH *(1093, 1296)*
FAMAGUSTA *(1571)*
FORTY-FIVE *(REB-1745)*
GIBRALTAR *(1704, 1779,*
1782-1783)
GÖTTINGEN *(1760)*
GREAT FIRE *(I-1666)*
GREAT TREK *(I-1835-1837)*
GRONINGEN *(1594, 1678)*
GUNPOWDER *(P-1605)*
HIROSHIMA *(I-1945)*
JERUSALEM *(c1400BC, 588BC,*
AD70, 637, 1099)
KIMBERLEY *(1899-1900)*
LADYSMITH *(1899-1900)*
LENINGRAD *(1941-1943)*
LONG MARCH *(I-1934-1935)*
MAGDEBURG *(1631, 1806)*
MONTARGIS *(1427)*
MONTAUBAN *(1621)*
PERPIGNAN *(1542, 1642)*
PHARISEES' *(R-90BC)*
SARAGOSSA *(1710, 1808, 1809)*
SCAPA FLOW *(I-1919)*
SILISTRIA *(1854)*
ST QUENTIN *(1557)*
STRALSUND *(1715)*
TARRAGONA *(1813)*
VICKSBURG *(1863)*

10

ADRIANOPLE *(1912-1913)*
BLACK DEATH *(I-14th C, 1665)*
CATO STREET *(P-1820)*
CHARLESTON *(1780, 1863-1865)*
COLCHESTER *(1648)*
COPENHAGEN *(1658, 1801, 1807)*
DOGGER BANK *(I-1904)*
GLOUCESTER *(1643)*
HANDSWORTH *(R-1985)*
HEIDELBERG *(1688)*
INDUSTRIAL *(REV-1760s-)*

LANDRECIES *(1712, 1794)*
LA ROCHELLE *(1573, 1628)*
LITTLE ROCK *(I-1957)*
LUXEMBOURG *(1795)*
MAESTRICHT *(1579, 1673, 1703,*
1748, 1793-1794)
MAGNA CARTA *(I-1215)*
MONTEVIDEO *(1807, 1814)*
NORE MUTINY *(I-1797)*
NOTTINGHAM *(R-1831)*
PHALSBOURG *(1814, 1815, 1870)*
PORT ARTHUR *(1904)*
PORTUGUESE *(REV-1641-1668)*
SEVASTOPOL *(1854-1855,*
1941-1942)
STALINGRAD *(1942-1943)*
STRASBOURG *(1870)*
THÉROUANNE *(1303, 1479, 1513)*
THIONVILLE *(1792)*

11

BASING HOUSE *(1643-1645)*
DIEN BIEN PHU *(1954)*
ENTEBBE RAID *(I-1976)*
GREAT PLAGUE *(I-1665)*
GREAT SCHISM *(I-1378-1417)*
JAMESON RAID *(I-1895)*
LONDONDERRY *(1689)*
MISSOLONGHI *(1822, 1823,*
1825-1826)
PEARL HARBOR *(I-1941)*
PONDICHERRY *(1748)*
SCHWEIDNITZ *(1762, 1807)*
SHARPEVILLE *(M-1960)*
ST BRICE'S DAY *(M-1002)*
STRANGEWAYS *(¶-1990)*
VINEGAR HILL *(REB-1798)*

12

BERGEN-OP-ZOOM *(1588, 1622,*
1747, 1814)
BLOODY SUNDAY *(I-1905, 1972)*

HISTORY – SIEGES, INCIDENTS & PLOTS

FREDRIKSHALD *(1718)*
HARPER'S FERRY *(I-1859)*
INDIAN MUTINY *(I-1857-1858)*
PHILLIPSBURG *(1644, 1676, 1688, 1734, 1799-1800)*
SAN SEBASTIAN *(1813)*
SERINGAPATAM *(1792, 1799)*
SIDNEY STREET *(¶-1911)*
THROGMORTON'S *(P-1584)*
VALENCIENNES *(1677, 1793, 1794)*
WESTERPLATTE *(1939)*

SPAGHETTTI HOUSE *(¶-1975)*
ST BARTHOLOMEW *(M-1572)*

14

BALCOMBE STREET *(¶-1975)*
BOSTON TEA PARTY *(I-1773)*
BROADWATER FARM *(R-1985)*
CONSTANTINOPLE *(1453)*
IRANIAN EMBASSY *(¶-1980)*
SOUTH SEA BUBBLE *(I-1720)*

13

CIUDAD RODRIGO *(1810, 1812)*
GENERAL STRIKE *(I-1926)*
LIBYAN EMBASSY *(¶-1984)*
REIGN OF TERROR *(I-1793-1794)*

15

EDINBURGH CASTLE *(1571)*
ST VALENTINE'S DAY *(M-1929)*
TENNIS COURT OATH *(I-1789)*
TIANANMEN SQUARE *(M-1989)*
WALL STREET CRASH *(I-1929)*

HISTORY

TREATIES & ACTS

All Treaties except: (A) = Act   (D) = Diet   (E) = Edict

3

ABO *(1743)*
GIN *(A-1751)*
RIO *(1947)*
TEA *(A-1773)*

4

JAYS *(1704)*
KIEL *(1814)*
LOAN *(A-1773)*
LUND *(1679)*
LYON *(1601)*
RIGA *(1921)*
RIOT *(A-1715)*
ROME *(1957)*
TEST *(A-1673)*

5

AIGUN *(1858)*
ARRAS *(1482, 1579)*
BADEN *(1713)*
BASLE *(1499, 1795)*
BLOIS *(1505)*
BREDA *(1667)*
DOVER *(1670)*
FLEIX *(1580)*
GHENT *(1814)*

HAGUE *(1720)*
INDIA *(A-1784, 1858, 1919, 1935)*
JASSY *(1792)*
MINES *(A-1842)*
NOYON *(1516)*
OUCHY *(1912)*
PARIS *(1814, 1856, 1857, 1898, 1762, 1783, 1952)*
RIPON *(1640)*

STAMP *(A-1765)*
SUGAR *(A-1764)*
UNION *(A-1536, 1707, 1800)*
WORMS *(D-1521) (1743)*

6

AMIENS *(1802)*
ANKARA *(1930)*
BALLOT *(A-1872)*
BERLIN *(1728, 1742)*
BJORKO *(1905)*
BRUGES *(1375)*
ÉCOUEN *(E-1559)*
FUSSEN *(1745)*
KARDIS *(1661)*
KNARED *(1613)*
LISBON *(1668)*
LONDON *(1518, 1604, 1827,*
　　　　　1834, 1839, 1913,
　　　　　1915)
LUBECK *(1629)*
MADRID *(1630)*
MUNICH *(1552)*
MUTINY *(A-1689)*
NANTES *(E-1598)*
OLMÜTZ *(1850)*
PASSAU *(1552)*
PRAGUE *(1635, 1866)*
QUEBEC *(A-1774)*
RAZDIN *(1681)*
REFORM *(A-1832, 1867)*
SALBAI *(1782)*
SENLIS *(1493)*
SÈVRES *(1920)*
SPEYER *(D-1529)*
TILSIT *(1807)*
TROYES *(1420, 1564)*
VERELA *(1790)*
VIENNA *(1642, 1725,*
　　　　　1731, 1738)
ZBOROV *(1649)*
ZÜRICH *(1859)*

7

ALTMARK *(1629)*
AUSTRIA *(1726)*
BERWICK *(1560)*
DRESDEN *(1745)*
ÉTAPLES *(1492)*
ETERNAL *(E-1577)*
FACTORY *(A-1819, 1833)*
GRANADA *(1500)*
HANOVER *(1725)*
JANUARY *(E-1562)*
KALISCH *(1813)*
LATERAN *(1929)*
LOCARNO *(1925)*
MIKULOV *(1621)*
NANKING *(1842)*
NEMOURS *(1585)*
NEUILLY *(1919)*
NONSUCH *(1585)*
POOR LAW *(A-1601)*
RAPALLO *(1920, 1922)*
RASTATT *(1714)*
REVENUE *(A-1764)*
RYSWICK *(1697)*
SEVILLE *(1729)*
SISTOVA *(1791)*
TESCHEN *(1779)*
TREASON *(A-1534, 1554,*
　　　　　1571, 1581)
TRIANON *(1920)*
UTRECHT *(1571, 1713)*
VERVINS *(1598)*
WEDMORE *(879)*
WINDSOR *(1506)*
ZURAVNO *(1676)*

8

ABORTION *(A-1967)*
AUGSBURG *(1555)*
BARWALDE *(1631)*
BELGRADE *(1739)*
BERGERAC *(1577)*
BRUSSOLO *(1610)*

HISTORY — TREATIES & ACTS

CHAMBORD *(1552)*
CHERASIO *(1631)*
CLEAN AIR *(A-1955)*
CORN LAWS *(A-1815)*
EQUAL PAY *(A-1970)*
KILKENNY *(A-1367)*
LAUSANNE *(1922)*
MARRIAGE *(A-1753)*
PUGACHEV *(1773)*
PYRÉNÉES *(1659)*
RICHMOND *(1562)*
ROSKILDE *(1658)*
STOLBOVO *(1617)*
TIENTSIN *(1858)*
UCCIALLI *(1889)*
VOLSTEAD *(A-1919)*
WAITANGI *(1840)*

9

ARANJUERG *(1752)*
BARCELONA *(1493)*
BRETIGNEY *(1360)*
BUCHAREST *(1913)*
COMPIÈGNE *(1635, 1918)*
EDINBURGH *(1560)*
EDUCATION *(A-1870, 1902, 1918, 1944)*
ENCLOSURE *(A-1795, 1812)*
EXCLUSION *(A-1679)*
FRANKFURT *(1871)*
GREENWICH *(1543)*
INDEMNITY *(A-1727)*
IRISH LAND *(A-1870)*
JOINVILLE *(1584)*
KARLOWITZ *(1699)*
LICENSING *(A-1872, 1988)*
LUNÉVILLE *(1801)*
PANMUNJON *(1953)*
PRESSBURG *(1806)*
ST GERMAIN *(1920)*
STOCKHOLM *(1641, 1671, 1721)*
SUPREMACY *(A-1534)*
TRIENNIAL *(A-1641, 1694)*

10

ANDRUSSOVO *(1667)*
COPENHAGEN *(1660)*
KONIGSBERG *(1656)*
LONGJUMEAU *(1568)*
MINORITIES *(A-1919, 1920)*
NAVIGATION *(A-1651)*
PARLIAMENT *(A-1911, 1949)*
PORTSMOUTH *(1905)*
QUARTERING *(A-1765, 1774)*
REGULATION *(A-1773)*
SAN STEFANO *(1878)*
SETTLEMENT *(A-1701)*
SEPTENNIAL *(A-1716)*
TOLERATION *(E-313) (A-1689)*
TRAVENTHAL *(1700)*
UNIFORMITY *(A-1549)*
VERSAILLES *(1756, 1757, 1759, 1783, 1919)*
WESTPHALIA *(1648)*

11

ALTRANSTÄDT *(1706)*
BANK CHARTER *(A-1844)*
CAT AND MOUSE *(A-1913)*
CORPORATION *(A-1661)*
DECLARATION *(A-1766)*
FRIEDEWALDE *(1551)*
INTOLERABLE *(A-1774)*
KELLOGG PACT *(1928)*
RESTITUTION *(E-1635)*
ROAD TRAFFIC *(A-1930)*
SOUTH AFRICA *(A-1909)*
TORDESILLAS *(1494)*
VEREENIGING *(1902)*
WALLINGFORD *(1153)*
WESTMINSTER *(1654, 1655, 1756, 1758)*
ZSITVA-TOROK *(1606)*

12

BILL OF RIGHTS *(A-1689, 1791)*
BREST-LITOVSK *(1918)*
CAMPO FORMINO *(1797)*
ETERNAL PEACE *(533)*
HABEAS CORPUS *(A-1679)*
HAMPTON COURT *(1562)*
NORTH AMERICA *(A-1867)*
SAN ILDEFONSO *(1778)*
TRADE DISPUTE *(A-1927)*
WÜSTERHAUSEN *(1726)*

13

AIX-LA-CHAPELLE *(1748)*
FONTAINEBLEAU *(1743)*
RACE RELATIONS *(A-1972)*

14

CONSTANTINOPLE *(1913)*
MEDINA DEL CAMPO *(1489)*

15

COMBINATION LAWS *(A-1799)*
MUNICH AGREEMENT *(1938)*

MYTHOLOGY

(A) = Arthurian   (E) = Egyptian   (I) = Indian   (P) = Persian
(R) = Roman   (S) = Scandinavian (Norse)/Teutonic
All others Greek, (GR) in joint entries only
(C) = Creature   (G) = Group   (L) = Location
¶ = Object   * = Alternative spelling/name

3

ASK (S)
BES (E)
DIA
DIS (R-L)
EOS
GEB (E)
HEL (S)
IDA (L)
INO
ION
KAY (A)
MUT (E)
NUN (E-L)
NUT (E)
OPS (R)
PAN
PAX (R)
SET (E)
SHU (E)
SIF (S)
SOL (R)
TIW (S)
ULL (S)

4

ABAS
ACIS
AGNI (I)
AJAX
AMON (E) *1
AMUN (E) *1
APIS (E-C)
ARES
ARGO ¶
  (ship)

ATUM (E)
AUGE
BALI (I)
BAST (E)
BIAS
BUTO (E)
CACA (R)
CETO
CIOS (L)
CLIO
  (Muse of
  History)
DEVI (I)
DIDO (R)
ECHO
ELIS (L)
ERIS
EROS
ERYX (L)
ETNA (L)
FREY (S)
GAEA
HEBE
HERA
HERO
IDAS
ILIA (R) *2
ILUS
IOLE
IRIS
ISIS (E)
ISSA
ITYS
JUNO (R)
KAMA (I)
LEDA
LETO
LOKI (S)

LUNA (R)
MAIA (Pleiad)
MARS (R)
MORS (R)
NEMI (R-L)
NIKE
NUMA (R)
NYSA (L)
ODIN (S) *3
OLEN
OSSA (L)
OTUS
PERI (P)
PTAH (E)
RAMA (I)
RHEA (E)
  (GR)
  (R) *2
ROME (R-L)
SATI (E)
SIVA (I)
SOMA (I)
STYX (L)
THOR (S)
TROS
TROY (L) *4
TYRO
YAMA (I)
YIMA (P)
YMIR (S)
ZEUS

5

ADITI (I)
AEAEA (L)
AEDON

AESIR (S)
AESON
AËTES
ALEUS
AMMON (E) *1
ANHUR (E)
ARDEA (R-L)
ARGOS (L)
ARGUS
ARION (C)
ATLAS
ATLAS (L)
ATTIS
AULIS (L)
BELUS
BENNU (E-C)
BITON
CACUS (R)
CERES (R)
CHAOS (L)
CHILO
CHIOS (L)
CIRCE
COEUS
CREON
CRETE (L)
CUPID (R)
DANAË
DELOS (L)
DIANA (R)
DIONE
DOLON
DORUS
DRYAD
ERATO
  (Muse of
  Love Poetry)
EURUS

FATES (G)
FLORA (R)
FRIGG (S)
GJÖLL (S-L)
GYGES (C)
HADES
HADES (L)
HELEN
HELLE
HETIS
HORAE (G)
HORUS (E)
HOURI (P)
HYDRA (C) *5
HYLAS
HYMEN
IDAEA
ILIUM (L) *4
INDRA (I)
IRENE
IXION
JANUS (R)
JASON
KHNUM (E)
KHONS (E)
LADON (C)
LAIUS
LAMIA
LAMUS
LARES (R-G)
LERNA (L)
LETHE (L)
LEUCE
LINUS
LYDIA (L)
MAERA (C)
MANES (R-G)
MANTO

MAZDA *(P)*
MEDEA
MEDUS
METIS
MIDAS
MINOS
MYSIA *(L)*
NAIAD
NAXOS *(L)*
NEITH *(E)*
NIOBE
NISUS
NJÖRD *(S)*
NORNS *(S-G)*
NOTUS
NYMPH
ORCUS *(R)*
ORCUS *(R-L)*
ORION
PALES *(R)*
PARIS
PERSE
PICUS *(R)*
PLUTO *(L)*
PRIAM
PYLUS *(L)*
REMUS *(R)*
RHODE
SATYR
SEBEK *(E)*
SEKER *(E)*
SHIVA *(I)*
SIBYL
SINIS
SINON
SIREN
SOLON
SURYA *(I)*
TALOS
TEGEA *(L)*
TEMPE *(L)*
TENES
THEBE
THOAS
THOTH *(E)*
THYIA

TIBER *(R-L)*
TITAN
TROAS *(L)*
TROLL *(S)*
TYCHE
USHAS *(I)*
VANIR *(S-G)*
VENUS *(R)*
VESTA *(R)*
VIDAR *(S)*
WODEN *(S)* *3
ZETES
ZOHAK *(P)*

6

ACAMAS
ADONIS
AEACUS
AEGEUS
AEGINA *(L)*
AENEAS
AEOLUS
AEROPE
AETHRA
AGENOR
AGLAIA *(Grace)*
ALCYON *(L)*
ALECTO
ALIPES ¶
  (winged sandals)
AMAZON
AMYCUS
ANUBIS *(E)*
ANUKET *(E)*
APHAIA
APOLLO
AQUILO *(R)*
ARICIA *(R-L)*
ARTHUR *(A)*
ASGARD *(S-L)*
ASOPUS
ATHENA *6
ATHENE *6
ATHENS *(L)*

ATREUS
ATTICA *(L)*
AUGIAS
AURORA *(R)*
AUSTER *(R)*
AVALON *(A-L)*
BALDER *(S)*
BALIAS *(C)*
BAUCIS
BOREAS
BRAHMA *(I)*
CADMUS
CALAIS
CANACE
CASTOR
CELEUS
CHARIS *(R)*
CHARON
CHIONE
CLAROS *(L)*
CLOTHO *(Fate)*
COTTUS *(C)*
CREUSA *7
CRONOS *8
CRONUS *8
CYBELE
CYNCUS
CYRENE
DANAID
DANAUS
DAPHNE
DELPHI *(L)*
DICTYS
DIDYMA *(L)*
DODONA *(L)*
DRYADS *(G)*
DRYOPE
DRYOPS
ECHION
EGERIA *(R)*
ELAINE *(A)*
ELATUS
EPEIUS
EREBOS *(L)* *9
EREBUS *(L)* *9
EUBOEA *(L)*

EUROPA
EVADNE
FAUNUS *(R)*
FENRIR *(S-C)*
FREYJA *(S)*
GAWAIN *(A)*
GERYON *(C)*
GLAUCE *7
GRACES *(G)* *10
GRAEAE *(G)*
GREECE *(L)*
HAEMON
HATHOR *(E)*
HEBRUS *(R-L)*
HECABE *11
HECATE
HECTOR
HECUBA *11
HELIOS
HELLEN
HERMES
HESTIA
HOENIR *(S)*
HYADES *(G)*
HYGEIA
HYLLUS
HYPNOS
IASION
ICARUS
IOLCUS *(L)*
ISMENE
ITHACA *(L)*
KHEPRI *(E)*
LATIUM *(R-L)*
LATONA *(R)*
LEMNOS *(L)*
LESBOS *(L)*
LICHAS
LYCAON
MAERAE *(G)*
MANASA *(I-L)*
MEDUSA *(Gorgon)*
MEGARA
MEMNON
MENTOR
MERLIN *(A)*

MYTHOLOGY

MEROPE *(Pleiad)*
MINYAE *(G)*
MOPSUS
NAIADS *(G)*
NELEUS
NEREID
NEREUS
NESTOR
OENEUS
OENONE
OGYGIA *(L)*
OILEUS
OSIRIS *(E)*
OTONIA
OTRERE
PALLAS
PAPHOS *(L)*
PARCAE *(R-G)*
PELEUS
PELIAS
PELION *(L)*
PELOPS
PENEUS
PERDIX
PERSES
PHAROS *(L)*
PHOCIS *(L)*
PHOCUS
PHOEBE
PHOLUS *(C)*
POLLUX *12*
POMONA *(R)*
PONTUS
PROCNE
PSYCHE
PYTHIA
PYTHON *(C)*
RAMNES *(R-G)*
RENPET *(E)*
RHESUS
RHODES *(L) *13*
RHODOS *(L) *13*
SATURN *(R)*
SATYRS *(G)*
SCARAB *(E-C)*
SCIRON

SCYLLA *(C)*
SCYROS *(L)*
SELENE
SELKET *(E)*
SESHAT *(E)*
SESTOS *(L)*
SICILY *(L)*
SIGEUM *(L)*
SILENI *(G)*
SIRENS *(G)*
SPARTA *(L)*
SPARTI *(G)*
SPHINX *(C)*
STHENO *(Gorgon)*
SYRINX
TALAUS
TEFNUT *(E)*
TELLUS *(R)*
TEREUS
TETHYS
THALES
THALIA
   (Grace)
   (Muse of
   Comedy)
THEBES *(L)*
THEMIS
THETIS
THRACE *(L)*
TIRYNS *(L)*
TITANS *(G)*
TITIES *(R-G)*
TITYUS
TMOLUS *(L)*
TRITON
TRITON *(L)*
TROLLS *(S-G)*
TURNUS *(R)*
TYDEUS
TYPHON *(C)*
UDAEUS
UPUAUT *(E)*
URANIA
   (Muse of
   Astronomy)
URANUS

VISHNU *(I)*
VULCAN *(R)*
XUTHUS
ZEPHYR *14*
ZETHUS

7

ABDERUS
ACASTUS
ACESTES *(R)*
ACHAEUS
ACHERON *(L)*
ACTAEON
ADMETUS
AEGAEON *(C) *15*
AETOLIA *(L)*
AHRIMAN *(P)*
ALCAEUS
ALCMENE
ALCYONE *(Pleiad)*
ALTHAEA
AMAZONS *(G)*
AMPHION
AMYCLAE *(L)*
AMYMONE *(L)*
ANTAEUS
ANTENOR
ANTEROS
ANTIOPE
ARACHNE
ARCADIA *(L)*
ARGOLIS *(L)*
ARIADNE
ARTEMIS
ASTYNAX
ATHAMAS
ATROPOS *(Fate)*
AVERNUS *(L)*
BACCHAE *(G) *16*
BACCHUS *(R)*
BIFRÖST *(S) ¶*
  (bridge)
BOEOTIA *(L)*
BONA DEA *(R)*

BRAURON *(L)*
BRISEIS
BRONTES
BROTEAS
CAELIAN *(R-L)*
  (Rome hill)
CAENEUS
CALCHAS
CALYDON *(L)*
CALYPSO
CAMELOT *(A-L)*
CECROPS
CELOENO *(Pleiad)*
CENTAUR *(C)*
CEPHEUS
CERCYON
CHEIRON
CHLORIS *(R)*
CISSEUS
CLEOBIS
CLOELIA *(R)*
CLYMENE
COCALUS
COCYTUS *(L)*
COLCHIS *(L)*
CORINTH *(L)*
CORONIS
CROESUS
CURATII *(R-G)*
CURETES *(G)*
CYCLOPS
CYLLENE *(L)*
CYTHERA *(L)*
DACTYLI *(G)*
DANAIDS *(G)*
DAPHNIS
DEIPYLE
DEMETER
DINDYMA *(L)*
ECHEMUS
ECHIDNE *(C)*
ELECTRA
ELECTRA *(Pleiad)*
ELEUSIS *(L)*
ELPENOR
ELYSIUM *(L)*

EMPUSAE *(G)*
ENIPEUS
EPAPHUS
EPHESUS *(L)*
EPIGONI *(G)*
ERGINUS
ERIGONE
ERYTHIA *(L)*
EUMAEUS
EURYALE *(Gorgon)*
EURYTUS *17
EUTERPE
  (Muse of
  Music &
  Lyric Poetry)
EVANDER *(R)*
FEBRUUS *(R)*
FERIDUN *(P)*
FORTUNA *(R)*
GALAHAD *(A)*
GALATEA
GLAUCUS
GORDIUS
GORGONS *(G)*
GRACCHI *(R-G)*
GUNGNIR *(S) ¶*
  (spear)
HARPIES *(G)*
HELENUS
HELICON *(L)*
HESIONE
HORATII *(R-G)*
HYPENOR
IAPETUS
ICARIUS
IGRAINE *(A)*
ILYTHIA
INACHUS
IOBATES
IPHITUS
JOCASTA
JUPITER *(R)*
JUTURNA *(R)*
LACONIA *(L)*
LAELAPS *(C)*
LAERTES

LAKSHMI *(I)*
LAOCOÖN
LAODICE
LARISSA *(L)*
LATINUS *(R)*
LEANDER
LUCERES *(R-G)*
LUCIFER *(S)*
LYDIANS *(G)*
LYNCEUS
LYSIPPE
MACARIA
MAENADS *(G) *16*
MAGAERA
MARSYAS
MEANDER *(L)*
MEGAEIA
MERCURY *(R)*
MIDGARD *(S-L)*
MILETUS
MINERVA *(R)*
MISENUS
MITHRAS *(P)*
MJOLNIR *(S) ¶*
  (hammer)
MORDRED *(A)*
MUSAEUS
MYCENAE *(L)*
NEMESIS
NEPHELE
NEPTUNE *(R)*
NEREIDS *(G)*
NICIPPE
NUMITOR *(R)*
NYMPHAE *(G)*
OCEANUS
OEAGRUS
OEDIPUS
OLYMPIA *(L)*
OLYMPUS *(L)*
OMPHALE
ORESTES
ORPHEUS
ORTHRUS *(C)*
ORTYGIA *(L)*
PANDION

PANDORA
PEGASUS *(C)*
PELORUS
PENATES *(R-G)*
PERSEUS
PETASUS *¶*
  (hat)
PHAEDRA
PHAETON
PHARAOH *(E)*
PHINEUS
PHOENIX
PHOENIX *(E-C)*
PHORCUS
PHRIXUS
PLEIONE
POLITES
POLYBUS
PRIAPUS
PROCRIS
PROETUS
PROTEUS
PYLADES
PYRRHUS *18
ROMULUS *(R)*
SABINES *(R-G)*
SABINUS *(R)*
SALMONE *(L)*
SAVITAR *(I)*
SCHERIA *(L)*
SEKHMET *(E)*
SILENUS
SIPYLUS *(L)*
STENTOR
STEROPE *(Pleiad)*
STRYMON *(L)*
STRYMOR
TARCHON *(R)*
TARPEIA *(R)*
TAYGETE *(Pleiad)*
TELAMON
TENEDOS *(L)*
THEBANS *(G)*
THESEUS
THYADES *(G)*
THYRSUS *¶ (wand)*

TROJANS *(G)*
ULYSSES *(R)*
VIMINAL *(R-L)*
  (Rome hill)
VIVIANE *(A)*
XANTHUS *(C)*
ZAGREUS

8

ABSYRTUS *19
ACHELOUS
ACHILLES
ACRISIUS
ADRASTUS
AEACIDES *(G)*
AGAMEDES
AGANIPPE *(L)*
ALCESTIS
ALCINOUS
ALCMAEON
AMALTHEA *(C)*
AMYTHAON
ANCHISES
ANTIGONE
APSYRTUS *19
ARETHUSA
ARETHUSA *(L)*
ARIMASPI *(G)*
ASCANIUS
ASTRAEUS
ASTYANAX
ATALANTA
ATLANTIS *(L)*
AVENTINE *(R-L)*
  (Rome hill)
BEBRYCES *(G)*
BEBRYCOS *(L)*
BRIAREUS *(C) *15*
CADUCEUS *¶ (staff)*
CALLIOPE
  (Muse of
  Epic Poetry)
CALLISTO
CAPANEUS

MYTHOLOGY

CASTALIA
CAUCASUS *(L)*
CENTAURS *(C-G)*
CEPHALUS
CERBERUS *(C)*
CHALYBES *(R-G)*
CHIMAERA *(C)* *20
CHIMEIRA *(C)* *20
CHRYSAOR
CHRYSEIS
CLOACINA *(R)*
CORNELIA *(R)*
CRETHEUS
CYCLOPES *(G)*
DAEDALUS
DAMOCLES
DANAIDES *(G)*
DARDANUS
DEIDAMIA
DEMOPHON
DESPOENA
DIOMEDES
DIONYSUS
DIOSCURI *(G)*
DIS PATER *(R)*
DRAUPNIR *(S) ¶ (ring)*
ENDYMION
ERIDANUS *(L)*
ERINNYES *(G)* *21
ERIPHYLE
ETEOCLES
EUMOLPUS
EURIDYCE
EURYNOME
EURYTION
FAVONIUS *(R)*
GANYMEDE
GIGANTES *(G)*
HARMONIA
HAROERIS *(E)*
HEIMDALL *(S)*
HELLENES *(G)*
HEMITHEA
HERACLES
HERCULES *(R)*
HERMIONE

HESPERUS
HORATIUS *(R)*
HYPERION
ILIONEUS
ILITHYIA
IPHICLES
JUVENTAS *(R)*
LABDACUS
LACHESIS *(Fate)*
LAKE NEMI *(R-L)*
LANCELOT *(A)*
LAODAMIA
LAOMEDON
LAPITHAE *(G)*
LAVINIUM *(R-L)*
LIBITINA *(R)*
LYCURGUS
LYSANDER
MACAREUS
MARPESSA
MELAMPUS
MELEAGER
MENELAUS
MESHKENT *(E)*
MILANION
MINOTAUR *(C)*
MOLOSSUS
MORPHEUS
MOUNT IDA *(L)*
MYRTILUS
NAUPLIUS
NAUSICCA
NEFERTUM *(E)*
NEKHEBET *(E)*
NUMICIUS *(R-L)*
NYCTINUS
ODYSSEUS
OECHALIA *(L)*
OENOMAUS
OENOPION
PACTOLUS *(L)*
PALAEMON
PALATINE *(R-L)*
   (Rome hill)
PANDARUS
PANOPEUS

PASIPHAË
PENELOPE
PENTHEUS
PERCIVAL *(A)*
PHILEMON
PHLEGYAS
PILUMNUS *(R)*
PITTACUS
PLEIADES *(G)*
POLYXENA
PORTUNUS *(R)*
POSEIDON
PSAMATHE
QUIRINAL *(R-L)*
   (Rome hill)
QUIRINUS *(R)*
RAMAYANA *(I)*
SARPEDON
SILVANUS *(R)*
SISYPHUS
SLEIPNIR *(S-C)*
SPARTANS
TANTALUS
TARENTUM *(R-L)*
TARPEIUS *(R)*
TARTARUS *(L)*
TELEPHUS
TEUTHRAS
THANATOS
THESPIUS
THESSALY *(L)*
THYESTES
TITANESS
TITHONUS
TVASHTAR *(I)*
VALHALLA *(S-L)*
VICTORIA *(R)*
ZEPHYRUS *14

9

ACROPOLIS *(L)*
AEGISTHUS
AGAMEMNON
AKHENATON *(E)*

ALBA LONGA *(R-L)*
ALCYONEUS
AMARAVATI *(I-L)*
AMENHOTEP *(E)*
AMPHIARUS
ANDROMEDA
APHRODITE
APOLLONIA *(L)*
AREOPAGUS *(L)*
ARGONAUTS *(G)*
ARISTAEUS
ASCLEPIUS
ASIA MINOR *(L)*
AUTOLYCUS
BASSAREUS
BHUTAPATI *(I)*
CALLIRHOË
CASSANDRA
CHARITIES *(G)* *10
CHARYBDIS *(C)*
CITHAERON *(L)*
CONSUALIA *(R)*
DEIANEIRA *17
DEIPHOBUS
DEUCALION
ELECTRYON
ENCELADUS
EPHIALTES
EPIDAURUS *(L)*
ESQUILINE *(R-L) (Rome hill)*
ETRUSCANS *(R-G)*
EUMENIDES *(G)* *21
EUPHORBUS
EXCALIBUR *(A)* ¶ *(sword)*
FAUSTULUS *(R)*
GUINEVERE *(A)*
HAMADRYAD
HARPALYCE
HIPPOCOÖN
HIPPOLYTA *22
HIPPOLYTE *22
HOLY GRAIL *(A)* ¶ *(chalice)*
IDOMENEUS
IPHIGENIA
LEUCIPPUS
LOTOPHAGI *(G)* *23

LYCOMEDES
LYRNESSUS *(L)*
MELPOMENE
 (Muse of Tragedy)
MENOECEUS
METANEIRA
MNEMOSYNE
MOUNT ERYX *(L)*
MOUNT ETNA *(L)*
MOUNT NYSA *(L)*
MOUNT OSSA *(L)*
MYRMIDONS *(G)* *24
NARCISSUS
NEFERTITI *(E)*
OCEANIDES *(G)*
OREITHYIA
PALAMEDES
PALINAURUS
PALLADIUM ¶ *(statue)*
PARNASSUS *(L)*
PATROCLUS
PAUSANIUS
PERIANDER
PIRITHOUS
POLYDORUS
POLYNICES
PRAJAPATI *(I)*
PYGMALION
RIVER STYX *(L)*
SALMONEUS
SARASVATI *(I)*
SCAMANDER
SCAMANDER *(L)*
STHENELUS
TEIRESIAS
TELCHINES *(G)*
THERSITES
TISIPHONE
TYNDAREUS
VALKYRIES *(S-G)*
YGGDRASIL *(S)* ¶ *(tree)*

10

AMPHITRION *25
AMPHITRITE

AMPHITRYON *25
ANDROMACHE
ANTILOCHUS
BACCHANTES *(G)*
BRIHASPATI *(I)*
CAPITOLINE *(R-L)*
 (Rome hill)
CASSIOPEIA
CHRYSIPPUS
CIMMERIANS *(G)*
CORNUCOPIA ¶ *(horn)*
CORYBANTES *(G)*
CRETAN BULL *(C)*
DRAVIDIANS *(I-G)*
EPIMETHEUS
ERECHTHEUS
EUPHROSYNE *(Grace)*
GAETULIANS *(R-G)*
HAMADRYADS *(G)*
HELLESPONT *(L)*
HEPHAESTUS
HESPERIDES *(G)*
HIPPOCRENE *(L)*
HIPPODAMIA *26
HIPPOLYTUS
HYACINTHUS
IPHIANASSA
LAKE TRITON *(L)*
LIBER PATER *(R)*
MENESTHEUS
MOUNT ATLAS *(L)*
MYRMIDONES *(G)* *24
NEMEAN LION *(C)*
ORCHOMENUS
PERIPHETES
PERSEPHONE
PETESUCHOS *(E-C)*
PHALANTHUS *(R)*
PHLEGETHON *(L)*
POLYDEUCES *12
POLYHYMNIA
 (Muse of Heroic Hymns)
POLYMESTER
POLYPHEMUS
PORPHYRION
PROCRUSTES

MYTHOLOGY

PROMETHEUS
PROSERPINA *(R)*
RHEA SILVIA *(R)* *2
RIVER GJÖLL *(S-L)*
RIVER LETHE *(L)*
RIVER TIBER *(R-L)*
ROUND TABLE *(A)* ¶
SCAEAN GATE *(L)*
STYMPHALUS *(L)*
TARQUINIUS *(R)*
TELEMACHUS
TELEPHASSA
TITANESSES *(G)*
TROPHONIUS
UNDERWORLD *(L)*

11

AESCULAPIUS *(R)*
AGATHYRSANS *(G)*
BELLEROPHON
BRITOMARTIS
CRESPHONTES
ERYSICHTHON
GOLDEN BOUGH ¶
GORDIAN KNOT ¶
HIPPODAMEIA *26
LAKE AVERNUS *(L)*
LOTUS EATERS *(G)* *23
MORGAN LE FAY *(A)*
MOUNT MANASA *(I-L)*
MOUNT PELION *(L)*
MOUNT TMOLUS *(L)*
NEOPTOLEMUS *18
PALLANTIDES *(G)*

PENTHESILEA
PHILOCTETES
RIVER HEBRUS *(R-L)*
SABINE WOMEN *(R-G)*
TELLUS MATER *(R)*
TERPSICHORE
  (Muse of Choral
  Song & Dance)
TROJAN HORSE ¶ *27
WOODEN HORSE ¶ *27

12

ACCA LARENTIA *(R)*
ANCUS MARTIUS *(R)*
CLYTEMNESTRA
DICTAEAN CAVE *(L)*
ERICHTHONIUS
GOLDEN APPLES ¶
GOLDEN FLEECE ¶
HYDRA OF LERNA *(C)* *5
HYPERBOREANS *(G)*
LAESTRYGONES *(G)*
MOUNT CYLLENE *(L)*
MOUNT DINDYMA *(L)*
MOUNT OLYMPUS *(L)*
MOUNT SIPYLUS *(L)*
PELOPONNESUS *(L)*
PERICLYMENUS
RHADAMANTHUS
RIVER ACHERON *(L)*
RIVER COCYTUS *(L)*
RIVER MEANDER *(L)*
RIVER STRYMON *(L)*
TARPEIAN ROCK *(L)*

13

AUGEAN STABLES *(L)*
CERYNEIAN HIND *(C)*
HALIRRHOTHIUS
NUMA POMPILIUS *(R)*
PARTHENOPAEUS
PONTUS EUXINUS *(L)*
RIVER ERIDANUS *(L)*
RIVER NUMICIUS *(R-L)*
RIVER PACTOLUS *(L)*
SIEGE PERILOUS *(A)* ¶ *(chair)*
SOW OF CROMMYUM *(C)*
VESTAL VIRGINS *(R-G)*

14

APPLE OF DISCORD ¶
CALYDONIAN BEAR *(C)*
CATTLE OF GERYON *(C-G)*
HECATONCHEIRES *(G)*
HERMAPHRODITUS
LAKE STYMPHALUS *(L)*
MOUNT CITHAERON *(L)*
MOUNT PARNASSUS *(L)*
RIVER SCAMANDER *(L)*
SERVIUS TULLIUS *(R)*
UTHER PENDRAGON *(A)*

15

CASTALIAN SPRING *(L)*
MARES OF DIOMEDES *(C-G)*
RIVER PHLEGETHON *(L)*
SWORD OF DAMOCLES ¶
TULLUS HOSTILIUS *(R)*

PARLIAMENTS

(A) = Austria   (AF) = Afghanistan   (BA) = Bangladesh
(BH) = Bhutan   (BO) = Botswana   (BR) = Britain   (BU) = Bulgaria
(C) = China   (CI) = Channel Islands   (D) = Denmark   (E) = Egypt
(EG) = East Germany (until 1990)   (ET) = Ethiopia   (F) = France
(FI) = Finland   (G) = Germany   (GR) = Greece   (H) = Hungary
(I) = Ireland   (IC) = Iceland   (IN) = India   (IOM) = Isle of Man
(IR) = Iran   (IS) = Israel   (IT) = Italy   (J) = Japan   (K) = Kenya
(LA) = Laos   (LI) = Liechtenstein   (M) = Malaysia   (MA) = Maldives
(MO) = Monaco   (MOÇ) = Moçambique   (MON) = Mongolia
(N) = Netherlands   (NE) = Nepal   (NO) = Norway   (P) = Poland
(R) = Russia   (S) = Sweden   (SA) = South Africa   (SM) = San Marino
(SP) = Spain   (SU) = Surinam   (SWA) = Swaziland   (SWI) = Switzerland
(SY) = Syria   (T) = Tanzania   (US) = USA   (Y) = Yugoslavia
(ZA) = Zambia   (ZI) = Zimbabwe
(v) = various   † = Party   ↑ = Inner power group   ¶ = Nickname of early
English parliament   * = Alternative name

3

ANC (SA) †
INP (I) †
MAD ¶
OUP (BR) †
SDP (BR) †
SLD (BR) †
SNP (BR) †

4

DÁIL (I) *1
DERG (ET)
DIET (v)
DUMA (R)
GOOD ¶
KANU (K) †
LONG ¶
RUMP ¶
SDLP (BR) †
SEJM (P)
TANU (T) †
UNIP (ZA) †

ZANU (ZI) †
ZAPU (ZI) †

5

AZANA (SP) †
BA'ATH (SY) †
CABAL ↑
DIANA (GR) †
JUNTA ↑
LIKUD (IS) †
PASOK (G) †
SHURA (E)
VOULI (G)
WHIGS (BR) †

6

ADDLED ¶
CORTES (SP)
DUNCES' ¶
GREENS (BR/v) †
JANATA (IN) †

JATIYA (BA) †
KOKKAI (J) †
LABOUR (BR/v) †
LÄNDER (G)
MAJLIS (IR/MA)
SEANAD (I) *2
SENATE (US/v)
SHENGO (ET)
STATEN (SU)
TORIES (BR) †
TSOGDU (BH)

7

ALTHING (IC)
CABINET (BR/v) ↑
DRUNKEN ¶
ECOLOGY (BR) †
FALANGE (SP) †
FRELIMO (MOÇ) †
INKATHA (SA) †
KNESSET (IS)
KREMLIN (R)
LAGTING (NO)

LANDTAG (LI)
MONGREL ¶
RIKSDAG (S)
SANGI-IN (J)
SHUGI-IN (J)
TYNWALD (IOM)
USELESS ¶

8

ALLIANCE (BR) †
CONGRESS (US/v)
　　　　　　(IN) †
FINE GAEL (I) †
GRATTAN'S ¶
LIBANDLA (SWA)
LIBERALS (BR/v) †
LOK SABHA (IN)
NATIONAL (BR/v) †
SINN FEIN (I) †
SOBRANJE (BU) *3
STATSRÅD (S)
STORTING (NO)
SUBRANIE (BU) *3

PARLIAMENTS

9

BAREBONES ¶
BUNDESRAT *(A/SWI/G)*
BUNDESTAG *(G)*
DEMOCRATS *(US/v)* †
EDUSKUNTA *(FI)*
FOLKETING *(D)*
ODELSTING *(NO)*
PANCHAYAT *(NE)*
PATHET LAO *(LA)* †
POLITBURO *(R)* ↑
PRESIDIUM *(R)* ↑
REGIERUNG *(LI)*
REICHSTAG *(G)*
SKUPSTINA *(Y)*
STAATSRAT *(EG)*
STÄNDERAT *(SWI)*
THE STATES *(CI)*
TORY PARTY *(BR)* †
WHIG PARTY *(BR)* †

10

BOLSHEVIKS *(R)* †
COMMUNISTS *(R/v)* †
DIRECTOIRE *(F)*
FIANNA FÁIL *(I)* †
GREEN PARTY *(BR/v)* †
LOYA JIRGAH *(AF)*
LOWER HOUSE *(v)*
MENSHEVIKS *(R)* †
OIREACHTAS *(I)*
PARLAMENTO *(IT)*
PARLIAMENT *(v)*
PENSIONARY ¶
PLAID CYMRU *(BR)* †
RAYJA SABHA *(IN)*
SANDANISTA *(NI)* †
SOCIALISTS *(v)*
SOLIDARITY *(P)* †
UPPER HOUSE *(v)*

11

DÁIL EIREANN *(I)* *1
DEWAN NEGARA *(M)*
DEWAN RAKYAT *(M)*
EERSTE KAMER *(N)*
HOUSE OF KEYS *(IOM)*
LABOUR PARTY *(BR/v)* †
MINISTERRAT *(EG)*
NATIONALRAT *(A/SWI)*
REPUBLICANS *(US/v)* †
STAR CHAMBER *(BR)* ↑
TROTSKYITES *(R)* †
TWEEDE KAMER *(N)*
VOLKSKAMMER *(EG)*

12

GREAT COUNCIL *(SM)*
HOUSE OF LORDS *(BR)*
INDEPENDENTS *(BR/v)* †
LIBERAL PARTY *(BR)* †
MEBYON KERNOW *(BR)* †
ORSZÁGGYÜLÉS *(H)*
POPULAR FRONT *(v)* †
WONDER-MAKING ¶
WORKERS' PARTY *(v)*

13

CONSERVATIVES *(BR)* †
FEDERAL SENATE *(v)*
HOUSE OF CHIEFS *(BO)*
NATIONAL FRONT *(BR)* †
PEOPLE'S KHURAL *(MO)*
SEANAD EIREANN *(I)* *2
SUPREME SOVIET *(R)*

14

COMMUNIST PARTY *(R/v)* †
COUNCIL OF STATE *(v)*
FEDERAL CHAMBER *(v)*
GENERAL COUNCIL *(v)*
HOUSE OF COMMONS *(GB/v)*
SCOTTISH LABOUR *(BR)* †
STATEN-GENERAAL *(N)*

15

COUNCIL OF EUROPE
FEDERAL ASSEMBY *(v)*
HOUSE OF ASSEMBLY *(SA/v)*
NATIONAL COUNCIL *(MO)*
PEOPLE'S ASSEMBLY *(v)*
PEOPLE'S CONGRESS *(C)*
SOCIAL DEMOCRATS *(GB/v)* †
ULSTER UNIONISTS *(BR)* †

PEOPLE

ANTIQUE-MAKERS

(C) = Clockmaker/watchmaker   (F) = Furniture-maker
(G) = Glassmaker   (P) = Potter/porcelain-maker   (S) = Silversmith/goldsmith

3

FOX *(F)*
LAW *(S)*

4

ADAM *(F)*
AULT *(P)*
BELL *(P)*
DAUM *(G)*
HOPE *(F)*
IVES *(C)*
KEAN *(P)*
KENT *(F)*
KNOX *(S)*
LAND *(C)*
LUND *(P)*
NAHL *(F)*
ROUX *(F)*
SWAN *(G)*
WALL *(P)*
WEBB *(G)*
WOOD *(P)*

5

BLOOR *(P)*
DUCHÉ *(P)*
ELERS *(P)*
ELLIS *(F)*
GALLÉ *(G)*
GROTH *(S)*
JACOB *(F)*
KNIBB *(C)*
KOCKS *(P)*

LEACH *(P)*
LE ROY *(C)*
MAROT *(F)*
MOSER *(S)*
MUDGE *(C)*
ODIOT *(S)*
OEBEN *(F)*
PETIT *(P)*
PHYFE *(F)*
PRATT *(P)*
QUARE *(C)*
SABIN *(F)*
SMITH *(S)*
SPODE *(P)*
STORR *(S)*
VEZZI *(P)*
WATTS *(P)*

6

ARNOUX *(P)*
BEILBY *(G)*
BELTER *(F)*
BOULLE *(F)*
CARVER *(F)*
DUBOIS *(P)*
DUTTON *(C)*
DWIGHT *(P)*
GILLOW *(F)*
GRICCI *(P)*
HUNGER *(P)*
JANSEN *(P)*
KAMBLI *(F)*
MINTON *(P)*
PAUZIÉ *(S)*
REVERE *(S)*
RHODES *(P)*

ROHLFS *(F)*
SEDDON *(F)*
TÉTARD *(S)*
TUCKER *(P)*
TURNER *(P)*
WISTAR *(G)*

7

AMELUNG *(G)*
ANDRIES *(P)*
ASTBURY *(P)*
BATEMAN *(S)*
BÖTTGER *(P)*
BRAMELD *(P)*
BREGUET *(C)*
CELLINI *(S)*
CHRISTY *(G)*
CRESPIN *(S)*
DESPREZ *(G)*
DE VRIES *(F)*
DOULTON *(P)*
DRESSER *(S)*
FABERGÉ *(S)*
FLÖTNER *(F)*
GARRARD *(S)*
GERMAIN *(S)*
GRENDEY *(F)*
HARLAND *(C)*
KÄNDLER *(P)*
KUNCKEL *(G)*
LALIQUE *(G)*
LESSORE *(P)*
MATTERN *(F)*
POTERAT *(P)*
RÖNTGEN *(F)*
SCHUPPE *(S)*

STEUBEN *(G)*
STIEGEL *(G)*
TIFFANY *(G)*
TOMPION *(C)*
WILLARD *(C)*

8

BIENNAIS *(S)*
BOLSOVER *(S)*
BREWSTER *(F)*
CHAFFERS *(P)*
CLÉRISSY *(P)*
CRESSENT *(F)*
DE MORGAN *(P)*
DUESBURY *(P)*
GAUDREAU *(F)*
KETTERER *(C)*
KIRCHNER *(P)*
KOEPPING *(G)*
LANNUIER *(F)*
MELCHIOR *(P)*
NESTFELL *(F)*
RANDOLPH *(F)*
RIESENER *(F)*
SALVIATI *(G)*
SHERATON *(F)*
SPENGLER *(P)*
SPRIMONT *(S)*
TINWORTH *(P)*
TOWNSEND *(F)*
VULLIAMY *(C)*
WEDGWOOD *(P)*
WHIELDON *(P)*
WILLAUME *(S)*

9

BRUSTOLON *(F)*
DANHAUSER *(F)*
DE LAMERIE *(S)*
DESMALTER *(F)*
INGERSOLL *(C)*
JAMNITZER *(S)*
MAJORELLE *(F)*
OPPENHEIM *(G)*
PUIFORCAT *(S)*
SCHNEIDER *(G)*
VERZELINI *(G)*
WINDMILLS *(C)*
ZESCHINER *(P)*

10

BREYSPAARK *(F)*
COOKWORTHY *(P)*
DELAHERCHE *(P)*
FROMANTEEL *(C)*
JAQUET-DROZ *(C)*
MEISSONIER *(S)*
RICHARDSON *(G)*

11

BILLINGSLEY *(P)*
CHAMBERLAIN *(P)*
CHIPPENDALE *(F)*
DELLA ROBBIA *(P)*
HEPPLEWHITE *(F)*
RAVENSCROFT *(G)*
RITTENHOUSE *(C)*
VAN EENHOORN *(P)*

13

VAN RISENBURGH *(F)*

PEOPLE

ARCHITECTS

¶ = Designer   NB: Double entry = two architects with same name

3

MAY *(Eltham Lodge, London)*
OUD *(Spangen, Rotterdam)*

4

ADAM *(Glasgow Infirmary)*
ASAM *(St John Nepomuk, Munich)*
BAHR *(Frauenkirche, Dresden)*
BUON *(Doge's Palace, Venice)*
EDGE *(Raynham Hall, nr Fakenham)*
EGAS *(Toledo Cathedral)*
KAHN *(Salk Institute, California)*

KENT *(Horse Guards Block, Whitehall)*
LOOS *(Scheu House, Vienna)*
NASH *(Royal Pavilion, Brighton)*
PACE *(University Chapel, Keele)*
RIED *(Wladislavttall, Prague)*
SHAW *(New Scotland Yard)*
WEBB *(Greenwich Royal Hospital)*
WOOD *(Royal Crescent, Bath)*
WREN *(St Paul's Cathedral, London)*

5

AALTO *(Finlandia Concert Hall, Helsinki)*

PEOPLE – ARCHITECTS

AKBAR *(Red Fort, Agra)*
BACON *(Lincoln Memorial, Washington)*
BARMA *(St Basil's Cathedral, Moscow)*
BARRY *(Houses of Parliament, London)*
BROWN ¶ *(Kew Gardens, London)*
CECIL *(Burghley House, Stamford)*
COSTA *('The Grand Plan', Brasilia)*
CRANE ¶
DANCE *(Mansion House, London)*
(Newgate Prison, London)
ELMES *(St George's Hall, Liverpool)*
GADDI *(Ponte Vecchio, Florence)*
GIBBS *(Radcliffe Camera, Oxford)*
GAUDÍ *(Church of the Sagrada Familia, Barcelona)*
HOBAN *(White House, Washington)*
HORTA *(Innovation Store, Brussels)*
JEHAN *(Taj Mahal, Agra)*
JONES *(Banqueting Hall, Whitehall)*
KNOTT *(County Hall, London)*
LE DUC *(various, Paris)*
LE VAU *(Palace of Versailles, nr Paris)*
LIPPI *(Villa Medici, Rome)*
LOCKE *(Bristol Cathedral)*
PAINE *(Wardour Castle, nr Shaftesbury)*
PIANO *(Centre Pompidou, Paris – with ROGERS)*
PONTI *(Pirelli Building, Milan)*
PUGIN *(Birmingham Cathedral)*
ROSSI *(General Staff HQ, Leningrad)*
SALVI *(Trevi Fountain, Rome)*
SCOTT *(Liverpool Cathedral)*
(St Pancras Station, London)
SINAN *(Shezade Mosque, Istanbul)*
SOANE *(Bank of England, London)*
SPEER *(Chancellery, Berlin)*
SUGAR *(Abbé St Denis, nr Paris)*
UTZON *(Sydney Opera House)*
VARDY *(Horse Guards, Whitehall)*
WYATT *(Theatre Royal, Drury Lane)*
(Radcliffe Observatory, Oxford)

6

ABADIE *(Sacré Coeur, Paris)*
ALESSI *(Palazzo Marino, Milan)*
ARCHER *(St John's Church, Westminster)*
BASEVI *(Fitzwilliam College, Cambridge)*
BOULÉE *(Tomb of Newton)*
BRUNEL *(Clifton Suspension Bridge, Bristol)*
(Thames Tunnel, London)
BURGES *(Cardiff Castle)*
BURTON *(Triumphal Arch, Hyde Park)*
CUBITT *(King's Cross Station, London)*
DOBSON *(Central Station, Newcastle)*
EIFFEL *(Eiffel Tower, Paris)*
FAVRAN *(Narbonne Cathedral)*
FLORIS *(Town Hall, Antwerp)*
GIOTTO *(Campanile, Florence)*
GODWIN *(White House, Chelsea)*
GREENE *(Gamble House, California)*
HANSEN *(Heinrichshof, Vienna)*
INWOOD *(St Pancras Church, London)*
LEDOUX *(Hôtel de Montmerena, Paris)*
LESCOT *(Louvre, Paris)*
MESSEL *(Wertheim Store, Berlin)*
MORRIS ¶
NEUTRA *(Lovell House, Los Angeles)*
PARLER *(Prague Cathedral)*
PAXTON *(Crystal Palace, London)*
PEARCE *(Parliament House, Dublin)*
RAMSEY *(Norwich Cathedral)*
ROGERS *(Centre Pompidou, Paris – with PIANO)*
ROMANO *(Mantua Cathedral)*
SALVIN *(Harlaxton Hall, nr Grantham)*
SERLIO *(Château d'Ancy le Franc, Burgundy)*
SHREVE *(Empire State Building, New York)*
SMIRKE *(British Museum, London)*
SOLARI *(Salzburg Cathedral)*
SPENCE *(Coventry Cathedral)*
STREET *(Royal Court of Justice, London)*

TALMAN *(Chatsworth House, nr Bakewell)*
TATLIN *(Tower of the 3rd International, Moscow)*
THYNNE *(Old Somerset House, London)*
VIGNON *(La Madeleine, Paris)*
VOYSEY ¶
WALLOT *(Reichstag Building, Berlin)*
WRIGHT *(Guggenheim, New York)*
YEVELE *(Canterbury Cathedral)*

7

ALBERTI *(Santa Maria Novella, Florence)*
BARKHIN *(Izvestia Building, Moscow)*
BATTARD *(Palais de Justice, Lyon)*
BEHRENS *(Turbine Hall, Berlin)*
BENTLEY *(Westminster Cathedral)*
BERNINI *(St Peter's, Rome)*
BOILEAU *(St Eugène, Paris)*
CORBETT *(YMCA Building, Manchester)*
DE SILOE *(Granada Cathedral)*
FERSTEL *(Votivkirche, Vienna)*
GARNIER *(Opéra, Paris)*
GÄRTNER *(Old Palace, Athens)*
GIBBERD *(Liverpool RC Cathedral)*
GIBBONS ¶
GILBERT *(Woolworth Building, New York)*
GIRAULT *(Petit Palais, Paris)*
GROPIUS *(Bauhaus, Dessau)*
GUARINI *(Palazzo Carignano, Turin)*
HADRIAN *(Tibur Villa)*
HOLLAND *(Carlton House, London)*
LATROBE *(Capitol, Washington)*
LUTYENS *(Viceroy's House, Delhi)*
MACHUCA *(New Palace, Alhambra, Granada)*
MADERNO *(Palazzo Barberini, Rome)*
MANSART *(Sante Marie de la Visitation, Paris)*
NEUMANN *(Würzburg Palace)*

OSTBERG *(City Hall, Stockholm)*
PEARSON *(Truro Cathedral)*
PERUZZI *(Villa Farnesina, Rome)*
RAPHAEL *(St Peter's, Rome)*
RINALDI *(Lenin Palace, Leningrad)*
SACCONI *(Victor Emmanuel II Monument, Rome)*
TELFORD *(Menai Suspension Bridge, Caernarfon)*
VENTURI *(Guild House, Philadelphia)*
VIGNOLA *(St Peter's, Rome)*
WALPOLE *(Strawberry Hill, Twickenham)*
WARDELL *(St Mary's Cathedral, Sydney)*
WASTELL *(King's College Chapel, Cambridge)*
WILKINS *(Downing College, Cambridge)*
WYNFORD *(Nave of Winchester Cathedral)*

8

AMMANATI *(Palazzo Pitti, Florence)*
BRAMANTE *(St Peter's, Rome)*
BULFINCH *(State House, Boston USA)*
CHAMBERS *(Somerset House, London)*
CUIJPERS *(Rijksmuseum, Amsterdam)*
DE BROSSE *(St Gervais, Paris)*
DI CAMBIO *(Santa Croce, Florence)*
HARDWICK *(Entrance of Euston Station, London)*
HITTORFF *(Gare du Nord, Paris)*
JOURDAIN *(Samaritaine, Paris)*
LANGHANS *(Brandenburg Gate, Berlin)*
LEONARDO ¶
MELNIKOV *(Rusakov Club, Moscow)*
PALLADIO *(San Giorgio Maggiore, Venice)*
PERRAULT *(Louvre, Paris)*
PIRANESI *(Santa Maria del Priorato, Rome)*

PEOPLE – ARCHITECTS

POELAERT *(Palais de Justice, Brussels)*
RUGGIERI *(Palazzo Pitti, Florence)*
SANGALLO *(Santo Spirito, Florence)*
SCAMOZZI *(Rocca Pisani, Lonigo)*
SMYTHSON *(Longleat House, nr Warminster)*
SOUFFLOT *(Panthéon, Paris)*
SPAVENTO *(Santa Salvatore, Venice)*
SULLIVAN *(Schlesinger-Mayor Store, Chicago)*
VANBRUGH *(Castle Howard, Malton)*
VISCONTI *(Louvre, Paris)*
WILLIAMS *(Daily Express Building, Fleet Street)*

9

BORROMINI *(Pallazo Falconieri, Rome)*
BOUCICAUT *(Bon Marché Store, Paris)*
BOURGEOIS *(Cité Moderne, Paris)*
BROGNIART *(La Bourse, Paris)*
CARPENTER *(Lancing College, nr Worthing)*
CHAMPNEYS *(Newnham College, Cambridge)*
COCKERELL *(Ashmolean Library, Oxford)*
DE CORMONT *(Amiens Cathedral)*
DE HERRERA *(Escorial, nr Madrid)*
DUQUESNEY *(Gare de l'Est, Paris)*
HAWKSMOOR *(Christ Church, Spitalfields, London)*
JEFFERSON *(Virginia University)*
JUSTINIAN *(Hagia Sophia, Constantinople)*
LEMERCIER *(Sorbonne Church, Paris)*
LENGINOUR *(Chester Cathedral)*
MACKMURDO ¶
NIEYMEYER *(Brasilia Cathedral)*
PUCHSPAUM *(St Stephen's, Vienna)*
RASTRELLI *(Winter Palace, Leningrad)*

VAN CAMPEN *(Royal Palace, Amsterdam)*
VESPASIAN *(Colosseum, Rome)*

10

BURLINGTON *(Chiswick House, London)*
DELLA PORTA *(St Peter's, Rome)*
DI VINCENZO *(San Petronio, Bologna)*
HODGKINSON *(Brunswick Centre, London)*
MACKINTOSH *(School of Art, Glasgow)*
MICHELOZZO *(Medici Palace, Florence)*
PIERMARINI *(La Scala, Milan)*
PÖPPELMANN *(Zwinger, Dresden)*
ROSSELLINO *(Pienza Cathedral)*
SAN MICHELI *(San Bernardino, Verona)*
SERVANDONI *(Saint-Sulpice, Paris)*
VILLANUEVA *(Prado, Madrid)*
WATERHOUSE *(National History Museum, London)*

11

APOLLODORUS *(Trajan's Column, Rome)*
BRETTINGHAM *(Holkham Hall, Wells, Norfolk)*
CHURRIGUERA *(Salamanca Cathedral)*
LE CORBUSIER *(Unité d'Habitation, Marseilles)*
MICHELANGELO *(St Peter's, Rome)*
VON ENSINGER *(Ulm Cathedral)*

12

AL-MUTAWAKKIL *(Great Mosque, Samarra)*
BRUNELLESCHI *(Florence Cathedral)*

13

WILLIAM OF SENS *(Canterbury Cathedral)*

14

MAURICE DE SULLY *(Notre Dame, Paris)*

15

LEONARDO DA VINCI ¶

PEOPLE

ARTISTS

(E) = Engraver/etcher/wood-carver   (F) = Art forger   (S) = Sculptor
*NB: A = Artist only used for joint entries   * = Alternative spelling/name*

3

APT
ARP
BOL
COX
DIX
DOU
LAM
MOR
RAY
UGO *(A/E)*
VOS

4

AVED
BOTH
CANO *(A/S)*

CARO *(S)*
CARR
CIMA
COLE
COOK
CUYP
DALI
DORÉ *(E)*
DUFY
ETTY
FEKE
GABO *(S)*
GILL *(A/S)*
GOYA *(A/E)*
GROS
HALS
HEEM
HONE
HUNT *1
JOHN

JUEL
KALF
KLEE *(A/E)*
KOCH
LELY
MAES
MASO
MIRÓ
NASH
OPIE
PETO
RENI
ROSA *(A/E)*
RUDE *(S)*
TROY
TUKE
TURA
VIEN
WEST
WITZ

WOOD
ZICK

5

ABBEY
ALLAN
APPEL
BACON
BALLA
BANKS *(S)*
BARRY
BARYE *(S)*
BLAKE *(A/E)*
BOEHM *(S)*
BOSCH
BOUTS
BROWN
BRUYN

BURRA
CARRA
COROT
COSTA
COTES
CROME
DANBY
DAVID
DEGAS
DEVIS
DOLCI
DÜRER *(A/E)*
ERNST
FOLEY
FOPPA
FRITH
GRECO *2
GROSZ
HAYEZ
HOOCH *3

PEOPLE – ARTISTS

HOOGH *3
ITTEN
KLIMT
LÉGER
LEWIS
LIPPI
LOTTO
LOWRY
LUINI
MANET
MENGS
METSU
MONET
MOORE (S)
MUCHA
MUNCH
NAVEZ
NICOL
NOLAN
NOTKE (A/E)
ORPEN
OUDRY
OUTIN
PALMA
PEALE
PENCZ (A/E)
PIERO
PIPER
POOLE
POZZO
PUGET (S)
PUVIS
REDON
RICCI
RILEY
RODIN (S)
ROSSO
RUNGE
SCOTT
STAËL
STEEN
SUVÉE
TACCA (S)
TOBEY
TONKS
VOUET

VRIES (S)
VROOM
WATTS
WHITE
ZOPPO

6

ALBANI
ANDREA *4
BARKER
BATONI
BEWICK (E)
BOUDIN
BRAQUE
BREGNO (S)
BUTLER (S)
CALLOT (E)
CANOVA (S)
CASSON
CIBBER (S)
CLAUDE
CLOUET
COELLO
COOPER
COPLEY
COSWAY
COTMAN
COYPEL
COZENS
CRESPI
DAWSON
DERAIN
DE WINT
DOBELL
DOBSON
DUCCIO
DURAND (E)
ERHART (S)
FILDES
FOSTER
FUSELI
GEDDES
GIOTTO
GIRTIN

GIULIO
GLEYRE
GLOVER
GOUJON (S)
GREUZE
GUARDI
HECKEL
HOUDON (S)
INGRES
JAGGER
KNIGHT
KRÜGER
LASZLO
LA TOUR
LEGROS
LESLIE
MARINI (S)
MARTIN
McEVOY
MERYON (E)
MILLET
MORRIS
MYTENS
OLIVER
OSTADE
PACHER (A/E)
PALMER
PANINI
PIETRO (A/S)
PISANO (S)
RAMSAY
RENOIR
RIBERA
RIVERA
ROBBIA (S) *5
ROMNEY
RUBENS
SACCHI (S)
SANDBY (E)
SERGEL (S)
SEURAT
SIGNAC
SISLEY
SLUTER (S)
SODOMA
STOMER

STRANG (A/E)
STUBBS
TANGUY
TATLIN (A/S)
TISSOT
TITIAN
TOCQUÉ
TROOST
TURNER
VAN LOO
VAN RYN *6
VASARI
VERNET
VERRIO
VERTUE (E)
VILLON
WALKER
WARHOL
WEENIX
WEYDEN *7
WILKIE
WILSON
WITTEL
WRIGHT
YEAMES

7

ALGARDI (S)
ALLSTON
AMIGONI
APPIANI
ASSELYN
AUDUBON
BALDUNG (A/E)
BARBARI (E)
BARLACH (S)
BAROCCI
BASSANO
BELLINI
BERCHEM
BERNINI (S)
BINGHAM
BÖCKLIN
BOLOGNA (S)

BONHEUR
BONNARD
BOUCHER (A/E)
BOURDON
BROUWER
BRUEGEL *8
CALVERT
CELLINI (S)
CÉZANNE
CHAGALL
CHARDIN
CIMABUE
CLODION (S)
COLLIER
CORINTH
COURBET
CRANACH (A/E)
DALZIEL
DAUMIER
DA VINCI *9
EL GRECO *2
EPSTEIN (S)
FERRARI
FLAXMAN
FOUQUET
GAUGUIN
GENTILE
GIBBONS (E)
GLEIZES
GUTHRIE
HARTUNG
HOBBEMA
HOCKNEY
HOGARTH (A/E)
HOKUSAI (A/E)
HOLBEIN
HOPPNER
ISRAËLS
KEATING (F)
KNELLER
LANCRET
LAURANA (S)
MACLISE
MAILLOL (S)
MARTINI
MATISSE

MEMLINC *10
MEMLING *10
MILLAIS
MORISOT
MORLAND
MURILLO
NATTIER (A/E)
ORCAGNA (A/S)
PARSONS
PASMORE
PHIDIAS (S)
PICABIA
PICASSO
PIGALLE (S)
PITTONI
POLLOCK
POURBUS
POUSSIN
POYNTER
PRADIER (S)
QUARTON
QUELLIN (E)
QUERCIA
RAEBURN
RAPHAEL
RIBALTA
ROUAULT (A/E)
SARGENT
SICKERT
SLEVOGT
SPENCER
STEVENS
STROZZI
TENIERS
TENNIEL
TERBURG *11
TIBALDI (A/S)
TIEPOLO
UCCELLO
UTRILLO
VALADON
VAN DYCK (A/E)
VAN EYCK
VAN GOGH
VERMEER
VISCHER (S)

WATTEAU
WOOTTON
WYNANTS
ZADKINE (S)
ZOFFANY
ZUCCARO

8

AGOSTINO (S)
AMMANATI (S)
ANNIGONI
ARMITAGE (S)
AVERCAMP
BACICCIO
BEAUMONT
BECKMANN
BELLOTTO
BERTOLDO
BRABAZON
BRANCUSI (S)
BRANGWYN
BREUGHEL *8
BRONZINO (S)
BRUEGHEL *8
CALLCOTT
CARPEAUX (S)
CARRACCI
CASTAGNO
CHANTREY (S)
CHRISTUS
COYSEVOX (S)
CRESWICK
DELAUNAY
DRYSDALE
EASTLAKE
FALCONET (S)
FIELDING
FRAMPTON (S)
GHIBERTI (S)
GIORDANO
GIOVANNI
GIRARDON (S)
GUERCINO
HEPWORTH (S)

HILLIARD
JORDAENS
KIRCHNER
LANDSEER (A/S)
LAWRENCE
LEONARDO *9
LOMBARDO (S)
MAGRITTE
MALEVICH
MANTEGNA
MARSHALL
MASACCIO
MONTAGNA
MUNNINGS
NEVINSON
PERUGINO
PIRANESI (E)
PISSARRO
PONTORMO
PURRMANN
PYNACKER
REYNOLDS
RICHARDS
ROSSETTI
ROTTMAYR
ROUSSEAU
RUISDAEL
SARACENI
SASSETTA
SCHLÜTER (S)
SERPOTTA
SERUSIER
SEVERINI
SOLIMENA
SPRANGER
TERBORCH *11
TOPOLSKI
VAN GOYEN
VERMEYEN
VERONESE
VITTORIA (S)
VIVARINI
VLAMINCK
VUILLARD
WHISTLER
ZURNURÁN

9

ACKERMANN
ANTONELLO
BAKHUISEN
BARTHOLDI (S)
BEARDSLEY
BECCAFUMI
BLOEMAERT
CANALETTO
CONSTABLE
CORREGGIO
DELACROIX
DELAROCHE
DONATELLO (A/S)
ELSHEIMER
FABRITIUS
FEUERBACH
FRAGONARD
GÉRICAULT
GHISLANDI
GIORGIONE
GRÜNEWALD
HONTHORST
KANDINSKY
KAUFFMANN
KOKOSCHKA
LANFRANCO
MESTROVIC (S)
MULTSCHER (S)
NICHOLSON
NOLLEKENS (S)
NORTHCOTE
PECHSTEIN
PIAZZETTA
PISANELLO
POLIAKOFF
REMBRANDT *6
ROUBILIAC (S)
SAENREDAM
SANSOVINO (S)
SIQUEIROS
STANFIELD
STANZIONE
THORNHILL
TISCHBEIN

PEOPLE – ARTISTS

VANDERLYN
VELASQUEZ *12
VELAZQUEZ *12

10

ALMA-TADEMA
ARCHIPENKO (S)
BANDINELLI (S)
BAUMEISTER
BERRUGUETE
BOTTICELLI
BOUGUEREAU
BURNE-JONES
CARAVAGGIO
CHAMPAIGNE
GIACOMETTI (S)
HOLMAN HUNT *1
KENNINGTON (A/S)
LIEBERMANN
LORENZETTI
MODIGLIANI
ORCHARDSON
PELLEGRINI
POLLAIUOLO (A/S)
POLYCLITUS (S)
PRAXITELES (S)
ROSSELLINO (S)
ROWLANDSON
SCHWITTERS
SEBASTIANO
SIGNORELLI

SQUARCIONE
SUTHERLAND
TINTORETTO
TORRIGIANO (S)
VANDERBANK
VAN DER GOES
VECCHIETTA (A/S)
VERROCCHIO (A/S)
WALDMÜLLER
WESSELMANN
WESTMACOTT (S)
WINSTANLEY (E)
ZUCCARELLI

11

BARTOLOMMEO
DELLA ROBBIA (S) *5
DOMENICHINO
FARQUHARSON
GENTILESCHI
PRIMATICCIO (A/S)
SCHEEMAKERS (S)
TERBRUGGHEN
THORNYCROFT (S)
THORVALDSEN
VAN MEEGEREN (F)
VIGÉE-LEBRUN

12

ALBERTINELLI
FANTIN-LATOUR

GAINSBOROUGH
GRANDMA MOSES
LICHTENSTEIN
MICHELANGELO (A/S)
PARMIGIANINO
PLEYDENWURFF
RYSSELBURGHE
SASSOFERRATO
VAN DER WEYDEN *7
WINTERHALTER

13

DUCHAMP-VILLON
SÁNCHEZ-COELLO

14

ANDREA DEL SARTO *4
THEOTOCOPOULOS *2
VALLAYER-COSTER

15

LEONARDO DA VINCI *9
MODERSOHN-BECKER
REMBRANDT VAN RYN *6
SCHMIDT-ROTTLUFF (E)
TOULOUSE-LAUTREC

PEOPLE

COMPOSERS

3

BAX
CUI
FRY
TYE

4

ADAM
ARNE
BACH
BART
BECK
BERG
BLOW
BOHM
BYRD
CAGE
FOSS
GADE
GAUL
IVES
KERN
LALO
LVOV
LYTE
MONO
ORFF
TOCH
WOLF

5

ABSIL
AGNEW
ALAIN
ALLAM

ANSON
AUBER
AURIC
BERIO
BINET
BIZET
BLISS
BLOCH
BOITO
COWEN
DANBY
DUFAY
DUKAS
DYSON
ELGAR
FALLA
FAURÉ
FRANZ
GLUCK
GRIEG
GROFÉ
HAYDN
HENZE
HOLST
HUBER
IBERT
KOVEN
LEHÁR
LISZT
LOEWE
LULLY
PARRY
RAVEL
REGER
RICCI
RIETI
ROSSI
SATIE
SOUSA
SPOHR

SUPPÉ
TOSTI
VERDI
WEBER
WEILL
WIDOR

6

ALFANO
ANSELL
ARNELL
ARNOLD
BARBER
BARTÓK
BENOÎT
BERLIN
BRAHMS
BRIDGE
BUSONI
CHOPIN
CLARKE
COATES
COWARD
CZERNY
DELIUS
DUPARC
DVOŘÁK
EISLER
ENESCO
FLOTOW
FOSTER
FRANCK
GERMAN
GLINKA
GOUNOD
HADLEY
HANDEL
HANSON

HUMMEL
JACOBI
KODÁLY
LIADOV
MAHLER
MINKUS
MOZART
PARKER
PLEYEL
PORTER
QUANTZ
RAMEAU
RUBBRA
SCHÜTZ
SEIBER
STRONG
TALLIS
THOMAS
VARÈSE
WAGNER
WALTON
WEBERN
WESLEY

7

ADDISON
ALABIEV
ALBÉNIZ
ARENSKY
BANTOCK
BARRAUD
BELLINI
BENNETT
BERGSMA
BERLIOZ
BORODIN
BRITTEN
COPLAND

CORELLI
DEBUSSY
DELIBES
FRANKEL
GIBBONS
GILBERT
HERBERT
IRELAND
JANÁČEK
JOACHIM
LAMBERT
MacCUNN
MALLING
MARTINU
MENOTTI
MILHAUD
NIELSON
NOVELLO
PEPUSCH
POULENC
PUCCINI
PURCELL
QUILTER
RODGERS
ROMBERG
ROSSINI
RUGGLES
SAUGUET
SINDING
SMETANA
STAINER
STRAUSS
TANSMAN
TARTINI
TIPPETT
TORELLI
VIVALDI
WALLACE
WEELKES
XENAKIS

8

AKIMENKO
ALBINONI
BLOMDAHL
BOUGHTON
BRUCKNER
CHABRIER
COUPERIN
DOHNÁNYI
GERSHWIN
GIORDANO
GLAZUNOV
GRAINGER
GRANADOS
HAMLISCH
HERSCHEL
HONEGGER
KETÈLBEY
MAILLART
MASCAGNI
MASSENET
MESSAGER
MESSIAEN
PAGANINI
PALMGREN
PHILIDOR
RAYBOULD
RESPIGHI
SCHNABEL
SCHUBERT
SCHUMANN
SCRIABIN
SIBELIUS
SONDHEIM
SPONTINI
STANFORD
SULLIVAN
TAVERNER
TELEMANN

PEOPLE – COMPOSERS

VICTORIA
WAGENAAR

9

ADDINSELL
BALAKIREV
BEETHOVEN
BERNSTEIN
BUXTEHUDE
CHERUBINI
DONIZETTI
DUNSTABLE
FITELBERG
GRUENBERG
HINDEMITH
LOCATELLI
MacDOWELL
MACKENZIE
MARINETTI
MAZZOCCHI
MEYERBEER
MONIUSZKO
OFFENBACH

PAISIELLO
PERGOLESI
PROKOFIEV
RODRIGUEZ
SCARLATTI
SCHÖNBERG
STEINBACH
STEINBERG
TOMMASINI

10

BLITZSTEIN
BOCCHERINI
FERRABOSCO
KABALEVSKY
MIASKOVSKY
MONTEVERDI
MUSSORGSKY
PALESTRINA
PENDERECKI
PONCHIELLI
RUBINSTEIN
SAINT-SAËNS

SKALKOTTAS
STRAVINSKY
VERSTOVSKY
VILLA-LOBOS
WALDTEUFEL
WILLIAMSON

11

BARING-GOULD
CHARPENTIER
DITTERSDORF
HUMPERDINCK
LEONCAVALLO
LLOYD WEBBER
MENDELSSOHN
NIEDERMEYER
RACHMANINOV
STOCKHAUSEN
TCHAIKOVSKY
WOLF-FERRARI

12

DALLAPICCOLA

KOUSSEVITSKY
ROSTROPOVICH
SHOSTAKOVICH

13

KHATCHATURIAN
ROUGET DE L'ISLE

14

JOSQUIN DES PRÉS
RIMSKY-KORSAKOV

15

ALBRECHTSBERGE
COLERIDGE-TAYLO
IPPOLITOV-IVANOV
SCHNEITZHOEFFER
VAUGHAN WILLIAMS

PEOPLE

CRIMINALS

(A) = Assassin-victim   (O) = Outlaw   (S) = Spy   (W) = War criminal
NB: Double entry = two criminals with same name

4

BELL
HARE *(with BURKE –
    Body-snatchers)*
HESS *(W)*

JUDD *(Phoenix Trunk
    Murders)*
KRAY
RUBY *(A-Oswald)*
RYAN *(Hungerford
    Massacre)*

SPOT

5

ALLEN

BIGGS *(Great Train Robbery)*
BLOOD
BLAKE *(S)*
BLUNT *(S)*
BRADY *(with HINDLEY – Moors Murders)*
BROOK *(Barn Murder)*
BURKE *(with HARE – Body-snatchers)*
DAVIS
ELLIS
EVANS
GODSE *(A-Gandhi)*
HAIGH *(Acid Bath Murders)*
HEATH
HINDS
JAMES *(O)*
JOYCE *(W-Lord Haw-Haw)*
KELLY *(O)* *(Machine-gun)*
MURAT
PEACE
PRIME
PROLL
SMITH *(Brides in the Bath Murders)*
WYNNE *(S)*
ZELLE *(S-Mata Hari)*

6

BAADER
BARBIE *(W)*
BARROW *(O-Clyde of Bonnie & Clyde)*
BOESKY
BONNEY *(O-Billy the Kid)*
BORDEN
CAPONE *(Scarface)*
CORDAY *(A-Marat)*
CORONA
COTTON

DAVIES
HITLER *(W)*
IVANOV *(S)*
LANDRU *(Bluebeard)*
MALONE
MANSON *('Family' Ritual Killings)*
MANUEL
NELSON *(Baby Face)*
OSWALD *(A-J Kennedy)*
PARKER *(O-Bonnie of Bonnie & Clyde)*
PETROV *(S)*
PHILBY *(S)*
STROUD *(Birdman of Alcatraz)*
TURPIN
WILSON *(Great Train Robbery)*

7

BENTLEY
BINGHAM *(S)*
BORMANN *(W)*
BOUVIER
BURGESS *(S)*
CALVERT
CASSIDY *(O-Butch)*
CHAPMAN *(A-Lennon)*
CRIPPEN
DE SALVO *(The Boston Strangler)*
DIAMOND *(Legs)*
EDWARDS *(Great Train Robbery)*
GILMORE
GOERING *(W)*
HIMMLER *(W)*
HINDLEY *(with BRADY – Moors Murders)*
LAFARGE
MACLEAN *(S)*
MANCINI *(Brighton Trunk Murder)*
McMAHON *(A-Mountbatten)*

McVICAR
McVITIE
MEINHOF
MENGELE *(W)*
MERRETT
NEILSON *(Black Panther)*
POULSON
RACHMAN
SANGRET *(Wigwam Murder)*
TETZNER
VASSALL *(S)*
VOLLMAN
WEBSTER

8

BYWATERS
CHESSMAN
CHRISTIE
EICHMANN *(W)*
GOEBBELS *(W)*
HANRATTY *(A6 Murder)*
HOLLIDAY *(O)*
LONSDALE *(S)*
MAYBRICK
MITCHELL *(Mad Axe-man)*
PERUGGIA
QUISLING *(W)*
SEADLUND
THOMPSON

9

CHARRIÈRE *(Papillon)*
DILLINGER
HAUPTMANN *(Lindbergh Kidnapping)*
NICHOLSON
PENKOVSKY *(S)*
STREICHER *(W)*
SUTCLIFFE *(The Yorkshire Ripper)*

10

MERRIFIELD
RIBBENTROP *(W)*

PEOPLE – CRIMINALS

11

WILKES-BOOTH *(A-Lincoln)*

12

SIRHAN SIRHAN *(A-R Kennedy)*

PEOPLE

ENTERTAINERS – ACTORS & ACTRESSES

*B = Baron   *D = Dame   *S = Sir   ¶ = Known by one name only

BOW *(8C)*
DAY *(7J, 8D)*
DEE *(9S)*
EGE *(8J)*
EVE *(9T)*
FOX *(8J, 9E, 11M)*
HAY *(7W)*
KEY *(8J)*
LEE *(8B, 10B, 14C)*
LOM *(10H)*
LOY *(8M)*
MIX *(6T)*
RAY *(7A, 9A)*
RIX *(8B) *S*
ROC *(11P)*
SIM *(9S, 11A)*
VAN *(8B)*
YIP *(8D)*

4

ABEL *(10W)*
ADAM *(10R)*

ALDA *(8A)*
AMES *(8L)*
ARIS *(7B)*
ARNT *(11C)*
AUER *(10M)*
BACH *(11B)*
BALL *(11L, 11V, 12N)*
BARA *(9T)*
BARI *(8L)*
BARR *(11P)*
BASS *(9A)*
BELL *(7A, 7T)*
BIRD *(8J)*
BOHT *(8J)*
BOND *(8W, 9D)*
BOYD *(11S, 11W)*
BRON *(11E)*
BURR *(11R)*
CAAN *(9J)*
CHER *¶*
COBB *(8L)*
COLE *(10G)*
COOK *(10E)*
COPE *(11K)*
CULP *(10R)*
DAHL *(10A)*

DALE *(7J)*
DALY *(8T)*
DEAN *(9J, 9P)*
DORS *(9D)*
DOWN *(14L)*
DREW *(9E)*
DUNN *(9C)*
EDDY *(10N)*
EGAN *(9P, 11R)*
ELAM *(8J)*
ELES *(10S)*
FALK *(9P)*
FARR *(9D)*
FAYE *(9A)*
FORD *(9G, 12H)*
GENN *(7L)*
GERE *(11R)*
GISH *(11L)*
GRAY *(9L, 10D, 11D)*
GREY *(12J)*
GYNT *(9G)*
HALE *(8A, 10S, 11B, 12G)*
HALL *(9H, 10P)*
HARE *(13R)*
HAWN *(10G)*

HIRD *(9T)*
HOLM *(7I)*
HOPE *(7B)*
HUNT *(10G)*
HURT *(8J)*
IDEN *(12R)*
IVES *(8B)*
JEAN *(10G)*
KAHN *(12M)*
KAYE *(9D, 10G)*
KEAN *(10E)*
KEEL *(10H)*
KEEN *(9D)*
KENT *(8J)*
KERR *(11D)*
KNOX *(13A)*
KWAN *(9N)*
KYDD *(7S)*
LADD *(8A, 10C)*
LAHR *(8B)*
LAKE *(12V)*
LANE *(10L)*
LANG *(10R)*
LAYE *(10E)*
LEON *(11V)*
LISI *(9V)*
LORD *(8J)*

LOTT *(11B)*
LOWE *(10A)*
LYNN *(9R)*
LYON *(7B, 7S)*
MAIN *(12M)*
MARX *(9C, 9G,*
9H, 9Z,
11G)
MAYO *(12V)*
MORE *(11K)*
MUIR *(8J)*
MUNI *(8P)*
NEAL *(12P)*
NEFF *(13H)*
NEIL *(14H)*
NERO *(10F)*
OWEN *(8B, 12R)*
PAGE *(13G)*
PECK *(11G)*
PENN *(8S)*
PYNE *(13F)*
RAFT *(10G)*
REED *(9D, 10O)*
REES *(12A)*
REID *(9B)*
RICE *(8J)*
RIGG *(9D)*
ROSS *(13K)*
ROTH *(11L)*
RUSH *(11B)*
RYAN *(8J, 9H,*
10R)
SABU ¶
SHAW *(10M, 10R)*
SHER *(10A)*
SIMS *(8J)*
SOUL *(9D)*
SWIT *(11L)*
SYMS *(10S)*
TATE *(10S)*
TATI *(11J)*
TEAL *(7R)*
THAW *(8J)*
TODD *(7A, 11R)*
TONE *(12F)*
TORN *(7R)*

TOTO ¶
TREE *(11H)* *S
WARD *(8B, 9S,*
10R)
WEBB *(11C)*
WELD *(11T)*
WEST *(7M, 8A,*
11T)
WILD *(8J)*
WING *(8A)*
WOOD *(11N)*
WRAY *(7F)*
YORK *(11M, 12S)*

5

ADAMS *(9E, 9T,*
10J)
ADLER *(11L)*
AIMÉE *(10A)*
AKINS *(11C)*
ALLEN *(10W, 11G,*
12P)
ANNIS *(14F)*
ARDEN *(8E)*
ARKIN *(9A)*
ARLEN *(12R)*
ARNAZ *(9D)*
ASHER *(9J)*
ASNER *(7E)*
ASTOR *(9M)*
AUTRY *(9G)*
AYRES *(8L)*
BAKER *(8T, 10C,*
11G, 12C,
12S) *S
BANKS *(11L)*
BARON *(10L)*
BARRY *(9G)*
BATES *(9A, 10R,*
13F)
BEENY
BEERY *(9N, 12W)*
BERLE *(11M)*
BEWES *(11R)*

BIXBY *(9B)*
BLACK *(10K)*
BLAKE *(11A)*
BLOOM *(11C)*
BLORE *(9E)*
BLYTH *(8A)*
BOLAM *(10J)*
BONDI *(11B)*
BOONE *(12R)*
BOOTH *(10E, 12A)*
BOWIE *(10D)*
BOYER *(12C)*
BRENT *(11G)*
BRETT *(11J)*
BROOK *(10C)*
BROWN *(9J)*
BRUCE *(10N, 11B)*
BRYAN *(9D)*
BUONO *(11V)*
BURKE *(11A)*
BURNS *(11G)*
BUSCH *(8M)*
BYRNE *(10P)*
CAINE *(12M)*
CAREY *(10J)*
CARNE *(9J)*
CARON *(11L)*
CHASE *(10C, 13L)*
CLARK *(9F, 11P)*
CLIFT *(15M)*
CLIVE *(7E)*
CLOSE *(10G)*
CONTE *(12R)*
CONTI *(8T)*
CORKE *(10F)*
CORRI *(13A)*
COSBY *(9B)*
COURT *(10H)*
CRAIG *(10W, 12M)*
CROSS *(8B)*
DALIO *(11M)*
DANCE *(12C)*
DARIN *(10B)*
DARRO *(12F)*
DAVIS *(9J, 10B,*
10S)

DELON *(10A)*
DENCH *(9J)* *D
DEREK *(7B, 9J)*
DONAT *(11R)*
DRAKE *(14G)*
DUFFY *(12P)*
DUNNE *(10I)*
DYALL *(14V)*
EATON *(12S)*
EBSEN *(10B)*
EGGAR *(13S)*
ELVEY *(12M)*
ESSEX *(10D)*
EVANS *(9D, 10B,*
10E *D,*
10L)
EWELL *(8T)*
FAITH *(9A)*
FIELD *(8S, 10B,*
10S, 15S)
FINCH *(10P)*
FLYNN *(10E, 12B)*
FONDA *(9J, 10H,*
10P)
FROBE *(9G)*
GABIN *(9J)*
GABLE *(10C)*
GABOR *(8E, 11Z)*
GARBO *(10G)*
GAUGE *(14A)*
GAUNT *(12W)*
GLESS *(11S)*
GOUGH *(12M)*
GOULD *(12E)*
GRANT *(8L, 9C,*
12D)
GROOM *(8S)*
GROUT *(10J)*
GWENN *(11E)*
HAGEN *(9J)*
HAIGH *(12K)*
HANDL *(10I)*
HANKS *(8T)*
HARDY *(11O, 11R)*
HAYES *(10H, 11M,*
13P)

275

HENIE *(10S)*
HINES *(11F, 12G)*
HODGE *(13P)*
HOWES *(10B, 13S)*
HULCE *(8T)*
IMRIE *(10C)*
INMAN *(9J)*
IRONS *(11J)*
JAFFE *(8S)*
JAMES *(8S, 14G)*
JASON *(10D)*
JAYNE *(13J)*
JOHNS *(11G, 11M, 14S)*
JONES *(10A, 10P, 12S, 13J)*
JOYCE *(11Y)*
KEACH *(10S)*
KEITH *(13P)*
KELLY *(9G, 9P, 10G)*
KLINE *(10K)*
KWOUK *(9B)*
LACEY *(11R)*
LAINE *(12F)*
LANGE *(9H, 12J)*
LANZA *(10M)*
LEACH *(13R)*
LEIGH *(10J, 11V)*
LENYA *(10L)*
LE ROY *(11M)*
LEWIS *(10J)*
LLOYD *(8S, 11H)*
LODGE *(10D)*
LOGAN *(12P)*
LOREN *(11S)*
LORRE *(10P)*
LUCAN *(11A)*
LUCAS *(12W)*
LUKAS *(9P)*
MADOC *(9R, 11P)*
MAGEE *(12P)*
MARCH *(12F)*
MARKS *(11A)*
MARSH *(9J, 11M, 13R)*

MASON *(10J)*
MAYNE *(10F)*
McCOY *(14S)*
MILES *(10S, 12B) *S*
MILLS *(9J *S, 11H, 11J)*
MOODY *(8R)*
MOORE *(10R, 11D, 12C, 14M)*
MORSE *(10B, 10H)*
MOUNT *(10P)*
MOWER *(12P)*
MUNRO *(10J)*
NAISH *(12J)*
NARES *(9O)*
NIMMO *(10D)*
NIMOY *(12L)*
NIVEN *(10D)*
NOLAN *(10L)*
NOLTE *(9N)*
NOVAK *(8K)*
OAKIE *(9J)*
OATES *(11W)*
O'HARA *(12M)*
OLAND *(11W)*
OLSEN *(8O)*
O'MARA *(9K)*
O'NEAL *(9R, 10T, 12P)*
O'SHEA *(9M, 11T)*
PAPAS *(10I)*
PARKS *(10L)*
PAYNE *(13L)*
PITTS *(9Z)*
POSTA *(13A)*
POWER *(11T)*
PRAED *(12M)*
PRICE *(11D, 12V)*
PRIOR *(12M)*
PRYOR *(12R)*
QUICK *(10D)*
QUINN *(12A)*
RAINS *(11C)*
RALPH *(11J)*
REEVE
RENZI *(8E)*

RIGBY *(12T)*
ROMAN *(9R)*
SACHS *(11A)*
SAINT *(13E)*
SAXON *(9J)*
SCOTT *(10T, 11G, 12G, 12J, 12Z, 13R)*
SEARS *(12H)*
SEGAL *(11G)*
SELBY *(9T)*
SETON *(10B) *S*
SHANE *(9P)*
SHEEN *(11M)*
SILVA *(10H)*
SIMON *(11S)*
SMITH *(8R, 11M, 12C) *S*
SOLON *(9E)*
STACK *(11R)*
STAFF *(10K)*
STAMP *(12T)*
STARK *(11G)*
STEEL *(12A)*
STING ¶
STOCK *(10N)*
STONE *(10L, 12M)*
STORM *(9G)*
TANDY *(12J)*
TERRY *(10E) *D*
TILLY *(8M)*
TOLER *(11S)*
TOPOL ¶
TORMÉ *(8M)*
TRACY *(8L, 12S)*
TULLY *(10S)*
TUTIN *(12D)*
URICH *(11R)*
VANCE *(11V)*
VEIDT *(11C)*
WAITE *(10R)*
WALSH *(8K)*
WAYNE *(9J)*
WELCH *(11R)*
WELLS *(9J)*
WHITE *(10C, 10P)*

WILDE *(11C)*
WYATT *(9J)*
WYMAN *(9J)*
YATES *(12P)*
YOUNG *(8G, 9A, 11R, 12L)*
ZUCCO *(11G)*

6.

ABBOTT *(9B)*
ADDAMS *(10D)*
AHERNE *(11B)*
AITKEN *(11M)*
ALBERT *(11E)*
ALTMAN *(10J)*
AMECHE *(9D)*
ANGELI *(10P)*
ANGERS *(11A)*
ANHOLT *(10T)*
ANKERS *(12E)*
ANSARA *(13M)*
ARLISS *(12G)*
ARNATT *(10J)*
ARNAUD *(12Y)*
ARNESS *(11J)*
ARNOLD *(12E)*
ARNOUL *(15F)*
ARTHUR *(10J)*
ATKINS *(11C, 12E)*
ATWILL *(12L)*
AUDRAN *(14S)*
AVALON *(13F)*
AYLMER *(11F) *S*
BACALL *(12L)*
BACKUS *(9J)*
BAILEY *(11P, 11R)*
BALSAM *(12M)*
BANNEN *(9I)*
BARDOT *(14B)*
BARKER *(9L, 10E)*
BARNES *(12B)*
BARRIE *(12A)*
BARRON *(10J, 11K)*
BARTOK *(9E)*

BAXTER *(10A, 12W)*
BEATTY *(12R, 12W)*
BENDIX *(13W)*
BENSON *(11F) *S*
BERGEN *(13C)*
BIRKIN *(10J)*
BISSET
BOGART *(14H)*
BOLGER *(9R)*
BOSLEY *(9T)*
BOWLES *(11P)*
BRANDO *(12M)*
BRAZZI *(13R)*
BRIERS *(13R)*
BRIGGS *(12J)*
BROLIN *(11J)*
BROOKS *(9R)*
BROWNE *(10J, 11C)*
BRYANT *(13M)*
BURTON *(13R)*
BYRNES *(9E)*
CADELL *(11S)*
CAGNEY *(11J)*
CALLOW *(11S)*
CANNON *(10D, 10E)*
CANTOR *(11E)*
CARNEY *(9A)*
CARSON *(10J, 12V, 13J)*
CARTER *(11L)*
CASSON *(11L) *S*
CHANEY *(9L)*
CHASEN *(13H)*
CHERRY *(11H)*
CHITTY *(10E)*
CLEESE *(10J)*
COBURN *(11J, 13C)*
COLMAN *(12R)*
CONNOR *(13K)*
COOGAN *(12J)*
COOMBS *(9P)*
COOPER *(10G, 12G) *D*
COTTEN *(12J)*
COWARD *(10N) *S*
CRABBE *(12B)*
CRAVEN *(11G)*
CROSBY *(10B)*

CRUISE *(9T)*
CULVER *(12R)*
CURRIE *(12F)*
CURTIS *(10T, 14J)*
CUSACK *(11C, 12S)*
DAILEY *(9D)*
DALTON *(13T)*
DAMONE *(9V)*
DARREN *(11J)*
DAVIES *(12R, 13W)*
DAWSON *(10A)*
DECKER *(11D)*
DEL RIO *(13D)*
DENHAM *(13M)*
DE NIRO *(12R)*
DE SICA *(14V)*
DEVANE *(13W)*
DEVINE *(10A)*
DE VITO *(11D)*
DEXTER *(10B)*
DIBLEY *(11J)*
DILLER *(13P)*
DOBSON *(11A)*
DUMONT *(14M)*
DUNCAN *(12A)*
DURBIN *(12D)*
EKBERG *(11A)*
EKLAND *(11B)*
ESMOND *(10C, 10J)*
FARGAS *(13A)*
FERRER *(9M, 10J)*
FIELDS *(8W, 12G) *D*
FINLAY *(11F)*
FISHER *(12C)*
FORMBY *(12G)*
FOSTER *(11B, 11J)*
FOWLDS *(11D)*
FOWLER *(11H)*
FRASER *(9L, 10B, 12R)*
FULLER *(12L)*
GAMBON *(13M)*
GARNER *(11J)*
GARSON *(11G)*
GAYNOR *(11J, 11M)*
GEESON *(10J, 11S)*
GEORGE *(11S)*

GIBSON *(9M, 11H)*
GLASER
GLOVER *(11B, 12J)*
GORCEY *(9L)*
GORDON *(10G, 10M, 11N, 12H)*
GORING *(12M)*
GRABLE *(11B)*
GRAVES *(11P)*
GREENE *(11L, 13R)*
GUYLER *(12D)*
GWYNNE *(10F)*
HAGMAN *(11L)*
HAMILL *(10M)*
HANLEY *(11J)*
HANNAH *(11D)*
HARDIN *(8T)*
HARLOW *(10J)*
HARPER *(12G, 13J, 13V)*
HARRIS *(11J, 13R)*
HARVEY *(9J, 14L)*
HAVERS *(11N)*
HAYDEN *(14S)*
HAYTER *(11J)*
HEDLEY *(10J)*
HEDREN *(11T)*
HEFLIN *(9V)*
HEMPEL *(13A)*
HENDRY *(9I)*
HENSON *(11N, 12G)*
HEPTON *(13B)*
HESTON *(14C)*
HILLER *(11W) *D*
HOBSON *(13V)*
HOLDEN *(9F, 13W)*
HOWARD *(12A, 12L, 12T)*
HOWERD *(13F)*
HUDSON *(10R)*
HUGHES *(11N, 11W)*
HUNTER *(9I, 9T, 13R)*
HUSSEY *(10R, 12O)*
HUSTON *(12W)*
HUTTON *(11B)*
INGRAM *(9R)*
IRVING *(11H) *S*
JACOBI *(11D)*

JARVIS *(12M)*
JESSEL *(12G)*
JOLSON *(8A)*
KARLIN *(12M)*
KEATON *(11D, 12B)*
KEELER *(10R)*
KENDAL *(14F)*
KOVACK *(11N)*
KRUGER *(11H)*
LAMARR *(10H)*
LAMOUR *(13D)*
LANDEN *(14D)*
LANDON *(13M)*
LATHAM *(12P)*
LAUREL *(10S)*
LAURIE *(10J, 11P)*
LAWSON *(11S, 13W)*
LAYTON *(12G)*
LEMMON *(10J)*
LENSKA *(10R)*
LESLIE *(10J)*
LESTER *(10M)*
LEVANT *(11O)*
LILLIE *(14B)*
LINDEN *(12J)*
LINDER *(9M)*
LIPMAN *(13M)*
LISTER *(11M)*
LONDON *(11J)*
LUGOSI *(10B)*
LUMLEY *(12J)*
LUPINO *(9I)*
MACKAY *(12F)*
MacNEE *(13P)*
MACRAE *(12D)*
MAGILL *(12R)*
MAJORS *(9L)*
MALDEN *(10K)*
MALONE *(13D)*
MARTIN *(10D, 10M, 15M, 15P)*
MARVIN *(9L)*
MASSEY *(10A, 13R)*
MATURE *(12V)*
McCREA *(10J)*
McEWAN *(15G)*

McKERN *(9L)*
MEDWIN *(13M)*
MENJOU *(13A)*
MERMAN *(11E)*
MIDLER *(11B)*
MIRREN *(11H)*
MONROE *(13M)*
MOREAU *(12J)*
MORELL *(11A)*
MORGAN *(11F, 11H, 14G)*
MORLEY *(12R)*
MORRIS *(10L, 13C)*
MORROW *(9V)*
MOSTEL *(10Z)*
MULLEN *(13B)*
MURPHY *(11A, 11B, 11E, 12G)*
MURRAY *(9D, 10B, 13B)*
MURTON *(12L)*
NAPIER *(10A)*
NEAGLE *(10A) *D*
NELSON *(8E, 10G)*
NEWLEY *(13A)*
NEWMAN *(10P, 11B, 13N)*
NEWTON *(12R)*
NOIRET *(14P)*
OBERON *(11M)*
O'BRIAN *(10H)*
O'BRIEN *(9P, 12E, 14M)*
OGILVY *(9I)*
O'KEEFE *(12D)*
O'TOOLE *(11P)*
OULTON *(11B)*
PACINO *(8A)*
PAGETT *(12N)*
PALMER *(11L, 14G)*
PARKER *(11C)*
PARTON *(11D)*
PICKUP *(12R)*
PITHEY *(13W)*
PORTER *(10E, 15N)*
POWELL *(10D, 10J, 12R)*
POWERS *(14S)*
PROWSE *(12J)*
PURDOM *(12E)*
QUALEN *(10J)*

QUAYLE *(10A, 10J,*
13A) *S
RAINER *(11L)*
REAGAN *(12R)*
REDMAN *(11J)*
REEVES *(11S, 14K)*
REINER *(10C)*
REMICK *(9L)*
RENNIE *(13M)*
RHODES *(10E, 14M)*
RIDGES *(13S)*
RIDLEY *(12A)*
RITTER *(9T, 12T)*
ROACHE *(13W)*
ROBSON *(9M, 11F) *D*
ROGERS *(9R, 10W, 12G)*
ROLAND *(13G)*
ROMAIN *(12Y)*
ROMERO *(11C)*
ROONEY *(12M)*
ROURKE *(12M)*
SALLIS *(11P)*
SCALES *(14P)*
SCHELL *(11M)*
SEWELL *(12G)*
SHARIF *(10O)*
SHINER *(12R)*
SIDNEY *(12S)*
SINDEN *(12D)*
SINGER *(14C)*
SLATER *(10J)*
SLOANE *(13E)*
SOMMER *(10E)*
SPACEK *(11S)*
STEELE *(11T, 13B)*
ST JOHN *(10J)*
STREEP *(11M)*
STRIDE *(10J)*
STUBBS *(9U)*
SUCHET *(11D)*
SUGDEN *(12M)*
SUZMAN *(11J)*
SWAYZE *(13P)*
TAFLER *(12S)*
TAUBER *(13R)*
TAYLOR *(12R, 15E)*

TEARLE *(13G) *S*
TEMPLE *(13S)*
TEWSON *(15G)*
THOMAS *(11T)*
THORNE *(12A)*
TOBIAS *(12G, 12O)*
TOMLIN *(10L)*
TOM MIX
TREVOR *(12C)*
TUCKER *(12S, 13F)*
TURNER *(10L, 14K)*
TURPIN *(9B)*
TWIGGY *¶*
TYZACK *(14M)*
URECAL *(13M)*
VALLEE *(10R)*
VARNEY *(9R)*
VAUGHN *(12R)*
VERNON *(13R)*
VOIGHT *(9J)*
WAGNER *(12R, 13L)*
WALKER *(10Z, 11C, 11N)*
WARNER *(8H, 10J, 11D)*
WATSON *(10J, 11W)*
WATTIS *(13R)*
WAXMAN *(8A)*
WEAVER *(12D, 15S)*
WELLES *(11O)*
WERNER *(11O)*
WHITTY *(9M) *D*
WILCOX *(11P)*
WILDER *(10G)*
WILLIS *(11B)*
WILSON *(12D, 13R)*
WILTON *(14P)*
WINGER *(11D)*
WISDOM *(12N)*
WOLFIT *(12D) *S*
WRIGHT *(10W, 12T)*
WYMARK *(13P)*
WYNTER *(10D)*
ZADORA *(9P)*

7

ABRAHAM *(14F)*

ACKLAND *(11J)*
AGUTTER *(12J)*
ALDO RAY
ALLGOOD *(11S)*
ALLYSON *(11J)*
ANDRESS *(13U)*
ANDREWS *(11D, 12H,*
12J, 14A)
ANN BELL
ANN TODD
ARLETTY *¶*
ASKWITH *(12R)*
ASTAIRE *(11F)*
AYKROYD *(10D)*
BABCOCK *(14B)*
BAINTER *(10F)*
BALFOUR *(14M)*
BASTEDO
BAYLDON *(15G)*
BEACHAM
BELLAMY *(12R)*
BEN ARIS
BEN LYON
BENNETT *(11J, 12H)*
BERGMAN *(13I)*
BERTISH *(14S)*
BLAKELY *(12C)*
BLESSED *(12B)*
BLETHYN *(13B)*
BLOCKER *(10D)*
BOB HOPE
BO DEREK
BOGARDE *(11D)*
BOTTOMS *(14T)*
BOUCHET *(14B)*
BRACKEN *(12E)*
BRANAGH *(14K)*
BRENNAN *(13W)*
BRIDGES *(11B, 11J, 12L)*
BRITTON *(11T)*
BRONSON *(14C)*
BRYNNER *(10Y)*
BURBAGE *(14R)*
BUTTONS *(10R)*
CALHERN *(12L)*
CALHOUN *(11R)*

CALVERT *(14P)*
CAMERON *(10R)*
CARGILL *(14P)*
CARROLL *(10L, 14D)*
CHAPLIN *(10S, 14C)* *S
CILENTO *(12D)*
COLBERT
COLLINS *(10R, 11J,*
12L, 14P)
COLONNA *(12J)*
COMPTON *(10F)*
CONKLIN *(14C)*
CONNERY *(11S, 12J)*
CONNORS *(12C)*
CORBETT *(13H)*
CRANHAM *(14K)*
CROSBIE *(14A)*
CUSHING *(12P)*
DALTREY *(12R)*
DANEMAN *(11P)*
DANIELL *(12H)*
DANIELS *(11B)*
DARNELL *(12L)*
DAVISON *(12P)*
DE HAVEN *(13G)*
DENEUVE
DENISON *(14M)*
DONOVAN *(12J)*
DOTRICE *(10R, 12K,*
14M)
DOUGLAS *(11K, 13A,*
13M, 14M)
DRESDEL *(12S)*
DUNAWAY *(11F)*
DURANTE *(12J)*
DUTTINE *(11J)*
ED ASNER
EDWARDS *(12G, 12V)*
EE CLIVE
ELLIOTT *(14D)*
ELPHICK *(14M)*
ESTRADA *(11E)*
FANTONI *(13S)*
FARRELL *(11M, 13G)*
FAWCETT *(13F)*
FAY WRAY

FELDMAN *(12M)*
FIRBANK *(10A)*
FLEMING *(13R)*
FORREST *(12S)*
FORSYTH *(13B)*
FRANCIS *(10J, 10K,*
11A, 14R)
FRAWLEY *(14W)*
FRICKER *(13B)*
GARDNER *(10A)*
GARLAND *(11J)*
GARRICK *(12D)*
GAZZARA *(10B)*
GIELGUD *(11J)* *S
GILBERT *(11J)*
GILMORE *(12S)*
GINGOLD *(15H)*
GLEASON *(13J)*
GODDARD *(11L, 15P)*
GODSELL *(12V)*
GRAHAME *(13G)*
GRANGER *(14S)*
GRAYSON *(14K)*
GREGORY *(12J)*
GREGSON *(11J)*
GUTHRIE *(11A)*
HACKMAN *(11G)*
HAMMOND *(10K)*
HANCOCK *(13S)*
HARDING *(10A)*
HAWKINS *(11J)*
HAWTREY *(14C)*
HAYWARD *(12S)*
HELMOND
HENREID *(11P)*
HEPBURN *(13A)*
HEYWOOD *(11A)*
HICKSON *(11J)*
HOFFMAN *(13D)*
HOMOLKA *(12O)*
HOPKINS *(9B, 14A)*
HORDERN *(14M)* *S
HOSKINS *(10B)*
HOUSTON *(11G, 12R,*
13D)
HOWELLS *(13U)*

HOWLETT *(11N)*
HULBERT *(11J)*
HUNTLEY *(14R)*
IAN HOLM
IRELAND *(11J)*
JACKSON *(13G)*
JACQUES *(13H)*
JAMESON *(13L)*
JANSSEN *(12D)*
JAYSTON *(14M)*
JENKINS *(11M)*
JILL DAY
JIM DALE
JOHNSON *(10D, 10K,*
10V, 12C) *D
JOURDAN *(12L)*
JURGENS *(11C)*
JUSTICE
KARLOFF *(12B)*
KENDALL *(10K, 11S)*
KENNEDY *(13A, 13G)*
KINNEAR *(10R)*
KITCHEN *(14M)*
KOSSOFF *(12D)*
KRISTEL *(13S)*
LANGDON *(12H)*
LAZENBY *(13G)*
LEO GENN
LIVESEY *(12R)*
LOMBARD *(13C)*
MacGRAW *(10A)*
MADDERN *(13V)*
MADONNA ¶
MAE WEST
MAGNANI *(11A)*
MAHARIS *(13G)*
MARSDEN *(10R)*
MATTHAU *(13W)*
MAXWELL *(11L)*
MAYNARD *(11B)*
McCOWEN *(11A)*
McGUIRE *(14D)*
McKENNA *(15V)*
McQUEEN *(12S)*
McSHANE *(10I)*
MERCIER *(13S)*

MICHELL *(12K)*
MILLAND *(10R)*
MINOGUE *(12K)*
MITCHUM *(13R)*
MONTAND *(11Y)*
MULLARD *(13A)*
NESBITT *(13D)*
NETTLES *(11J)*
NEVILLE *(11J)*
NICHOLS *(12D)*
NOVARRO *(12R)*
O'CONNOR *(10U, 13D)*
OLIVIER *(15L) *B*
ORCHARD *(13J)*
PALANCE *(11J)*
PALUZZI *(14L)*
PARKINS *(14B)*
PATRICK *(12N)*
PEPPARD *(13G)*
PERKINS *(14A)*
PERREAU *(11G)*
PERTWEE *(10J, 11B)*
PETROVA *(11O)*
PHOENIX *(10P)*
PICKLES *(14W)*
PIDGEON *(13W)*
PLUMMER
POITIER *(13S)*
POLLARD *(9S)*
PORTMAN *(11E)*
PRESLEY *(12E)*
PRESTON *(13R)*
PRINGLE *(12B)*
PROVINE *(14D)*
QUILLEY *(13D)*
QUINTEN *(12C)*
RANDALL *(11J, 11T,*
 13L)
RANDELL *(10R)*
RAYMOND *(11G)*
RAY TEAL
REDFORD *(13R)*
RENALDO *(13D)*
RICHARD *(12C, 12W)*
RINGHAM *(11J)*
RIP TORN

RITCHIE *(11J)*
ROBARDS *(12J)*
ROBERTS *(13R)*
ROBESON *(11P)*
RODGERS *(12A)*
RUGGLES *(14C)*
RUSSELL *(11J, 15R)*
SAM KYDD
SANDERS *(13G)*
SARGENT *(11D)*
SAVALAS *(12T)*
SELLARS
SELLECK *(10T)*
SELLERS *(12P)*
SEYMOUR *(11A, 11J)*
SHATNER *(14W)*
SHEARER *(12M, 12N)*
SHELLEY *(14B)*
SHIELDS *(13A, 13B)*
SIDDONS *(12S)*
SILVERA *(13C)*
SILVERS *(11P)*
SIMMONS *(11J)*
SINATRA *(12F)*
SKELTON *(10R)*
SOTHERN *(10A)*
STEIGER *(10R)*
STEWART *(12J)*
STEVENS *(13C, 13R,*
 13S)
STRITCH *(13E)*
SUE LYON
SWANSON *(13G)*
TAMBLYN *(11R)*
TEMPEST *(12M) *D*
THORSON *(12L)*
TIERNEY *(11G)*
TIMOTHY
TOM BELL
TRAVERS *(11B)*
ULLMANN *(10L)*
USTINOV *(12P) *S*
VALLONE *(10R)*
VAN DYKE *(11D)*
VAUGHAN *(12P)*
VENTHAM *(12W)*

WALLACH *(10E)*
WALTERS *(12J, 14T)*
WARRICK *(11R)*
WATFORD *(11G)*
WATLING *(11J)*
WELLAND *(12C)*
WHITING *(14L)*
WHITMAN *(13S)*
WIDMARK *(14R)*
WILDING *(14M)*
WILL HAY
WINDSOR *(12F, 14B)*
WINKLER *(12H)*
WINTERS *(14S)*
WITHERS *(13G)*
WOOLLEY *(12M)*
YARDLEY *(14S)*

8

ADAM WEST
ALAN ALDA
ALAN HALE
ALAN LADD
ALBRIGHT *(14H)*
AL JOLSON
AL PACINO
ALVARADO *(11D)*
AL WAXMAN
ANDERSON *(12J, 13E,*
 *14J *D,*
 14W, 15B)
ANNA WING
ANN BLYTH
ARBUCKLE *(13F)*
ASHCROFT *(13P) *D*
BADDELEY *(14A)*
BANCROFT *(12A)*
BANERJEE *(14V)*
BANKHEAD
BASEHART *(15R)*
BASINGER *(11K)*
BEN CROSS
BENEDICT *(12D, 13B)*
BERT LAHR

PEOPLE – ENTERTAINERS – ACTORS & ACTRESSES

BICKFORD *(15C)*
BILL OWEN
BLACKMAN *(13H)*
BLONDELL *(12J)*
BOBBY VAN
BORGNINE *(14E)*
BRAMBELL *(15W)*
BRESSLAW *(15B)*
BRIAN RIX *S*
BROMBERG *(15J)*
BRUCE LEE
BUCHANAN *(12J, 13E)*
BURL IVES
BURT WARD
CALDICOT *(15R)*
CAPUCINE ¶
CARRILLO *(11L)*
CARTERET *(12A)*
CAVANAGH *(12P)*
CAZENOVE
CHAKIRIS *(14G)*
CHANDLER *(12J, 13H)*
CHANNING *(13C)*
CHARISSE *(11C)*
CHRISTIE *(13J)*
CLARA BOW
CLEMENTS *(12J) *S*
COLLEANO *(13B)*
COLLINGE
CONNOLLY *(14W)*
COSTELLO *(11L)*
CRAWFORD *(12J, 15M)*
CRIBBINS *(15B)*
CUMMINGS *(14R)*
DANIELLE *(15S)*
DAVID YIP
DAY-LEWIS *(14D)*
DE LA TOUR *(15F)*
DESMONDE *(13J)*
DIETRICH *(15M)*
DIFFRING *(13A)*
DONNELLY *(12R)*
DORIS DAY
DRESSLER *(13M)*
DREYFUSS *(15R)*
EASTWOOD *(13C)*

ED NELSON
ERICKSON *(12L)*
EVA GABOR
EVA RENZI
EVE ARDEN
FIELDING *(15F)*
FLANNERY *(13S)*
FONTAINE *(12J)*
FORSYTHE *(12J)*
FRANKLYN *(15W)*
GASCOINE *(12J)*
GIG YOUNG
GOLDBERG *(14W)*
GOODYEAR *(13J)*
GRANTHAM *(14L)*
GRENFELL *(13J)*
GRIFFITH *(12H)*
GUARDINO *(13H)*
GUINNESS *(12A) *S*
HAGGERTY *(11D)*
HALLIDAY *(12J)*
HAMILTON *(14G)*
HARRISON *(11R) *S*
HARTNELL *(15W)*
HAYWORTH *(12R)*
HB WARNER
HELPMANN *(14R) *S*
HEMMINGS *(13D)*
HOLLIDAY *(12J)*
HOLLOWAY *(15S)*
HOUSEMAN *(12J)*
JACK ELAM
JACK LORD
JACK WILD
JAMES FOX
JANET KEY
JEAN BOHT
JEAN KENT
JEAN MUIR
JEFFRIES *(14L)*
JOAN RICE
JOAN SIMS
JOHN BIRD
JOHN HURT
JOHN RYAN
JOHN THAW

JULIE EGE
KAY WALSH
KELLAWAY *(13C)*
KIM NOVAK
KINGSLEY *(11B)*
LANGFORD *(14B)*
LANSBURY *(14A)*
LAUGHTON *(15C)*
LAVENDER *(11I)*
LAVERICK *(12J)*
LAWRENCE
LEE GRANT
LEE J COBB
LEE TRACY
LEIGHTON
LEON AMES
LEW AYRES
LOCKHART *(12G)*
LOCKWOOD *(13J)*
LYNN BARI
MACLAINE *(15S)*
MACREADY *(14G)*
MAE BUSCH
MATTHEWS *(10A, 14J, 15F)*
McCALLUM *(13D)*
McDOWALL *(13B, 13R)*
McGOOHAN *(15P)*
McKELLEN *(11I) *S*
McKENZIE *(13J)*
McLAGLEN *(14V)*
MEG TILLY
MEL TORMÉ
MERCOURI *(14M)*
MEREDITH *(15B)*
MINNELLI *(12L)*
MITCHELL *(14W)*
MYRNA LOY
NICHOLAS *(12P)*
NICHOLLS *(11S)*
O'FARRELL
OLE OLSEN
PAUL MUNI
PENTELOW *(14A)*
PERCIVAL *(13L)*
PHILLIPS *(12S, 14L)*

PICKFORD *(12M)*
PRENTISS *(13P)*
RAFFERTY *(13C)*
RAMPLING
RATHBONE *(13B)*
RAY SMITH
REDGRAVE *(12L,*
15M *S,
15V)
REYNOLDS *(12B, 14D)*
ROBINSON *(15E)*
RON MOODY
ROSSITER *(15L)*
ROWLANDS *(13P)*
SAM GROOM
SAM JAFFE
SARRAZIN *(15M)*
SCHEIDER *(11R)*
SCHRODER *(13R)*
SCOFIELD *(13J)*
SEAN PENN
SHEPHERD *(14C)*
SHERIDAN *(11A, 13D)*
SID FIELD
SID JAMES
SIGNORET *(14S)*
SPINETTI *(14V)*
STALLONE
STANDING *(11G *S,*
12J)
STANWYCK *(15B)*
STEADMAN *(14A)*
STERLING *(11J)*
SUE LLOYD
TALMADGE *(13N)*
THOMPSON *(12J)*
THOMSETT *(13S)*
THORBURN *(12J)*
THORNTON *(13F)*
TINGWELL *(15C)*
TOM BAKER
TOM CONTI
TOM EWELL
TOM HANKS
TOM HULCE
TRAVOLTA *(12J)*

TREACHER *(12B)*
TY HARDIN
TYNE DALY
URQUHART *(14R)*
VAN CLEEF *(11L)*
VAN DOREN *(13M)*
VILLIERS *(13J)*
WARD BOND
WATERMAN *(14D)*
WC FIELDS
WHEATLEY *(12A)*
WHITELAW *(14B)*
WILLIAMS *(13S, 14E,*
15K, 15M)
WINFIELD *(12P)*
WOODWARD *(14E, 14J)*

9

ADAM FAITH
ALAN ARKIN
ALAN BATES
ALAN YOUNG
ALEXANDER *(13J)*
ALFIE BASS
ALICE FAYE
ANDERSSON *(13B)*
ANDREW RAY
ARMSTRONG *(15R)*
ART CARNEY
BARKWORTH *(14P)*
BARRYMORE *(13D, 13J,*
14E, 15L)
BEL GEDDES
BEN TURPIN
BERNHARDT *(14S)*
BERYL REID
BILL BIXBY
BILL COSBY
BO HOPKINS
BUD ABBOTT
BURT KWOUK
CARDINALE
CARRADINE *(13J, 14D)*
CARY GRANT

CHEVALIER
CHICO MARX
CHURCHILL *(14D, 14S)*
CLIVE DUNN
COLBOURNE
COURTENAY *(12T)*
CRUTCHLEY
DALE EVANS
DAN DAILEY
DANNY KAYE
DAVENPORT *(14H, 14N)*
DAVID SOUL
DEREK BOND
DEREK FARR
DESI ARNAZ
DIANA DORS
DIANA RIGG
DIANE KEEN
DICKINSON *(14A, 15S)*
DON AMECHE
DON MURRAY
DONNA REED
DORA BRYAN
EDD BYRNES
EDDINGTON *(13P)*
EDIE ADAMS
EDWARD FOX
ELLEN DREW
ERIC BLORE
EVA BARTOK
EWEN SOLON
FAIRBANKS
FAIRCHILD *(15M)*
FAITHFULL
FAY HOLDEN
FERNANDEL ¶
FRED CLARK
FREDERICK *(14L)*
FULLERTON *(14F)*
GALE STORM
GENE AUTRY
GENE BARRY
GENE KELLY
GERT FROBE
GLENN FORD
GREENWOOD *(13J)*

PEOPLE – ENTERTAINERS – ACTORS & ACTRESSES

GRETA GYNT
GUILLAUME *(15R)*
GUMMO MARX
HAMPSHIRE *(14S)*
HARDWICKE *(15C)* *S
HARPO MARX
HAWTHORNE *(14N)*
HELEN RYAN
HENDERSON *(12D)*
HOPE LANGE
HUNNICUTT *(14G)*
HUNTZ HALL
HYDE-WHITE
IAN BANNEN
IAN HENDRY
IAN HUNTER
IAN OGILVY
IDA LUPINO
JACK OAKIE
JAMES CAAN
JAMES DEAN
JANE ASHER
JANE FONDA
JANE WYATT
JANE WYMAN
JAN HARVEY
JEAN GABIN
JEAN HAGEN
JEAN MARSH
JIM BACKUS
JOAN DAVIS
JOE E BROWN
JOHN DEREK
JOHN INMAN
JOHN MILLS *S
JOHN SAXON
JOHN WAYNE
JOHN WELLS
JON VOIGHT
JUDI DENCH *D
JUDY CARNE
KATE O'MARA
KELLERMAN *(14S)*
KERCHEVAL *(12K)*
LANCASTER *(13B)*
LAPOTAIRE *(13J)*

LEE MAJORS
LEE MARVIN
LEE REMICK
LEO GORCEY
LEO McKERN
LEX BARKER
LILLICRAP
LINDA GRAY
LIZ FRASER
LON CHANEY
LYNDHURST
MacARTHUR *(14J)*
MACDONALD *(13A)*
MacMURRAY *(13F)*
MANSFIELD *(14J)*
MARY ASTOR
MAX LINDER
MAY ROBSON
MAY WHITTY *D
MEL FERRER
MEL GIBSON
MILO O'SHEA
MOOREHEAD *(14A)*
NANCY KWAN
NETTLETON *(13L)*
NICHOLSON *(13J)*
NICK NOLTE
NOAH BEERY
O'SULLIVAN
OWEN NARES
PAT COOMBS
PAT O'BRIEN
PAUL KELLY
PAUL LUKAS
PAUL SHANE
PETER DEAN
PETER EGAN
PETER FALK
PIA ZADORA
PLEASENCE *(15D)*
PLOWRIGHT *(13J)*
PRINCIPAL
RALPH LYNN
RAY BOLGER
RAY BROOKS
REG VARNEY

REX INGRAM
ROBERTSON *(13D, 14C)*
ROY ROGERS
RUTH MADOC
RUTH ROMAN
RYAN O'NEAL
SANDERSON *(13J)*
SANDRA DEE
SCHNEIDER *(13R)*
SHEILA SIM
SIMON WARD
SLAUGHTER *(12T)*
SMETHURST *(13J)*
ST CLEMENT *(12P)*
STOCKWELL *(13D)*
STREISAND *(15B)*
STRUTHERS *(14S)*
SU POLLARD
TAB HUNTER
TAYLFORTH
TEX RITTER
THEDA BARA
THORA HIRD
THORNDIKE *(14S)* *D
TOM BOSLEY
TOM CRUISE
TOMLINSON *(14D)*
TONY ADAMS
TONY SELBY
TREVOR EVE
TROUGHTON
UNA STUBBS
VALENTINE *(14K)*
VALENTINO
VAN HEFLIN
VAN PATTEN *(13D, 14J)*
VIC DAMONE
VIC MORROW
VIRNA LISI
WATERSTON *(12S)*
WHITFIELD *(13J)*
ZASU PITTS
ZEPPO MARX
ZIMBALIST *(14E)*

AE MATTHEWS
ALAIN DELON
ALAN NAPIER
ALI MacGRAW
ALLAN JONES
ANDY DEVINE
ANNA DAWSON
ANNA MASSEY
ANNA NEAGLE *D
ANNA QUAYLE
ANNE BAXTER
ANN FIRBANK
ANN HARDING
ANN-MARGRET
ANN SOTHERN
ANOUK AIMÉE
ANTONY SHER
ARLENE DAHL
ARTHUR LOWE
AVA GARDNER
BARRY EVANS
BARRY MORSE
BECKINSALE
BÉLA LUGOSI
BELINDA LEE
BELLINGHAM (15L)
BEN GAZZARA
BERNARD LEE
BETTE DAVIS
BETTY FIELD
BILL FRASER
BILL MURRAY
BING CROSBY
BOBBY DARIN
BOBBY HOWES
BOB HOSKINS
BRAD DEXTER
BRUCE SETON *S
BUDDY EBSEN
CARL ESMOND
CARL REINER
CARMICHAEL (13I)
CAROL WHITE
CASSAVETES (14J)

CELIA IMRIE
CHERYL LADD
CHEVY CHASE
CLARK GABLE
CLIVE BROOK
COLIN BAKER
DANA WYNTER
DAN AYKROYD
DAN BLOCKER
DAVID BOWIE
DAVID ESSEX
DAVID JASON
DAVID LODGE
DAVID NIVEN
DAWN ADDAMS
DEAN MARTIN
DEREK NIMMO
DIANA QUICK
DICK POWELL
DONALD GRAY
DON JOHNSON
DRINKWATER (15C)
DULCIE GRAY
DYAN CANNON
EDITH EVANS *D
EDMUND KEAN
EDWIN BOOTH
ELISHA COOK
ELI WALLACH
ELKE SOMMER
ELLEN TERRY *D
ERIC BARKER
ERIC PORTER
ERIK CHITTY
ERIK RHODES
ERROL FLYNN
ESMA CANNON
EVELYN LAYE
FAY BAINTER
FAY COMPTON
FERDY MAYNE
FIONA CORKE
FITZGERALD (15B)
FRANCO NERO
FRED GWYNNE
GALE GORDON

GARETH HUNT
GARY COOPER
GENE NELSON
GENE WILDER
GEORGE COLE
GEORGE RAFT
GLENN CLOSE
GLORIA JEAN
GOLDIE HAWN
GORDEN KAYE
GRACE KELLY
GRETA GARBO
HASSELHOFF (15D)
HAZEL COURT
HEDY LAMARR
HELEN HAYES
HELEN MORSE
HENRY FONDA
HENRY SILVA
HERBERT LOM
HOWARD KEEL
HUGH O'BRIAN
IAN McSHANE
IRENE DUNNE
IRENE HANDL
IRENE PAPAS
JACK CARSON
JACK HEDLEY
JACK LEMMON
JACK WARNER
JACK WATSON
JAMES BOLAM
JAMES GROUT
JAMES MASON
JANE BIRKIN
JANE POWELL
JANET LEIGH
JANET MUNRO
JAN FRANCIS
JEAN ARTHUR
JEAN HARLOW
JERRY LEWIS
JILL BROWNE
JILL ESMOND
JILL ST JOHN
JOAN LESLIE

PEOPLE – ENTERTAINERS – ACTORS & ACTRESSES

JOEL McCREA
JOHN ALTMAN
JOHN BARRON
JOHN CLEESE
JOHN LAURIE
JOHN QUALEN
JOHN QUAYLE
JOHN SLATER
JOHN STRIDE
JON PERTWEE
JOSÉ FERRER
JOYCE CAREY
JUDY GEESON
JULIE ADAMS
KAREN BLACK
KARL MALDEN
KATHY STAFF
KAY FRANCIS
KAY HAMMOND
KAY JOHNSON
KAY KENDALL
KEVIN KLINE
LANA MORRIS
LANA TURNER
LANCHESTER (14E)
LARRY PARKS
LE MESURIER (14J)
LEO CARROLL
LEWIS STONE
LILY TOMLIN
LINDA EVANS
LIV ULLMANN
LLOYD NOLAN
LOTTE LENYA
LUPINO LANE
LYNDA BARON
MARIO LANZA
MARK HAMILL
MARK LESTER
MARTIN SHAW
MARY GORDON
MARY MARTIN
MISCHA AUER
MONTGOMERY
NELSON EDDY
NIGEL BRUCE

NIGEL STOCK
NOËL COWARD *S
OLIVER REED
OMAR SHARIF
PAT PHOENIX
PAUL NEWMAN
PEARL WHITE
PEGGY MOUNT
PENHALIGON (15S)
PENNINGTON
PETER BYRNE
PETER FINCH
PETER FONDA
PETER JONES
PETER LORRE
PIER ANGELI
PORTER HALL
RACHEL WARD
RAF VALLONE
RALPH BATES
RALPH WAITE
RAY COLLINS
RAY MILLAND
RED BUTTONS
RED SKELTON
RICHARDSON (13I,
    15R) *S
ROBERT CULP
ROBERT LANG
ROBERT RYAN
ROBERT SHAW
ROCK HUDSON
ROD CAMERON
ROD STEIGER
ROGER MOORE
RONALD ADAM
RON RANDELL
ROSSINGTON (14J)
ROY DOTRICE
ROY KINNEAR
ROY MARSDEN
RUBY KEELER
RUDY VALLEE
RULA LENSKA
RUTHERFORD *D
RUTH HUSSEY

SALLY FIELD
SAMMY DAVIS
SANDOR ELES
SARAH MILES
SHARON TATE
SONJA HENIE
SONNIE HALE
STACY KEACH
STAN LAUREL
STEPHENSON (15H)
SUSAN TULLY
SUTHERLAND
SYD CHAPLIN
SYLVIA SIMS
TATUM O'NEAL
TERRY SCOTT
TOM SELLECK
TONY ANHOLT
TONY CURTIS
TUSHINGHAM (14R)
UNA O'CONNOR
VAN JOHNSON
WADDINGTON (14B)
WALTER ABEL
WENDY CRAIG
WILLIAMSON (15N)
WILL ROGERS
WILL WRIGHT
WOODY ALLEN
YUL BRYNNER
ZENA WALKER
ZERO MOSTEL
ZETTERLING (13M)

11

ALASTAIR SIM
ALEC McCOWEN
ALFRED BURKE
ALFRED MARKS
AMANDA BLAKE
ANDRÉ MORELL
ANDREW SACHS
ANITA DOBSON
ANITA EKBERG

ANNA MAGNANI
ANNE FRANCIS
ANNE HEYWOOD
ANNE SEYMOUR
ANN SHERIDAN
ARLO GUTHRIE
ARTHUR LUCAN
AUDIE MURPHY
AVRIL ANGERS
BADEN-SEMPER *(15N)*
BARBARA BACH
BARBARA HALE
BARBARA LOTT
BARBARA RUSH
BARRACLOUGH *(14R)*
BARRY FOSTER
BARRY NEWMAN
BARTHOLOMEW
BEAU BRIDGES
BEBE DANIELS
BEN KINGSLEY
BETTE MIDLER
BETTY GRABLE
BETTY HUTTON
BEULAH BONDI
BILL MAYNARD
BILL PERTWEE
BILL TRAVERS
BRENDA BRUCE
BRIAN AHERNE
BRIAN GLOVER
BRIAN MURPHY
BRIAN OULTON
BRITT EKLAND
BRUCE WILLIS
BUTTERWORTH
CECIL PARKER
CESAR ROMERO
CHAMBERLAIN
CHARLES ARNT
CLAIRE BLOOM
CLAUDE AKINS
CLAUDE RAINS
CLIFTON WEBB
CLINT WALKER
CONRAD VEIDT

CORAL ATKINS
CORAL BROWNE
CORNEL WILDE
COURTNEIDGE **D*
CRUICKSHANK
CURT JURGENS
CUTHBERTSON *(15l)*
CYD CHARISSE
CYRIL CUSACK
DANA ANDREWS
DAN HAGGERTY
DANNY DE VITO
DARYL HANNAH
DAVID SUCHET
DAVID WARNER
DEBORAH KERR
DEBRA WINGER
DE HAVILLAND
DENNIS PRICE
DEREK FOWLDS
DIANA DECKER
DIANE KEATON
DICK SARGENT
DICK VAN DYKE
DIRK BOGARDE
DOLLY PARTON
DOLORES GRAY
DON ALVARADO
DUDLEY MOORE
EDDIE ALBERT
EDDIE CANTOR
EDDIE MURPHY
EDMUND GWENN
ELEANOR BRON
ERIC PORTMAN
ERIK ESTRADA
ETHEL MERMAN
FAYE DUNAWAY
FELIX AYLMER **S*
FLORA ROBSON **D*
FRANK BENSON **S*
FRANK FINLAY
FRANK MORGAN
FRAZER HINES
FRED ASTAIRE
GEMMA CRAVEN

GENE HACKMAN
GENE RAYMOND
GENE TIERNEY
GEORGE BAKER
GEORGE BRENT
GEORGE BURNS
GEORGE SEGAL
GEORGE ZUCCO
GIGI PERREAU
GLYN HOUSTON
GORDON SCOTT
GRACIE ALLEN
GRAHAM STARK
GREENSTREET
GREER GARSON
GREGORY PECK
GROUCHO MARX
GWEN WATFORD
GUY STANDING **S*
HARDY KRUGER
HAROLD LLOYD
HARRY FOWLER
HAYLEY MILLS
HELEN CHERRY
HELEN MIRREN
HELEN MORGAN
HENRY GIBSON
HENRY IRVING **S*
HERBERT TREE **S*
IAN LAVENDER
IAN McKELLEN **S*
JACK HAWKINS
JACK HULBERT
JACK PALANCE
JACK WATLING
JACQUES TATI
JAMES ARNESS
JAMES BROLIN
JAMES CAGNEY
JAMES COBURN
JAMES DARREN
JAMES GARNER
JAMES HAYTER
JANE RUSSELL
JANE SEYMOUR
JANET DIBLEY

JANET GAYNOR
JANET SUZMAN
JAN STERLING
JEAN SIMMONS
JEFF BRIDGES
JENNY HANLEY
JEREMY BRETT
JEREMY IRONS
JESSIE RALPH
JILL BENNETT
JILL IRELAND
JIMMY HANLEY
JOAN BENNETT
JOAN COLLINS
JOAN HICKSON
JOAN RANDALL
JODIE FOSTER
JOHN DUTTINE
JOHN GIELGUD *S
JOHN GILBERT
JOHN GREGSON
JOHN IRELAND
JOHN NETTLES
JOHN NEVILLE
JOHN RINGHAM
JOSS ACKLAND
JOYCE REDMAN
JUDY GARLAND
JULIA FOSTER
JULIE HARRIS
JULIE LONDON
JULIET MILLS
JUNE ALLYSON
JUNE RITCHIE
KEITH BARRON
KENNETH COPE
KENNETH MORE
KIM BASINGER
KIRK DOUGLAS
LARRY HAGMAN
LEE VAN CLEEF
LEO CARRILLO
LESLIE BANKS
LESLIE CARON
LEWIS CASSON *S
LILLIAN GISH

LILLIAN ROTH
LILLI PALMER
LIZA GODDARD
LOIS MAXWELL
LORETTA SWIT
LORNE GREENE
LOU COSTELLO
LUCILLE BALL
LUISE RAINER
LUTHER ADLER
LYNDA CARTER
MAGGIE SMITH
MARCEL DALIO
MARIA AITKEN
MARIA SCHELL
MARION MARSH
MARTIN SHEEN
MASTROIANNI
MEGS JENKINS
MELVYN HAYES
MERLE OBERON
MERVYN JOHNS
MERVYN LE ROY
MERYL STREEP
MICHAEL J FOX
MICHAEL YORK
MIKE FARRELL
MILTON BERLE
MITZI GAYNOR
MOIRA LISTER
NANCY KOVACK
NANCY WALKER
NATALIE WOOD
NERYS HUGHES
NICKY HENSON
NIGEL HAVERS
NOELE GORDON
NOËL HOWLETT
OLGA PETROVA
OLIVER HARDY
ORSON WELLES
OSCAR LEVANT
OSKAR WERNER
PATRICIA ROC
PATRICK BARR
PAULA WILCOX

PAUL DANEMAN
PAUL HENREID
PAUL ROBESON
PEARL BAILEY
PETER BOWLES
PETER GRAVES
PETER O'TOOLE
PETER SALLIS
PETULA CLARK
PHILIP MADOC
PHIL SILVERS
PIGOTT-SMITH (14T)
PIPER LAURIE
RAQUEL WELCH
RAYMOND BURR
REX HARRISON *S
RICHARD EGAN
RICHARD GERE
RICHARD TODD
ROBERT DONAT
ROBERT HARDY
ROBERT STACK
ROBERT URICH
ROBERT YOUNG
ROBIN BAILEY
RODNEY BEWES
ROLAND YOUNG
RONALD LACEY
RORY CALHOUN
ROY SCHEIDER
RUSS TAMBLYN
RUTH WARRICK
SALLY GEESON
SARA ALLGOOD
SCHILDKRAUT
SEAN CONNERY
SHARON GLESS
SIDNEY TOLER
SILVERHEELS (14J)
SIMON CADELL
SIMON CALLOW
SIMONE SIMON
SISSY SPACEK
SONDERGAARD (15G)
SOPHIA LOREN
STEPHEN BOYD

STEVE REEVES
SUE NICHOLLS
SUMMERFIELD
SUSAN GEORGE
SUZY KENDALL
TERRY-THOMAS
TESSIE O'SHEA
TIMOTHY WEST
TIPPI HEDREN
TOMMY STEELE
TONY BRITTON
TONY RANDALL
TUESDAY WELD
TYRONE POWER
VALERIE LEON
VICTOR BUONO
VINCENT BALL
VIVIAN VANCE
VIVIEN LEIGH
VON STROHEIM
WARNER OLAND
WARREN OATES
WEISSMULLER
WENDY HILLER *D
WENDY HUGHES
WILLIAM BOYD
WYLIE WATSON
YOOTHA JOYCE
YVES MONTAND
ZSA ZSA GABOR

12

ALAN WHEATLEY
ALEC GUINNESS *S
AMANDA BARRIE
ANGELA THORNE
ANGHARAD REES
ANNA CARTERET
ANNE BANCROFT
ANTHONY BOOTH
ANTHONY QUINN
ANTHONY STEEL
ANTON RODGERS
ARCHIE DUNCAN

ARNOLD RIDLEY
ARTHUR HOWARD
ATTENBOROUGH *S
BERNARD MILES *S
BILL TREACHER
BINNIE BARNES
BORIS KARLOFF
BRIAN BLESSED
BRYAN PRINGLE
BURT REYNOLDS
BUSTER CRABBE
BUSTER KEATON
CARRIE FISHER
CARROLL BAKER
C AUBREY SMITH *S
CELIA JOHNSON *D
CHARLES BOYER
CHARLES DANCE
CHRIS QUINTEN
CHUCK CONNORS
CLAIRE TREVOR
CLAYTON MOORE
CLIFF RICHARD
COLIN BLAKELY
COLIN WELLAND
DANDY NICHOLS
DAVID GARRICK
DAVID JANSSEN
DAVID KOSSOFF
DEANNA DURBIN
DEANNAH GRANT
DEBORAH GRANT
DENNIS O'KEEFE
DENNIS WEAVER
DERYCK GUYLER
DIANE CILENTO
DIRK BENEDICT
DONALD SINDEN
DONALD WOLFIT *S
DON HENDERSON
DOOLEY WILSON
DOROTHY TUTIN
DUNCAN MACRAE
EDDIE BRACKEN
EDMOND O'BRIEN
EDMUND PURDOM

EDWARD ARNOLD
EILEEN ATKINS
ELLIOTT GOULD
ELVIS PRESLEY
EVELYN ANKERS
FINLAY CURRIE
FRANCHOT TONE
FRANKIE DARRO
FRANKIE LAINE
FRANK SINATRA
FRANK WINDSOR
FREDRIC MARCH
FULTON MACKAY
GENE LOCKHART
GEORGE ARLISS
GEORGE C SCOTT
GEORGE FORMBY
GEORGE JESSEL
GEORGE LAYTON
GEORGE MURPHY
GEORGE SEWELL
GEORGE TOBIAS
GEORGINA HALE
GERALD HARPER
GINGER ROGERS
GLADYS COOPER *D
GLADYS HENSON
GLYNN EDWARDS
GRACIE FIELDS *D
GREGORY HINES
HANNAH GORDON
HARRISON FORD
HARRY ANDREWS
HARRY LANGDON
HEATHER SEARS
HENRY DANIELL
HENRY WINKLER
HUGH GRIFFITH
HYWEL BENNETT
JACK BUCHANAN
JACKIE COOGAN
JACK THOMPSON
JAMES GREGORY
JAMES STEWART
JANETTE SCOTT
JASON CONNERY

PEOPLE – ENTERTAINERS – ACTORS & ACTRESSES

JASON DONOVAN
JASON ROBARDS
J CARROL NAISH
JEAN ANDERSON
JEANNE MOREAU
JEFF CHANDLER
JENNIE LINDEN
JENNIFER GREY
JENNY AGUTTER
JERRY COLONNA
JESSICA LANGE
JESSICA TANDY
JILL GASCOINE
JIMMY DURANTE
JOAN BLONDELL
JOAN CRAWFORD
JOAN FONTAINE
JOANNA LUMLEY
JOHN CLEMENTS *S
JOHN FORSYTHE
JOHN HALLIDAY
JOHN HOUSEMAN
JOHNNY BRIGGS
JOHN STANDING
JOHN TRAVOLTA
JOSEPH COTTEN
JUDY HOLLIDAY
JULIAN GLOVER
JULIE ANDREWS
JULIET PROWSE
JULIE WALTERS
JUNE LAVERICK
JUNE THORBURN
KAREN DOTRICE
KEITH MICHELL
KEN KERCHEVAL
KENNETH HAIGH
KYLIE MINOGUE
LAUREN BACALL
LEIF ERICKSON
LEONARD NIMOY
LESLIE FULLER
LESLIE HOWARD
LEWIS COLLINS
LINDA DARNELL
LINDA THORSON

LIONEL ATWILL
LIONEL MURTON
LIZA MINNELLI
LLOYD BRIDGES
LOLLOBRIGIDA
LORETTA YOUNG
LOUIS CALHERN
LOUIS JOURDAN
LYNN REDGRAVE
MADELINE KAHN
MARIA TEMPEST *D
MARIUS GORING
MARJORIE MAIN
MARLON BRANDO
MARTIN BALSAM
MARTIN JARVIS
MARTY FELDMAN
MARY PICKFORD
MAUREEN O'HARA
MAUREEN PRIOR
MAURICE ELVEY
MICHAEL CAINE
MICHAEL CRAIG
MICHAEL GOUGH
MICHAEL PRAED
MICKEY ROONEY
MICKEY ROURKE
MILBURN STONE
MIRIAM KARLIN
MOIRA SHEARER
MOLLIE SUGDEN
MONTY WOOLLEY
NICHOLAS BALL
NICOLA PAGETT
NIGEL PATRICK
NORMAN WISDOM
NORMA SHEARER
OLIVER TOBIAS
OLIVIA HUSSEY
OSCAR HOMOLKA
PAM ST CLEMENT
PATRICIA NEAL
PATRICK ALLEN
PATRICK DUFFY
PATRICK MAGEE
PATRICK MOWER

PATRICK O'NEAL
PAUL CAVANAGH
PAULINE YATES
PAUL NICHOLAS
PAUL SCOFIELD
PAUL WINFIELD
PETER CUSHING
PETER DAVISON
PETER SELLERS
PETER USTINOV *S
PETER VAUGHAN
PHILIP LATHAM
PHYLLIS LOGAN
RALPH BELLAMY
RAMON NOVARRO
REGINALD OWEN
RENÉE HOUSTON
RICHARD ARLEN
RICHARD BOONE
RICHARD CONTE
RICHARD PRYOR
RITA HAYWORTH
ROBERT BEATTY
ROBERT DE NIRO
ROBERT MORLEY
ROBERT NEWTON
ROBERT POWELL
ROBERT TAYLOR
ROBERT VAUGHN
ROBERT WAGNER
ROBIN ASKWITH
ROGER DALTREY
ROGER LIVESEY
RONALD COLMAN
RONALD CULVER
RONALD FRASER
RONALD MAGILL
RONALD PICKUP
RONALD REAGAN
RONALD SHINER
ROSALIND IDEN
RUPERT DAVIES
RUTH DONNELLY
SAM WATERSTON
SARAH SIDDONS
SHIRLEY EATON

SHIRLEY JONES
SIAN PHILLIPS
SIDNEY TAFLER
SINEAD CUSACK
SONIA DRESDEL
SOPHIE TUCKER
SPENCER TRACY
STANLEY BAKER *S
STEVE FORREST
STEVE McQUEEN
SUSAN GILMORE
SUSAN HAYWARD
SUSANNAH YORK
SYLVIA SIDNEY
TELLY SAVALAS
TERENCE RIGBY
TERENCE STAMP
TERESA WRIGHT
THELMA RITTER
TOD SLAUGHTER
TOM COURTENAY
TREVOR HOWARD
VANDA GODSELL
VERONICA LAKE
VICTOR MATURE
VINCE EDWARDS
VINCENT PRICE
VIOLET CARSON
VIRGINIA MAYO
WALLACE BEERY
WALTER HUSTON
WANDA VENTHAM
WARNER BAXTER
WARREN BEATTY
WENDY RICHARD
WHITSUN-JONES
WILLIAM GAUNT
WILLIAM LUCAS
YVONNE ARNAUD
YVONNE ROMAIN
ZACHARY SCOTT

13

ADOLPHE MENJOU
ADRIENNE CORRI

ADRIENNE POSTA
AIMI MACDONALD
ALEXANDER KNOX
ANGELA DOUGLAS
ANOUSKA HEMPEL
ANTHONY NEWLEY
ANTHONY QUAYLE *S
ANTON DIFFRING
ANTONIO FARGAS
ARTHUR KENNEDY
ARTHUR MULLARD
ARTHUR SHIELDS
AUDREY HEPBURN
BARBARA MULLEN
BARBARA MURRAY
BARBARA STEELE
BASIL RATHBONE
BERNARD HEPTON
BETTY McDOWALL
BIBI ANDERSSON
BILLY BENEDICT
BONAR COLLEANO
BRENDA BLETHYN
BRENDA FRICKER
BRIGIT FORSYTH
BROOKE SHIELDS
BURT LANCASTER
CANDICE BERGEN
CARMEN SILVERA
CAROL CHANNING
CAROLE LOMBARD
CECIL KELLAWAY
CHARLES COBURN
CHESTER MORRIS
CHIPS RAFFERTY
CLINT EASTWOOD
CONNIE STEVENS
DALE ROBERTSON
DAVID HEMMINGS
DEAN STOCKWELL
DENNIS QUILLEY
DERREN NESBITT
DICK VAN PATTEN
DINAH SHERIDAN
DOLORES DEL RIO
DONALD HOUSTON

DONALD O'CONNOR
DOROTHY LAMOUR
DOROTHY MALONE
DREW BARRYMORE
DUNCAN RENALDO
DUSTIN HOFFMAN
EDDIE ANDERSON
EDGAR BUCHANAN
ELAINE STRITCH
EVA MARIE SAINT
EVERETT SLOANE
FARRAH FAWCETT
FATTY ARBUCKLE
FLORENCE BATES
FORREST TUCKER
FRANKIE AVALON
FRANKIE HOWERD
FRANK THORNTON
FREDERICK PYNE
FRED MacMURRAY
GEORGE KENNEDY
GEORGE LAZENBY
GEORGE MAHARIS
GEORGE PEPPARD
GEORGE SANDERS
GERALDINE PAGE
GILBERT ROLAND
GLENDA FARRELL
GLENDA JACKSON
GLORIA DE HAVEN
GLORIA GRAHAME
GLORIA SWANSON
GODFREY TEARLE *S
GOOGIE WITHERS
GORDON JACKSON
HARRY GUARDINO
HARRY H CORBETT
HATTIE JACQUES
HEATHER CHASEN
HELEN CHANDLER
HILDEGARD NEFF
HONOR BLACKMAN
IAN CARMICHAEL
IAN RICHARDSON
INGRID BERGMAN
JACKIE GLEASON

PEOPLE – ENTERTAINERS – ACTORS & ACTRESSES

JACK NICHOLSON
JACK SMETHURST
JAMES VILLIERS
JANE LAPOTAIRE
JEAN ALEXANDER
JEANNIE CARSON
JENNIFER JAYNE
JENNIFER JONES
JENNY SEAGROVE
JERRY DESMONDE
JESSICA HARPER
JOAN GREENWOOD
JOAN PLOWRIGHT
JOAN SANDERSON
JOHN BARRYMORE
JOHN CARRADINE
JOYCE GRENFELL
JULIA LOCKWOOD
JULIA McKENZIE
JULIAN ORCHARD
JULIE CHRISTIE
JULIE GOODYEAR
JUNE WHITFIELD
KATHARINE ROSS
KENNETH CONNOR
KRISTOFFERSON
LANCE PERCIVAL
LAURENCE PAYNE
LESLIE RANDALL
LINDSAY WAGNER
LOIS NETTLETON
LORRAINE CHASE
LOUISE JAMESON
MacCORKINDALE
MAI ZETTERLING
MAMIE VAN DOREN
MARIE DRESSLER
MARILYN MONROE
MAUREEN LIPMAN
MAURICE DENHAM
MELVYN DOUGLAS
MICHAEL ANSARA
MICHAEL BRYANT
MICHAEL GAMBON
MICHAEL LANDON
MICHAEL MEDWIN

MICHAEL RENNIE
MINERVA URECAL
NANETTE NEWMAN
NORMA TALMADGE
PATRICIA HAYES
PATRICIA HODGE
PATRICK MacNEE
PATRICK SWAYZE
PATRICK WYMARK
PATSY ROWLANDS
PAULA PRENTISS
PAUL EDDINGTON
PEGGY ASHCROFT *D
PENELOPE KEITH
PHYLLIS DILLER
RACHEL ROBERTS
RANDOLPH SCOTT
RAYMOND MASSEY
REGINALD MARSH
RHONDA FLEMING
RICHARD BRIERS
RICHARD BURTON
RICHARD GREENE
RICHARD HARRIS
RICHARD TAUBER
RICHARD VERNON
RICHARD WATTIS
RICHARD WILSON
RICKY SCHRODER
ROBERT MITCHUM
ROBERT PRESTON
ROBERT REDFORD
ROBERTSON HARE
RODDY McDOWALL
ROMY SCHNEIDER
RONNIE STEVENS
ROSEMARY LEACH
ROSSANO BRAZZI
RUSSELL HUNTER
SALLY ANN HOWES
SALLY THOMSETT
SAMANTHA EGGAR
SERGIO FANTONI
SHEILA HANCOCK
SHEILA MERCIER
SHIRLEY TEMPLE

SIDNEY POITIER
SIMON WILLIAMS
STANLEY RIDGES
STELLA STEVENS
STUART WHITMAN
SUSAN FLANNERY
SYLVIA KRISTEL
TIMOTHY DALTON
URSULA ANDRESS
URSULA HOWELLS
VALERIE HARPER
VALERIE HOBSON
VICTOR MADDERN
WALTER BRENNAN
WALTER MATTHAU
WALTER PIDGEON
WENSLEY PITHEY
WILFRID LAWSON
WILLIAM BENDIX
WILLIAM DEVANE
WILLIAM HOLDEN
WILLIAM ROACHE
WINDSOR DAVIES

14

AGNES MOOREHEAD
ALEXANDER GAUGE
ALISON STEADMAN
ANGELA BADDELEY
ANGELA LANSBURY
ANGIE DICKINSON
ANNETTE CROSBIE
ANTHONY ANDREWS
ANTHONY HOPKINS
ANTHONY PERKINS
ARTHUR PENTELOW
BARBARA BABCOCK
BARBARA BOUCHET
BARBARA PARKINS
BARBARA SHELLEY
BARBARA WINDSOR
BEATRICE LILLIE
BILLIE WHITELAW
BILL WADDINGTON

BONNIE LANGFORD	JAMIE LEE CURTIS	PHYLLIS CALVERT
BRIGITTE BARDOT	JANE ROSSINGTON	PRUNELLA SCALES
CAMPBELL SINGER	JAYNE MANSFIELD	RAYMOND FRANCIS
CHARLES BRONSON	JAY SILVERHEELS	RAYMOND HUNTLEY
CHARLES HAWTREY	JESSIE MATTHEWS	RICHARD BURBAGE
CHARLES RUGGLES	JOANNE WOODWARD	RICHARD WIDMARK
CHARLIE CHAPLIN *S	JOHN CASSAVETES	RITA TUSHINGHAM
CHARLTON HESTON	JOHN LE MESURIER	ROBERT CUMMINGS
CHESTER CONKLIN	JOYCE VAN PATTEN	ROBERT HELPMANN *S
CHRISTOPHER LEE	JUDITH ANDERSON *D	ROBERT URQUHART
CLIFF ROBERTSON	KAREN VALENTINE	ROY BARRACLOUGH
CYBILL SHEPHERD	KATHLEEN TURNER	SALLY KELLERMAN
DANIEL DAY-LEWIS	KATHRYN GRAYSON	SALLY STRUTHERS
DAVID CARRADINE	KENNETH BRANAGH	SARAH BERNHARDT
DAVID TOMLINSON	KENNETH CRANHAM	SARAH CHURCHILL
DEBBIE REYNOLDS	KYNASTON REEVES	SCHWARZENEGGER
DENHOLM ELLIOTT	LAURENCE HARVEY	SHELLEY WINTERS
DENNIS WATERMAN	LEONARD WHITING	SIMONE SIGNORET
DIAHANN CARROLL	LESLEY-ANNE DOWN	STEFANIE POWERS
DIANA CHURCHILL	LESLIE GRANTHAM	STÉPHANE AUDRAN
DINSDALE LANDEN	LESLIE PHILLIPS	STEPHEN YARDLEY
DOROTHY McGUIRE	LIONEL JEFFRIES	STERLING HAYDEN
DOROTHY PROVINE	LUCIANA PALUZZI	STEWART GRANGER
EDWARD WOODWARD	LYNNE FREDERICK	STRATFORD JOHNS
EFREM ZIMBALIST	MARGARET DUMONT	SUSAN HAMPSHIRE
ELSA LANCHESTER	MARGARET O'BRIEN	SUZANNE BERTISH
ERNEST BORGNINE	MARGARET TYZACK	SYBIL THORNDIKE *D
ESTHER WILLIAMS	MARJORIE RHODES	SYLVESTER McCOY
ETHEL BARRYMORE	MARY TYLER MOORE	THORLEY WALTERS
FELICITY KENDAL	MELINA MERCOURI	TIMOTHY BOTTOMS
FIONA FULLERTON	MICHAEL BALFOUR	TIM PIGOTT-SMITH
F MURRAY ABRAHAM	MICHAEL DENISON	VALENTINE DYALL
FRANCESCA ANNIS	MICHAEL DOUGLAS	VICTOR BANERJEE
GABRIELLE DRAKE	MICHAEL ELPHICK	VICTOR McLAGLEN
GARFIELD MORGAN	MICHAEL HORDERN *S	VICTOR SPINETTI
GAYLE HUNNICUTT	MICHAEL JAYSTON	VITTORIO DE SICA
GEOFFREY PALMER	MICHAEL KITCHEN	WALTER CONNOLLY
GEORGE CHAKIRIS	MICHAEL WILDING	WARNER ANDERSON
GEORGE HAMILTON	MICHELE DOTRICE	WARREN MITCHELL
GEORGE MACREADY	NIGEL DAVENPORT	WHOOPI GOLDBERG
GERALDINE JAMES	NIGEL HAWTHORNE	WILFRED PICKLES
HARDIE ALBRIGHT	PATRICK CARGILL	WILLIAM FRAWLEY
HARRY DAVENPORT	PAULINE COLLINS	WILLIAM SHATNER
HILDEGARDE NEIL	PENELOPE WILTON	
HUMPHREY BOGART	PETER BARKWORTH	
JAMES MacARTHUR	PHILIPPE NOIRET	

15

BARBARA ANDERSON
BARBARA STANWYCK
BARBRA STREISAND
BARRY FITZGERALD
BERNARD BRESSLAW
BERNARD CRIBBINS
BURGESS MEREDITH
CAROL DRINKWATER
CEDRIC HARDWICKE *S
CHARLES BICKFORD
CHARLES LAUGHTON
CHARLES TINGWELL
DAVID HASSELHOFF
DONALD PLEASENCE
EDWARD G ROBINSON
ELIZABETH TAYLOR
FENELLA FIELDING
FRANCES DE LA TOUR
FRANCIS MATTHEWS
FRANÇOISE ARNOUL
GALE SONDERGAARD

GEOFFREY BAYLDON
GERALDINE McEWAN
HENRY STEPHENSON
HERMOINE GINGOLD
IAIN CUTHBERTSON
J EDWARD BROMBERG
JOSEPHINE TEWSON
KENNETH WILLIAMS
LAURENCE OLIVIER *B
LEONARD ROSSITER
LIONEL BARRYMORE
LYNDA BELLINGHAM
MARLENE DIETRICH
MICHAEL CRAWFORD
MICHAEL REDGRAVE *S
MICHAEL SARRAZIN
MICHAEL WILLIAMS
MILLICENT MARTIN
MONTGOMERY CLIFT
MORGAN FAIRCHILD
NICOL WILLIAMSON
NINA BADEN-SEMPER
NYREE DAWN PORTER

PAMELA SUE MARTIN
PATRICK McGOOHAN
PAULETTE GODDARD
RALPH RICHARDSON *S
RICHARD BASEHART
RICHARD CALDICOT
RICHARD DREYFUSS
ROBERT ARMSTRONG
ROBERT GUILLAUME
ROSALIND RUSSELL
SANDRA DICKINSON
SHIRLEY ANN FIELD
SHIRLEY MACLAINE
SIGOURNEY WEAVER
STANLEY HOLLOWAY
SUSAN PENHALIGON
SUZANNE DANIELLE
VANESSA REDGRAVE
VIRGINIA McKENNA
WILFRED BRAMBELL
WILLIAM FRANKLYN
WILLIAM HARTNELL

PEOPLE

ENTERTAINERS – CLASSICAL PERFORMERS

(B) = Ballet-dancer/choreographer   (C) = Conductor   (O) = Opera-singer
Musicians: (BA) = Bass player   (CE) = Cellist   (CL) = Clarinettist
(FL) = Flautist   (G) = Guitarist   (HA) = Harpist   (HO) = Horn player
(L) = Lutanist   (OB) = Oboist   (OR) = Organist   (P) = Pianist
(VA) = Viola player   (VC) = Violoncellist   (VI) = Violinist
NB: F = Female

3

SUK *(VI)*

4

AUER *(VI)*
BEST *(OR)*
BUTT *(O) F*
BYRD *(OR)*
CULP *(O) F*
DUNN *(VI)*
DYER *(O) F*
FOLI *(O)*
HALL *(C)*
HESS *(P) F*
HILL *(O) F*
KURZ *(O) F*
LEVI *(C)*
LIND *(O) F*
MÖDL *(O) F*
NAGY *(B)*
NONI *(O) F*
PARK *(B) F*
PYNE *(O) F*
RALF *(O)*
RIES *(VI)*
SENA *(C)*
VOGL *(O)*
WALL *(B)*
WOOD *(C)*
WYSS *(O) F*

5

ABACO *(VI)*
ACKTÉ *(O) F*
ADAMS *(O)*
ALARD *(VI)*
ALLIN *(BA)*
AMATI *(VI)*
ANDRÉ *(C)*
ARRAU *(P)*
BAKER *(O) F*
BOEHM *(FL)*
BOULT *(C)*
BRAIN *(HO)*
BREAM *(G)*
BRUCH *(C)*
BÜLOW *(C)*
CROSS *(O) F*
DU PRÉ *(CE) F*
EREDE *(C)*
EVANS *(O)*
GEDDA *(O)*
GIGLI *(O)*
GOBBI *(O)*
GRISI *(B) F,*
   (O) F
HALLÉ *(C)*
HAMEL *(B) F*
JORDÁ *(C)*
LABAN *(B)*
LANZA *(O)*
MEILI *(O) F*
MELBA *(O) F*

MUNCH *(C)*
OGDON *(P)*
PATEY *(O) F*
PATTI *(O) F*
PEARS *(O)*
PETIT *(B)*
PINZA *(O)*
RAISA *(O) F*
RANKL *(C)*
SLEEP *(B)*
SOLTI *(C)*
SPOHR *(VI)*
STEAR *(O)*
STERN *(VI)*
SZELL *(C)*
TEYTE *(O) F*
TUDOR *(B)*
VIÑES *(P)*
YSAŸE *(VI)*

6

ABBOTT *(O) F*
ACHRON *(VI)*
ALBANI *(O) F*
ALCOCK *(OR)*
ASHTON *(B)*
BARATI *(CE)*
BÉRIOT *(VI)*
BOCHSA *(HA)*
BOULEZ *(C)*
CALLAS *(O) F*
CARRON *(O)*

CARUSO *(O)*
CASALS *(CE)*
COATES *(O) F*
DANIAS *(B)*
DAWSON *(O)*
DOWELL *(B) F*
DRAPER *(CL)*
DUNCAN *(B) F*
ENESCO *(VI)*
FARRAR *(O) F*
FOKINE *(B)*
GALWAY *(FL)*
HEMPEL *(O) F*
HEROLD *(O)*
ITURBI *(C)*
JACOBI *(C)*
JANSEN *(O)*
KEMBLE *(O) F*
KIPNIS *(O)*
KÖHLER *(P) F*
LUSSAN *(O) F*
MORRIS *(O) F*
PAPINI *(VI)*
PREVIN *(C)*
QUANTZ *(FL)*
RATTLE *(C)*
REEVES *(O)*
REINER *(C)*
SCHIPA *(O)*
SIBLEY *(B) F*
SLADEN *(O) F*
SQUIRE *(CE)*
TALLIS *(OR)*

TAUBER *(O)*
TERTIS *(VA)*
VALOIS *(B)* F
WELDON *(O)* F
WENDON *(O)*

7

AGUJARI *(O)* F
BAZZINI *(VI)*
BEECHAM *(C)*
BUJONES *(B)*
CABALLÉ *(O)* F
CARREÑO *(P)* F
CORELLI *(VI)*
D'ARANYI *(VI)* F
DEERING *(OR)*
DESMOND *(O)* F
DOMINGO *(O)*
DOWLAND *(L)*
FARRELL *(B)* F
FERRIER *(O)* F
FONTEYN *(B)* F
GIBBONS *(OR)*
GREGORY *(B)* F
HAMMOND *(O)* F
KARAJAN *(C)*
LAMBERT *(C)*
LEHMANN *(O)* F
MARKOVA *(B)* F
MARTINS *(B)*
MATTERS *(O)*
MENUHIN *(P)* F,
      (VI)
MILKINA *(PI)* F
NIKISCH *(C)*
NUREYEV *(B)*
PAVLOVA *(B)* F
RAMBERT *(B)* F
ROBBINS *(B)*
ROBESON *(O)*
SARGENT *(C)*
SCHWARZ *(C)*
SEGOVIA *(G)*
SEYMOUR *(B)* F

STABILE *(O)*
STAMITZ *(VI)*
TEBALDI *(O)* F
THIBAUD *(VI)*
TIBBETT *(O)*
TRAUBEL *(O)* F
ULANOVA *(B)* F
WALLACE *(O)*

8

ANSERMET *(C)*
BACKHAUS *(P)*
BERINGER *(P)*
BJÖRLING *(O)*
BLAGROVE *(VI)*
BODANSKY *(C)*
BORGATTI *(O)*
CARRERAS *(O)*
CARRODUS *(VI)*
EGLEVSKY *(B)*
FLAGSTAD *(O)* F
FOURNIER *(VC)*
GOOSSENS *(HA)* F,
      (OB)
GORDEYEV *(B)*
GRANADOS *(P)*
HABANECK *(VI)*
HERRMANN *(C)*
HOROWITZ *(P)*
KIRKLAND *(B)* F
KREISLER *(VI)*
KREUTZER *(VI)*
LABLACHE *(O)*
MARÉCHAL *(CE)*
MILSTEIN *(VI)*
NIJINSKY *(B)*
PAGANINI *(VI)*
RAISBECK *(O)* F
ROBINSON *(C)*
ROTHWELL *(C)*,
      (OB) F
SMALLENS *(C)*
STEPHENS *(O)* F
STERLING *(O)* F
TE KANAWA *(O)* F

VASILIEV *(B)*
WILLIAMS *(G)*

9

ASHKENAZY *(P)*
BARENBOIM *(P)*
BERNSTEIN *(C)*
BRANNIGAN *(O)*
BURROUGHS *(O)*
CAMPANINI *(O)*
CHALIAPIN *(O)*
DIAGHILEV *(B)*
FARINELLI *(O)*
FRANSELLA *(FL)*
HAUSEGGER *(C)*
KARSAVINA *(B)* F
KLEMPERER *(C)*
MANTOVANI *(C)*
McCORMACK *(O)*
NORDQUIST *(C)*
OLCZEWSKA *(O)* F
PAVAROTTI *(O)*
STEINBACH *(C)*
STOKOWSKI *(C)*
TALLCHIEF *(B)* F
TORTELIER *(CE)*
TOSCANINI *(C)*
WHITEHILL *(O)*
ZIMBALIST *(VI)*

10

AROLDINGEN *(B)* F
BALANCHINE *(B)*
BARBIROLLI *(C)*
BATTISTINI *(O)*
BILLINGTON *(O)* F
BORTOLUZZI *(B)*
CHEVILLARD *(C)*
DEMESSIEUX *(OR)*
FISTOULARI *(C)*
GALLI-CURCI *(O)* F
KONDRASHIN *(C)*

MANCINELLI *(C)*
PADEREWSKI *(P)*
RUBINSTEIN *(P)*
STRADIVARI *(VI)*
SUTHERLAND *(O) F*
TAGLIAVINI *(O)*
TETRAZZINI *(O) F*
VIEUXTEMPS *(VI)*

HOOGSTRATEN *(C)*
LESCHETIZKY *(P)*
LLOYD WEBBER *(CE)*
PERSICHETTI *(C)*
SCHWARZKOPF *(O) F*
STILES-ALLEN *(O) F*
STOCKHAUSEN *(HA),*
                (O)

13

HAMILTON-SMITH *(O) F*
HOLLINGSWORTH *(C)*

14

BAHR-MILDENBURG *(O) F*

11

BARYSHNIKOV *(B)*
FURTWÄNGLER *(C)*

12

KOUSSEVITSKY *(C)*
ROSTROPOVICH *(CE)*

PEOPLE

ENTERTAINERS – DIRECTORS

All American except: (A) = Austrian   (AU) = Australian   (BR) = British
(CA) = Canadian   (CZ) = Czechoslovakian   (F) = French
(G) = German   (GR) = Greek   (H) = Hungarian   (I) = Italian
(J) = Japanese   (P) = Polish   (RO) = Romanian   (RU) = Russian
(S) = Swedish
NB: American (US) only shown for double entry under one surname

3

BOX *(BR)*
DAY *(BR)*
LEE
RAY

4

AUER *(H)*
BAVA *(I)*

FORD
GLEN *(BR)*
GOLD *(BR)*
HALL
HILL
KING
LANG *(G,*
        US)
LEAN *(BR)*
LORD
MANN
PENN

RANK *(BR)*
REED *(BR)*
RICH *(BR)*
RITT
ROEG *(BR)*
ROSS
TATI *(F)*
TODD *(BR)*
TORS *(H)*
WISE
WOOD

5

ALLEN
AMATO *(I)*
APTED *(BR)*
ASHBY
BACON
CAPRA *(I)*
CARNE *(F)*
CLAIR *(F)*
CLINE
CUKOR

DONEN
FORDE *(BR)*
FOSSE
FREED
GUEST *(BR)*
HAWKS
JOFFE *(BR)*
KAZAN
KORDA *(H)*
LLOYD *(BR)*
LOACH *(BR)*
LOSEY

PEOPLE – ENTERTAINERS – DIRECTORS

LUBIN
LUMET
MAYER
MEYER
MOXEY *(BR)*
PABST *(G)*
PONTI *(I)*
RELPH *(BR)*
ROACH
ROZSA *(H)*
SEITZ
SHARP *(AU)*
STARK
STONE
VADIM *(F)*
VIDOR
WALSH
WHALE
WYLER
YATES *(BR)*
YOUNG *(BR)*
ZUKOR *(H)*

6

ABBOTT
ALTMAN
BALCON *(BR)*
BARTON
BEATTY
BENTON
BERMAN *(BR, US)*
BROOKS
BUTLER
CASTLE
CIMINO
CONWAY
CORMAN
CURTIZ *(H)*
DASSIN
DE SICA *(I)*
DISNEY
DONNER *(BR, US)*

FORBES *(BR)*
FORMAN *(CZ)*
GODARD *(F)*
HERZOG *(G)*
HILLER *(CA)*
HUGHES *(BR, US)*
HUSTON
KRAMER
LANDAU
LANDIS
LEISEN
LESTER
LEVINE
LITVAK *(RU)*
MILLER *(BR)*
NORMAN *(BR)*
OPHULS *(G)*
PICHEL
POTTER
POWELL *(BR)*
RENOIR *(F)*
ROBSON
ROGERS *(BR)*
ROSSEN
RYDELL
SIEGEL
THOMAS *(BR)*
THORPE
TROTTI
VARNEL *(F)*
WALLIS
WANGER
WARHOL
WELLES
WHELAN
WILCOX *(BR)*
WILDER *(A/H)*
WINNER *(BR)*
ZANUCK
ZELNIK *(RO)*

7

AHLBERG *(S)*
ALDRICH

ANNAKIN *(BR)*
ASQUITH *(BR)*
BERGMAN *(S)*
BORZAGE
CHABROL *(F)*
CHOMSKY
CLAYTON *(BR)*
CLÉMENT *(F)*
COCTEAU *(F)*
COPPOLA
DEARDEN
DeMILLE
DMYTRYK *(CA)*
EDWARDS
FELLINI *(I)*
FLEMING
GARNETT
GILBERT *(BR)*
GOLDWYN
JEWISON *(CA)*
JOHNSON
KARLSON
KUBRICK
LEACOCK *(BR)*
LEONARD
McCAREY
NEILSON
NICHOLS
POLLACK
PUTTNAM *(BR)*
RADFORD *(BR)*
REDFORD
RESNAIS *(F)*
RICHTER *(G)*
ROBBINS
RUSSELL *(BR)*
SENNETT
SHERMAN
SIODMAK
SPIEGEL *(P)*
STEVENS
STURGES
VAN DYKE
WELLMAN

8

ANDERSON *(BR)*
AVILDSEN
BEAUDINE
BEAUMONT
BERKELEY
BOULTING *(BR)*
BRACKETT
BROCCOLI
BROWNLOW *(BR)*
CRICHTON *(BR)*
DIETERLE *(G)*
FRIEDKIN
GOULDING *(BR)*
GRIFFITH
HAMILTON *(BR)*
HATHAWAY
ICHIKAWA *(J)*
JEFFRIES *(BR)*
KEIGHLEY
KERSHNER
KUROSAWA *(J)*
LEVINSON
LUBITSCH *(G)*
McLAGLEN
MINNELLI
MULLIGAN
POLANSKI *(F/P)*
SANDRICH
SCORSESE
SELZNICK
SPELLING
STALLONE
SUSSKIND
THALBERG
TRUFFAUT *(F)*
VISCONTI *(I)*

9

ANTONIONI *(I)*
BERNHARDT *(G)*
CARSTAIRS *(BR)*
FLEISCHER

GOLDSTONE
HITCHCOCK (BR)
MAMOULIAN (RU)
MILESTONE
NEGULESCO (RO)
PASTERNAK (H)
PECKINPAH
PREMINGER (A)
REINHARDT (A)
ROSENBERG
SCHAFFNER
SCHNEIDER
SPIELBERG
STEVENSON (BR)
STROMBERG

WANAMAKER
YOSHIMURA (J)
ZINNEMANN (A)

10

BERTOLUCCI (I)
EISENSTEIN (RU)
MANKIEWICZ
RICHARDSON (BR)
SILLIPHANT
SODERBERGH
ZEFFIRELLI (I)

11

BOGDANOVICH
COSTA-GAVRAS (GR)
PRESSBURGER (H)
SCHLESINGER (BR)
SHAUGHNESSY (BR)
SPRINGSTEEN

12

ATTENBOROUGH (BR)
MORE O'FERRALL (BR)
SCHERTZINGER
VON STERNBERG (A)

PEOPLE

ENTERTAINERS − POPULAR SINGERS & MUSICIANS

† = Group   ¶ = Known by one name only

3

ABC †
A-HA †
ANT (7A)
DAY (8D)
DEE (7D, 7J, 7K)
DIO †
ELO †
FOX †, (11S)
GUN †
JAM †
KIM (7A)
LEE (7D, 8B, 8L,
   8P, 9B)

MAY (8S)
MUD †
PнD †
POP (7I)
RAY (10J)
REA (8C)
ROE (8T)
ROS (10E)
ROY (8H)
SKY †
TEX (6J)
UFO †
URE (8M)
VEE (8B)
WAH! †

WHO †
XTC †
YES †

4

ABBA †
AC/DC †
ANKA (8P)
BAEZ (8J)
BALL (9K)
BAND †
BASS (12F)
BATT (8M)

BEAT †
BECK (8J)
BELL (10M, 13M)
BILK (9A)
BLUE (9B)
BONN (8I)
BONO ¶
BROS †
BUSH (8K)
BYRD (11C)
CARA (9I)
CARR (9P, 9V)
CARS †
CASH (10J)
CASS (8M)

CHER ¶
CHIC †
COLE (11N)
COMO (9P)
CULT †
CURE †
DANA ¶
DAWN †
DEAN (9J, 10H)
DENE (9T)
DEVO †
DION ¶
DODD (7K)
DUNN (9C)
DURY (7I)

EDDY *(9D, 10N)*
FAME *(11G)*
FAWN *(9J)*
FIRM *†*
FORD *(9E, 11C)*
FOXX *(8I, 11C)*
FRED *(8J)*
FREE *†*
FURY *(9B)*
GAYE *(10M)*
GETZ *(8S)*
GIBB *(8A, 9B, 9R, 11M)*
GORE *(10L)*
GRAY *(9D)*
HALL *(9D)*
HEBB *(9B)*
HERD *†*
HILL *(9B, 9V)*
HOLT *(8J)*
HUNT *(10M)*
IDOL *(9B)*
INXS *†*
IVES *(8B)*
JETS *†*
JOEL *(9B)*
JOHN *(9E)*
KANE *(8E)*
KAYE *(9D)*
KEEL *(10H)*
KHAN *(9C)*
KIDD *(10J)*
KING *(6B, 8B, 9H, 10C, 10E, 11S, 12J)*
KITT *(10E)*
KUNZ *(11C)*
LANG *(7D)*
LAST *(9J)*
LIND *(7B)*
LINX *†*
LOBO *¶*
LOSS *(7J)*
LOVE *(9G)*
LULU *¶*
LYNN *(8V)*

MANN *(10J)*
MONK *(14T)*
MOON *(9K)*
MOVE *†*
NAIL *(9J)*
NASH *(10J)*
NEIL *¶*
NENA *¶*
NEWS *†*
NICE *†*
OPUS *†*
PACE *(8T)*
PAGE *(9P)*
PARK *(9S)*
PARR *(8J)*
PAUL *(8O, 9B)*
PIAF *(9E)*
PINE *(12C)*
PIPS *†*
REED *(7L)*
REID *(8N)*
RICH *(9B, 11C)*
ROSS *(9A, 9D)*
ROY C
ROZA *(8L)*
RUSH *†, (12J)*
RUTS *†*
RYAN *(8P, 9B, 10M)*
SADE *¶*
SANG *(12S)*
SHAW *(9A, 10S)*
SLIK *†*
SOUL *(9D)*
STYX *†*
SWAN *(9B)*
TAMS *†*
THEM *†*
TOTO *†*
TOYS *†*
T REX *†*
TRIO *†*
VEGA *(11S)*
WARD *(9A, 13C)*
WEBB *(9M)*
WEST *(9K)*

WHAM! *†*
WOOD *(7R)*

5

ABBOT *(9R)*
ALARM *†*
ALLEN *(12C)*
AUGER *(10B)*
AUTRY *(9G)*
AVONS *†*
BAKER *(11G)*
BARRY *(8L, 9J)*
BASIE *(10C)*
BASIL *(9T)*
BERRY *(9D, 9M, 9N, 10C)*
BIGGS *(10B)*
BLACK *(10C)*
BLOOM *(10B)*
BLYTH *(8A)*
BONDS *(11G)*
BOONE *(8P)*
BOOTH *(12W)*
BOWIE *(10D)*
BRAGG *(10B)*
BREAD *†*
BRENT *(9T)*
BROWN *(8J, 8S, 10J, 11A)*
BRUCE *(9J, 10T)*
BYRDS *†*
CAMEO *†*
CLARK *(11P)*
CLASH *†*
CLIFF *(10J)*
CLINE *(10P)*
COGAN *(9A)*
COOKE *(8S)*
CREAM *†*
CRUSH *(10B)*
DARIN *(10B)*
DARTS *†*
DAVID *(7F)*
DAVIS *(10M, 10S, 11B, 12S)*

DEENE *(10C)*
DIXON *(8R)*
DOLAN *(8J)*
DOLCE *(8J)*
DOORS *†*
DUFFY *(12S)*
DUSTY *(9S)*
DYLAN *(8B)*
ELLIS *(12S)*
ESSEX *(10D)*
EVANS *(12M)*
EXILE *†*
FACES *†*
FAGIN *(8J)*
FAITH *(9A, 10P)*
FALCO *†*
FELIX *(10J)*
FERRY *(10B)*
FLACK *(12R)*
FLOYD *(10E)*
FOCUS *†*
FORDE *(12F)*
GAYLE *(12C)*
GOONS *†*
GORMÉ *(10E)*
GRANT *(9E)*
GRECO *(10B)*
GREEN *(7A)*
HALEY *(9B)*
HARDY *(14F)*
HARRY *(11D)*
HAYES *(10I)*
HEATH *(10T)*
HEINZ *¶*
HELLO *†*
HENRY *(13C)*
HINES *(9E)*
HOLLY *(10B)*
HORNE *(9L)*
HUTCH *¶*
HYNDE *(13S)*
IRWIN *(11B)*
JACKS *(10T)*
JAMES *(10J, 10T)*
JAPAN *†*
JARRE *(15J)*

JONES *(8T, 9A, 9P,*
10A, 10B, 10G,
10J, 11H, 12S)
KAMEN *(9N)*
KELLY *(9G)*
KENNY †
KINKS †
KIRBY *(10K)*
KRUPA *(9G)*
LAINE *(9C, 12F)*
LANZA *(10M)*
LE BON *(10S)*
LEWIS *(9H, 10L,*
11R, 13J)
LLOYD *(10M)*
LOCKE *(11J)*
LOGAN *(10J, 11J)*
LOPEZ *(10T)*
LOTIS *(11D)*
LUMAN *(8B)*
LYDON *(9J)*
LYMON *(12F)*
LYNCH *(10K)*
MARIE *(10K)*
MAYNE *(12C)*
McCOY *(8V)*
MILES *(9J)*
MILLS *(8M, 11H, 14S)*
MOJOS †
MONEY *(9Z)*
MONRO *(9M)*
MOONE *(11M)*
MOORE *(9G, 11D)*
MOYET *(11A)*
MR BIG †
NOBLE *(11D)*
NOONE *(10P)*
NUMAN *(9G)*
OATES *(9J)*
OCEAN *(10B)*
O'JAYS †
PAIGE *(11E)*
PARIS *(9R)*
PAYNE *(10F)*
PEERS *(11D)*
PETTY *(8T)*

PILOT †
POOLE *(10B)*
PRADO *(10P)*
PRICE *(9A, 10L)*
PROBY *(7P)*
QUEEN †
RACEY †
RAWLS *(8L)*
REDDY *(10H)*
REGAN *(9J)*
RILEY *(13J)*
ROMEO *(9M)*
ROSSO *(9N)*
RUFUS †
SARNE *(9M)*
SAXON †
SAYER *(8L)*
SCOTT *(9J, 10L)*
SHAND *(10J)*
SIMON *(9P, 10C)*
SKIDS †
SLADE †
SMITH *(7O, 10J, 11B)*
SOUTH *(8J)*
SPACE †
STARR *(8K, 10E, 10R)*
STEAM †
STING ¶
SWANN *(11D)*
SWEET †
TATUM *(8A)*
TEMPO *(9N)*
TOPOL ¶
TORMÉ *(8M)*
TOYAH ¶
TRACY *(11A)*
TRENT *(11J)*
TRUTH †
TYLER *(11B)*
TYMES †
VALLI *(12F)*
WAITE *(9J)*
WALSH *(8J)*
WATTS *(12C)*
WELLS *(9M)*
WELSH *(9A, 10B)*

WHITE *(10B)*
WILDE *(8K, 10M)*
WINGS †
WYLIE *(9P)*
WYMAN *(9B)*
YAZOO †
YOUNG *(9N, 9P, 10J,*
10K, 11L)
ZAGER *(12M)*
ZZ TOP †

6

ALMOND *(10M)*
ALPERT *(10H)*
ANGELS †
ARNOLD *(8P)*
ATKINS *(10C)*
ATWELL *(14W)*
AVALON *(13F)*
BAILEY *(11P)*
BALDRY *(14L)*
BARBER *(11C)*
BASSEY *(13S)*
BB KING
BECHET *(12S)*
BENSON *(12G)*
BENTON *(11B)*
BERLIN †
BIRKIN *(10J)*
BLAKEY *(9A)*
BONEY M †
BOWLLY *(8A)*
BREWER *(12T)*
BROOKS *(11E)*
BURDON *(10E)*
CANNON *(12F)*
CANTOR *(11E)*
CARMEN *(10E)*
CARNEY *(10K)*
COCKER *(9J)*
COMETS †
CONRAD *(10J)*
CONWAY *(10R)*
COOPER *(11A)*
COTTON *(11B)*

COWARD *(10N)*
CRAMER *(11F)*
CREOLE *(9K)*
CROSBY *(10B)*
CUTLER *(10A)*
DAMNED †
DAMONE *(9V)*
DARREN *(11J)*
DAVIES *(9R, 10D)*
DAWSON *(11P)*
DEKKER *(13D)*
DENVER *(10J, 10K)*
DE PAUL *(12L)*
DISTEL *(11S)*
DIVINE ¶
DOLLAR †
DOMINO *(10F)*
DORSEY *(9L, 11T)*
DR HOOK †
DUNCAN *(12J)*
DUNDAS *(11D)*
DUPREE *(11S)*
DURHAM *(12J)*
EAGLES †
EASTON *(12S)*
EQUALS †
EUROPE †
FABIAN ¶
FAMILY †
FENTON *(11S)*
FERRER *(10J)*
FIELDS *(12G)*
FISHER *(11E)*
FORMBY *(12G)*
FUREYS †
GALWAY *(11J)*
GASKIN *(13B)*
GAYNOR *(12G)*
GELDOF *(9B)*
GENTRY *(12B)*
GIBSON *(9D, 11W)*
GILLAN †
GITANA *(12G)*
GO WEST †
GRACIE *(13C)*
GRAHAM *(10J)*

HANSON *(10J)*
HARDIN *(9T)*
HARLEY *(11S)*
HARRIS *(9J, 10P, 10R, 11A, 13R)*
HERMAN *(11W)*
HILTON *(12R)*
HODGES *(12J)*
HOLDER *(11N)*
HOOKER *(13J)*
HOPKIN *(10M)*
HORTON *(12J)*
HUNTER *(9T)*
HYLAND *(11B)*
IFIELD *(11F)*
JAGGER *(10M)*
JOE TEX
JOLSON *(8A)*
JOPLIN *(11J, 11S)*
KEPURA *(9J)*
KNIGHT *(12G)*
KRAMER *(12B)*
LAUDER *(11H)*
LAUPER *(11C)*
LENNON *(10J, 12J)*
LENNOX *(11A)*
LESTER *(11K)*
LEYTON *(10J)*
LIMAHL ¶
LIMMIE ¶
LINDON *(12M)*
LONDON *(11J, 12L)*
LOVICH *(10L)*
LYNOTT *(10P)*
MACRAE *(12G)*
MAI TAI †
MARINI *(12M)*
MARLEY *(9B)*
MARTIN *(9R, 10D, 10M, 10T, 15M)*
MARVIN *(9L, 10H)*
MATHIS *(12J)*
McCRAE *(12G)*
McLEAN *(9D)*
McTELL *(11R)*
MEEHAN *(10T)*

MELVIN *(12H)*
MENDES *(12S)*
MERMAN *(11E)*
MILLER *(9N, 10G, 11G, 11R)*
MILLIE ¶
MINGUS *(13C)*
MINOTT *(11S)*
MONROE *(11G)*
MONTEZ *(11C)*
MORGAN *(10J, 11H)*
MORRIS *(10L)*
MORTON *(15J)*
MOTORS †
MURPHY *(10R)*
MURRAY *(10R)*
NELSON *(10R, 11S)*
NEWLEY *(13A)*
NICOLE ¶
NOLANS †
OFARIM *(9A, 12E)*
OLIVER ¶
OSMOND *(11D, 11M)*
OUR KID †
PALMER *(12R)*
PARKER *(13C)*
PARTON *(11D)*
PEARLS †
PIGBAG †
PITNEY *(10G)*
POGUES †
POLICE †
POWELL *(10C)*
PRINCE ¶
QUATRO *(10S)*
RAINEY *(8M)*
RAYDIO †
RED BOX †
REEVES *(9J, 12M)*
RICHIE *(12L)*
RIDDLE *(12N)*
RITTER *(9T)*
ROGERS *(11J, 11K, 12G)*
ROWLES *(10J)*
RUFFIN *(11J)*
RUMOUR †

RYDELL (11B)
SAILOR †
SAMMES (10M)
SAVAGE (10E)
SCAGGS (9B)
SEDAKA (10N)
SEEGER (10P)
SHARPE (11R)
SIFFRE (10L)
SIMONE (10N)
SLEDGE (11P)
SMITHS †
SMOKIE †
SPARKS †
SPEARS (14B)
STATON (11C)
STEELE (11T)
SUMMER (11D)
SYLVIA ¶
TAYLOR (11J, 11R)
TEMPLE (13S)
THOMAS (11R, 12E)
TILLEY (11V)
TRACIE ¶
TRANS-X †
TRENET (13C)
TROGGS †
TUCKER (11T, 12S)
TURNER (9I, 10J, 10T)
TWEETS †
TWITTY (12C)
UK SUBS †
ULLMAN (12T)
VALENS (13R)
VALLEE (10R)
VAPORS †
VINTON (11B)
VIPERS †
VISAGE †
WALKER (10J, 11S, 12J)
WALLER (10F)
WATERS (11E, 11M)
WEEDON (10B)
WESTON (9K)
WILSON (10M, 12D, 12J)
WISDOM (12N)

WONDER (12S)
WOOLEY (10S)
WRIGHT (10R)
WYNTER (10M)
ZAMFIR (13G)

7

ADAM ANT
AL GREEN
AMAZULU †
AMERICA †
ANDREWS (12C)
ANDY KIM
ANIMALS †
ARCHIES †
ARRIVAL †
ASTAIRE (11F)
BAND AID †
BANGLES †
BAUHAUS †
BEATLES †
BEE GEES †
BENATAR (10P)
BENNETT (11T, 12C)
BLONDIE †
BOB LIND
BON JOVI †
BOSWELL (10E)
BOX TOPS †
BRANDON (13J)
BROONZY (14B)
BRUBECK (11D)
BUGGLES †
CALVERT (12E)
CARROLL (13R)
CASSIDY (12D)
CASUALS †
CHARLES (10R, 11T)
CHECKER (13C)
CHICAGO †
CLAPTON (11E)
CLOONEY (15R)
COCHRAN (12E)
COLEMAN (14O)

COLLINS (11J, 11P)
COLONNA (12J)
CORNELL (10D, 11L)
DAKOTAS †
DALTREY (12R)
DANIELS (12B)
DAVE DEE
DE BURGH (12C)
DEE C LEE
DELRONS †
DIAMOND (11N)
DICKSON (14B)
DONEGAN (13L)
DON LANG
DONOVAN ¶, (12J)
DOOLIES †
DOUGLAS (11C, 12C)
DURANTE (12J)
DYNASTY †
EDMUNDS (11D)
EDWARDS (12T)
ELLIMAN (13Y)
ERASURE †
ESTEFAN (13G)
FARLOWE (12C)
FONTANA (12W)
FRANCIS (13C)
FR DAVID
FREEMAN (10B)
GABRIEL (12P)
GAP BAND †
GARRETT (11L)
GENESIS †
GEORDIE †
GLITTER (11G)
GOODIES †
GOODMAN (12B)
GOODWIN (10R)
GUTHRIE (11A, 11G, 12W)
HANCOCK (13H)
HAWKINS (14C)
HAYWARD (13J)
HENDRIX (11J)
HEYWARD (11N)
HOLIDAY (13B)

303

HOLLIES †
HOPKINS *(15L)*
HOUSTON *(14W)*
IAN DURY
IGGY POP
IT BITES †
JACKSON *(10J, 12J,*
14M, 15J)
JESTERS †
JOE LOSS
JOEY DEE
JOHNSON *(11M, 12H,*
12T, 13J, 13L)
JUSTICE *(12J)*
KEN DODD
KERSHAW *(10N)*
KIKI DEE
LOCKLIN *(11H)*
LOGGINS *(12K)*
LOU REED
LUVVERS †
MacCOLL *(13K)*
MADNESS †
MADONNA ¶
MALCOLM *(11C)*
MANCINI *(12H)*
MANILOW *(12B)*
MARBLES †
MARCELS †
MARILYN ¶
MARKHAM *(14P)*
MARSDEN *(12G)*
MARTELL *(11L)*
MARTINO *(9A)*
MATHIEU *(15M)*
MAUGHAN *(12S)*
MAURIAT *(11P)*
McGUIRE *(12B)*
McLAREN *(14M)*
MELANIE ¶
MERCURY *(14F)*
MERSEYS †
MICHAEL *(13G)*
MICHELL *(12K)*
MINOGUE *(12K)*
MIRANDA *(13C)*

MOMENTS †
MONKEES †
MONSOON †
NATASHA ¶
NILSSON ¶
O'CONNOR *(10D, 12H)*
OC SMITH
ODYSSEY †
ORBISON *(10R)*
ORLANDO *(11T)*
OSMONDS †
OTTAWAN †
OUTLAWS †
PEARSON *(13J)*
PENROSE *(14C)*
PEPPERS †
PERKINS *(11C)*
PICKETT *(13W)*
PIGLETS †
PINKIES †
PIRATES †
PJ PROBY
POLLARD *(9S)*
PRESLEY *(12E)*
PRESTON *(11M, 12B,*
13J)
PROVINE *(14D)*
PUCKETT *(11G)*
RAH BAND †
RAINBOW †
RAMONES †
RAMRODS †
RATTLES †
REDBONE †
REDDING *(11O)*
REGENTS †
REPLAYS †
RICHARD *(12C, 12K)*
RICHMAN *(15J)*
ROBBINS *(11K, 12M)*
ROBERTS *(14M)*
ROBESON *(11P)*
RODGERS *(13J, 14C)*
ROLLINS *(12S)*
ROUSSOS *(12D)*
ROY WOOD

RUSSELL *(13P)*
SAD CAFÉ †
SANTANA †
SAVALAS *(12T)*
SECOMBE *(12H)*
SEEKERS †
SELLERS *(12P)*
SHADOWS †
SHANNON ¶, *(10D)*
SHAPIRO *(12H)*
SHARKEY *(14F)*
SHELDON *(11D)*
SHELTON *(11A)*
SHERBET †
SHERMAN *(12A)*
SINATRA *(12F, 12N)*
SINITTA ¶
SOS BAND †
SQUEEZE †
SQUIRES *(14D)*
STEVENS *(10C, 10R,*
12A, 12R,
13C, 13S)
STEWART *(10R, 11A,*
11D, 15J)
STRAWBS †
SYLVIAN *(12D)*
SYREETA ¶
TAVARES †
TERRELL *(12T)*
TIKORAM *(13T)*
TONIGHT †
TRAFFIC †
TRAMMPS †
TURTLES †
TWINKLE ¶
VALANCE *(12R)*
VALENTE *(15C)*
VAN DYKE *(12L)*
VAUGHAN *(12S, 14F,*
14M)
VINCENT *(11G)*
WAILERS †
WAKELIN *(13J)*
WALLACE *(13N)*
WALTERS *(13T)*

WARWICK (13D)
WEAVERS †
WEDLOCK (11F)
WHISTLE †
WINTERS (11R)
WINWOOD (12S)
WIZZARD †
WOMBLES †
WURZELS †
WYNETTE (12T)
ZEIGLER (11A)
ZODIACS †
ZOMBIES †

8

ADDERLEY
AL BOWLLY
AL JOLSON
ALLISONS †
ALL-STARS †
ANDERSON (13M)
ANDY GIBB
ANN BLYTH
ART TATUM
AZNAVOUR (15C)
BANSHEES †
BEN E KING
BENNY LEE
BIG THREE †
BLUE MINK †
BOBBY VEE
BOB DYLAN
BOB LUMAN
BUCHANAN (12J)
BURL IVES
BURNETTE (14J)
BYGRAVES (11M)
CAMPBELL (12G)
CARLISLE (13E)
CASCADES †
CHAMPION (13H)
CHIFFONS †
CHI-LITES †
CHRIS REA

CHRISTIE †, (11L)
COASTERS †
COLTRANE (12J)
COOLIDGE (12R)
COSTELLO (13E)
CRAWFORD (13R)
CREW CUTS †
CRICKETS †
CRYSTALS †
DIAMONDS †
DIETRICH (15M)
DOONICAN (11V)
DORIS DAY
DREAMERS †
DRIFTERS †
DRISCOLL (13J)
ECKSTINE (13B)
EDEN KANE
FENTONES †
FIVE STAR †
FLANAGAN (11B)
FLANDERS (15M)
FLOATERS †
FORTUNES †
FOUR ACES †
FOURMOST †
FOUR TOPS †
FRAMPTON (13P)
FRANKLIN (14A)
GARDINER (13B)
GARRITTY (15F)
HAMILTON (12R, 14G)
HARRISON (12N, 14G)
HARRY ROY
HAWKWIND †
HEATWAVE †
HOLLIDAY (15M)
HOLLOWAY (15S)
HONEYBUS †
HOTSHOTS †
IGLESIAS (13J)
INEZ FOXX
INK SPOTS †
ISSY BONN
JACKSONS †
JEFF BECK

JOAN BAEZ
JOE BROWN
JOE DOLAN
JOE DOLCE
JOE FAGIN
JOE SOUTH
JOE WALSH
JOHN FRED
JOHN HOLT
JOHN PARR
KATE BUSH
KAY STARR
KIM WILDE
KNOPFLER (12M)
LAWRENCE (13K, 13S)
LEANDROS (13V)
LEAPY LEE
LEN BARRY
LEO SAYER
LIBERACE ¶
LIPPS INC †
LITA ROZA
LOU RAWLS
MAMA CASS
MA RAINEY
MATCHBOX †
MATTHEWS (14J)
MAX ROMEO
MAYFIELD (14C)
McKELLAR (15K)
McKENZIE (13S)
MEAT LOAF †
MEL TORMÉ
MIDGE URE
MIKE BATT
MIRACLES †
MITCHELL (11G, 12J)
MIXTURES †
MORRISON (11V)
MR MISTER †
MRS MILLS
MUDLARKS †
MULLIGAN (13G)
NAZARETH †
NEIL REID
NEWBEATS †

NEW ORDER †
NEW WORLD †
NICHOLAS (12P)
OLDFIELD (12M)
OLYMPICS †
OSBOURNE (12O)
OWEN PAUL
PAT BOONE
PAUL ANKA
PAUL RYAN
PEDDLERS †
PEGGY LEE
PETERSON (13O)
PHARAOHS †
PHILLIPS (11S, 14E)
PIONEERS †
PIRANHAS †
PLATTERS †
PP ARNOLD
PRINCESS ¶
PUSSYCAT †
RAFFERTY (13G)
REG DIXON
REPARATA ¶
REYNOLDS (14D)
RIPERTON (14M)
ROBINSON (11T, 14S)
ROCKWELL ¶
RONETTES †
RONSTADT (13L)
RUBETTES †
SAKAMOTO (11K)
SAM BROWN
SAM COOKE
SARSTEDT (13P, 13R)
SCAFFOLD †
SEMPRINI ¶
SHAKATAK †
SHALAMAR †
SHEARING (14G)
SHERIDAN (12M)
SIMON MAY
SIOUXSIE ¶
SKELLERN (13P)
SOFT CELL †
SPECIALS †

SPINNERS †
STAFFORD (10J)
STAN GETZ
STARDUST (13A)
ST PETERS
STRATTON (14E)
SUPREMES †
SURFARIS †
SURVIVOR †
TALK TALK †
TED HEATH
THOM PACE
THURSTON (13B)
TIGHT FIT †
TOM JONES
TOMMY ROE
TOM PETTY
TORNADOS †
TOURISTS †
TOY DOLLS †
TRAVOLTA (12J)
ULTRAVOX †
UMILIANI (13P)
UNION GAP †
VANDROSS (14L)
VANGELIS ¶
VAN HALEN †
VAN McCOY
VENTURES †
VERA LYNN
WATERMAN (14D)
WHISPERS †
WILLIAMS (11D, 12A,
            12H, 12I,
            12J, 13D,
            13M, 15D,
            15M)
ZAVARONI (12L)

9

ABI OFARIM
ACKER BILK
ADAM FAITH
ALAN PRICE
ALED JONES
ALEX WELSH

ALMA COGAN
AL MARTINO
ANITA WARD
ANNIE ROSS
ARMSTRONG (14L)
ART BLAKEY
ARTIE SHAW
BACHELORS †
BADFINGER †
BARRY BLUE
BARRY GIBB
BARRY RYAN
BEACH BOYS †
BELAFONTE (14H)
BENNY HILL
BIG BOPPER
BILL HALEY
BILL WYMAN
BILLY FURY
BILLY IDOL
BILLY JOEL
BILLY PAUL
BILLY SWAN
BLACK LACE †
BLUEBELLS †
BLUENOTES †
BLUNSTONE (14C)
BOBBY HEBB
BOB GELDOF
BOB MARLEY
BO DIDDLEY
BOW WOW WOW †
BOY GEORGE
BOZ SCAGGS
BRENDA LEE
BRIGHTMAN (14S)
BUCKS FIZZ †
BUDDY RICH
BUZZCOCKS †
CHAKA KHAN
CHEVALIER (15A)
CLEO LAINE
CLIVE DUNN
COVINGTON (14J)
CRUSADERS †
CUFFLINKS †

DANKWORTH *(15J)*
DANNY KAYE
DARYL HALL
DAVE BERRY
DAVID SOUL
DIANA ROSS
DIXIE CUPS †
DOBIE GRAY
DON GIBSON
DON McLEAN
DUANE EDDY
DUBLINERS †
EARL HINES
EASYBEATS †
EDDY GRANT
EDITH PIAF
ELLINGTON *(12R, 13D)*
ELTON JOHN
EMILE FORD
FAITHFULL
FELICIANO *(13J)*
FOREIGNER †
FOUR PREPS †
GARFUNKEL *(12A)*
GARY MOORE
GARY NUMAN
GENE AUTRY
GENE KELLY
GENE KRUPA
GEOFF LOVE
GILLESPIE *(14D)*
GOLDSBORO *(14B)*
GRAPPELLI
GREENBAUM *(15N)*
GREYHOUND †
HAZLEWOOD *(12L)*
HENDERSON *(12J)*
HETTY KING
HOCKRIDGE *(15E)*
HOT BUTTER †
HUEY LEWIS
IKE TURNER
IRENE CARA
IVY LEAGUE †
JACK BRUCE
JACK SCOTT

JAMES FAWN
JAMES LAST
JAN KEPURA
JANKOWSKI *(14H)*
JEFFERSON ¶
JET HARRIS
JIMMY DEAN
JIMMY NAIL
JIM REEVES
JOAN REGAN
JOE COCKER
JOHN BARRY
JOHN LYDON
JOHN MILES
JOHN OATES
JOHN WAITE
KEITH MOON
KEITH WEST
KEMPFAERT *(13B)*
KENNY BALL
KID CREOLE
KIM WESTON
KRAFTWERK †
LANDSCAPE †
LEE DORSEY
LEE MARVIN
LENA HORNE
LIGHTFOOT *(14T, 15G)*
LITTLE EVA
LOOSE ENDS †
LOS BRAVOS †
LYTTELTON
MANTOVANI ¶
MARILLION †
MARMALADE †
MARTI WEBB
MARY WELLS
MATT MONRO
McCARTNEY *(13P)*
McCORMACK *(13J)*
McPHATTER *(14C)*
MEL AND KIM †
MEN AT WORK †
MIGIL FIVE †
MIKE BERRY
MIKE SARNE

MORRICONE *(14E)*
MOTORHEAD †
MOUSKOURI *(13N)*
NED MILLER
NEIL YOUNG
NICK BERRY
NICK KAMEN
NINI ROSSO
NINO TEMPO
O'SULLIVAN
PAPER LACE †
PARKINSON *(14J)*
PARTRIDGE *(12D)*
PATTI PAGE
PAUL SIMON
PAUL YOUNG
PEARL CARR
PERRY COMO
PETE WYLIE
PINK FLOYD †
PONI-TAILS †
RAINWATER *(15M)*
RAY DAVIES
RAY MARTIN
REAL THING †
REINHARDT *(15D)*
ROBERTSON *(11B)*
ROBIN GIBB
ROSE ROYCE †
ROXY MUSIC †
RUSS ABBOT
RYAN PARIS
SCORPIONS †
SEARCHERS †
SHIRELLES †
SHONDELLS †
SIMON PARK
SIMPLY RED †
SLIM DUSTY
SPOTNICKS †
STAPLETON *(14C)*
STATUS QUO †
STEELY DAN †
STRAY CATS †
STREISAND *(15B)*
SU POLLARD

307

SYLVESTER ¶, (15V)
TAB HUNTER
TEAGARDEN (13J)
TEENAGERS †
TERRY DENE
TEX RITTER
THIN LIZZY †
TILLOTSON (15J)
TIM HARDIN
TONI BASIL
TONY BRENT
TOWNSHEND (13P)
TREMELOES †
UPSETTERS †
VALENTINE (15D)
VANDELLAS †
VIC DAMONE
VIKKI CARR
VINCE HILL
WHITFIELD (14D)
WHITTAKER (14R)
YARDBIRDS †
YELLOW DOG †
ZACHARIAS (15H)
ZOOT MONEY

10

ADGE CUTLER
ALLAN JONES
AMEN CORNER †
APPLEJACKS †
ART OF NOISE †
BAD MANNERS †
BANANARAMA †
BARRY BIGGS
BARRY WHITE
BELLE STARS †
BERT WEEDON
BIG COUNTRY †
BILLY BRAGG
BILLY OCEAN
BING CROSBY
BLANCMANGE †
BLOCKHEADS †
BOB AND EARL †

BOBBY BLOOM
BOBBY CRUSH
BOBBY DARIN
BRIAN AUGER
BRIAN JONES
BRIAN POOLE
BRUCE WELSH
BRYAN FERRY
BUDDY GRECO
BUDDY HOLLY
BUD FREEMAN
CANNED HEAT †
CARAVELLES †
CARLY SIMON
CARMICHAEL (15H)
CAROL DEENE
CAROLE KING
CARPENTERS †
CAT STEVENS
CHECKMATES †
CHET ATKINS
CHICORY TIP †
CHORDETTES †
CHUCK BERRY
CILLA BLACK
COMMODORES †
COMMUNARDS †
COUNT BASIE
COZY POWELL
DAVE DAVIES
DAVID BOWIE
DAVID ESSEX
DEAN MARTIN
DEEP PURPLE †
DEF LEPPARD †
DEL SHANNON
DES O'CONNOR
DON CORNELL
DR FEELGOOD
DURAN DURAN †
EARTHA KITT
EDDIE FLOYD
EDMUNDO ROS
EDNA SAVAGE
EDWIN STARR
ERIC BURDON

ERIC CARMEN
EURYTHMICS †
EVE BOSWELL
EVELYN KING
EYDIE GORMÉ
FATS DOMINO
FATS WALLER
FITZGERALD (14E)
FREDA PAYNE
GAINSBOURG (15S)
GARY MILLER
GENE PITNEY
GRACE JONES
HANK MARVIN
HARDCASTLE (14P)
HAZELL DEAN
HELEN REDDY
HERB ALPERT
HIGHWAYMEN †
HONEYCOMBS †
HOWARD KEEL
HURRICANES †
IRON MAIDEN †
ISAAC HAYES
JAKI GRAHAM
JAMES BROWN
JAN AND DEAN †
JANE BIRKIN
JANE MORGAN
JESS CONRAD
JETHRO TULL †
JIMMY CLIFF
JIMMY JAMES
JIMMY JONES
JIMMY LOGAN
JIMMY SHAND
JIMMY SMITH
JIMMY YOUNG
JOAN TURNER
JOE JACKSON
JOHN DENVER
JOHN HANSON
JOHN LENNON
JOHN LEYTON
JOHNNIE RAY
JOHNNY KIDD

JOHNNY MANN
JOHNNY NASH
JOHN ROWLES
JOHN WALKER
JOSÉ FERRER
JO STAFFORD
JUDGE DREAD
JULIE FELIX
KAJAGOOGOO †
KALIN TWINS †
KAREN YOUNG
KARL DENVER
KATE CARNEY
KATHY KIRBY
KELLY MARIE
KENNY LYNCH
LABI SIFFRE
LAMBRETTAS †
LENA LOVICH
LESLEY GORE
LILY MORRIS
LINDA LEWIS
LINDA SCOTT
LIQUID GOLD †
LLOYD PRICE
LOUDERMILK (15J)
LOVE AFFAIR †
MACKINTOSH (13K)
MAGGIE BELL
MARC ALMOND
MARIE LLOYD
MARIO LANZA
MARION RYAN
MARI WILSON
MARK WYNTER
MARSHA HUNT
MARTINDALE (14W)
MARTY WILDE
MARVIN GAYE
MARY HOPKIN
MARY MARTIN
MATT BIANCO †
MELACHRINO
MICK JAGGER
MIKE SAMMES
MILES DAVIS

MONTENEGRO (14H)
MONTGOMERY
MOODY BLUES †
MÖTLEY CRÜE †
MUNGO JERRY †
NEIL SEDAKA
NELSON EDDY
NEW EDITION †
NEW SEEKERS †
NEWTON-JOHN
NIK KERSHAW
NINA SIMONE
NOËL COWARD
PACEMAKERS †
PAT BENATAR
PATSY CLINE
PERCY FAITH
PEREZ PRADO
PETER NOONE
PETE SEEGER
PHIL HARRIS
PHIL LYNOTT
PRETENDERS †
RACING CARS †
RAM JAM BAND †
RAY CHARLES
RAY STEVENS
RICK NELSON
RINGO STARR
ROD STEWART
ROLF HARRIS
RON GOODWIN
ROSE MURPHY
ROY ORBISON
RUBY MURRAY
RUBY WRIGHT
RUDY VALLEE
RUSS CONWAY
SAM AND DAVE †
SAMMY DAVIS
SAM THE SHAM
SANDIE SHAW
SANDPIPERS †
SEX PISTOLS †
SHANGRI-LAS †
SHEB WOOLEY

SIMON LE BON
SINGING NUN
SMALL FACES †
SOMERVILLE (15J)
STARGAZERS †
STRANGLERS †
STYLISTICS †
SUPERTRAMP †
SUZI QUATRO
TEDDY BEARS †
TERRY JACKS
THIRD WORLD †
TINA TURNER
TOMMY BRUCE
TOMMY JAMES
TOM TOM CLUB †
TONY MARTIN
TONY MEEHAN
TRINI LOPEZ
UNDERTONES †
VANITY FARE †
WASHINGTON (14G,
                    15D)
WAVELENGTH †
WHITESNAKE †
WILLIAMSON

11

ALICE COOPER
ALISON MOYET
AMII STEWART
ANDY STEWART
ANITA HARRIS
ANNE SHELTON
ANNE ZEIGLER
ANNIE LENNOX
ARLO GUTHRIE
ARMATRADING (15J)
ARTHUR BROWN
ARTHUR TRACY
BA ROBERTSON
BEIDERBECKE (14B)
BESSIE SMITH
BIG DEE IRWIN

BIG ROLL BAND †
BILLIE DAVIS
BILLY COTTON
BOBBY RYDELL
BOBBY VINTON
BONNIE TYLER
BRIAN HYLAND
BRONSKI BEAT †
BROOK BENTON
BUD FLANAGAN
CANDI STATON
CARL DOUGLAS
CARL MALCOLM
CARL PERKINS
CHACKSFIELD
CHARLIE BYRD
CHARLIE FOXX
CHARLIE KUNZ
CHARLIE RICH
CHAS AND DAVE †
CHINA CRISIS †
CHRIS BARBER
CHRIS MONTEZ
CLINTON FORD
CULTURE CLUB †
CYNDI LAUPER
DAVE BRUBECK
DAVE EDMUNDS
DAVE STEWART
DAVID DUNDAS
DAVID PARTON
DEAD OR ALIVE †
DEBBIE HARRY
DENNIS LOTIS
DENNIS NOBLE
DEPECHE MODE †
DIRE STRAITS †
DOLLY PARTON
DONALD PEERS
DONALD SWANN
DONNA SUMMER
DONNY OSMOND
DON WILLIAMS
DOUG SHELDON
EDDIE CANTOR
EDDIE FISHER

ELAINE PAIGE
ELKIE BROOKS
ERIC CLAPTON
ETHEL MERMAN
ETHEL WATERS
FATBACK BAND †
FLOYD CRAMER
FOUNDATIONS †
FOUR PENNIES †
FOUR SEASONS †
FRANK IFIELD
FRED ASTAIRE
FRED WEDLOCK
FUN BOY THREE †
GARY GLITTER
GARY PUCKETT
GARY US BONDS
GENERATION X †
GENE VINCENT
GEORGIE FAME
GERRY MONROE
GINGER BAKER
GLENN MILLER
GLITTER BAND †
GUY MITCHELL
GWEN GUTHRIE
HANK LOCKLIN
HARRY LAUDER
HAYLEY MILLS
HELEN MORGAN
HILLTOPPERS †
HOWARD JONES
HUMAN LEAGUE †
HUMPERDINCK
IMAGINATION †
JACKIE TRENT
JACKSON FIVE †
JAMES DARREN
JAMES GALWAY
JAMES TAYLOR
JANIS JOPLIN
JIMI HENDRIX
JIMMY RUFFIN
JOHNNY LOGAN
JORDONAIRES †
JOSEPH LOCKE

JUDAS PRIEST †
JUDY COLLINS
JUDY GARLAND
JULIE LONDON
JULIE ROGERS
KATE ROBBINS
KAYE SISTERS †
KENNY ROGERS
KETTY LESTER
KILLING JOKE †
KYU SAKAMOTO
LEIF GARRETT
LENA MARTELL
LESTER YOUNG
LINDISFARNE †
LOU CHRISTIE
LYNN CORNELL
MAGGIE MOONE
MANFRED MANN †
MARIE OSMOND
MARVELETTES †
MARV JOHNSON
MAURICE GIBB
MAX BYGRAVES
MERSEYBEATS †
MIKE PRESTON
MINDBENDERS †
MISTINGUETT ¶
MODERNAIRES †
MUDDY WATERS
NAPOLEON XIV
NAT KING COLE
NEIL DIAMOND
NICK HEYWARD
NODDY HOLDER
OHIO EXPRESS †
ORANGE JUICE †
OTIS REDDING
OVERLANDERS †
PAUL MAURIAT
PAUL ROBESON
PEARL BAILEY
PERCY SLEDGE
PETER DAWSON
PET SHOP BOYS †
PHIL COLLINS

PILTDOWN MEN †
PLAYBOY BAND †
POPPY FAMILY †
PROCOL HARUM †
QUANTUM JUMP †
RALPH McTELL
RAMSEY LEWIS
R DEAN TAYLOR
ROCKY SHARPE
ROGER MILLER
RUBY WINTERS
RUFUS THOMAS
SACHA DISTEL
SAINTE-MARIE
SAMANTHA FOX
SANDY NELSON
SCOTT JOPLIN
SCOTT WALKER
SHANE FENTON
SID PHILLIPS
SIMON DUPREE
SIMPLE MINDS †
SLIM WHITMAN
SOLOMON KING
SPRINGFIELD
SPRINGSTEEN
STEPPENWOLF †
STEVE HARLEY
SUGAR MINOTT
SUZANNE VEGA
T CONNECTION †
TEMPTATIONS †
TINA CHARLES
TOMMY DORSEY
TOMMY STEELE
TOMMY TUCKER
TOM ROBINSON
TONY BENNETT
TONY ORLANDO
VAL DOONICAN
VAN MORRISON
VESTA TILLEY
WAYNE GIBSON
WHITE PLAINS †
WITHERSPOON
WOODY HERMAN

12

ALLAN SHERMAN
ANDY WILLIAMS
APRIL STEVENS
ART GARFUNKEL
BARRY MANILOW
BARRY McGUIRE
BENNY GOODMAN
BILLY DANIELS
BILLY J KRAMER
BILLY PRESTON
BLACK SABBATH †
BOB AND MARCIA †
BOBBIE GENTRY
BOOMTOWN RATS †
BOYSTOWN GANG †
CHARLESWORTH
CHARLIE WATTS
CHESNEY ALLEN
CHRIS ANDREWS
CHRIS DE BURGH
CHRIS FARLOWE
CLARICE MAYNE
CLIFF BENNETT
CLIFF RICHARD
COCKNEY REBEL †
CONWAY TWITTY
COURTNEY PINE
CRAIG DOUGLAS
CRYPT-KICKERS †
CRYSTAL GAYLE
DAVID CASSIDY
DAVID SYLVIAN
DEMIS ROUSSOS
DON PARTRIDGE
DOOLEY WILSON
DOROTHY MOORE
DREAMWEAVERS †
EDDIE CALVERT
EDDIE COCHRAN
ELVIS PRESLEY
ESTHER OFARIM
EVELYN THOMAS
FIDDLER'S DRAM †
FIRST EDITION †

FLEETWOOD MAC †
FLORRIE FORDE
FLOWERPOT MEN †
FONTELLA BASS
FOUR FRESHMEN †
FRANKIE LAINE
FRANKIE LYMON
FRANKIE VALLI
FRANK SINATRA
FREDDY CANNON
GEORGE BENSON
GEORGE FORMBY
GEORGE McCRAE
GERRY MARSDEN
GERTIE GITANA
GINGER ROGERS
GLADYS KNIGHT
GLEN CAMPBELL
GLORIA GAYNOR
GORDON MACRAE
GRACIE FIELDS
GRATEFUL DEAD †
GUYS AND DOLLS †
HANK WILLIAMS
HAROLD MELVIN
HARRY SECOMBE
HAZEL O'CONNOR
HELEN SHAPIRO
HENRY MANCINI
HOLLY JOHNSON
HOT CHOCOLATE †
HOUSEMARTINS †
IRIS WILLIAMS
JACK BUCHANAN
JACKIE WILSON
JANET JACKSON
JASON DONOVAN
JENNIFER RUSH
JERRY COLONNA
JIMMY DURANTE
JIMMY JUSTICE
JOE HENDERSON
JOHN COLTRANE
JOHNNY DUNCAN
JOHNNY HODGES
JOHNNY HORTON

JOHNNY MATHIS
JOHN TRAVOLTA
JOHN WILLIAMS
JONATHAN KING
JONI MITCHELL
JUDITH DURHAM
JULIAN LENNON
JUNIOR WALKER
KEITH MICHELL
KEITH RICHARD
KENNY LOGGINS
KING BROTHERS †
KINGSTON TRIO †
KYLIE MINOGUE
LAURIE LONDON
LEE HAZLEWOOD
LENA ZAVARONI
LEROY VAN DYKE
LIONEL RICHIE
LYNSEY DE PAUL
MARINO MARINI
MARK KNOPFLER
MARK SHERIDAN
MARTHA REEVES
MARTY ROBBINS
MAUREEN EVANS
MEDICINE HEAD †
MICHAEL ZAGER
MIDNIGHT STAR †
MIKE OLDFIELD
MIKI AND GRIFF †
MILLIE LINDON
MODERN LOVERS †
MUSICAL YOUTH †
NANCY SINATRA
NELSON RIDDLE
NOËL HARRISON
NORMAN WISDOM
OZZY OSBOURNE
PAUL AND PAULA †
PAUL NICHOLAS
PETER GABRIEL
PETERS AND LEE †
PETER SELLERS
PLASTIC PENNY †
POWER STATION †

PRETTY THINGS †
RAY ELLINGTON
RICKY STEVENS
RICKY VALANCE
RITA COOLIDGE
ROBERTA FLACK
ROBERT PALMER
ROGER DALTREY
RONNIE HILTON
RUSS HAMILTON
SAMANTHA SANG
SARAH VAUGHAN
SECRET AFFAIR †
SERGIO MENDES
SHEENA EASTON
SHIRLEY ELLIS
SHIRLEY JONES
SHOCKING BLUE †
SHOWSTOPPERS †
SIDNEY BECHET
SISTER SLEDGE †
SKEETER DAVIS
SONNY AND CHER †
SONNY ROLLINS
SOPHIE TUCKER
SPENCER DAVIS
SPRINGFIELDS †
STEELEYE SPAN †
STEPHEN DUFFY
STEVE WINWOOD
STEVIE WONDER
ST LOUIS UNION †
STYLE COUNCIL †
SUNSHINE BAND †
SUSAN MAUGHAN
TALKING HEADS †
TAMMI TERRELL
TAMMY WYNETTE
TEDDY JOHNSON
TELLY SAVALAS
TERESA BREWER
THE YOUNG ONES †
THREE DEGREES †
TOMMY EDWARDS
TRACEY ULLMAN
VERNONS GIRLS †

WAYNE FONTANA
WEATHER GIRLS †
WEBSTER BOOTH
WOODY GUTHRIE
YOUNG RASCALS †

13

ALVIN STARDUST
ALTERED IMAGES †
ANTHONY NEWLEY
ATOMIC ROOSTER †
BARBARA GASKIN
BARRON KNIGHTS †
BERT KEMPFAERT
BILLIE HOLIDAY
BILLY ECKSTINE
BOBBY THURSTON
BORIS GARDINER
BROOK BROTHERS †
CARMEN MIRANDA
CHARLES TRENET
CHARLIE GRACIE
CHARLIE MINGUS
CHARLIE PARKER
CHRISSIE HYNDE
CHUBBY CHECKER
CLARENCE HENRY
CLIFFORD T WARD
CONNIE FRANCIS
CONNIE STEVENS
DANNY WILLIAMS
DAVE CLARK FIVE †
DEEP RIVER BOYS †
DESMOND DEKKER
DIONNE WARWICK
DUKE ELLINGTON
ELSIE CARLISLE
ELVIS COSTELLO
FAT LARRY'S BAND †
FLYING LIZARDS †
FLYING PICKETS †
FRANKIE AVALON
GEORGE MICHAEL
GEORGHE ZAMFIR

GERRY MULLIGAN
GERRY RAFFERTY
GLORIA ESTEFAN
HARRY CHAMPION
HEARTBREAKERS †
HERBIE HANCOCK
ISLEY BROTHERS †
JACK TEAGARDEN
JEANNIE C RILEY
JERRY LEE LEWIS
JIMMIE RODGERS
JOHN LEE HOOKER
JOHN McCORMACK
JOHNNY BRANDON
JOHNNY JOHNSON
JOHNNY PEARSON
JOHNNY PRESTON
JOHNNY WAKELIN
JOSÉ FELICIANO
JULIE DRISCOLL
JULIO IGLESIAS
JUSTIN HAYWARD
KATIE LAWRENCE
KEN MACKINTOSH
KIRSTY MacCOLL
LAURIE JOHNSON
LINDA RONSTADT
LITTLE RICHARD
LONNIE DONEGAN
LOVIN' SPOONFUL †
MADELEINE BELL
MAGIC LANTERNS †
MASON WILLIAMS
MILLS BROTHERS †
MODERN ROMANCE †
MODERN TALKING †
MOIRA ANDERSON
MOTT THE HOOPLE †
NANA MOUSKOURI
NELLIE WALLACE
OLLIE AND GERRY †
OSCAR PETERSON
PAUL McCARTNEY
PEE WEE RUSSELL
PETER FRAMPTON
PETER SARSTEDT

PETER SKELLERN
PETE TOWNSHEND
PICKETTY WITCH †
PIERO UMILIANI
RANDY CRAWFORD
REO SPEEDWAGON †
RICHARD HARRIS
RITCHIE VALENS
ROBIN SARSTEDT
ROCKIN' BERRIES †
ROLLING STONES †
RONNIE CARROLL
SCOTT McKENZIE
SHAKIN' STEVENS
SHIRLEY BASSEY
SHIRLEY TEMPLE
SHOWADDYWADDY †
SPANDAU BALLET †
STEALER'S WHEEL †
STEVE LAWRENCE
TEARS FOR FEARS †
THOMPSON TWINS †
THREE DOG NIGHT †
TINITA TIKORAM
TREVOR WALTERS
TWISTED SISTER †
VICKY LEANDROS
VILLAGE PEOPLE †
WILSON PICKETT
YVONNE ELLIMAN
ZAGER AND EVANS †

14

ADAM AND THE ANTS †
ALTHIA AND DONNA †
ANDREWS SISTERS †
ARETHA FRANKLIN
BARBARA DICKSON
BAY CITY ROLLERS †
BIG BILL BROONZY
BILLIE JO SPEARS
BIX BEIDERBECKE
BOBBY GOLDSBORO

CHARLES PENROSE
CLODAGH RODGERS
CLYDE McPHATTER
COLIN BLUNSTONE
CURTIS MAYFIELD
CYRIL STAPLETON
DAVID WHITFIELD
DEBBIE REYNOLDS
DENNIS WATERMAN
DIZZY GILLESPIE
DOOBIE BROTHERS †
DOROTHY PROVINE
DOROTHY SQUIRES
DORSEY BROTHERS †
ELLA FITZGERALD
ENNIO MORRICONE
ESTHER PHILLIPS
EUGENE STRATTON
EVERLY BROTHERS †
FAIRWEATHER-LOW
FEARGAL SHARKEY
FIFTH DIMENSION †
FRANÇOISE HARDY
FRANKIE VAUGHAN
FREDDIE MERCURY
GENO WASHINGTON
GEORGE HAMILTON
GEORGE HARRISON
GEORGE SHEARING
GIBSON BROTHERS †
GODLEY AND CREME †
HARRY BELAFONTE
HAYSI FANTAYZEE †
HERMAN'S HERMITS †
HORST JANKOWSKI
HUGO MONTENEGRO
JESSIE MATTHEWS
JIMMY PARKINSON
JOHN BARRY SEVEN †
JOHNNY BURNETTE
JON AND VANGELIS †
JULIE COVINGTON
KOOL AND THE GANG †
LONG JOHN BALDRY
LORD ROCKINGHAM
LOUIS ARMSTRONG

LUTHER VANDROSS
MALCOLM McLAREN
MALCOLM ROBERTS
MALCOLM VAUGHAN
McGUIRE SISTERS †
MICHAEL JACKSON
NASHVILLE TEENS †
ORNETTE COLEMAN
PAUL HARDCASTLE
PEACHES AND HERB †
PETER AND GORDON †
PIGMEAT MARKHAM
PLASTIC ONO BAND †
POINTER SISTERS †
PUBLIC IMAGE LTD †
RENÉE AND RENATO †
ROCKSTEADY CREW †
ROGER WHITTAKER
ROOFTOP SINGERS †
SARAH BRIGHTMAN
SCRITTI POLITTI †
SHAKY AND BONNIE †
SMOKEY ROBINSON
STEPHANIE MILLS
SWEET SENSATION †
SWING OUT SISTER †
TERRY LIGHTFOOT
THELONIOUS MONK
WALKER BROTHERS †
WHITNEY HOUSTON

WINIFRED ATWELL
WINK MARTINDALE

15

ALBERT CHEVALIER
BARBRA STREISAND
BELLAMY BROTHERS †
BEVERLEY SISTERS †
BIG BEN BANJO BAND †
CAPTAIN SENSIBLE
CATERINA VALENTE
CHARLES AZNAVOUR
CLASSIC NOUVEAUX †
DELTA RHYTHM BOYS †
DENIECE WILLIAMS
DETROIT EMERALDS †
DETROIT SPINNERS †
DICKIE VALENTINE
DINAH WASHINGTON
DJANGO REINHARDT
EDMUND HOCKRIDGE
FREDDIE GARRITTY
GORDON LIGHTFOOT
HELMUT ZACHARIAS
HOAGY CARMICHAEL
JEAN-MICHEL JARRE
JELLY ROLL MORTON
JERMAINE JACKSON

JERMAINE STEWART
JIMMY SOMERVILLE
JOAN ARMATRADING
JOHN D LOUDERMILK
JOHNNY DANKWORTH
JOHNNY TILLOTSON
JONATHAN RICHMAN
KENNETH McKELLAR
LIGHTNIN' HOPKINS
MARLENE DIETRICH
MARVIN RAINWATER
MAURICE WILLIAMS
McGUINNESS FLINT †
MICHAEL FLANDERS
MICHAEL HOLLIDAY
MIDDLE OF THE ROAD †
MILLICENT MARTIN
MIRIELLE MATHIEU
NORMAN GREENBAUM
PARTRIDGE FAMILY †
PLASTIC BERTRAND
PSYCHEDELIC FURS †
RAY PARKER JUNIOR
ROSEMARY CLOONEY
SERGE GAINSBOURG
STANLEY HOLLOWAY
TEMPERANCE SEVEN †
UNIT FOUR PLUS TWO †
VICTOR SYLVESTER
WOMACK AND WOMACK †

PEOPLE

ENTERTAINERS –
TELEVISION & RADIO PERSONALITIES

(A) = Artist   *(C)* = Comedian(s)/comédienne   *(DJ)* = Disc jockey
(E) = Entertainer   *(I)* = Impressionist/impersonator   *(M)* = Magician
(N) = Newsreader/reporter   *(P)* = Presenter/host   *(PA)* = Panellist
(PU) = Puppeteer   *(SP)* = Sports commentator   *(V)* = Ventriloquist
(W) = Weather forecaster
*S = Sir

3

COX *(6D-P)*
    (7M-SP)
DAY *(8R-N/P) *S*
DEE *(8S-DJ/P)*
FRY *(10S-C)*
GEE *(9D-C/I)*
HAY *(7A-SP)*
JAY *(8P-N/P)*
KAY *(E-8K)*
RAY *(6T-C)*
    (8R-P)
ROY *(8D-C)*
WAX *(7R-C)*

4

ADIE *(8K-N)*
ALAN *(7R-V)*
BALL *(9B-C)*
    (10J-P)
BOYD *(9T-P)*
CANT *(9B-P)*
CASH *(8D-DJ)*
CASS *(9D-N)*
COLE *(8J-N)*
    (9S-N)
COOK *(7S-P)*
    (9P-C)
    (9R-P)
DELL *(8A-DJ)*

DODD *(7K-C)*
DUNN *(8J-DJ)*
FALK *(11B-P)*
FISH *(11M-W)*
FORD *(8A-N)*
GALL *(9S-N)*
GOLD *(9J-C)*
GRAY *(9E-C)*
    (10M-P)
HALE *(10G-C)*
HALL *(9T-V)*
    (10S-P/SP)
HANN *(10J-P)*
HART *(8T-A)*
HASS *(8H-P)*
    (9L-P)
HILL *(9B-C)*
    (9J-P/SP)
HUDD *(7R-C)*
HULL *(7R-PU)*
HUNT *(9J-SP)*
ICKE *(9D-P/SP)*
IDLE *(8E-C)*
JUDD *(10L-P)*
KERR *(10G-P)*
KING *(8D-C)*
    (12J-P)
KNOX *(9T-C)*
LONG *(10J-DJ)*
LOWE *(7T-SP)*
    (9C-N)
MAYO *(9S-DJ/P)*

MUIR *(9F-PA)*
OWEN *(8N-P)*
PACE *(10N-C)*
PEEL *(8J-DJ)*
PYKE *(10M-P)*
RACE *(9S-P)*
READ *(6A-C)*
    (8M-DJ)
REES *(7K-N)*
REID *(8M-C)*
RICE *(10A-P)*
ROSS *(8N-P)*
    (12J-P)
SNOW *(9P-N)*
TIDY *(8B-A)*
TODD *(7B-C)*
TOOK *(9B-P)*
TUSA *(8J-N)*
VINE *(9D-P/SP)*
WADE *(12V-SP)*
WALL *(7M-C)*
WATT *(7J-SP)*
WEST *(9P-SP)*
WISE *(9E-C)*
WOOD *(12V-C)*

5

ABBOT *(9R-C)*
ALLEN *(12C-C)*
ASKEY *(11A-C)*

ASPEL *(12M-P)*
BAKER *(10H-C)*
    12R-N/P)
BANKS *(9J-P)*
BATES *(10S-DJ)*
BATEY *(10D-P)*
BENNY *(9J-C)*
BLACK *(10C-P)*
BLAIR *(11L-E/P)*
BLIGH *(12J-P)*
BORGE *(11V-C)*
BOUGH *(10F-P)*
BOWEN *(8J-C/P)*
BRAGG *(11M-P)*
BROWN *(10F-I)*
    (10J-I)
    (11D-C)
BRUCE *(8K-SP)*
    (10L-C)
BUERK *(12M-N)*
BURKE *(10J-P)*
BURNS *(11G-P)*
BUZZI *(9R-C)*
CAINE *(10M-P)*
CHASE *(12C-C)*
CLARK *(10C-SP)*
COOKE *(13A-P)*
CRANE *(9A-P)*
CRYER *(10B-C/PA)*
DALBY *(15B-SP)*
DARKE *(8I-SP)*
DAVEY *(12B-W)*

DAVRO *(10B-C/l)*
DENIS *(11A-P)*
   (13M-P)
DRAKE *(12C-C)*
ELTON *(8B-C)*
EMERY *(9D-C)*
EMNEY *(9F-C)*
EVANS *(11N-C)*
EWART *(8T-N)*
FREUD *(9E-P)*
FROST *(10D-P)*
FYFFE *(9W-C)*
GILES *(9B-W)*
GOONS *(C)*
GRANT *(12R-P)*
GREEN *(9T-SP)*
   (10B-P/PA)
GREGG *(9A-P)*
GROOM *(10S-P)*
GUBBA *(9T-SP)*
HANDS *(11J-N)*
HENRY *(10L-C)*
HORNE *(12K-C/P)*
JAMES *(10C-P)*
   (10J-C)
JANES *(14C-SP)*
JEWEL *(10J-C)*
JONES *(8A-SP)*
   (9C-P)
   (10P-P/PA)
   (10P-SP)
   (10S-P)
   (10T-C)
JUNOR *(10P-P)*
KELLY *(10C-P)*
   (10H-P)
   (12B-PA)
   (12M-P)
KLEIN *(11R-C)*
LAKER *(8J-SP)*
LARGE *(10E-C)*
LA RUE *(10D-E/l)*
LEWIS *(9T-SP)*
   (11M-N)
LLOYD *(10C-SP)*
LYNAM *(12D-P/SP)*

McGEE *(11D-P)*
MILES *(12M-P)*
MOORE *(8R-DJ)*
   (10B-P/SP)
   (11D-C)
   (12P-P)
NEGUS *(11A-P)*
NERVO *(10J-C)*
NIXON *(10D-M)*
ODDIE *(9B-C)*
PALIN *(12M-C)*
PARRY *(9A-SP)*
PERRY *(9F-SP)*
PLATT *(8K-C)*
RIDER *(10S-P/SP)*
ROBEY *(11G-C)*
ROWAN *(8D-C)*
SACHS *(12L-P)*
SAYLE *(11A-C)*
SCOTT *(9J-W)*
   (11B-SP)
   (11S-P)
SERLE *(10C-P)*
SMITH *(8M-C)*
   (9M-DJ/P)
   (10G-N)
SYKES *(9E-C)*
TULLY *(9M-N)*
WEEKS *(9A-SP)*
WOGAN *(10T-P)*
WOLFF *(10H-P)*
WOODS *(10P-N)*
WORTH *(10H-C)*
YOUNG *(10J-DJ/P)*
   (11M-P)

6

ALLISS *(11P-SP)*
AL READ *(C)*
ARCHER *(14G-N)*
ARLOTT *(10J-SP)*
BARKER *(12R-C)*
BARNES *(11C-N)*
BAXTER *(13R-P)*
   (13S-C)

BEADLE *(12J-P)*
BENAUD *(12R-SP)*
BERMAN *(13S-C)*
BRADEN *(13B-P)*
BROUGH *(11P-V)*
BURNET *(14A-N)* *S
BUTLER *(11B-SP)*
CAESAR *(9S-C)*
CANNON *(11T-C)*
CARSON *(11F-C)*
CARTER *(10J-P)*
CASTLE *(9R-E/P)*
CLARKE *(8O-P)*
CLEESE *(10J-C)*
CLOUGH *(12G-N)*
COOPER *(11T-C/M)*
   (12J-P)
COSIER *(10T-SP)*
CRAVEN *(10J-N/P)*
CULLEN *(11S-N)*
DAVIES *(9D-SP)*
   (11B-SP)
   (12D-P/SP)
DAWSON *(9L-C/P)*
DENNIS *(9L-C/l)*
DOC COX *(P)*
DOUGAL *(12R-N)*
EMBERG *(11B-C)*
FOSTER *(13B-SP)*
FRENCH *(10D-C)*
GARDEN *(12G-C)*
GREENE *(11S-P)*
   (12H-P)
GUYLER *(12D-C)*
HARBEN *(12P-P)*
HARRIS *(10R-A/E)*
   (11K-V)
HARVEY *(12A-N)*
HAYNES *(12A-C)*
HAYTON *(12P-N)*
HEARNE *(13R-C)*
HEINEY *(10P-P)*
HELVIN *(11M-P)*
HEMERY *(11D-SP)*
HOBDAY *(11P-N)*
HOBLEY *(14M-P)*

HOWARD *(14M-P)*
HOWERD *(13F-C)*
HUGHES *(10G-SP)*
JENSEN *(11D-DJ)*
JUNKIN *(10J-C/PA)*
KRAMER *(10J-SP)*
LAURIE *(10H-C)*
LAWLEY *(9S-N/P)*
LIDELL *(11A-N)*
LITTLE *(9S-C)*
MARTIN *(10D-C)*
MAYALL *(9R-C)*
MILLER *(9M-C)*
MINTER *(10A-SP)*
MODLEY *(12A-C)*
MODLIN *(11M-P)*
MORGAN *(11C-P/SP)*
MORRIS *(10M-P)*
 (12J-P)
MOTSON *(10J-SP)*
MURRAY *(10C-C)*
 (10P-DJ/P)
 (11J-P)
MURROW *(8E-N)*
NOAKES *(10J-P)*
NORDEN *(11D-P/PA)*
NORMAN *(11B-P)*
OAKSEY *(10J-SP)*
OLIVER *(9V-C)*
PARKIN *(13L-N)*
PAXMAN *(12J-P)*
PETERS *(12S-P)*
PILGER *(10J-N)*
POWELL *(11P-DJ)*
 (11S-C)
PULMAN *(10J-SP)*
PURVES *(11P-P)*
RAYNER *(12C-P/PA)*
RIPPON *(12A-N/P)*
RIVERS *(10J-C)*
ROGERS *(9T-C/P)*
RUDNER *(10R-C)*
SABIDO *(9K-N)*
SADLER *(11B-N)*
SAVILE *(11J-DJ/P)* *S
SCULLY *(10H-P)*

SNAGGE *(10J-N/SP)*
ST JOHN *(9I-P/SP)*
STUART *(11M-N)*
SUCHET *(10J-N)*
TED RAY *(C)*
TRAVIS *(13D-DJ)*
WALDEN *(11B-P)*
WALKER *(9R-C/P)*
 (12M-SP)
WALTON *(10K-SP)*
WARING *(11E-SP)*
WATERS *(11D-C)*
 (11E-C)
WELSBY *(11E-P/SP)*
WILCOX *(13D-P)*
WILLIS *(9B-SP)*
 (12W-W)
WILMOT *(10G-C/I)*
WILSON *(9B-P/SP)*
 (12J-SP)
 (13F-W)
WILTON *(10R-C)*
WISDOM *(12N-C)*
WRIGHT *(11S-DJ)*

7

ADAMSON *(11T-SP)*
ALEX HAY *(SP)*
ANDREWS *(13E-P/SP)*
BARNETT *(13I-PA)*
BELLAMY *(12D-P)*
BENNETT *(13L-C/P)*
BENTINE *(14M-C)*
BERGLAS *(12D-M)*
BIGGINS *(P)*
BLOFELD *(12H-SP)*
BOB TODD *(C)*
BOTTING *(13L-P)*
BRANDON *(11T-DJ)*
BREMNER *(11R-C/I)*
BRINTON *(10T-N)*
BROMLEY *(12P-SP)*
BRUNSON *(14M-N)*
BURNETT *(11P-DJ)*

CAMSELL *(13G-P)*
CARROTT *(13J-C)*
CARTHEW *(14A-N)*
CHAPMAN *(13G-C)*
CHEGWIN *(12K-DJ/P)*
CHESTER *(14C-C/DJ)*
CLIFTON *(13B-C)*
COLEMAN *(12D-P/SP)*
COLLIER *(13N-C)*
CORBETT *(12H-PU)*
 (13R-C)
 (14M-PU)
CRICKET *(12J-C)*
CURTOIS *(12B-N)*
DANIELS *(11P-M)*
DELANEY *(12F-P)*
DIAMOND *(11A-P)*
DIGANCE *(14R-C)*
DIMMOCK *(12P-P/SP)*
DOUGLAS *(11J-C)*
DRABBLE *(11P-P)*
EDMONDS *(11N-DJ/P)*
EDWARDS *(12J-C)*
ENGLISH *(13A-C)*
EVERETT *(12K-DJ/P)*
EVERTON *(12C-SP)*
FELDMAN *(12M-C)*
FORDYCE *(12K-DJ/P)*
FORSYTH *(12B-E/P)*
FREEMAN *(11A-DJ)*
 (11J-P)
FRINTON *(14F-C)*
GOODIES *(C)*
GOODWIN *(10K-C)*
GOSLING *(10R-P)*
GRAYSON *(12L-C/P)*
GREAVES *(12J-P/SP)*
HANCOCK *(11T-C)*
HANDLEY *(12T-C)*
HARDING *(11M-C)*
 (14G-PA)
HOLNESS *(10B-P)*
HOLLAND *(12J-P)*
HOUSEGO *(11F-P)*
JACKLIN *(11T-SP)*
JACKSON *(11J-DJ)*

JIM WATT *(SP)*
KARNEHM *(11J-SP)*
KENDALL *(14K-N/P)*
KEN DODD *(C)*
KENNEDY *(12S-P)*
    (14L-P)
KEN REES *(N)*
KERSHAW *(11A-DJ)*
KETTLEY *(11J-W)*
LAIDLAW *(13R-SP)*
LANNING *(11D-SP)*
LINDLEY *(12J-SP)*
MACLEAN *(10D-C)*
MARK COX *(SP)*
MASKELL *(10D-SP)*
MATTHEW *(12B-DJ)*
MAX WALL *(C)*
McGOWAN *(12C-P)*
MURDOCH *(14R-C)*
NEWHART *(10B-C)*
O'CONNOR *(10D-E/P)*
    (10T-C/P)
PARSONS *(15N-P)*
PEEBLES *(11A-DJ)*
PHILBIN *(13M-P)*
PICKLES *(14W-P)*
PLOMLEY *(10R-P)*
RANTZEN *(13E-P)*
RAY ALAN *(V)*
REDFERN *(13A-P)*
REDHEAD *(12B-N)*
ROD HULL *(PU)*
ROY HUDD *(C)*
RUBY WAX *(C)*
RUSHTON *(13W-PA)*
SECOMBE *(12H-C/P) *S*
SELLERS *(12P-C)*
SIMPSON *(11J-N)*
SISSONS *(12P-N/P)*
SPENCER *(11J-SP)*
ST CLAIR *(11I-P)*
STEWART *(9E-DJ)*
    (15A-N)
STILGOE *(14R-C/P)*
SUE COOK *(P)*
SWANTON *(9E-SP)*

TARBUCK *(12J-C)*
TARRANT *(12C-P)*
TED LOWE *(SP)*
THROWER *(13D-N)*
TIMPSON *(11J-N)*
TRINDER *(12T-C)*
TRUEMAN *(11F-SP)*
VAUGHAN *(13N-P)*
VINCENT *(13R-DJ)*
WARRISS *(10B-C)*
WEBSTER *(11M-N)*
WHEELER *(12J-C)*
    (14C-N)
    *(15M-PA) *S*
WHICKER *(11A-P)*
WIDLAKE *(12B-P)*
WINFREY *(12O-P)*
WINTERS *(11M-C)*
    (13B-C)
WORSNIP *(11G-P)*
YARWOOD *(11M-C/I)*

8

ALAN DELL *(DJ)*
ANNA FORD *(N)*
ANN JONES *(SP)*
ATKINSON *(13R-C)*
BAKEWELL *(12J-P)*
BEN ELTON *(C)*
BENJAMIN *(15F-P)*
BILL TIDY *(A)*
BOARDMAN *(12S-C)*
BYGRAVES *(11M-E/P)*
CAMPBELL *(13G-N)*
    (15P-PA)
CAVANAGH *(13P-C/I)*
CHALMERS *(14J-P)*
COLTRANE *(14R-C)*
CONNOLLY *(13B-C)*
CRADDOCK *(13F-P)*
    (14J-P)
CROWTHER *(14L-P)*
DAN ROWAN *(C)*
DAVE KING *(C)*

DAVIDSON *(11J-C)*
DEREK ROY *(C)*
DIMBLEBY *(13D-P)*
    (15R-P)
DINENAGE *(12F-P)*
ED MURROW *(N)*
ERIC IDLE *(C)*
FLANAGAN *(11B-C)*
FLETCHER *(13C-C)*
FRINDALL *(12B-SP)*
GRAVENEY *(11T-SP)*
HAMILTON *(13D-DJ)*
HANRAHAN *(13B-N)*
HANS HASS *(P)*
IAN DARKE *(SP)*
JIM BOWEN *(C/P)*
JIM LAKER *(SP)*
JOHN COLE *(N)*
JOHN DUNN *(DJ)*
JOHN PEEL *(DJ)*
JOHNSTON *(13B-P/SP)*
JOHN TUSA *(N)*
KAREN KAY *(E)*
KATE ADIE *(N)*
KEN BRUCE *(SP)*
KEN PLATT *(C)*
KRANKIES *(C)*
KRONKITE *(14W-N)*
LEUCHARS *(12A-N)*
MARSHALL *(14A-PA)*
    (14H-SP)
McDONALD *(14T-N)*
MEL SMITH *(C)*
METCALFE *(12J-P)*
MIKE READ *(DJ)*
MIKE REID *(C)*
MILLIGAN *(13S-C)*
MITCHELL *(14L-P)*
MONTEITH *(13K-C)*
NAUGHTON *(15C-C)*
NICK OWEN *(P)*
NICK ROSS *(P)*
OZ CLARKE *(P)*
PETER JAY *(N/P)*
PETTIFER *(14J-N/P)*
RAY MOORE *(DJ)*

ROBIN DAY *(N/P)* **S*
ROBIN RAY *(P)*
ROBINSON *(12A-P)*
      (14R-P)
SAUNDERS *(C)*
SERGEANT *(12J-N)*
SIMON DEE *(DJ/P)*
SINSTADT *(14G-SP)*
STENNETT *(12S-C)*
THOMPSON *(12E-C)*
      (14J-N)
TIM EWART *(N)*
WEISKOPF *(11T-SP)*
WHITELEY *(15R-P)*
WILLIAMS *(12A-P)*
      (14D-SP)
      (14G-SP)
WITCHELL *(N)*

9

ALAN PARRY *(SP)*
ALAN WEEKS *(SP)*
ANDY CRANE *(P)*
ANNE GREGG *(P)*
ARMSTRONG *(14F-N)*
      (15P-N)
BARRYMORE *(P)*
BARRY TOOK *(P)*
BENNY HILL *(C)*
BILL GILES *(W)*
BILL ODDIE *(C)*
BLACKBURN *(13T-DJ)*
BOBBY BALL *(C)*
BOB WILLIS *(SP)*
BOB WILSON *(SP)*
BOSANQUET *(N)*
BRANDRETH *(14G-P)*
BRIAN CANT *(P)*
CAROLGEES *(12B-P)*
CARPENTER *(14H-P/SP)*
CHRIS LOWE *(N)*
CLAY JONES *(P)*
CLITHEROE *(14J-C)*
CRAZY GANG *(C)*
DAI DAVIES *(SP)*

DAVID CASS *(N)*
DAVID ICKE *(P/SP)*
DAVID VINE *(P/SP)*
DeCOURCEY *(14R-V)*
DICK EMERY *(C)*
DUSTIN GEE *(C/I)*
EDDIE GRAY *(C)*
ED STEWART *(DJ)*
EMMA FREUD *(P)*
ERIC SYKES *(C)*
ERNIE WISE *(C)*
EW SWANTON *(SP)*
FRANK MUIR *(PA)*
FRED EMNEY *(C)*
FRED PERRY *(SP)*
GASCOIGNE *(15B-P)*
HENDERSON *(15D-C)*
HUMPHRIES *(13J-N)*
      (14B-C/I)
HUNNIFORD *(15G-P)*
IAN ST JOHN *(P/SP)*
JACK BENNY *(C)*
JACK SCOTT *(W)*
JAMES HUNT *(SP)*
JEFF BANKS *(P)*
JIMMY GOLD *(C)*
JIMMY HILL *(P/SP)*
KIM SABIDO *(N)*
KNOX-MAWER *(13J-P)*
LES DAWSON *(C/P)*
LES DENNIS *(C/I)*
LONGHURST *(14H-SP)*
LOTTE HASS *(P)*
MacGREGOR *(12S-N)*
MAGNUSSON *(15M-P)*
MARK TULLY *(N)*
MAX MILLER *(C)*
McCASKILL *(12I-W)*
McCORMACK *(13M-SP)*
McCRIRICK *(13J-SP)*
McPHERSON *(15A-SP)*
MIKE SMITH *(DJ/P)*
MONKHOUSE *(12B-C/P)*
MOORCROFT *(15A-SP)*
MORECAMBE *(13E-C)*
NICHOLSON *(N)*

O'SULLEVAN *(14P-SP)*
PARKINSON *(P)*
PETER COOK *(C)*
PETER SNOW *(N)*
PETER WEST *(SP)*
PICKERING *(12R-SP)*
RHYS-JONES *(14G-C)*
RIK MAYALL *(C)*
ROBERTSON *(12M-SP)*
      (13M-P)
ROGER COOK *(P)*
ROSENTHAL *(12J-SP)*
ROY CASTLE *(E/P)*
ROY WALKER *(C/P)*
RUSS ABBOT *(C)*
SANDY GALL *(N)*
SCHOFIELD *(P)*
SHANDLING *(14G-SP)*
SID CAESAR *(C)*
SIMON COLE *(N)*
SIMON MAYO *(DJ/P)*
SINGLETON *(12V-P)*
STEVE RACE *(P)*
SUE LAWLEY *(N/P)*
SYD LITTLE *(C)*
TEDDY KNOX *(C)*
TED ROGERS *(C/P)*
TERRY HALL *(V)*
TOMMY BOYD *(P)*
TONY GREEN *(SP)*
TONY GUBBA *(SP)*
TONY LEWIS *(SP)*
TRETHOWAN *(12I-N)*
VIC OLIVER *(C)*
WILL FYFFE *(C)*

10

ALAN MINTER *(SP)*
ANNEKA RICE *(P)*
BARRY CRYER *(C/PA)*
BENNY GREEN *(P)*
BEN WARRISS *(C)*
BOBBY DAVRO *(C/I)*
BOB HOLNESS *(P)*

BOB NEWHART *(C)*
BRIAN MOORE *(P/SP)*
BRIGHTWELL *(SP)*
CHIC MURRAY *(C)*
CHRIS KELLY *(P)*
CHRIS SERLE *(P)*
CILLA BLACK *(P)*
CLIVE CLARK *(SP)*
CLIVE JAMES *(P)*
CLIVE LLOYD *(SP)*
DAN MASKELL *(SP)*
DANNY LA RUE *(E/I)*
DAVID FROST *(P)*
DAVID NIXON *(M)*
DAWN FRENCH *(C)*
DEREK BATEY *(P)*
DES O'CONNOR *(E/P)*
DICK MARTIN *(C)*
DON MACLEAN *(C)*
FAITH BROWN *(I)*
FRANK BOUGH *(P)*
GAMBACCINI *(14P-DJ)*
GARETH HALE *(C)*
GARY WILMOT *(C/I)*
GILES SMITH *(N)*
GRAHAM KERR *(P)*
GWYN HUGHES *(SP)*
HARGREAVES *(14J-P)*
HARRY WORTH *(C)*
HEINZ WOLFF *(P)*
HENRY KELLY *(P)*
HONEYCOMBE *(N/P)*
HUGH LAURIE *(C)*
HUGH SCULLY *(P)*
HYLDA BAKER *(C)*
JACK KRAMER *(SP)*
JAMES BURKE *(P)*
JANET BROWN *(I)*
JANICE LONG *(DJ)*
JIMMY JAMES *(C)*
JIMMY JEWEL *(C)*
JIMMY NERVO *(C)*
JIMMY YOUNG *(DJ/P)*
JOAN RIVERS *(C)*
JOHN ARLOTT *(SP)*
JOHN CARTER *(P)*

JOHN CLEESE *(C)*
JOHN CRAVEN *(N/P)*
JOHN JUNKIN *(C/PA)*
JOHN MOTSON *(SP)*
JOHN NOAKES *(P)*
JOHNNY BALL *(P)*
JOHN OAKSEY *(SP)*
JOHN PILGER *(N)*
JOHN PULMAN *(SP)*
JOHN SNAGGE *(N/SP)*
JOHN SUCHET *(N)*
JUDITH HANN *(P)*
KEN GOODWIN *(C)*
KENT WALTON *(SP)*
KILROY-SILK *(P)*
LENNY BRUCE *(C)*
LENNY HENRY *(C)*
LESLEY JUDD *(P)*
MacPHERSON *(15S-P)*
MAGNUS PYKE *(P)*
MARTI CAINE *(P)*
MICHELMORE *(15C-P)*
MIKE MORRIS *(P)*
MURIEL GRAY *(P)*
NORMAN PACE *(C)*
PAUL HEINEY *(P)*
PENNY JUNOR *(P)*
PETE MURRAY *(DJ/P)*
PETER JONES *(P/PA, SP)*
PETER WOODS *(N)*
RAY GOSLING *(P)*
RITA RUDNER *(C)*
ROBB WILTON *(C)*
ROLF HARRIS *(A/E)*
ROY PLOMLEY *(P)*
SIMON BATES *(DJ)*
SIMON GROOM *(P)*
SOMERVILLE *(15J-N)*
STEPHEN FRY *(C)*
STEPHENSON *(C)*
STEVE JONES *(P)*
STUART HALL *(P/SP)*
TERRY JONES *(C)*
TERRY WOGAN *(P)*
TIM BRINTON *(N)*

TITCHMARSH *(14A-P)*
TOM O'CONNOR *(C/P)*
TONY COSIER *(SP)*

11

ALAN FREEMAN *(DJ)*
ALAN WHICKER *(P)*
ALEXEI SAYLE *(C)*
ALVAR LIDELL *(N)*
ANDY KERSHAW *(DJ)*
ANDY PEEBLES *(DJ)*
ANNE DIAMOND *(P)*
ARMAND DENIS *(P)*
ARTHUR ASKEY *(C)*
ARTHUR NEGUS *(P)*
BARRY DAVIES *(SP)*
BARRY NORMAN *(P)*
BELLA EMBERG *(C)*
BERNARD FALK *(P)*
BRENT SADLER *(N)*
BRIAN BUTLER *(SP)*
BRIAN WALDEN *(P)*
BROUGH SCOTT *(SP)*
BUD FLANAGAN *(C)*
CAROL BARNES *(N)*
CLIFF MORGAN *(P/SP)*
DAVE LANNING *(SP)*
DAVID HEMERY *(SP)*
DAVID JENSEN *(DJ)*
DEBBIE McGEE *(P)*
DENIS NORDEN *(P/PA)*
DORIS WATERS *(C)*
DUDLEY MOORE *(C)*
DUGGIE BROWN *(C)*
EDDIE WARING *(SP)*
ELSIE WATERS *(C)*
ELTON WELSBY *(P/SP)*
FRANK CARSON *(C)*
FRED HOUSEGO *(P)*
FRED TRUEMAN *(SP)*
GEORGE ROBEY *(C)*
GLENDENNING *(SP)*
GLYN WORSNIP *(P)*
GORDON BURNS *(P)*

ISLA ST CLAIR *(P)*
JACK DOUGLAS *(C)*
JACK JACKSON *(DJ)*
JACK KARNEHM *(SP)*
JENNI MURRAY *(P)*
JIM DAVIDSON *(C)*
JIMMY SAVILE *(DJ/P) *S*
JOHN FREEMAN *(P)*
JOHN KETTLEY *(W)*
JOHN SIMPSON *(N)*
JOHN SPENCER *(SP)*
JOHN TIMPSON *(N)*
KEITH HARRIS *(V)*
LIONEL BLAIR *(E/P)*
MARIE HELVIN *(P)*
MARK WEBSTER *(N)*
MARTYN LEWIS *(N)*
MAX BYGRAVES *(E/P)*
MEADOWCROFT *(SP)*
MELVYN BRAGG *(P)*
MICHAEL FISH *(W)*
MIKE HARDING *(C)*
MIKE WINTERS *(C)*
MIKE YARWOOD *(C/I)*
MOIRA STUART *(N)*
MONTY MODLIN *(P)*
MURIEL YOUNG *(P)*
NIGHTINGALE *(15A-DJ)*
NOËL EDMONDS *(DJ/P)*
NORMAN EVANS *(C)*
PAUL BURNETT *(DJ)*
PAUL DANIELS *(M)*
PETER ALLISS *(SP)*
PETER BROUGH *(V)*
PETER HOBDAY *(N)*
PETER POWELL *(DJ)*
PETER PURVES *(P)*
PHIL DRABBLE *(P)*
PRENDEVILLE *(P)*
ROBERT KLEIN *(C)*
RORY BREMNER *(C/I)*
SANDY POWELL *(C)*
SARAH CULLEN *(N)*
SARAH GREENE *(P)*
SELINA SCOTT *(P)*
STEVE WRIGHT *(DJ)*

TOM GRAVENEY *(SP)*
TOM WEISKOPF *(SP)*
TOMMY CANNON *(C)*
TOMMY COOPER *(C/M)*
TONY ADAMSON *(SP)*
TONY BRANDON *(DJ)*
TONY HANCOCK *(C)*
TONY JACKLIN *(SP)*
VICTOR BORGE *(C)*

12

ALUN WILLIAMS *(P)*
ANDREW HARVEY *(N)*
ANGELA RIPPON *(N/P)*
ANNE LEUCHARS *(N)*
ANNE ROBINSON *(P)*
ARTHUR HAYNES *(C)*
ARTHUR MODLEY *(C)*
ATTENBOROUGH *(P) *S*
BARBARA KELLY *(PA)*
BERNARD DAVEY *(W)*
BILL FRINDALL *(SP)*
BOB CAROLGEES *(P)*
BOB MONKHOUSE *(C/P)*
BRIAN CURTOIS *(N)*
BRIAN MATTHEW *(DJ)*
BRIAN REDHEAD *(N)*
BRIAN WIDLAKE *(P)*
BROOKE-TAYLOR *(15T-C)*
BRUCE FORSYTH *(E/P)*
CATHY McGOWAN *(P)*
CHARLIE CHASE *(C)*
CHARLIE DRAKE *(C)*
CHESNEY ALLEN *(C)*
CHRIS TARRANT *(P)*
CLAIRE RAYNER *(P/PA)*
CLIVE EVERTON *(SP)*
DAVID BELLAMY *(P)*
DAVID BERGLAS *(M)*
DAVID COLEMAN *(P/SP)*
DERYCK GUYLER *(C)*
DESMOND LYNAM *(P/SP)*
DICKIE DAVIES *(P/SP)*
EMMA THOMPSON *(C)*
FRANK DELANEY *(P)*

FRED DINENAGE *(P)*
GORDON CLOUGH *(N)*
GRAEME GARDEN *(C)*
HARRY CORBETT *(PU)*
HARRY SECOMBE *(C/P) *S*
HENRY BLOFELD *(SP)*
HUGHIE GREENE *(P)*
IAN McCASKILL *(W)*
IAN TRETHOWAN *(N)*
JASMINE BLIGH *(P)*
JEAN METCALFE *(P)*
JEREMY BEADLE *(P)*
JEREMY PAXMAN *(P)*
JIMMY CRICKET *(C)*
JIMMY EDWARDS *(C)*
JIMMY GREAVES *(P/SP)*
JIMMY LINDLEY *(SP)*
JIMMY TARBUCK *(C)*
JIMMY WHEELER *(C)*
JIM ROSENTHAL *(SP)*
JOAN BAKEWELL *(P)*
JOHNNY MORRIS *(P)*
JOHN SERGEANT *(N)*
JONATHAN KING *(P)*
JONATHAN ROSS *(P)*
JOOLS HOLLAND *(P)*
JOSEPH COOPER *(P)*
JULIAN WILSON *(SP)*
KEITH CHEGWIN *(DJ/P)*
KEITH FORDYCE *(DJ/P)*
KENNETH HORNE *(C/P)*
KENNY EVERETT *(DJ/P)*
LARRY GRAYSON *(C/P)*
LEONARD SACHS *(P)*
MARTY FELDMAN *(C)*
MATTHEW KELLY *(P)*
MAX ROBERTSON *(SP)*
MICHAEL ASPEL *(P)*
MICHAEL BUERK *(N)*
MICHAEL MILES *(P)*
MICHAEL PALIN *(C)*
MURRAY WALKER *(SP)*
NORMAN WISDOM *(C)*
OPRAH WINFREY *(P)*
PATRICK MOORE *(P)*
PETER BROMLEY *(SP)*

PETER DIMMOCK *(P/SP)*
PETER SELLERS *(C)*
PETER SISSONS *(N/P)*
PHILIP HARBEN *(P)*
PHILIP HAYTON *(N)*
RICHARD BAKER *(N/P)*
RICHIE BENAUD *(SP)*
ROBERT DOUGAL *(N)*
RONNIE BARKER *(C)*
RON PICKERING *(SP)*
RUSSELL GRANT *(P)*
SARAH KENNEDY *(P)*
STAN BOARDMAN *(C)*
STAN STENNETT *(C)*
STARMER-SMITH *(SP)*
STREET-PORTER *(P)*
SYLVIA PETERS *(P)*
TOMMY HANDLEY *(C)*
TOMMY TRINDER *(C)*
VAL SINGLETON *(P)*
VICTORIA WOOD *(C)*
VIRGINIA WADE *(SP)*
WINCEY WILLIS *(W)*
WOLSTENHOLME *(SP)*

13

ALISTAIR COOKE *(P)*
ANTHEA REDFERN *(P)*
ARTHUR ENGLISH *(C)*
BERNARD BRADEN *(P)*
BERNIE CLIFTON *(C)*
BERNIE WINTERS *(C)*
BILLY CONNOLLY *(C)*
BRENDAN FOSTER *(SP)*
BRIAN JOHNSTON *(P/SP)*
CYRIL FLETCHER *(C)*
DANVERS-WALKER *(N)*
DAVE LEE TRAVIS *(DJ)*
DAVID DIMBLEBY *(P)*
DAVID HAMILTON *(DJ)*
DEBBIE THROWER *(N)*
DESMOND WILCOX *(P)*
EAMONN ANDREWS *(P/SP)*
ERIC MORECAMBE *(C)*

ESTHER RANTZEN *(P)*
FANNY CRADDOCK *(P)*
FRANCIS WILSON *(W)*
FRANKIE HOWERD *(C)*
GAVIN CAMPBELL *(N)*
GEORGE CAMSELL *(P)*
GRAHAM CHAPMAN *(C)*
ISOBEL BARNETT *(PA)*
JASPER CARROTT *(C)*
JOHN HUMPHRIES *(N)*
JOHN McCRIRICK *(SP)*
JUNE KNOX-MAWER *(P)*
KELLY MONTEITH *(C)*
LENNIE BENNETT *(C/P)*
LEONARD PARKIN *(N)*
LOUISE BOTTING *(P)*
MAGGIE PHILBIN *(P)*
MARK McCORMACK *(SP)*
MARTIN-JENKINS *(SP)*
MICHAELA DENIS *(P)*
MICK ROBERTSON *(P)*
NORMAN COLLIER *(C)*
NORMAN VAUGHAN *(P)*
PETER CAVANAGH *(C/I)*
RAYMOND BAXTER *(P)*
RENTON LAIDLAW *(SP)*
RICHARD HEARNE *(C)*
ROBBIE VINCENT *(DJ)*
RONNIE CORBETT *(C)*
ROWAN ATKINSON *(C)*
SHELLEY BERMAN *(C)*
SPIKE MILLIGAN *(C)*
STANLEY BAXTER *(C)*
TONY BLACKBURN *(DJ)*
VAUGHAN-THOMAS *(P)*
WILLIE RUSHTON *(PA)*

14

ALAN TITCHMARSH *(P)*
ALASTAIR BURNET *(N)* *S
ANTHONY CARTHEW *(N)*
ARTHUR MARSHALL *(PA)*
BARRY HUMPHRIES *(C/I)*
CHARLES WHEELER *(N)*

CHARLIE CHESTER *(C/DJ)*
CHRISTINE JANES *(SP)*
DORIAN WILLIAMS *(SP)*
FIONA ARMSTRONG *(N)*
FREDDIE FRINTON *(C)*
GARRY SHANDLING *(C)*
GEOFFREY ARCHER *(N)*
GERALD SINSTADT *(SP)*
GERALD WILLIAMS *(SP)*
GILBERT HARDING *(PA)*
GRIFF RHYS-JONES *(C)*
GYLES BRANDRETH *(P)*
HARRY CARPENTER *(P/SP)*
HENRY LONGHURST *(SP)*
HOWARD MARSHALL *(SP)*
JACK HARGREAVES *(P)*
JEREMY THOMPSON *(N)*
JIM MEADOWCROFT *(SP)*
JIMMY CLITHEROE *(C)*
JOHNNY CRADDOCK *(P)*
JUDITH CHALMERS *(P)*
JULIAN PETTIFER *(N/P)*
KENNETH KENDALL *(N/P)*
LESLIE CROWTHER *(P)*
LESLIE MITCHELL *(P)*
LUDOVIC KENNEDY *(P)*
MARGARET HOWARD *(P)*
MATTHEW CORBETT *(PU)*
McDONALD HOBLEY *(P)*
MICHAEL BENTINE *(C)*
MICHAEL BRUNSON *(N)*
MIRIAM STOPPARD *(P)*
PAUL GAMBACCINI *(DJ)*
PETER O'SULLEVAN *(SP)*

RICHARD DIGANCE *(C)*
RICHARD MURDOCH *(C)*
RICHARD STILGOE *(C/P)*
ROBBIE COLTRANE *(C)*
ROBERT ROBINSON *(P)*
ROGER DeCOURCEY *(V)*
TREVOR McDONALD *(N)*
WALTER KRONKITE *(N)*
WILFRED PICKLES *(P)*

15

ADRIAN MOORCROFT *(SP)*
ALASTAIR STEWART *(N)*
ANNE NIGHTINGALE *(DJ)*
ARCHIE McPHERSON *(SP)*
BAMBER GASCOIGNE *(P)*
BARRINGTON DALBY *(SP)*
CHARLIE NAUGHTON *(C)*
DICKIE HENDERSON *(C)*
FLOELLA BENJAMIN *(P)*
GLORIA HUNNIFORD *(P)*
JULIA SOMERVILLE *(N)*
MAGNUS MAGNUSSON *(P)*
MORTIMER WHEELER *(PA)* *S
NICHOLAS PARSONS *(P)*
PAMELA ARMSTRONG *(N)*
PATRICK CAMPBELL *(PA)*
RICHARD DIMBLEBY *(P)*
RICHARD WHITELEY *(P)*
SANDY MacPHERSON *(P)*
TIM BROOKE-TAYLOR *(C)*

PEOPLE

EXPLORERS

All explorers except: (AS) = Astronaut   (AV) = Aviation pioneer
(M) = Mountaineer
* = Alternative spelling

3

CÃO *(R Congo)*

4

BEAN *(AS)*
BYRD *(AV-N & S Poles)*
CANO *(Pacific)*
CARR *(AS)*
COOK *(Australia/NZ)*
DIAS *(Cape of Good Hope) *1*
DIAZ *(Cape of Good Hope) *1*
EYRE *(L Eyre)*
HUNT *(M-Everest)*
MOCK *(AV-round-the-world flight)*
MUNK *(NE Canada)*
PAEZ *(Blue Nile)*
PARK *(R Niger)*
POLO *(Asia)*
POST *(AV-round-the-world flight)*
RIDE *(AS)*
ROSS *(Antarctica)*
SOTO *(Mexico)*

5

BAKER *(L Albert)*
BARTH *(Sudan)*
BOONE *(R Mississippi)*
BROWN *(AV-Atlantic, with ALCOCK)*
BURKE *(Australia, with WILLS)*
CABOT *(Newfoundland)*
        (S America)
DAVIS *(Davis Str)*
DESIO *(M-K2)*

DRAKE *(S America/Pacific)*
FUCHS *(Antarctica)*
GLENN *(AS)*
IRWIN *(AS)*
KIZIM *(AS)*
MEYER *(M-Kilimanjaro)*
OATES *(S Pole)*
OJEDA *(Brazil/Venezuela)*
PARRY *(N Greenland)*
PEARY *(N Pole)*
POGUE *(AS)*
POPOV *(AS)*
RAZIN *(R Volga)*
REMEK *(AS)*
RURIK *(R Dnieper)*
SCOTT *(S Pole)*
        (AS)
        (AV-longest solo flight)
SMITH *(AV-Britain-Australia)*
SOLIS *(R Plate)*
SPEKE *(Nile source/L Tanganyika,*
        with BURTON)
STURT *(R Darling)*
TITOV *(AS)*
WHITE *(AS)*
WILLS *(Australia, with BURKE)*
YOUNG *(AS)*

6

ALCOCK *(AV-Atlantic, with BROWN)*
ALDRIN *(AS)*
ANDERS *(AS)*
BAFFIN *(Baffin Is/Bay)*
BALBOA *(Panama)*
BALMAT *(M-Mont Blanc)*
BERING *(Alaska/Bering Str)*

BORMAN *(AS)*
BURTON *(Mecca/L Victoria/*
L Tanganyika, with SPEKE)
CERNAN *(AS)*
COLSON *(Simpson Des)*
CONRAD *(AS)*
COOPER *(AS)*
CORTES *(Mexico)*
DA GAMA *(Natal/Malabar Coast)*
DARWIN *(Galapagos Is)*
DE WITT *(N Australia)*
GIBSON *(AS)*
GORDON *(AS)*
HASTON *(M-Everest)*
HUDSON *(Hudson R/Bay)*
JOLIET *(L Huron/L Erie)*
LEONOV *(AS)*
LOVELL *(AS)*
NANSEN *(Arctic)*
PINZÓN *(Brazil)*
RYUMIN *(AS)*
SERRÃO *(E Indies)*
TASMAN *(Tasmania/NZ)*
VOLKOV *(AS)*
WILKES *(Antarctica)*
WRIGHT *(AV-first flight)*
XAVIER *(W Pacific)*
YEAGER *(AV-supersonic flight)*

GRECHKO *(AS)*
GRISSOM *(AS)*
HILLARY *(M-Everest)*
HOUTMAN *(SW Australia)*
JOHNSON *(AV-England-Australia)*
KOMAROV *(AS)*
KUBASOV *(AS)*
LA SALLE *(Ohio R)*
MANAROV *(AS)*
MANNING *(Lhasa)*
PACCARD *(M-Mont Blanc)*
PAULHAN *(AV-London-Manchester)*
PICCARD *(Marianas Trench)*
PIZARRO *(Pacific/Peru)*
RALEIGH *(Virginia)*
SCHIRRA *(AS)*
SHEPARD *(AS)*
STANLEY *(Congo)*
SWIGERT *(AS)*
TENZING *(M-Everest)*
TRISTÃO *(R Senegal)*
WEDDELL *(Weddell Sea)*
WHYMPER *(M-Matterhorn)*
WRANGEL *(Coast of Siberia)*

8

ABALAKOV *(M-Communism)*
ALVARADO *(Guatemala)*
AMUNDSEN *(NW Passage/S Pole)*
CAMPBELL *(Limpopo source)*
CARTERET *(Pacific)*
COLUMBUS *(W Indies)*
ERICSSON *(Newfoundland)*
FLINDERS *(SE Australia)*
FRANKLIN *(N Canada)*
HUMBOLDT *(S America/Russia)*
JEFFRIES *(AV-balloon flight, with*
BLANCHARD)
JOURDAIN *(E Indies)*
MAGELLAN *(Moluccas/Magellan Str)*
MARCHAND *(Ivory Coast)*
McDIVITT *(AS)*
MOLLISON *(AV-Australia-England)*
PALGRAVE *(Arabia)*

7

ALVAREZ *(Ethiopia)*
BARENTS *(Barents Sea/Spitzbergen)*
BLÉRIOT *(AV-English Channel)*
CAILLIÉ *(Timbuktu)*
CARTIER *(St Lawrence R)*
CHAFFEE *(AS)*
COLLINS *(AS)*
CRIPPEN *(AS)*
CROZIER *(N Canada)*
DAMPIER *(New Guinea)*
FAWCETT *(Amazon tributaries)*
FIENNES *(Poles)*
GAGARIN *(AS)*
GILBERT *(Newfoundland)*

PEOPLE – EXPLORERS

POPOVICH *(AS)*
RICKMERS *(M-Lenin)*
SCHOUTEN *(Cape Horn)*
SOLOVYOV *(AS)*
STAFFORD *(AS)*
SVERDRUP *(Arctic)*
VESPUCCI *(Florida)*
ZEPPELIN *(AV-airship flight)*

COMPAGNONI *(M-K2)*
ERIK THE RED *(Greenland)*
McCANDLESS *(AS)*
PRZEWALSKI *(Gobi Des)*
SAVITSKAYA *(AS)*
SHACKLETON *(Coast of Antarctica)*
TERESHKOVA *(AS)*
ZURBRIGGEN *(M-Aconcagua)*

9

ARMSTRONG *(AS)*
BLANCHARD *(AV-balloon flight, with JEFFRIES)*
BONINGTON *(M-Eiger/Everest)*
CASTELNAU *(L Titicaca)*
CHAMPLAIN *(E Canada)*
FROBISHER *(N Canada)*
HEYERDAHL *(Pacific)*
JANTSZOON *(NE Australia)*
LACEDELLI *(M-K2)*
LINDBERGH *(AV-Atlantic)*
MACKENZIE *(W Canada)*
MACKINDER *(M-Kenya)*
MIDDLETON *(Sumatra/Java)*
ROMANENKO *(AS)*
VANCOUVER *(Vancouver Is)*
VERRAZANO *(Coast of N America)*
YELISEYEV *(AS)*

11

LIVINGSTONE *(Victoria Falls)*
MONTGOLFIER *(AV-balloon flight)*
SCHWEICKART *(AS)*

12

BOUGAINVILLE *(Pacific)*
YOUNGHUSBAND *(Manchuria)*

13

HERRLIGKOFFER *(M-Nanga Parbat)*
VON RICHTHOFEN *(China/Japan)*

14

BELLINGSHAUSEN *(Coast of Antarctica)*
KINGSFORD SMITH *(AV-Pacific)*
WRIGHT BROTHERS *(AV-first flight)*

10

BARRINGTON *(M-Eiger)*
CHANCELLOR *(Moscow/White Sea)*

PEOPLE

MILITARY LEADERS

(A) = Airman   (S) = Soldier   (SA) = Sailor
(AF) = African   (AM) = American (North & South)   (AS) = Asian
(AU) = Australian   (B) = British   (E) = European   (I) = Irish   (R) = Roman
* = Alternative spelling/name

3

LEE *(AM-S)*
NEY *(E-S)*
OKU *(AS-S)*
OTT *(E-S)*
PAU *(E-S)*

4

ALBA *(E-S) *1*
ALVA *(E-S) *1*
BART *(E-S)*
BEGG *(B-SA)*
BOCK *(E-S)*
BOSE *(AS-S)*
BYNG *(B-S, B-SA)*
DAUN *(E-S)*
DIAZ *(E-S)*
DILL *(B-S)*
FOCH *(E-S)*
FOIX *(E-S)*
GIAP *(AS-S)*
GORT *(B-S)*
HAIG *(B-S)*
HOLK *(E-S)*
HOOD *(AM-S, B-SA)*
HOWE *(B-S, B-SA)*
HULL *(B-S)*
JODL *(E-S)*
JUIN *(E-S)*
KING *(AM-SA)*

LACY *(E-S)*
LAKE *(B-S)*
LEEB *(E-S)*
MACK *(E-S)*
MINA *(E-S)*
MOLA *(E-S)*
MONK *(B-S/SA) *2*
NIEL *(E-S)*
NOGI *(AS-S)*
PENN *(B-SA)*
PILE *(B-S)*
POLK *(AM-S)*
POPE *(AM-S)*
RAIS *(E-S)*
RAPP *(E-S)*
RÖHM *(E-S)*
ROON *(E-S)*
ROSE *(B-S)*
ROSS *(B-S)*
SAXE *(E-S)*
SLIM *(B-S)*
SPEE *(E-SA)*
TITO *(E-S)*
TOGO *(AS-SA)*
TOJO *(AS-S)*
UDET *(E-A)*
WOOD *(B-S, B-SA)*

5

ABBAS *(AS-S)*
AKBAR *(AS-S)*
ALLEN *(AM-S)*
ANDRÉ *(B-S)*

ANSON *(B-SA)*
ARNIM *(E-S)*
ASHBY *(AM-S)*
BABUR *(AS-S)*
BADER *(B-A)*
BAIRD *(B-S)*
BALCK *(E-S)*
BANKS *(AM-S)*
BIRON *(E-S)*
BLAKE *(B-SA)*
BLIGH *(B-SA)*
BOTHA *(AF-S)*
BOYLE *(B-A, I-S)*
BRAGG *(AM-S)*
BROKE *(B-SA)*
BRUCE *(B-S)*
BRUNE *(E-S)*
BUELL *(AM-S)*
BÜLOW *(E-S)*
CLARK *(AM-S)*
CLIVE *(B-S)*
CONDÉ *(E-S)*
COWAN *(B-SA)*
CROOK *(AM-S)*
DAYAN *(AS-S)*
DE WET *(AF-S)*
DEWEY *(AM-SA)*
DORIA *(E-SA)*
DRAKE *(B-SA)*
EARLY *(AM-S)*
ELBÉE *(E-S)*
EL CID *(E-S)*
EUGEN *(E-S)*
EWELL *(AM-S)*
GATES *(AM-S)*

GOUGH *(B-S)*
GRANT *(AM-S, B-S)*
HARDY *(B-SA)*
HAWKE *(B-SA)*
HOCHE *(E-S)*
HUGER *(AM-S)*
ISMAY *(B-S)*
JONES *(AM-SA)*
JUNOT *(E-S)*
KEITH *(B-SA)*
KEYES *(B-SA)*
KLUCK *(E-S)*
KLUGE *(E-S)*
KONEV *(AS-S)*
LALLY *(E-S)*
LEESE *(B-S)*
LEMAN *(E-S)*
LEWIN *(B-SA)*
LUCAN *(B-S)*
MAHAN *(AM-SA)*
MAUDE *(B-S)*
MEADE *(AM-S)*
MERCY *(E-S)*
MODEL *(E-S)*
MONCK *(B-S/SA) *2*
MOORE *(B-S)*
MURAT *(E-S)*
ORLOV *(AS-S)*
OSMAN *(AS-S)*
OYAMA *(AS-S)*
PARMA *(E-S)*
PERRY *(AM-SA)*
POUND *(B-SA)*
PRICE *(B-SA)*
PRIDE *(B-S)*

PEOPLE – MILITARY LEADERS

ROOKE *(B-SA)*
SCOTT *(AM-S)*
SELIM *(AS-S)*
SMITH *(B-SA)*
SMUTS *(AF-S)*
SOULT *(E-S)*
STARK *(AM-S)*
SUCRE *(AM-S)*
SULLA *(R-S)*
TILLY *(E-S)*
TOVEY *(B-SA)*
TROMP *(E-SA)*
TRYON *(B-SA)*
WHITE *(B-S)*
WOLFE *(B-S)*
WREDE *(E-S)*

6

AETIUS *(R-S)*
ANDERS *(E-S)*
ARGYLL *(B-S)*
ARNOLD *(AM-S,*
AM-SA)
AUMALE *(E-S)*
BAYARD *(E-S)*
BEATTY *(B-SA)*
BENBOW *(B-SA)*
BISHOP *(AM-A)*
BOISOT *(E-SA)*
BULLER *(B-S)*
BULNES *(AM-S)*
CAESAR *(R-S)*
CARNOT *(E-S)*
CARVER *(B-S)*
CHANZY *(E-S)*
CONRAD *(E-S)*
CORTES *(E-S)*
CRONJE *(AF-S)*
CUSTER *(AM-S)*
DARIUS *(AS-S)*
DARLAN *(E-SA)*
DAVOUT *(E-S)*
DESAIX *(E-S)*
DÖNITZ *(E-SA) *3*

DOUHET *(E-A)*
DUFOUR *(E-S)*
DUNDEE *(B-S)*
DUNOIS *(E-S)*
EUGENE *(E-S)*
FISHER *(B-SA)*
FRANCO *(E-S)*
FRASER *(B-SA)*
FRENCH *(B-S)*
FRUNZE *(AS-S)*
FULLER *(B-S)*
GIBSON *(B-A)*
GINKEL *(E-S)*
GIRAUD *(E-S)*
GORDON *(B-S)*
GÖRING *(E-A) *4*
GRANBY *(B-S)*
GREENE *(AM-S)*
HALDER *(E-S)*
HALSEY *(AM-SA)*
HARRIS *(B-A)*
HIPPER *(E-SA)*
HITLER *(E-S)*
HOOKER *(AM-S)*
HOPTON *(B-S)*
HOWARD *(B-SA)*
HUGHES *(B-SA)*
HUNTLY *(B-S)*
JOFFRE *(E-S)*
JOMINI *(E-S)*
JUAREZ *(AM-S)*
KEARNY *(AM-S)*
KEITEL *(E-S)*
KEPPEL *(B-SA)*
KLÉBER *(E-S)*
KLEIST *(E-S)*
KOENIG *(E-S)*
KONIEV *(AS-S)*
KRUGER *(AF-S)*
KUROKI *(AS-S)*
LANNES *(E-S)*
LAUDON *(E-S)*
MANGIN *(E-S)*
MARIUS *(R-S)*
MOLTKE *(E-S)*
MONCEY *(E-S)*

MOREAU *(E-S)*
MORGAN *(AM-S)*
MURRAY *(B-S)*
NAGUMO *(AS-SA)*
NAPIER *(B-S,*
B-SA)
NELSON *(B-SA)*
NIMITZ *(AM-SA)*
OUTRAM *(B-S)*
PARKER *(B-S)*
PATTON *(AM-S)*
PAULUS *(E-S)*
PELLEW *(B-SA)*
PÉTAIN *(E-S)*
PICTON *(B-S)*
PLUMER *(B-S)*
POMPEY *(R-S)*
PORTAL *(B-A)*
PORTER *(AM-SA)*
PUTNIK *(E-S)*
RAEDER *(E-SA)*
RAGLAN *(B-S)*
RAMSAY *(B-SA)*
RODNEY *(B-SA)*
ROGERS *(AM-S)*
ROMMEL *(E-S)*
RUPERT *(E-S/SA)*
RUYTER *(E-SA)*
SCHEER *(E-SA)*
SCIPIO *(R-S)*
SEECKT *(E-S)*
SHOVEL *(B-SA)*
SIVAJI *(AS-S)*
SPAATZ *(AM-A)*
STUART *(AM-S)*
SUCHET *(E-S)*
SUMTER *(AM-S)*
TAYLOR *(AM-S)*
TEDDER *(B-A)*
THOMAS *(AM-S)*
TRAJAN *(R-S)*
TROCHU *(E-S)*
TYRONE *(I-S)*
WALLER *(B-S)*
WAVELL *(B-S)*
WILSON *(B-S)*

XERXES *(AS-S)*
ZHUKOV *(AS-S)*

7

AGRIPPA *(R-S)*
ALLENBY *(B-S)*
AMHERST *(B-S)*
APRAXIN *(AS-S)*
ATATÜRK *(AS-S) *5*
BAYAZID *(AS-S)*
BAZAINE *(E-S)*
BENEDEK *(E-S)*
BERWICK *(B-S)*
BIGEARD *(E-S)*
BLÜCHER *(E-S)*
BOLIVAR *(AM-S)*
BOSQUET *(E-S)*
BOURBON *(E-S)*
BRADLEY *(AM-S)*
BROGLIE *(E-S)*
BUCKNER *(AM-S)*
BUDENNY *(AS-S)*
BURNABY *(B-S)*
CABRERA *(E-S)*
CADORNA *(E-S)*
CANARIS *(E-SA)*
CHUIKOV *(AS-S)*
CLINTON *(B-S)*
CORDOBA *(E-S)*
COURBET *(E-SA)*
CRADOCK *(B-S)*
DECATUR *(AM-SA)*
DE LA REY *(AF-S)*
DENIKIN *(AS-S)*
DOENITZ *(E-SA) *3*
DON JUAN *(E-S/SA)*
DOWDING *(B-A)*
DREYFUS *(E-S)*
DUPLEIX *(E-S)*
EXMOUTH *(B-SA)*
FAIRFAX *(B-S)*
FORREST *(AM-S)*
FRITSCH *(E-S)*
GAMELIN *(E-S)*

GARNIER *(E-SA)*
GEORGES *(E-S)*
GEORGEY *(E-S)*
GODUNOV *(AS-S)*
GOERING *(E-A) *4*
GONZAGA *(E-S)*
GOURAUD *(E-S)*
GRAVINA *(E-SA)*
GROUCHY *(E-S)*
GUEVARA *(AM-S)*
HALLECK *(AM-S)*
HAMPTON *(AM-S)*
HARDING *(B-S)*
HOEPNER *(E-S)*
JACKSON *(AM-S)*
JOUBERT *(AF-S)*
JOURDAN *(E-S)*
KOLCHAK *(AS-S)*
KOPRULU *(AS-S)*
KUTUSOV *(AS-S)*
LAMBERT *(B-S)*
LECLERC *(E-S)*
LEOPOLD *(E-S)*
LINCOLN *(AM-S)*
LIN PIAO *(AS-S)*
LYAUTEY *(E-S)*
MAKAROV *(AS-SA)*
MARMONT *(E-S)*
MARWITZ *(E-S)*
MASSÉNA *(E-S)*
METAXAS *(E-S)*
METHUEN *(B-S)*
MORTIER *(E-S)*
NIVELLE *(E-S)*
ORMONDE *(B-S)*
OUDINOT *(E-S)*
PESCARA *(E-S)*
PHILLIP *(B-SA)*
PICKETT *(AM-S)*
PIZARRO *(E-S)*
POLLOCK *(B-SA)*
PONTIAC *(AM-S)*
RACOCZY *(E-S)*
REGULUS *(R-S)*
ROBERTS *(B-S)*
SARRAIL *(E-S)*

SEYMOUR *(B-SA)*
SHERMAN *(AM-S)*
SPINOLA *(E-S)*
STEUBEN *(E-S)*
STUDENT *(E-S)*
STURDEE *(B-SA)*
SUVOROV *(AS-S)*
TIRPITZ *(E-SA)*
TURENNE *(E-S)*
VENDÔME *(E-S)*
VILLARS *(E-S)*
WALLACE *(AM-S)*
WEYGAND *(E-S)*
WINGATE *(B-S)*
WRANGEL *(AS-S)*
WÜRMSER *(E-S)*

8

ALBRECHT *(E-S)*
ALEKSEEV *(AS-S)*
ALVAREDO *(E-S)*
ALVINCZY *(E-S)*
ANDERSON *(AM-S)*
ANGLESEY *(B-S)*
ANTHOINE *(E-S)*
AUGEREAU *(E-S)*
AUGUSTUS *(E-S, R-S)*
BADOGLIO *(E-S)*
BEAULIEU *(E-S)*
BERNHARD *(E-S)*
BERTHIER *(E-S)*
BERTRAND *(E-S)*
BIRDWOOD *(B-S)*
BLOMBERG *(E-S)*
BOSCAWEN *(B-SA)*
BOURBAKI *(E-S)*
BOURMONT *(E-S)*
BRUSILOV *(AS-S)*
BUCHANAN *(AM-SA)*
BURGOYNE *(B-S)*
BURNSIDE *(AM-S)*
CAMPBELL *(B-S)*
CARDIGAN *(B-S)*

CARRANZA *(AM-S)*
CASTRIES *(E-S)*
CETEWAYO *(AF-S)*
CHESHIRE *(B-A)*
COCHRANE *(B-SA)*
CROMWELL *(B-S)*
DE GAULLE *(E-S)*
DUQUESNE *(E-SA)*
ELWORTHY *(B-A)*
EXELMANS *(E-S)*
FARRAGUT *(AM-SA)*
FREYBERG *(AU-S)*
GALLIÉNI *(E-S)*
GALTIERI *(AM-S)*
GRAZIANI *(E-S)*
GUDERIAN *(E-S)*
GUYNEMER *(E-A)*
HAMILCAR *(AF-S)*
HAMILTON *(B-S)*
HANNIBAL *(AF-S)*
HAVELOCK *(B-S)*
HOFFMANN *(E-S)*
IRONSIDE *(B-S)*
JELLICOE *(B-SA)*
JOHNSTON *(AM-S)*
KORNILOV *(AS-S)*
LANREZAC *(E-S)*
LAWRENCE *(B-S)*
LEFEBVRE *(E-S)*
LOSSBERG *(E-S)*
LUCULLUS *(R-S)*
MacMAHON *(I-S)*
MANSFELD *(E-S)*
MANSTEIN *(E-S)*
MARCHAND *(E-S)*
MARSHALL *(AM-S)*
MAUNOURY *(E-S)*
McCREERY *(B-S)*
MITCHELL *(AM-A)*
MITSCHER *(AM-SA)*
MONMOUTH *(B-S)*
MONTCALM *(E-S)*
MONTROSE *(B-S)*
MOROSINI *(E-SA)*
MOULTRIE *(AM-S)*
MOUNTJOY *(B-S)*

PEOPLE – MILITARY LEADERS

MURAVIEV *(AS-S)*
NAPOLEON *(E-S) *6*
O'HIGGINS *(AM-S)*
PERIGNON *(E-S)*
PERSHING *(AM-S)*
POTEMKIN *(AS-S)*
RADETSKY *(E-S)*
SAUMAREY *(B-SA)*
SCHÖRNER *(E-S)*
SEYDLITZ *(E-S)*
SHERIDAN *(AM-S)*
SHUN CHIH *(AS-S)*
SIKORSKI *(E-S)*
SKOBELEV *(AS-S)*
SPRUANCE *(AM-SA)*
STILICHO *(R-S)*
STILWELL *(AM-S)*
STRACHAN *(B-SA)*
SULEIMAN *(AS-S)*
SULLIVAN *(AM-S)*
TECUMSEH *(AM-S)*
TERAUCHI *(AS-S)*
THE MADHI *(AF-S)*
WOLSELEY *(B-S)*
YAMAGATA *(AS-S)*
YAMAMOTO *(AS-SA)*
ZEITZLER *(E-S)*

9

ALBEMARLE *(B-S)*
ALEXANDER *(B-S, E-S)*
ANGOULÊME *(E-S)*
ANTONESCU *(E-S)*
BAGRATION *(AS-S)*
BARATIERI *(E-S)*
BERESFORD *(B-SA)*
BERTHELOT *(E-S)*
BESSIÈRES *(E-S)*
BONAPARTE *(E-S) *6*
BOUFFLERS *(E-S)*
BOULANGER *(E-S)*
BRUNSWICK *(E-S)*
CAMBRIDGE *(B-S)*

CAMBRONNE *(E-S)*
CANROBERT *(E-S)*
CASTELNAU *(E-S)*
CAVAIGNAC *(E-S)*
CHENNAULT *(AM-SA)*
CONINGHAM *(B-SA)*
CONNAUGHT *(B-S)*
DIEBITSCH *(E-S) *7*
DOOLITTLE *(AM-SA)*
DUCKWORTH *(B-SA)*
DUMOURIEZ *(E-S)*
DUNDONALD *(B-SA)*
ESPARTERO *(E-S)*
FREDERICK *(E-S)*
GARIBALDI *(E-S)*
GNEISENAU *(E-S)*
GRENVILLE *(B-SA)*
HASDRUBAL *(AF-S)*
HIDEYOSHI *(AS-S)*
IVANOVICH *(E-S) *7*
KITCHENER *(B-S)*
LAFAYETTE *(E-S)*
LA MARMORA *(E-S)*
MacARTHUR *(AM-S)*
MACDONALD *(E-S)*
MACKENSEN *(E-S)*
MARCELLUS *(R-S)*
McCLELLAN *(AM-S)*
MENSHEKOV *(AS-S)*
MILTIADES *(E-S)*
NADIR SHAH *(AS-S)*
NANA SAHIB *(AS-S)*
NEWCASTLE *(B-S)*
NICHOLSON *(B-S)*
NUNGESSER *(E-SA)*
OLDCASTLE *(B-S)*
PEMBERTON *(AM-S)*
PRETORIUS *(AF-S)*
RAWLINSON *(B-S)*
REICHENAU *(E-S)*
ROBERTSON *(B-S)*
RUNDSTEDT *(E-S)*
RUPPRECHT *(E-S)*
SAN MARTIN *(AM-S)*
SANTA ANNA *(AM-S)*
SANTA CRUZ *(E-SA)*

SCHOMBERG *(E-S)*
STEINMETZ *(E-S)*
ST VINCENT *(B-SA)*
TOURVILLE *(E-SA)*
TOWNSHEND *(B-S)*
TRENCHARD *(B-A)*
VORONTSOV *(AS-S)*
WALDERSEE *(E-S)*
WELLESLEY *(B-S) *8*
WITZLEBEN *(E-S)*
YAMASHITA *(AS-S)*

10

ABD EL-KADER *(AF-S)*
ABERCROMBY *(B-S)*
ALANBROOKE *(B-S)*
AUCHINLECK *(B-S)*
BEAUREGARD *(AM-S)*
BELLEGARDE *(E-S)*
BERNADOTTE *(E-S)*
CHELSMFORD *(B-S)*
CLAUSEWITZ *(E-S)*
CODRINGTON *(B-SA)*
CORNWALLIS *(B-S)*
CRAZY HORSE *(AM-S)*
CUMBERLAND *(B-S)*
CUNNINGHAM *(B-SA)*
EISENHOWER *(AM-S)*
ENVER PASHA *(AS-S)*
FALKENHAYN *(E-S)*
GUILLAUMAT *(E-S)*
HILL-NORTON *(B-SA)*
HINDENBERG *(E-S)*
KELLERMANN *(E-S)*
KESSELRING *(E-S)*
KUBLAI KHAN *(AS-S)*
KUROPATKIN *(AS-S)*
L'OUVERTURE *(AM-S)*
LUDENDORFF *(E-S)*
LUXEMBOURG *(E-S)*
MANCHESTER *(B-S)*
MANNERHEIM *(E-S)*
MAO TSE-TUNG *(AS-S)*
MAXIMILIAN *(E-S)*

MEHEMET ALI *(E-S)*
MONTGOMERY *(B-S)*
MOUNTEVANS *(B-SA)*
MULEY HACEN *(E-S)*
OCHTERLONY *(B-S)*
OGLETHORPE *(B-S)*
RICHTHOFEN *(E-A)*
SCHLIEFFEN *(E-S)*
SOKOLOVSKY *(AS-S)*
SOMERVILLE *(B-SA)*
TANTIA TOPI *(AS-S)*
TIMOSHENKO *(AS-S)*
VASILEVSKY *(AS-S)*
VILLENEUVE *(E-SA)*
VOROSHILOV *(AS-S)*
WASHINGTON *(AM-S)*
WELLINGTON *(B-S)* *8

STRATHNAIRN *(B-S)*
TORSTENSSON *(E-S)*
WALLENSTEIN *(E-S)*

12

BRECKINRIDGE *(AM-S)*
EICHELBERGER *(AM-S)*
GOUVION-ST-CYR *(E-S)*
IBRAHIM PASHA *(AS-S)*
KEMAL ATATÜRK *(AS-S)* *5
LEIGH MALLORY *(B-SA)*
MONTECUCCOLI *(E-S)*
PRINCE EUGENE *(E-S)*
PRINCE RUPERT *(E-S/SA)*
RICKENBACKER *(AM-A)*
SHAPOSHNIKOV *(AS-S)*
TUKHACHEVSKY *(AS-S)*

11

ALBUQUERQUE *(E-S)*
ALVENSLEBEN *(E-S)*
BADEN-POWELL *(B-S)*
BEAUHARNAIS *(E-S)*
BRAUCHITSCH *(E-S)*
CHODKIEWITZ *(E-S)*
COLLINGWOOD *(B-SA)*
CONSTANTINE *(R-S)*
ELPHINSTONE *(B-SA)*
EPAMINONDAS *(E-S)*
GENGHIS KHAN *(AS-S)*
KURIBAYASHI *(AS-S)*
LAMORICIÈRE *(E-S)*
LIDDELL HART *(B-S)*
MARLBOROUGH *(B-S)*
MONTMORENCY *(E-S)*
MOUNTBATTEN *(B-S/SA)*
MÜNCHHAUSEN *(E-S)*
PONIATOWSKI *(E-S)*
RENNENKAMPF *(AS-S)*
ROKOSSOVSKI *(AS-S)*
SAINT-ARNAUD *(E-S)*
SCHARNHORST *(E-S)*
SCHWARZKOPF *(AM-S)*
SITTING BULL *(AM-S)*

13

CHIANG KAI-SHEK *(AS-S)*
FABIUS MAXIMUS *(R-S)*
FRIEDRICH KARL *(E-S)*
LETTOW-VORBECK *(E-S)*
PETER THE GREAT *(AS-S)*
PRIMO DE RIVERA *(E-S)*
SCHWARZENBERG *(E-S)*
STRAUSSENBERG *(E-S)*

14

BARCLAY DE TOLLY *(AS-S)*
CHÂTEAU-RENAULT *(E-SA)*
ROZHDESTVENSKI *(AS-SA)*
VERDY DU VERNOIS *(E-S)*
WINDISCH-GRAETZ *(E-S)*

15

CASSIUS LONGINUS *(R-S)*
MAURICE OF NASSAU *(E-S)*
NAPIER OF MAGDALA *(B-S)*
ROCHEJACQUELEIN *(E-S)*

PEOPLE

POLITICIANS & LEADERS – BRITAIN

† = Prime minister

3

EDE
FOX
GOW
JAY
PYM

4

BENN
BUTE †
CARR
CAVE
COOK
EDEN †
FOOT
GREY †
HART
HILL
HOGG
HOWE
HURD
JUDD
KING
LANE
LONG
LUCE
NOTT
ORME
OWEN
PEEL †
PITT †
REES
WEBB

5

ALTON

AMERY
ASTOR
BAKER
BEITH
BEVAN
BEVIN
BROWN
BURKE
CECIL
CREWE
DERBY †
EGGAR
GOULD
GRIGG
HEATH †
HOARE
LEVER
LLOYD
MAJOR †
MASON
MOORE
NEAVE
NORTH †
PEART
PRIOR
SHORE
SHORT
SMITH
STEEL
STRAW
YOUNG

6

ASHLEY
ATKINS
ATTLEE †
BARBER

BIFFEN
BOYSON
BRIGHT
BROOKE
BUTLER
CASTLE
CLARKE
COBDEN
CRIPPS
CURRIE
CURZON
DALTON
DU CANN
ECCLES
ENNALS
FOWLER
FRANKS
GEDDES
GUMMER
HARDIE
HAVERS
HEALEY
HEFFER
HOWARD
HOWELL
JENKIN
JOSEPH
LAMONT
LAWSON
MACKAY
MAYHEW
MELLOR
MOSLEY
MULLEY
NEWTON
ONSLOW
PATTEN
PELHAM †
POWELL

RIDLEY
RIPPON
ROBENS
SANDYS
SILKIN
SOAMES
TEBBIT
THOMAS
THORPE
VARLEY
WALKER
WILSON †

7

ADDISON
ASHDOWN
ASQUITH †
BALDWIN †
BALFOUR †
BOATENG
BOOTHBY
BRITTAN
CANNING †
CHALKER
CHANNON
CHATHAM †
DALYELL
DENNING
EDWARDS
GILMOUR
GRAFTON †
GRIMOND
HALDANE
HALIFAX
JENKINS
JOPLING
KAUFMAN

KINNOCK
MACLEOD
MARPLES
NABARRO
PAISLEY
PROFUMO
RIFKIND
RODGERS
RUDDOCK
RUSSELL †
SCARMAN
SKINNER
SNOWDEN
STEWART
TAPSELL
VIGGERS
WAKEHAM
WALPOLE †
YOUNGER

8

ABERDEEN †
ANDERSON
BELSTEAD
BONAR LAW †
BRABAZON
BROUGHAM
CROSLAND
CROSSMAN
DISRAELI †
DUNWOODY
GODERICH †
HAILSHAM
HARCOURT
JELLICOE
LANSBURY
MAUDLING

MITCHELL
MORRISON
MOYNIHAN
PERCEVAL †
PORTILLO
PORTLAND †
PRENTICE
PRESCOTT
ROSEBERY †
SHINWELL
SIDMOUTH †
STANHOPE
THATCHER †
WHITELAW
WILLIAMS

9

BEVERIDGE
BONDFIELD
BOTTOMLEY
CALLAGHAN †
CHURCHILL †
CHUTER-EDE
CONCANNON
CRITCHLEY
DONALDSON
FAIRBAIRN
GAITSKELL
GLADSTONE †
GREENWOOD
GRENVILLE †
HENDERSON
HESELTINE
HUSKISSON
KITCHENER
LIVERPOOL †

LYTTELTON
MACDONALD †
MacGREGOR
MacLENNAN
MACMILLAN †
MELBOURNE †
MOLYNEAUX
NEWCASTLE †
OPPENHEIM
PARKINSON
PASSFIELD
SALISBURY †
SHELBURNE †
TOWNSHEND
TREFGARNE
WINTERTON
WOLFENDEN

10

CARRINGTON
CUNNINGHAM
DEVONSHIRE †
ELWYN-JONES
EWART-BIGGS
HATTERSLEY
LENNOX-BOYD
ORMSBY-GORE
PALMERSTON †
ROCKINGHAM †
STONEHOUSE
TWEEDMOUTH
WADDINGTON
WALDEGRAVE
WEATHERILL
WELLINGTON †
WILMINGTON †

11

BEAVERBROOK
BUTLER-SLOSS
CASTLEREAGH
CHAMBERLAIN †
DOUGLAS-HOME †
HORE-BELISHA
LIVINGSTONE
LLOYD GEORGE †
MAYBRAY-KING
SELWYN-LLOYD
TRUMPINGTON
WILBERFORCE

12

BEAUMONT-DARK
BONHAM-CARTER
GORDON WALKER
McNAIR-WILSON
THORNEYCROFT

13

BOYD-CARPENTER

14

HEATHCOAT-AMORY

15

CAMPBELL-SAVOURS

PEOPLE

POLITICIANS & LEADERS – WORLD

(A) = Australia (ALB) = Albania (ALG) = Algeria (AR) = Argentina
(AU) = Austria (B) = Belgium (BA) = Bangladesh (BUL) = Bulgaria
(BUR) = Burma (C) = China (CA) = Canada (CH) = Chile
(CO) = Congo (CU) = Cuba (CY) = Cyprus (CZ) = Czechoslovakia
(D) = Denmark (E) = Egypt (EG) = East Germany (F) = France
(FI) = Finland (G) = Germany (GH) = Ghana (GR) = Greece
(H) = Hungary (HA) = Haiti (I) = Irish Republic (IC) = Iceland
(IN) = India (IND) = Indonesia (IQ) = Iraq (IR) = Iran (IS) = Israel
(IT) = Italy (J) = Japan (JO) = Jordan (K) = Kenya (KA) = Kampuchea
(LE) = Lebanon (LI) = Libya (M) = Malaysia (MA) = Malta
(MAL) = Malawi (ME) = Mexico (MO) = Mongolia (N) = Netherlands
(NIC) = Nicaragua (NIG) = Nigeria (NK) = North Korea (NO) = Norway
(NZ) = New Zealand (P) = Portugal (PAK) = Pakistan (PAL) = Palestine
(PAN) = Panama (PE) = Peru (PH) = Philippines (PO) = Poland
(PR) = Prussia (R) = Russia (RO) = Romania (S) = Sweden
(SA) = South Africa (SI) = Singapore (SK) = South Korea (SP) = Spain
(SR) = Sri Lanka (SU) = Sudan (SW) = Switzerland (SY) = Syria
(T) = Turkey (TA) = Tanzania (U) = Uganda
(US) = United States († = US president) (V) = Vietnam
(WG) = West Germany (Y) = Yugoslavia (Z) = Zambia (ZA) = Zaïre
(ZI) = Zimbabwe
NB: Former countries' names are used, where relevant

3

AGT *(N)*
LIE *(NO)*

4

AMIN *(U)*
BLUM *(SA)*
BUSH *(US)* †
COOK *(A)*
COTY *(F)*
FORD *(US)* †

HOLT *(A)*
HULL *(US)*
KING *(US)*
KIRK *(NZ)*
KOHL *(WG)*
MEIR *(IS)*
MORO *(IT)*
NAGY *(H)*
ÖZAL *(T)*
POLK *(US)* †
RHEE *(SK)*
RUSK *(US)*
TAFT *(US)* †
TITO *(Y)*

TOJO *(J)*
VLOK *(SA)*

5

ADAMS *(US)* †
AGNEW *(US)*
ASSAD *(SY)*
BAKER *(US)*
BANDA *(MAL)*
BEGIN *(IS)*
BERIA *(R)*
BOTHA *(SA)*

CLARK *(CA)*
DAYAN *(IS)*
DESAI *(IN)*
DE WET *(SA)*
DREES *(N)*
EBRET *(G)*
EVREN *(T)*
GRANT *(US)* †
HAVEL *(CZ)*
HAWKE *(A)*
HAYES *(US)* †
HOXHA *(ALB)*
HUSAK *(CZ)*
JONAS *(AU)*

KAIFU *(J)*
LANGE *(NZ)*
LAVAL *(F)*
LENIN *(R)*
LODGE *(US)*
LYNCH *(I)*
MALAN *(SA)*
MBOYA *(K)*
MENEM *(AR)*
NEHRU *(IN)*
NIXON *(US)* †
NKOMO *(ZI)*
OBOTE *(U)*
PALME *(S)*

PERES (IS)
PERÓN (AR)
RABIN (IS)
SADAT (E)
SILVA (P)
SINGH (IN)
SMITH (ZI)
SMUTS (SA)
SPAAK (B)
STOPH (EG)
THANT (BUR)
TYLER (US) †
VANCE (US)
VILLA (ME)

6

AQUINO (PH)
ARAFAT (PAL)
ARTHUR (US) †
AURIOL (F)
BASHIR (SU)
BHUTTO (PAK)
BRANDT (WG)
CARTER (US) †
CASTRO (CU)
CHIRAC (F)
COATES (NZ)
DUBCEK (CZ)
DULLES (US)
ERHARD (WG)
ESHKOL (IS)
FADDEN (A)
FRANCO (SP)
FRASER (A,
  NZ)
FUKUDA (J)
GANDHI (IN)
GRIVAS (GR)
HERTER (US)
HITLER (G)
HOOVER (US) †
JUÁREZ (ME)
KAUNDA (Z)
KRENTZ (EG)

KRUGER (SA)
MARCOS (PH)
MOBUTU (ZA)
MODROW (EG)
MONROE (US) †
MUGABE (ZI)
NASSER (E)
NÉMETH (H)
ORTEGA (NIC)
PÉTAIN (F)
PIERCE (US) †
POL POT (KA)
QUAYLE (US)
REAGAN (US) †
ROCARD (F)
ROGERS (US)
SHAMIR (IS)
SHULTZ (US)
SOARES (P)
STALIN (R)
SUZUKI (J)
TAYLOR (US) †
TRUMAN (US) †
WALESA (PO)
WILSON (US) †
ZAPATA (ME)

7

ACHESON (US)
ALLENDE (CH)
ATATÜRK (T)
AZIKIWE (NIG)
BATISTA (CU)
BORMANN (G)
CAETANO (P)
COLLINS (I)
DE KLERK (SA)
DUKAKIS (US)
EYSKENS (B)
GADDAFI (LI)
GEMAYEL (LE)
GROMYKO (R)
HARDING (US) †
HAUGHEY (I)

HERTZOG (SA)
HIMMLER (G)
HUSSEIN (IQ,
  JO)
JACKSON (US) †
JOHNSON (US) †
KENNEDY (US) †
KOSYGIN (R)
LINCOLN (US) †
LUBBERS (N)
LUMUMBA (CO)
MADISON (US) †
MANDELA (SA)
MARTENS (B)
MENZIES (A)
MIKOYAN (R)
MINTOFF (MA)
MOLOTOV (R)
MONDALE (US)
MUBARAK (E)
MULDOON (NZ)
NKRUMAH (GH)
NORIEGA (PAN)
NYERERE (TA)
PARNELL (I)
PEARSON (CA)
SALAZAR (P)
SCHMIDT (WG)
SHASTRI (IN)
SUHARTO (IND)
TROTSKY (R)
TRUDEAU (CA)
VORSTER (SA)
WALLACE (US)
WHITLAM (A)
YELTSIN (R)
ZHIVKOV (BUL)

8

ADENAUER (WG)
ALFONSIN (AR)
ANDROPOV (R)
AYUB KHAN (PAK)
BATMUNKH (MO)

BEN BELLA (ALG)
BISMARCK (PR)
BREZHNEV (R)
BUCHANAN (US) †
BULGANIN (R)
CARLSSON (S)
CHAMORRO (NIC)
COOLIDGE (US) †
COSGRAVE (I)
COSTELLO (I)
DALADIER (F)
DE GAULLE (F)
DE VALERA (I)
DOLLFUSS (AU)
DUVALIER (HA)
FILLMORE (US) †
GARFIELD (US) †
GENSCHER (WG)
GOEBBELS (G)
GONZÁLEZ (SP)
HARRISON (US) †
HOLYOAKE (NZ)
HONECKER (EG)
HUMPHREY (US)
KEKKONEN (FI)
KENYATTA (K)
KHOMEINI (IR)
KOIVISTO (FI)
LIGACHEV (R)
MAKARIOS (CY)
MALENKOV (R)
MARKOVIC (Y)
MARSHALL (US)
McCARTHY (US)
McKINLEY (US) †
MULRONEY (CA)
MUSEVENI (U)
MUZOREWA (ZI)
NAPOLEON (F)
O'HIGGINS (CH)
PINOCHET (CH)
PODGORNY (R)
POINCARÉ (F)
POMPIDOU (F)
QUISLING (NO)
SCHLÜTER (D)

ULBRICHT *(EG)*
VAN BUREN *(US)* †
VERWOERD *(SA)*
WALDHEIM *(AU)*
WELENSKY *(ZI)*

9

ANDREOTTI *(IT)*
BEN-GURION *(IS)*
CEAUSESCU *(RO)*
CHERNENKO *(R)*
CHOU EN-LAI *(C)*
CLEVELAND *(US)* †
DELAMURAZ *(SW)*
GARIBALDI *(IT)*
GORBACHEV *(R)*
HO CHI-MINH *(V)*
JEFFERSON *(US)* †
KIM IL-SUNG *(NK)*
KISSINGER *(US)*
LA GUARDIA *(US)*
MUSSOLINI *(IT)*
ROH TAE-WOO *(SK)*
ROOSEVELT *(US)* †
STEVENSON *(US)*
SUN YAT-SEN *(C)*
TINDEMANS *(B)*
VASSILIOU *(CY)*

10

BRUNDTLAND *(NO)*
CLEMENCEAU *(F)*
EISENHOWER *(US)* †
FITZGERALD *(I)*
HINDENBURG *(G)*
JARUZELSKI *(PO)*
KARAMANLIS *(GR)*
KHRUSHCHEV *(R)*
LEE KUAN YEW *(SI)*
LIU SHAO-CH'I *(C)*
MAO TSE-TUNG *(C)*
MAZOWIECKI *(PO)*
METTERNICK *(AU)*
MITTERRAND *(F)*
PADEREWSKI *(PO)*
PAPANDREOU *(GR)*
RAFSANJANI *(IR)*
RIBBENTROP *(G)*
TALLEYRAND *(F)*
VOROSHILOV *(R)*
WASHINGTON *(US)* †
WEINBERGER *(US)*

11

ABDUL RAHMAN *(M)*
DIEFENBAKER *(CA)*

ROBESPIERRE *(F)*
ROCKEFELLER *(US)*
TZANNETAKIS *(GR)*

12

BANDARANAIKE *(SR)*
DENG XIAO-PING *(C)*
HAMMARSKJÖLD *(S)*
KEMAL ATATÜRK *(T)*
SHEVARDNADZE *(R)*

13

CHIANG KAI-SHEK *(C)*
MACKENZIE KING *(CA)*
MUJIBUR RAHMAN *(BA)*
SADDAM HUSSEIN *(IQ)*

14

FINNBOGADÓTTIR *(IC)*
PÉREZ DE CUÉLLAR *(PE*

15

GISCARD D'ÉSTAING *(F)*

PEOPLE

RELIGIOUS LEADERS

(AC) = Archbishop of Canterbury   (C) = Cardinal   (MI) = Missionary/
evangelist   (MO) = Monk   (P) = Pope   (R) = Rabbi
* = Alternative spelling/name

3

FOX *(Quakers)*
HUS *(Hussites) *1*
LEE *(Shakers)*
LEO *(P)*
ODO *(AC)*
SIN *(C)*

4

BEDE *(MO)*
DALY
EDDY *(Christian Science)*
HUME *(C)*
HUSS *(Hussites) *1*
KEMP *(AC)*
KENT
KNOX
LANG *(AC)*
LAUD *(AC)*
MANI *(Manichaeism)*
MOON *(Moonies)*
PAUL *(P)*
PIUS *(P)*
POLE *(AC)*
RYAN
TAIT *(AC)*
TUTU
WAKE *(AC)*

5

ABBOT *(AC)*
BACON *(MO)*

BOOTH *(Salvation Army)*
BRUNO *(MO-Carthusians)*
CAIUS *(P)*
CAREY *(AC)*
CONON *(P)*
DARBY *(Plymouth Brethren)*
DONUS *(P)*
EAMES
FELIX *(P)*
GLEMP *(C)*
JESUS *(Christianity) *2*
KEBLE
LINUS *(P)*
NANAK *(Sikhism)*
PETER *(P)*
PUSEY *(Puseyites)*
SMITH *(Mormons)*
SMYTH *(Baptists)*
SOPER
URBAN *(P)*
VARAH *(Samaritans)*
YOUNG *(Mormons)*

6

ADRIAN *(P)*
AGATHO *(P)*
ANSELM *(AC)*
BECKET *(AC) *3*
BENSON *(AC)*
BLANCH
BOESAK
BUNGAY *(MO)*
CALVIN *(Calvinists)*
COGGAN *(AC)*

DAMIEN *(MI)*
DEVINE
EUGENE *(P)*
FABIAN *(P)*
FISHER *(AC)*
GRAHAM *(MI)*
HEENAN *(C)*
HILARY *(P)*
HOWLEY *(AC)*
IRVING *(Irvingites)*
JULIUS *(P)*
LANDUS *(P)*
LAO-TZU *(Taoism)*
LOYOLA *(Jesuits) *4*
LUCIUS *(P)*
LUTHER *(Reformation)*
MARCUS *(P)*
MARTIN *(P)*
MILLER *(Seventh Day Adventists)*
MORTON *(AC)*
NEWMAN *(C)*
OTUNGA *(C)*
RAMSEY *(AC)*
RUNCIE *(AC)*
SECKER *(AC)*
SIXTUS *(P)*
SUMNER *(AC)*
TEMPLE *(AC)*
TERESA *(MI) *5*
THOMAS *(Christadelphians)*
VICTOR *(P)*
WARHAM *(AC)*
WESLEY *(Methodists)*
WOLSEY *(C)*
WYCLIF *(Lollards) *6*

PEOPLE – RELIGIOUS LEADERS

7

ANTERUS *(P)*
AQUINAS *(MO)* *7
AYLWARD *(MI)*
BERNARD *(MO-Cistercians)*
CLAYTON *(Toc H)*
CLEMENT *(P)*
COLLINS
CONNELL
CRANMER *(AC)*
DAMASUS *(P)*
DOMINIC *(MO-Dominicans)*
DUNSTAN *(AC)*
ERASMUS *(Humanists)*
ERASTUS *(Erastians)*
FRANCIS *(MO-Franciscans)* *8
GAUTAMA *(Buddhism)*
GREGORY *(P)*
HABGOOD
HUBBARD
HYGINUS *(P)*
JENKINS
LEONARD
LONGLEY *(AC)*
MANNING *(C)*
MARINUS *(P)*
McMAHON
Ó FIAICH *(C)*
PAISLEY
PASCHAL *(P)*
PONTIAN *(P)*
ROMANUS *(P)*
RUSSELL *(Jehovah's
        Witnesses)*
SANKARA *(Hinduism)*
SERGIUS *(P)*
SOTERUS *(P)*
STEPHEN *(P)*
STIGAND *(AC)*
THERESA *(MI)* *5
TOMÁŠEK *(C)*
WORLOCK
ZACHARY *(P)*
ZOSIMUS *(P)*
ZWINGLI *(Zwinglianists)*

8

AGAPETUS *(P)*
ANICETUS *(P)*
BANCROFT *(AC)*
BENEDICT *(MO-Benedictines)*
        (P)
BONIFACE *(P)*
CALIXTUS *(P)*
CUTHBERT *(AC)*
DAVIDSON *(AC)*
EUSEBIUS *(P)*
FORMOSUS *(P)*
GELASIUS *(P)*
HONORIUS *(P)*
IGNATIUS *(MO)*
INNOCENT *(P)*
JOHN PAUL *(P)*
KHOMEINI
LANFRANC *(AC)*
LEFEBVRE
LIBERIUS *(P)*
MAKARIOS
MOHAMMED *(Islam)*
NICHOLAS *(P)*
PELAGIUS *(P)*
RASPUTIN *(MO)*
SHEPPARD
SIRICIUS *(P)*
STAFFORD *(AC)*
THEODORE *(P)*
VIGILIUS *(P)*
VITALIAN *(P)*
WHITGIFT *(AC)*
WYCLIFFE *(Lollards)* *6

9

ADEODATUS *(P)*
ALEXANDER *(P)*
ANACLETUS *(P)*
AUGUSTINE *(AC)*
CELESTINE *(P)*
CONFUCIUS *(Confucianism)*
DIONYSIUS *(P)*

EUTYCHIAN *(P)*
EVARISTUS *(P)*
HORMISDAS *(P)*
MARCELLUS *(P)*
MILTIADES *(P)*
MUGGLETON *(Muggletonians)*
OLDCASTLE *(Lollards)*
RICHELIEU *(C)*
SEVERINUS *(P)*
SILVERIUS *(P)*
SISSINIUS *(P)*
SYLVESTER *(P)*
SYMMACHUS *(P)*
TILLOTSON *(AC)*
VALENTINE *(P)*
ZOROASTER *(Zoroastrians)* *9

10

ANASTASIUS *(P)*
HUDDLESTON
JAKOBOVITS *(R)*
SABINIANUS *(P)*
SCHWEITZER *(MI)*
SIMPLICIUS *(P)*
SWEDENBORG *(Swedenborgians)*
VARDHAMANA *(Jainism)*
ZEPHYRINUS *(P)*

11

CONSTANTINE *(P)*
ELEUTHERIUS *(P)*
JESUS CHRIST *(Christianity)* *2
MARCELLINUS *(P)*
ROSENCREUTZ *(Rosicrucians)*
TELESPHORUS *(P)*
ZARATHUSTRA *(Zoroastrians)* *9

12

DE WINCHELSEA *(AC)*
MOTHER TERESA *(MI)* *5

13

MANNERS-SUTTON *(AC)*
MOTHER THERESA *(MI)* *5
THOMAS À BECKET *(AC)* *3
THOMAS AQUINAS *(MO)* *7

14

IGNATIUS LOYOLA *(Jesuits)* *4

15

FRANCIS OF ASSISI *(Franciscans)* *8

PEOPLE

SAINTS

= Alternative name

3

ITA
IVO *(Lawyers)*
LEO *1
ODO

4

ANNE *(Canada, Housewives)*
BEDE
CHAD
ELMO *2
ELOI *(Jewellers)*
ERIC *(Sweden)*
JOHN
JUDE
LUKE *(Artists, Brewers, Physicians)*
MARK
MARY
OLAF *(Norway)*
PAUL
REMI
SAVA
ZITA *(Domestic servants)*

5

AGNES
AIDAN
ALBAN
AMAND *(Innkeepers & wine merchants)*
ASAPH
ASGAR *(Denmark)*
BASIL
BRUNO

CLARE *(Television)*
DAVID *(Poets, Wales)*
DENIS *(France)*
GILES
HELEN
HILDA
JAMES *(Labourers, Spain)*
LOUIS *(Barbers)*
MUNGO *(Glasgow)*
ODILO
PETER
PIRAN
SABAS
SILAS
SIMON
ULRIC
VITUS *(Comedians)*

6

ADRIAN *(Soldiers)*
AGATHA *(Bell-founders, Nurses)*
ALBERT *(Scientists)*
ANDREW *(Greece, Russia, Scotland)*
ANSELM
ANTONY
CANUTE *(Denmark)*
CLAUDE *(Sculptors)*
DYSMAS *(Funeral directors)*
EDMUND
FIACRE *(Cab-drivers)*
GEORGE *(England, Farmers, Portugal, Scouts, Soldiers)*

GODRIC
HUBERT *(Hunters)*
JEROME *(Librarians)*
JOSEPH *(Belgium,*
Canada,
Carpenters,
Workers)
JUSTIN
LUCIAN
MARTHA *(Cooks,*
Dieticians)
MONICA
NINIAN
OSWALD
PHILIP
PHOCAS *(Gardeners)*
ROBERT *3
SIMEON
SOPHIA
TERESA *(Spain)* *4
(Airmen,
France) *5
THOMAS *(Architects)*
URSULA

7

ADJUTOR *(Yachtsmen)*
ALEXIUS *(Nurses)*
AMBROSE
ANTHONY *(Grave-diggers)*
BARBARA *(Architects, Gunners,*
Miners)
BERNARD
BRENDAN *(Sailors)*
BRIDGET *(Scholars, Sweden)*
CASIMIR *(Poland)*
CASSIAN *(Secretaries)*
CECILIA *(Musicians & singers, Poets)*
CLEMENT
COLETTE
COLUMBA *(Scotland)*
CRISPIN *(Shoemakers)*
CYPRIAN
DOMINIC *(Astronomers)*

DUNSTAN *(Blacksmiths, Goldsmiths,*
Metal-workers, Musicians
& singers)
ELIGIUS *(Blacksmiths, Jewellers)*
ERASMUS *(Sailors)* *2
EULALIA *(Sailors)*
EUSTACE
FLORIAN *(Firemen)*
FRANCIS *(Authors & journalists)* *6
(Italy) *7
(RC missionaries) *8
GABRIEL *(Postal, radio & television*
workers)
GREGORY *(Musicians & singers,*
Teachers) *9
ISIDORE *(Farmers)*
LEONARD *(Prisoners)*
MATTHEW *(Accountants,*
Tax-collectors)
MAURICE *(Infantrymen)*
MICHAEL *(Germany, Grocers,*
Paratroopers, Policemen)
NORBERT
PASCHAL
PATRICK *(Ireland)*
RAPHAEL *(Nurses, Physicians,*
Travellers)
SERGIUS
STEPHEN *(Bricklayers, Hungary)*
SWITHIN
THÉRÈSA *4, *5
THÉRÈSE *(Florists)*
TIMOTHY
VINCENT *(Portugal, Wine-growers)*
WILFRID

8

BARNABAS
BENEDICT *(Speleologists)*
BONIFACE *(Germany)*
CAMILLUS *(Nurses)*
COLUMBAN
CUTHBERT *(Sailors)*
DOROTHEA *(Florists, Gardeners)*

PEOPLE – SAINTS

GENESIUS *(Actors, Lawyers, Secretaries)*
GERTRUDE *(West Indies)*
IGNATIUS *(Soldiers)*
INNOCENT
LAWRENCE *(Cooks)*
MARGARET
MATTHIAS
NICHOLAS *(Bakers, Children, Greece, Pawnbrokers, Russia, Travellers)*
PERPETUA
THEODORE
VENERIUS *(Lighthouse-keepers)*
VERONICA
WINIFRED

9

APOLLONIA *(Dentists)*
AUGUSTINE *(Brewers, Printers, Theologians)*
BERNADINE *(Advertising)*
CATHERINE *(Students, Teachers, Wheelwrights)*
DEUSDEDIT
FERDINAND *(Engineers)*
HOMOBONUS *(Tailors)*
HONORATUS *(Bakers)*
JOAN OF ARC *(France, Soldiers)*
JOHN BOSCO *(Editors)*
JOHN OF GOD *(Book-sellers, Nurses, Printers)*
KENTIGERN *(Glasgow)*
PANTALEON *(Physicians)*
PROCOPIUS *(Czechoslovakia)*
SEBASTIAN *(Archers, Atheletes, Soldiers)*
THADDAEUS
VALENTINE
WENCESLAS *(Czechoslovakia)*
WILLIBALD
ZACHARIAS

10

ANASTASIUS *(Goldsmiths, Metal-workers)*
ATHANASIUS
BERNADETTE
BERNARDINO *(Bankers)*
FRUMENTIUS
SIMON PETER
STANISLAUS *(Poland)*
THOMAS MORE *(Lawyers)*
WILLIBRORD *(Netherlands)*

11

BARTHOLOMEW
CHRISTOPHER *(Motorists, Sailors, Travellers)*
LEO THE GREAT *1*

12

THOMAS BECKET *10*

13

FRANCIS XAVIER *(RC missionaries)* *8*
JOHN OF NEPUMUK *(Czechoslovakia)*
PETER GONZALES *(Sailors)*
TERESA OF AVILA *(Spain)* *4*
THOMAS À BECKET *10*
THOMAS AQUINAS *(Philosophers, Students)*
VINCENT FERRER *(Builders)*

14

ANTHONY OF PADUA *(Portugal, Travellers)*
FRANCIS DE SALES *(Authors & journalists)* *6*
JOHN THE BAPTIST

NICHOLAS OF MYRA *(Brewers)*
OUR LADY OF GRACE *(Motor-cyclists)*

FRANCIS OF ASSISI *(Italy, Merchants)* *7
GREGORY THE GREAT *(Musicians & singers, Teachers)* *9
JOSEPH CUPERTINO *(Airmen)*
ROBERT OF MOLESME *3
TERESA OF LISIEUX *(Airmen, France)* *5

15

COSMAS AND DAMIAN *(Barbers, Physicians, Surgeons)*

PEOPLE

SCIENTISTS

*(A) = Astronomer   (B) = Botanist/naturalist   (C) = Chemist/biologist
(I) = Inventor   (M) = Mathematician   (P) = Physicist*

3

GED *(I-stereotyping)*
KAY *(I-flying shuttle)*
LEE *(I-knitting machine)*
OHM *(P)*
RAY *(B)*

4

AIRY *(A)*
ABEL *(M)*
BAER *(C)*
BELL *(I-telephone)*
BENZ *(I-car engine)*
BEST *(C)*
BIRÓ *(I-ball-point pen)*
BODE *(A)*
BOHR *(P)*
BOND *(A)*

BORN *(P)*
BOSE *(B/P)*
BOYS *(I-radio-micrometer)*
COHN *(B)*
COLT *(I-revolver)*
COUÉ *(C)*
DAVY *(C/I-miner's lamp)*
DREW *(I-scotch tape)*
GOLD *(A)*
GRAY *(B)*
HAHN *(C/P)*
HALE *(A)*
HOLT *(I-combine harvester)*
HOWE *(I-sewing machine)*
HUNT *(I-safety-pin)*
IVES *(I-halftone engraving)*
KLIC *(I-rotogravure)*
KOCH *(C)*

LAND *(I-polaroid camera)*
LAUE *(P)*
MACH *(P)*
OTIS *(I-passenger lift)*
OTTO *(I-4-stroke engine)*
PONS *(A)*
RABI *(P)*
RYLE *(A)*
SWAN *(I-bromide paper)*
TAMM *(P)*
TODD *(C)*
TULL *(I-seed drill)*
UREY *(P)*
VENN *(M)*
VERY *(I-flare signal)*
WATT *(I-condensing steam engine)*
YALE *(I-cylinder lock)*
YANG *(P)*
ZENO *(M)*

PEOPLE – SCIENTISTS

5

ADAMS *(A)*
AIKEN *(I-digital computer)*
AMICI *(A)*
ASTON *(C)*
BACON *(A/I-magnifying glass)*
BAILY *(A)*
BAIRD *(I-mechanical television)*
BANKS *(B)*
BAUMÉ *(I-hydrometer)*
BLACK *(C/P)*
BLOCH *(P)*
BOOLE *(M)*
BOOTH *(I-vacuum cleaner)*
BOSCH *(C)*
BOTHE *(P)*
BOYLE *(C/P)*
BRAGG *(P)*
BRAHE *(A)*
BROWN *(B)*
CARRÉ *(I-refrigerator)*
CHAIN *(C)*
COOKE *(P)*
CRICK *(C)*
CURIE *(C/P)*
DALEN *(P)*
DEBYE *(C/P)*
DEWAR *(I-vacuum flask)*
DIRAC *(M/P)*
DYSON *(A)*
ENCKE *(A)*
EULER *(M)*
FERMI *(P)*
FRANK *(P)*
FREGE *(M)*
GABOR *(I-holograph)*
GALLE *(A)*
GAUSS *(A/M)*
GIBBS *(P)*
GÖDEL *(M)*
HABER *(C)*
HARDY *(M)*

HENRY *(P)*
HERTZ *(P)*
HOOKE *(A/P)*
HOYLE *(A)*
HYATT *(I-celluloid)*
JEANS *(A/M)*
JOULE *(P)*
KLEIN *(M)*
KOWAL *(A)*
KREBS *(C)*
LIBBY *(C)*
LODGE *(P)*
MAGEE *(I-parking meter)*
MAXIM *(I-machine-gun)*
MAYER *(P)*
MONGE *(M)*
MOORE *(A)*
MORSE *(I-telegraph)*
NOBEL *(C/I-dynamite)*
NOBLE *(P)*
PAPIN *(I-pressure cooker)*
PASCH *(I-safety match)*
PAULI *(P)*
RAMAN *(P)*
REBER *(A)*
RITTY *(I-cash register)*
ROMER *(P)*
ROSSE *(A)*
SAGAN *(A)*
SEGRÉ *(P)*
SHORT *(I-loudspeaker)*
SMITH *(I-ship's propeller)*
SODDY *(C)*
STAHL *(C/P)*
TATUM *(C)*
TESLA *(I-high-frequency coil)*
VOLTA *(I/P-electric battery)*
WEBER *(C)*
WHITE *(B)*
YOUNG *(P)*

6

AGNESI *(M)*
ALFVÉN *(A/P)*

AMPÈRE *(P)*
ASPDIN *(I-Portland cement)*
BAEYER *(C)*
BARROW *(M)*
BOLYAI *(M)*
BONNET *(B)*
BRAMAH *(I-hydraulic press)*
BRIGGS *(M)*
BUFFON *(M)*
BUNSEN *(C/I-bunsen burner)*
CANTOR *(M)*
CAUCHY *(M)*
CAYLEY *(I-glider) (M)*
CLAUDE *(I-tubular neon light)*
CONWAY *(M)*
CRAMER *(M)*
CUGNOT *(I-steam car)*
DALTON *(C)*
DARWIN *(B)*
DE BARY *(B)*
DIESEL *(I-diesel engine)*
DONATI *(A)*
DREYER *(A)*
DUNLOP *(I-pneumatic tyre)*
ECKERT *(I-electronic computer, with MAUCHLY)*
EDISON *(I-phonograph)*
ENGLER *(B)*
EUCLID *(M)*
FERMAT *(M)*
FLOREY *(C)*
FRISCH *(P)*
FULLER *(I-solar battery, with PEARSON) (I-geodesic dome)*
FULTON *(I-torpedo)*
GALOIS *(M)*
GALTON *(C/I-finger-printing)*

GEIGER (I-Geiger counter)
GRAHAM (P)
GUNTER (M)
HALLEY (A)
HEVESY (C)
HOOKER (B)
HUBBLE (A)
HUGHES (I-microphone)
ISSARO (C)
JACOBI (M)
OLIOT (P)
ORDAN (M)
JUDSON (I-zip-fastener)
KALMUS (I-Technicolor)
KELVIN (P)
KEPLER (A/M)
LANDAU (P)
LENOIR (I-internal combustion engine)
LIEBIG (C)
LOOMIS (A/M)
LOVELL (A)
LOWELL (A)
MAIMAN (I-laser)
MARKOV (M)
McADAM (I-macadamised road surface)
MENDEL (B)
MÜLLER (C)
NAPIER (M)
NEWTON (A/M/P)
NIEPCE (I-permanent photograph)
PAPPUS (M)
PASCAL (M)
PEIRCE (M)
PENNEY (P)
PETERS (I-equal area projection)
PINCUS (I-contraceptive pill)
PLANCK (M/P)
RAMSAY (C)
RAMSEY (M)

SANGER (C)
SAVERY (I-steam pump)
SCHICK (I-electric razor)
SHOLES (I-typewriter)
SINGER (I-practical sewing machine)
SLOANE (B)
SPERRY (I-gyro-compass)
SPÖRER (A)
STEFAN (P)
STEVIN (M)
STIFEL (M)
STOKES (M/P)
TALBOT (I-calotype photographic process)
TAYLOR (M)
TELLER (P)
THALES (A/M)
TOWNES (I-maser)
WALLIS (I-'bouncing bomb')
WALTON (I-linoleum) (P)
WATSON (C)
WESSEL (M)
WIENER (M)
WILSON (P)
WÖHLER (C)
WRIGHT (I-aeroplane)
YUKAWA (P)

7

AUDUBON (B)
BABBAGE (M)
BANTING (C)
BARDEEN (I-transistor, with BRATTAIN & SHOCKLEY)
BATESON (C)
BATTANI (A)
BEHRING (C)
BELLAMY (B)
BERGIUS (C)

BISSELL (I-carpet sweeper)
BOYD-ORR (C)
BRAILLE (I-'reading' system for the blind)
BURBANK (B)
CARDANO (M)
CASSINI (A)
CELSIUS (A/P)
CHARLES (P)
CORRENS (B)
COULOMB (P)
CROOKES (P)
DAIMLER (I-car engine pioneer)
DE VRIES (B)
DICKSON (I-terylene, with WHINFIELD)
DOPPLER (P)
EASTMAN (I-roll-film)
EHRLICH (C)
EICHLER (B)
EUDOXUS (A)
FARADAY (C/I-dynamo)
FLEMING (C)
FOURIER (M/P)
FRESNEL (P)
GALILEO (A/M/P)
GALVANI (P)
GATLING (I-rapid-fire gun)
GILBERT (P)
GLIDDEN (I-barbed wire)
GODDARD (P)
HALDANE (C)
HERMITE (M)
HILBERT (M)
HUGGINS (A)
HUYGENS (A/M/P)
JANSSEN (A)
KENDALL (C)
KOROLEV (P)
KOZIREV (A)
LALANDE (A)
LAMARCK (B)
LAMBERT (A/M)

345

PEOPLE – SCIENTISTS

LANGLEY *(A)*
LANSTON *(I-monotype)*
LAPLACE *(A/M)*
LOCKYER *(A)*
LUMIÈRE *(I-cine-camera)*
LYSENKO *(C)*
MARCONI *(I-wireless)*
MAUCHLY *(I-electronic
    computer,
    with ECKERT)*
MAXWELL *(M/P)*
MESSIER *(A)*
MOISSAN *(C)*
MOSELEY *(P)*
MURDOCK *(I-gas
    lighting)*
NEILSON *(I-blast
    furnace)*
NEUMANN *(M)*
OERSTED *(P)*
PARSONS *(I-turbine
    steam-ship)*
PASTEUR *(C)*
PAULING *(C)*
PEARSON *(I-solar
    battery,
    with FULLER)*
POISSON *(M)*
POULSEN *(I-tape-
    recorder)*
PRANDTL *(P)*
PTOLEMY *(A/M)*
RÉAUMUR *(P)*
RIEMANN *(M)*
RÖNTGEN *(P)*
RUSSELL *(M)*
SANDAGE *(A)*
SCHEELE *(C)*
SCHMIDT *(A)*
SEABORG *(P)*
SEMENOV *(P)*
SHAPLEY *(A/P)*
SIEMENS *(P)*
STANLEY *(I-electric
    transformer)*
SWINTON *(I-tank)*

THENARD *(C)*
THOMSON *(P)*
VAVILOV *(B)*
WALLACE *(B)*
    (P)
WHEELER *(I-electric fan)*
WHITNEY *(I-cotton gin)*
WHITTLE *(I-jet engine)*
WILKINS *(C)*
ZIEGLER *(C)*
ZÖLLNER *(A/P)*

8

ÅNGSTRÖM *(A/P)*
APPLETON *(P)*
AVOGADRO *(P)*
BEAUFORT *(I-wind scale)*
BERLINER *(I-gramophone)*
BESSEMER *(I-steel converter)*
BIRDSEYE *(I-frozen food process)*
BRATTAIN *(I-transistor, with
    BARDEEN &
    SHOCKLEY)*
BREWSTER *(I-kaleidoscope)*
BROWNING *(I-automatic rifle)*
BUSHNELL *(I-submarine)*
CHADWICK *(P)*
CHERWELL *(P)*
CLAUSIUS *(P)*
CROMPTON *(I-spinning mule)*
DAGUERRE *(I-daguerrotype)*
DEDEKIND *(M)*
DE MOIVRE *(M)*
DE MORGAN *(M)*
EINSTEIN *(M/P)*
FOUCAULT *(I-gyroscope)*
FRANKLIN *(I-lightning conductor)*
GASSENDI *(P)*
GILLETTE *(I-safety razor)*
GOLDMARK *(I-LP record)*
GOODYEAR *(I-vulcanised rubber)*
GUERICKE *(P)*
HAMILTON *(M)*
HARRISON *(I-chronometer)*
HERSCHEL *(A)*

IPATIEFF *(P)*
JACQUARD *(I-Jacquard loom)*
KLAPROTH *(C)*
LAGRANGE *(A/M)*
LANGMUIR *(C)*
LAWRENCE *(P)*
LEGENDRE *(M)*
LEIBNITZ *(M)*
LEMAÎTRE *(A)*
LEONARDO *(C/M)*
LINNAEUS *(B)*
LONSDALE *(P)*
McMILLAN *(P)*
MERCATOR *(I-cylindrical world projection)*
MERSENNE *(M)*
MICHELIN *(I-car tyre)*
MULLIKEN *(C/P)*
NEWCOMEN *(I-steam engine)*
OLIPHANT *(P)*
OUGHTRED *(I-slide rule)*
PLANTSON *(I-dental plate)*
POINCARÉ *(M)*
PONCELET *(M)*
RAYLEIGH *(P)*
RHETICUS *(A/M)*
ROBINSON *(C)*
SABATIER *(C)*
SAKHAROV *(P)*
SHOCKLEY *(I-transistor, with BARDEEN & BRATTAIN)*
SHRAPNEL *(I-shrapnel shell)*
SIKORSKY *(I-practical helicopter)*
STIRLING *(M)*
STURGEON *(I-electro-magnet)*
THOMPSON *(P)*
TOMBAUGH *(A)*
VAN ALLEN *(P)*
VON BRAUN *(P)*
WATERMAN *(I-fountain pen)*
WEISMANN *(C)*
WOODWARD *(C)*
ZEPPELIN *(I-rigid airship)*
ZERNICKE *(P)*
ZWORYKIN *(I-standard television)*

9

ALBUZJANI *(M)*
ARKWRIGHT *(I-spinning-frame)*
ARMSTRONG *(I-hydraulic crane)*
ARRHENIUS *(C/P)*
BAEKELAND *(I-Bakelite)*
BECQUEREL *(P)*
BERNOULLI *(M)*
BERZELIUS *(C)*
BLANCHARD *(I-parachute)*
BRONOWSKI *(M)*
BURROUGHS *(I-commercial adding machine)*
CALLENDER *(P)*
CAROTHERS *(I-nylon)*
CAVENDISH *(P)*
CHERENKOV *(P)*
COCKCROFT *(P)*
COCKERELL *(I-hovercraft)*
CONDORCET *(M)*
CRONSTEDT *(C)*
D'ALEMBERT *(M)*
DAUBENTON *(B)*
DAVENPORT *(P)*
DESARGUES *(M)*
DESCARTES *(M)*
DIRICHLET *(M)*
EDDINGTON *(A/M)*
ENDLICHER *(B)*
FABRICIUS *(A)*
FESSENDEN *(I-radio-telephone)*
FIBONACCI *(M)*
FLAMSTEED *(A)*
GASCOIGNE *(I-micrometer)*
GAY-LUSSAC *(C/P)*
GUTENBERG *(I-printing press)*
HEAVISIDE *(P)*
HELMHOLTZ *(P)*
JOHANNSEN *(C)*
KRONECKER *(M)*
KURCHATOV *(P)*
LAVOISIER *(C)*
LECLANCHÉ *(C)*
LEVERRIER *(A)*
LOMONOSOV *(A)*

PEOPLE – SCIENTISTS

MACINTOSH *(I-waterproof clothing)*
MACLAURIN *(M)*
MACMILLAN *(I-bicycle)*
McCORMICK *(I-reaping machine)*
NICHOLSON *(C)*
OLDENBURG *(P)*
PELLETIER *(C)*
PICKERING *(A)*
PONIATOFF *(I-videotape recording)*
PRIESTLEY *(C)*
RAMANUJAN *(M)*
REMINGTON *(I-advanced typewriter)*
SCHLEIDEN *(B)*
STEINMETZ *(P)*
STEVENSON *(I-lighthouse light
systems)*
STROMEYER *(C)*
SYLVESTER *(M)*
VAUQUELIN *(C)*
WHINFIELD *(I-terylene, with
DICKSON)*
WHITEHEAD *(M)*
WHITWORTH *(I-Whitworth
screw-thread)*
ZSIGMONDY *(C)*

10

ANAXAGORAS *(M)*
ARCHIMEDES *(M)*
BARKHAUSEN *(P)*
BERNOULLIS *(M)*
CANNIZZARO *(C)*
CARTWRIGHT *(I-power loom)*
COPERNICUS *(A/M)*
DE LA CIERVA *(I-autogyro)*
DEMOCRITUS *(M)*
DIOPHANTUS *(M)*
FAHRENHEIT *(I-mercury thermometer)*
FARNSWORTH *(I-electrical television)*
FITZGERALD *(P)*
HARGREAVES *(I-spinning jenny)*
HARRINGTON *(I-water closet)*
HEISENBERG *(P)*
HIPPARCHUS *(A/M)*
INGENHOUSZ *(B/P)*

KOLMOGOROV *(M)*
LANCHESTER *(I-disc-brake)*
LIPPERSHEY *(I-telescope)*
MENDELEYEV *(C)*
NICOMACHUS *(M)*
PYTHAGORAS *(M)*
RUTHERFORD *(P)*
SENEFELDER *(I-lithography)*
SOMMERFELD *(P)*
STEPHENSON *(I-locomotive)*
SWAMMERDAM *(B)*
TORRICELLI *(I-barometer)*
TREVITHICK *(I-steam carriage)*
WATSON-WATT *(I-radar)*
WHEATSTONE *(P)*
WHITEHOUSE *(M)*

11

ARISTARCHUS *(A/M)*
BASKERVILLE *(I-advanced printing
type)*
GOLDSCHMIDT *(C)*
HERTZSPRUNG *(A)*
HINSHELWOOD *(C)*
KALASHNIKOV *(I-Kalashnikov rifle)*
LEEUWENHOEK *(P)*
LOBACHEVSKI *(M)*
MÈGE-MOURIÉS *(I-margarine)*
MONTGOLFIER *(I-air balloon)*
OMAR KHAYYÁM *(A/M)*
OPPENHEIMER *(P)*
SCHRÖDINGER *(P)*
TSIOLKOVSKY *(P)*
VAN DER WAALS *(P)*
WEIERSTRASS *(M)*

12

AL-KHOWARIZMI *(M)*
AMBARTSUMIAN *(A/P)*
ERATOSTHENES *(A/M)*
FRIESE-GREENE *(I-motion picture)*
MERGENTHALER *(I-linotype)*
SCHIAPERELLI *(A)*
WESTINGHOUSE *(I-air-brake)*

13

BRANDENBURGER *(l-cellophane)*
CHANDRASEKHAR *(A)*
REGIOMONTANUS *(A/M)*

14

GALILEO GALILEI *(A/M/P)*

15

LEONARDO DA VINCI *(C/M)*

PEOPLE

SPORTSPEOPLE – ATHLETES

3

COE *(12S)*
SLY *(8W)*

4

BAYI *(11F)*
BECK *(10V)*
BILE *(8A)*
BUDD *(8Z)*
CRAM *(9S)*
CRUZ *(11J)*
DRUT *(7G)*
DUNN *(9P)*
HILL *(8M)*
KOCH *(10M)*
KULA *(10D)*
KUTS *(12V)*
MAFE *(7A)*
RAND *(8M)*
RONO *(9H)*
ROWE *(10A)*
RYUN *(7J)*
WADE *(10K)*

5

BANKS *(11W)*
BEYER *(8U)*
BINNS *(10K)*
BLACK *(10C,*
10R)
BOARD *(12L)*
BOYLE *(12R)*
BOXER *(14C)*
CAPES *(10G)*
CLARK *(11E)*
COLON *(10M)*
CRABB *(10S)*
ERANG *(12M)*
FALCK *(14H)*
FELKE *(10P)*
FUCHS *(9R)*
FUDGE *(10P)*
HAYES *(8H)*
HINES *(8J)*
HYMAN *(12D)*
KEINO *(8K)*
KEOGH *(10L)*
KINCH *(8B)*
LANDY *(9J)*

LEWIS *(9C)*
LYNCH *(11A)*
MOSES *(7E)*
NURMI *(10P)*
OAKES *(9J)*
OBENG *(11E)*
OVETT *(10S)*
OWENS *(10J)*
PIRIE *(11G)*
PRESS *(10I,*
11T)
PRICE *(11B)*
REGIS *(9J)*
SHARP *(12C)*
SMITH *(11C,*
11T)
SNELL *(10P)*
STOCK *(10K)*
VIREN *(10L)*
WAITZ *(10G)*
WELLS *(10A)*

6

AOUITA *(10S)*

BEAMON *(9B)*
BIKILA *(11A)*
BORZOV *(13V)*
CLARKE *(9R)*
COATES *(12D)*
CONNER *(11K)*
DAVIES *(10L)*
DECKER
(see SLANEY)
FOSTER *(10G,*
13B)
HEMERY *(11D)*
HOOPER *(11B)*
JENNER *(11B)*
MARKIN *(12V)*
McKEAN *(9T)*
MENNEA *(12P)*
MILLER *(12L)*
MORROW *(14B)*
MURRAY *(12Y)*
NAYLOR *(10M)*
NEMETH *(12A)*
NIHILL *(10P)*
OERTER *(8A)*
OTTLEY *(11D)*
PACKER *(9A)*

349

PEOPLE – SPORTSPEOPLE – ATHLETES

PASCOE *(10A)*
PETERS *(10M)*
SEDYKH *(11Y)*
SLANEY *(10M)*
STRONG *(13S)*
TOOMEY *(10B)*
TULLOH *(11B)*
WALKER *(10J)*
WARDEN *(15C)*
WESSIG *(10G)*
YIFTER *(12M)*

7

ADE MAFE
AKABUSI *(12K)*
AKII-BUA *(11J)*
ASHFORD *(13E)*
BACKLEY *(12S)*
BECCALI *(12L)*
BEDFORD *(12D)*
BENNETT *(11T,*
  14A)
BIGNALL
 (see RAND)
BRAGINA *(14L)*
BRASHER *(12C)*
ED MOSES
ELLIOTT *(11H,*
  12P)
FOSBURY *(11D)*
GUNNELL *(12S)*
GUY DRUT
JACKSON *(12C)*
JENKINS *(12D)*
JIM RYUN
JOHNSON *(10B,*
  12R)
KINGDOM *(12R)*
LERWILL *(11A)*
LIDDELL *(11E)*
MATHIAS *(10B)*
PETKOVA *(12M)*
QUARRIE *(10D)*
RIDGEON *(10J)*

RUDOLPH *(12W)*
SANEYEV *(13V)*
SCHMIDT *(15W)*
SHORTER *(12F)*
SIMEONI *(11S)*
STECHER *(13R)*
TANCRED *(11B)*
ZATOPEK *(11E)*

8

ABDI BILE
ABRAHAMS *(14H)*
AL OERTER
BEV KINCH
BOB HAYES
CHATAWAY *(13C)*
CHRISTIE *(15L)*
CRAWFORD *(14H)*
IBBOTSON *(13D)*
JIM HINES
KIP KEINO
LANNAMAN *(13S)*
MARY RAND
MIKE HILL
NEHEMIAH *(15R)*
POLYAKOV
THOMPSON *(11D,*
  13D)
UDO BEYER
WENDY SLY
ZOLA BUDD

9

ANN PACKER
BANNISTER *(14R)*
BOB BEAMON
CARL LEWIS
HENRY RONO
JOHN LANDY
JOHN REGIS
JUDY OAKES
KAZANKINA

McFARLANE *(13M)*
MOORCROFT *(14D)*
PAULA DUNN
PUTTEMANS *(14E)*
RON CLARKE
RUTH FUCHS
SANDERSON *(14T)*
SLUPIANEK *(14I)*
SMALLWOOD *(14K)*
STEVE CRAM
SZEWINSKA *(14I)*
TKACHENKO
TOM McKEAN
VESELKOVA
WHITBREAD *(15F)*
WOHLHUTER *(13R)*
WOODERSON *(15S)*

10

ALAN PASCOE
ALLAN WELLS
ARTHUR ROWE
BEN JOHNSON
BILL TOOMEY
BOB MATHIAS
BRIGHTWELL
CHRIS BLACK
CIERPINSKI
DAINIS KULA
DON QUARRIE
GEOFF CAPES
GERD WESSIG
GREG FOSTER
GRETE WAITZ
HOYTE-SMITH
IRINA PRESS
JESSE OWENS
JOHN WALKER
JON RIDGEON
JUANTORENA
KATHY BINNS
KEITH STOCK
KIRSTY WADE
KONCHELLAH *(15B)*

LASSE VIREN
LINDA KEOGH
LYNN DAVIES
MALINOWSKI
MARK NAYLOR
MARIA COLON
MARITA KOCH
MARY PETERS
MARY SLANEY
PAAVO NURMI
PAULA FUDGE
PAUL NIHILL
PETER SNELL
PETRA FELKE
OLIZARENKO
ROGER BLACK
SAID AOUITA
STEVE CRABB
STEVE OVETT
VOLKER BECK

JOHN AKII-BUA
KEITH CONNER
KOZAKIEWICZ
PONOMARYEVA
RASHCHUPKIN
SARA SIMEONI
TAMARA PRESS
TODD BENNETT
TOMMIE SMITH
WESSINGHAGE
WILLIE BANKS
YURIY SEDYKH

13

BRENDAN FOSTER
CHRIS CHATAWAY
DALEY THOMPSON
DEREK IBBOTSON
EVELYN ASHFORD
MIKE McFARLANE
RENATE STECHER
RICK WOHLHUTER
SHIRLEY STRONG
SONIA LANNAMAN
VALERIY BORZOV
VIKTOR SANEYEV

12

ANGELA NEMETH
BLANKERS-KOEN
CAMERON SHARP
CHRIS BRASHER
COLIN JACKSON
DAVID BEDFORD
DAVID JENKINS
DENNIS COATES
DOROTHY HYMAN
FRANK SHORTER
KRISS AKABUSI
LILLIAN BOARD
LOUISE MILLER
LUIGI BECCALI
MARIA PETKOVA
MICHAEL ERANG
MIRUTS YIFTER
PETER ELLIOTT
PIETRO MENNEA
RAELENE BOYLE
RAFER JOHNSON
ROGER KINGDOM
SALLY GUNNELL
SEBASTIAN COE
STEVE BACKLEY
VIKTOR MARKIN
VLADIMIR KUTS
WILMA RUDOLPH
YVONNE MURRAY

14

AINSLEY BENNETT
BOBBY-JOE MORROW
CHRISTINA BOXER
DAVID MOORCROFT
EMILE PUTTEMANS
HAROLD ABRAHAMS
HASLEY CRAWFORD
HILDEGARD FALCK
ILONA SLUPIANEK
IRENA SZEWINSKA
KATHY SMALLWOOD
LUDMILA BRAGINA
ROGER BANNISTER
TESSA SANDERSON

11

ABEBE BIKILA
ALAN LERWILL
ANDREA LYNCH
BERWYN PRICE
BILL TANCRED
BRIAN HOOPER
BRISCO-HOOKS
BRUCE JENNER
BRUCE TULLOH
CALVIN SMITH
DAVID HEMERY
DAVID OTTLEY
DICK FOSBURY
DON THOMPSON
ELLERY CLARK
EMIL ZATOPEK
ERIC LIDDELL
ERNEST OBENG
FILBERT BAYI
GORDON PIRIE
HERB ELLIOTT
JOAQUIM CRUZ

15

BILLY KONCHELLAH
CHRISTINE WARDEN
FATIMA WHITBREAD
GRIFFITHS-JOYNER
LINFORD CHRISTIE
RENALDO NEHEMIAH
SYDNEY WOODERSON
WOLFGANG SCHMIDT

PEOPLE

SPORTSPEOPLE – BOXERS

= Alternative name

3

ALI (11M) *1

4

BAER (7M)
BENN (9N)
CLAY (11C) *1
CRUZ (9S)
DUNN (11R)
FARR (9T)
HART (10M)
HOPE (11M)
TATE (8J)
WATT (7W)

5

BRUNO (10F)
BURNS (10T)
CURRY (8D)
DURAN (12R)
ELLIS (10J)
GOMEZ (13W)
LOUIS (8J)
MAGRI (12C)
MARSH (10T)
MILLS (12F)
MOORE (11A)
ORTIZ (11C)
SMITH (10J)
TIGER (9D)
TYSON (9M)

6

BODELL (10J)
BUGNER (9J)

CONTEH (10J)
COOPER (11H)
DOWNES (11T)
GRAHAM (11H)
HAGLER (12M)
HEARNS (12T)
HOLMES (11L)
KAYLOR (10M)
LISTON (11S)
LONDON (10J, 11B)
MINTER (10A)
NELSON (12A)
NORTON (9K)
SIBSON (10T)
SPINKS (10L, 11T, 13M)
TUNNEY (10G)
TURPIN (14R)
WALKER (11B)
WEAVER (10M)

7

ANDRIES (13D)
BENITEZ (14W)
BERBICK (13T)
CARNERA (12P)
CHARLES (13E)
COCKELL (10D)
COETZEE (13G)
CORBETT (12J)
COWDELL (10P)
DEMPSEY (11J)
DOUGLAS (13B)
ERSKINE (10J)
FOREMAN (13G)

FRAZIER (10J)
GARDNER (12J)
JIM WATT
JOHNSON (11J, 13M)
LEONARD (15S)
MAX BAER
McGOWAN (13W)
NAPOLES (11J)
SHARKEY (11J)
STRACEY (12J)
TERRELL (12E)
WALCOTT (10J)
WILLARD (11J)

8

BRADDOCK (13J)
BUCHANAN (11K)
DON CURRY
FINNEGAN (13C)
JEFFRIES (13J)
JOE LOUIS
JOHN TATE
MARCIANO (13R)
McGUIGAN (13B)
PALOMINO (14C)
ROBINSON
SULLIVAN (12J)
WINSTONE (14H)
WOODCOCK (13B)

9

DICK TIGER
HOLYFIELD
HONEYGHAN (14L)

JOE BUGNER
JOHANNSON
KEN NORTON
McALINDEN (14D)
MIKE TYSON
NIGEL BENN
PATTERSON (14F)
SCHMELING (12M)
STEVE CRUZ
TOMMY FARR

10

ALAN MINTER
CARPENTIER
DON COCKELL
FRANK BRUNO
GENE TUNNEY
JACK BODELL
JACK LONDON
JAMES SMITH
JIMMY ELLIS
JOE ERSKINE
JOE FRAZIER
JOE WALCOTT
JOHN CONTEH
LEON SPINKS
MARK KAYLOR
MARVIN HART
MIKE WEAVER
PAT COWDELL
TERRY MARSH
TOMMY BURNS
TONY SIBSON

11

ARCHIE MOORE
BILLY WALKER

BRIAN LONDON
CARLOS ORTIZ
CASSIUS CLAY *1
FITZSIMMONS (14B)
HENRY COOPER
HEROL GRAHAM
JACK DEMPSEY
JACK JOHNSON
JACK SHARKEY
JESS WILLARD
JOSÉ NAPOLES
KEN BUCHANAN
LARRY HOLMES
MAURICE HOPE
MUHAMMAD ALI *1
RICHARD DUNN
SONNY LISTON
TERRY DOWNES
TERRY SPINKS
WITHERSPOON (14T)

CHARLIE MAGRI
ERNIE TERRELL
FREDDIE MILLS
JAMES CORBETT
JOHN H STRACEY
JOHN L GARDNER
JOHN SULLIVAN
MARVIN HAGLER
MAX SCHMELING
PRIMO CARNERA
ROBERTO DURAN
THOMAS HEARNS

JAMES JEFFRIES
MARVIN JOHNSON
MICHAEL SPINKS
ROCKY MARCIANO
TREVOR BERBICK
WALTER McGOWAN
WILFREDO GOMEZ

14

BOB FITZSIMMONS
CARLOS PALOMINO
DANNY McALINDEN
FLOYD PATTERSON
HOWARD WINSTONE
LLOYD HONEYGHAN
RANDOLPH TURPIN
TIM WITHERSPOON
WILFRED BENITEZ

13

BARRY McGUIGAN
BRUCE WOODCOCK
BUSTER DOUGLAS
CHRIS FINNEGAN
DENNIS ANDRIES
EZZARD CHARLES
GEORGE FOREMAN
GERRIE COETZEE
JAMES BRADDOCK

12

AZUMAH NELSON

15

SUGAR RAY LEONARD

PEOPLE

SPORTSPEOPLE – CRICKETERS

All played for England except: (A) = Australia   (I) = India   (NZ) = New Zealand
(P) = Pakistan   (SA) = South Africa   (WI) = West Indies

3

FRY (5C)
MAY (8P)
OLD (8C)

4

AMES (10L)
BOON (9D-A)
COOK (8N)

HALL (7W-WI)
HICK (10G)
LAMB (9A)
LOCK (8T)
MEAD (6C)

NASH (11M)
RICE (9C-SA)
ROSE (9B)
SNOW (8J)
TATE (11M)

VOCE (8B)
WOOD (9B,
10G-A)

PEOPLE – SPORTSPEOPLE – CRICKETERS

5

AGNEW *(9J)*
ALLEN *(10G)*
AMISS *(10D)*
ATHEY *(9B)*
BROAD *(10C)*
CAPEL *(10D)*
CB FRY
CLOSE *(10B)*
CROWE *(11M-NZ)*
DUJON *(13G-WI)*
EVANS *(12G)*
GIBBS *(10L-WI)*
GOOCH *(11G)*
GOWER *(10D)*
GRACE *(7W)*
GRIEG *(9T)*
GROUT *(10W-A)*
HIGGS *(8K)*
HOBBS *(9J)*
JESTY *(11T)*
JONES *(9D-A)*
KNOTT *(9A)*
LAKER *(8J)*
LAWRY *(9B-A)*
LEVER *(9J)*
LEWIS *(9T, 10C)*
LLOYD *(10C-WI)*
LOGIE *(8G-WI)*
LYNCH *(10M-WI)*
MARKS *(8V)*
MARSH *(11G, 11R-A)*
MOXON *(11M)*
PARKS *(8J)*
ROOPE *(11G)*
SLACK *(9W)*
SMALL *(14G)*
SMITH *(9M, 10R)*
TYSON *(10F)*
WALSH *(13C-WI)*
WAUGH *(10S-A)*

6

ALLOTT *(10P)*
ARNOLD *(11G)*
BAILEY *(12T)*
BEDSER *(10A, 10E)*
BENAUD *(12R-A)*
BISHOP *(9I-WI)*
BORDER *(11A-A)*
BOTHAM *(9I)*
CONNER *(14C-WI)*
COWANS *(12N)*
CP MEAD
DANIEL *(11W-WI)*
DEXTER *(9T)*
DILLEY *(12G)*
EDRICH *(10B, 10J)*
FENDER *(11P)*
FOSTER *(10N)*
FOWLER *(12G)*
FRASER *(11A)*
GARNER *(10J-WI)*
HADLEE *(13R-NZ)*
HARVEY *(10N-A)*
HAYNES *(13D-WI)*
HUGHES *(10M-A)*
HUTTON *(9L)*
INSOLE *(10D)*
KANHAI *(11R-WI)*
LAWSON *(11G-A)*
LILLIE *(12D-A)*
LOADER *(11P)*
MILLER *(11K-A)*
ONTONG *(12R-SA)*
PARKER *(10P)*
PULLAR *(11G)*
RADLEY *(11C-NZ)*
RHODES *(13W)*
SELVEY *(10M)*
SOBERS *(11G-WI)*
TAVARÉ *(11C)*
TAYLOR *(9B)*
TITMUS *(10F)*
VERITY *(12H)*

WARNER *(12P)*
WILLEY *(11P)*
WILLIS *(9B)*

7

AMBROSE *(14C-WI)*
ARAN LAL *(I)*
ASIF DIN *(I)*
BARNETT *(10K)*
BOYCOTT *(12G)*
BRADMAN *(10D-A)*
BUTCHER *(13R-WI)*
CLINTON *(14G)*
COMPTON *(12D)*
CONGDON *(10B-NZ)*
COWDREY *(12C)*
DENNESS *(11M)*
DOWNTON *(11P)*
EDMONDS *(11P)*
ELLISON *(14R)*
EMBUREY *(11J)*
GATTING *(11M)*
GIFFORD *(13N)*
HAMMOND *(12W)*
HENDREN *(12P)*
HOLDING *(14M-WI)*
JACKMAN *(12R)*
JARDINE *(14D)*
LARKINS *(12W)*
LARWOOD *(13H)*
MALCOLM *(12D)*
MILBURN *(12C)*
NEWPORT *(11P)*
PARFITT *(12P)*
PRINGLE *(12D)*
PROCTER *(11M-SA)*
RANDALL *(12D)*
ROBERTS *(11A-WI)*
ROEBUCK *(12P)*
RUSSELL *(11J)*
STATHAM *(12B)*
STEWART *(11A, 11M)*
THOMSON *(11J-A)*

TRUEMAN *(11F)*
WALCOTT *(12C-WI)*
WES HALL *(WI)*
WG GRACE
WG WOOLLEY *(12F)*
WOOLMER *(10B)*
WORRELL *(12F-WI)*
YARDLEY *(13N)*

8

ALDERMAN *(13T-A)*
ATHERTON *(12M)*
BAIRSTOW *(13D)*
BAPTISTE *(14E-WI)*
BENJAMIN *(WI)*
BILL VOCE
BREARLEY *(12M)*
CHAPPELL *(11I-A, 12G-A)*
CHRIS OLD
ENGINEER *(14F-I)*
FLETCHER *(13K)*
GAVASKAR *(13S-I)*
GRAVENEY *(11T, 13D)*
GUS LOGIE *(WI)*
HEMMINGS *(13E)*
JIM LAKER
JIM PARKS
JOHN SNOW
KAPIL DEV *(I)*
KEN HIGGS
LINDWALL *(11R-A)*
MADAN LAL *(I)*
MARSHALL *(15M-WI)*
NICK COOK
PETER MAY
PONSFORD *(15W-A)*
RICHARDS *(11V-WI, 12J, 13B-SA)*
ROBINSON *(11T)*
SHEPHERD *(12J)*

SHEPPARD *(13D)*
SUBBA ROW *(13R-I)*
SURRIDGE *(14S)*
TONY LOCK
VIC MARKS

9

ALAN KNOTT
ALLAN LAMB
ASIF IQBAL *(P)*
BARRY WOOD
BILL ATHEY
BILL LAWRY *(A)*
BOB TAYLOR
BOB WILLIS
BRIAN ROSE
CLIVE RICE *(SA)*
DAVID BOON *(A)*
DEAN JONES *(A)*
DeFREITAS
D'OLIVEIRA *(14B)*
GREENIDGE *(15G-WI)*
GRIFFITHS *(WI)*
IAN BISHOP *(WI)*
IAN BOTHAM
IMRAN KHAN *(P)*
JACK HOBBS
JOHN AGNEW
JOHN LEVER
LEN HUTTON
LUCKHURST *(14B)*
MIKE SMITH
PATTERSON *(WI)*
SAINSBURY *(14P)*
SRIKKANTH *(I)*
SUTCLIFFE
TED DEXTER
TENDULKAR *(15S-I)*
TONY GREIG
TONY LEWIS
UNDERWOOD *(14D)*
WASIM BARI *(P)*
WILF SLACK

10

ABDUL QADIR *(P)*
ALEC BEDSER
AZHARUDDIN *(I)*
BARRINGTON *(13K)*
BEV CONGDON *(NZ)*
BILL EDRICH
BISHEN BEDI *(I)*
BOB WOOLMER
BRIAN CLOSE
CHRIS BROAD
CHRIS LEWIS
CLIVE LLOYD *(WI)*
DAVID CAPEL
DAVID GOWER
DENIS AMISS
DON BRADMAN *(A)*
DOUG INSOLE
ERIC BEDSER
FRANK TYSON
FRED TITMUS
GRAEME HICK
GRAHAM WOOD *(A)*
GREATBATCH *(14M-NZ)*
GUBBY ALLEN
JOEL GARNER
JOHN EDRICH
KIM BARNETT
LANCE GIBBS *(WI)*
LESLIE AMES
MERV HUGHES *(A)*
MIKE SELVEY
MONTE LYNCH *(WI)*
NEIL FOSTER
NEIL HARVEY *(A)*
PAUL ALLOTT
PAUL PARKER
RICHARDSON *(WI)*
ROBIN SMITH
SHACKLETON *(15D)*
STEVE WAUGH *(A)*
VENGSARKAR *(15D-I)*
WALLY GROUT *(A)*
WASIM AKRAM *(P)*

PEOPLE – SPORTSPEOPLE – CRICKETERS

11

ALLAN BORDER *(A)*
ANDY ROBERTS *(WI)*
ANGUS FRASER
CHRIS TAVARÉ
CLIVE RADLEY *(NZ)*
CONSTANTINE *(WI)*
FAIRBROTHER *(15N)*
FRED TRUEMAN
GARRY SOBERS *(WI)*
GEOFF ARNOLD
GEOFF LAWSON *(A)*
GEOFF PULLAR
GRAHAM GOOCH
GRAHAM MARSH
GRAHAM ROOPE
IAN CHAPPELL *(A)*
ILLINGWORTH *(14R)*
JACK RUSSELL
JEFF THOMSON *(A)*
JOHN EMBUREY
KEITH MILLER *(A)*
MALCOLM NASH
MARTIN CROWE *(NZ)*
MARTIN MOXON
MAURICE TATE
MIKE DENNESS
MIKE GATTING
MIKE PROCTER *(SA)*
PAUL DOWNTON
PERCY FENDER
PETER LOADER
PETER WILLEY
PHIL EDMONDS
PHIL NEWPORT
RAVI SHASTRI *(I)*
RAY LINDWALL *(A)*
RODNEY MARSH *(A)*
ROHAN KANHAI *(WI)*
TIM ROBINSON
TOM GRAVENEY
TREVOR JESTY
VIV RICHARDS *(WI)*
WAYNE DANIEL *(WI)*
YOUNIS AHMED *(P)*

ZAHEER ABBAS *(P)*

12

BRIAN STATHAM
CHETAN SHARMA *(I)*
CHRIS COWDREY
CLIVE WALCOTT *(WI)*
COLIN COWDREY
COLIN MILBURN
DENIS COMPTON
DENNIS LILLIE *(A)*
DEREK RANDALL
DEREK PRINGLE
DEVON MALCOLM
FRANK WOOLLEY
FRANK WORRELL *(WI)*
GEOFF BOYCOTT
GODFREY EVANS
GRAEME FOWLER
GRAHAM DILLEY
GREG CHAPPELL *(A)*
HEDLEY VERITY
INTIKHAB ALAM *(P)*
JACK RICHARDS
JAVED MIANDAD *(P)*
JOHN SHEPHERD
KALLICHARRAN *(WI)*
MIKE ATHERTON
MIKE BREARLEY
NORMAN COWANS
PATSY HENDREN
PELHAM WARNER
PETER PARFITT
PETER ROEBUCK
RICHIE BENAUD *(A)*
ROBIN JACKMAN
RODNEY ONTONG *(SA)*
SARFRAZ NAWAZ *(P)*
TREVOR BAILEY
WALLY HAMMOND
WAYNE LARKINS

13

BARRY RICHARDS *(SA)*

CHANDRASEKHAR *(I)*
COURTNEY WALSH *(WI)*
DAVID BAIRSTOW
DAVID GRAVENEY
DAVID SHEPPARD
DESMOND HAYNES *(WI)*
EDDIE HEMMINGS
GEOFFREY DUJON *(WI)*
HANIF MOHAMMED *(P)*
HAROLD LARWOOD
KEITH FLETCHER
KEN BARRINGTON
MUDASSAR NASAR *(P)*
NORMAN GIFFORD
NORMAN YARDLEY
RAMAN SUBBA ROW *(I)*
RICHARD HADLEE *(NZ)*
ROLAND BUTCHER *(WI)*
SADIQ MOHAMMAD *(P)*
SUNIL GAVASKAR *(I)*
TERRY ALDERMAN
WILFRED RHODES

14

BASIL D'OLIVEIRA
BRIAN LUCKHURST
CARDIGAN CONNER *(WI)*
CURTLEY AMBROSE *(WI)*
DEREK UNDERWOOD
DOUGLAS JARDINE
ELDINE BAPTISTE *(WI)*
FAROUK ENGINEER *(I)*
GLADSTONE SMALL
GRAHAME CLINTON
MARK GREATBATCH *(NZ)*
MICHAEL HOLDING *(WI)*
PETER SAINSBURY
RAY ILLINGWORTH
RICHARD ELLISON
STUART SURRIDGE

15

DEREK SHACKLETON

DILIP VENGSARKAR *(I)*
GORDON GREENIDGE *(WI)*
MALCOLM MARSHALL *(WI)*

NEIL FAIRBROTHER
SACHIN TENDULKAR *(I)*
WILLIAM PONSFORD *(A)*

PEOPLE

SPORTSPEOPLE – FOOTBALLERS

All from British Isles except: (E) = European   (SA) = South American

3

LAW *(8D)*
LEE *(8S,*
   10F)
SIX *(9D-E)*
URE *(6I)*

4

BALL *(8A)*
BELL *(9C)*
BEST *(10G)*
BOND *(8J)*
CARR *(10W)*
DEAN *(9D)*
DIDI *(SA)*
GRAY *(9E)*
HILL *(9J)*
HOWE *(7D)*
HUNT *(9R)*
JACK *(9D)*
KOPA *(11R-E)*
NEAL *(8P)*
PELE *(SA)*
REES *(10R)*

REID *(9P)*
RICE *(7P)*
RUSH *(7I)*
SWAN *(9P)*
TODD *(9C)*
VAVA *(SA)*
WARK *(8J)*
WEBB *(8N)*
ZOFF *(8D-E)*

5

ALLEN *(9C,*
   11R)
ASTLE *(9J)*
BAKER *(8J)*
BANKS *(11G)*
BONDS *(10B)*
BRADY *(9L)*
BURNS *(10K)*
BYRNE *(10R)*
COHEN *(11G)*
DIXON *(8L,*
   10K)
DRAKE *(8T)*
ELDER *(9A)*

GILES *(11J)*
HURST *(10G)*
JAMES *(9A,*
   13L)
JONES *(10C)*
MARSH *(11R)*
MILLS *(9M)*
MOORE *(10B)*
NEILL *(10T)*
NURSE *(8M)*
PAINE *(10T)*
REGIS *(12C)*
REVIE *(8D)*
RIOCH *(10B)*
SMITH *(10B,*
   10T)
SWIFT *(10F)*
VILLA *(10R-SA)*
WHITE *(9J)*
WOODS *(10C)*
YOUNG *(11G)*

6

A'COURT *(10A)*
ALBERT *(13F-E)*

BARESI *(12F-E)*
BARNES *(10J)*
BASTIN *(11C)*
BAXTER *(9J)*
BONIEK *(14Z-E)*
BOWLES *(10S)*
BUCHAN *(12M,*
   13C)
CARTER *(11R)*
CLARKE *(11A)*
CLOUGH *(11B,*
   11N)
CROOKS *(11G)*
CRUYFF *(12J-E)*
CULLIS *(10S)*
CURRIE *(10T)*
DOUGAN *(11D)*
FINNEY *(9T)*
GEORGE *(13C)*
GULLIT *(10R-E)*
HARRIS *(9R)*
HAYNES *(12J)*
HODDLE *(11G)*
HUGHES *(11E)*
HUNTER *(12N)*
IAN URE
JORDAN *(9J)*

PEOPLE – SPORTSPEOPLE – FOOTBALLERS

KEEGAN *(11K)*
KELSEY *(10J)*
LABONE *(11B)*
LAWTON *(11T)*
MACARI *(9L)*
MACKAY *(10D)*
MARTIN *(11A)*
MEDWIN *(11T)*
MERCER *(9J)*
MÜLLER *(10G-E)*
NORMAN *(13M)*
O'LEARY *(11D)*
O'NEILL *(12M)*
OSGOOD *(11P)*
PARKES *(10P)*
PEARCE *(12S)*
PETERS *(12M)*
PUSKAS *(12F-E)*
RAMSEY *(9A)*
RATTIN *(SA)*
RIVERA *(12G-E)*
ROBSON *(11B)*
SANSOM *(11K)*
SEAMAN *(11D)*
SPRAKE *(10G)*
STILES *(11N)*
ST JOHN *(9I)*
SUAREZ *(10L-E)*
TAYLOR *(11T)*
VOLLER *(10R-E)*
WADDLE *(11C)*
WATSON *(10D)*
WILSON *(9B,
9R)*
WRIGHT *(11B)*
YASHIN *(9L-E)*
YORATH *(11T)*

7

ADAMSON *(12J)*
ARDILES *(12O-SA)*
BARTRAM *(10S)*
BENTLEY *(10R)*
BINGHAM *(12B)*

BLOKHIN *(11O-E)*
BONETTI *(12P)*
BREMNER *(12B)*
BUTCHER *(12T)*
CHANNON *(11M)*
CHARLES *(11J)*
CHIVERS *(13M)*
COPPELL *(12S)*
DON HOWE
DOUGLAS *(12B)*
EASTHAM *(13G)*
EDWARDS *(13D)*
ENGLAND *(11M)*
EUSEBIO *(E)*
FASHANU *(11J)*
FLOWERS *(10R)*
FRANCIS *(12G,
13T)*
GEMMILL *(13A)*
GENTILE *(14C-E)*
GREAVES *(12J)*
HAPGOOD *(12E)*
HATELEY *(11M)*
IAN RUSH
JEZZARD *(14B)*
KENDALL *(13H)*
KENNEDY *(10R)*
KNOWLES *(12C)*
LAUDRUP *(14M-E)*
LIDDELL *(12B)*
LINEKER *(11G)*
LORIMER *(12P)*
MARINER *(11P)*
MANNION *(11W)*
McILROY *(12J,
12S)*
MERRICK *(10G)*
MILBURN *(13J)*
MULLERY *(11A)*
NICHOLL *(12C)*
PAT RICE
PLATINI *(13M-E)*
POINTER *(10R)*
QUIXALL *(13A)*
RADFORD *(11J)*
SCOULAR *(12J)*

SHANKLY *(11B)*
SHILTON *(12P)*
SOUNESS *(13G)*
TOSHACK *(11J)*
WILKINS *(10R)*

8

ALAN BALL
ANDERSON *(11V)*
ARMFIELD *(13J)*
BROOKING *(14T)*
CANTWELL *(12N)*
CHARLTON *(12J,
13B)*
CLEMENCE *(11R)*
DALGLISH *(13K)*
DENIS LAW
DINO ZOFF *(E)*
DON REVIE
HARTFORD *(11A)*
JENNINGS *(11P)*
JOE BAKER
JOHN BOND
JOHNSTON *(10M)*
JOHN WARK
LEE DIXON
MARADONA *(13D-SA)*
MATTHEWS *(15S)*
MEL NURSE
MEREDITH *(13B)*
NEIL WEBB
NICHOLAS *(13P,
15C)*
PERRYMAN *(13S)*
PHIL NEAL
RIVELINO *(SA)*
SAMMY LEE
SIMONSEN *(13A-E)*
SOUTHALL *(15N)*
STRACHAN *(14G)*
TED DRAKE
THOMPSON *(12P)*
VENABLES *(13T)*
WOODCOCK *(12T)*

ALEX ELDER
ALEX JAMES
ALF RAMSEY
ALLCHURCH *(13I)*
BEARDSLEY *(14P)*
BOB WILSON
BROADBENT *(14P)*
CALLAGHAN *(12I)*
COLIN BELL
COLIN TODD
DAVID JACK
DICKINSON *(14J)*
DIDIER SIX *(E)*
DI STEFANO *(E)*
DITCHBURN *(12T)*
DIXIE DEAN
EDDIE GRAY
GASCOIGNE *(13P)*
IAN ST JOHN
JEFF ASTLE
JOE JORDAN
JOE MERCER
JIM BAXTER
JIMMY HILL
JOHNSTONE *(15W)*
JOHN WHITE
LEV YASHIN *(E)*
LIAM BRADY
LOFTHOUSE *(12N)*
LOU MACARI
MACDONALD
McDERMOTT *(14T)*
McFARLAND *(12R)*
McLINTOCK *(14F)*
MICK MILLS
MORTENSEN *(13S)*
PETER REID
PETER SWAN
RAY WILSON
ROGER HUNT
RON HARRIS
SCHILLACI *(E)*
SPRINGETT *(12R)*
STAPLETON *(14F)*

SUMMERBEE *(13M)*
TOM FINNEY
VAN BASTEN *(14M-E)*
WHITESIDE *(15N)*

ALAN A'COURT
BILLY BONDS
BOBBY MOORE
BOBBY SMITH
BRUCE RIOCH
CHRIS WOODS
CLIFF JONES
CLIVE ALLEN
DAVE MACKAY
DAVE WATSON
FRANCIS LEE
FRANK SWIFT
GARY SPRAKE
GEOFF HURST
GEORGE BEST
GERD MÜLLER *(E)*
GIL MERRICK
GROBBELAAR *(15B)*
HUTCHINSON *(15T)*
JACK KELSEY
JOHN BARNES
KENNY BURNS
KERRY DIXON
LUIS SUAREZ *(E)*
MO JOHNSTON
PHIL PARKES
RAY KENNEDY
RAY POINTER
RAY WILKINS
RICKY VILLA *(SA)*
ROGER BYRNE
RON FLOWERS
RONNIE REES
ROY BENTLEY
RUDI VOLLER *(E)*
RUMMENIGGE *(E)*
RUUD GULLIT
SAM BARTRAM

SHACKLETON *(13L)*
STAN BOWLES
STAN CULLIS
TERRY NEILL
TERRY PAINE
TOMMY SMITH
TONY CURRIE
WILLIE CARR

ALAN MULLERY
ALLAN CLARKE
ALVIN MARTIN
ASA HARTFORD
BECKENBAUER *(E)*
BILL SHANKLY
BILLY WRIGHT
BOBBY ROBSON
BRIAN CLOUGH
BRIAN LABONE
BRYAN ROBSON
CHRIS WADDLE
CLIFF BASTIN
DAVID O'LEARY
DAVID SEAMAN
DEREK DOUGAN
EMLYN HUGHES
GARTH CROOKS
GARY LINEKER
GEORGE COHEN
GEORGE YOUNG
GLENN HODDLE
GORDON BANKS
JOHN CHARLES
JOHN FASHANU
JOHNNY GILES
JOHN RADFORD
JOHN TOSHACK
KENNY SANSOM
KEVIN KEEGAN
MARK HATELEY
MIKE CHANNON
MIKE ENGLAND
NIGEL CLOUGH
NOBBY STILES

PEOPLE – SPORTSPEOPLE – FOOTBALLERS

OLEG BLOKHIN *(E)*
PAT JENNINGS
PAUL MARINER
PETER OSGOOD
RAICH CARTER
RAY CLEMENCE
RAYMOND KOPA
RODNEY MARSH
RONNIE ALLEN
TERRY MEDWIN
TERRY YORATH
TOMMY LAWTON
TOMMY TAYLOR
VIV ANDERSON
WILF MANNION

12

BILLY BINGHAM
BILLY BREMNER
BILLY LIDDELL
BLANCHFLOWER
BRYAN DOUGLAS
CHRIS NICHOLL
CYRIL KNOWLES
CYRILLE REGIS
EDDIE HAPGOOD
FERENC PUSKAS *(E)*
FRANCO BARESI *(E)*
GERRY FRANCIS
GIANNI RIVERA *(E)*
IAN CALLAGHAN
JACK CHARLTON
JIMMY ADAMSON
JIMMY GREAVES
JIMMY McILROY
JIMMY SCOULAR
JOHANN CRUYFF *(E)*

JOHNNY HAYNES
MARTIN BUCHAN
MARTIN O'NEILL
MARTIN PETERS
NAT LOFTHOUSE
NOEL CANTWELL
NORMAN HUNTER
OSSIE ARDILES *(SA)*
PETER BONETTI
PETER LORIMER
PETER SHILTON
PHIL THOMPSON
RON SPRINGETT
ROY McFARLAND
SAMMY McILROY
STEVE COPPELL
STUART PEARCE
TED DITCHBURN
TERRY BUTCHER
TONY WOODCOCK

13

ALBERT QUIXALL
ALLAN SIMONSEN *(E)*
ARCHIE GEMMILL
BILLY MEREDITH
BOBBY CHARLTON
CHARLIE BUCHAN
CHARLIE GEORGE
DIEGO MARADONA *(SA)*
DUNCAN EDWARDS
FLORIAN ALBERT *(E)*
GEORGE EASTHAM
GRAEME SOUNESS
HOWARD KENDALL
IVOR ALLCHURCH
JACKIE MILBURN
JIMMY ARMFIELD

KENNY DALGLISH
LEIGHTON JAMES
LEN SHACKELTON
MARTIN CHIVERS
MAURICE NORMAN
MICHEL PLATINI *(E)*
MIKE SUMMERBEE
PAUL GASCOIGNE
PETER NICHOLAS
STAN MORTENSEN
STEVE PERRYMAN
TERRY VENABLES
TREVOR FRANCIS

14

BEDFORD JEZZARD
CLAUDIO GENTILE *(E)*
FRANK McLINTOCK
FRANK STAPLETON
GORDON STRACHAN
JIMMY DICKINSON
MARCO VAN BASTEN *(E)*
MICHAEL LAUDRUP *(E)*
PETER BEARDSLEY
PETER BROADBENT
TERRY McDERMOTT
TREVOR BROOKING
ZBIGNIEV BONIEK *(E)*

15

BRUCE GROBBELAAR
CHARLIE NICHOLAS
NEVILLE SOUTHALL
NORMAN WHITESIDE
STANLEY MATTHEWS
TOMMY HUTCHINSON
WILLIE JOHNSTONE

CRITICAL

PEOPLE

SPORTSPEOPLE – GENERAL

(B) = Badminton   (BA) = Baseball   (BO) = Bowls   (C) = Cycling
(D) = Darts   (G) = Gymnastics   (H) = Hockey
(I) = Ice-skating/speed-skating   (J) = Judo   (MP) = Modern Pentathlon
(R) = Rowing   (RS) = Rifle-shooting   (S) = Swimming/diving
(SK) = Skiing   (SN) = Snooker/billiards   (SQ) = Squash
(TT) = Table-tennis

3

DAY *(7P-TT)*
FOX *(6J-MP)*
KIM *(8N-G)*
LEE *(9S-SN)*
MEO *(7T-SN)*
RAE *(9J-SN)*

4

BELL *(10M-SK)*
BOND *(9N-SN)*
COBB *(6T-BA)*
DEAN *(15C-I)*
FORD *(11B-I)*
HUNT *(9G-SQ)*
LOWE *(8J-D)*
REES *(12L-D)*
ROSE *(8P-BA)*
ROWE *(9D-TT,*
   12R-TT)
RUTH *(8B-BA)*
RYAN *(9N-BA)*
VANA *(11B-TT)*
WITT *(12K-I)*
WOOD *(10W-BO)*

5

AARON *(9H-BA)*
ADAMA *(9N-J)*
BARNA *(11V-TT)*
BLACK *(8I-S)*
CROFT *(9J-S)*
CURRY *(9J-I)*
DANDO *(12S-G)*
DAVIS *(8J-SN,*
   9F-SN,
   10S-SN)
DEVOY *(10S-SQ)*
DRAGO *(9T-SN)*
ENDER *(13K-S)*
GILKS *(12G-B)*
GOULD *(10S-S)*
HENIE *(10S-I)*
JACKS *(10B-J)*
JONES *(8A-TT)*
KERLY *(9S-H)*
KILLY *(15J-SK)*
LEACH *(11J-TT)*
LEWIS *(11H-S)*
MAHRE *(9P-SK)*
PERRY *(9F-TT,*
   9N-B)
PREAN *(9C-TT)*
ROCHE *(12S-C)*
SPITZ *(9M-S)*
TOMBA *(12A-SK)*
VIRGO *(9J-SN)*
WHITE *(10J-SN)*

6

BARNES *(13C-TT)*
BRIGGS *(11K-J)*
BRYANT *(11D-BO)*
BURTON *(11B-C)*
CONWAY *(12J-I)*
COOPER *(13M-RS)*
DAVIES *(13S-S)*
DELLER *(11K-D)*
FOULDS *(10N-SN)*
FRASER *(10D-S)*
GEORGE *(11B-D)*
GERRIG *(9L-BA)*
HARRIS *(9R-C)*
HAYDON
  (see JONES)
HEIDEN *(10E-I)*
HENDRY *(13S-SN)*
JIM FOX *(MP)*
KORBUT *(10O-G)*
LEMOND *(10G-C)*
MERCKX *(11E-C)*
PARKER *(10J-TT)*
PHELPS *(11B-S)*
PORTER *(10H-C)*
PULMAN *(10J-SN)*
TAYLOR *(12D-SN)*
THORNE *(12W-SN)*
TOWLER *(11D-I)*
TY COBB *(BA)*
WILKIE *(11D-S)*
WILSON *(11J-D)*

7

ALLCOCK *(11T-BO)*
BRISTOW *(11E-D)*
COUSINS *(12R-I)*
DOUGLAS *(14D-TT)*
EDWARDS *(12E-SK)*
FLOWERS *(14M-D)*
GOODHEW *(13D-S)*
GRINHAM *(11J-S)*
HALLETT *(11M-SN)*
HARTONO *(11R-B)*
HIGGINS *(11A-SN)*
HINAULT *(14B-C)*
JACKSON *(13D-I)*
JOHNSON *(10J-SN)*
KLAMMER *(12F-SK)*
KNOWLES *(11T-SN)*
LINDRUM *(13H-SN,*
   13W-SN)
PARROTT *(11J-SN)*
PAUL DAY *(TT)*
REARDON *(10R-SN)*
RODNINA *(12I-SK)*
SIMPSON *(12T-C)*
SPENCER *(11J-SN)*
STEVENS *(11K-SN)*
THOMSON *(11A-BO)*
TONY MEO *(SN)*
TORVILL *(12J-I)*
WATTANA *(12J-SN)*
WEBSTER *(11J-B)*
ZEITSEV *(I)*

361

PEOPLE – SPORTSPEOPLE – GENERAL

8

ANDERSEN *(13G-S)*
ANDERSON *(11B-D)*
ANN JONES *(TT)*
ANQUETIL *(15J-C)*
BABE RUTH *(BA)*
BERGMANN *(15R-TT)*
CHAPERON *(11B-SN)*
CHARLTON *(13E-SN)*
COMANECI *(13N-G)*
DiMAGGIO *(11J-BA)*
IAN BLACK *(S)*
JOE DAVIS *(S)*
JOHN LOWE *(D)*
LUDGROVE *(13L-S)*
MOUNTJOY *(12D-SN)*
NELLI KIM *(G)*
PETE ROSE *(BA)*
REDGRAVE *(13S-R)*
STENMARK *(15I-SK)*
THORBURN *(13C-SN)*
TREDGETT *(12M-B)*
WALLISER *(13M-SK)*
WILLIAMS *(11R-SN,*
14E-S)

9

CARL PREAN *(TT)*
CASLAVSKA *(13V-G)*
DIANA ROWE *(TT)*
FRED DAVIS *(SN)*
FRED PERRY *(TT)*
GEOFF HUNT *(SQ)*
GRIFFITHS *(14T-SN)*
HANK AARON *(BA)*
JACKIE RAE *(SN)*
JOHN CURRY *(I)*
JOHN VIRGO *(SN)*
JUNE CROFT *(S)*
LAZARENKO *(14C-D)*
LOU GERRIG *(BA)*
MARK SPITZ *(S)*
MOORHOUSE *(15A-S)*
NEIL ADAMS *(J)*

NIGEL BOND *(SN)*
NOLAN RYAN *(BA)*
NORA PERRY *(B)*
PHIL MAHRE *(SK)*
REG HARRIS *(C)*
SEAN KERLY *(H)*
SYDNEY LEE *(SN)*
TONY DRAGO *(SN)*
WERBENUIK *(13B-SN)*

10

BARRINGTON *(15J-SQ)*
BRIAN JACKS *(J)*
DAWN FRASER *(S)*
ERIC HEIDEN *(I)*
GREG LEMOND *(C)*
HARDCASTLE *(15S-S)*
HAMMERSLEY
 (see PARKER)
HUGH PORTER *(C)*
JILL PARKER *(TT)*
JIMMY WHITE *(SN)*
JOE JOHNSON *(SN)*
JOHN PULMAN *(SN)*
MARTIN BELL *(SK)*
NEIL FOULDS *(SN)*
OLGA KORBUT *(G)*
QAMAR ZAMAN *(SQ)*
RAY REARDON *(SN)*
RUTHERFORD *(G)*
SHANE GOULD *(S)*
SKOBLIKOVA *(I)*
SONJA HENIE *(I)*
STEVE DAVIS *(SN)*
SUSAN DEVOY *(SQ)*
WILLIE WOOD *(BO)*
ZURBRIGGEN *(SK)*

11

ALEX HIGGINS *(SN)*
ANDY THOMSON *(BO)*

BERNARD FORD *(I)*
BERYL BURTON *(C)*
BOB ANDERSON *(D)*
BOBBY GEORGE *(D)*
BOB CHAPERON *(SN)*
BOHUMIL VANA *(TT)*
BRIAN PHELPS *(S)*
DAVID BRYANT *(BO)*
DAVID WILKIE *(S)*
DIANE TOWLER *(I)*
EDDIE MERCKX *(C)*
ERIC BRISTOW *(D)*
HAYLEY LEWIS *(S)*
JANE WEBSTER *(B)*
JOCKY WILSON *(D)*
JOE DiMAGGIO *(BA)*
JOHNNY LEACH *(TT)*
JOHN PARROTT *(SN)*
JOHN SPENCER *(SN)*
JUDY GRINHAM *(S)*
KAREN BRIGGS *(J)*
KEITH DELLER *(D)*
KIRK STEVENS *(SN)*
LONSBOROUGH *(S)*
MIKE HALLETT *(SN)*
REX WILLIAMS *(SN)*
RUDY HARTONO *(B)*
TONY ALLCOCK *(BO)*
TONY KNOWLES *(SN)*
TOURISCHEVA *(G)*
VIKTOR BARNA *(TT)*
WEISSMULLER *(S)*

12

ALBERTO TOMBA *(SK)*
DENNIS TAYLOR *(SN)*
DOUG MOUNTJOY *(SN)*
EDDIE EDWARDS *(SK)*
FRANZ KLAMMER *(SK)*
GILLIAN GILKS *(B)*
IRINA RODNINA *(I)*
JAHANGIR KHAN *(SQ)*
JAMES WATTANA *(SN)*
JAYNE TORVILL *(I)*
JOANNE CONWAY *(I)*

KATARINA WITT *(I)*
LEIGHTON REES *(D)*
MIKE TREDGETT *(B)*
ROBIN COUSINS *(I)*
ROSALIND ROWE *(TT)*
STEPHEN ROCHE *(C)*
SUZANNE DANDO *(G)*
TOMMY SIMPSON *(C)*
WILLIE THORNE *(SN)*

13

BILL WERBENUIK *(SN)*
CHESTER BARNES *(TT)*
CLIFF THORBURN *(SN)*
DONALD JACKSON *(I)*
DUNCAN GOODHEW *(S)*

EDDIE CHARLTON *(SN)*
GRETA ANDERSEN *(S)*
HORACE LINDRUM *(SN)*
KORNELIA ENDER *(S)*
LINDA LUDGROVE *(S)*
MALCOLM COOPER *(RS)*
MARIE WALLISER *(SK)*
NADIA COMANECI *(G)*
SHARRON DAVIES *(S)*
STEPHEN HENDRY *(SN)*
STEVE REDGRAVE *(R)*
VERA CASLAVSKA *(G)*
WALTER LINDRUM *(SN)*

14

BERNARD HINAULT *(C)*

CLIFF LAZARENKO *(D)*
DESMOND DOUGLAS *(TT)*
ESTHER WILLIAMS *(S)*
MAUREEN FLOWERS *(D)*
TERRY GRIFFITHS *(SN)*

15

ADRIAN MOORHOUSE *(S)*
CHRISTOPHER DEAN *(I)*
INGEMAR STENMARK *(SK)*
JACQUES ANQUETIL *(C)*
JEAN-CLAUDE KILLY *(SK)*
JONAH BARRINGTON *(SQ)*
RICHARD BERGMANN *(TT)*
SARAH HARDCASTLE *(S)*

PEOPLE

SPORTSPEOPLE – GOLFERS

3

RAY *(9E)*
WAY *(7P)*

4

AOKI *(8I)*
BEAN *(8A)*
BECK *(8C)*
HUNT *(11B)*
KITE *(7T)*
LEMA *(8T)*

LYLE *(9S)*
MIZE *(9L)*
OGLE *(9B)*
PARK *(10W)*
PATE *(9J)*
REES *(7D)*
TWAY *(7B)*

5

AARON *(10T)*
BRAND *(11G)*
BRAID *(10J)*

BROWN *(8K)*
CLARK *(11H)*
COLES *(9N)*
DARCY *(11E)*
FALDO *(9N)*
FLOYD *(8R)*
GREEN *(11H)*
HAGEN *(11W)*
HOGAN *(8B)*
IRWIN *(9H)*
JAMES *(9M)*
JONES *(10B)*
LOCKE *(10B)*
MARSH *(11G)*

NAGLE *(8K)*
NORTH *(9A)*
SMYTH *(8D)*
SNEAD *(8S)*

6

ALLISS *(11P)*
ARMOUR *(11T)*
BARNES *(11B)*
BOXALL *(13R)*
BREWER *(9G)*
CASPER *(11B)*

COTTON *(11H, 12T)*
GRAHAM *(11D)*
HORTON *(11T)*
LANGER *(14B)*
MILLER *(12J)*
MORRIS *(9T)*
NELSON *(11L)*
NORMAN *(10G)*
PALMER *(12A)*
PINERO *(12M)*
PLAYER *(10G)*
ROGERS *(10B)*
SUTTON *(9H)*

PEOPLE – SPORTSPEOPLE – GOLFERS

TAYLOR *(10J)*
VARDON *(11H)*
WATSON *(9T)*

7

BOB TWAY
CHARLES *(10B)*
DAI REES
FEHERTY *(12D)*
GARRIDO *(14A)*
JACKLIN *(11T)*
LITTLER *(11G)*
O'CONNOR *(14C)*
McNULTY *(11M)*
PAUL WAY
SANDERS *(11D)*
SARAZEN *(11G)*
STADLER *(12C)*
STEWART *(13P)*
STRANGE *(13C)*
THOMSON *(12P)*
TOM KITE
TREVINO *(10L)*
VICENZO
WADKINS *(12L)*
WOOSNAM *(10I)*
ZOELLER *(12F)*

8

ANDY BEAN
BAIOCCHI *(12H)*
BEN HOGAN
CHIP BECK
CRENSHAW *(11B)*
DES SMYTH
FAULKNER *(11M)*
ISAO AOKI
KEL NAGLE
KEN BROWN
LONGMUIR *(12B)*
NAKAMURA *(13T)*
NICKLAUS *(12J)*

OLAZABAL
RAFFERTY *(13R)*
RAY FLOYD
SAM SNEAD
TONY LEMA
TORRANCE *(11S)*
WEISKOPF *(11T)*

9

ANDY NORTH
BONALLACK *(13M)*
BRETT OGLE
EDWARD RAY
FERNANDEZ
GALLACHER
GAY BREWER
HALE IRWIN
HAL SUTTON
JERRY PATE
LARRY MIZE
MARK JAMES
NEIL COLES
NICK FALDO
SANDY LYLE
TOM MORRIS
TOM WATSON

10

BILL ROGERS
BOBBY JONES
BOBBY LOCKE
BOB CHARLES
GARY PLAYER
GREG NORMAN
IAN WOOSNAM
JAMES BRAID
JOHN TAYLOR
LEE TREVINO
OOSTERHUIS *(15P)*
TOMMY AARON
WILLIE PARK

11

BALLESTEROS *(15S)*
BEN CRENSHAW
BERNARD HUNT
BILLY CASPER
BRIAN BARNES
DAVID GRAHAM
DOUG SANDERS
EAMONN DARCY
GENE LITTLER
GENE SARAZEN
GORDON BRAND
GRAHAM MARSH
HARRY VARDON
HENRY COTTON
HOWARD CLARK
HUBERT GREEN
LARRY NELSON
MARK McNULTY
MAX FAULKNER
PETER ALLISS
SAM TORRANCE
TOMMY ARMOUR
TOMMY HORTON
TOM WEISKOPF
TONY JACKLIN
WALTER HAGEN

12

ARNOLD PALMER
BILL LONGMUIR
CALCAVECCHIA
CRAIG STADLER
DAVID FEHERTY
FUZZY ZOELLER
HUGH BAIOCCHI
JACK NICKLAUS
JOHNNY MILLER
LANNY WADKINS
MANUEL PINERO
PAYNE STEWART
PETER THOMSON
THOMAS COTTON

PEOPLE

SPORTSPEOPLE – JOCKEYS

(N) = National hunt jockeys   (S) = Showjumpers/eventers

3

FOX *(10F, 10R)*
MAC *(11E-S)*

4

CARR *(9H)*
COOK *(8P)*
DURR *(11F)*
HEAD *(10F)*
HIDE *(9E)*
IVES *(8T)*
LENG *(12V-S)*
LOWE *(9J)*
REID *(8J)*
TODD *(8M-S)*
TUCK *(8P-N)*
WYER *(10L-N)*

5

BARRY *(8R-N)*
BERRY *(10F-N)*
BURKE *(9J-N)*
DWYER *(9M-N)*
EDGAR *(8E-S, 8T-S)*
GREEN *(12L-S)*
HILLS *(12M, 12R)*
KEITH *(11D)*
LEWIS *(10G)*
MEADE *(12R-S)*
MOORE *(8A-S, 10G)*
MUNRO *(9A)*
PYRAH *(12M-S)*
QUINN *(12R)*
ROUSE *(10B)*
SMITH *(9D, 10T-N, 11H-S, 11R-S)*

SMYTH *(8R)*
STACK *(10T-N)*
STARK *(8I-S)*
ST CYR *(10H-S)*
WRAGG *(10H)*

6

ARCHER *(10F)*
BROOME *(11D-S)*
BUCKLE *(11F)*
CARSON *(12W)*
COAKES *(11M-S)*
DAVIES *(9B-N)*
EDDERY *(9P, 10P)*
FARGIS *(9J-S)*
HUNTER *(11J-S)*
KINANE *(11T-N)*
KLIMKE *(12R-S)*
KNIGHT *(11S-N)*
MACKEN *(11E-S)*
MERCER *(9J)*

MELLOR *(10S-N)*
MOLONY *(9T-N)*
MURRAY *(10T)*
NEWNES *(10B)*
O'NEILL *(11J-N)*
PITMAN *(13R-N)*
RIMELL *(10F)*
SMIRKE *(13C)*
SMYTHE *(9P-S)*
TAAFFE *(9P-N)*
TAYLOR *(11B)*
UTTLEY *(11J-N)*
WINTER *(10F-N)*

7

BARCLAY *(12S)*
BAYLISS *(13R-S)*
BRADLEY *(15C-S)*
BUCKLEY *(10P-N)*
CAUTHEN *(12S)*
DETTORI *(14F)*
FENWICK *(14C-N)*

FRANCIS *(11D-N)*
GIFFORD *(11J-N)*
HOLGATE
(see LENG)
JOHNSON *(12E)*
KINNANE *(14M)*
LINDLEY *(12J)*
McMAHON *(12P-S)*
PIGGOTT *(13L)*
RAYMOND *(12B)*
ROBERTS *(14M)*
SKELTON *(11N-S)*
STARKEY *(15G)*
THORNER *(13G-N)*
TINKLER *(10K)*
WILLCOX *(13S-S)*
WINKLER *(11H-S)*

8

ANN MOORE *(S)*
ASMUSSEN *(12C)*
BRABAZON *(14A-N)*
BREASLEY *(14S)*
CARBERRY *(13T-N)*
CHAMPION *(11B-N)*
COCHRANE *(11R)*
DAVIDSON *(13B-S)*
DONOGHUE *(13S)*
DUFFIELD *(14G)*
DUNWOODY *(15R-N)*
EARNSHAW *(14R-N)*
FLETCHER *(13B-N)*
FRANCOME *(12J-N)*
IAN STARK *(S)*
JOHN REID
KELLAWAY *(12P-N)*
LIZ EDGAR *(S)*
MARK TODD *(S)*
MARSHALL *(13B-N)*
McCARRON *(13C)*
PAUL COOK
PAUL TUCK *(N)*
PHILLIPS *(12M-S)*
RICHARDS *(14G)*

ROBINSON *(14W-N)*
RON BARRY *(N)*
RON SMYTH
SAUNDERS *(12D-N)*
SWINBURN *(14W)*
TED EDGAR *(S)*
TONY IVES
WHITAKER *(12J,
15M)*

9

ALAN MUNRO
BOB DAVIES *(N)*
BRODERICK *(14P-N)*
BROOKSHAW *(12T-N)*
DOUG SMITH
EDDIE HIDE
HARRY CARR
JIMMY LOWE
JOE FARGIS *(S)*
JOE MERCER
JOHN BURKE *(N)*
JOHNSTONE *(12R)*
LLEWELLYN *(14H-S)*
MARK DWYER *(N)*
PAT EDDERY
PAT SMYTHE *(S)*
PAT TAAFFE *(N)*
POINCELET *(14R)*
SCUDAMORE *(14P-N)*
SHOEMAKER *(15W)*
TIM MOLONY *(N)*

10

BILL NEWNES
BRIAN ROUSE
CHEVALLIER *(S)*
DOWDESWELL *(14J-N)*
FRANK BERRY *(N)*
FRED ARCHER
FREDDIE FOX
FREDDY HEAD

FRED RIMELL *(N)*
FRED WINTER *(N)*
GEOFF LEWIS
HARRY WRAGG
HENRI ST CYR *(S)*
HUTCHINSON *(13R)*
KIM TINKLER
LORCAN WYER *(N)*
PAT BUCKLEY *(N)*
PAUL EDDERY
RICHARD FOX
STAN MELLOR *(N)*
TOMMY SMITH *(N)*
TOMMY STACK *(N)*
TONY MURRAY
WILLIAMSON *(14B)*

11

BIDDLECOMBE *(N)*
BOB CHAMPION *(N)*
BRIAN TAYLOR
DAVID BROOME *(S)*
DICK FRANCIS *(N)*
DRUMMOND-HAY *(S)*
DUNCAN KEITH
EDDIE MACKEN *(S)*
EMMA-JANE MAC *(S)*
FRANK BUCKLE
FRANKIE DURR
GEORGE MOORE
HANS WINKLER *(S)*
HARVEY SMITH *(S)*
JANET HUNTER *(S)*
JIMMY UTTLEY *(N)*
JONJO O'NEILL *(N)*
JOSH GIFFORD *(N)*
NICK SKELTON *(S)*
PRIOR-PALMER
(see GREEN)
RAY COCHRANE
ROBERT SMITH *(S)*
SAINT-MARTIN *(15Y)*
SMITH-ECCLES *(N)*
STEVE KNIGHT *(N)*
TOMMY KINANE *(N)*

BRUCE RAYMOND
CASH ASMUSSEN
DICK SAUNDERS *(N)*
ERNIE JOHNSON
JIMMY LINDLEY
JOHN FRANCOME *(N)*
JOHN WHITAKER *(S)*
LUCINDA GREEN *(S)*
MALCOLM PYRAH *(S)*
MARION COAKES *(S)*
MARK PHILLIPS *(S)*
MICHAEL HILLS
PADDY McMAHON *(S)*
PAUL KELLAWAY *(N)*
PRINCESS ANNE *(S)*
RAE JOHNSTONE
RAINER KLIMKE *(S)*
RICHARD HILLS
RICHARD MEADE *(S)*
RICHARD QUINN
SANDY BARCLAY
SCHOCKEMÖHLE *(S)*
STEVE CAUTHEN

TIM BROOKSHAW *(N)*
VIRGINIA LENG *(S)*
WILLIE CARSON

13

BRIAN FLETCHER *(N)*
BRYAN MARSHALL *(N)*
BRUCE DAVIDSON *(S)*
CHARLIE SMIRKE
CHRIS McCARRON
GRAHAM THORNER *(N)*
LESTER PIGGOTT
RACHEL BAYLISS *(S)*
RICHARD PITMAN *(N)*
RON HUTCHINSON
SHEILA WILLCOX *(S)*
STEVE DONOGHUE
TOMMY CARBERRY *(N)*

14

AUBREY BRABAZON *(N)*
BILL WILLIAMSON

CHARLIE FENWICK *(N)*
FRANKIE DETTORI
GEORGE DUFFIELD
GORDON RICHARDS
HARRY LLEWELLYN *(S)*
JACK DOWDESWELL *(N)*
MICHAEL KINNANE
MICHAEL ROBERTS
PADDY BRODERICK *(N)*
PETER SCUDAMORE *(N)*
ROBERT EARNSHAW *(N)*
ROGER POINCELET
SCOBIE BREASLEY
WALTER SWINBURN
WILLIE ROBINSON *(N)*

15

CAROLINE BRADLEY *(S)*
GREVILLE STARKEY
MICHAEL WHITAKER *(S)*
RICHARD DUNWOODY *(N)*
WILLIE SHOEMAKER
YVES SAINT-MARTIN

PEOPLE

SPORTSPEOPLE – RACING-DRIVERS

(R) = Rally-driver   (S) = Speed-record breaker

3	BELL *(9D)*	MOSS *(12S)*	BEHRA *(9J)*	LAUDA *(9N)*
DON *(7K-S)*	COBB *(8J-S)*	PACE *(10C)*	CLARK *(8J, 10R-R)*	NOBLE *(12R-S)*
	HILL *(8P, 10G)*			PROST *(10A)*
4	HUNT *(9J)*	5	FRERE *(9P)*	RINDT *(11J)*
	ICKX *(9J)*		HULME *(10D)*	ROHRL *(11W-R)*
AMON *(9C)*	MASS *(10J)*	ALESI *(9J)*	JONES *(9A)*	SENNA *(11A)*
			KLING *(9C)*	VARZI *(12A)*

PEOPLE – SPORTSPEOPLE – RACING-DRIVERS

6

ARFONS *(9A-S)*
ARNOUX *(10R)*
ASCARI *(13A)*
BERGER *(13G)*
BROOKS *(10T)*
CHIRON *(11L)*
EKLUND *(9P-R)*
ELFORD *(9V-R)*
EYSTON *(12G-S)*
FANGIO *(10J)*
FARINA *(14G)*
GURNEY *(9D)*
HARPER *(11P-R)*
LIGIER *(9G)*
PALMER *(14J)*
PARKES *(10M)*
PIQUET *(12N)*
PIRONI *(12D)*
REVSON *(11P)*
ROSIER *(11L)*
SCHELL *(11H)*
TAMBAY *(13P)*
THOMAS *(11P-S)*
WATSON *(10J)*
WISDOM *(10A-R)*

7

BANDINI *(14L)*
BARRETT *(11S-S)*
BENOIST *(13R)*
BONNIER *(9J)*
BOUTSEN *(14T)*
BRABHAM *(11J)*
BRUNDLE *(13M)*
COLLINS *(12P)*
FAGIOLI *(12L)*
GINTHER *(13R)*
HOPKIRK *(12P-R)*
IRELAND *(12I)*
KAYE DON *(S)*
LAFITTE *(14J)*
MAKINEN *(11T-R)*

MANSELL *(12N)*
McLAREN *(12B)*
MIKKOLA *(12H-R)*
NILSSON *(13G)*
PARNELL *(10R)*
PATRESE *(15R)*
ROSBERG *(11K)*
SEGRAVE *(12H-S)*
SIFFERT *(13J)*
STEWART *(13J)*
SUMMERS *(13R-S)*
SURTEES *(11J)*
VATANEN *(10A-R)*
WARWICK *(12D)*

8

AALTONEN *(13R-R)*
ALBORETO *(15M)*
ANDRETTI *(13M)*
BELTOISE
CAMPBELL *(14D-S,*
15M-S)
CARLSSON *(12E-R)*
GABELICH *(12G-S)*
GONZALEZ *(12J)*
HAILWOOD *(12M)*
HAWTHORN *(12M)*
JIM CLARK
JOHN COBB *(S)*
NUVOLARI *(13T)*
PETERSON *(14R)*
PHIL HILL
SENECHAL *(14R)*
VON TRIPS

9

AIRIKKALA *(15P-R)*
ALAN JONES
ART ARFONS *(S)*
BLOMQVIST *(13S-R)*
BREEDLOVE *(14C-S)*
CARL KLING

CHRIS AMON
DAN GURNEY
DE ANGELIS *(13E)*
DEPAILLER
DEREK BELL
GUY LIGIER
JABOUILLE
JACKY ICKX
JAMES HUNT
JEAN ALESI
JEAN BEHRA
JO BONNIER
KANKKUNEN *(13J-R)*
NIKI LAUDA
PAUL FRERE
PER EKLUND *(R)*
REGAZZONI *(13C)*
REUTEMANN *(15C)*
RODRIGUEZ *(14P)*
ROSEMEYER *(14B)*
SALVADORI *(12R)*
SCHECKTER *(13J)*
VIC ELFORD *(R)*
VILLORESI *(14L)*
WALDEGARD *(14B-R)*

10

ALAIN PROST
ANNE WISDOM *(R)*
ARI VATANEN *(R)*
CARACCIOLA
CARLOS PACE
DENNY HULME
FITTIPALDI
GRAHAM HILL
JOCHEN MASS
JOHN WATSON
JUAN FANGIO
MIKE PARKES
REG PARNELL
RENÉ ARNOUX
ROGER CLARK *(R)*
SODERSTRÖM *(15B-R)*
TONY BROOKS
VILLENEUVE

11

AYRTON SENNA
HARRY SCHELL
JACK BRABHAM
JOCHEN RINDT
JOHN SURTEES
KEKE ROSBERG
LOUIS CHIRON
LOUIS ROSIER
PARRY THOMAS *(S)*
PETER HARPER *(R)*
PETER REVSON
STAN BARRETT *(S)*
TIMO MAKINEN *(R)*
TRINTIGNANT
WALTER ROHRL *(R)*

12

ACHILLE VARZI
AITKEN-WALKER *(R)*
BRUCE McLAREN
DEREK WARWICK
DIDIER PIRONI
ERIK CARLSSON *(R)*
GARY GABELICH *(S)*
GEORGE EYSTON *(S)*
HANNU MIKKOLA *(R)*
HENRY SEGRAVE *(S)*
INNES IRELAND

JOSÉ GONZALEZ
LUIGI FAGIOLI
MIKE HAILWOOD
MIKE HAWTHORN
MOSS-CARLSSON *(15P-R)*
NELSON PIQUET
NIGEL MANSELL
PADDY HOPKIRK *(R)*
PETER COLLINS
RICHARD NOBLE *(S)*
ROY SALVADORI
SHUTTLEWORTH
STIRLING MOSS

13

ALBERTO ASCARI
ANTONIO ASCARI
CLAY REGAZZONI
ELIO DE ANGELIS
GERHARD BERGER
GUNNAR NILSSON
JACKIE STEWART
JODY SCHECKTER
JOSEPH SIFFERT
JUHA KANKKUNEN *(R)*
MARIO ANDRETTI
MARTIN BRUNDLE
PATRICK TAMBAY
RAUNO AALTONEN *(R)*
RICHIE GINTHER

ROBERT BENOIST
ROBERT SUMMERS *(S)*
STIG BLOMQVIST *(R)*
TAZIO NUVOLARI

14

BERND ROSEMEYER
BJÖRN WALDEGARD *(R)*
CRAIG BREEDLOVE *(S)*
DONALD CAMPBELL *(S)*
GIUSEPPE FARINA
JACQUES LAFITTE
JONATHAN PALMER
LORENZO BANDINI
LUIGI VILLORESI
PEDRO RODRIGUEZ
ROBERT SENECHAL
RONNIE PETERSON
THIERRY BOUTSEN

15

BENGT SODERSTRÖM *(R)*
CARLOS REUTEMANN
MALCOLM CAMPBELL *(S)*
MICHELE ALBORETO
PAT MOSS-CARLSSON *(R)*
PENTTI AIRIKKALA *(R)*
RICCARDO PATRESE

PEOPLE

SPORTSPEOPLE – RUGBY-PLAYERS

All from British Isles except: (A) = Australian   (AR) = Argentinian
(F) = French   (NZ) = New Zealand   (SA) = South African

3

FOX *(8G-NZ)*
OTI *(8C)*

4

ELLA *(8M-A)*
EMYS *(10A)*
GRAY *(7K-NZ)*
HARE *(9D)*
JOHN *(9B)*
KOCH *(9C-SA)*
MASO *(6J-F)*
MIAS *(10L-F)*
RING *(8M)*
SHAW *(8M-NZ)*

5

CHAMP *(9E-F)*
DAUGA *(11B-F)*
DEANS *(10C)*
ELLIS *(8J-SA)*
GOING *(8S-NZ)*
HADEN *(9A-NZ)*
JEEPS *(11D)*
JONES *(8K)*
LYDON *(7J)*
MEADS *(10C-NZ)*
MOORE *(10B)*
PORTA *(9H-AR)*
PRICE *(11G)*
RIVES *(15J-F)*
SCOTT *(8B-NZ)*
SELLA *(13P-F)*

SHARP *(12R)*
SMITH *(8I,*
11A)
WHITE *(10D)*
YOUNG *(10D)*

6

BLANCO *(11S-F)*
CALDER *(12F)*
COTTON *(10F)*
CRONIN *(12D)*
DAVIES *(12G,*
12M,
14J)
DOOLEY *(10W)*
GERBER *(11D-SA)*
GIBSON *(10M)*
HANLEY *(12E)*
HOLMES *(11T)*
IRVINE *(10A)*
JARDEN *(9R-NZ)*
JO MASO *(F)*
LYNAGH *(13M-A)*
MORGAN *(11C)*
MULLIN *(13B)*
MURPHY *(11K)*
NATHAN *(10W-NZ)*
OFFIAH *(12M)*
PROBYN *(10J)*
PULLIN *(10J)*
SKRÉLA *(F)*
TANNER *(11H)*
TEAGUE *(10M)*
TUKALO *(10I)*
UTTLEY *(11R)*
WILSON *(9S-NZ)*

7

ACKFORD *(11P)*
BENNETT *(11P)*
CAMPESE *(12D-A)*
CARLING *(11W)*
DUCKHAM *(12D)*
DU PREEZ *(11F-SA)*
EDWARDS *(13G)*
GREGORY *(11A)*
GUSCOTT *(13J)*
HIPWELL *(11J-A)*
JACKSON *(12P)*
JEFFREY *(11J)*
JO LYDON
KEN GRAY *(NZ)*
KIERNAN *(10T)*
LENIHAN *(12D)*
LOCHORE *(12B-NZ)*
McBRIDE
O'REILLY *(11T)*
PROSSER *(10R)*
RENDALL *(11P)*
TOPLISS *(11D)*
TREMAIN *(10K-NZ)*
WHEELER *(12P)*

8

ANDERSON *(14W)*
BEAUMONT *(12B)*
BOB SCOTT *(NZ)*
CHALMERS *(12C)*
CHRIS OTI
GRANT FOX *(NZ)*
HASTINGS *(13G,*
13S)
IAN SMITH

JAN ELLIS *(SA)*
KEN JONES
MARK ELLA *(A)*
MARK RING
MARK SHAW *(NZ)*
POIDEVIN *(13S-A)*
SCHUSTER *(12J-NZ)*
SHELFORD *(13W-NZ)*
SID GOING *(NZ)*
SLATTERY *(14F)*
WILLIAMS *(10J,*
　　　　　11J)

9

ANDY HADEN *(NZ)*
ARMSTRONG *(13G)*
BARRY JOHN
CATCHPOLE *(12K-A)*
CHRIS KOCH *(SA)*
DUSTY HARE
ERIC CHAMP *(F)*
GALLACHER *(13J)*
GRIFFITHS *(13M)*
HUGO PORTA *(AR)*
LOVERIDGE *(13D-NZ)*
RON JARDEN *(NZ)*
SPANGHERO *(15W-F)*
STU WILSON *(NZ)*
UNDERWOOD *(13R)*

10

ANDY IRVINE
ARTHUR EMYS
BRIAN MOORE
COLIN DEANS
COLIN MEADS *(NZ)*
DAVID YOUNG
DEREK WHITE
FITZGERALD *(15D)*
FRAN COTTON
IVAN TUKALO
JEFF PROBYN
JJ WILLIAMS
JOHN PULLIN

KEL TREMAIN *(NZ)*
LUCIEN MIAS *(F)*
McLAUGHLAN *(13I)*
McLOUGHLIN *(13R)*
MIKE GIBSON
MIKE TEAGUE
RAY PROSSER
TOM KIERNAN
VILLEPREUX *(F)*
WADE DOOLEY
WAKA NATHAN *(NZ)*

11

ANDY GREGORY
ARTHUR SMITH
BENOIT DAUGA *(F)*
BUTTERFIELD *(15J)*
CLIFF MORGAN
DANIE GERBER *(SA)*
DAVE TOPLISS
DICKIE JEEPS
FRIK DU PREEZ *(SA)*
GRAHAM PRICE
HAYDN TANNER
JOHN HIPWELL *(A)*
JOHN JEFFREY
JPR WILLIAMS
KEVIN MURPHY
KIRKPATRICK *(14I-NZ)*
PAUL ACKFORD
PAUL RENDALL
PHIL BENNETT
ROGER UTTLEY
SERGE BLANCO *(F)*
TERRY HOLMES
TONY O'REILLY
WILL CARLING

12

BILL BEAUMONT
BRIAN LOCHORE *(NZ)*
CRAY CHALMERS
DAMIAN CRONIN
DAVID CAMPESE *(A)*

DAVID DUCKHAM
DONAL LENIHAN
ELLERY HANLEY
FINLAY CALDER
GERALD DAVIES
JOHN SCHUSTER
KEN CATCHPOLE *(A)*
MARTIN OFFIAH
MERVYN DAVIES
PETER JACKSON
PETER WHEELER
RICHARD SHARP
WINTERBOTTOM

13

BRENDAN MULLIN
DAVE LOVERIDGE *(NZ)*
GARETH EDWARDS
GARY ARMSTRONG
GAVIN HASTINGS
IAN McLAUGHLAN
JEREMY GUSCOTT
JOHN GALLAGHER
MICHAEL LYNAGH *(A)*
MIKE GRIFFITHS
PHILIPPE SELLA *(F)*
RAY McLOUGHLIN
RORY UNDERWOOD
SCOTT HASTINGS
SIMON POIDEVIN *(A)*
WAYNE SHELFORD *(NZ)*

14

FERGUS SLATTERY
IAN KIRKPATRICK *(NZ)*
JONATHON DAVIES
WILLIE ANDERSON

15

DAVID FITZGERALD
JEAN-PIERRE RIVES *(F)*
JEFF BUTTERFIELD
WALTER SPANGHERO *(F)*

PEOPLE

SPORTSPEOPLE – TENNIS-PLAYERS

3

COX *(7M)*
DOD *(9L)*
FRY *(10S)*
PAZ *(11M)*

4

ASHE *(10A)*
BORG *(9B)*
CASE *(8R)*
CASH *(7P)*
DURR *(13F)*
GRAF *(10S)*
HARD *(11D)*
HART *(9D)*
HOAD *(7L)*
KING *(14B)*
LUTZ *(7B)*
NOAH *(11Y)*
RYAN *(13E)*
WADE *(12V)*

5

BATES *(11J)*
BUDGE *(11D)*
BUENO *(10M)*
CHANG *(12M)*
COURT *(13M)*
CROFT *(12A)*
DURIE *(7J)*
EVERT *(10C)*
FIBAK *(11W)*
GOMER *(9S)*
HOBBS *(9A)*
JANES *(15C)*

JAVER *(12M)*
JONES *(8A)*
KODES *(8J)*
KRIEK *(10J)*
LAVER *(8R)*
LENDL *(9I)*
LEWIS *(10C)*
LLOYD *(9J,*
10D)
MAYER *(10S)*
MOODY *(15H)*
MORAN *(11G)*
OKKER *(8T)*
OSUNA *(11R)*
PAISH *(10G)*
PERRY *(9F)*
PETRA *(9Y)*
PILIC *(10N)*
ROCHE *(9T)*
ROUND *(12D)*
SELES *(11M)*
SMITH *(9S,*
see COURT)
STOVE *(10B)*
VILAS *(14G)*

6

AGASSI *(11A)*
AUSTIN *(10J,*
11B,
11T)
BAILEY *(11C)*
BARKER *(9S)*
BECKER *(11B)*
BROUGH *(12L)*
BUXTON *(12A)*
CASALS *(11R)*
CASTLE *(12A)*

CAWLEY *(12E)*
COOPER *(12A)*
CURRAN *(11K)*
DROBNY *(14J)*
EDBERG *(12S)*
FRASER *(11N)*
GIBSON *(12A)*
HEWITT *(9B)*
JARRYD *(12A)*
KRAMER *(10J)*
MARBLE *(11A)*
OLMEDO *(10A)*
RICHEY *(11N)*
SEIXAS *(9V)*
STOLLE *(10F)*
SUKOVA *(12H)*
SUSMAN *(11K)*
TANNER *(12R)*
TAYLOR *(11R)*
TEGART *(10J)*
TILDEN *(10B)*
TIRIAC *(9I)*
TRUMAN
(see JANES)
WILSON *(11B)*

7

BOB LUTZ
BOROTRA *(11J)*
CONNORS *(12J)*
EMERSON *(10R)*
FLEMING *(12P)*
JO DURIE
LACOSTE *(11R)*
LECONTE *(12H)*
LENGLEN *(14S)*
LEW HOAD
MARK COX

MASTERS *(12G)*
MAYOTTE *(10T)*
McENROE *(11J)*
McNAMEE *(11P)*
MOFFITT
(see KING)
MOTTRAM *(13B)*
NASTASE *(11I)*
ORANTES *(13M)*
PAT CASH
RAMIREZ *(12R)*
SAMPRAS *(11P)*
SANCHEZ *(14A)*
SANTANA *(13M)*
SEDGMAN *(12F)*
SHRIVER *(10P)*
TRABERT *(11T)*

8

AMRITRAJ *(13V)*
ANN JONES
CAPRIATI
CONNOLLY *(15M)*
DAVIDSON *(12O)*
DRYSDALE *(13C)*
FLETCHER *(11K)*
GARRISON *(12Z)*
GONZALES *(14P)*
JAN KODES
McKINLEY *(13C)*
McMILLAN *(12F)*
McNAMARA *(13P)*
MORTIMER *(14A)*
NEWCOMBE *(12J)*
PASARELL *(15C)*
ROD LAVER
ROSEWALL *(11K)*
ROSS CASE
SABATINI

SANGSTER *(12M)*
STOCKTON *(12D)*
TOM OKKER
TURNBULL *(13W)*
WILANDER *(12M)*

9

ANNE HOBBS
BJÖRN BORG
BOB HEWITT
DORIS HART
FRED PERRY
GOOLAGONG
  (see CAWLEY)
GOTTFRIED *(14B)*
ION TIRIAC
IVAN LENDL
JOHN LLOYD
LOOSEMORE *(14S)*
LOTTIE DOD
METREVELI *(13A)*
SARA GOMER
STAN SMITH
SUE BARKER
TONY ROCHE
VIC SEIXAS
YVON PETRA

10

ALEX OLMEDO
ARTHUR ASHE
BETTY STOVE
BILL TILDEN
CHRIS EVERT
CHRIS LEWIS
DAVID LLOYD
FRED STOLLE
GEOFF PAISH
GERULAITIS *(15V)*
JACK KRAMER
JOHAN KRIEK
JOHN AUSTIN

JUDY TEGART
MANDLIKOVA *(14H)*
MARIA BUENO
NICKI PILIC
PAM SHRIVER
ROY EMERSON
SANDY MAYER
SHIRLEY FRY
STEFFI GRAF
TIM MAYOTTE
WILLS-MOODY *(15H)*

11

ALICE MARBLE
ANDRE AGASSI
BOBBY WILSON
BORIS BECKER
BUNNY AUSTIN
CHRIS BAILEY
DARLENE HARD
DONALD BUDGE
GUSSIE MORAN
ILIE NASTASE
JEAN BOROTRA
JEREMY BATES
JOHN McENROE
KAREN SUSMAN
KEN FLETCHER
KEN ROSEWALL
KEVIN CURRAN
KÖHDE-KILSCH
MERCEDES PAZ
MONICA SELES
NANCY RICHEY
NAVRATILOVA
NEALE FRASER
PAUL McNAMEE
PETE SAMPRAS
PIETRANGELI
RAFAEL OSUNA
RENÉ LACOSTE
ROGER TAYLOR
ROSIE CASALS
TONY TRABERT

TRACY AUSTIN
VAN RENSBURG
WOJTEK FIBAK
YANNICK NOAH

12

ALTHEA GIBSON
ANDERS JARRYD
ANDREW CASTLE
ANGELA BUXTON
ANNABEL CROFT
ASHLEY COOPER
DICK STOCKTON
DOROTHY ROUND
EVONNE CAWLEY
FRANK SEDGMAN
FREW McMILLAN
GEOFF MASTERS
HELENA SUKOVA
HENRI LECONTE
JIMMY CONNORS
JOHN NEWCOMBE
LOUISE BROUGH
MATS WILANDER
MICHAEL CHANG
MIKE SANGSTER
MONIQUE JAVER
OWEN DAVIDSON
PETER FLEMING
RAOUL RAMIREZ
ROSCOE TANNER
STEFAN EDBERG
VIRGINIA WADE
ZINA GARRISON

13

ALEX METREVELI
BUSTER MOTTRAM
CHUCK McKINLEY
CLIFF DRYSDALE
ELIZABETH RYAN
FRANÇOISE DURR
MANUEL ORANTES

MANUEL SANTANA
MARGARET COURT
PETER McNAMARA
VIJAY AMRITRAJ
WENDY TURNBULL

14

ANGELA MORTIMER

ARANTXA SANCHEZ
BILLIE-JEAN KING
BRIAN GOTTFRIED
CHRISTINE JANES
GUILLERMO VILAS
HANA MANDLIKOVA
JAROSLAV DROBNY
PANCHO GONZALES
SARAH LOOSEMORE

SUZANNE LENGLEN

15

CHARLIE PASARELL
HELEN WILLS-MOODY
MAUREEN CONNOLLY
VITAS GERULAITIS

PEOPLE

WRITERS

(D) = Dramatist   (E) = Essayist/historian   (P) = Poet
NB: (A) = Author/Authoress, only used for joint entries
* = Famous pseudonym/† = real name

3	**AMIS**	**GREY**	**LIVY** *(E)*	**SAND** **2*
	BABE *(D)*	**GUNN** *(P)*	**LOOS**	**SHAW** *(A)*
ADE	**BAUM**	**HALL** *(D)*	**LYLY** *(A/D/P)*	*(D/E)*
ECO	**BEHN** *(A/D)*	**HARE** *(D)*	**MANN** *(A/E)*	**SNOW**
FRY *(D)*	**BÖLL**	**HART** *(D)*	**MUIR** *(P)*	**TATE** *(P)*
GAY *(D/P)*	**BOLT** *(D)*	**HILL**	**NASH** *(P)*	**TODD**
HAY *(P)*	**BOND**	**HOGG** *(P)*	**OVID** *(P)*	**URIS**
KEE *(E)*	**BUCK**	**HOOD** *(P)*	**OWEN** *(D)*	**VEGA** *(D/P)*
KYD *(D)*	**CARY**	**HOPE**	*(P)*	**WAIN** *(A/P)*
LEE	**COOK**	**HUGO**	**PAGE** *(D)*	**WARD** **3*
NIN	**DAHL**	**HUME** *(E)*	**POPE** *(E/P)*	**WEBB**
POE *(A/P)*	**DUNN** *(A/P)*	**HUNT** *(P)*	**PUZO**	**WEST**
PYE *(P)*	**FORD** *(A/D/P)*	**HYNE**	**READ**	**WOOD** *(A)*
PYM	**GALT**	**JONG**	**RHYS**	*(D)*
TYL *(D)*	**GEMS** *(D)*	**KAYE**	**ROSS** *(P)*	**WOUK**
	GIDE *(A/D)*	**KENT**	**ROTH**	**WREN**
4	**GORE** *(A/D)*	**KING**	**ROWE** *(D/P)*	**WYSS**
	GRAY *(D)*	**LAMB** *(E/P)*	**SADE**	**ZOLA**
ABSE *(P)*	*(P)*	**LEAR** *(P)*	**SAKI** **1*	

ADAMS *(A)*
      (E)
AIKEN *(P)*
ALBEE *(D)*
ALGER
ARDEN *(D)*
AUDEN *(D/P)*
AWDRY
BACON *(E)*
BANKS
BARTH
BATES
BEHAN *(D)*
BENÉT *(A/P)*
BEYLE †4
BLAIR *(A/E)* †5
BLAKE *(A)* †6
      (P)
BLOCH
BRAGG
BRUNA
BURKE *(E)*
BURNS *(P)*
BYATT
BYRON *(P)*
CAMUS *(A/D)*
CAPEK *(D)*
CAREW *(P)*
CAREY
CHASE
CLARE *(P)*
CLARK
COHEN *(P)*
COOKE *(E)*
CRAIG
CRANE *(A/P)*
DANTE *(P)*
DEFOE
DONNE *(P)*
DOYLE
DUMAS
EDGAR *(D)*
EDSON
ELIOT *(A)*
      (D/P)

EXTON *(D)*
FLINT *(P)*
FRAYN *(D)*
FRIEL *(D)*
FROST *(P)*
GENET *(A/D)*
GLOAG
GOGOL *(A/D)*
GORKI *(A/D)*
GOSSE *(E/P)*
GRASS *(A/D)*
GRIMM
HALEY
HARDY *(A/P)*
HARTE
HAVEL *(D)*
HEINE *(E/P)*
HENRY *7
HENTY
HESSE *(A/P)*
HEYER
HINES
HOMER *(P)*
HULME *(E/P)*
IBSEN *(D)*
INNES
IRWIN
JACOB
JAMES
JARRY *(D)*
JOHNS
JONES *(P)*
JOYCE
KAFKA
KEATS *(P)*
KEEFE *(D)*
KESEY
KEYES
KLEIN *(P)*
KOPIT *(D)*
LEIGH *(D)*
LEVIN *(E)*
LEWIS
LODGE *(A)*
      (D/P)
LOFTS

LOGUE *(P)*
LORCA *(D/P)*
LOWRY
LYALL
MAGEE
MAMET *(D)*
MARSH
MILNE *(A/D/P)*
MOORE
MUNRO †1
NASHE *(D)*
NEWBY
NIVEN
NOBBS
NOYES *(P)*
ODETS *(D)*
O'HARA
ORCZY
ORTON *(D)*
OTWAY *(D)*
OUIDA *8
PAINE *(E)*
PATON
PEAKE
PÉGUY *(E/P)*
PEPYS *(E)*
PLATH *(P)*
PLATO *(E)*
POUND *(P)*
POWYS
PRIOR *(P)*
RAINE *(P)*
READE *(A/D)*
RILKE *(P)*
SACHS *(D)*
SAGAN
SCOTT *(A/P)*
      (A)
SEGAL
SELBY
SHUTE
SIMMS
SIMON *(A)*
      (D)
SMITH *(A)*
      (A/D)
      (P)

SPARK
SPYRI
STAËL
STEEL
STEIN
STOUT
STOWE
SWIFT *(A/E/P)*
SYNGE *(D)*
TASSO *(D/P)*
TWAIN *9
UDALL *(D)*
VERNE
VIDAL *(A/E)*
VIGNY *(A/D/P)*
WAUGH
WELLS
WHITE
WILDE *(D/P)*
WOLFE *(P)*
WOOLF
WYATT *(P)*
YEATS *(D/P)*
YERBY
YONGE
ZWEIG

ALCOTT
ALDISS
AMBLER
ANSTEY
ARCHER
ARNOLD *(P)*
AROUET *(A/D/E)* †10
ASCHAM *(E)*
ASIMOV
AUSTEN
AUSTIN *(P)*
BAGLEY
BALZAC
BARAKA *(D)*
BARHAM *(A/P)*
BARNES *(A)*
      (P)

PEOPLE – WRITERS

BAROJA *(A/E)*
BARRIE *(A/D)*
BECQUE *(D)*
BELLOC *(E/P)*
BELLOW
BENSON
BESANT
BIERCE *(A/P)*
BINCHY
BINYON *(P)*
BLYTON
BORGES *(A/E)*
BORROW
BRAINE
BRECHT *(D/P)*
BRETON *(E/P)*
BRIDIE *(D)*
BRONTË
BROOKE *(P)*
BROWNE †3
BRYANT *(E)*
BUCHAN
BUNYAN
BURNEY
BURTON *(E)*
BUTLER *(A)*
   (P)
CABELL
CAPOTE
CARVER *(A/P)*
CATHER
CAVAFY *(P) *11*
CIBBER *(D/P)*
CLARKE
CLEARY
CONDON
CONRAD
COONEY *(D)*
COOPER
COWARD *(D)*
COWPER *(P)*
CRABBE *(P)*
CRONIN
DANIEL *(P)*
DAUDET
DAVIES *(P)*

DE VERE *(P)*
DRYDEN *(D/P)*
DUNBAR *(P)*
ÉLUARD *(P)*
EMPSON *(P)*
EUSDEN *(P)*
EVELYN *(E)*
FARRAR
FOUQUÉ
FOWLES
FRANCE
FRASER
FRISCH *(A/D)*
FUGARD *(D)*
FULLER *(A/P)*
GALTON *(D)*
GIBBON *(E)*
GOETHE *(D/P)*
GORDON
GRAHAM
GRAVES *(A/E/P)*
GREENE
HAILEY
HANLEY
HARRIS
HELLER
HEMANS *(P)*
HESIOD *(P)*
HILTON
HOBBES *(E)*
HOLMAN *(D)*
HOLMES *(E/P)*
HORACE *(P)*
HUGHES *(A)*
   (P)
IRVING *(A/E)*
   (A)
JEROME *(A/D)*
JONSON *(D/P)*
KEEFFE *(D)*
KELLER *(A/P)*
KIRKUP
KLEIST *(D)*
KRANTZ
LANDOR *(P)*
LARKIN *(P)*

LEASOR
LEVINE *(P)*
LINNEY *(D)*
LIVELY
LONDON
LOWELL *(P)*
LUCIAN *(P)*
LUDLUM
MAILER
MALORY
McBAIN
McEWAN
McKUEN *(P)*
MERCER *(D)*
MILLER *(A)*
   (D)
MILTON *(P)*
MOONEY
MORGAN *(A/D)*
MORRIS *(P)*
MROZEK *(D)*
NERVAL *(E/P)*
NESBIT
NEWMAN *(A/D)*
   (E)
O'BRIEN
O'CASEY *(D)*
O'NEILL *(D)*
ORWELL *(A/E) *5*
PARKER *(A)*
   (E)
PARKIN
PASCAL *(E)*
PETÖFI *(P)*
PINDAR *(P)*
PINERO *(D)*
PINTER *(D)*
PLAIDY
PORTER †7
   (A)
   (P)
POTTER *(A)*
   (D)
POWELL
PROUST
RACINE *(D)*

RIDLEY *(D)*
ROWLEY *(D)*
RUDKIN *(D)*
RUNYON
RUSKIN *(E)*
SALTEN
SAPPER *12
SAPPHO *(P)*
SARDOU *(D)*
SARTRE *(A/D/E)*
SAVAGE *(P)*
SAYERS
SENECA *(D)*
SEWELL
SHANGE *(D)*
SHARPE
SIDNEY *(P)*
SINGER
SMILES *(E)*
SPRING
STEELE *(D/E)*
STERNE
STOKER
STOREY *(D)*
SYMONS
TAGORE *(P)*
TAYLOR *(D)*
   (E)
TERSON *(D)*
THOMAS *(A)*
   (D/P)
   (D)
   (P)
TOLLER *(D/P)*
UNDSET
UPDIKE
UTTLEY
VALÉRY *(E/P)*
VIRGIL *(P)*
WALLER *(P)*
WALTON *(E)*
WANDOR *(D)*
WARTON *(P)*
WELDON
WERFEL *(A/P)*
WESKER *(D)*

WIGGIN
WILCOX *(P)*
WILDER *(A/D)*
WILLIS *(A/D)*
WILSON *(A)*
        (D)
WOTTON *(P)*
WRIGHT *(A/E)*
        (P)

7

ACKROYD *(A/E)*
ADDISON *(E)*
ALCAEUS *(P)*
ALVAREZ *(P)*
ANOUILH *(D)*
ARBUZOV *(D)*
ARIOSTO *(D/P)*
ARRABAL *(A/D)*
ASHBERY *(P)*
BAGNOLD
BALCHIN
BALDWIN *(A/D)*
BARSTOW
BECKETT *(A/D/P)*
BEDDOES *(P)*
BENNETT *(A)*
        (D)
BENTLEY
BERNARD *(D)*
BIGGERS
BLUNDEN *(E/P)*
BOSWELL *(E)*
BRENTON *(D)*
BRIDGES *(P)*
BÜCHNER *(D)*
BURGESS
BURNETT
CAEDMON *(P)*
CAMERON *(E)*
        (P)
CAMPION *(P)*
CANNING
CARLYLE *(E)*
CARROLL *(A/P)* *13

CHAPMAN *(D)*
        (P)
CHAUCER *(P)*
CHEKHOV *(D)*
CLAVELL
CLELAND
CLEMENS †9
CLEMENT *(D)*
COBBETT *(E)*
COCTEAU *(D/P)*
COETZEE
COLETTE
COLLINS
COOKSON
CORELLI
CREASEY
CURTEIS *(D)*
DEEPING
DELANEY *(D)*
DELEDDA
DELILLO
DICKENS
DIDEROT *(D/E)*
DODGSON *(A/P)* †13
DOUGLAS *(P)*
DOWLING *(P)*
DRABBLE
DRAYTON *(P)*
DREISER
DUHAMEL *(A/E)*
DUNSANY *(A/D)*
DURRELL
ELLMANN *(E)*
EMERSON *(E/P)*
ENRIGHT *(A/P)*
ERCILLA *(P)*
FEYDEAU *(D)*
FIRBANK
FLECKER *(P)*
FLEMING
FOLLETT
FORSTER
FORSYTH
FOSCOLO *(P)*
FRANCIS
FRENEAU *(P)*

GALLICO
GARDNER
GASKELL
GAUTIER *(A/P)*
GIBBONS
GILBERT *(D)*
GISSING
GOLDING
GOLDMAN
GOLDONI *(D)*
GOODMAN *(A/D)*
GOOLDEN
GRAHAME
HAGGARD
HAMMETT
HAMPTON *(D)*
HARTLEY
HARWOOD *(D)*
HAZLITT *(E)*
HELLMAN *(A/D)*
HERBERT *(A/D/E)*
        (A)
        (P)
HERRICK *(P)*
HEYWOOD *(D/E)*
HIBBERT
HIGGINS
HILLIER
HODGSON *(P)*
HOLBERG *(D/P)*
HOLROYD
HOPKINS *(P)*
HORNUNG
HOUSMAN *(P)*
HOWATCH
HUBBELL *(P)*
IONESCO *(D)*
IRELAND *(P)*
JACKSON *(P)*
JANSSON
JIMÉNEZ *(P)*
JOHNSON *(A)*
        (E/P)
KASTNER
KAUFMAN *(D)*
KAVAFIS *(P)* †11

PEOPLE – WRITERS

KEATING
KENNEDY *(E)*
KEROUAC
KIMMINS *(D)*
KIPLING *(A/P)*
LABICHE *(D)*
LEACOCK
LE CARRÉ *14
LEONARD *(D)*
LESSING
LINDSAY *(P)*
LOFTING
MACLEAN
MANNING
MARLOWE *(D/P)*
MARQUEZ
MARQUIS *(A/P)*
MARRYAT
MARVELL *(P)*
MASTERS
MAUGHAM *(A/D)*
MAURIAC
MAUROIS *(A/E)*
McGOUGH *(P)*
McGRATH *(D)*
McNEILE †12
MENCKEN *(E)*
MISHIMA *(A/D/P)*
MITFORD
MOLIÈRE *(D)* *15
MORAVIA
MUMFORD
MURDOCH
NABOKOV
NAIPAUL
NEWBOLT *(P)*
NICHOLS *(D)*
OSBORNE *(D)*
PATMORE *(P)*
PEACOCK *(A/P)*
PLAUTUS *(D)*
PREBBLE
PUSHKIN *(A/D/P)*
PYNCHON
QUENEAU *(A/P)*
RANSOME

RAPHAEL
RENDELL
RIDDELL *(P)*
RIMBAUD *(P)*
ROBBINS
ROBERTS
ROLLAND *(A/E)*
ROMAINS *(E/P)*
ROSTAND *(D)*
RUSHDIE
RUSSELL *(E)*
SAROYAN *(A/D)*
SASSOON *(P)*
SEYMOUR
SHAFFER *(D)*
SHELDON
SHELLEY *(A)*
(P)
SHEPARD *(D)*
SHERMAN *(D)*
SIMENON
SIMPSON *(D)*
SITWELL *(A)*
(A/P)
SKELTON *(P)*
SOUTHEY *(P)*
SPENDER *(P)*
SPENSER *(P)*
STEVENS *(P)*
STEWART
SURTEES
TERENCE *(D)*
THEROUX
THESPIS *(P)*
THOMSON *(P)*
THOREAU *(E/P)*
THURBER
THWAITE *(P)*
TOLKIEN
TOLSTOY
TOMALIN *(P)*
TOYNBEE *(E)*
TRAVERS *(A)*
(D)
USTINOV *(D)*
VAN VOGT

VAUGHAN *(P)*
VICENTE *(D)*
VINAVER *(D)*
WALLACE
WALPOLE *(A)*
(E/P)
WEBSTER *(D)*
WHARTON
WHITING *(D)*
WHITMAN *(P)*
WIELAND *(A/P)*
WYNDHAM

8

ALLBEURY
ANDERSEN
ANDERSON
APULEIUS *(E)*
BANVILLE *(D/P)*
BARBUSSE
BEAUMONT *(D)*
BEAUVOIR *(A/E)*
BEERBOHM
BENCHLEY
BETJEMAN *(P)*
BJÖRNSON *(A/D)*
BRADBURY
BROOKNER
BROWNING *(P)*
BRUNHOFF
CALDWELL
CAMPBELL *(P)*
CARTLAND
CATULLUS *(P)*
CHANDLER
CHRISTIE *(A/D)*
CONGREVE *(D/P)*
COOLIDGE
CORNWELL †14
CROMPTON
CUMMINGS *(P)*
D'AVENANT *(D/P)*
DAY-LEWIS *(A *6/P)*
DEIGHTON
DE LA MARE *(A/P)*

DISRAELI
DONLEAVY
DUDEVANT †2
ETHEREGE (D)
FARQUHAR (D)
FAULKNER
FIELDING (A/D)
FLANNERY (D)
FLAUBERT
FLETCHER (D)
(P)
FORESTER
FREELING
GARFIELD
GINSBERG (P)
GONCOURT
GREVILLE (P)
HASTINGS (A)
(D)
HEINLEIN
HUYSMANS
JENNINGS (P)
KÁLIDÁSA (D)
KAVANAGH
KAWABATA
KENEALLY
KINGSLEY
KOESTLER (A/E)
KOTZEBUE (D)
LAGERLÖF
LANGLAND (P)
LAWRENCE (A/P)
(E)
LEOPARDI (P)
LOCKHART (E)
LONGFORD
LOVELACE (P)
MACAULAY (A/P)
(E)
MacINNES (A/P)
MacNEICE (P)
MALLARMÉ (P)
MARIVAUX (D)
MARQUAND
MELVILLE
MENANDER (D/P)

MEREDITH (A/P)
MICHELET (E)
MICHENER
MITCHELL
MOORCOCK
MORTIMER (A/D)
NEKRASOV (P)
PALGRAVE (P)
PERELMAN
PERRAULT
PETRARCH (P)
POQUELIN (D) †15
QUENNELL (E)
RABELAIS
RATTIGAN (D)
REMARQUE
RICHARDS
ROSSETTI (P)
ROUSSEAU (E)
RUNEBERG (P)
SABATINI
SALINGER
SANDBURG (P)
SCHILLER (D/P)
SHADWELL (D)
SHERIDAN (D)
SHERRIFF (A/D)
SILLITOE
SINCLAIR
SMOLLETT
SPILLANE
STAFFORD (P)
STENDHAL *4
STOPPARD (D)
STRACHEY (A/E)
SUCKLING (D/P)
TEASDALE (P)
TENNYSON (P)
TIBULLUS (P)
TRAHERNE (P)
TREMBLAY (A/D)
TROLLOPE
TULSI DAS (P)
TURGENEV (A/D)
VANBRUGH (D)
VERLAINE (P)

VOLTAIRE (A/D/E) *10
VONNEGUT
WAMBAUGH
WEDEKIND (D)
WEDGWOOD (E)
WHEATLEY
WHITTIER (P)
WILLIAMS (D)
(P)
XENOPHON (E)

9

AESCHYLUS (D)
AINSWORTH
AKHMATOVA (P)
ALDINGTON (A/E/P)
ALLINGHAM (A)
(P)
ARBUTHNOT (E)
ARISTOTLE (E)
AYCKBOURN (D)
BERESFORD
BLACKMORE
BLEASDALE (D)
BOCCACCIO (A/P)
BRICKHILL
BRIGHOUSE (D)
BURROUGHS
CAECILIUS (P)
CALVERLEY (P)
CERVANTES
CHARRIÈRE
CHARTERIS
CHURCHILL (D)
(E)
COLERIDGE (P)
CORNEILLE (D)
CRESSWELL
D'ANNUNZIO (A/D/P)
DE FILIPPO (D)
DE LA RAMÉE †8
DE LA ROCHE
DE QUINCEY (E)
DICKINSON (P)

DU MAURIER
DURBRIDGE *(D)*
ECKERMANN
EDGEWORTH
EURIPIDES *(D)*
FORRESTER
FROISSART *(E/P)*
GIRAUDOUX *(A/D)*
GLANVILLE
GOLDSMITH *(A/D/P)*
GONCHAROV
GROSSMITH
HAUPTMANN *(D)*
HAWTHORNE
HEMINGWAY
HIGHSMITH
HÖLDERLIN *(P)*
HOUSEHOLD
INNAURATO *(D)*
ISHERWOOD
KLOPSTOCK *(P)*
LA BRUYÈRE
LA FRENAIS *(D)*
LAMARTINE *(E/P)*
LAMPEDUSA
LERMONTOV *(P)*
LINKLATER
LLEWELLYN
LUCRETIUS *(P)*
LYTTELTON *(P)*
MACDONALD
MACKENZIE
MANKOWITZ *(A/D)*
MANSFIELD
MARTINEAU
MASEFIELD *(P)*
MASSINGER *(D)*
METALIOUS
MIDDLETON *(D)*
MONSARRAT
MONTAIGNE *(E)*
NICHOLSON *(P)*
O'FLAHERTY
OSTROVSKY *(D)*
PARKINSON *(E)*
PASTERNAK

POLIAKOFF *(D)*
POMERANCE *(D)*
PRIESTLEY *(A/D)*
PRITCHETT *(A/E)*
RADCLIFFE
ROCHESTER
ROSENTHAL *(D)*
SACKVILLE *(P)*
SCHREINER
SHENSTONE *(P)*
SHOLOKHOV
SIMONIDES *(P)*
SLAUGHTER
SOPHOCLES *(D)*
SOUTHWELL *(P)*
STACPOOLE
STEINBECK
STEVENSON *(A/E/P)*
SWINBURNE *(P)*
THACKERAY
UNGARETTI *(P)*
VERHAEREN *(P)*
VITTORINI
WERGELAND *(D/P)*
WHITEHEAD *(A/P)*
WODEHOUSE
WYCHERLEY *(D)*
YANKOWITZ *(D)*

10

BAINBRIDGE
BALLANTYNE
BAUDELAIRE *(P)*
BUCKERIDGE
CHATTERTON *(P)*
CHESTERTON *(A/E/P)*
CLAUDIANUS *(P)*
DOSTOEVSKY
DRINKWATER *(D/E/P)*
DÜRRENMATT *(A/D)*
FITZGERALD *(A)*
(E/P)
GALSWORTHY *(A/D)*
KESSELRING *(D)*

LA FONTAINE *(A/P)*
LAGERKVIST *(A/D/P)*
LONGFELLOW *(P)*
MacDIARMID *(P)*
MAUPASSANT
MAYAKOVSKY *(P)*
McGONAGALL *(P)*
MUGGERIDGE *(E)*
PIRANDELLO *(A/D)*
PROPERTIUS *(P)*
RICHARDSON
SCHNITZLER *(A/D)*
STRINDBERG *(A/D/P)*
TARKINGTON *(A/D)*
THEOCRITUS *(P)*
THUCYDIDES *(E)*
VAN DER POST
VANSITTART
WATERHOUSE *(A/D)*
WILLIAMSON
WORDSWORTH *(P)*
XENOPHANES *(E)*

11

ANZENGRÜBER *(A/D)*
APOLLINAIRE *(P)*
ARCHILOCHUS *(P)*
BARING-GOULD
BACCHYLIDES *(P)*
BLESSINGTON
CALLIMACHUS *(P)*
CASTIGLIONE *(E/P)*
DELDERFIELD
DION CASSIUS *(E)*
DOUGLAS-HOME *(D)*
EICHENDORFF *(A/E/P)*
GRILLPARZER *(D/P)*
KAZANTZAKIS *(A/P)*
MAETERLINCK *(D/P)*
MONTHERLANT *(A/D)*
OMAR KHAYYÁM *(P)*
O'SHAUGNESSY *(P)*
PÉREZ GALDÓS *(A/D)*
SHAKESPEARE *(D/P)*

SIENKIEWICZ
STREATFEILD
YEVTUSHENKO *(P)*

12

ARISTOPHANES *(D)*
BEAUMARCHAIS *(D)*
BLASCO IBÁÑEZ
BRACKENRIDGE *(A/D)*
BULWER-LYTTON *(A/D/E)*
FEUCHTWANGER *(A/D)*
HOFMANNSTHAL *(D/P)*
MARTIN DU GARD
QUILLER-COUCH *(E/P)*

ROBBE-GRILLET
SAINT-EXUPÉRY
SOLZHENITSYN

13

CHATEAUBRIAND *(E)*
CSOKONAI VITEZ *(P)*
HARISHCHANDRA *(E/P)*
SACKVILLE-WEST *(A/P)*
TIRSO DE MOLINA *(D)*

14

BRILLAT-SAVARIN *(E)*

COMPTON-BURNETT
GRIMMELSHAUSEN
LECONTE DE LISLE *(P)*
MANNING-SANDERS
OEHLENSCHLÄGER *(D/P)*
SULLY-PRUDHOMME *(P)*
TAYLOR BRADFORD
ZORRILLA Y MORAL *(P)*

15

BARRETT-BROWNING *(P)*
DIODORUS SICULUS *(E)*
GRANVILLE BARKER *(D)*

SPORT

RACEHORSES

(F) = Flat   (N) = National hunt   (S) = Showjumping/equestrianism

3

ESB *(N)*
OXO *(N)*

4

BULA *(N)*
CROW *(N)*
MELD *(F)*
TEAL *(N)*
TROY *(F)*

5

ANGLO *(N)*
ARKLE *(N)*
AYALA *(N)*
DANTE *(F)*
LADAS *(F)*
PIAFF *(S)*
PINZA *(F)*
PSALM *(S)*
RELKO *(F)*
RIBOT *(F)*
TRIGO *(F)*
UNITE *(F)*

6

ALIYSA *(F)*
BIG BEN *(S)*
DAHLIA *(F)*
DARIUS *(F)*
DIOMED *(F)*
EMPREY *(F)*

GRUNDY *(F)*
HENBIT *(F)*
LUCIUS *(N)*
MR WHAT *(N)*
MY LOVE *(F)*
NIMBUS *(F)*
PHILCO *(S)*
RED RUM *(N)*
RIBERO *(F)*
ROCKET *(S)*
SAGACE *(F)*
SIR KEN *(N)*
SUNDEW *(N)*
TULYAR *(F)*
VIRAGO *(F)*

7

ALLEGED *(F)*
BUSTINO *(F)*
CAUGHOO *(N)*
DAWN RUN *(N)*
DEISTER *(S)*
DOUBLET *(S)*
ECLIPSE *(N)*
GAY TRIP *(N)*
GRITTAR *(N)*
KAHYASI *(F)*
KILMORE *(N)*
MAHMOUD *(F)*
MORSTON *(F)*
MR FRISK *(N)*
NASHWAN *(F)*
PARTHIA *(F)*
PHAR LAP *(F)*
PSIDIUM *(F)*
RIBOCCO *(F)*

ROBERTO *(F)*
RUBSTIC *(N)*
SECRETO *(F)*
SHADEED *(F)*
SHERGAR *(F)*
SIR IVOR *(F)*
SPECIFY *(N)*
ST PADDY *(F)*
TEENOSO *(F)*
WEST TIP *(N)*

8

AFFIRMED *(F)*
ALDANITI *(N)*
BEN NEVIS *(N)*
BLAKENEY *(F)*
CHARISMA *(S)*
COLUMBUS *(S)*
CORBIÈRE *(N)*
CREPELLO *(F)*
FLANAGAN *(S)*
FOINAVON *(N)*
GALCADOR *(F)*
HYPERION *(F)*
JAY TRUMP *(N)*
LARKSPUR *(F)*
LAVANDIN *(F)*
MAN OF WAR *(F)*
MILL REEF *(F)*
MR SOFTEE *(S)*
NIJINSKY *(F)*
NONOALCO *(F)*
RAG TRADE *(N)*
RYAN'S SON *(S)*
STROLLER *(S)*
WELL TO DO *(N)*

9

BEETHOVEN *(S)*
BOOMERANG *(S)*
EARLY MIST *(N)*
FOXHUNTER *(S)*
HIGHCLERE *(F)*
LANZAROTE *(N)*
L'ESCARGOT *(N)*
MANIFESTO *(N)*
MILL HOUSE *(N)*
OH SO SHARP *(F)*
PERSIMMON *(F)*
PHIL DRAKE *(F)*
PRICELESS *(S)*
RHINEGOLD *(F)*
SEA BIRD II *(F)*
SEA PIGEON *(N)*
TAP ON WOOD *(F)*
WHAT A MYTH *(N)*

10

BELLA PAOLA *(F)*
FREEBOOTER *(N)*
HALLO DANDY *(N)*
HARD RIDDEN *(F)*
MERRYMAN II *(N)*
MONKSFIELD *(N)*
NICKEL COIN *(N)*
NIGHT NURSE *(N)*
PEARL DIVER *(F)*
PERSIAN WAR *(N)*
POCAHONTAS *(F)*
QUARE TIMES *(N)*
SANGLAMORE *(F)*
SANTA CLAUS *(F)*
SEE YOU THEN *(N)*

SLIP ANCHOR *(F)*
SNOW KNIGHT *(F)*
TEAM SPIRIT *(N)*
THE THINKER *(N)*
WINDSOR LAD *(F)*

11

ALLEZ FRANCE *(F)*
CHARLOTTOWN *(F)*
CORNISHMAN V *(S)*
COTTAGE RAKE *(N)*
DUNFERMLINE *(F)*
EL GRAN SEÑOR *(F)*
HERRINGBONE *(F)*
LAST SUSPECT *(N)*
MOON MADNESS *(F)*
NEVER SAY DIE *(F)*
ROYAL PALACE *(F)*
RUSSIAN HERO *(N)*
SECRETARIAT *(F)*
SHAHRASTANI *(F)*
SUN PRINCESS *(F)*
THE MINSTREL *(F)*

12

ARCTIC PRINCE *(F)*
COMMANCHE RUN *(F)*
DANCING BRAVE *(F)*
DESERT ORCHID *(N)*
DON'T FORGET ME *(F)*
GOLDEN FLEECE *(F)*
GOLDEN MILLER *(N)*
ÎLE DE BOURBON *(F)*
MAORI VENTURE *(N)*
NATIVE DANCER *(F)*
PETITE ETOILE *(F)*
QUEST FOR FAME *(F)*
RAINBOW QUEST *(F)*
RED ALLIGATOR *(N)*
REYNOLDSTOWN *(N)*
RHYME 'N' REASON *(N)*
STRAIGHT DEAL *(F)*

13

A TOUCH OF CLASS *(S)*
CAPTAIN CUTTLE *(F)*
EXHIBITIONIST *(F)*

LITTLE POLVEIR *(N)*
LOVELY COTTAGE *(N)*
TUDOR MINSTREL *(F)*

14

CAPTAIN CHRISTY *(N)*
COMEDY OF ERRORS *(N)*
DIAMOND JUBILEE *(F)*
FORGIVE 'N' FORGET *(N)*
MERELY-A-MONARCH *(S)*
NICOLAUS SILVER *(N)*
NORTHERN DANCER *(F)*
REFERENCE POINT *(F)*
SHEILA'S COTTAGE *(N)*
SHIRLEY HEIGHTS *(F)*

15

BRIGADIER GERARD *(F)*
BURROUGH HILL LAD *(N)*
HIGHLAND WEDDING *(N)*
MASTER CRAFTSMAN *(S)*
PRIVY COUNCILLOR *(F)*

SPORT

SPORTS COMPETITIONS

(A) = Athletics   (AF) = American football   (B) = Badminton
(BA) = Baseball   (BO) = Bowls   (BX) = Boxing   (C) = Cricket
(CY) = Cycling   (D) = Darts   (EF) = Eton Fives
(EQ) = Equestrianism/showjumping   (F) = Football   (FE) = Fencing
(FL) = Flying/gliding   (G) = Golf   (GR) = Greyhound-racing   (H) = Hockey
(HR) = Horse-racing   (IH) = Ice-hockey   (L) = Lacrosse
(MC) = Motorcycle-racing   (MR) = Motor-racing/rallying   (P) = Polo
(R) = Rugby   (RS) = Rifle-shooting   (RT) = Real Tennis   (RW) = Rowing
(S) = Swimming   (SN) = Snooker   (T) = Tennis   (TT) = Table-tennis
(Y) = Yachting
(v) = various sports

3

PGA *(G)*

4

EBOR *(HR)*
OAKS *(HR)*
OPEN *(G)*

5

ASHES *(C)*
DERBY *(HR)*
FA CUP *(F)*

6

FA VASE *(F)*
LE MANS *(MR)*
US OPEN *(G/T)*

7

GOLD CUP *(HR)*
LINCOLN *(HR)*

MILK CUP *(F)*
ROUS CUP *(F)*
SKOL CUP *(F)*
ST LEGER *(HR)*
THE OPEN *(G)*
UBER CUP *(B)*
UEFA CUP *(F)*
VOLK CUP *(GL)*

8

BOAT RACE *(RW)*
DAVIS CUP *(T)*
GUCCI CUP *(EQ)*
KING'S CUP *(T)*
MILK RACE *(CY)*
OLYMPICS *(A/v)*
POT BLACK *(SN)*
ROSE BOWL *(AF)*
RYDER CUP *(G)*
SIMOD CUP *(F)*
THE ASHES *(C)*
WELSH CUP *(F)*
WORLD CUP *(F/v)*

9

CURRIE CUP *(R)*
CURTIS CUP *(G)*
DREAM MILE *(A)*
LEAGUE CUP *(F/R)*
QUEEN'S CUP *(P)*
SUPERBOWL *(AF)*
TALBOT CUP *(BO)*
THAMES CUP *(RW)*
THOMAS CUP *(B)*
US MASTERS *(G)*
WALKER CUP *(G)*
WIMBLEDON *(T)*
WYFOLD CUP *(RW)*
ZENITH CUP *(F)*

10

AMATEUR CUP *(F)*
DUNHILL CUP *(G)*
FRENCH OAKS *(HR)*
FRENCH OPEN *(T)*
NATIONS CUP *(SH)*
STANLEY CUP *(IH)*
TWINING CUP *(SH)*

11

ADMIRAL'S CUP *(Y)*
AMERICA'S CUP *(Y)*
BATHURST CUP *(RT)*
BREEDERS' CUP *(HR)*
BRITISH OPEN *(G)*
CALCUTTA CUP *(R)*
CESAREWITCH *(HR)*
EUROPEAN CUP *(F/A)*
FASTNET RACE *(Y)*
GILLETTE CUP *(C)*
GOODWOOD CUP *(HR)*
HARRISON CUP *(P)*
IROQUOIS CUP *(L)*
KINNAIRD CUP *(EF)*
KOLAPORE CUP *(RS)*
LADA CLASSIC *(SN)*
MILLE MIGLIA *(MR)*
PRIX DU DIANE *(HR)*
QUEEN'S PRIZE *(RF)*
RANJI TROPHY *(C)*
SAFARI RALLY *(MR)*
SCOTTISH CUP *(F)*
SHELL SHIELD *(C)*
SHELL TROPHY *(C)*
TARGA FLIORA *(MR)*
THE OLYMPICS *(A/v)*
TRIPLE CROWN *(R)*
WATERLOO CUP *(BO)*
WIGHTMAN CUP *(T)*
WORLD SERIES *(BA)*

12

AMERICAN BOWL *(AF)*
ASCOT GOLD CUP *(HR)*
BRITISH DERBY *(EQ)*
CHALLENGE CUP *(R)*
CORBILLON CUP *(TT)*
EBOR HANDICAP *(HR)*
HENRY LEAF CUP *(RT)*
HOSPITALS' CUP *(R)*
INDIANAPOLIS *(MR)*
MIDDLETON CUP *(B)*

OLYMPIC GAMES *(A/v)*
SAVAGE SHIELD *(FE)*
TEXACO TROPHY *(C)*
TOUR DE FRANCE *(CY)*
WORLD MASTERS *(D)*

13

BELMONT STAKES *(HR)*
BOLOGNA TROPHY *(S)*
BUDWEISER BOWL *(AF)*
CHARITY SHIELD *(F)*
CORNHILL TESTS *(C)*
CORONATION CUP *(HR)*
DIAMOND SCULLS *(RW)*
DOUGLAS TROPHY *(FL)*
DUNLOP MASTERS *(G)*
ECLIPSE STAKES *(HR)*
FEDERATION CUP *(T)*
GRAND NATIONAL *(HR)*
HENLEY REGATTA *(RW)*
JULES RIMET CUP *(F)*
KENTUCKY DERBY *(HR)*
LANCOME TROPHY *(G)*
NAT WEST TROPHY *(C)*
OXFORD TORPIDS *(RW)*
PILKINGTON CUP *(R)*
SCURRY GOLD CUP *(GR)*
SWAYTHLING CUP *(TT)*
TOURIST TROPHY *(MC)*
VOLVO WORLD CUP *(EQ)*

14

AUSTRALIAN OPEN *(T)*
BRABAZON TROPHY *(G)*
BUDWEISER DERBY *(HR)*
CAMBRIDGE LENTS *(RW)*
CAMBRIDGESHIRE *(HR)*
CHAMPION HURDLE *(HR)*
COVENTRY STAKES *(HR)*
COWDRAY PARK CUP *(P)*
EMSLEY CARR MILE *(A)*
FIVE NATIONS CUP *(R)*
GIMCRACK STAKES *(HR)*
GREYHOUND DERBY *(GR)*

SPORT – SPORTS COMPETITIONS

HICKSTEAD DERBY *(EQ)*
INTER-CITIES CUP *(F)*
LITTLEWOODS CUP *(F)*
LONDON MARATHON *(A)*
RUNFURLY SHIELD *(R)*

15

CHAMPIONS' TROPHY *(H)*
CONSTRUCTORS' CUP *(MR)*
LINCOLN HANDICAP *(HR)*
LOMBARD/RAC RALLY *(MR)*

MIDDLESEX SEVENS *(R)*
MONTE CARLO RALLY *(MR)*
PARIS-DAKAR RALLY *(MR)*
PGA CHAMPIONSHIP *(G)*
PREAKNESS STAKES *(HR)*
SCHNEIDER TROPHY *(FL)*
SHEFFIELD SHIELD *(C)*
SHERPA VAN TROPHY *(F)*
THOUSAND GUINEAS *(HR)*
WBA CHAMPIONSHIP *(BX)*
WBC CHAMPIONSHIP *(BX)*
WINGFIELD SCULLS *(RW)*
WOOLWICH MASTERS *(BO)*

SPORT

SPORTS TEAMS – FOOTBALL

*All England/Wales except: (E) = Europe   (I) = Ireland   (S) = Scottish League
(SA) = South America   (US) = USA
† = Common abbreviation/nickname*

3

AYR *(S)*
QPR †
WBA †

4

AJAX *(E)*
ARDS *(I)*
BURY
CITY †
HIBS *(S)* †
HULL
YORK

5

ALLOA *(S)*
CLYDE *(S)*
CREWE
DERBY
LAZIO *(E)*
LEEDS
LUTON
RAITH *(S)*
SPURS †
STOKE
VILLA †
WIGAN

6

AC ROMA *(E)*
ALBION *(S)*
BOLTON
CELTIC *(S)*
DUNDEE *(S)*
EXETER
FOREST †
FORFAR *(S)*
FULHAM
HEARTS *(S)* †
HONVED *(E)*
MAN UTD †
MONACO *(E)*

MORTON *(S)*
NAPOLI *(E)*
OLDHAM
ORIENT †
OXFORD
PALACE †
ROVERS †
SANTOS *(SA)*
UNITED †
WOLVES †

7

AC MILAN *(E)*
AIRDRIE *(S)*

ARSENAL
BENFICA *(E)*
BERWICK *(S)*
BRECHIN *(S)*
BURNLEY
CARDIFF
CHELSEA
CHESTER
COLOGNE *(E)*
EVERTON
FALKIRK
FC MALMO *(E)*
FC PORTO *(E)*
GRIMSBY
HALIFAX

IPSWICH
LINCOLN
MAN CITY †
NORWICH
PARTICK *(S)*
PRESTON
RANGERS *(S)*
READING
SWANSEA
SWINDON
TORQUAY
WALSALL
WATFORD
WEST HAM
WREXHAM

8

ABERDEEN *(S)*
ARBROATH *(S)*
BARNSLEY
BESIKTAS *(E)*
BRADFORD
BRIGHTON
CARLISLE
CHARLTON
COVENTRY
EAST FIFE
FC TWENTE *(E)*
HAMILTON *(S)*
HEREFORD
HULL CITY
JUVENTUS *(E)*
KATOWICE *(E)*
LINFIELD *(I)*
MILLWALL
MONTROSE *(S)*
PLYMOUTH
PORT VALE
ROCHDALE
SÃO PAULO *(SA)*
SOUTHEND
STIRLING *(S)*
ST MIRREN *(S)*
TRANMERE

VALENCIA *(E)*
WEST BROM †
YORK CITY

9

ALDERSHOT
AYR UNITED *(S)*
BALLYMENA *(I)*
BARCELONA *(E)*
BLACKBURN
BLACKPOOL
BOHEMIANS *(I)*
BRENTFORD
CAMBRIDGE
CLYDEBANK *(S)*
DONCASTER
DUMBARTON *(S)*
EINTRACHT *(E)*
FEYENOORD *(E)*
GLENTORAN *(I)*
HIBERNIAN *(S)*
LEICESTER
LINGFIELD *(I)*
LIVERPOOL
LUTON TOWN
MAIDSTONE
MANSFIELD
MAN UNITED †
NEWCASTLE
ROTHERHAM
SAMPDORIA *(E)*
ST ÉTIENNE *(E)*
STOCKPORT
STOKE CITY
STRANRAER
SV HAMBURG *(E)*
TOTTENHAM
WANDERERS †
WEDNESDAY †
WIMBLEDON

10

ANDERLECHT *(E)*

ASTON VILLA
BIRMINGHAM
DARLINGTON
DYNAMO KIEV *(E)*
EXETER CITY
GILLINGHAM
GOTHENBURG *(E)*
HARTLEPOOL
INTER MILAN *(E)*
KILMARNOCK *(S)*
MEADOWBANK *(S)*
MOTHERWELL *(S)*
OLYMPIAKOS *(E)*
PORTSMOUTH
QUEEN'S PARK *(S)*
REAL MADRID *(E)*
RIVER PLATE *(SA)*
SCUNTHORPE
SHREWSBURY
SUNDERLAND

11

BOURNEMOUTH
BRECHIN CITY *(S)*
BRISTOL CITY
CARDIFF CITY
CHESTER CITY
COWDENBEATH *(S)*
DERBY COUNTY
DUKLA PRAGUE *(E)*
DUNFERMLINE *(S)*
FERENCVAROS *(E)*
GRIMSBY TOWN
HALIFAX TOWN
IPSWICH TOWN
LEEDS UNITED
LINCOLN CITY
NORTHAMPTON
NORWICH CITY
NOTTS COUNTY †
NOTTS FOREST †
RAITH ROVERS
SCARBOROUGH
SOUTHAMPTON

ST JOHNSTONE
SWANSEA CITY
SWINDON TOWN
UJPEST DOZSA *(E)*

STENHOUSEMUIR *(S)*
TORQUAY UNITED
WEST HAM UNITED
WIGAN ATHLETIC

12

ALBION ROVERS *(S)*
BAYERN MUNICH *(E)*
BRADFORD CITY
CHESTERFIELD
COVENTRY CITY
DUNDEE UNITED *(S)*
EAST STIRLING *(S)*
GRASSHOPPERS *(E)*
HUDDERSFIELD
LEYTON ORIENT
MOSCOW DYNAMO *(E)*
OXFORD UNITED
PETERBOROUGH
PSV EINDHOVEN *(E)*
REAL SOCIEDAD *(E)*
WEST BROMWICH

13

AIRDRIEONIANS *(S)*
ALLOA ATHLETIC *(S)*
BRISTOL ROVERS
CARL ZEISS JENA *(E)*
CRYSTAL PALACE
DINAMO TBILISI *(E)*
DYNAMO DRESDEN *(E)*
GLASGOW CELTIC *(S)*
INDEPENDIENTE *(SA)*
LEGIA WARSZAWA *(E)*
LEICESTER CITY
MAIDSTONE TOWN
MANSFIELD TOWN
MIDDLESBROUGH
MOSCOW SPARTAK *(E)*
NEW YORK COSMOS *(US)*
PANATHINAIKOS *(E)*
SPARTAK MOSCOW *(E)*
STANDARD LIÈGE *(E)*

14

ATLETICO BILBAO *(E)*
ATLETICO MADRID *(E)*
BERWICK RANGERS *(S)*
BIRMINGHAM CITY
CARLISLE UNITED
CREWE ALEXANDRA
FORFAR ATHLETIC *(S)*
GLASGOW RANGERS *(S)*
HEREFORD UNITED
MANCHESTER CITY
OLDHAM ATHLETIC
PARIS ST GERMAIN *(E)*
PARTICK THISTLE *(S)*
PLYMOUTH ARGYLE
SHREWSBURY TOWN
SOUTHEND UNITED
SPORTING LISBON *(E)*
STIRLING ALBION *(S)*
TRANMERE ROVERS
ZENIT LENINGRAD *(E)*

15

BLACKBURN ROVERS
BOLTON WANDERERS
CAMBRIDGE UNITED
DONCASTER ROVERS
NEWCASTLE UNITED
NORTHAMPTON TOWN
PRESTON NORTH END
QUEEN OF THE SOUTH *(S)*
RED STAR BELGRADE *(E)*
SCARBOROUGH TOWN
SHEFFIELD UNITED
STEAVA BUCHAREST *(E)*
STOCKPORT COUNTY
TAMPA BAY ROWDIES *(US)*

SPORT

SPORTS TEAMS – RUGBY

(L) = Rugby League   (N) = National side
† = National nickname

3
AYR

4
BATH
KENT
HULL *(L)*
SALE
YORK *(L)*

5
DEVON
FYLDE
ITALY *(N)*
JAPAN *(N)*
KELSO
KIWIS *†*
  (New Zealand)
LEEDS *(L)*
LEIGH *(L)*
LIONS *†*
  (Britain)
NEATH
PUMAS *†*
  (Argentina)
RUGBY
WALES *(N)*
WASPS
WIGAN *(L)*

6
BARROW *(L)*
BATLEY *(L)*

DURHAM
EXETER
FRANCE *(N)*
FULHAM *(L)*
HAVANT
HULL KR *(L)*
OLDHAM *(L)*
ORRELL
OXFORD
SURREY
WIDNES *(L)*

7
BEDFORD
BRISTOL
CARDIFF
CHORLEY *(L)*
ENGLAND *(N)*
HALIFAX *(L)*
HUNSLET *(L)*
IRELAND *(N)*
MAESTEG
MELROSE
MOSELEY
ROMANIA *(N)*
SALFORD *(L)*
SWANSEA
SWINTON *(L)*

8
ABERAVON
ASPATRIA
BRIDGEND
CHESHIRE

CORNWALL
COVENTRY
DEWSBURY *(L)*
EBBW VALE
GOSFORTH
HEREFORD
KEIGHLEY *(L)*
LLANELLI
MIDLANDS
RICHMOND
SARACENS
SCOTLAND *(N)*
SOMERSET
ST HELENS *(L)*
TYNEDALE
WATERLOO

9
CAMBRIDGE
DONCASTER *(L)*
HAMPSHIRE
LEICESTER
MET POLICE
MIDDLESEX
SHEFFIELD *(L)*
WAKEFIELD *(L)*
WALLABIES *†*
  (Australia)
YORKSHIRE

10
BLACKHEATH
CASTLEFORD *(L)*
CUMBERLAND

GLOUCESTER
HARLEQUINS
LANCASHIRE
NOTTINGHAM
PONTYPRIDD
SPRINGBOKS *†*
  (South Africa)
VALE OF LUNE
WARRINGTON *(L)*
WHITEHAVEN *(L)*

11
ABERTILLERY
LONDON IRISH
LONDON WELSH
ROSSLYN PARK

12
EAST MIDLANDS
FEATHERSTONE *(L)*
WARWICKSHIRE

13
NORTH MIDLANDS
STAFFORDSHIRE

14
LONDON SCOTTISH
NORTHUMBERLAND

SPORT

SPORTS VENUES – FOOTBALL GROUNDS

*¶ = National stadium   * = Alternative name*

3

DEN *(Millwall) *1*
NÉP *(Hungary) ¶*

4

DELL *(Southampton) *2*

5

DA LUZ *(Benfica)*
IBROX *(Rangers) *3*
INÖNÜ *(Besiktas Istanbul)*
KIROV *(Zenit Leningrad)*
LEGIA *(Legia Warszawa)*
LENIN *(Spartak Moscow)*

6

ATOCHA *(San Sebastian)*
BESCOT *(Walsall)*
BOSUIL *(Antwerp)*
HEYSEL *(Belgium) ¶*
NECKAR *(Stuttgart)*
PRATER *(Austria) ¶*
TA'QALI *(Malta) ¶*
THE DEN *(Millwall) *1*
VALLEY *(Charlton) *4*

7

ANFIELD *(Liverpool)*
BAYVIEW *(East Fife)*
BISLETT *(Oslo)*
BOGHEAD *(Dumbarton)*
CAMP NOU *(Barcelona) *5*
DALL'ARA *(Bologna)*

ELM PARK *(Reading)*
FIR PARK *(Motherwell)*
JULISKA *(Dukla Prague)*
NOU CAMP *(Barcelona) *5*
SAN SIRO *(AC Milan)*
         (Inter Milan)
STRAHOV *(Czechoslovakia) ¶*
THE DELL *(Southampton) *2*
ULLEVÅL *(Norway) ¶*
WEMBLEY *(England) ¶*

8

BELLE VUE *(Doncaster Rovers)*
BERNABEU *(Real Madrid)*
COMUNALE *(Juventus)*
DEEPDALE *(Preston NE)*
DENS PARK *(Dundee)*
FEETHAMS *(Darlington)*
FIRS PARK *(East Stirling)*
FLAMINIO *(Lazio Rome)*
GIGG LANE *(Bury)*
HIGHBURY *(Arsenal)*
HOME PARK *(Plymouth Argyle)*
MARACAÑA *(Brazil) ¶*
MILLMOOR *(Rotherham Utd)*
MOLINEUX *(Wolves)*
MOSS ROSE *(Chester City)*
PARKHEAD *(Celtic)*
SAN MAMÉS *(Bilbao)*
SPOTLAND *(Rochdale)*
TURF MOOR *(Burnley)*
VALE PARK *(Port Vale)*
WANKDORF *(Switzerland) ¶*

9

DEAN COURT *(Bournemouth)*
EWOOD PARK *(Blackburn Rovers)*

FIELD MILL *(Mansfield Town)*
GAY MEADOW *(Shrewsbury Town)*
GLEBE PARK *(Brechin City)*
HAWTHORNS *(WBA) *6*
LEEDS ROAD *(Huddersfield Town)*
LINKS PARK *(Montrose)*
MAINE ROAD *(Manchester City)*
MANOR PARK *(Oxford Utd)*
NYA ULLEVI *(Gothenburg)*
OCHILVIEW *(Stenhousemuir)*
PLAINMOOR *(Torquay Utd)*
ROKER PARK *(Sunderland)*
ROOTS HALL *(Southend Utd)*
RUGBY PARK *(Kilmarnock)*
STAIR PARK *(Stranraer)*
ST ANDREWS *(Birmingham City)*
THE VALLEY *(Charlton) *4*
UPTON PARK *(West Ham Utd)*
VILLA PARK *(Aston Villa)*

10

ASHTON GATE *(Bristol City)*
CARROW ROAD *(Norwich City)*
CITY GROUND *(Notts Forest)*
EASTER ROAD *(Hibernian)*
EDGELY PARK *(Stockport Co)*
ELLAND ROAD *(Leeds Utd)*
GRESTY ROAD *(Crewe Alex)*
LOFTUS ROAD *(QPR)*
LONDON ROAD *(Peterborough Utd)*
LOVE STREET *(St Mirren)*
MEADOW LANE *(Notts County)*
NINIAN PARK *(Cardiff)*
(Wales) ¶
PLOUGH LANE *(Wimbledon)*
SEAMER ROAD *(Scarborough)*
SHAY GROUND *(Halifax)*
SINCIL BANK *(Lincoln City)*
STARKS PARK *(Raith Rovers)*
TYNECASTLE *(Hearts) *7*
VETCH FIELD *(Swansea City)*

11

BRAMALL LANE *(Sheffield Utd)*
BRUNO PLACHE *(Lokomotive Leipzig)*
BRUNTON PARK *(Carlisle Utd)*
BURNDEN PARK *(Bolton Wand)*
CENTRAL PARK *(Cowdenbeath)*
CLIFTONHILL *(Albion Rovers)*
DOUGLAS PARK *(Hamilton Acad)*
EAST END PARK *(Dunfermline Ath)*
EDGAR STREET *(Hereford Utd)*
FIRHILL PARK *(Partick Thistle)*
FRATTON PARK *(Portsmouth)*
GRIFFIN PARK *(Brentford)*
HAMPDEN PARK *(Queen's Park)*
(Scotland) ¶
IDRAETSPARK *(Denmark) ¶*
OAKWELL PARK *(Barnsley)*
OLD TRAFFORD *(Manchester Utd)*
PORTMAN ROAD *(Ipswich Town)*
PRENTON PARK *(Tranmere Rovers)*
ST JAMES PARK *(Exeter City)*
(Newcastle Utd)
STATION PARK *(Forfar Ath)*
TWERTON PARK *(Bristol Rovers)*
WINDSOR PARK *(Linfield)*
(N Ireland) ¶

12

ABBEY STADIUM *(Cambridge Utd)*
ANNFIELD PARK *(Stirling Alb)*
AYRESOME PARK *(Middlesbrough)*
BLUNDELL PARK *(Grimsby Town)*
BOUNDARY PARK *(Oldham Ath)*
BRISBANE ROAD *(Leyton Orient)*
COLD BLOW LANE *(Millwall) *1*
COUNTY GROUND *(Northampton Town)*
(Swindon Town)
GAYFIELD PARK *(Arbroath)*
GLANFORD PARK *(Scunthorpe Utd)*
GOODISON PARK *(Everton)*
HILLSBOROUGH *(Sheffield Wed)*
IBROX STADIUM *(Rangers) *3*
KILBOWIE PARK *(Clydebank)*

SPORT – SPORTS VENUES – FOOTBALL GROUNDS

SELHURST PARK *(Crystal Palace)*
SOMERSET PARK *(Ayr Utd)*
THE HAWTHORNS *(WBA) *6*
VALLEY PARADE *(Bradford City)*
VICARAGE ROAD *(Watford)*

13

CAPPIELOW PARK *(Morton)*
CRAVEN COTTAGE *(Fulham)*
DALYMOUNT PARK *(Bohemians)*
(Ireland) ¶
FILBERT STREET *(Leicester City)*
HIGHFIELD ROAD *(Coventry City)*
McDIARMID PARK *(St Johnstone)*
PITTODRIE PARK *(Aberdeen)*
TANNADICE PARK *(Dundee Utd)*
VASILIJ LEVSKI *(Bulgaria)* ¶
WATLING STREET *(Maidstone Utd)*
WHITE HART LANE *(Spurs)*

14

BASEBALL GROUND *(Derby Co)*

BLOOMFIELD ROAD *(Blackpool)*
BOOTHFERRY PARK *(Hull City)*
BROCKVILLE PARK *(Falkirk)*
BROOMFIELD PARK *(Airdrie)*
GIUSEPPE MEAZZA *(Milan)*
KENILWORTH ROAD *(Luton Town)*
PALMERSTON PARK *(Queen of the
South)*
PARC DES PRINCES *(Paris St
Germain)*
*(Racing Club
de Paris)*
(France) ¶
RECREATION PARK *(Alloa Ath)*
SHIELFIELD PARK *(Berwick Rangers)*
STAMFORD BRIDGE *(Chelsea)*
TYNECASTLE PARK *(Hearts) *7*
VICTORIA GROUND *(Hartlepool)*
(Stoke City)

15

BOOTHAM CRESCENT *(York City)*
SPRINGFIELD PARK *(Wigan Ath)*

SPORT

SPORTS VENUES – GENERAL

(A) = Athletics   (B) = Badminton   (BO) = Bowls   (BX) = Boxing
(C) = Cricket   (CQ) = Croquet   (CY) = Cycling   (D) = Darts
(EQ) = Equestrianism/showjumping   (G) = Golf   (GF) = Gaelic Football
(GR) = Greyhound racing   (H) = Hockey   (HU) = Hurling   (J) = Judo
(MC) = Motor-cycling   (MR) = Motor-racing   (P) = Polo   (RO) = Rowing
(RT) = Real Tennis   (RU) = Rugby   (SH) = Shooting   (SN) = Snooker
(SP) = Speedway   (SQ) = Squash   (T) = Tennis   (TO) = Tobogganing
(v) = various

3

PAU *(MR)*
RIO *(MR)*
RYE *(G)*
SPA *(MR)*

4

AVUS *(MR)*
BRNO *(MC, MR)*
ENNA *(MR)*
FUJI *(MR)*
NIAZ *(C)*
OSLO *(A)*
OVAL *(C)*
WACA *(C)*

5.

ABLIS *(MR)*
ASSEN *(MC)*
CROFT *(MR)*
DACCA *(C)*
DIJON *(MR)*
DRING *(C)*
GABBA *(C)*
GOFFS *(SN)*
IMOLA *(MR)*
IQBAL *(C)*
JEREZ *(MR)*

LORD'S *(C)*
MONZA *(MC, MR)*
OLNEY *(Pancake Race)*
TROON *(G)*

6.

BELFRY *(G)*
BISLEY *(SH)*
BOURDA *(C)*
HENLEY *(RO)*
IMATRA *(MC)*
JARAMA *(MR)*
LA MOYE *(G)*
LE MANS *(MR)*
LYDDEN *(MR)*
MISANO *(MR)*
MONACO *(MR)*
OPORTO *(MR)*
OXFORD *(SP)*
RHEIMS *(MR)*
SUZUKA *(MC, MR)*
SYDNEY *(C)*
ZOLDER *(MR)*

7

ACHÈRES *(MR)*
AUGUSTA *(G)*

BRAEMAR *(Highland Games)*
CANFORD *(RT)*
CATFORD *(GR)*
CHEPAUK *(C)*
DAYTONA *(MC, MR)*
DETROIT *(MR)*
DRENTHE *(MR)*
DUNDROD *(MC, MR)*
ESTORIL *(MR)*
FENNERS *(C)*
FIR PARK *(MR)*
HEXAGON *(SN)*
HOYLAKE *(G)*
KYALAMI *(MR)*
MADONIE *(MR)*
NUGELLO *(MR)*
PESCARA *(MR)*
PHOENIX *(MR)*
SEBRING *(MR)*
THE WACA *(C)*
TRIPOLI *(MR)*
WEMBLEY *(v)*
ZELTWEG *(MR)*

8

ADELAIDE *(C, MR)*
BELLE VUE *(GR, SP)*
BRISBANE *(C)*
BURGHLEY *(EQ)*

CRUCIBLE *(SN)*
EDEN PARK *(C)*
FERNDOWN *(G)*
LAKESIDE *(D)*
LAS VEGAS *(BX, MR)*
LINDRICK *(G)*
MONTREAL *(MR)*
MOOR PARK *(G)*
NEWLANDS *(C)*
NIVELLES *(MR)*
SALZBURG *(MR)*
SANDWICH *(G)*
SELANGOR *(MR)*
ST JOVITE *(MR)*
ST MORITZ *(TO)*
ST PIERRE *(G)*
THE GABBA *(C)*
THE PARKS *(C)*
THRUXTON *(MR)*
VIDARBHA *(C)*
WATERLOO *(BO)*

9

BADMINTON *(EQ)*
BARCELONA *(MR)*
BOCA RATON *(T)*
BRABOURNE *(C)*
CROKE PARK *(G, HU)*
EDGBASTON *(C)*
ELLIS PARK *(C)*
GATESHEAD *(A)*
GREEN PARK *(C)*
GUILDHALL *(BO, SN)*
HALL GREEN *(G)*
HARRINGAY *(GR)*
HICKSTEAD *(EQ)*
INGLISTON *(MR)*
KARNATAKA *(C)*
LONG BEACH *(MR)*
MELBOURNE *(C)*
MONTLHÉRY *(MR)*
MUIRFIELD *(G)*
NORISRING *(MR)*
PERRY BARR *(G)*

PRESTWICK *(G)*
RIVERSIDE *(MR)*
ST ANDREWS *(G)*
THE BELFRY *(G)*
TURNBERRY *(G)*
WENTWORTH *(G)*
WHITE CITY *(A, GR)*
WIMBLEDON *(T)*
ZANDVOORT *(MR)*

10

ALBERT HALL *(BX, T)*
ANDERSDORP *(MR)*
BONNEVILLE *(MR)*
BREMGARTEN *(MR)*
BROOKLANDS *(MR)*
BROUGH PARK *(G)*
CARNOUSTIE *(G)*
EAST LONDON *(MR)*
GLENEAGLES *(G)*
HEADINGLEY *(C)*
HOCKENHEIM *(MC, MR)*
HURLINGHAM *(CQ, SQ)*
IFFLEY ROAD *(A)*
INTERLAGOS *(MR)*
KIRKISTOWN *(MR)*
LILLESHALL *(B, CY)*
McLEAN PARK *(C)*
MONTE CARLO *(MR)*
OULTON PARK *(MC, MR)*
PAUL RICARD *(MR)*
QUEEN'S CLUB *(SQ, T)*
RAWALPINDI *(C)*
ROEHAMPTON *(CQ, RU)*
SABINA PARK *(C)*
SNETTERTON *(MR)*
TWICKENHAM *(RU)*
VALLELUNGA *(MR)*

11

BLAIRGOWRIE *(G)*
BRAND'S HATCH *(MR)*

CADWELL PARK *(MR)*
CASTLE COMBE *(MC, MR)*
COWDRAY PARK *(P)*
EDEN GARDENS *(C)*
ELKHART LAKE *(MR)*
FETEH MAIDEN *(C)*
FOREST HILLS *(T)*
FORO ITALICO *(T)*
HUNGARORING *(MR)*
MALLORY PARK *(MR)*
MOSPORT PARK *(MR)*
MOTSPUR PARK *(H)*
MURRAYFIELD *(RU)*
NÜRBURGRING *(MR)*
OLD TRAFFORD *(C, RU)*
PORTMARNOCK *(G)*
ROSSLYN PARK *(RU)*
SACHSENRING *(MC)*
SILVERSTONE *(MR)*
SUNNINGDALE *(G)*
TRENT BRIDGE *(C)*
WALTHAMSTOW *(G)*
WALTON HEATH *(G)*
WATKINS GLEN *(MR)*

12

BASIN RESERVE *(C)*
INDIANAPOLIS *(MR)*
MONDELLO PARK *(MR)*
ROLAND GARROS *(T)*
THE BERKSHIRE *(G)*

13

CAESAR'S PALACE *(MR)*
CRYSTAL PALACE *(A, J)*
DONINGTON PARK *(MR)*
LANSDOWNE CLUB *(SQ)*
LANSDOWNE ROAD *(RU)*
LYTHAM ST ANNES *(G)*
ROYAL ABERDEEN *(G)*
ROYAL BIRKDALE *(G)*
ROYAL ST DAVID'S *(G)*

ST GEORGE'S PARK *(C)*
WOOLLOONGABBA *(C)*
WOLVERHAMPTON *(G)*

ROYAL LIVERPOOL *(G)*
ROYAL PORTHCAWL *(G)*
ROYAL ST GEORGE'S *(G)*

14

FEROZ SHAH KOTLA *(C)*
FLUSHING MEADOW *(T)*
OSTERREICHRING *(MR)*
PARC DES PRINCES *(RU)*

15

CARDIFF ARMS PARK *(RU)*
LAWRENCE GARDENS *(C)*
ROYAL COUNTY DOWN *(G)*
ROYAL NORTH DEVON *(G)*

SPORT

SPORTS VENUES – RACECOURSES

All in Britain except: (AU) = Australia   (F) = France   (HK) = Hong Kong
(IR) = Ireland   (IT) = Italy   (US) = United States

3

AYR

4

BATH
EVRY *(F)*
NAAS *(IR)*
YORK

5

ASCOT
EPSOM
KELSO

NAVAN *(IR)*
PERTH
RIPON
SLIGO *(IR)*

6

GALWAY *(IR)*
HEXHAM
LAUREL *(US)*
LUDLOW
MALLOW *(IR)*
REDCAR
SHA TIN *(HK)*
THIRSK
TRALEE *(IR)*

7

AINTREE
AUTEUIL *(F)*
CARTMEL
CHESTER
CLONMEL *(IR)*
CURRAGH *(IR)*
DUNDALK *(IR)*
LAYTOWN *(IR)*
NEWBURY
PIMLICO *(US)*
SAN SIRO *(IT)*
TAUNTON
THURLES *(IR)*
WARWICK
WINDSOR
WEXFORD *(IR)*

8

AQUEDUCT *(US)*
BEVERLEY
BRIGHTON
CARLISLE
CHEPSTOW
FAKENHAM
GOODWOOD
HEREFORD
LIMERICK *(IR)*
LISTOWEL *(IR)*
PLUMPTON
RANDWICK *(AU)*
SARATOGA *(US)*
WETHERBY
YARMOUTH

SPORT – SPORTS VENUES – RACECOURSES

9

CAPANELLE *(IT)*
CATTERICK
CHANTILLY *(F)*
DEAUVILLE *(F)*
DONCASTER
DOWN ROYAL *(IR)*
EDINBURGH
KEENELAND *(US)*
KILBEGGAN *(IR)*
KILLARNEY *(IR)*
LEICESTER
LONGCHAMP *(F)*
NEWCASTLE
NEWMARKET
ROSCOMMON *(IR)*
SALISBURY
SOUTHWELL
STRATFORD
TOWCESTER
UTTOXETER
WINCANTON
WORCESTER

10

BALLINROBE *(IR)*
CHELTENHAM
FAIRY HOUSE *(IR)*
FLEMINGTON *(AU)*
FOLKESTONE
GOWRAN PARK *(IR)*
HUNTINGDON
NOTTINGHAM
PONTEFRACT
SANTA ANITA *(US)*
SEDGEFIELD
THE CURRAGH *(IR)*

11

BANGOR-ON-DEE
BELLEWSTOWN *(IR)*
BELMONT PARK *(US)*
DOWNPATRICK *(IR)*
HAPPY VALLEY *(HK)*
HAYDOCK PARK
KEMPTON PARK
MARKET RASEN

NEWTON ABBOT
PHOENIX PARK *(IR)*
PUNCHESTOWN *(IR)*
SANDOWN PARK

12

CAGNES-SUR-MER *(F)*
FONTWELL PARK
HAMILTON PARK
LEOPARDSTOWN *(IR)*

13

ARLINGTON PARK *(US)*
HOLLYWOOD PARK *(US)*
LINGFIELD PARK
WOLVERHAMPTON

14

CHURCHILL DOWNS *(US)*
DEVON AND EXETER
GULFSTREAM PARK *(US)*

TRANSPORT

AIR – AIRCRAFT & AIRLINES

(AS) = Airship   (H) = Helicopter
¶ = Airline

3

ATI ¶
 (Italy)
BAC
BAₑ
BAF ¶
 (Britain)
BEA ¶
 (Britain)
BIA ¶
 (Britain)
BMA ¶
 (Britain)
CSA ¶
 (Czechoslovakia)
EAA
GAF
IAI
JAL ¶
 (Japan)
JAT ¶
 (Yugoslavia)
KLM ¶
 (Netherlands)
LAN ¶
 (Chile)
LAP ¶
 (Paraguay)
LET
LOT ¶
 (Poland)
MAS ¶
 (Malaysia)
MBB *(H)*
MIG
MIL *(H)*
PIA ¶
 (Pakistan)

PUP
SAA ¶
 (S Africa)
SAS ¶
 (Scandinavia)
SIA ¶
 (Singapore)
TAP ¶
 (Portugal)
THY ¶
 (Turkey)
TWA ¶
 (USA)
UAL ¶
 (USA)
UTA ¶
 (France)
VFW

4

AERO
ALIA ¶
 (Jordan)
AVRO
B CAL ¶
 (Britain)
BEAR
BEDE
BELL *(H)*
BOAC ¶
 (Britain)
BWIA ¶
 (Trinidad & Tobago)
CAAC ¶
 (China)
CASA
EL AL ¶
 (Israel)

FIAT
FORD
FUJI
FURY
HARP *(H)*
HART
HAWK
HIND
LAMA *(H)*
LYNX *(H)*
NAMC
NORD
PUMA *(H)*
RYAN
SAAB
SIAI
SKUA
SPAD
UTVA
VEGA
ZERO

5

AIR UK ¶
 (Britain)
AKRON *(AS)*
AVIAN
AZTEC
BARON
BEECH
CAMEL
COMET
CP AIR ¶
 (Canada)
DELTA
FOUND
GATES

GOTHA
HARKE *(H)*
HELIO
HOMER *(H)*
JODEL
KAMAN *(H)*
KAMOV *(H)*
KANIA
LAKER ¶
 (Britain)
MALEV ¶
 (Hungary)
MAXIM
ORION ¶
 (Britain)
PAN AM ¶
 (USA)
PFLAZ
PIPER
POTEZ
ROBIN
SABRE
SHARK *(H)*
SHORT
STUKA
TAROM ¶
 (Romania)
TAUBE
US AIR ¶
 (USA)
VARIG ¶
 (Brazil)
VIASA ¶
 (Venezuela)
VICTA

6

AGUSTA *(H)*

TRANSPORT – AIR – AIRCRAFT & AIRLINES

AIRBUS
APACHE
ARIANA ¶
  (Afghanistan)
AVIACO ¶
  (Spain)
BADGER
BEAGLE
BENSEN
BERIEV
BOEING
BÖLKOW
BOSTON
BRYMON ¶
  (Britain)
CESSNA
CIERVA
CONAIR ¶
  (Denmark)
CONDOR
DAKOTA
DAN-AIR ¶
  (Britain)
DINFIA
EDGLEY
FAIREY
FARMAN
FOKKER
FULMAR
GARDAN
GARUDA ¶
  (Indonesia)
HAWKER
HERALD
HILLER (H)
HUGHES (H)
HUNTER
IBERIA ¶
  (Spain)
ITAVIA ¶
  (Italy)
JAGUAR
LAWSON
LUXAIR ¶
  (Luxembourg)
MACCHI

MARTIN
METEOR
MIRAGE
NAVAJO
NIMROD
NORFLY ¶
  (Norway)
NORMAN
OPTICA
OSPREY
QANTAS ¶
  (Australia)
SABENA ¶
  (Belgium)
SAUDIA ¶
  (Saudi Arabia)
SHORTS
SUKHOI
TAYLOR
TOMCAT
VALMET
VICTOR
VIRGIN ¶
  (Britain)
VOUGHT
VULCAN
WESSEX

7

ANTONOV
BENNETT
BRANIFF ¶
  (USA)
BRANTLY
BRISTOL
BRISTOW (H)
BRIT AIR ¶
  (Britain)
CAPRONI
CHINOOK (H)
CONVAIR
CORSAIR
DAUPHIN (H)
DORNIER
DOUGLAS

EMBRAER
ENSTROM (H)
EUROAIR ¶
  (Britain)
FIJI AIR ¶
  (Fiji)
FINNAIR ¶
  (Finland)
FOLLAND
GAZELLE (H)
GLOSTER
GOSHAWK
GRUMMAN
GULF AIR ¶
  (Gulf states)
HALIFAX
HARRIER
HEINKEL
HELLCAT
HUNTING
HUSTLER
IRAN AIR ¶
  (Iran)
JAVELIN
JETSTAR
JUNKERS
LINCOLN
LISUNOV
MERCKLE
MIKOYAN
MONARCH ¶
  (Britain)
MUSTANG
OLYMPIC ¶
  (Greece)
PANAVIA
PENHOËT
PHANTOM
PIAGGIO
PILATUS
PROCTOR
RYANAIR ¶
  (Ireland)
SCANAIR ¶
  (Sweden)
SCINTEX

SEAHAWK (H)
SEA KING (H)
SEPECAT
SKYHAWK
SKYSHIP (AS)
SOPWITH
SPANTAX ¶
  (Spain)
STEALTH
TARRANT
TEMPEST
TORNADO
TRIDENT
TRISTAR
TUPOLEV
TYPHOON
VALIANT
VAMPIRE
VICKERS
WARDAIR ¶
  (Canada)

8

AER ARANN ¶
  (Ireland)
AEROFLOT ¶
  (Russia)
AIR INDIA ¶
  (India)
AIR INTER ¶
  (France)
AIR LANKA ¶
  (Sri Lanka)
AIR MALTA ¶
  (Malta)
AIR ZAÏRE ¶
  (Zaïre)
ALITALIA ¶
  (Italy)
ALOUETTE (H)
BELLANCA
BRABAZON
CATALINA
CHEROKEE

CHEYENNE
CHIPMUNK
COMANCHE
COMMANDO
CONCORDE
CONQUEST
CORVETTE
DASSAULT
EGYPTAIR ¶
  (Egypt)
ETENDARD
FOURNIER
GUARDIAN
HERCULES
ILYUSHIN
IROQUOIS (H)
ISLANDER
JUMBO JET
KAWASAKI
LYSANDER
LOCKHEED
LOGANAIR ¶
  (Britain)
MacREADY
MEXICANA ¶
  (Mexico)
MOSQUITO
NORTHROP
PIASECKI
ROCKWELL
SAUNDERS
SIKORSKY (H)
SKYCRANE (H)
SPITFIRE
STIRLING
SWISSAIR ¶
  (Switzerland)
TOMAHAWK
TRANSALL
TUNIS AIR ¶
  (Tunisia)
VANGUARD
VISCOUNT
WESTLAND (H)
YAKOVLEV
ZEPPELIN (AS)

9

AER LINGUS ¶
(Ireland)
AIR ALSACE ¶
(France)
AIR CANADA ¶
(Canada)
AIR ÉCOSSE ¶
(Britain)
AIR EUROPE ¶
(Britain)
AIR FRANCE ¶
(France)
AIR NIPPON ¶
(Japan)
BEARDMORE
BLACKBURN
BRITANNIA ¶
(Britain)
BUCCANEER
DRAGONFLY (H)
FAIRCHILD
FOCKE-WOLF
GLADIATOR
HURRICANE
INTERFLUG ¶
(E Germany)
KAWANISHI
KOREAN AIR ¶
(S Korea)
LANCASTER
LATÉCOÈRE
LIBERATOR
LIGHTNING
LINJEFLYG ¶
(Sweden)
LUFTHANSA ¶
(W Germany)
MAERSK AIR ¶
(Denmark)
MARTINAIR ¶
(Netherlands)
McDONNELL
PEREGRINE
SEADRAGON (H)

SEASPRITE (H)
SKYKNIGHT
SWORDFISH
TIGER MOTH
VIGILANTE
WHIRLWIND (H)

10

AEROMEXICO ¶
(Mexico)
AGUSTA-BELL (H)
AIR AFRIQUE ¶
(Ivory Coast)
AIR ALGÉRIE ¶
(Algeria)
AIR JAMAICA ¶
(Jamaica)
AVRO-VULCAN
BEECHCRAFT
BORDELAISE
CONNECTAIR ¶
(Britain)
FELLOWSHIP
FRIENDSHIP
HINDENBURG (AS)
HORNET MOTH
ICELANDAIR ¶
(Iceland)
MANCHESTER
MCD DOUGLAS
MIDDLE EAST ¶
(Lebanon)
MITSUBISHI
ROTORCRAFT (H)
SEA HARRIER
SHACKLETON
SUNDERLAND
SWEARINGEN
TRADEWINDS ¶
(Britain)
TRANS WORLD ¶
(USA)
WELLINGTON

11

AIR BOTSWANA ¶
(Botswana)
BEAUFIGHTER
CONTINENTAL ¶
(USA)
DE HAVILLAND
GRASSHOPPER (H)
HANDLEY PAGE
HUMMINGBIRD
MERCHANTMAN
SUD-AVIATION
THAI AIRWAYS ¶
(Thailand)
THUNDERBOLT

12

AÉROSPATIALE
ARROW AIRWAYS ¶
(Britain)
GRAF ZEPPELIN (AS)
IRAQI AIRWAYS ¶
(Iraq)
KENYA AIRWAYS ¶
(Kenya)
MANX AIRLINES ¶
(Britain)
OBERLERCHNER
TURBO TRAINER
WESTLAND-BELL (H)
WORLD AIRWAYS ¶
(USA)

13

AIR ATLANTIQUE ¶
(Britain)
AIR NEW ZEALAND ¶
(New Zealand)
ANGLO AIRLINES ¶
(Britain)
BRITTEN-NORMAN
BRYMON AIRWAYS ¶
(Britain)

TRANSPORT — AIR – AIRCRAFT & AIRLINES

CATHAY PACIFIC ¶
(Hong Kong)
CYPRUS AIRWAYS ¶
(Cyprus)
DELTA AIR LINES ¶
(USA)
KUWAIT AIRWAYS ¶
(Kuwait)
MESSERSCHMITT
NORTH AMERICAN
PEOPLE EXPRESS ¶
(USA)
ROYAL AIR MAROC ¶
(Morocco)
SUPER FORTRESS
SUPER STALLION
TURBO SARATOGA

14

AERO ARGENTINES ¶
(Argentina)

BRITISH AIRWAYS ¶
(Britain)
BRITISH MIDLAND ¶
(Britain)
CHANNEL EXPRESS ¶
(Britain)
FLYING FORTRESS
HAWKER SIDDELEY
NIGERIA AIRWAYS ¶
(Nigeria)
OLYMPIC AIRWAYS ¶
(Greece)
PACIFIC WESTERN ¶
(Canada)
STRATOFORTRESS
UGANDA AIRLINES ¶
(Uganda)
UNITED AIRLINES ¶
(USA)
VIRGIN ATLANTIC ¶
(Britain)

15

BRITISH AIRTOURS ¶
(Britain)
DASSAULT-BREGUET
EASTERN AIRLINES ¶
(USA)
FLYING TIGER LINE ¶
(USA)
GENERAL DYNAMICS
IMPERIAL AIRWAYS ¶
(Britain)
SAVIOA-MARCHETTI
STERLING AIRWAYS ¶
(Denmark)
TÜRK HAVA YOLLARI ¶
(Turkey)
WESTERN AIRLINES ¶
(USA)

TRANSPORT

AIR – AIRPORTS – BRITISH ISLES

(H) = Heliport only

4

CORK
DYCE *(Aberdeen)*
EDAY *(Orkneys)*
HURN *(Bournemouth)*
LYDD
MONA *(Holyhead)*

REEF *(Tiree)*
WICK

5

BOURN *(nr Cambridge)*
LEWIS *(Hebrides)*

LUTON
SCONE *(Perth)*
SLEAP *(nr Wem)*
SPEKE *(Liverpool)*

6

BARROW

BARTON *(Manchester)*
BODMIN
CROSBY *(Carlisle)*
EXETER
FETLAR *(Shetlands)*
FILTON *(nr Bristol)*
FLOTTA *(Orkneys)*
JERSEY
KEMBLE *(nr Cirencester)*
RHOOSE *(Cardiff)*
SANDAY *(Orkneys)*
SIBSON *(Peterborough)*
ST JUST *(nr Land's End)*
SYWELL *(Northampton)*
THURSO
TRESCO *(H-Scillies)*
ULCEBY *(Grimsby)*
VALLEY *(nr Holyhead)*
WESTON *(H-Weston-super-Mare)*
YEOVIL

7

BRISTOL
CLACTON
GATWICK *(London)*
IPSWICH
LYNEHAM *(nr Swindon)*
MANSTON *(nr Ramsgate)*
NORWICH
PAISLEY *(Glasgow)*
PORTLAW *(Waterford)*
REDHILL
SCATSTA *(Shetlands)*
SHANNON *(nr Limerick)*
SHOBDON *(nr Leominster)*
ST MARY'S *(Scillies)*
SWANSEA
WESTRAY *(Orkneys)*
WHALSAY *(Shetlands)*

8

BAGINTON *(Coventry)*
CARNMORE *(Galway)*

CULDROSE *(Helston)*
DALCROSS *(Inverness)*
EGLINTON *(Londonderry)*
FAIR ISLE
FAIROAKS *(nr Woking)*
GUERNSEY
HATFIELD
HAWARDEN *(Chester)*
HEATHROW *(London)*
HUCKNALL
KIRKWALL
LEUCHARS *(St Andrews)*
LULSGATE *(Bristol)*
NORTH BAY *(Barra, Hebrides)*
OLD SARUM *(Salisbury)*
PENZANCE *(H)*
PORTLAND *(H)*
ROTHESAY *(H-Bute)*
SEETHING *(nr Norwich)*
SHOREHAM *(Brighton/Worthing)*
SOUTHEND
ST ANGELO *(Enniskillen)*
STANSTED *(London)*
ST MAWGAN *(Newquay)*
STOLPORT *(London City)*
STRONSAY *(Orkneys)*
SUMBURGH *(Shetlands)*
SYDENHAM *(Belfast Harbour)*
TEESSIDE *(nr Darlington)*
THE BLAYE *(Alderney)*
THRUXTON *(nr Andover)*
TINGWALL *(Lerwick, Shetlands)*
WESTLAND *(H-London)*
WICKENBY *(Market Rasen)*

9

BATTERSEA *(H-London)*
CAMBRIDGE
CHALGROVE *(nr Oxford)*
CONINGTON *(Peterborough)*

CRANFIELD *(nr Bedford)*
DONCASTER
EASTLEIGH *(Southampton)*
LEAVESDEN *(nr Watford)*
LEICESTER
PORT ELLEN *(Islay)*
PRESTWICK *(Ayr)*
ROBOROUGH *(Plymouth)*
ROCHESTER
STAVERTON *(Cheltenham/ Gloucester)*
STORNOWAY *(Hebrides)*
TURNHOUSE *(Edinburgh)*
YEOVILTON *(nr Yeovil)*

10

ABBOTSINCH *(Glasgow)*
ALDERGROVE *(Belfast)*
BALIVANICH *(Benbecula, Hebrides)*
BALTASOUND *(Unst, Shetlands)*
BIGGIN HILL *(nr Westerham)*
BIRMINGHAM
BLACKBUSHE *(nr Camberley)*
CHICHESTER
DUNKESWELL *(nr Honiton)*
KIDLINGTON *(Oxford)*
MANCHESTER
NORTH DENES *(Gt Yarmouth)*
NOTTINGHAM
RONALDSWAY *(Isle of Man)*
STAPLEFORD *(nr Brentford)*
WEST FREUGH *(Dumfries)*

11

BRIZE NORTON *(nr Oxford)*
COLLINSTOWN *(Dublin)*
CUMBERNAULD
FARNBOROUGH
INGOLDMELLS *(Skegness)*
ISLE OF WIGHT *(Bembridge)*
LEE-ON-SOLENT
NEWTOWNARDS
PAPA WESTRAY *(Orkneys)*
SQUIRE'S GATE *(Blackpool)*
WOOLSINGTON *(Newcastle)*

12

EAST MIDLANDS *(nr Derby)*
MACHRIHANISH *(Kintyre)*
NETHERTHORPE *(nr Worksop)*

13

HAVERFORDWEST
LEEDS/BRADFORD
RIVERSIDE PARK *(Dundee)*

14

GREENHAM COMMON *(Newbury)*
HALFPENNY GREEN *(nr Bridgnorth)*
NORTH RONALDSAY *(Orkneys)*
WIGTOWN/BALDOON

15

ASHAIG/BROADFORD *(Isle of Skye)*

TRANSPORT

AIR – AIRPORTS – WORLD

3

KOS

4

BELP *(Berne)*
FARO *(Algarve)*
LUQA *(Malta)*
ORLY *(Paris)*
PISA
PRAT *(Barcelona)*
PULA
RIEM *(Munich)*
SEEB *(Oman)*
VIAS *(Buviers)*

5

CAIRO
ESSEY *(Nancy)*
IBIZA
ITAMI *(Osaka)*
LOGAN *(Boston)*
LUNGI *(Freetown)*
LUXOR
LUZON *(Manila)*
MAHON *(Minorca)*
O'HARE *(Chicago)*
PALAM *(Delhi)*
PALMA *(Majorca)*
PERTH
SOFIA
TEGEL *(Berlin)*
TILLE *(Beauvais)*
ZANTE

6

BENINA *(Benghazi)*

CHANGI *(Singapore)*
CHANIA *(Crete)*
DEURNE *(Antwerp)*
DORVAL *(Montreal)*
DULLES *(Washington DC)*
DUM DUM *(Calcutta)*
EZEIZA *(Buenos Aires)*
FINDEL *(Luxembourg)*
GALEAO *(Rio de Janeiro)*
GANDER *(Newfoundland)*
GERONA
HANEDA *(Tokyo)*
HARARE
JEDDAH
KLOTEN *(Zürich)*
KOTOKA *(Accra)*
KUWAIT
LINATE *(Milan)*
LUSAKA
MALAGA
NAPLES
NARITA *(Tokyo)*
NASSAU
NEWARK *(New York)*
OKECIE *(Warsaw)*
OSTEND
OTTAWA
PAPHOS *(Cyprus)*
RUZYNÉ *(Prague)*
SADDAM *(Baghdad)*
SUBANG *(Kuala Lumpur)*
VANTAA *(Helsinki)*

7

ALGHERO *(Sardinia)*
ALMEIRIA
ANTALYA
ARLANDA *(Stockholm)*

ATHINAI *(Athens)*
BAHRAIN
BARAJAS *(Madrid)*
BILLUND *(Jutland)*
BLAGNAC *(Toulouse)*
CAUMONT *(Avignon)*
DF MALAN *(Cape Town)*
ESBJERG *(Jutland)*
FORNEBU *(Oslo)*
FUNCHAL *(Madeira)*
HOUSTON
KASTRUP *(Copenhagen)*
KERKYRA *(Corfu)*
LARNACA *(Cyprus)*
LASINIA *(Oran)*
LESQUIN *(Lille)*
MIRABEL *(Montreal)*
NICOSIA *(Cyprus)*
SATOLAS *(Lyon)*
TANGIER

8

ABU DHABI
ALICANTE
ARRECIFE *(Lanzarote)*
AUCKLAND
CANBERRA
COINTRIN *(Geneva)*
DAMASCUS
DON MUANG *(Bangkok)*
ENTZHEIM *(Strasbourg)*
ESSENDON *(Melbourne)*
GABORONE
IDLEWILD *(interim name of JF KENNEDY)*
JAN SMUTS *(Johannesburg)*
LISBONNE *(Lisbon)*
MALPENSA *(Milan)*

MEHRABAD *(Tehran)*
MERIGNAC *(Bordeaux)*
MONASTIR *(Tunis)*
PARADISI *(Rhodes)*
RONGOTAI *(Wellington)*
SALZBURG
SCHIPHOL *(Amsterdam)*
WINNIPEG
ZAVENTEM *(Brussels)*

9

BEN GURION *(Tel Aviv)*
BULLTOFTA *(Malmo)*
COTE D'AZUR *(Nice)*
DOWNSVIEW *(Toronto)*
DUBROVNIK
EINDHOVEN
FIUMICINO *(Rome)*
GUARULHOS *(São Paulo)*
HERAKLION *(Crete)*
HEWANORRA *(St Lucia)*
HUNG-CHAIO *(Shanghai)*
INNSBRUCK
JF KENNEDY *(New York)*
KEFALONIA
KEMAYORAN *(Djakarta)*
LA GUARDIA *(New York)*
LAS PALMAS *(Gran Canaria)*
LE BOURGET *(Paris)*
LENINGRAD
LE TOUQUET *(Boulogne)*
LOS RODEOS *(Tenerife)*
MARCO POLO *(Venice)*
MARIGNANE *(Marseilles)*
REYKJAVIK
SANTA CRUZ *(Bombay)*
SCHWECHAT *(Vienna)*
TEMPELHOF *(Berlin)*
VANCOUVER

10

AMON CARTER *(Fort Worth/Dallas)*
DÜSSELDORF

GARDERMOEN *(Oslo)*
HARTSFIELD *(Atlanta)*
HELLENIKON *(Athens)*
LOS ANGELES
LOUIS BOTHA *(Durban)*
MINGALADON *(Rangoon)*
PUERTO RICO
SCHONEFELD *(Berlin)*
TULLMARINE *(Melbourne)*
WELLINGTON

11

DAR-ES-SALAAM
FUHLSBÜTTEL *(Hamburg)*
JORGE CHAVET *(Lima)*

12

BENITO JUÁREZ *(Mexico City)*
ECHTERDINGEN *(Stuttgart)*
JOMO KENYATTA *(Nairobi)*
METROPOLITAN *(Detroit)*
NORMAN MANLEY *(Kingston)*
SAN FRANCISCO
SHEREMETYEVO *(Moscow)*
THESSALONIKI
ZESTIENHOVEN *(Rotterdam)*

13

CHÂTEAU BOUGON *(Nantes)*
CHIANG KAI-SHEK *(Taipei)*
FRANKFURT MAIN

14

BASEL-MULHOUSEN *(Basle)*
BEIJING CAPITAL *(Peking)*
KINGSFORD SMITH *(Sydney)*

15

CHARLES DE GAULLE *(Paris)*
LEONARDO DA VINCI *(Rome)*
MURTALA MUHAMMED *(Lagos)*

TRANSPORT

LAND – CARS

(AC) = AC   (A-H) = Austin-Healey   (ALV) = Alvis
(AM) = Aston Martin   (AR) = Alfa Romeo
(A-S) = Armstrong-Siddeley   (AUD) = Audi   (AUS) = Austin
(BEN) = Bentley   (BR) = Bristol   (BU) = Buick
(CAD) = Cadillac   (CH) = Chevrolet   (CHR) = Chrysler   (CIT) = Citroën
(DA) = Daimler   (DAC) = Dacia   (DAI) = Daihatsu   (DO) = Dodge
(FER) = Ferrari   (FI) = Fiat   (F-N) = Frazer-Nash   (FOR) = Ford
(FSO) = FSO   (HIL) = Hillman   (HON) = Honda   (HUD) = Hudson
(HUM) = Humber   (HY) = Hyundai   (IS) = Isuzu
(JAG) = Jaguar   (JEN) = Jensen   (JOW) = Jowett
(LAM) = Lamborghini   (LAN) = Lancia   (LAD) = Lada   (LIN) = Lincoln
(LOT) = Lotus   (MAS) = Maserati   (MAZ) = Mazda
(M-B) = Mercedes-Benz   (MER) = Mercury   (MG) = MG
(MIT) = Mitsubishi   (MO) = Morris   (MOR) = Morgan
(NIS) = Nissan (Datsun)   (OLD) = Oldsmobile   (OP) = Opel
(PAN) = Panther   (PEU) = Peugeot   (PLY) = Plymouth   (PON) = Pontiac
(POR) = Porsche   (REL) = Reliant   (REN) = Renault   (RIL) = Riley
(R-R) = Rolls-Royce   (ROV) = Rover   (SA) = Saab   (SE) = Seat
(SIM) = Simca   (SIN) = Singer   (SK) = Skoda   (ST) = Standard
(STU) = Studebaker   (SUB) = Subaru   (SUN) = Sunbeam   (SUZ) = Suzuki
(TAL) = Talbot   (TOY) = Toyota   (TRI) = Triumph   (TVR) = TVR
(VAU) = Vauxhall   (VOL) = Volvo   (VW) = Volkswagen
(WOL) = Wolseley   (YUG) = Yugo
¶ = Make

3

ACE (AC)
BMW ¶
BRM ¶
CRX (HON)
DAF ¶
ELF (RIL)
FSO ¶
IMP (HIL)
LNA (CIT)

MGA (MG)
MGB (MG)
MGC (MG)
NSU ¶
REX (SUB)
TVR ¶
UNO (FI)
ZIL ¶

4

ALFA (AR)
ALTO (SUZ)
ARNA (AR)
AUDI ¶
BÉBÉ (PEU)
BENZ ¶
BETA (LAN)
BORA (MAS)
CITY (HON)

CLIO (REN)
COLT (MIT)
DART (DA,
   DO)
DINO (FER,
   FI)
ELAN (LOT)
ETNA (LOT)
FORD ¶
FURY (PLY)
GOLF (VW)

HAWK (HUM)
INDY (MAS)
ISIS (MOR)
ITAL (MO)
JAZZ (HON)
LADA ¶
LUCE (MAZ)
LYNX (MER)
MAXI (AUS)
MINI (AUS,
   MO)

TRANSPORT – LAND – CARS

MINX *(HIL)*
NIVA *(LAD)*
NOVA *(CH, VAU)*
OMNI *(DO)*
OPEL *¶*
POLO *(VW)*
PONY *(FOR, HY)*
RIVA *(LAD)*
RUBY *(AUS)*
SAAB *¶*
SANA *(YUG)*
SEAT *¶*
STAG *(TRI)*
TIPO *(FI)*
VEGA *(CH)*
VELO *(M-B)*
VISA *(CIT)*
VIVA *(VAU)*
WASP *(WOL)*
YUGO *¶*

CIVIC *(HON)*
COBRA *(AC, FOR)*
COMBI *(SA)*
COMET *(MER)*
CORSA *(OP)*
COSMO *(MAZ)*
CROMA *(FI)*
CROWN *(TOY)*
C-TYPE *(JAG)*
DACIA *¶*
DEDRA *(LAN)*
DELTA *(LAN, OLD)*
DENEM *(DAC)*
DERBY *(VW)*
DEVON *(AUS)*
DODGE *¶*
DOLLY *(CIT)*
D-TYPE *(JAG)*
DYANE *(CIT)*
ECLAT *(LOT)*
EDSEL *(FOR)*
ELITE *(LOT)*
E-TYPE *(JAG)*
EXCEL *(LOT)*
FUEGO *(REN)*
GAMMA *(LAN)*
HUSKY *(HIL)*
IBIZA *(SE)*
ISUZU *¶*
JALPA *(LAM)*
JETTA *(VW)*
JUSTY *(SUB)*
KAPPA *(LAN)*
KARIF *(MAS)*
LASER *(FOR)*
LE CAR *(REN)*
LEONE *(SUB)*
LOTUS *¶*
MAGNA *(MG)*
MANTA *(OP)*
MARK X *(JAG)*
MAZDA *¶*
MERAK *(MAS)*
MERIT *(VAU)*

METRO *(AUS)*
MICRA *(NIS)*
MINOR *(MO)*
MONZA *(OP)*
MUIRA *(LAM)*
NUOVA *(FI)*
OMEGA *(OLD, OP)*
ORION *(FOR)*
PANDA *(FI)*
PILOT *(FOR, ROV)*
PINTO *(FOR)*
RAPID *(SK)*
REGAL *(BU)*
RILEY *¶*
RITMO *(FI)*
ROBIN *(REL)*
SABLE *(MER)*
SABRE *(REL)*
SAMBA *(TAL)*
SCOUT *(DA)*
SEVEN *(AUS)*
SIGMA *(MIT)*
SIMCA *¶*
SKODA *¶*
SPEED *(ROV)*
SPORT *(SA)*
SUNNY *(NIS)*
SUPRA *(TOY)*
SWIFT *(SUZ)*
TAMAR *(TVR)*
TEMPO *(FOR)*
THEMA *(LAN)*
TIGER *(SUN)*
TODAY *(HON)*
TOPAZ *(MER)*
TREVI *(LAN)*
VELOX *(VAU)*
VOGUE *(SIN)*
VOLVO *¶*

6

ACCORD *(HON)*

ALLARD *¶*
ALPINE *(REN, SUN, TAL)*
AMAZON *(VOL)*
ANGLIA *(FOR)*
ARONDE *(SIM)*
ARTENA *(LAN)*
ASCONA *(OP)*
ASTURA *(LAN)*
AUSTIN *¶*
BEETLE *(VW)*
BEL AIR *(CH)*
BIG SIX *(VAU)*
BOBCAT *(MER)*
CALAIS *(OLD)*
CAMARO *(CH)*
CARINA *(TOY)*
CEDRIC *(NIS)*
CELICA *(TOY)*
CHERRY *(NIS)*
CHUMMY *(AUS)*
CONSUL *(FOR)*
CORDIA *(MIT)*
CORONA *(TOY)*
COUGAR *(MER)*
COWLEY *(MOR)*
CRESTA *(VAU)*
CUSTOM *(DO, FOR)*
DELAGE *¶*
DE SOTO *¶*
DOMINO *(DAI)*
DORSET *(AUS)*
ENSIGN *(ST)*
ESCORT *(FOR)*
ESPADA *(LAM)*
ESPRIT *(LOT)*
EUROPA *(FER, LOT)*
FALCON *(FOR)*
FARINA *(AUS)*
FIESTA *(FOR)*
FLAVIA *(LAN)*
FULVIA *(LAN)*
FUTURA *(FOR)*

5

ACECA *(AC)*
ALPHA *(LAN)*
ALVIS *¶*
APPIA *(LAN)*
ARDEA *(LAN)*
ARIES *(DO)*
ARROW *(PLY)*
ASPEN *(DO)*
ASTRA *(VAU)*
ASTRE *(PON)*
AVANT *(AUD, CIT)*
BUICK *¶*
CADET *(VAU)*
CAMRY *(TOY)*
CAPRI *(FOR, MER)*
CAROL *(MAZ)*

GALANT *(MIT)*
GHIBLI *(MAS)*
GIULIA *(AR)*
GLORIA *(NIS)*
GROSSE *(M-B)*
HEALEY *¶*
HERALD *(TRI)*
HORNET *(WOL)*
HUMBER *¶*
HUNTER *(HIL,*
SIN)
IMPALA *(CH)*
JAGUAR *¶*
JENSEN *¶*
JOWETT *¶*
KADETT *(OP)*
KITTEN *(REL)*
KNIGHT *(DA)*
LAMBDA *(LAN)*
LANCER *(MIT)*
LANCIA *¶*
LAUREL *(NIS)*
LEGACY *(SUB)*
LEGEND *(HON)*
LE MANS *(PON,*
SIN)
LIGIER *¶*
LITTLE *(CH)*
MAGNUM *(VAU)*
MALAGA *(SE)*
MALIBU *(CH)*
MARINA *(MO)*
MAXIMA *(NIS)*
MERKUR *(MER)*
METEOR *(MER,*
ROV)
MIDGET *(MG)*
MINICA *(MIT)*
MIRADA *(DO)*
MIRAGE *(MIT)*
MODEL T *(FOR)*
MONACO *(DO,*
RIL)
MORGAN *¶*
OXFORD *(MO)*
PASSAT *(VW)*

PIAZZA *(IS)*
POLARA *(DO)*
PREVIA *(TOY)*
PRISMA *(LAN)*
PROTON *¶*
PULSAR *(NIS)*
RAPIER *(SUN)*
RED RAM *(DO)*
REGATA *(FI)*
REGENT *(OP)*
REGINA *(DA)*
REKORD *(OP)*
RENOWN *(TR)*
RIALTO *(REL)*
ROYALE *(VAU)*
SAMARA *(LAD)*
SENIOR *(DO)*
SENTRA *(NIS)*
SHADOW *(DO)*
SHELBY *(DO)*
SIERRA *(FOR)*
SILVIA *(NIS)*
SINGER *¶*
SOARER *(TOY)*
SOLARA *(TAL)*
SONATA *(HY)*
SONETT *(SA)*
SPIRIT *(NIS)*
SPRINT *(CH)*
SPRITE *(A-H)*
SQUIRE *(FOR)*
STANZA *(NIS)*
STRADA *(FI)*
SUBARU *¶*
SUZUKI *¶*
TAGORA *(TAL)*
TALBOT *¶,*
(SUN)
TAUNUS *(FOR)*
TAURUS *(FOR)*
TEMPRA *(FI)*
TERCEL *(TOY)*
TOLEDO *(TRI)*
TOYOTA *¶*
TREDIA *(MIT)*
TROFEO *(OLD)*

TUSCAN *(TVR)*
VELOCE *(AR)*
VICTOR *(VAU)*
VIKING *(OLD)*
VIOLET *(NIS)*
VIRAGE *(AM)*
VITARA *(SUZ)*
VOLARE *(PLY)*
WYVERN *(VAU)*
ZEPHYR *(FOR)*
ZODIAC *(FOR)*

7

ACCLAIM *(TRI)*
ADELPHI *(RIL)*
ADMIRAL *(OP)*
AIRLINE *(REN)*
ALFASUD *(AR)*
ALFETTA *(AR)*
ALLANTE *(CAD)*
ALLEGRO *(AUS)*
AMERICA *(FER)*
APRILIA *(LAN)*
ARGENTA *(FI)*
AURELIA *(LAN)*
AVENGER *(CHR,*
HIL,
TAL)
BALILLA *(FI)*
BALLADE *(HON)*
BELMONT *(VAU)*
BENTLEY *¶*
BERETTA *(CH)*
BITURBO *(MAS)*
BRIGAND *(BR)*
BRISTOL *¶*
BUGATTI *¶*
CALIBRA *(VAU)*
CAPELLA *(MAZ)*
CARIOCA *(VOL)*
CARLTON *(VAU)*
CARRERA *(POR)*
CELESTE *(MIT)*
CENTURY *(BU,*
TOY)

CHAMADE *(REN)*
CHARADE *(DAI)*
CHARGER *(DO)*
CITROËN *¶*
CLASSIC *(FOR)*
CORDOBA *(CHR)*
COROLLA *(TOY)*
CORONET *(DO)*
CORRADO *(VW)*
CORSAIR *(FOR)*
CORSICA *(CH)*
CORTINA *(FOR)*
CORVAIR *(CH)*
CRICKET *(PLY)*
CUTLASS *(OLD)*
DAIMLER *¶*
DAYTONA *(DO,*
(FER)
DELMONT *(OLD)*
DE VILLE *(CAD,*
PAN)
DIALPHA *(LAN)*
ELECTRA *(BU)*
ESTELLE *(SK)*
FAMILIA *(MAZ)*
FAVORIT *(SK)*
FERRARI *¶*
FIRENZA *(OLD,*
VAU)
FLORIDE *(REN)*
FREGATE *(REN)*
GALAXIE *(FOR)*
GAZELLE *(SIN)*
GRANADA *(FOR)*
HILLMAN *¶*
HORIZON *(CHR,*
PLY,
TAL)
HYUNDAI *¶*
INTEGRA *(HON)*
INVICTA *¶*
JAVELIN *(JOW)*
JETFIRE *(OLD)*
JUPITER *(JOW)*
KAPITAN *(OP)*
KHAMSIN *(MAS)*

TRANSPORT – LAND – CARS

KYALAMI *(MAS)*
LAGONDA ¶,
    (AM)
LA SALLE *(CAD)*
LeBARON *(CHR)*
LEOPARD *(NIS)*
LE SABRE *(BU)*
LINCOLN ¶
MAESTRO *(AUS)*
MARQUIS *(MER)*
MERCURY ¶
MONARCH *(MER)*
MONDIAL *(FER)*
MONTEGO *(AUS)*
MUSTANG *(FOR)*
NEWPORT *(CHR)*
OAKLAND *(PON)*
OLYMPIA *(OP)*
PACKARD ¶
PANHARD ¶
PANTHER ¶
PENNANT *(ST)*
PEUGEOT ¶
PHANTOM *(R-R)*
PHOENIX *(PON)*
POLONEZ *(FSO)*
PONTIAC ¶
POPULAR *(FOR)*
PORSCHE ¶
PRAIRIE *(NIS)*
PREFECT *(FOR)*
PRELUDE *(HON)*
PREMIER *(REN)*
PRIMERA *(NIS)*
PUBLICA *(TOY)*
PULLMAN *(HUM)*
QUATTRO *(AUD)*
QUINTET *(HON)*
REGENCY *(DA)*
RELIANT ¶
RENAULT ¶
RIVIERA *(BU)*
SANTANA *(VW,*
    SUZ)
SAPPORO *(MIT)*
SAVANNA *(REN)*

SCEPTRE *(HUM)*
SCORPIO *(FOR)*
SENATOR *(OP,*
    VAU)
SEVILLE *(CAD)*
SKYHAWK *(BU)*
SKYLARK *(BU)*
SKYLINE *(NIS)*
SPECIAL *(BU)*
STARION *(MIT)*
STARLET *(TOY)*
STELLAR *(HY)*
STRATOS *(LAN)*
ST REGIS *(DO)*
SUNBEAM ¶
SUNBIRD *(PON)*
TEMPEST *(PON)*
TORPEDO *(PON)*
TOWN CAR *(LIN)*
VALIANT *(PLY)*
VANTAGE *(AM)*
VANWALL ¶
VENTORA *(VAU)*
VENTURA *(PON)*
VETTURA *(FER)*
VICEROY *(VAU)*
VITESSE *(ROV,*
    TRI)
VOLANTE *(AM)*
WEEKEND *(FI)*
WILD CAT *(BU)*

8

APPLAUSE *(DAI)*
ATLANTIC *(AUS)*
BLUEBIRD *(NIS)*
BREVETTI *(FI)*
CADILLAC ¶
CAMARGUE *(R-R)*
CARLSSON *(SA)*
CATALINA *(PON)*
CAVALIER *(CH,*
    VAU)
CHARMANT *(DAI)*
CHEVELLE *(CH)*

CHEVETTE *(CH,*
    VAU)
CHRYSLER ¶
CIMARRON *(CAD)*
CITATION *(CH)*
CONCERTO *(HON)*
CONQUEST *(CH,*
    DA)
CORNICHE *(BEN,*
    R-R)
CORVETTE *(CH)*
COUNTACH *(LAM)*
CRESSIDA *(TOY)*
DAIHATSU ¶
DAUPHINE *(REN)*
DEBONAIR *(MIT)*
DELAHAYE ¶
DE LOREAN ¶
DiLAMBDA *(LAN)*
DIPLOMAT *(DO,*
    OP)
DOLOMITE *(TRI)*
ELDORADO *(CAD)*
FAIRLADY *(NIS)*
FAIRLANE *(FOR)*
FAIRMONT *(FOR)*
FIREBIRD *(PON)*
FLAMINIA *(LAN)*
FOUR-FOUR *(MOR)*
GRAN FURY *(PLY)*
GREY LADY *(ALV)*
HEREFORD *(AUS)*
IMPERIAL *(CHR)*
KALLISTA *(PAN)*
LIGHT SIX *(VAU)*
MAGNETTE *(MG)*
MAJESTIC *(DA)*
MARBELLA *(SE)*
MASERATI ¶
MAVERICK *(FOR)*
MERCEDES ¶
MINI CITY *(AUS)*
MINI MOKE *(AUS)*
MISTRALE *(MAS)*
MONTEREY *(MER)*
MONTREAL *(AR)*

MONTROSE *(MAZ)*
MULSANNE *(BEN)*
PARK LANE *(MER)*
PLUS FOUR *(MOR)*
PLYMOUTH ¶
PRESTIGE *(CIT)*
PRINCESS *(AUS)*
ROADSTER *(TRI)*
SAPPHIRE *(A-S)*
SCIMITAR *(REL)*
SCIROCCO *(VW)*
SOMERSET *(AUS,*
BU)
SPECTRUM *(CH)*
SPITFIRE *(TRI)*
SPRINTER *(TOY)*
STANDARD ¶
STERLING *(ROV)*
STILETTO *(SUN)*
SUNDANCE *(PLY)*
SUPERIOR *(CH)*
TIPO ZERO *(FI)*
TOPOLINO *(FI)*
TORONADO *(BU,*
OLD)
TRiKAPPA *(LAN)*
VANGUARD *(ST)*
VAUXHALL ¶
VISCOUNT *(VAU)*
WAYFARER *(DO)*
WOLSELEY ¶

9

ALFA ROMEO ¶
AUTO UNION ¶
BABY GRAND *(CH)*
BARRACUDA *(PLY)*
BELVEDERE *(PLY)*
BRITANNIA *(BR)*
CAMBRIDGE *(AUS)*
CARAVELLE *(PLY,*
REN)
CELEBRITY *(CH,*
VAU)

CHEVROLET ¶
CHIEFTAIN *(PON)*
COMMODORE *(OP)*
DOUBLE-SIX *(DA)*
FLEETWOOD *(CAD)*
GIULIETTA *(AR)*
GRAND PRIX *(PON)*
HAMPSHIRE *(AUS)*
HURRICANE *(A-S)*
INTEGRALE *(LAN)*
MARQUETTE *(BU)*
MAYFLOWER *(TRI)*
METRO CITY *(AUS)*
MIRAFIORI *(FI)*
MONTCLAIR *(MER)*
NEW YORKER *(CHR)*
PRESIDENT *(NIS)*
ROADPACER *(MAZ)*
SHEERLINE *(AUS)*
SOVEREIGN *(DA,*
JAG)
STAR CHIEF *(PON)*
SUPERFAST *(FER)*
TRAVELLER *(MO)*

10

AMBASSADOR *(AUS)*
BERLINETTA *(FER)*
BONNEVILLE *(PON)*
COLT MIRAGE *(MIT)*
COUNTRYMAN *(AUS)*
CROWN EIGHT *(TOY)*
CROWN ROYAL *(TOY)*
CUNNINGHAM ¶
FOUR-NINETY *(CH)*
FRAZER-NASH ¶
GOLDEN HAWK *(STU)*
JUVAQUATRE *(REN)*
LANCHESTER ¶
LAUBFROSCH *(OP)*
MINI-COOPER *(AUS,*
MO)
MITSUBISHI ¶
MONTE CARLO *(CH,*
LAN)

OLDSMOBILE ¶
PARISIENNE *(PON)*
PATHFINDER *(RIL)*
ROADMASTER *(BU)*
ROAD RUNNER *(PLY)*
ROLLS-ROYCE ¶
SILVER DAWN *(R-R)*
SILVER SPUR *(R-R)*
STUDEBAKER ¶
SUPER SNIPE *(HUM)*
TERRAPLANE *(HUD)*
TESTAROSSA *(FER)*
VERSAILLES *(LIN)*
VOLKSWAGEN ¶

11

ASTON MARTIN ¶
BEAUFIGHTER *(BR)*
CALIFORNIAN *(HIL)*
CELICA SUPRA *(TOY)*
CONTINENTAL *(LIN)*
FIFTH AVENUE *(CHR)*
FLIGHT SWEEP *(PLY)*
GALANT SIGMA *(MIT)*
GRAN TURISMO *(SA)*
INTERCEPTOR *(JEN)*
KARMANN GHIA *(VW)*
LAMBORGHINI ¶
LANCER FIORE *(MIT)*
MEADOWBROOK *(DO)*
MINI MAYFAIR *(AUS)*
NINETY-EIGHT *(OLD)*
PRINCE HENRY *(VAU)*
QUADRILETTE *(PEU)*
REINASTELLA *(REN)*
SILVER CLOUD *(R-R)*
SILVER GHOST *(R-R)*
STREAMLINER *(PON)*
SUPER BEETLE *(VW)*
TARGA FLORIO *(F-N)*
THUNDERBIRD *(FOR)*
WESTMINSTER *(AUS)*

TRANSPORT – LAND – CARS

AUSTIN-HEALEY ¶
COMET CYCLONE *(MER)*
COSMOPOLITAN *(LIN)*
CUTLASS CIERA *(OLD)*
DE DION BOUTON ¶
GRAND MARQUIS *(MER)*
HISPANO-SUIZA ¶
JENSEN-HEALEY ¶
LOTUS-CORTINA *(FOR)*
MERCEDES-BENZ ¶
METRO CLUBMAN *(AUS)*
METROPOLITAN *(AUS)*
SILVER SHADOW *(R-R)*
SILVER SPIRIT *(R-R)*
SILVER STREAK *(PON)*
SILVER WRAITH *(R-R)*
SUPER AMERICA *(FER)*
TREVI VOLUMEX *(LAN)*

CROWN VICTORIA *(FOR)*
DAIMLER-JAGUAR ¶

ESCORT ECLIPSE *(FOR)*
MAJESTIC MAJOR *(DA)*
MINI TRAVELLER *(AUS, MO)*
REGATA COMFORT *(FI)*
REGATA WEEKEND *(FI)*
TRACTION AVANT *(CIT)*
VANTAGE ZAGATO *(AM)*

14

ACCORD AERODECK *(HON)*
CUTLASS SUPREME *(OLD)*
SIERRA COSWORTH *(FOR)*
SIERRA SAPPHIRE *(FOR)*
SUPERMIRAFIORI *(FI)*
VANTAGE VOLANTE *(AM)*

15

ACCORD EXECUTIVE *(HON)*
BERLINETTA BOXER *(FER)*
DAUPHINE GORDINI *(REN)*
MARQUIS BROUGHAM *(MER)*
PANHARD-LEVASSOR ¶

TRANSPORT

LAND – TRUCKS & VANS

(AEC) = AEC (AUS) = Austin (BED) = Bedford/Vauxhall
(CH) = Chevrolet (COM) = Commer (DAC) = Dacia
(DAF) = DAF (DAI) = Daihatsu (FI) = Fiat (FOR) = Ford
(IS) = Isuzu (IV) = Iveco (LEY) = Leyland or Leyland/DAF
(L-R) = Land-Rover (MAN) = MAN (M-B) = Mercedes-Benz
(MIT) = Mitsubishi (NIS) = Nissan (PEG) = Pegaso
(RAN) = Range-Rover (SCA) = Scania (SUZ) = Suzuki (TAL) = Talbot
(THO) = Thornycroft (TOY) = Toyota (VOL) = Volvo
(VW) = Volkswagen
† = 'Off-road' model ¶ = Make

3

AEC *¶*
AWD *¶*
COB *(COM)*
DAF *¶*
ERF *¶*
GUY *¶*
MAN *¶*

4

FIAT *¶*
FORD *¶*
HINO *¶*
JEEP *¶*
LIAZ *¶*
MACK *¶*
MIDI *(BED)*
SISU *¶*
TARO *(VW)*

5

ANTAR *(THO)*
BRUIN *(CH)*

CADDY *(VW)*
CARGO *(FOR)*
DACIA *¶*
DAILY *(IV)*
DODGE *¶*
EXTRA *(REN)*
FODEN *¶*
GIPSY *(AUS)*
HIACE *(TOY)*
ISUZU *¶*
IVECO *¶*
KAMAZ *¶*
RHINO *(SUZ) †*
SETRA *¶*
VOGUE *(RAN) †*
VOLVO *¶*

6

AUSTIN *¶*
BEAGLE *(BED)*
COMMER *¶*
DENNIS *¶*
DUCATO *(FI)*
DUSTER *(DAC) †*
ESPACE *(REN)*
MAGNUM *(REN)*

MASTER *(REN)*
PATROL *(NIS) †*
PEGASO *¶*
RANCHO *(TAL) †*
RASCAL *(BED)*
SCANIA *¶*
SEDDON *¶*
SHERPA *(LEY)*
SHOGUN *(MIT) †*
SUZUKI *¶*
THAMES *(FOR)*
TOYOTA *¶*
TRAFIC *(REN)*
TROJAN *¶*
TRONER *(PEG)*
VITARA *(SUZ)*

7

BEDFORD *¶*
BRISTOL *¶*
CABSTAR *(NIS)*
CRUISER *(LEY)*
EXPRESS *(TAL)*
KARRIER *(COM)*
LEYLAND *¶*
MAMMOTH *(AEC)*

MASTIFF *(LEY)*
OSHKOSH *¶*
PRAIRIE *(NIS) †*
RENAULT *¶*
SANTANA *(SUZ) †*
TRANSIT *(FOR)*
TROOPER *(IS) †*
VANETTE *(NIS)*

8

ASTRAMAX *(BED)*
BRADFORD *¶*
DAIHATSU *¶*
FOURTRAK *(DAI) †*
KENWORTH *¶*
MAXICODE *(REN)*
MERCEDES *¶*
SCAMMELL *¶*
SHOWTRAC *(SCA)*
SPORTRAK *(DAI) †*

9

CATTLEMAN *(DAF)*
CHEVROLET *¶*

411

TRANSPORT — LAND — TRUCKS & VANS

COMMANDER *(MAN)*
DISCOVERY *(L-R)* †
DORMOBILE *(BED)*
FREIGHTER *(LEY)*
LAND-ROVER ¶
ROADTRAIN *(LEY)*
TURBOSTAR *(IV)*

LOUISVILLE *(FOR)*
POWERLINER *(M-B)*
RANGE-ROVER ¶
ROADRUNNER *(LEY)*
SPACE WAGON *(MIT)* †
VOLKSWAGEN ¶

12

GLOBETROTTER *(VOL)*
MAGIRUS DEUTZ ¶
MAMMOTH MAJOR *(AEC)*
MERCEDES-BENZ ¶
SPACE CRUISER *(TOY)* †
THAMES TRADER *(FOR)*

10

HIGHWAYMAN *(SCA)*
LEYLAND/DAF ¶

11

FLEETMASTER *(FOD)*
LANDCRUISER *(TOY)* †
THORNYCROFT ¶

14

SEDDON ATKINSON ¶

TRANSPORT

RAIL — LONDON UNDERGROUND

† = Docklands Light Railway

4

BANK
OVAL

5

ANGEL
ONGAR
UPNEY

6

BALHAM
DEBDEN

EPPING
EUSTON
LEYTON
MORDEN
PINNER
POPLAR †
TEMPLE

7

ALDGATE
ALDWYCH
ARSENAL
BARKING
BOROUGH
BOW ROAD
BRIXTON

CHESHAM
CROXLEY
EAST HAM
EDGWARE
ELM PARK
FAIRLOP
HOLBORN
KILBURN
MILE END
NEASDEN
OAKWOOD
PIMLICO
RUISLIP
ST PAUL'S
WAPPING
WATFORD
WEST HAM

8

ALPERTON
AMERSHAM
BARBICAN
BURNT OAK
CHIGWELL
EASTCOTE
HAINAULT
HEATHROW
HIGHGATE
ICKENHAM
LOUGHTON
MONUMENT
MOORGATE
MOOR PARK
MUDCHUTE †

NEW CROSS
NORTHOLT
OSTERLEY
PERIVALE
PLAISTOW
RICHMOND
ROYAL OAK
SHADWELL
STANMORE
UXBRIDGE
VAUXHALL
VICTORIA
WANSTEAD
WATERLOO
WOODFORD

9

ACTON TOWN
ALL SAINTS †
BAYSWATER
BECONTREE
BOW CHURCH †
CHALK FARM
COLINDALE
EAST ACTON
ESSEX ROAD
GANTS HILL
GREENFORD
GREEN PARK
HAMPSTEAD
HARLESDEN
KINGSBURY
LIMEHOUSE †
MAIDA VALE
NORTHWOOD
OLD STREET
PARK ROYAL
QUEENSWAY
REDBRIDGE
SOUTHGATE
SOUTH QUAY †
STOCKWELL
ST PANCRAS
STRATFORD
TOWER HILL
UPMINSTER
UPTON PARK
WEST ACTON
WESTFERRY †
WHITE CITY
WIMBLEDON
WOOD GREEN

10

ARNOS GROVE
BOND STREET
BRENT CROSS
CAMDEN TOWN
CANONS PARK

DEVONS ROAD †
DOLLIS HILL
EARL'S COURT
EAST PUTNEY
EMBANKMENT
FARRINGDON
GRANGE HILL
HANGER LANE
HERON QUAYS †
HIGH BARNET
HILLINGDON
HORNCHURCH
KENNINGTON
KENSINGTON
KEW GARDENS
KING'S CROSS
MANOR HOUSE
MARBLE ARCH
MARYLEBONE
NORTH ACTON
NORTH WEALD
PADDINGTON
QUEENSBURY
QUEEN'S PARK
SHOREDITCH
TOOTING BEC
WEST HARROW

11

ALDGATE EAST
BAKER STREET
BARKINGSIDE
BARON'S COURT
BELSIZE PARK
BLACKFRIARS
BOSTON MANOR
BOUNDS GREEN
CHORLEYWOOD
COCKFOSTERS
DRAYTON PARK
EDGWARE ROAD
GUNNERSBURY
HAMMERSMITH
HATTON CROSS

HOLLAND PARK
KENSAL GREEN
KENTISH TOWN
KILBURY PARK
LATIMER ROAD
LEYTONSTONE
NEWBURY PARK
NORTH EALING
NORTHFIELDS
NORTH HARROW
PRESTON ROAD
RAYNERS LANE
REGENT'S PARK
ROTHERHITHE
SNARESBROOK
SOUTH EALING
SOUTHFIELDS
SOUTH HARROW
ST JOHN'S WOOD
SUDBURY HILL
SUDBURY TOWN
SURREY DOCKS
THEYDON BOIS
TUFNELL PARK
WEMBLEY PARK
WESTMINSTER
WEST RUISLIP
WHITECHAPEL

12

BETHNAL GREEN
BROMLEY BY-BOW
CANNON STREET
CHANCERY LANE
CHARING CROSS
CHISWICK PARK
CLAPHAM NORTH
CLAPHAM SOUTH
COLLIER'S WOOD
COVENT GARDEN
CROSSHARBOUR †
DAGENHAM EAST
EALING COMMON
EAST FINCHLEY

TRANSPORT — RAIL – LONDON UNDERGROUND

EUSTON SQUARE
FINCHLEY ROAD
FINSBURY PARK
GOLDERS GREEN
GOLDHAWK ROAD
GOODGE STREET
HOLLOWAY ROAD
HOUNSLOW EAST
LAMBETH NORTH
LONDON BRIDGE
MANSION HOUSE
MILL HILL EAST
NEW CROSS GATE
OXFORD CIRCUS
PARSONS GREEN
PUTNEY BRIDGE
RODING VALLEY
RUISLIP MANOR
SEVEN SISTERS
SLOANE SQUARE
SOUTH RUISLIP
STEPNEY GREEN
ST JAMES'S PARK
SWISS COTTAGE
TURNHAM GREEN
TURNPIKE LANE
WARREN STREET
WEST BROMPTON

WEST FINCHLEY
WOODSIDE PARK

13

BUCKHURST HILL
CLAPHAM COMMON
HENDON CENTRAL
ISLAND GARDENS †
KNIGHTSBRIDGE
LADBROKE GROVE
LANCASTER GATE
NORTHWICK PARK
RICKMANSWORTH
RUSSELL SQUARE
SHEPHERD'S BUSH
SOUTH WOODFORD
STAMFORD BROOK
TOTTENHAM HALE
TOWER GATEWAY †
WARWICK AVENUE
WEST HAMPSTEAD
WEST INDIA QUAY †
WIMBLEDON PARK

14

BLACKHORSE ROAD

CALEDONIAN ROAD
EALING BROADWAY
FULHAM BROADWAY
GLOUCESTER ROAD
HYDE PARK CORNER
NORTHWOOD HILLS
RUISLIP GARDENS
SOUTH WIMBLEDON
WESTBOURNE PARK
WEST KENSINGTON
WILLESDEN GREEN

15

FINCHLEY CENTRAL
HARROW-ON-THE-HILL
HOUNSLOW CENTRAL
LEICESTER SQUARE
LIVERPOOL STREET
NOTTING HILL GATE
RAVENSCOURT PARK
SOUTH KENSINGTON
STONEBRIDGE PARK
TOOTING BROADWAY
UPMINSTER BRIDGE

TRANSPORT

RAIL – STATIONS & TRAINS

All stations except: (B) = Bridge   (TR) = Train   (TU) = Tunnel

3

BOX *(TU)*
TAY *(B)*

5

ABBEY *(St Albans)*
ADLER *(TR)*
FORTH *(B)*

6

CASTLE *(Northampton)*
EUSTON *(London)*
FRIARY *(Plymouth)*
PRIORY *(Dover)*
PUTNEY *(B)*
ROCKET *(TR)*
SEIKAN *(TU-Japan)*
SEVERN *(TU)*
THORPE *(Norwich)*
TOTLEY *(TU)*

7

BANK TOP *(Darlington)*
BLÜCHER *(TR)*
CHANNEL *(TU)*
CHELSEA *(B)*
CITADEL *(Carlisle)*
INVICTA *(TR)*
MALLARD *(TR)*
MIDLAND *(Chesterfield,
Nottingham)*
PARAGON *(Hull)*

3 (column 2)

PARKWAY *(Bristol,
Didcot)*
SIMPLON *(TU-Alps)*
ST JOHN'S *(Bedford)*

8

BUTE ROAD *(Cardiff)*
CONNOLLY *(Dublin)*
EXCHANGE *(Liverpool)*
GOTTHARD *(TU-Alps)*
LANSDOWN *(Cheltenham)*
OSHIMIZU *(TU-Japan)*
SNOW HILL *(Birmingham,
London)*
ST DAVID'S *(Exeter)*
ST LAZARE *(Paris)*
VAUXHALL *(Gt Yarmouth)*
VICTORIA *(London,
Manchester,
Southend)*
WALLGATE *(Wigan)*
WATERLOO *(London)*
WAVERLEY *(Edinburgh)*

9

BRIDGE END *(Belfast)*
DEANSGATE *(Manchester)*
HAYMARKET *(Edinburgh)*
HUEY P LONG *(B-USA)*
NEW STREET *(Birmingham)*
RIVERSIDE *(Tilbury)*
SHRUB HILL *(Worcester)*
STANDEDGE *(TU)*
ST PANCRAS *(London)*

TRANSPORT – RAIL – STATIONS & TRAINS

10

BEDMINSTER *(Bristol)*
DEVON BELLE *(TR)*
DORCHESTER *(TR)*
GARE DE L'EST *(Paris)*
GARE DE LYON *(Paris)*
GARE DU NORD *(Paris)*
HIGH STREET *(Swansea)*
HUNGERFORD *(B)*
KING'S CROSS *(London)*
LIME STREET *(Liverpool)*
LOCOMOTION *(TR)*
LONDON ROAD *(Guildford,*
Leicester)
MARYLEBONE *(London)*
MOOR STREET *(Birmingham)*
PADDINGTON *(London)*
PICCADILLY *(London,*
Manchester)
ST BOTOLPH'S *(Colchester)*

11

ATTERCLIFFE *(Sheffield)*
BLACKFRIARS *(B)*
(London)
BROAD STREET *(London)*
EVENING STAR *(TR)*
JAMES STREET *(Liverpool)*
LE TRAIN BLEU *(TR)*
QUEEN STREET *(Cardiff,*
Glasgow)

TEMPLE MEADS *(Bristol)*
TRENT VALLEY *(Nuneaton)*
WOODHEAD NEW *(TU)*

12

AMIENS STREET *(Dublin)*
CANNON STREET *(London)*
CHARING CROSS *(London)*
GRAND CENTRAL *(New York)*
LAWRENCE HILL *(Bristol)*
LONDON BRIDGE *(London)*
MONTPARNASSE *(Paris)*
PUFFING BILLY *(TR)*

13

BRIGHTON BELLE *(TR)*
FORSTER SQUARE *(Bradford)*
ORIENT EXPRESS *(TR)*
PARKESTON QUAY *(Harwich)*

14

FLYING SCOTSMAN *(TR)*
HOLBORN VIADUCT *(London)*

15

CLAPHAM JUNCTION *(London)*
FENCHURCH STREET *(London)*
LIVERPOOL STREET *(London)*

SEA – SHIPS

All general ships except: (AC) = Aircraft-carrier   (BR) = Blue Riband holder
(L) = Line   (R) = Raft   (S) = Submarine   (SP) = Speedboat
(T) = Tanker   (Y) = Yacht
* = Alternative name

3

ESK
REX *(BR)*

4

AJAX
DRUM *(Y-Le Bon)*
FRAM *(Amundsen,*
        Nansen)
GJÖA *(Amundsen)*
HOOD
IOWA
LION
NINA *(Columbus)*
QE II
TAKU *(S)*
VEGA *(Y-Greenpeace)*

5

CAIRO
EAGLE
EGYPT
EMDEN
GREEK *(L)*
HELLE
JUNYO *(AC)*
MAINE
P AND O *(L)*
PASHA *(Drake)*
PINTA *(Columbus)*
SEINE
STARK

TIGER
UPTON

6

AFFRAY *(S)*
ARDENT
BARHAM
BEAGLE *(Darwin)*
BOUNTY *(Bligh)*
BREMEN *(BR)*
CUNARD *(L)*
CUXTON
DARING
EREBUS *(Franklin,*
        Ross)
EUROPA *(BR)*
EXETER
FRANCE *(renamed*
        NORWAY)
FRENCH *(L)*
HERMES *(AC)*
JUDITH *(Drake)*
NIMITZ *(AC)*
NORWAY
PUEBLO
RENOWN *(S)*
RODNEY
SCHEER *1
STRUMA
SYDNEY
SYNETA *(T)*
TERROR *(Franklin)*
THERON *(Fuchs)*
THETIS *(S)*
TIGRIS *(Heyerdahl)*

TRITON *(S)*
VIKING *(Nansen)*
YAMATO

7

ALTMARK
AMERICA *(Y)*
ARIZONA
ATHENIA
BELFAST
BRISTOL
COSSACK
CURAÇAO
DUNEDIN
GABRIEL *(Frobisher)*
GLASGOW
IVANHOE
KON-TIKI *(R-Heyerdahl)*
LIBERTY *(Y)*
MATTHEW *(J Cabot)*
MEMPHIS
MICHAEL *(Frobisher)*
MONITOR
NORFOLK *(Flinders)*
PELICAN *(renamed*
        GOLDEN HIND
        – Drake)
POLARIS *(S-series)*
REPULSE *(S)*
REVENGE *(S)*
SEALINK *(L)*
SHEMARA *(Y-Docker)*
SUHAILI *(Y-Knox-Johnston)*
SULTANA
TIRPITZ

TITANIC
VALIANT *(S-series)*
VICTORY *(Nelson)*
WARRIOR

VITTORIA *(Magellan)*
WARSPITE *(S)*
YORKTOWN *(AC)*

8

ACHILLES
AMETHYST
ANTELOPE
ARK ROYAL *(AC)*
BELGRANO *2
BISMARCK
BLUEBIRD *(SP-Campbell)*
CANBERRA
CHANDRIS *(L)*
COVENTRY
DAUPHINE *(Verrazano)*
FEARLESS
FORTRESS
GOOD HOPE
GRAF SPEE *3
HIMALAYA
INTREPID
IRON DUKE
MARIGOLD *(Drake)*
MARY ROSE
MERRIMAC
MISSOURI
MONMOUTH
MONTROSE *(Crippen
           case)*
NAUTILUS *(S)*
ROYAL OAK
SARATOGA *(AC)*
SAVANNAH
SCORPION *(S)*
SEYDLITZ
SHAMROCK *(Y-Lipton)*
SOBERTON
SPLENDID *(S)*
SQUIRREL *(Gilbert)*
THRESHER *(S)*
UPHOLDER *(S)*
VANGUARD *(Nelson)*

9

ADVENTURE *(Cook)*
BRITANNIA *(Y-Royal Family)*
CHRISTINA *(Y-Onassis)*
CHURCHILL *(S)*
CUTTY SARK
DISCOVERY *(Scott)*
EDINBURGH
ELIZABETH *(Drake)*
ENDEAVOUR *(Cook,
           Shackleton)*
ENDURANCE
GNEISENAU
GULLIVER G *(Y-Francis)*
HAMPSHIRE
ITALY MARU
JERVIS BAY
LUSITANIA *(BR)*
MAYFLOWER *(Pilgrim
           Fathers)*
NEW JERSEY
NORMANDIE *(BR)*
QUEEN MARY *(BR)*
RAMILLIES
RED FUNNEL *(L)*
SHEFFIELD
STOCKHOLM
TÉMÉRAIRE
TERRA NOVA *(Scott)*
TRUCULENT *(S)*
WHITE STAR *(L)*

10

AMOCO CADIZ *(T)*
BIRKENHEAD
BIRMINGHAM
BUCENTAURE

CUMBERLAND
DEVONSHIRE
DISCOVERIE *(Hudson)*
ENTERPRISE *(AC)*
FORMIDABLE
GOLDEN HIND *(Drake)*
INVINCIBLE *(AC)*
LISBON MARU
LIVELY LADY *(Y-Rose)*
MANCHESTER
MAURETANIA *(BR)*
NEW ZEALAND *(Y)*
PRINZ EUGEN
REDOUTABLE *(Villeneuve)*
RESOLUTION *(S)*
⠀⠀⠀⠀⠀⠀⠀⠀⠀*(Cook)*
ROYAL DUTCH *(L)*
SANTA MARIA *(Columbus)*
SIR GALAHAD
VINDICTIVE

11

ANDREA DORIA
AUSTRALIA II *(Y)*
DORSETSHIRE
DREADNOUGHT *(S,*
⠀⠀⠀⠀⠀⠀⠀⠀⠀*S-series)*
EXXON VALDEZ *(T)*
FORFARSHIRE *(Darling rescue)*
GIPSY MOTH IV *(Y-Chichester)*
ILLUSTRIOUS *(AC)*
MARY CELESTE *4
MISS ENGLAND *(SP-Segrave)*
ROYAL GEORGE
SCHARNHORST
SIR TRISTRAM
SOUTHAMPTON

12

ACHILLE LAURO
ARANDORA STAR
BRITISH STEEL *(Y-Blyth)*
GREAT BRITAIN
GREAT EASTERN
GREAT WESTERN
INVESTIGATOR *(Flinders)*
MARIE CELESTE *4
MORNING CLOUD *(Y-Heath)*
SEAWISE GIANT *(T)*
TORREY CANYON *(T)*
UNITED STATES *(BR)*
⠀⠀⠀⠀⠀⠀⠀⠀⠀⠀⠀*(L)*

13

ADMIRAL SCHEER *1
CHRISTOS BITAS *(T)*
KOWLOON BRIDGE *(T)*
PRINCE OF WALES
WHITE CRUSADER *(Y)*

14

GREAT BRITAIN II *(Y-Blyth)*
HOLLAND-AMERICA *(L)*
QUEEN ELIZABETH
RAINBOW WARRIOR *(Greenpeace)*
ROYAL ROTTERDAM *(L)*
VITTORIO VENETO

15

ADMIRAL GRAF SPEE *3
CHARLOTTE DUNDAS
EXPRESS CRUSADER *(Y-James)*
GENERAL BELGRANO *2
ROBERTSON'S GOLLY *(Y-Francis)*
STARS AND STRIPES *(Y)*

TRANSPORT

SPACE – SPACECRAFT

All general spacecraft except: (AS) = Artificial satellite   (L) = Launcher
(M) = Module   (MB) = Moon buggy   (SS) = Space station

3

OGO *(AS)*
OSO *(AS)*
SMM *(AS)*

4

ANIK *(AS)*
AZUR *(AS)*
ECHO *(AS)*
HEOS *(AS)*
LUNA
MARS
NOVA
ZOND

5

AEROS *(AS)*
ARIEL *(AS)*
ATLAS
EAGLE *(M)*
EKRAN *(L)*
INSAT *(AS)*
LUNIK
OFFEQ

SOYUZ
TIROS *(AS)*
TITAN
TV-SAT *(AS)*

6

APOLLO
ARIANE
COSMOS *(AS)*
GEMINI
GIOTTO
HELIOS
HUBBLE
PHOBOS
RANGER
REDUGA *(L)*
SALYUT *(SS)*
SATURN
SKYLAB *(SS)*
VENERA
VIKING
VOSTOK

7

ADVANCE

FOUNDER
LANDSAT *(AS)*
MARINER
MOLNIYA
ORBITER
PIONEER
PROGNOZ *(AS)*
SPUTNIK *(AS)*
TELSTAR *(AS)*
VOSKHOD
VOYAGER

8

ATLANTIS
COLUMBIA
EUTELSAT *(AS)*
EXPLORER *(AS)*
GORIZONT *(L)*
INTELSAT *(AS)*
LUNOKHOD *(MB)*
MAGELLAN
METEOSAT *(AS)*
PROGRESS *(AS)*
SAN MARCO
SPACELAB *(SS)*
SPACENET *(AS)*

SURVEYOR
THOR-ABLE

9

ARYABHATA *(AS)*
ATLAS-ABLE
EARLY BIRD *(AS)*

10

CHALLENGER
DISCOVERER *(AS)*
FRIENDSHIP
SHINSEI SSI *(AS)*

11

INTERCOSMOS

12

LUNAR ORBITER
PIONEER VENUS

INDEX

All main subjects in bold